D1229727

ARISTOTLE
XVI

LCL 317

ARISTOTLE

PROBLEMS
BOOKS XXII–XXXVIII

WITH AN ENGLISH TRANSLATION BY

W. S. HETT

RHETORICA AD ALEXANDRUM

WITH AN ENGLISH TRANSLATION BY

H. RACKHAM

HARVARD UNIVERSITY PRESS
CAMBRIDGE, MASSACHUSETTS
LONDON, ENGLAND

First published 1937
Revised and reprinted 1957
Reprinted 1965, 1983, 1994, 2001

LOEB CLASSICAL LIBRARY® is a registered trademark
of the President and Fellows of Harvard College

ISBN 0-674-99350-0

Printed in Great Britain by St Edmundsbury Press Ltd,
Bury St Edmunds, Suffolk, on acid-free paper.
Bound by Hunter & Foulis Ltd, Edinburgh, Scotland.

CONTENTS

PROBLEMS

CONTENTS

RHETORICA AD ALEXANDRUM

ARISTOTLE'S
PHYSICAL PROBLEMS

ΑΡΙΣΤΟΤΕΛΟΥΣ
ΦΥΣΙΚΑ ΠΡΟΒΛΗΜΑΤΑ
ΚΑΤ' ΕΙΔΟΣ ΣΥΝΑΓΩΓΗΣ

ΚΒ

ΟΣΑ ΠΕΡΙ ΟΠΩΡΑΝ

Διὰ τί τὴν ὀπώραν ὕστερον ἢ πρότερον φαγοῦσιν 1
οὐκ ἀνάλογος[1] τοῖς αὐτοῖς ὁ ὄγκος τῆς πληρώσεως
γίνεται; ἢ ὅτι βαρυτέρα ἐστὶν ἡ ὀπώρα πολὺ τῶν
σιτίων; δηλοῖ δὲ τὰ σῦκα, ἐὰν ὕστατα βρωθῇ·
10 τελευταῖα γὰρ ἐμεῖται. ἐὰν μὲν οὖν πρῶτα, διὰ
βάρος κάτω πορευόμενα εὐρυχωρίαν ἄνω ποιεῖ,
ὥστε ῥᾳδίως δέχεσθαι τὸν ὄγκον τῶν σιτίων.
ἀνάπαλιν δὲ εἰσελθόντα τὰ σιτία, διὰ τὸ μὴ κάτω
φέρεσθαι, ταχὺ τοῦ ἄνω κενοῦ προσλαμβάνει.

Διὰ τί τῶν γλυκέων ὄντων ὁμοιοτέρων ἡμῖν ἢ 2
15 τῶν δριμέων, θᾶττον πληρούμεθα ὑπὸ τῶν γλυκέων; εἰκὸς δὲ ἦν ἧττον· ὑπὸ γὰρ τῶν ὁμοίων
ἧττον ἦν εἰκὸς πληροῦσθαι. ἢ ὅτι οὐχ ὁμοίως τό
τε ἀγγεῖον πληροῦται ταχύ, ἐξ οὗ πληρούμεθα,

---

[1] ἀνάλογος most mss. : ἀνάλογον Ruelle.

ARISTOTLE'S
PHYSICAL PROBLEMS
ARRANGED ACCORDING TO THEIR CONTENTS

BOOK XXII

PROBLEMS CONCERNING FRUIT

WHY is it that the quantity of food needed to pro- 1
duce satiety is not proportionate in the same persons,
but varies according to whether they eat fruit after
or before a meal ? Is it because fruit is much heavier
than the same volume of solid food ? Figs prove
this, if they are eaten last ; for they are vomited
last. If, then, they are eaten first, owing to their
weight they sink down and leave plenty of room
above, so as to admit easily the volume of solid food.
Conversely, when the solid food enters, because it
does not travel downwards, it quickly fills the upper
empty space.

Why is it that, although sweet food is more like 2
our bodies than bitter, we are much more quickly
sated by sweet food ? It might seem natural that
we should be less so ; for it is natural that we should
be less easily sated with what is like us. Is it because
the receptacle from which we are sated and the body
which is nourished are not filled equally quickly, but

930 a

καὶ τὸ τρεφόμενον, ἀλλ' ἐνίοτε ἡ μὲν κοιλία πλήρης
ἐστίν, οἷον τῶν διψώντων, τὸ δὲ δίψος οὐδὲν ἧττόν
20 ἐστιν. οὐ γὰρ τῷ ταύτην εἶναι πλήρη παυόμεθα
διψῶντες, ἀλλὰ τῷ ἕκαστον τῶν τοῦ σώματος τὸ
αὑτῷ οἰκεῖον ἐσπακέναι, καὶ ὅταν ἐκεῖνα ἀπολάβῃ
ἱκανῶς, τότε παυόμεθα διψῶντες. καὶ πεινῶντες
δὲ ὡσαύτως.

Διὰ τί θᾶττον πληρούμεθα ἀπὸ τῶν γλυκέων ἢ 3
25 ἀπὸ τῶν δριμέων; ἢ ὅτι θᾶττον παυόμεθα ἐπιθυμοῦντες τῶν γλυκέων; ἢ ὡς μὲν ἡ κοιλία
πληροῦται, οὕτω καὶ ἡμεῖς ὑπὸ τῶν γλυκέων,
οὐχ ὁμολογεῖται, ὅτι δὲ ἡ ἐπιθυμία θᾶττον ὑπ'
αὐτῶν πληροῦται, τοῦτ' ἂν εἴη λεκτέον; ἢ ὅτι ἡ
μὲν ἐπιθυμία, ὡς ἁπλῶς εἰπεῖν, ἔστι μὲν ἔνδεια,
30 καὶ ὅταν μηκέτι ἔχωμεν τροφὴν ἢ ὀλίγην; τὰ
μὲν οὖν δριμέα οὐκ ἔστι τρόφιμα, ἀλλὰ τροφὴν
μὲν ὀλίγην ἔχει, τὸ δὲ περίττωμα πολύ. εἰκότως
οὖν πολλὰ ταῦτα ζητοῦμεν ἐσθίειν καὶ οὐκ ἐμ-
πιπλάμεθα αὐτῶν[1] τὴν ἐπιθυμίαν, διὰ τὸ ἔτι
προσδεῖσθαι τροφῆς, ταῦτα δὲ μὴ ἔχειν τροφήν.
35 τὰ δὲ γλυκέα ἅπαντά ἐστι τροφή, καὶ ἀπὸ μικρῶν
τοιούτων πολλὴν λαμβάνει τὸ σῶμα. ὅταν οὖν
ἀπολάβῃ πολλὴν τροφήν, οὐκέτι δύναται ἐσθίειν
διὰ τὸ μὴ ὑποφέρειν. εἰκότως οὖν θᾶττον ὑπὸ
τῶν γλυκέων πληρούμεθα.

Διὰ τί τὰ περικάρπια καὶ τὰ κρέα, καὶ ὅσα 4
930 b τοιαῦτα ἐν τοῖς ἀσκοῖς ἄσηπτα γίνεται ὅταν
σφόδρα φυσηθῶσι, καὶ τὰ ἐν τοῖς ἀκριβῶς περιπωματιζομένοις ὡσαύτως; ἢ διότι σήπεται μὲν
κινούμενα πάντα, τὰ δὲ πλήρη ἀκίνητα; ἀδύνατον
γὰρ ἄνευ κενοῦ κινηθῆναι, ταῦτα δὲ πλήρη.

[1] αὐτῶν Ruelle.

4

sometimes the stomach may be full, as in the case of the thirsty, but their thirst is no less ? For we do not cease being thirsty because the stomach is full, but because each part of the body has drawn in its own proper food, and when all these have taken what they require, then we cease to be thirsty. The same is true with hunger.

Why are we more quickly sated with sweet than 3 with bitter foods ? Is it because we cease to crave for the sweet more quickly ? Or while it is not generally admitted that we become sated as our stomach is filled with sweet foods, yet might it not be said that our desire is more quickly satisfied by them ? Or is it because desire, to describe it in simple terms, is a form of want, and arises when we no longer have sustenance or only a little ? Now bitter things are not nutritive ; they contain little nutriment but much waste product. Naturally, therefore, we seek to eat them in large quantities, and do not satisfy our desire with them, because we still require nourishment and bitter things do not contain it. But all sweet things are nourishment, and the body derives much nourishment from a few of them. But when it has absorbed a large quantity of nourishment, it can no longer eat because it can no longer tolerate it. Naturally, therefore, we are more quickly sated by the sweet.

Why is it that fruits and meat and all similar things 4 which are put in leather bottles remain without decaying, when the bottles are fully blown up, and that the same thing happens in vessels whose lids are tightly sealed ? Is it because movement is the cause of decay, and when the containers are full there is no movement ? For movement is impossible without an empty space and these are full.

5 Διὰ τί μετὰ τὰ σαπρὰ τῶν περικαρπίων ὁ οἶνος 5
πικρὸς φαίνεται πινόμενος; ἢ ὅτι τὴν πικρότητα
ἔχει ἡ σαπρότης ἡ τοιαύτη; τὸ οὖν ἐπιμένον ἐπὶ
τῇ γλώττῃ, μιγνύμενον τῷ πόματι καὶ διαχεόμενον
πικρὸν ποιεῖ τὸ πόμα. αὐτὸ δὲ καθ᾽ αὑτὸ ἧττον
10 φαίνεται ἐσθιόμενον διὰ τὸ πολλῶν ἅπτεσθαι καὶ
εἰς μικρὰ διανενεμῆσθαι τὸν τοιοῦτον χυμόν.

Διὰ τί τὰ τραγήματα ἐδεστέον; ἢ ἕνεκα τοῦ 6
πιεῖν ἱκανόν; οὐ γὰρ μόνον ποτέον τῆς δίψης
χάριν τῆς ἐπὶ τοῖς σιτίοις, ἀλλὰ καὶ μετὰ τὸ σιτίον.

15 Διὰ τί τὰ ὀπτὰ κάρυα ψυχθέντα χείρω γίνεται, 7
καὶ ὁ ἄρτος δὲ καὶ ὁ βάλανος καὶ πολλὰ τῶν
τοιούτων, θερμανθέντα δὲ πάλιν βελτίω; ἢ διότι
ψυχθέντος μὲν πέπηγεν ὁ χυμός, ἀναχλιανθέντος
δὲ πάλιν χεῖται; ἡ δὲ ἡδονὴ γίνεται διὰ τὸν
χυμόν.

20 Διὰ τί ἐπὶ τῇ ἀπολαύσει τῆς ὀπώρας, οἷον σύκων 8
καὶ τῶν τοιούτων, ἢ οἶνον ἄκρατον δεῖ ἐπιπίνειν
ἢ ὕδωρ; ταῦτα δὲ ἐναντία. ἢ ὅτι ἡ ὀπώρα καὶ
θερμή ἐστι καὶ ὑγρὰ διὰ τὴν γένεσιν; ἔχει γὰρ
πολὺ πῦρ καὶ ὑγρότητα, ὥστε διὰ μὲν τὸ πῦρ οἷον
25 ζέσιν ποιεῖ ὁ χυμὸς εἴσω, ὅπερ ἔξω τὸ γλεῦκος
ποιεῖ. ἧττον δὲ ἔχει δύναμιν καὶ τὰ ἄλλα τὰ
ἀκρόδρυα. τὸ δὲ τῆς ὑγρότητος πλῆθος ἀπεψίαν
ποιεῖ. τὸ μὲν οὖν ὕδωρ διὰ τὴν ψυχρότητα
σβεννύει τὴν ζέσιν, ὁ δὲ οἶνος διὰ τὴν θερμότητα
ὡς ἐπὶ τὸ πολύ· ὥσπερ γὰρ πῦρ ἐνίοτε πυρός, ἐὰν
30 ᾖ ἔλαττον, ἀφαιρεῖται τὴν ἰσχύν. μᾶλλον δὲ τῇ
θερμότητι πεπτικός ἐστι τῆς ὑγρότητος, καὶ διὰ
βάρος κατακρατεῖ τῶν τῆς ζέσεως ἐπιπολασμῶν.

Διὰ τί τῶν ἰσχάδων γλυκύταται αἱ δίχα ἐσχι- 9
σμέναι, οὔτε δὲ αἱ πολυσχιδεῖς οὔτε αἱ ἀσχιδεῖς;
6

Why does wine when drunk after eating rotten 5
fruit taste bitter ? Is it because there is an element of
bitterness in such rottenness ? That which remains
on the tongue, when mixed with the drink and penetrating it, makes it bitter. The fruit itself when eaten
seems less bitter because juice of this kind touches
many parts, and so is divided into small particles.

Why should one eat dried fruits ? Is it in order 6
that we may drink enough ? For one must drink,
not merely because of the thirst which arises while
eating solid food, but also after solid food.

Why are roasted nuts less pleasant when they are 7
cold, as also are bread, acorns, and many similar
things, but much pleasanter when they are hot ? Is
it because when they are cold the juice is congealed,
but flows again when they are warmed ? And the
pleasure is due to the juice.

Why should one pour unmixed wine or water over 8
figs and the like for the real enjoyment of the fruit ?
For these are opposites. Is it because fruit is both
warm and moist because of its origin ? For it contains much heat and moisture, so that owing to the
heat the juice produces a form of boiling within, just
as must does outside. The other class, namely the
hard-shelled fruits, have this power in a less degree.
But the quantity of moisture causes a difficulty of
concoction. The water, then, because of its coldness
extinguishes the boiling, but the wine generally does
so by its warmth ; just as a fire sometimes takes away
the strength of a fire, if it is smaller. Wine, then, by
its heat more easily causes the concoction of the
moisture, and owing to its weight it prevails over the
surface of the boiling.

Why are the sweetest dried figs those which are 9
divided in half, and neither the much-divided nor

930 b ἢ διότι ἐκ μὲν τῶν πολυσχιδῶν διαπέπνευκεν καὶ
35 ἐξίκμακεν μετὰ τοῦ ὑγροῦ τὸ πλεῖστον τοῦ γλυκέος, ἐν δὲ ταῖς μεμυκυίαις πλεῖον τὸ ὑδατῶδές
ἐστι διὰ τὸ μὴ ἠτμικέναι; αἱ δὲ ἐσχισμέναι μέν,
μὴ εἰς πολλὰ δέ, ἀμφοτέρων τούτων ἐκτός εἰσι
τῶν παθημάτων.

Διὰ τί ταῖς καμίνοις ξηραινόμενα[1] τὰ σῦκα 10
931 a σκληρότερα γίνεται, ἐὰν ψυχθῇ ἐν τῇ καμίνῳ, ἢ
ἂν ἐξαιρεθέντα ψυχθῇ; ἢ ὅτι ἐν μὲν τῇ καμίνῳ
ἐξατμίζει πᾶν τὸ ὑγρὸν ὑπὸ τοῦ θερμοῦ, ἔξω δὲ
περιεστηκὼς ὁ ἀὴρ ψύχων κωλύει τὸ ὑγρὸν ἐξιέναι
5 καὶ συνίστασθαι; μᾶλλον γὰρ ἐξατμίζει. ἔστι δὲ
τὰ μὲν ξηρὰ σκληρά, τὰ δὲ ὑγρὰ μαλακά.

Διὰ τί παρὰ τὰ στρυφνὰ ὁ οἶνος καὶ τὸ ὕδωρ 11
φαίνεται γλυκύτερα, οἷον ἐάν τις βαλάνους ἢ
μύρτα ἤ τι τῶν τοιούτων διατράγῃ; ἢ εἰκότως,
καθάπερ καὶ ἐπὶ τῶν ἄλλων; πᾶν γὰρ τὸ αὐτὸ
10 παρὰ τὸ ἐναντίον μᾶλλον φαίνεται, οἱ δὲ τῶν ἐναντίων χυμοὶ ἀντικείμενοί πώς εἰσιν. ἢ ὅτι, καθάπερ
ἐπὶ τῶν βαπτομένων, ὑπὸ τῶν στρυφνῶν ἡ γλῶττα
προδιεργάζεται καὶ τοὺς πόρους ἀνοίγεται, ὥστε
μᾶλλον διιέναι τὸ γλυκύ; καὶ γὰρ τὰ βαπτόμενα
τούτου ἕνεκεν προβρέχουσιν ἐν τοῖς στρυφνοῖς,
15 τῷ διεργασθὲν μᾶλλον δέχεσθαι τὴν βαφήν.

Διὰ τί τὰ γλυκέα ἧττον δοκεῖ γλυκέα εἶναι 12
θερμὰ ὄντα ἢ ὅταν ψυχθῇ; πότερον ὅτι ἅμα δύο
αἰσθήσεις γίνονται ἀμφοῖν, ὥστε ἡ τοῦ θερμοῦ
ἐκκρούει τὴν ἑτέραν; ἢ ὅτι καὶ τὸ γλεῦκος
20 θερμόν; ὥσπερ οὖν πῦρ γίνεται ἐπὶ πῦρ. κωλύει

---

[1] ξηραινόμενα Sylburgh : ψυχόμενα Ruelle.

the undivided ? Is it because in the case of much-divided figs most of the sweetness has escaped and evaporated with the moisture, but in those which are closed up there is more moisture because it has not evaporated ? Figs divided in half, and not into many portions, escape both these results.

Why is it that figs which are dried in ovens 10 grow harder if they are cooled in an oven than if they are taken out and cooled ? Is it because in the oven all the moisture evaporates under the influence of the heat, but outside the surrounding air which cools them prevents the moisture from escaping and congealing ? For there is more evaporation (in the former case). Now dry things are hard and wet ones soft.

Why do wine and water seem sweeter when taken 11 with sour food ; for instance if one eats acorns or myrtle-berries or anything of the kind ? Or is this natural, as in all other cases ? For the identity of a thing becomes more obvious when contrasted with its opposite, and the flavours of opposites are in a sense antithetic. Or is it that, as in the case of things dyed, the tongue has been already worked upon by what is sour and opens its pores, so that the sweet penetrates more ? This is why they soak things which are to be dyed in sour liquid beforehand, so that by having been worked upon the material may take the dye more easily.

Why do sweet foods taste less sweet when they are 12 hot than when they have been cooled ? Is it because there are two separate sensations of the two qualities occurring at the same time, so that the sensation of the hot drives out the other ? Or is it because sweetness is hot ? In that case it is like adding fire to fire.

οὖν ἡ θερμότης. ἢ ὅτι τὸ πῦρ ἀφαιρεῖται τὰς
δυνάμεις ἀπάντων διὰ τὸ κινητικὸν εἶναι; ἐγγυτέρω οὖν τοῦ μεταβάλλειν ἐστὶ θερμὰ ὄντα,
ἀποψυχθέντα δὲ ἕστηκεν.

Διὰ τί ποτε τὰ ἄχυρα τὰ μὲν σκληρὰ πέττει, τὰ 13
δὲ πεπεμμένα οὐ σήπει; ἢ ὅτι τὰ ἄχυρα θερμόν τε
25 καὶ ὁλκόν ἐστιν; τῇ μὲν οὖν θερμότητι πέττει,
τῷ δὲ ὁλκὸν εἶναι τὸν ἰχῶρα τὸν σηπόμενον δέχεται·
διὸ οὐ σήπει.

Διὰ τί τὰ σῦκα μαλακὰ καὶ γλυκέα ὄντα λυ- 14
μαίνεται τοὺς ὀδόντας; ἢ διὰ τὴν γλισχρότητα
προσέρχεται τοῖς οὔλοις, καὶ παρεμπίπτει διὰ
30 τῶν ὀδόντων εἰς τὰ διὰ μέσου διὰ τὸ μαλακὰ εἶναι,
καὶ σῆψιν ποιεῖ ταχέως ἅτε θερμὰ ὄντα; τάχα
δὲ ἴσως καὶ διὰ τὴν σκληρότητα τῶν κεγχραμίδων
ἐν τῇ τούτων κατεργασίᾳ πονοῦσι ταχέως οἱ
ὀδόντες.

So the heat prevents (the sensation of sweet). Or is it because fire takes away the power of anything because it produces movement? Hot things, then, are nearer to a state of change, but when cooled they become stationary again.

Why does chaff ripen hard fruit but does not rot 13 what is already ripe? Is it because chaff is hot and absorbent? It ripens by its heat, but being absorbent it takes up the rotting liquid; hence the fruit does not decay.

Why do figs which are soft and sweet damage the 14 teeth? Do they attack the gums because they are glutinous, and pass into the spaces between the teeth because they are soft, and produce decay quickly because they are hot? Perhaps also the teeth soon suffer in dealing with them owing to the hardness of the small seeds they contain.

ΚΓ

ΟΣΑ ΠΕΡΙ ΤΟ ΑΛΜΥΡΟΝ ΥΔΩΡ ΚΑΙ ΘΑΛΑΤΤΑΝ

35 Διὰ τί τὸ κῦμα οὐκ ἐπιγελᾷ ἐν τοῖς βαθέσι 1
πελάγεσιν, ἀλλ᾽ ἐν τοῖς μικροῖς καὶ βραχέσιν; ἢ
ὅτι τὸ μικρὸν ὑγρὸν φερόμενον μᾶλλον διαιρεῖται
ὑπὸ τοῦ πνεύματος ἢ τὸ πολύ;

Διὰ τί τὰ κύματα πρότερον φοιτᾷ ἐνίοτε τῶν 2
ἀνέμων; ἢ ὅτι πρὸς τῇ ἀρχῇ τοῦ πνεύματος ἡ
931 b θάλαττα ὠσθεῖσα πρώτη τὴν ἐχομένην ἀεὶ ταὐτὸν
ποιεῖ; διόπερ οὔσης αὐτῆς συνεχοῦς καθάπερ μιᾷ
πληγῇ συνεχεῖ πάσαις γίνεται. τὸ δὲ ἐν ἑνὶ
χρόνῳ γίνεται, ὥστε συμβαίνει τήν τε πρώτην
καὶ τὴν ἐσχάτην ἅμα κινεῖσθαι. ὁ δὲ ἀὴρ οὐ
5 πάσχει τοῦτο, ὅτι οὔτε ἐστὶν ἓν σῶμα συνεχές, τῷ
πολλὰς πάντοθεν ἀντικρούσεις λαμβάνειν, αἳ πολλάκις κωλύουσι τὴν πρώτην καὶ νεανικωτάτην
κίνησιν, τήν τε θάλασσαν οὐ ποιοῦσι τοῦτο διὰ
τὸ βαρυτέραν καὶ δυσκινητοτέραν αὐτοῦ εἶναι.

Διὰ τί τὰ πλοῖα γέμειν δοκεῖ μᾶλλον ἐν τῷ 3
10 λιμένι ἢ ἐν τῷ πελάγει, καὶ θεῖ δὲ θᾶττον ἐκ τοῦ
πελάγους πρὸς τὴν γῆν ἢ ἀπὸ τῆς γῆς εἰς τὸ
πέλαγος; ἢ ὅτι τὸ πλέον ὕδωρ ἀντερείδει μᾶλλον

BOOK XXIII

Problems connected with Salt Water and the Sea

Why do not the waves ripple in deep seas, but only 1 in small and shallow ones? Is it because a small quantity of water as it is carried along is more divided by the wind than a large quantity?

Why do the waves sometimes move before the 2 winds reach them? Is it because near the source of the wind the sea being driven along first continually produces the same effect on the part next to it? Consequently, as the sea is continuous, all parts are affected as if by one continuous blow. But this action is simultaneous, so that the first and last parts are moved at the same time. The air does not suffer the same effect, because it is not one continuous body, for it receives many contrary impulses from all quarters, which often check the first and the most vigorous movement, but they do not produce this effect on the sea, because it is heavier and more difficult to move than the air.

Why is it that ships appear more heavily laden in 3 harbour than they do in the open sea, and run faster from the sea towards the land than from the land towards the sea? Is it because the larger quantity of water offers more resistance than the small

13

τοῦ¹ ὀλίγου, ἐν δὲ τῷ ὀλίγῳ δέδυκεν διὰ τὸ κρατεῖν
αὐτοῦ μᾶλλον; ὠθεῖ γὰρ κάτωθεν τὸ ὕδωρ ἄνω.
15 ἐν μὲν οὖν τῷ λιμένι ὀλίγη ἐστὶν ἡ θάλασσα, ἐν δὲ
τῷ πελάγει βαθεῖα. ὥστε καὶ ἄγειν πλέον δόξει
ἐν τῷ λιμένι καὶ κινήσεται χαλεπώτερον διὰ τὸ
δεδυκέναι μᾶλλον καὶ ἧττον ἀντερείδειν τὸ ὕδωρ.
ἐν τῷ πελάγει δὲ τἀναντία τούτων ἐστίν.

Διὰ τί, ὅταν τι ῥιφθῇ εἰς τὴν θάλατταν κυμαί- 4
20 νουσαν, οἷον ἡ ἄγκυρα, γαλήνη γίνεται; ἢ διότι
ἵσταται ἡ θάλαττα τῷ φερομένῳ, μεθ' οὗ ἀὴρ
συγκαταφέρεται, ὃς ἐπ' εὐθείας κάτω φερόμενος
καὶ ἐνταῦθα ἐπισπασθεὶς συνεπισπᾶται τὸ ἐκ
πλαγίου κινοῦν τὴν θάλατταν; ὁ δὲ κλύδων τῆς
θαλάττης οὐκ ἄνωθεν κάτω γίνεται ἀλλ' ἐπιπολῆς·
25 οὗ λήξαντος γαλήνη γίνεται. ἔτι συνιοῦσα ἡ
θάλασσα εἰς τὰ διαστάντα τῷ φερομένῳ δίνην
ποιεῖ. ἡ δὲ δίνη κύκλῳ φέρεται. ἐπεὶ δὲ ἡ
εὐθεῖα τοῦ κύκλου κατὰ σημεῖον ἅπτεται, τὰ δὲ
κύματα ἐπ' εὐθείας λοξῆς φέρεται, συμβαίνοι ἂν
αὐτὰ τοῦ ἐξωτάτου τῆς δίνης κατὰ σημεῖον
30 ἅπτεσθαι, διά τε τὰ εἰρημένα καὶ διὰ τὴν τῆς
δίνης φοράν, ἢ προσιοῦσα ἀπωθεῖται αὐτά. ἀκύμου
δὲ ὄντος τοῦ κατ' αὐτὴν τόπου, γαλήνην ἐν τῇ
ῥήξει αὐτῆς συμβαίνει γίνεσθαι, ὅτι συγκαταβὰς
ὁ ἀὴρ τῷ ἐνεχθέντι κάτω, ἀναφερόμενος καὶ ὠθῶν
ἄνω τὴν θάλατταν καθάπερ πομφολυγοῖ αὐτήν·
35 ἡ γὰρ πομφόλυξ ὑγροῦ ὑπ' ἀέρος κάτωθεν ἀν-
ωθουμένου ἐστίν. πομφόλυξ δὲ πᾶσα λεία καὶ
γαληνός ἐστιν. σημεῖα δὲ τῶν εἰρημένων ἐστί·

---

¹ ἐκ τοῦ Ruelle.

quantity, and in the small quantity the ship sinks because it exercises more influence over it? For it thrusts the water up from below. Now in harbour the sea is shallow, but in the open sea it is deep. So that the ship in harbour will appear to be carrying more, and will move with greater difficulty, because it has sunk farther and the water supports it less. But in the open sea the opposite of this is true.

Why is it that, when any object, such as an anchor, 4 is thrown into a rough sea, a calm ensues? Is it because the sea is steadied by the moving object, with which air is carried down; the air travelling downwards in a straight line and drawn in that direction draws with it the sidelong force which moves the sea? Now the sea wave does not travel down from above but along the surface; when this force ceases, a calm ensues. Now the sea coming in to fill the gap created by the travelling body makes an eddy, and an eddy travels in a circle. But, since a straight line touches a circle at a point, and the movement of the wave is in an oblique straight line, it would follow that the waves touch the outside of the eddy at a point, both for the reasons already given and owing to the movement of the eddy, which, as it moves, repels the waves. As the place where the eddy is is free from waves, a calm must occur at the point where the surface is broken, because the air which was carried downwards with the moving object travels upwards again, and thrusting the sea upwards, as it were, produces bubbles on it; for the bubble consists of the moisture thrust up by the air from below. Every bubble is smooth and calm. There is proof of what has been said; a little later the sea

μετέωρος γὰρ ἡ κατὰ τὸ ἐνεχθὲν κάτω θάλαττα
τῆς πέριξ γίνεται μικρὸν ὕστερον.

Διὰ τί ἐνίοτε πλοῖα θέοντα ἐν τῇ θαλάττῃ εὐδίας 5
932 a καταπίνεται καὶ ἀφανῆ γίνεται, ὥστε μηδὲ ναυάγιον
ἀναπλεῖν; ἢ ὅταν ἀντρώδης τόπος ἐν τῇ ὑπὸ τὴν
θάλατταν γῇ ῥαγῇ, ἅμα εἰς τὴν θάλατταν καὶ ἔσω
ἀκολουθεῖ τῇ τοῦ πνεύματος φορᾷ; ὁμοίως δὲ καὶ
5 πάντῃ φερομένη κύκλῳ φέρεται κάτω. τοῦτο δέ
ἐστι δῖνος. τὰ δὲ περὶ Μεσήνην ἐν τῷ πορθμῷ
πάσχει μὲν τοῦτο διὰ τὸν ῥοῦν (γίνονται γὰρ αἱ
δῖναι ὑπὸ τούτου) καὶ καταπίνεται εἰς βυθὸν διὰ
ταῦτά τε, καὶ ὅτι ἡ θάλαττα βαθεῖά τε καὶ ἡ γῆ
ὕπαντρος μέχρι πόρρω. φέρουσιν οὖν εἰς ταῦτα
10 ἀποβιαζόμεναι αἱ δῖναι· διὸ οὐκ ἀναπλεῖ αὐτόθι τὰ
ναυάγια. ὁ δὲ ῥοῦς γίνεται, ὅταν παυσαμένου τοῦ
προτέρου ἀντιπνεύσῃ ἐπὶ τῆς θαλάττης ῥεούσης τῷ
προτέρῳ πνεύματι, μάλιστα δὲ ὅταν νότος ἀντιπνεύσῃ. ἀντιπνέοντα γὰρ ἀλλήλοις τὰ ῥεύματα
παρεκθλίβεται ὥσπερ ἐν τοῖς ποταμοῖς, καὶ γίνονται
15 αἱ δῖναι. φέρεται δὲ ἑλιττομένη ἡ ἀρχὴ τῆς κινήσεως ἄνωθεν ἰσχυρὰ οὖσα. ἐπεὶ οὖν εἰς πλάγιον
οὐκ ἔστιν ὁρμᾶν (ἀντωθεῖται γὰρ ὑπ' ἀλλήλων),
ἀνάγκη εἰς βάθος ὠθεῖσθαι, ὥστε καὶ ὃ ἂν ληφθῇ
ὑπὸ τῆς δίνης, κἀνάγκη συγκαταφέρεσθαι. διὸ
ἀνάσιμα τὰ πλοῖα ποιοῦνται· ἤδη γὰρ ὀρθόν ποτε
20 μνημονεύεται καταποθέν.

Διὰ τί ἡ θάλαττα λευκοτέρα ἡ ἐν τῷ Πόντῳ ἢ 6
ἡ ἐν τῷ Αἰγαίῳ; πότερον διὰ τὴν ἀνάκλασιν τῆς
16

over the spot where the object has been thrown in rises to a higher level than the surrounding water.

Why is it that sometimes craft travelling on the 5 sea in fine weather are sunk and completely disappear, so that no wreckage even comes to the surface ? Is it because when a spot in the ground underneath the sea breaks and forms a hollow, they follow the movement of the air down into the sea and into the hollow ? Similarly the sea travelling in a circle in every direction is carried below. This is a whirlpool. Ships in the Straits of Messina suffer thus because of the stream (which is the cause of whirlpools), and they are swallowed up into the depths, both for this reason and because the sea is deep and the ground beneath it full of hollows to a great distance. The eddies overpower the ships and carry them into the hollows ; that is why no wrecks rise from there. A current is formed when after the cessation of the former wind from one direction it blows in the opposite direction over a sea which is running under the influence of the previous wind, and particularly when the south wind is the contrary wind. For the currents blowing in opposite directions thrust each other aside, just as they do in rivers, and eddies are formed. But the original movement from above travels round and round because it is strong. Since, then, they cannot move obliquely (for they are repelled by each other), they must be driven downwards, so that anything caught by the eddy must be carried down with it. This is why ships are made with the ends turned up ; for it is recollected that sometimes one with straight ends has been swallowed up.

Why is the water in the Pontus whiter than that 6 in the Aegean ? Is it due to the refraction of the

932 a

ὄψεως τὴν γινομένην ἀπὸ τῆς θαλάττης εἰς τὸν
ἀέρα; ὁ μὲν γὰρ περὶ τὸν Πόντον ἀὴρ παχὺς καὶ
25 λευκός, ὥστε καὶ τῆς θαλάττης ἡ ἐπιφάνεια τοιαύτη
φαίνεται, ὁ δὲ ἐν τῷ Αἰγαίῳ κυανοῦς διὰ τὸ μέχρι
πόρρω εἶναι καθαρός, ὥστε καὶ ἡ θάλαττα ἀντ-
αυγοῦσα τοιαύτη φαίνεται. ἢ ὅτι πᾶσαι αἱ λίμναι
λευκότεραι τῆς θαλάττης; ὁ δὲ Πόντος ἐστὶ
λιμνώδης διὰ τὸ πολλοὺς ποταμοὺς εἰς αὐτὸν ῥεῖν.
30 αἱ δὲ λίμναι διαλευκότεραι τῆς θαλάττης καὶ τῶν
ποταμῶν· γράφουσι γοῦν οἱ γραφεῖς τοὺς μὲν ποταμοὺς ὠχρούς, τὴν δὲ θάλατταν κυανέαν. ἢ ὅτι διὰ
μὲν τοῦ ποτίμου οὐ¹ διέρχεται ταχὺ ἡ ὄψις, καὶ
ἀνακλᾶται πρὸς τὸν ἀέρα, ἀπὸ δὲ τῆς θαλάσσης
οὔτ' ἄνω ἀνακλᾶται διὰ τὸ μὴ λεῖον εἶναι τὸ ὕδωρ·
35 κάτω δὲ ἀποκάμνει βαδίζουσα· διὸ μέλαινα φαίνεται; ἐν δὲ τοῖς λιμνώδεσιν ἐπιπολῆς ὄντος τοῦ
ποτίμου, κάτω δὲ τοῦ ἁλμυροῦ, οὐ διέρχεται, ἀλλὰ
ἀνακλᾶται πρὸς τὴν αὐγήν· διὸ φαίνεται λευκὴ ἡ
ἐπιφάνεια αὐτῆς.

Διὰ τί ἡ θάλαττα τοῦ ποτίμου ὕδατος ἧττον 7
932 b ψυχρά, καὶ τὰ ἁλυκὰ τῶν γλυκέων; πότερον ὅτι
πυκνότερον ἡ θάλαττα καὶ μᾶλλον σῶμα; τὰ δὲ
τοιαῦτα ἧττον ψύχεται, ὥσπερ καὶ θερμαίνεται
μᾶλλον· σωστικωτέρα γὰρ τοῦ θερμοῦ διὰ τὴν
5 πυκνότητα. ἢ ὅτι λιπαρωτέρα ἡ θάλαττα; διὸ
καὶ οὐ σβέννυσι τὴν φλόγα. ὁμοίως καὶ ἐπὶ τῶν
ἄλλων. τὸ δὲ λιπαρώτερον θερμότερον. ἢ ὅτι γῆς
πολὺ ἔχει, ὥστε ξηρότερον; τὸ δὲ ξηρότερον
θερμότερον.

Διὰ τί θάλαττα εὐδιοπτοτέρα τοῦ ποτίμου, παχυ- 8
τέρα οὖσα; λεπτότερον γὰρ τὸ πότιμον τοῦ

18

sight which takes place from the sea into the air ? For the air in the Pontus is thick and white, so that the surface of the sea wears the same appearance, but the air in the Aegean seems blue because it is clear for such a long distance, so that the sea reflecting it seems similar. Is it because all lakes are whiter than the sea ? And the Pontus resembles a lake because many rivers flow into it. Lakes, indeed, are whiter than both sea and rivers ; so painters paint their rivers a pale colour, but the sea blue. Or is it because the vision does not easily penetrate fresh water, and is refracted to the air, but from the sea it is not refracted because the water is not smooth ; but the sight in penetrating below grows weary ; and so the sea appears black ? But in water resembling a lake, as the fresh water is on the surface and the salt water beneath, it does not penetrate, but is refracted towards the daylight ; consequently its surface appears to be white.

Why is the sea less cold than fresh water, and 7 brackish less cold than sweet water ? Is it because the sea is denser and contains more solid matter ? Such things cool less, just as they also grow more hot ; for they conserve heat more easily owing to their density. Or is it because sea-water is more fatty, and so does not extinguish the flame ? The same thing is true of other substances. For what is more fatty is warmer. Or is it because it contains much earth, and so is drier ? For the dry is also warmer.

Why is the sea more transparent than fresh water, 8 although it is denser ? For fresh water is lighter

---

¹ The ᴍs. has οὐ in the wrong place, as shown by the translation of Th. G.

932 b

10 ἁλμυροῦ. ἢ οὐ τὸ λεπτὸν αἴτιον, ἀλλ' εὐθυωρίαι
τῶν πόρων πλεῖσται καὶ μέγισταί εἰσιν; τὸ μὲν
οὖν πότιμον πυκνὸν διὰ λεπτομέρειάν ἐστιν, τὸ δὲ
ἁλμυρὸν μεγάλα ἔχει τὰ διάκενα. ἢ ὅτι καθαρώ-
τερον ἡ θάλαττα; γῇ μὲν γὰρ οὐκ ἔστιν, ἡ δὲ
ἄμμος βαρεῖα οὖσα ὑφίσταται. τὰ δὲ πότιμα
15 γεώδη. αὕτη¹ δὲ ἐν τῷ μεταξὺ φερομένη ἀνα-
θολοῦται ταχύ.

Διὰ τί ἐν τοῖς βορείοις εὐδιοπτοτέρα ἡ θάλαττα 9
ἢ ἐν τοῖς νοτίοις; ἢ ὅτι ἐν τῇ γαλήνῃ χρῶμα ἔχει
ἡ θάλαττα; λιπαρὸν γὰρ ἔνεστιν ἐν τῷ ἁλμυρῷ
χυμῷ. σημεῖον δέ· ἐκκρίνεται γὰρ ἔλαιον ἐν ταῖς
20 ἀλέαις. εὐδίας οὖν οὔσης καὶ ἀλεεινοτέρας τῆς
θαλάττης διὰ κουφότητα ἐπανθεῖ ἄνω ὁ τοιοῦτος
χυμός. τοῖς δὲ βορείοις ἧττον διὰ τὸ ψῦχος. ἔστιν
δὲ τὸ ὕδωρ εὐδιοπτότερον τοῦ ἐλαίου· τὸ γὰρ ἔλαιον
χρῶμα ἔχει, τὸ δὲ ὕδωρ ἄχροον παρεμφαινόμενον
σαφεστέραν ποιεῖ τὴν ἔμφασιν.

25 Διὰ τί λουσάμενοι τῇ θαλάττῃ θᾶττον ξηραί- 1
νονται, βαρυτέρᾳ οὔσῃ τῶν ποτίμων; ἢ ὅτι
παχυτέρα καὶ γεώδης ἡ θάλαττα; ὀλίγον οὖν
ἔχουσα τὸ ὑγρὸν ξηραίνεται θᾶττον.

Διὰ τί τὰ κύματα ἀνεμώδη; ἢ ὅτι σημεῖά ἐστι 1
30 πνεύματος ἐσομένου; ἔστι γὰρ τὸ πνεῦμα σύνωσις
ἀέρος. ἢ διὰ τὸ ἀεὶ προωθεῖσθαι γίνεται; προωθεῖ
δὲ οὐ συνεχές πω ὂν τὸ πνεῦμα, ἀλλὰ ἀρχόμενον.
τὸ μὲν δὴ πρῶτον ὥσπερ προεμαράνθη, ἄλλο δὲ
τοῦτο προέωσε καὶ ἄλλην πυκνότητα ἤγαγεν καὶ
35 ἀπεμαράνθη. ὥστε δῆλον, ὅταν ἤδη τὸ προωθού-
μενον παρῇ, ὅτι ἥξει καὶ τὸ κινοῦν· ἀρχόμενον γὰρ
τοῦτο ποιεῖ.

¹ αὕτη Forster : αὐτὴ Ruelle.

20

than salt water. Or is the lightness not the cause,
but the fact that the direct passages through it are
many and very large ? In that case fresh water is
dense because of the smallness of its parts, while
salt water contains large empty spaces. Or is it
because the sea is purer ? For there is no earth in
it and the sand being heavy lies at the bottom. But
fresh water is earthy. And the earth moving in the
middle of it is quickly stirred into mud.

Why is the sea more transparent in the north than 9
in the south ? Is it because the sea has colour in a
calm ? For there is a greasy element in brackish
liquid. There is evidence for this ; for in the warm
weather oil is exuded. So, when the sea is calm and
warmer, juice of this kind rises to the surface owing
to its lightness. This is less true in the north because
of the cold. For water is more easily transparent
than oil ; for oil has colour, but water appearing
colourless gives a clearer picture.

Why do those who wash in the sea get dry more 10
quickly, seeing that it is heavier than fresh water ?
Is it because the sea is denser and earthy ? So as it
contains but little moisture it dries more quickly.

Why do waves imply wind ? Is it because they 11
prove that the wind is coming ? For wind is a thrusting together of the air. Does wind arise because the
air is continually being thrust forward ? But the
wind thrusts the air forward when it is not yet blowing continuously, but is only beginning to do so. So
the first breath so to speak dies away, but it has
thrust forward another breath and driven on another
mass of air and then died away. So that it is clear,
when what is thrust forward is present, that which
sets it moving will also follow ; for it causes this
effect when it begins to blow.

Διὰ τί τὸ κῦμα προεκπίπτει τοῦ πνεύματος; ἢ 12
ὅτι οὐχ ἅμα παύεται τὸ πνεῦμα [τὸ] πνέον καὶ ἡ
θάλαττα κυμαίνουσα, ἀλλ᾽ ὕστερον ἡ θάλαττα;
933 a ἐνδέχεται γὰρ τὸ κινῆσαν πνεῦμα φθαρῆναι πρὸ τοῦ
γενέσθαι αἰσθητόν. ὥστε οὐ πρότερον τὸ κῦμα
πνεύματος, ἀλλὰ τὸ μὲν λανθάνει, τὸ δὲ οὔ. ἢ οὐχὶ
τὰ πνεύματα ἅμα πανταχοῦ πνεῖ, ἀλλ᾽ ὅθεν ἡ ἀρχὴ
5 πρότερον; ἅμα δὲ πνεῖ καὶ τὴν πλησίον θάλατταν
κινεῖ, αὕτη δὲ τὴν ἐχομένην· καὶ οὕτως ἂν ἐνδέχοιτο
πρότερον τὸ κῦμα ἐκπίπτειν. ὑπὸ γὰρ τῆς θαλάσσης καὶ οὐχ ὑπὸ τοῦ πνεύματος ἡ κίνησις, ἡ θάττων
τοῦ ἀέρος, ἡ τῆς θαλάττης.

Διὰ τί ἐν τῇ θαλάττῃ μᾶλλον νεῖν δύνανται ἢ ἐν 13
10 τοῖς ποταμοῖς; ἢ ὅτι ὁ νέων ἀεὶ ἐπιστηριζόμενος
ἐν τῷ ὕδατι νεῖ, ἐν δὲ τῷ σωματωδεστέρῳ μᾶλλον
ἀποστηρίζεσθαι δυνάμεθα, σωματωδέστερον δέ ἐστι
τὸ θαλάττιον ὕδωρ τοῦ ποταμίου· παχύτερον γάρ
ἐστι καὶ μᾶλλον ἀντερείδειν δυνάμενον.

Διὰ τί ποτε ἐν τῇ θαλάττῃ πλείω χρόνον δια- 14
15 τελεῖν δύνανται ἢ ἐν τῷ ποταμῷ; ἢ διότι τὸ
ποτάμιον ὕδωρ λεπτόν ἐστιν; μᾶλλον οὖν παρ-
εισδυόμενον πνίγει.

Διὰ τί ἡ μὲν θάλαττα κάεται, τὸ δὲ ὕδωρ οὔ; 15
ἢ κάεται μὲν κἀκεῖνο, ἡ δὲ θάλαττα ἧττον σβέννυσι
τὸ πῦρ διὰ τὸ λιπαρωτέρα εἶναι; σημεῖον δὲ ὅτι
20 λιπαρωτέρα· ἀπὸ γὰρ τῶν ἁλῶν ἔλαιον ἀφαιρεῖται.
ἢ καὶ ἧττον δύνανται οἱ πόροι ἁρμόττειν τῷ πυρὶ
διὰ τὸ παχύτεροι εἶναι, καὶ μᾶλλόν γε δή, ἅτε καὶ
τῶν ἁλῶν ἐνυπαρχόντων; ὥσπερ οὖν τὸ ξηρὸν τοῦ

---

[a] Presumably Aristotle only means that sea-water burns in
the sense that it does not easily extinguish fire.

Why does the wave break before the wind reaches 12
it ? Is it because the wind which is blowing and
the rough sea do not stop simultaneously, but the
sea dies down afterwards ? Possibly the wind which
produced the movement dies down before it is felt.
So that the wave does not come before the wind, but
the latter is not noticed, while the former is. Or is
it true that the wind does not blow simultaneously in
all places, but that it blows earlier at its point of origin ? But it blows and ruffles the sea in its neighbourhood at the same time, and this ruffles the sea next
to it ; in this way it would be possible for the wave
to break in front of the wind. For the movement is due
to the sea and not to the wind, being the movement
of the sea which travels faster than that of the air.

Why is it easier to swim in the sea than in rivers ? 13
Is it because the swimmer swims by continually
supporting himself against the water, and we can
gain more support in water which contains more solid
matter ? For sea-water contains more solid matter
than river-water. For it is denser and more capable
of offering resistance.

Why can one spend longer time in the sea than in 14
the river ? Is it because river-water is rare ? Hence
it penetrates more easily into the body and produces
suffocation.

Why is it that sea-water burns,[a] whereas river-water 15
does not ? Or does the latter also burn, but the sea
is less apt to quench the fire because it is oily ? We
have proof that it is more oily ; for oil is extracted
from sea-salt. Or can the passages in sea-water less
easily adjust themselves to the fire, because they are
thicker, and all the more is this true because salt is
present ? So just as the dry is less easily quenched

933 a

ὑγροῦ ἧττον σβεστικόν, καὶ τὸ ξηρὸν μᾶλλον κατὰ
λόγον καυστικόν ἐστιν καὶ ἕτερον ἑτέρου μᾶλλον,
25 τῷ ἐγγυτέρω τοῦ θερμοῦ εἶναι, τὸ ξηρότερον δὲ τῇ
θαλάττῃ· ἄμφω δὲ ταῦτα μᾶλλον ὑπάρχει.

Διὰ τί ἀπὸ μὲν τῆς θαλάττης οὐκ ἀποπνεῖ ἔωθεν 16
ψυχρόν, ἀπὸ δὲ τῶν ποταμῶν; ἢ ὅτι ἡ μὲν θάλαττά ἐστιν ἐν ἀναπεπταμένοις τόποις, οἱ δὲ
30 ποταμοὶ ἐν στενοῖς; ἡ μὲν οὖν ἀπὸ τῆς θαλάττης
αὔρα εἰς πολὺν τόπον σκίδναται, ὥστε εἶναι ἀ-
σθενής, ἡ δὲ ἀπὸ τῶν ποταμῶν ἀθρόως φέρεται καὶ
μᾶλλον ἰσχύει, διὸ μᾶλλον εἰκότως φαίνεται ψυχρά.
ἢ οὐ τοῦτό ἐστιν αἴτιον, ἀλλ' οἱ μὲν ποταμοὶ ψυχροί
εἰσιν, ἡ δὲ θάλαττα οὔτε θερμὴ οὔτε ψυχρά; γί-
35 νεται δὲ ἡ αὔρα καὶ ἡ ἀναπνοὴ θερμαινομένων ἢ
ψυχομένων τῶν ὑγρῶν· ὁπότερον γὰρ ἂν τούτων
πάσχῃ, ἐξαεροῦται, ἐξαερουμένου δὲ τοῦ ὕδατος ὁ
ἀὴρ ὁ γινόμενος φέρεται, ὅ ἐστιν αὔρα. τὸ μὲν οὖν
ἀπὸ τῶν ψυχρῶν ψυχρὸν εἰκότως ἀποπνεῖ, τὸ δὲ
40 ἀπὸ τῶν σφόδρα θερμῶν ἀποπνέον ψύχεται καὶ
γίνεται ψυχρόν. τοὺς μὲν οὖν ποταμοὺς ψυχροὺς
933 b ἅπαντας εὕροι τις ἄν, ἡ δὲ θάλαττα οὔτε ψυχρὰ
οὔτε θερμὴ σφόδρα ἐστίν. οὔτε οὖν τὸ ἀποπνέον
ψυχρὸν ἀπ' αὐτῆς ἐστί, διὰ τὸ μὴ ψυχρὰν εἶναι,
οὔτε ψύχεται ταχύ, διὰ τὸ μὴ θερμὴν εἶναι σφόδρα.

5 Διὰ τί ἐν τοῖς μείζοσι πελάγεσι βραδύτερον καθ- 17
ίσταται κύματα ἢ ἐν τοῖς βραχέσιν; ἢ ὅτι ἐκ τῆς
πολλῆς κινήσεως βραδύτερον καθίσταται πᾶν ἢ ἐκ
τῆς ὀλίγης; ἐν δὲ τοῖς μεγάλοις πελάγεσι πλείων
ἡ ἄμπωτις γίνεται ἢ ἐν τοῖς βραχέσιν. οὐθὲν οὖν
10 ἄλογον τὸ πλεῖον βραδύτερον καθίστασθαι.

Διὰ τί τὸ ἁλμυρὸν ὕδωρ ψυχρὸν μὲν οὐ πότιμον, 18

24

than the wet, and the dry is more easily burned, so the drier a thing is the more easily it is burned, because it is more allied to the hot, but the drier water is that in the sea ; but both these qualities (heat and dryness) are more present in the sea.

Why is it that the wind blowing from the sea in the 16 morning is not cold, but from the river it is ? Is it because the sea is in exposed places, but rivers are in enclosed country ? Consequently the breeze from the sea is scattered over a wide area, so that it is weak, whereas the breeze from the rivers travels with concentrated force and so is stronger, so that naturally it seems colder. Or is this not the reason, but is it because rivers are cold, whereas the sea is neither hot nor cold ? Now breezes and exhalations arise from wet bodies when these are growing either hot or cold ; whichever of these phenomena is taking place, there is evaporation, and when evaporation of water occurs the air which is caused travels, and this constitutes a breeze. What, then, arises from cold water naturally blows cold, and that from very hot water cools and becomes cold. Now one would find that all rivers are cold, but the sea is neither cold nor very hot. So the breeze blowing from it is not cold because it is not itself cold, nor does it cool quickly because it is not very hot.

Why do the waves subside more slowly in wider, 17 open seas than in shallow ones ? Is it because everything subsides more slowly after violent movement than after slight movement ? So in wide, open seas the tide is greater than it is in shallow seas. There is, therefore, nothing surprising in the fact that the larger mass of water subsides more slowly.

Why is salt water not drinkable when it is cold, 18

θερμαινόμενον δὲ μᾶλλον γίνεται πότιμον, καὶ
θερμὸν δὲ ὂν καὶ ἀποψυχόμενον; ἢ διότι εἰς τὸ
ἐναντίον ἀπὸ τοῦ ἐναντίου πέφυκεν μεταβάλλειν;
15 ἔστι δὲ τὸ πότιμον τῷ ἁλμυρῷ ἀντικείμενον· καὶ
θερμαινομένου μὲν ἀφέψεται τὸ ἁλμυρόν, ψυχομένου δὲ ὑφίσταται.

Διὰ τί τὰ πρὸς τῇ θαλάττῃ ὡς ἐπὶ τὸ πολὺ 19
ὕδατα γλυκέα [ὕδατα] ἀλλ' οὐχ ἁλμυρά; ἢ διὰ τὸ
ποτιμώτερα διηθούμενα γίνεσθαι; διηθεῖται δὲ τὸ
20 ἐγγύτερον τῆς θαλάττης μᾶλλον.

Διὰ τί τὸ ἁλμυρὸν ὕδωρ οὐκ ἀπόρρυτόν ἐστιν; 20
ἢ διότι τὸ μὲν βαρὺ στάσιμον; τὸ δὲ ἁλμυρὸν
βαρύ· διὸ καὶ τὰ θερμὰ μόνα τῶν ἁλμυρῶν
ὑδάτων ἀπόρρυτά ἐστιν. ἔχει γὰρ κουφότητα
25 ἐν αὑτοῖς, ἢ κρατεῖ τῆς κατὰ τὴν ἁλμυρίδα
βαρύτητος· τὸ γὰρ θερμὸν κουφότερόν ἐστιν.
ἔτι τὰ μὲν ἀπόρρυτα διηθεῖται διὰ τῆς γῆς·
ἠθουμένων δὲ ἀεὶ μάλιστα ὑφίσταται τὸ παχύτατον καὶ βαρύτατον, ἐκκρίνεται δὲ τὸ κοῦφον
καὶ καθαρόν· ἔστι γὰρ τὸ μὲν ἁλμυρὸν βαρύ, τὸ
δὲ γλυκὺ κοῦφον. διόπερ ἐστὶ γλυκέα τὰ ἀπόρ-
30 ρυτα. τὸ δ' αὐτὸ αἴτιόν ἐστι καὶ διὰ τί τὸ
ἁλμυρὸν ὕδωρ κινούμενον καὶ μεταβάλλον γλυκύτερον γίνεται· κουφότερον γὰρ καὶ ἀσθενέστερον διὰ
τὴν κίνησιν γίνεται.

Διὰ τί ἐν τῇ Λιβύῃ ἐὰν ὀρύξῃ τις παρὰ τὴν 21
θάλατταν, τὸ πρῶτον πότιμον, εἶθ' ἁλμυρὸν γίνεται
35 ταχύ, ἐν δὲ τοῖς ἄλλοις τόποις ἧττον ποιεῖ τοῦτο;
πότερον ὅτι τὸ μὲν πρῶτον τὸ ὑπάρχον ὕδωρ ἐν τῷ
τόπῳ καὶ τὸ πεπεμμένον ὑπὸ τῆς γῆς ἐστιν, ὅταν
δὲ χρονισθῇ, ἡ θάλαττα προσδιηθουμένη διὰ τὸ
πρόσφατον εἶναι ποιεῖ ἁλμυρώτερον; ἐν δὲ τοῖς

but more drinkable when it is heated, when it is hot and when it is cooling ? Is it because it is natural for it to change from one extreme to the other ? Now the drinkable is the opposite of the briny ; and the brine is boiled out when it is heated, but is precipitated when it grows cold.

Why is it that, generally speaking, water near the 19 sea is sweet and not brackish ? Is it because it becomes more drinkable through percolation? And that which is near the sea percolates more.

Why does not salt water flow easily ? Is it because 20 what is heavy tends to be stationary ? Now salt water is heavy ; so that salt water only flows easily when it is hot. For hot things contain a lightness in themselves, which masters the heaviness due to the salt ; for what is hot is lighter. Moreover, water which flows easily percolates through the earth ; and, as it percolates, the densest and heaviest part remains behind, while the light and pure part is separated. For salt water is heavy and fresh water light. This is why water which flows easily is fresh. The same cause explains why salt water becomes sweeter by moving and changing its position ; for it becomes lighter and less strong because of the movement.

Why is it in Libya, if one digs by the seashore, 21 the water one comes to first is drinkable, but soon becomes brackish, whereas in other places it becomes less so ? Is it because at first the water is what was there beforehand and has been concocted by the earth, but, as time goes on, the sea percolates and makes it more salt because it is new ? But in other

933 b

ἄλλοις ἢ οὐκ ἔχει ἢ πολὺ ὕδωρ διὰ τὸ μὴ ξηραίνε-
40 σθαι τὸν τόπον.

934 a Διὰ τί τοὺς ἅλας θᾶττον τήκει τὸ ἁλμυρὸν ὕδωρ 22
ἢ τὸ πότιμον; ἢ διότι τὸ μὲν τήκεσθαί ἐστι τὸ ὑπὸ
τοῦ ὑγροῦ ἢ θερμοῦ εἰσιόντος διαιρεῖσθαι, ὥστε
ὑγρὸν εἶναι; οὐ τήκει δὲ ἢ τὰ ὅλως μὴ δυνάμενα
5 εἰσιέναι, ἢ τὰ οὕτως ὥστε μὴ θιγγάνειν. μόλις δὲ
τήκει τὰ ῥᾳδίως διεξιόντα· τὰ δ᾽ ἐπιόντα βιαζόμενα,
ταῦτα τάχιστα διαιρεῖ. οὐκ εἰσέρχεται δὲ τὰ λίαν
μεγαλομερῆ· ὑπερέχει γὰρ τῶν πόρων. τὰ δὲ
μικρομερέστερα διέρχεται οὐ ψαυόμενα. ἔστι δὲ τὸ
μὲν πότιμον λεπτόν, τὸ δὲ ἁλμυρὸν παχύτερον, ὥστε
10 τὸ μὲν ῥᾳδίως διὰ λεπτότητα διαδῦνον μόλις τήκει,
τὸ δὲ εἰσέρχεται μέν, ἧττον δὲ διὰ τὸ μεγαλο-
μερέστερον εἶναι διαρρεῖ,[1] καὶ βιάζεται θᾶττον.

Διὰ τί τὸ ὕδωρ ἧττον φαίνεται λευκόν, ἐὰν 23
κινῆται, οἷον καὶ ἡ φρίκη; διὸ καὶ Ὅμηρος
15 ἀρχομένου φησὶ τοῦ πνεύματος "μελάνει δέ τε
πόντος ὑπ᾽ αὐτοῦ." ἢ διὰ δύο αἰτίας, ἐγγύθεν μὲν
τῆς ὄψεως οὔσης, διὰ τὸ διιέναι τὴν ὄψιν μᾶλλον
ἠρεμοῦντος, κινουμένου δὲ μὴ εὐθυπορεῖν· τὸ δὲ
διαφανὲς λευκὸν φαίνεται. δι᾽ οὗ γὰρ μὴ διέρχεται
20 ἡ ὄψις, μέλαν φησὶν εἶναι. διὸ καὶ ὁ ἀὴρ πόρρωθεν
μέλας φαίνεται, ὁ δὲ ἐγγὺς λευκός, καὶ θαλάττης
τὸ μὲν ἐγγὺς λευκόν, τὸ δὲ πόρρωθεν κυανοῦν καὶ
μέλαν. πόρρωθεν δέ, κινουμένης πως τῆς ὄψεως,

---

[1] διαρρεῖ Forster, διαιρεῖ Ruelle.

[a] This translation is dubious, and the sentence does not
seem to be to the point.

places either there is no water or much, because the place is not dried.[a]

Why does salt water dissolve salt more quickly 22 than fresh water ? Is it because melting consists of disintegration due to the entrance of either moisture or heat, so that it liquefies ? Substances which cannot penetrate at all do not cause melting, nor do those which are such that they cannot touch the substance. Substances which pass through easily scarcely produce any melting ; but those which make the most violent attack, produce the most rapid disintegration. Substances with large particles do not penetrate, for they are too big for the passages ; those with smaller parts pass through without touching. Now fresh water is rare, but salt water is denser, so that the former passing through easily owing to its lightness melts very little, while the latter can penetrate, but owing to the size of its parts flows through less easily, and so more readily forces its way.

Why does water appear less light in colour, if it is 23 set in motion, as, for instance, a ripple ? This is why Homer says when the wind arises " The sea is made black by it."[b] Is it due to two causes ; first because, when the sight is near by, it can penetrate more easily when it is at rest, but does not travel on a straight path, when it is moving, and the transparent seems light in colour ? That through which the sight does not pass Homer declares to be black. So the air from a distance seems black, but white from near by ; the sea also from near by seems white, but dark blue or black from a distance. Secondly, from a distance when the sight is moving in any way,

[b] *Iliad*, vii. 64.

934 a

καὶ τῷ διανακλᾶσθαι ἀθρόον τὴν ὄψιν, ἐὰν ἠρεμῇ,
πρὸς τὸ φῶς, κινουμένου δὲ μὴ δύνασθαι.

25 Διὰ τί ἐν τοῖς βαθέσι πελάγεσι τὸ κῦμα οὐκ 24
ἐπιγελᾷ, ἀλλ' ἐν τοῖς μικροῖς; πότερον ὅτι τὸ
μικρὸν φερόμενον ὕδωρ διαιρεῖται ὑπὸ τοῦ ἀέρος
μᾶλλον ἢ τὸ πολύ; διὸ θραύεται πατάξαν μᾶλλον.
ἐν μὲν οὖν τῷ βαθεῖ πολὺ τὸ κινούμενον, ἐν δὲ τῷ
βραχεῖ ὀλίγον.

30 Διὰ τί οἱ πρὸς νότον τόποι ἁλυκώτερα τὰ ὕδατα 25
ἔχουσιν; ἢ διὰ τὸ τὴν θάλατταν ὑπὸ νότου ὠθεῖσθαι ὑπὸ τὴν γῆν κεράννυται;

Διὰ τί τῶν ὑδάτων τὸ ἁλμυρὸν ἐπὶ τῷ γλυκεῖ 26
οἴνῳ μᾶλλον ἐπιπολάζει ἢ ἐπὶ τῷ αὐστηρῷ;
35 πότερον ὅτι μᾶλλον ἔχει γῆν ὁ γλυκύς, ὥσπερ
ἡ ἀσταφίς; ἢ ὅτι βαρύτερος καὶ γλισχρότερος ὁ
γλυκύς, ὥσθ' ἧττον μίγνυται, μὴ μιγνύμενος δὲ
ἐφίσταται.

Διὰ τί ὅλως ἐφίσταται γεῶδες ὄν; ἡ γὰρ οἰκεία 27
φορὰ κάτω. πότερον ὅτι μᾶλλον ἔχει γῆν ὁ
934 b γλυκύς; ἢ διὰ τὴν θερμότητα, καθάπερ οἱ ἅλες;
ὅμοιον γὰρ ἐξανθήματι. ἢ δι' ἄλλην αἰτίαν; εἰ
γὰρ οὐ διὰ τοῦτο καὶ ἐπὶ τῷ γλυκεῖ μᾶλλον, οὐκ
ἄλογον· θερμότατος γάρ.

Διὰ τί τὰ κύματα πρότερον φοιτᾷ ἐνίοτε τῶν 28
5 ἀνέμων; ἢ διότι καὶ τελευτᾷ ὕστερον; τὸ γὰρ
πρῶτον πνεῦμα ὡσανεὶ προδιαλύεται τοῦ ὠσθέντος
κύματος· ἀφικνεῖται δὲ οὐκ αὐτὸ τὸ πρῶτον ὠσθέν,
ἀλλ' ἀεὶ ἡ ὦσις γίνεται τοῦ ἐχομένου.

Διὰ τί αἱ κυματωδέστεραι γαῖ στερραὶ γίνονται 29

ᵃ Quite out of place here. The sentence must have come
from the previous problem.

the sight is refracted in a mass towards the light if the water is still, but this is impossible when the water is moving.

Why does not the wave make ripples in deep water, 24 while it does in shallow ? Is it because when a small body of water is travelling it is more easily broken up by the air than a large body ? Consequently as it strikes it more it is broken up. But in deep water the mass moved is large, but in shallow water small.

Why do places which face the south have more 25 brackish water ? Is it because the sea is driven beneath the earth by the south wind, and so becomes mixed ?

Why does salt water rest on the surface of sweet 26 wine, rather than of dry wine ? Is it because sweet wine, such as raisin wine, contains more earth ? Or is it because sweet wine is heavier and more viscous, so that the salt does not mix readily, and as it does not mix remains on the surface ?

Why, speaking generally, does salt, which is an 27 earthy substance, remain on the surface ? For its natural tendency is downwards. (Is it because the sweet contains more earth ?) [a] Is it owing to the heat, as in the case of salt ? For it is like an efflorescence. Or is it for another reason ? It is not unreasonable if this is not the reason why it floats more on sweet wine; for this is the warmest wine.

Why do waves sometimes begin to travel before the 28 wind reaches them ? Is it for the same reason that they die down after the wind ? For the first wind is, so to speak, dispersed before the wave which it has driven ; and it is not the wave which is first driven which comes, but the thrust continually affects the water which is next to it.

Why does ground which is more subject to the 29 breaking of the waves often become solid—as solid as

934 b

10 πολλάκις οὕτως σφόδρα ὥσπερ ἠδαφισμέναι; καὶ
ἡ μὲν κυματώδης γῆ στερεά, ἡ δὲ ἄπωθεν χαῦνος.
ἢ διότι ἡ μικρὰ ἄμμος οὐ πόρρωθεν ἐκβάλλεται ὑπὸ
τοῦ κύματος, ἀλλὰ ἡ μείζων μᾶλλον; ὥσπερ καὶ
τῇ χειρὶ βάλλειν πόρρω οὐ τὸ ἐλάχιστον μάλιστα
15 δυνατόν. ἔπειτα πολλῶν κυκωμένων τὰ ἐλάχιστα
ἐμπίπτοντα πυκνοῖ. ἡ δὲ τοῦ κύματος λωφῶντος
κίνησις ἐδαφίζει, κινεῖ δὲ οὐκέτι. διὰ μὲν οὖν τὸ
μὴ τὰ μικρότατα πόρρω δύνασθαι πηδᾶν, ἐκ μικρῶν
σφόδρα συντέθειται· διὰ δὲ τὸ πολλάκις κινεῖσθαι
συνεχὲς γίνεται πιπτούσης ἄμμου, ἕως ἂν συν-
20 αρμόσῃ· διὰ δὲ τὸ κῦμα τὸ τελευταῖον ἐδαφίζεται,
καὶ τὸ ἠρέμα ὑγρὸν συγκολλᾷ. ἡ δὲ πόρρω ξηρά
τε οὖσα διίσταται, καὶ ἐκ μειζόνων ἐστὶ λιθιδίων
καὶ ἀνεδάφιστος.

Διὰ τί τῆς θαλάσσης τὰ ἄνω τῶν ἐν τῷ βάθει 3
ἁλμυρώτερα καὶ θερμότερα; ὁμοίως δὲ καὶ ἐν τοῖς
25 φρέασι τοῖς ποτίμοις τὸ ἐπιπολῆς ἁλμυρώτερον τοῦ
εἰς βάθος· καίτοι ἔδει τὸ κατωτέρω· βαρύτερον γὰρ
τὸ ἁλμυρόν. ἢ διότι ὁ ἥλιος καὶ ὁ ἀὴρ ἀνάγει ἀεὶ
τὸ ἐλαφρότατον ἀπὸ τῶν ὑγρῶν; τὸ δὲ ποτιμώ-
τερον ἀεὶ κουφότερον, μᾶλλον δὲ ἀπάγει ἀπὸ τῶν
30 ἐγγυτέρων τόπων. ὥστε καὶ τῆς θαλάττης ἀπὸ
τῶν ἐπιπολῆς καὶ τῶν ποτίμων ἀνάγκη τὸ λειπό-
μενον ἁλμυρώτερον εἶναι, ἀφ' ὧν ἀνῆκται, ἢ ἀφ'
ὧν μηθὲν ἢ ἔλαττον.[1] διὰ τοῦτο δὲ καὶ θερμότερα
τὰ ἄνω· τὸ γὰρ ἁλμυρὸν θερμότερον τοῦ ποτίμου.
διὸ καὶ φασί τινες τῶν ἡρακλειτιζόντων ἐκ μὲν

---

[1] τὸ γλυκύ Ruelle.

if it were beaten for levelling ? And why is ground where the waves break hard, whereas farther away it is spongy ? Is it because small grains of sand are not thrown to any distance by the waves, but the larger ones are, just as it is impossible to throw what is very small to any distance with the hand ? So when many particles are mixed together the smallest fall through and become solid. Now the movement of the receding wave makes these level, but no longer shifts them. Owing to the fact that the smallest grains cannot leap very far, there is a compact mass of small grains ; and because it is in frequent motion, it becomes continuous as the sand falls, until each grain fits into its place ; and it is levelled by the last wave, and the slight moisture welds it together. But the ground farther away being dry breaks up, and consists of larger grains and is not flattened out.

Why are the upper parts of the sea more salt and 30 warmer than the parts at the bottom ? In the same way in fresh-water wells, the surface is more salt than the water below. Yet the water below ought to be more salt ; for salt water is heavier. Is it because the sun and the air are always drawing up the lightest part of the liquid ? Now the fresher water is always lighter, and the sun and the air exercise more attraction over parts nearer to them. So that both in the sea and in fresh water that which remains on the surface from which the attraction takes place, must be more salt than that from which little or nothing has been drawn. For the same reason the upper parts must be warmer ; for the salt is warmer than the fresh. This is why some of the followers of Heracleitus say that stones and earth

934 b

35 τοῦ ποτίμου ξηραινομένου καὶ πηγνυμένου λίθους
γίνεσθαι καὶ γῆν, ἐκ δὲ τῆς θαλάττης τὸν ἥλιον
ἀναθυμιᾶσθαι.

Διὰ τί τῆς θαλάττης τὰ πρὸς τῇ γῇ γλυκύτερά 31
ἐστιν; ἢ διότι ἐν τῇ κινήσει μᾶλλόν ἐστιν; κινούμενον δὲ τὸ ἁλμυρὸν γλυκύτερον γίνεται. ἢ ὅτι
935 a καὶ ἐν τῷ βάθει ἁλμυρώτερόν ἐστι τὸ ὕδωρ, τὰ δὲ
πρὸς τῇ γῇ ἧττόν ἐστι βαθέα. διὸ καὶ τἀγχιβαθῆ
ἁλμυρά ἐστι καὶ οὐχ ὁμοίως γλυκέα. τούτου δ'
αἴτιον, ὅτι βαρὺ ὂν τὸ ἁλμυρὸν φέρεται μᾶλλον εἰς
βάθος.

5 Διὰ τί ἡ θάλαττα μόνον τῶν ὑδάτων κάεται, τὰ 32
δὲ πότιμα καὶ ποτάμια οὔ; πότερον ὅτι γῆν
πολλὴν ἔχει; δηλοῦσι δὲ οἱ ἅλες. ἢ διότι λιπαρά;
δηλοῖ δὲ τὸ ἐν τοῖς ἅλασιν ὑφιστάμενον ἔλαιον.

Διὰ τί ἐν ταῖς λίμναις ἄμμος οὐ γίνεται ἢ ἧττον 33
10 ἢ ἐν τῇ θαλάττῃ καὶ τοῖς ποταμοῖς; ἢ ὅτι ἐν τῇ
θαλάττῃ πέτραι γίνονται, καὶ ἡ γῆ ἐκκέκαυται
μάλιστα; ἡ δὲ ἄμμος ἐστὶ πέτρα ἐψηγμένη εἰς
μικρὰ καὶ ἐλάχιστα μόρια. ψύχεται δὲ διὰ τὴν
πληγὴν τῶν κυμάτων. ἐν δὲ ταῖς λίμναις οὐ
γίνονται ὁμοίως πέτραι καθαραί, οὐδὲ θραύονται
15 ὁμοίως διὰ τὸ μὴ γίνεσθαι κύματα ὁμοίως. ἐν δὲ
τοῖς ποταμοῖς μᾶλλον, ὅτι τὴν μὲν γῆν κατα-
φέρουσιν, τὰς δὲ πέτρας τῇ πληγῇ θραύουσιν.

Διὰ τί, ὅταν ἡ λίμνη ἢ κοπάσῃ ἢ ξηρὰ γένηται, 34
ἀποκάεται ὁ σῖτος ἐν τῷ πεδίῳ μᾶλλον; πότερον
20 ὅτι τὸ ὑγρὸν τὸ ἐν τῇ λίμνῃ ἀπατμίζον τῇ ἀτμίδι
θερμαίνει τὸν ἀέρα, ὥστε ἐλάττους καὶ ἀσθενεστέρους ποιεῖ τοὺς πάγους ἢ ἐν τοῖς κοίλοις καὶ
προσελώδεσι τόποις; ἢ ἐκ τῆς γῆς, ὥσπερ λέ-

are formed by the drying and solidification of fresh water, and that the sun produces evaporation from the sea.

Why are the parts of the sea which are nearer the 31 land sweeter ? Is it because they are more in motion ? And when the salt element moves it becomes sweeter. Or is it because the water down below is more salt, and that near the land is less deep ? So also deep places near the shore are salt and not so sweet. This is due to the fact that the salt element being heavier is carried down to the depths.

[a] Why is sea-water the only kind of water which 32 burns, whereas fresh water and river-water do not ? Is it because it contains much earth ? Salt proves this. Or is it because it is oily ? The sediment of oil which is found in salt proves its existence.

Why is there no sand in lakes or at any rate less 33 than in the sea or in rivers ? Is it because there are rocks in the sea, and the earth has been extracted from them by burning ? But sand is rock ground into small and tiny particles. It is ground by the striking of the waves. But in lakes there are not bare rocks of this kind, nor are they broken up in the same way, because there are not waves to the same extent. But in rivers there is more sand because they carry down the earth with them, and break up the rocks by striking them.

Why is it that when a lake becomes exhausted or 34 dry the corn in the adjoining plain is more likely to be frost-bitten ? Is it because the moisture which evaporates in the lake warms the air by evaporation, so that it makes frosts less and weaker than in hollow and marshy spots ? Or does the cold arise, as men

[a] *Cf.* Problem 15.

935 a

γεται, τὰ ψύχη ἄρχεται καὶ λανθάνει εἰσδυόμενα·
ξηρᾶς οὖν οὔσης τῆς λίμνης, διὰ πλείονος τόπου ἡ
25 ψυχρότης πλείων προσπίπτουσα πήγνυσι καὶ ἀπο-
κάει μᾶλλον. ἐν δὲ ταῖς τοιαύταις χώραις τὰ ψύχη
κάτωθεν γίνεται, ὥσπερ καὶ δοκεῖ. καίτοι ἡ γῆ
θερμὴ τοῦ χειμῶνος· ἀλλὰ διὰ τὸ ἔφυγρον εἶναι
κατέψυκται τὸ ἐπιπολῆς θερμὸν τὸ ἐν τῇ γῇ. τὸ
30 γὰρ ὑγρὸν οὔτε οὕτω πόρρω ἐστὶν ὥστε μὴ ψύχεσθαι, διὰ τὴν ἐνοῦσαν θερμότητα ἐν τοῖς ὑγροῖς,
οὔτε οὕτως ὀλίγον ὥστε μηθὲν ἰσχύειν, διὰ τὸ
διάβροχον εἶναι τὴν γῆν. οἷον οὖν διὰ τὴν ψύξιν
αὐτοῦ συμβαίνει ἐπὶ κρυστάλλου περιπατεῖν καὶ
οἰκεῖν.

Διὰ τί ἡ θάλαττα ἁλμυρὰ καὶ πικρά ἐστιν; ἢ 35
35 ὅτι ἐν τῇ θαλάττῃ πλείους εἰσὶν οἱ χυμοί; καὶ γὰρ
τὸ ἁλμυρὸν καὶ τὸ πικρὸν ἅμα φαίνεται.

Διὰ τί τὰ ἐν τῇ θαλάττῃ ὄστρακα καὶ λίθοι 36
στρογγύλα γίνεται; ἢ ὅτι ὁμοίως περιθραυόμενα
935 b τὰ ἔσχατα εἰς τὸ στρογγύλον σχῆμα ἔρχεται;
τούτου γὰρ τὸ ἔσχατον ὅμοιον, ἡ δὲ θάλαττα πάντη
κινοῦσα ὁμοίως περιθραύει.

Διὰ τί ἐνιαχοῦ, ἐάν τις ὀρύξῃ παρὰ τὴν θάλατταν, 37
τὸ μὲν πρῶτον πότιμόν ἐστιν ὕδωρ, εἶθ᾽ ἁλμυρὸν
5 γίνεται; ἢ ὅτι αὐτῆς ἐστι τῆς θαλάττης τῆς
διηθούσης ὑπὸ τὴν γῆν τὸ ὕδωρ; εἰκότως οὖν
τὸ πρῶτόν ἐστι γλυκύ· ἐλαφρότερον γάρ ἐστι τὸ
γλυκὺ τοῦ ἁλυκοῦ, καὶ ἡ θάλαττα ἔχει τι τοῦ
γλυκέος, ὃ μιχθὲν τῇ γῇ μᾶλλον ἐπιπολάζει. τὸ
δὲ ἁλυκὸν διὰ τὸ βάρος καὶ διὰ τὸ τμητικὸν εἶναι
10 κάτω φέρεται. εἴτε οὖν οὕτως εἴτε κατὰ τὰς
φλέβας ἐκ τῆς ἠπείρου ῥεῖ ἐπὶ τὴν θάλατταν τὸ
γλυκὺ ὕδωρ, εἰκότως ἂν ἐπιπολῆς εἴη τῆς θαλάττης,

36

say, from the earth and penetrate without being noticed ? So when the lake is dry, greater cold spreads over a wider area and hardens and freezes more easily. In such places the cold comes from below as is popularly believed. Yet the ground is warm in winter ; but owing to the moisture the superficial heat on the ground is chilled. For the moisture is neither far enough away to prevent its becoming cold, owing to the warmth which exists in all liquids, nor is it so slight as to have no effect, because the earth is soaked. For instance it is due to the cold that one can walk and dwell upon ice.

Why is the sea salt and bitter ? Is it because there 35 are more juices in the sea ? For saltness and bitterness go together.

Why do shells and stones become round in the sea ? 36 Is it because their extremities being broken off equally assume a round shape ? For this is the only shape in which the outer surface is the same all over and the sea moving objects in every direction breaks off the extremities equally all round.

Why is it that in some places, if one digs near the 37 sea, the water is at first fresh, and then becomes salt ? Is it because the water consists of the sea itself which percolates beneath the earth ? Naturally, therefore, the water on top is sweet ; for sweet water is lighter than salt water, and the sea contains some element of sweetness, which when mixed with earth comes more to the surface. But the salt element, owing to its weight and because it is easily penetrated, is carried downwards. Either, then, in this way or through the veins (in the earth) the sweet water flows from the land into the sea, so that naturally it would rest on the surface of the sea, which is mingled with it. But

ἢ μίγνυται αὐτῇ. ἀνοιχθέντων δὲ τῶν πόρων,
ὕστερον διὰ πλῆθος τὸ ἁλυκὸν κρατοῦν τοιοῦτο πᾶν
ποιεῖ. συμβαίνει γὰρ πεφραγμένων τῶν ἄνω πόρων
15 ἄλλην ὁδὸν ζητεῖν τὸ ἐπιρρέον, ἀνοιχθέντων δὲ
ἐνταῦθα πᾶν φέρεσθαι, καθάπερ ἐπὶ τῶν τοῦ
σώματος φλεβῶν.

Διὰ τί ἡ θάλαττα οὖσα βαρυτέρα τοῦ ποτίμου 38
ὕδατος μᾶλλόν ἐστιν εὐδίοπτος; πότερον ὅτι
λιπαρωτέρα; τὸ δὲ ἔλαιον ἐπιχυθὲν ποιεῖ μᾶλλον
20 εὐδίοπτον. ἔχουσα δὲ ἐν αὑτῇ λίπος εἰκότως
μᾶλλον εὐδίοπτός ἐστιν. ἢ οὐχ ἅπαν τὸ ἐλαφρότερον καὶ εὐδιοπτότερον; αὐτὸ γὰρ τὸ ἔλαιον
ἐλαφρότερον τοῦ ὕδατος, εὐδιοπτότερον δὲ οὔ. ἢ
οὐκ εὐδιοπτότερόν ἐστιν, ἀλλὰ φαίνεται; τὸ γὰρ
πότιμον ὕδωρ ἀπὸ τῆς γῆς ἢ ἀπὸ ρευμάτων ἐστίν,
25 ἡ δὲ πηγὴ συναφίησι μετὰ τοῦ ὕδατος καὶ γῆν,
ὥστε τῷ μὴ καθαρὰ εἶναι τὰ ρεύματα συγκατάγει
τὴν γῆν καὶ ἰλύν. αὕτη οὖν ἐστιν ἡ αἰτία τοῦ
ἧττον εἶναι εὐδίοπτον.

Διὰ τί οἱ νέοντες ἐν τῇ θαλάττῃ λαπαροὶ γίνονται; 39
εἰ γὰρ ὅτι πονοῦσι, καὶ οἱ τροχιζόμενοι ἰσχυρὸν
30 πονοῦσι πόνον καὶ οὐ λαπάττονται. ἢ ὅτι οὐ πᾶς
πόνος ποιεῖ λάπαξιν, ἀλλ᾽ ὁ μὴ ποιῶν σύντηξιν; ἡ
δὲ ἐν τῇ θαλάττῃ διατριβὴ καὶ ὅλως δοκεῖ βρωτι-
κωτέρους ποιεῖν καὶ λαπαρούς· θερμή τε γάρ ἐστι
καὶ ξηρὰ ἡ ἀπ᾽ αὐτῆς ἀτμίς.

Διὰ τί Παῖσα[1] λίμνη πότιμος οὖσα πλύνει καὶ 40
35 ρύπτει τὰ ἱμάτια; πλύνει μὲν γὰρ τὸ γλυκύ,
ρύπτει δὲ τὸ πικρόν, ἅμα δὲ οὐχ οἷόν τε ἔχειν ταῦτα.

---

[1] πᾶσα Ruelle: but Th. G. renders Lacus Paesa and the
reference below to " this lake " seems to make the alteration
certain.

when the passages are opened, later on the salt element owing to its quantity overpowers the other and makes it all salt. For when the upper passages are clogged, the water flowing in must seek another path, but when they are opened, all travels by that channel, as happens with the veins of the body.

Why is the sea, seeing that it is heavier than fresh 38 water, more transparent? Is it because it is more oily? Oil poured on to water makes it more transparent. As, therefore, it has oil in it, the sea-water is naturally more transparent. Or is not everything which is lighter more transparent? For oil is lighter than water, but is not more transparent. Or is sea-water not really more transparent, but only seems to be so? For fresh water comes from the land or from streams, and the source sends out earth together with the water, so that the streams not being pure carry down earth and mud with them. This is the reason why fresh water is less transparent.

Why do those who swim in the sea have their 39 bowels opened? If it were due to exercise, then those who go in for violent running also take violent exercise, but their bowels are not opened. Is it because not every form of exercise opens the bowels, but only that which does not produce wasting? Now time spent in the sea seems to make men hungry as well as to open the bowels; for the evaporation from it is both warm and dry.

Why does Lake Paesa, of which the water is drink- 40 able, wash and scour clothes? For what is sweet washes, and what is bitter scours, and the water cannot possess both qualities at once. Or is it a fact

936 a ἢ οὐ τῷ πικρὸν εἶναι οὐθὲν ῥύπτει, ἀλλ' ἡ γλι-
σχρότης ῥυπτικόν; διὸ καὶ τὰ ἀκροκώλια καὶ ὅσα
μυξώδη τοιαῦτα, ὥστε καὶ τῶν πικρῶν ὅσα τούτου
μετέχει. ἐν δὲ τῇ λίμνῃ ταύτῃ συμβέβηκεν τοῦτο,
ὥστε τῆς νιτρώδους δυνάμεως τὸ μὲν πικρὸν
ἐκκεκαῦσθαι, ἐμμένειν δὲ τὸ λιπαρὸν καὶ γλίσχρον.
τούτῳ μὲν οὖν ῥύπτει, πλύνει δὲ τῷ ποτίμῳ αὐτῆς.

5 Διὰ τί τὸ γαληνίζον τῆς θαλάττης λευκὸν φαί- 4
νεται, τὸ δὲ κατάφορον μέλαν; ἢ ὅτι τὸ ἧττον
ὁρώμενον μελάντερον μᾶλλον φαίνεται; ἧττον δὲ
φαίνεται τὸ κινούμενον τοῦ ἠρεμοῦντος. ἢ διότι τὸ
μὲν διαφαινόμενον λευκόν, τὸ δὲ μὴ διαφαινόμενον
10 μέλαν; ἧττον δὲ διαφαίνεται τὸ κινούμενον.

that nothing cleanses by being bitter, but that it is viscosity which is the cleansing quality ? Hence it is the hooves and those parts which contain mucus, which are cleansing, so that bitter things which contain this quality are also cleansing. Now it is the case in this lake that the bitter part of the nitrous quality is burned out, and the oily and viscous element remains. By this quality it cleanses, and it washes because it is fresh water.

Why does the sea when calm seem white, while it 41 looks black while it is moving ? Is it because that which is less seen always appears darker ? Now that which is moving is less visible than that which is at rest. Or is it because the transparent is white, and the opaque black ? And what is moving is less transparent.

ΚΔ

926 a

ΟΣΑ ΠΕΡΙ ΤΑ ΘΕΡΜΑ ΥΔΑΤΑ

Διὰ τί τὸ θερμὸν ὕδωρ, ἐὰν ἐπικεχρισμένοι ὦσιν 1
ἐλαίῳ, ἧττον θερμόν ἐστι καταχεόμενον, τοῦ ἐλαίου
15 θερμοῦ ὄντος; ἢ διὰ τὸ λεαίνειν ὀλισθαίνει καὶ
ἧττον ἐνδύνει;

Διὰ τί τὰ ὕδατα ἐν τοῖς φρέασι μετὰ μεσημβρίαν 2
γίνεται τοῦ θέρους θερμά; ἢ διότι τηνικαῦτα ἤδη
κεκράτηκεν τὸ θερμὸν τὸν ἀέρα; πρὸ μεσημβρίας
δὲ τὸ θερμὸν λύει τε τὸ ψυχρὸν καὶ παύει· οὐχ ἅμα
20 δὲ πέπαυται καὶ κρατεῖ. ἀλλ᾽ ὅταν ἐπιχρονίσῃ.

Διὰ τί τὸ ὕδωρ θερμότερον ἐνίοτε τῆς φλογὸς 3
γινόμενον οὐ κατακάει τὰ ξύλα, ἡ δὲ φλὸξ κατακάει; ἢ ὅτι ἡ μὲν φλὸξ λεπτομερές, καὶ τὸ ἀπ᾽
αὐτῆς πνεῦμα, τὸ δὲ ὕδωρ μεγαλομερές, ὥστε οὐκ
25 εἰσδύεται· ἡ δὲ φλὸξ καὶ τὸ ἀπὸ τῶν ἀνθράκων
διὰ λεπτότητα εἰσιὸν διαλύει.

Διὰ τί τὸ μὲν ὕδωρ τὸ ζέον οὐ τήκει, ἡ δὲ κοιλία 4
τήκει; πότερον ὅτι τὸ μὲν θερμὸν τὸ ἐν τῇ κοιλίᾳ
εἰσέρχεται διὰ λεπτότητα, τὸ δὲ ὕδωρ οὐκ εἰσέρχεται διὰ παχύτητα; ἢ διότι καὶ τὰ ἄλλα κωλύει

42

BOOK XXIV

Problems connected with Hot Water

Why is it that if men are smeared with oil, water 1
feels less hot when poured over them, although oil
is hot ? Is it because owing to the smoothness the
water slips down and penetrates less ?

Why is it that after midday in summer the water 2
in cisterns becomes hot ? Is it because by that time
the heat has mastered the air ? Before midday the
heat is employed in thawing the cold and checking it.
But the cold does not cease at the same moment as
the heat gains the mastery, but only after some time
has elapsed.

Why does not hot water, of which the temperature 3
is sometimes higher than that of flame, scorch wood,
whereas the flame does ? Is it because flame consists
of light parts, and so does the vapour proceeding
from it, whereas water consists of large particles, so
that it does not penetrate ? But flame and the
vapour from coals penetrate because of their rarity,
and disintegrate the wood.

Why is it that boiling water does not cause melting, 4
whereas the stomach does ? Is it because the heat
in the stomach penetrates because of its rarity,
but water does not penetrate because it is dense ?
Or is it because the liquid prevents all else from

43

936 a

30 τήκεσθαι τὸ ὑγρόν; οὐθὲν γὰρ ἐν ὑγρῷ τήκεται. ἐν δὲ τῇ κοιλίᾳ τὸ ὑγρὸν εἰς τὴν κύστιν ὑπονοστοῦν οὕτω λύει.

Διὰ τί τῶν ἀγγείων ὁ πυθμὴν οὐ κάει ἐνόντος 5 τοῦ ὕδατος καὶ ζέοντος, ἀλλὰ καὶ φέρουσι τοῦ πυθμένος ἐχόμενοι, ἐξαιρεθέντος δὲ κάει; ἢ ὅτι 35 σβέννυται τὸ ἐγγινόμενον θερμὸν ἐν τῷ πυθμένι ὑπὸ τοῦ ὕδατος; διὸ καὶ οὐ τήκεται τὰ τηκτά, ἂν μὴ ψόφος ἐμπέσῃ.

Διὰ τί οὐχ ὑπερζεῖ τοῦ χειμῶνος ὁμοίως καὶ τοῦ 6 θέρους τὸ ὕδωρ, οὐ μόνον ὁμοίως θερμαινόμενον ἀλλὰ καὶ μᾶλλον, καὶ ὁμοίως θερμὸν ὂν καὶ ἔτι

936 b μᾶλλον; ἢ διότι ἡ ὑπέρζεσίς ἐστιν ἡ ἀναβολὴ τῶν πομφολύγων; τὸ μὲν οὖν ὕδωρ αὐτὸ θερμαίνεται τότε οὐθὲν ἧττον ἢ τοῦ θέρους,[1] αἱ δὲ πομφόλυγες αἴρεσθαι οὐ δύνανται ὁμοίως διὰ τὸ τὸν περιέχοντα 5 ἀέρα εἶναι ψυχρόν, ἀλλὰ ἐλάττους τε τὰ μεγέθη αἴρονται ὑπὸ τοῦ ψύχους θλιβόμεναι, καὶ δια- κόπτοντος τοῦ ἀέρος ταχὺ διαπίπτουσιν, ὥστε ἐλάττους τε τῷ ὄγκῳ καὶ τῷ πλήθει γίνονται τοῦ χειμῶνος, τοῦ δὲ θέρους τοὐναντίον. ἡ δὲ ὑπέρ- ζεσις γίνεται διὰ τὸ πλῆθος καὶ τὸ μέγεθος τοῦ ἀφροῦ.

10 Διὰ τί τὸ μὲν θερμὸν ὕδωρ ῥυτιδοῖ, τὸ δὲ πῦρ 7 θερμὸν ὂν οὔ; ἢ ὅτι τὸ μὲν πῦρ ποιεῖ πνεῦμα, ὥστε ὀγκοῖ; περιτείνεται γὰρ τὸ δέρμα. ἡ δὲ κάμψις ῥυτίς ἐστιν.

Διὰ τί τῶν ἀγγείων οἱ πυθμένες θερμαινομένου 8 τοῦ ὕδατος, ἕως ἂν ᾖ ψυχρὸν τὸ ὕδωρ, θερμότεροί 15 εἰσιν; ἢ διότι ψυχροῦ μὲν ἔτι ὄντος τοῦ ὕδατος

---

[1] θέρους Bonitz: ψύχους Ruelle.

[a] The Greek of the last sentence as it stands is untrans-

44

melting ? For nothing melts in liquid. But in the stomach the liquid sinks into the bladder, and so allows the melting to take place.

Why does not the bottom of a vessel burn when 5 there is boiling water in it, but one can hold it by the bottom and carry it, but when the water is removed it burns ? Is it because the heat engendered in the bottom is extinguished by the water ? This is why soluble substances do not melt if water is poured over them.[a]

Why does not water boil over in winter as much as 6 it does in summer, not only when it is subjected to heat for as long or even longer, but even when it is equally or more hot ? Is it because boiling over is due to the upward thrust of bubbles ? The water itself gets no less hot in winter than in summer, but the bubbles cannot rise to the same extent because the surrounding air is cold, but are smaller in size because they are compressed by the cold when they rise, and as the air breaks them up they quickly burst, so that they are less both in size and in number in the winter, but in the summer it is just the opposite. Boiling over is due to the extent and size of the froth.

Why does hot water cause wrinkles, but fire which 7 is hot does not ? Is it because fire produces a breath, so that it inflates ? For the outer covering is thus stretched, but it is the creasing of the skin that causes wrinkles.

When water is heated in a vessel why does the 8 bottom of the vessel get hotter, while the water is still cold ? Is it because, the water being still cold,

latable. The rendering here given is a translation of the Latin version of Th. G.

936 b

ἐγκατακλείεται τὸ θερμὸν καὶ ἀντιπεριίσταται εἴσω,
κωλυόμενον ἐξιέναι, ὅταν δὲ διαθερμανθῇ τὸ ἐνὸν
ὕδωρ, οὐκέτι ἀποστέγοντος ἀλλὰ διαπνέοντος καὶ
ἐλάττονος γινομένου τοῦ πυρός, ψυχρότερος γίνεται
20 ὁ πυθμήν, ὁμοίως ὥσπερ καὶ τὰ βαλανεῖα· καὶ γὰρ
ταῦτα τοῦ χειμῶνος θερμότερα ἢ τοῦ θέρους διὰ τὸ
ἐγκατακλείεσθαι τὸ θερμὸν ἐν τῷ χειμῶνι μᾶλλον
ἢ ἐν τῷ θέρει ὑπὸ τοῦ περιέχοντος ἀέρος ὄντος
ψυχροῦ.

Διὰ τί τὸ μὲν ὕδωρ ζέον οὐκ ἐκπαφλάζει, τὸ δὲ 9
ἔτνος καὶ ἡ φακῆ; καίτοι κουφότερον τὸ ὕδωρ
25 τούτων, τὰ δὲ κοῦφα ῥᾷον ῥῖψαι πόρρω. ποιεῖ δὲ
καὶ τὸ ἀργύριον ταὐτό, καὶ τοῦτο καθαιρόμενον· διὸ
οἱ ἐν τῷ ἀργυροκοπείῳ καλλύνοντες κερδαίνουσιν·
τὸ γὰρ διαρριπτούμενον συγκαλλύνοντες λαμβάνουσι τὰ λείψανα. ἢ διότι ποιεῖ μὲν τὸν ἐκ-
παφλασμὸν τὸ θερμὸν ἐξατμίζον καὶ βιαζόμενον τὰ
30 ἀντικρούοντα τῇ κατὰ φύσιν αὐτοῦ φορᾷ; τὸ μὲν
οὖν ὕδωρ διὰ κουφότητα καὶ λεπτότητα οὐκ ἀπο-
βιάζεται, ὥστε οὐκ ἀθροίζεται πολὺ θερμόν, ἀλλὰ
πρὶν ἁλισθῆναι φθάνει διακόψαν τὸ ἀεὶ προσελθόν.
τὰ δὲ ἔχοντα ἐν αὑτοῖς σῶμα, οἷον τὰ ῥοφήματα ἢ
35 ὁ ἄργυρος, διὰ βάρος τὸ σωματοειδὲς ἔχοντα πολύ,
καὶ ἀνταπωθοῦντα διὰ τὸ ἀποβιάζεσθαι βίᾳ, ἐξιόντος ἀποσφαιρίζεται ᾗ ἂν κρατήσῃ τὸ θερμόν· οὐ
γὰρ δίεισι διὰ πυκνότητα, ἀλλὰ κρατεῖ, ἕως ἂν ὑπὸ
τοῦ ἐπιρρέοντος θερμοῦ ἀπορριφθῇ. γίνεται δὲ
πληγή, οὐκ ὦσις, διὰ τὸ ταχὺ φέρεσθαι τὸ θερμὸν
κάτωθεν ἄνω.

937 a Διὰ τί τὰ μὲν ὀλίγον χρόνον ἐν τῷ θερμῷ βρεχό- 10
μενα ἀνοιδεῖ, τὰ δὲ πολὺν συμπίπτει καὶ γίνεται
ῥυσά; ἢ διότι τὸ θερμὸν ἐκ πεπηγότος ὑγρὸν

46

the heat is enclosed within and compressed, being prevented from escaping, but, when the water within grows hot all through, as the fire no longer holds the heat but escapes and becomes less, the bottom becomes cooler, just as it does in baths? They get hotter in winter than they do in summer because in the winter the heat is more confined than it is in the summer by the surrounding air which is cold.

Why does not boiling water boil over, whereas pea- 9 soup and lentil-soup does? And yet water is lighter than these and it is easier to throw light particles a long distance. Silver acts in the same way, when it is being refined; sweepers in the mint gain from this, for they sweep up what is scattered about and collect what is left. Or is it because the heat vaporizes and causes boiling over by exerting force on what opposes its own natural impetus? Water is not forced out because of its lightness and fineness, so that not much heat is collected, but before it masses together the heat which is continually passing in cuts its way through. But anything which has body, like porridge or silver, having a large solid element owing to its weight, and making a counterthrust because it is always having force applied to it, whenever the heat masters it, forms circular bubbles as it goes out; for owing to its density it cannot escape, but establishes a mastery, until it is cast out by the influx of the heat; so it is not a thrust but a blow, because the heat from below is travelling rapidly upwards.

Why is it that things which are soaked in hot 10 water for a short time swell, while those which are soaked for a long time shrink and grow wrinkled? Is it because the heat produces moisture in place of

47

937 a

ποιεῖ, ἐκ δὲ ὑγροῦ πνεῦμα, τὰ δὲ πυκνὰ ἀραιοῖ; τὸ
5 μὲν οὖν πρῶτον θερμαῖνον τὰ πεπηγότα ὑγρότερα
ποιεῖ, καὶ ἐξ ὑγρῶν πνευματοποιοῦν ὀγκηρὰ ποιεῖ
διαχέον· ὅταν δὲ μᾶλλον θερμαίνῃ τὸ πέριξ, ἀραιὸν
ποιεῖ, ὥστε ἀποπνεῖται ἡ ἀτμίς, καὶ τὸ ὑγρὸν
ξηραινόμενον συμπίπτειν ποιεῖ τοὺς ὄγκους. συμπιπτόντων δὲ ῥυσοῦται τὸ πέριξ δέρμα πάντων.
10 ᾗ δὲ ἀνωμάλως, ταύτῃ ῥυσὸν γίνεται.

Διὰ τί ὑπὸ τῶν θερμῶν ὑδάτων μᾶλλον ἢ ὑπὸ 11
τῶν ψυχρῶν πήγνυνται λίθοι; πότερον ὅτι τῇ τοῦ
ὑγροῦ ἐκλείψει γίνεται λίθος, μᾶλλον δὲ ὑπὸ τοῦ
θερμοῦ ἢ τοῦ ψυχροῦ ἐκλείπει τὸ ὑγρόν, καὶ ἀπο-
15 λιθοῦται δὴ διὰ τὸ θερμόν, καθάπερ καὶ Ἐμπεδοκλῆς φησὶ τάς τε πέτρας καὶ τοὺς λίθους διὰ[1] τὰ
θερμὰ τῶν ὑδάτων γίνεσθαι; ἢ τὸ θερμὸν ἀπο-
λιθοῖ· καὶ ὑπὸ τοῦ ψυχροῦ δὲ λιθοῦται διὰ τὸ τὴν
ὑπερβολὴν τοῦ πάγου τὸ ὑγρὸν ἀναλίσκουσαν σκλη-
ρύνειν; δῆλον οὖν ἐκ τῆς ὑπερβολῆς καὶ τὸ ἁπλῶς.

20 Διὰ τί ἐν τῷ θερμῷ ὕδατι, ἐὰν τὸν πόδα ἔχῃ τις, 12
ἠρεμοῦντος μὲν ἧσσον δοκεῖ εἶναι θερμόν, ἐὰν δὲ
κινηθῇ, θερμότερον; ἢ ὥσπερ καὶ ἐπὶ τοῦ σώματος,
ἐὰν ἐν τῷ πνεύματι τροχάζῃ τις, ἀεὶ ὁ προϊστάμενος
ἀὴρ ψυχρότερος; εἰς δὲ τὸ πορρώτερον ἀεὶ ἰὼν[2]
μᾶλλον αἰσθάνεται.

25 Διὰ τί ἐν τῷ ἡλίῳ μᾶλλον ἢ τῇ σκιᾷ τὰ θερμὰ 13
ψύχεται; πότερον ὅτι τὸ θερμὸν τὸ ἔλαττον ὑπὸ
τοῦ πλείονος φθείρεται; ἢ ὅτι ἐν μὲν τῇ σκιᾷ τὸ
ψυχρὸν περιεστηκὸς θλίβει τὸ ἐνὸν θερμὸν καὶ οὐκ
ἐᾷ ἐπεξιέναι, ὅπερ καὶ τοῖς θνήσκουσι ποιεῖ τὸ
30 ψυχρὸν προσχεόμενον; ἐγκατακλείει γὰρ τὸ θερμὸν
καὶ κωλύει ἐξιέναι· καὶ ὅλως τοῦ χειμῶνος ἅπασι

---

[1] διὰ Forster : καὶ Ruelle.
[2] ἀεὶ ἰὼν Bonitz : εἰσιὼν Ruelle.

what is solid, and vapour instead of liquid, and refines what is dense ? That which causes heat at first makes what is solid wetter, and as it vaporizes what is wet it penetrates and makes it swell, but when it has heated the envelope more, it rarefies it, so that the vapour escapes, and the wet becoming dry causes the swelling to subside. When it subsides, the surrounding skin always becomes wrinkled. Where the subsidence is uneven, there the wrinkles appear.

Why are stones hardened more easily by hot water 11 than by cold ? Is it because stones are formed by failure of moisture, and the moisture fails by heat rather than by cold, and the formation of stones is due to heat, just as Empedocles says that rocks and stones are due to hot water ? Or does heat produce stones, but stone is also produced by cold because the excess of frost exhausts the moisture and hardens it ? Evidently, then, this hardening is simply due to excess.

Why is it that if one holds a foot in hot water, 12 it seems less hot while the foot is still, but hotter if it is moved ? Is it similar to the experience of the body, if one runs in the wind, the air which is in contact with it being increasingly colder? The farther one continues to go the more one is conscious of it.

Why do hot things cool more quickly in the sun 13 than in the shade ? Is it because the less heat is destroyed by the greater ? Or is it because in the shade the surrounding cold compresses the heat within and does not allow it to escape, which also happens with the dying when cold water is poured over them ? For the cold water confines the heat, and prevents it from escaping. Generally speaking,

937 a

συμβαίνει τὰ ἔσωθεν θερμότερα· ἐν δὲ τῷ ἡλίῳ
οὐδενὸς ἀντιφράττοντος φέρεται καὶ θᾶττον ἀπολείπει.

Διὰ τί τὸ ἐν τῷ ἡλίῳ θερμαινόμενον ὕδωρ ὥστε 14
35 λούεσθαι οὐκ ἔστιν ὑγιεινότερον; πότερον ὅτι διὰ
τὸ ψύχεσθαι; καὶ ἔτι ἐπὶ τῷ σώματι ὂν[1] φρίττειν
ποιεῖ. ἢ ποιεῖ μὲν καὶ τοῦτο, ἀλλὰ κἂν πολλάκις
λούηταί τις, νοσερόν ἐστιν; τὸ μὲν γὰρ θερμὸν
ὅλως πεπτικόν ἐστι καὶ ξηραντικόν, τὸ δὲ ψυχρὸν
937 b σταλτικόν, ὥστε ἄμφω ποιεῖ τι ἀγαθόν. διὸ καὶ τὸ
ὕδωρ καὶ τὸ ψυχρὸν λουομένοις καὶ τὸ θερμὸν τὸ
ὑπὸ τοῦ πυρὸς χρήσιμον· τὸ δὲ ὑπὸ τοῦ ἡλίου διὰ
τὴν ἀσθένειαν τῆς θερμότητος οὐδέτερον τούτων
ποιεῖ, ἀλλὰ ὑγραίνει ὥσπερ τὸ τῆς σελήνης φῶς.

5 Διὰ τί τὸ ἐν τῷ ἡλίῳ θερμανθὲν ὕδωρ οὐκ ἀγα- 15
θόν; ἢ ὅτι τὰ ψυχόμενα ῥιγοῦν ποιεῖ;

Διὰ τί τὰ ἐν Μαγνησίᾳ καὶ τὰ ἐν Ἀταρνεῖ θερμὰ 16
πότιμά ἐστιν; ἢ διότι ἐμβάλλει ὕδωρ πλεῖον
ἀπορρέοντι τῷ θερμῷ, οὗ ἡ μὲν ἁλμυρότης ἀφανί-
10 ζεται, ἡ δὲ θερμότης διαμένει;

Διὰ τί ἐν Μαγνησίᾳ τὰ θερμὰ τοῦ μὲν θερμὰ 17
εἶναι ἐπαύσατο, ἁλμυρὸν δὲ ἦν τὸ ὕδωρ; ἢ πλεῖον
ἐπεχύθη ἅμα ψυχρὸν ἐπὶ τὰς πηγὰς ἀλλότριον, καὶ
ἐναπέσβεσε τὴν θερμότητα; ἡ δὲ γῆ ἁλμυρὰ μὲν
15 ἦν, θερμὴ δὲ οὔ, διὰ τὸ πλῆθος τοῦ ὕδατος τοῦ
ἐμβάλλοντος. ὅμοιον οὖν συνέβη τῷ διὰ τῆς τέφρας
ὕδατι ἠθουμένῳ· καὶ γὰρ τοῦτο διὰ θέρμης ἠθού-
μενον ἐκείνην μὲν καταψύχει, καὶ αὐτὸ ψυχρὸν
γίνεται, ἁλμυρόν τε καὶ πικρὸν διὰ τὴν τέφραν
ἐστίν. ἐπεὶ δὲ τὸ προσιὸν ἠλλοτριωμένον ἐστίν, δι'

[1] ἐπὶ τῷ σώματι ὂν Forster : ἐπεὶ τὸ σωμάτιον Ruelle.

in winter internal heat is always greater, but in the sun, as there is nothing to oppose it, it moves and soon vanishes.

Why is water heated in the sun not more healthy 14 for washing ? Does it, because it is cooling, also cause shivering while it is still on the surface of the body ? Does it have this effect and also is liable to produce disease, if one washes in it often ? For hot water, generally speaking, readily causes concoction and has a drying effect, but cold water produces contraction, so that each produces a good effect. Hence both cold water and water heated by fire are useful to men bathing, but water heated by the sun owing to the weakness of the heat does no good either way, but merely produces moisture like the light of the moon.

Why is not water heated by the sun good ? Is it 15 because that which is cooling produces shivering ?

Why is the hot water in Magnesia and Atarneus 16 drinkable ? Is it because, as the hot water flows out, more flows into it, so that its salt disappears, but its heat remains ?

Why did the hot springs in Magnesia cease to be 17 hot, but yet the water remained brackish ? [a] Did more cold water from another source flow into the springs at the same time, and quench the heat ? For the earth was salt but not hot, owing to the quantity of water flowing into it. The same thing happens to water which percolates through ashes. For this passing through the hot coal cools it and itself becomes cold, and also brackish and bitter owing to the ashes. But when the water which flows in becomes different in character, the heat which exists

[a] This is an unsatisfactory Problem. Its sense is doubtful and it does not agree with Problem 16.

20 ἄλλην αἰτίαν ἐκράτησεν ἡ θερμότης ἐνοῦσα ἐν τῇ
γῇ τῆς ψυχρότητος τοῦ ὕδατος δι᾽ ὀλιγότητα, καὶ
ἐγένετο πάλιν θερμά.

Διὰ τί τὰ ὅλα τῶν θερμῶν ὑδάτων ἁλμυρά; ἢ 1
διότι τὰ πολλὰ διὰ γῆς ἠθεῖται στυπτηριώδους
(δηλοῖ δὲ ἡ ὀσμὴ αὐτῶν) κεκαυμένης δέ; ἡ δὲ
25 τέφρα πάντων ἁλμυρὰ καὶ θείου ὄζει. διὸ καὶ
συγκάει οὕτως ὥσπερ ὁ κεραυνός. πολλὰ οὖν
θερμά ἐστιν ἀπὸ ἐπισημάνσεως κεραυνῶν.

Διὰ τί τὰ θερμὰ λουτρὰ ἱερά; ἢ ὅτι ἀπὸ τῶν 1
ἱερωτάτων γίνονται, θείου καὶ κεραυνοῦ;

in the earth for a different reason masters the coldness of the water owing to its small quantity and the water again becomes hot.

Why are hot springs always salt ? Is it because 18 they usually percolate through astringent earth (their smell proves this) which has been burned ? All ashes are brackish and smell of sulphur. This is why they burn like a thunderbolt. Many hot springs are due to the stroke of thunderbolts.

Why are hot bathing-pools sacred ? Is it because 19 they are caused by two very sacred things, sulphur and thunderbolts ?

ΚΕ

ΟΣΑ ΠΕΡΙ ΤΟΝ ΑΕΡΑ

Διὰ τί ἐν τοῖς ἀσκοῖς τοῖς πεφυσημένοις ἐν- 1
απολαμβανόμενα τὰ μέλη πόνον παρέχει; πότερον
διὰ τὴν πίεσιν τοῦ ἀέρος; ὥσπερ γὰρ οὐδὲ τοῖς
ἔξωθεν πιέζουσι τὸν ἀσκὸν ἐνδίδωσιν ὁ ἀήρ, ἀλλ᾽
35 ἀπωθεῖ, οὕτω καὶ τὰ ἐντὸς ἐναπολαμβανόμενα
θλίβει ὁ ἀήρ. ἢ διότι βίᾳ κατέχεται καὶ πεπί-
ληται; ἔξω οὖν πάντη ὁρμῶν κατὰ φύσιν προσ-
απερείδεται πρὸς τὸ ἐντὸς ἀπειλημμένον σῶμα.

Διὰ τί ἐν τοῖς ἕλεσι τοῖς παρὰ τοὺς ποταμοὺς 2
γίνονται οἱ καλούμενοι βούμυκοι, οὓς μυθολογοῦσιν
938 a ταύρους ἱεροὺς εἶναι τοῦ θεοῦ; ἔστι δὲ τὸ γινόμενον ψόφος ὅμοιος φωνῇ ταύρου, ὥστε αἱ βόες
οὕτω διατίθενται ἀκούουσαι ὥσπερ ταύρου μυκω-
μένου. ἢ ὅτι ὅσοι ποταμοὶ λιμνάζουσιν εἰς ἕλη,
[ἢ ὅσα ἕλη λιμνάζονται,] ἢ ὑπὸ θαλάττης ἀντι-
5 κρούονται, ἢ τὸ πνεῦμα ἀφιᾶσιν ἀθροώτερον, ἐν
τοῖς τοιούτοις γίνεται τοῦτο; αἴτιον δὲ ὅτι αἱ
κοιλίαι τῆς γῆς γίνονται. οὕτως οὖν κλυζόμενον
τὸ ὕδωρ, διὰ τὸ ἐνεῖναι ῥεῦμα ἐν τῇ τοιαύτῃ
λιμνασίᾳ, ἀπωθεῖται τὸν ἀέρα διὰ στενοῦ εἰς
εὐρυτέραν κοιλίαν, οἷον εἴ τις εἰς ἀμφορέα κενὸν

BOOK XXV

PROBLEMS CONNECTED WITH AIR

WHY is it that limbs suffer pain if they are enclosed 1
in inflated wineskins ? Is it due to the pressure
of the air ? The air does not give way to outside
pressure on the wineskin, but repels it ; just in the
same way the air compresses what is enclosed in it.
Or is it because the air is confined by force and compressed ? Consequently as the air has a natural impetus in every direction it must exert pressure on the
enclosed body.

Why do the so-called " ox bellowings " [a] occur in 2
marshes by the banks of rivers, which are due according to legend to the sacred bulls of the God ?
The phenomenon is a sound similar to that made by a
bull, so that cows are affected by it in the same way
as when they hear a bull bellowing. Does this occur
in places where the rivers stagnate in marshes, or
are repelled by the sea, or give off an unusually large
quantity of wind ? The reason is that hollows are
formed in the earth. So as the water wells up (there
is always a flow in marshy ground of this kind) it
forces the air through a narrow passage into a wider
hollow, just as if one made a sound through the neck

[a] Aristotle explains (*Meteor.* 368 a) that earthquakes are
due to the movement of air beneath the earth. When this
movement is insufficient to produce earth tremors it causes a
sound which men describe as " lowing."

¹⁰ κατὰ τὸ στόμιον ποιοῖ ψόφον, μυκήματι ὅμοιον
γίνεται· καὶ γὰρ ἡ μύκησις διὰ τοῦτο γίνεται τὸ
σχῆμα τοῖς βουσίν. πολλὰς δὲ καὶ ἀτόπους φωνὰς
ποιοῦσι τὰ σχήματα τῶν κοιλιῶν ἀνώμαλα ὄντα,
ἐπεὶ καὶ ἀμφορέως τὸν πύνδακα ἐάν τις ἀφελὼν
¹⁵ διὰ τοῦ πυθμένος τρίβῃ ἕλκων ἔσω καὶ ἔξω,¹ ψόφον
ποιεῖ, ὥστε φεύγειν τὰ θηρία, ὅταν οἱ ὀπωροφύλακες
κατασκευάσωσιν αὐτό.

Διὰ τί ὁ ἀὴρ οὐχ ὑγρός, ἁπτόμενος τοῦ ὕδατος; 3
τῶν γὰρ ἄλλων οὐθὲν ὅ τι οὐχ ὑγρόν, ἂν ἅψηται.
ἢ διότι τὸ ἔσχατον αὐτῶν ἅμα, τὸ δὲ ἐπίπεδον
²⁰ ἑκατέρου² ἕτερον; τὰ μὲν οὖν ἄλλα βαρύτερα, ὁ
δὲ ἀὴρ οὐ ῥέπει κατωτέρω τοῦ ἐσχάτου. ἅπτεται
μὲν οὖν, ὅτι οὐθὲν μεταξύ, οὐ βρέχεται δέ, ὅτι ἀεὶ
ἄνωθεν τοῦ ὕδατος.

Διὰ τί μέσων νυκτῶν καὶ μεσημβρίας μάλιστα 4
εὐδία γίνεται; ἢ διότι ἡ νηνεμία ἐστὶν ἀέρος
²⁵ στάσις, ἕστηκε δὲ μάλιστα ὅταν κρατῇ ἢ κρατῆται,
μαχόμενος δὲ κινεῖται; κρατεῖ μὲν οὖν μάλιστα
μέσων νυκτῶν, κρατεῖται δὲ μεσημβρίας· τοτὲ μὲν
γὰρ ὁ ἥλιος πορρωτάτω, τοτὲ δὲ ἐγγυτάτω γίνεται.
ἔτι ἄρχεται τὰ πνεύματα ἢ περὶ ἔω ἢ περὶ δυσμάς,
³⁰ λήγει δὲ τὸ μὲν ἕωθεν, ὅταν κρατηθῇ, τὸ δὲ ἀπὸ
δυσμῶν, ὅταν παύσηται κρατῶν. συμβαίνει οὖν
τὰ μὲν μεσημβρίας παύεσθαι, τὰ δὲ μέσων νυκτῶν.

Διὰ τί ὑποφαυσκούσης ἔω καὶ ἤδη πρωῒ μᾶλλόν 5
ἐστι ψῦχος ἢ τῆς νυκτός, ἐγγυτέρω ὄντος τοῦ ἡλίου

---

¹ The ms. has here the words εἰ τρίψει διὰ τοῦ καταδήματος.
It seems better to omit them, as they can add nothing to
the sense and κατάδημα is otherwise unknown.
² οὐχ add. Ruelle.

into an empty jar, and makes a sound like bellowing ; for it is through a passage of similar shape that the bellowing of bulls is produced. Shapes of hollow spaces which are irregular produce many strange noises. When one takes off the lid of a jar and rubs it over the bottom drawing it in and out, it makes enough noise to frighten animals, when the watchers of the fruit do it.

Why does not the air become moist, when in 3 contact with water ? There is no other substance which does not become moist, if in contact with water. Is it because the limit of each substance meets the other, but the surface of each remains distinct ? So all other substances are heavier, but the air does not sink below the limit of the water. It touches it, then, in the sense that there is nothing between them, but the air does not grow wet because it is always above the water.

Why does a calm most often occur at midnight 4 and midday ? Is it because an absence of wind is due to the stationary position of the air, and it is most stationary when it is either exercising or submitting to most control, but when it is struggling it moves ? Now it exercises most control at midnight, and submits to control most at midday ; for at the former hour the sun is farthest away, and at the latter the sun is nearest. Moreover, the wind rises either at sunrise or at sunset, and the wind which rises at dawn dies down when it passes under control, and that which rises at sunset dies down when it ceases to exercise control. So the former falls at midday and the latter at midnight.

Why is it that, when the day is just dawning and it is 5 still early, the cold is greater than at night, although

57

938 a

ἡμῶν; ἢ ὅτι πρὸς ἡμέραν δρόσος καὶ πάχνη
35 πίπτει, ταῦτα δέ ἐστι ψυχρά· ὥσπερ οὖν ῥανθέντος
τοῦ παντὸς τόπου ὑγρῷ ψυχρῷ γίνεται κατάψυξις.

Διὰ τί ἐν τῷ Πόντῳ καὶ ψύχη μάλιστα καὶ
πνίγη; ἢ διὰ τὴν παχύτητα τοῦ ἀέρος; τοῦ μὲν
γὰρ χειμῶνος οὐ δύναται διαθερμαίνεσθαι, τοῦ
938 b θέρους δέ, ὅταν θερμανθῇ, κάει διὰ τὴν παχύτητα.
ἡ δὲ αὐτὴ αἰτία καὶ διότι τὰ ἑλώδη τοῦ μὲν
χειμῶνος ψυχρά, τοῦ δὲ θέρους θερμά. ἢ διὰ τὴν
τοῦ ἡλίου φοράν; τοῦ μὲν γὰρ χειμῶνος πόρρω
γίνεται, τοῦ δὲ θέρους ἐγγύς.
5 Διὰ τί τῆς νυκτὸς αἰθρία μᾶλλον ἢ μεθ' ἡμέραν;
ἢ καὶ τοῦ πνεύματος καὶ τῆς ταραχῆς ὁ ἥλιος
αἴτιος; ταῦτα γὰρ κινήσεώς τινος γενομένης συμβαίνει γίνεσθαι. αἴτιον τοίνυν τὸ θερμόν. ὅταν
οὖν τοῦτο μὴ παρῇ, ἠρεμεῖ τὸ πᾶν, καὶ αἱρομένου
10 τοῦ ἡλίου μᾶλλον ἢ τοὐναντίον· καὶ τὸ '' μήποτ'
ἀπ' ἠπείρου '' τοῦτ' ἐστίν, ὅτι οὗ πλείστη κίνησις,
ἐκεῖ ἥκιστα ἄν τι μένοι καὶ συσταίη, μὴ ὁμαλοῦ
ὄντος καὶ κρατοῦντος τοῦ συνισταμένου. τοῦ μὲν
δὴ χειμῶνος ἡ θάλαττα τοιοῦτον, τοῦ δὲ θέρους
ἡ γῆ.

Διὰ τί, ὅταν διαχυθῇ τὸ ὑγρὸν εἰς ἀσκούς, οὐ
15 μόνον τὸ ὑγρὸν δέχεται ὁ πίθος μετὰ τῶν ἀσκῶν,
ἀλλὰ καὶ ἄλλο προσλαμβάνει; ἢ ὅτι ἐν τῷ ὑγρῷ
ἐνυπάρχει ὁ ἀήρ; οὗτος οὖν ὅταν μὲν ἐν τῷ
πίθῳ ἐνῇ, οὐ δύναται ἐκκρίνεσθαι διὰ τὸ μέγεθος
τοῦ πίθου· ἐκ γὰρ τοῦ μείζονος χαλεπώτερον
ἐκθλῖψαι ὁτιοῦν καὶ ὑγρὸν καὶ πνεῦμα, ὥσπερ καὶ
ἐκ τῶν σπόγγων. ὅταν δὲ μερίζηται εἰς μικρὰ

the sun is nearer to us at that hour ? Is it because
dew and hoar-frost fall towards day, and these are
cold ? So when every place is sprinkled with cold
moisture chill comes.

Why do both cold and stifling heat occur most 6
commonly in Pontus ? Is it owing to the density of
the air ? For in winter it cannot get heated through,
and in summer, when it is heated, it burns because of
its density. The same cause explains why marshy
districts are cold in winter, and hot in summer. Or is
it due to the travelling of the sun ? For in the winter
it is far away, and in summer near by.

Why is the sky clearer at night than in the day- 7
time ? Is the sun the cause of the wind and of the
disturbance ? For these things occur as the result
of movement. Heat, then, is the cause. When heat
is absent, everything is at rest, and this is more true
when the sun is rising than when it is sinking. The
proverb " Do not fear a cloud from the mainland in
winter " [a] means that where there is most movement
there also would be the least static conditions, as
that which causes stability is irregular and does not
exercise control. In the winter this is the nature of
the sea, in summer of the land.

Why is it that when liquid is poured from a jar into 8
wineskins the jar will not merely hold the liquid and
the skins, but also has room for more ? Is it because
there is air in the liquid ? So when the liquid is in
the jar, the air cannot escape owing to the size of the
jar, for it is more difficult to drive anything, whether
liquid or air, out of a larger vessel, as we can see in the
case of sponges. But when it is divided into smaller

[a] Only part of the proverb is given here ; for the whole
cf. 947 a 7.

20 ἐκθλίβεται ἐκ τοῦ ἀσκοῦ μετὰ τοῦ ἐνόντος, ὥσθ'
ἡ τοῦ ἀέρος χώρα κενὴ γίνεται, διὸ καὶ τοὺς
ἀσκοὺς καὶ ἔτι ἄλλο ὑγρὸν δέχεται ὁ πίθος. καὶ
μᾶλλον ἐπὶ τοῦ οἴνου τοῦτο γίνεται, ὅτι πλείων
ἀὴρ ἐν τῷ οἴνῳ ἔνεστιν ἢ ἐν τῷ ὕδατι. ὅμοιον δὲ
25 τούτῳ καὶ τὸ ταὐτὸ ἀγγεῖον τήν τε κονίαν καὶ τὸ
ὕδωρ χωρεῖν ἅμα, ὅσον ἑκάτερον χωρὶς ἐγχεόμενον.
ἔοικεν γὰρ πολλὰ εἶναι τὰ διάκενα τῆς τέφρας.
ἅτε οὖν λεπτότερον τὸ ὕδωρ διαδύνει μᾶλλον καὶ
συσσάττει ἤδη, ὥστε πυκνοῦσθαι, καὶ διὰ τὸ παρ'
ἕκαστον τῶν μερῶν εἶναι τὴν σάξιν (μᾶλλον γὰρ
30 σάττεται κατὰ μικρὸν σαττόμενον ἅπαν ἢ ἀθρόον),
τούτου δὲ γινομένου ὑποκαταβαίνειν τὴν κονίαν·
ἅμα δὲ καὶ ἡ τέφρα εἰς αὑτὴν δέχεται τὸ ὑγρὸν
διὰ τὸ ἔχειν κοιλίας. ἡ δὲ βαλλομένη τέφρα εἰς
τὸ ὕδωρ θερμὴ οὖσα τέμνει αὐτὸ καὶ ἐξαεροῖ. καὶ
35 πρότερον δὲ ὕδατος ἐγχυθέντος καὶ ὕστερον
κονίας ἐμπιπτούσης τὸ αὐτὸ γίνεται, ὥστε καὶ τὸ
ὕδωρ ἔχοι ἂν κοιλίας καὶ διάκενα αὐτὸ ἐν αὑτῷ.
ἢ οὐ τὸ ὕδωρ τὸ δεχόμενον τὴν κονίαν, ἀλλ' ἡ
κονία τὸ ὕδωρ; τὸ γὰρ λεπτομερέστερον εἰκὸς
εἶναι τὸ εἰσιόν. ἔτι καὶ ἐκ τῆς πείρας δῆλον.
939 a ὅταν γὰρ ἐπιπάττηται ἡ τέφρα, καθ' ὃν ἂν τόπον
ἐπιπάττηται, εἰς τοῦτον συρρεῖ τὸ ἄλλο ὕδωρ·
ἔδει δὲ τὸ ἐναντίον, εἴπερ ἦν τὸ ὕδωρ τὸ δεχόμενον.
ἢ οὐ συμβαίνει τοῦτο, ἐὰν πρότερον ἐγχυθῇ τὸ
ὕδωρ καὶ σφόδρα διαμεστώσῃ; ἀλλ' ἐὰν ὁτιοῦν
5 ἐπιβληθῇ, ὑπερχεῖται. ἐὰν δ' ἅπαξ ὑπερχυθῇ καὶ
ἐπιπέσῃ ἡ τέφρα, ἤδη συμβαίνει· ἡ γὰρ τέφρα ἦν
δεχομένη. ταὐτὸ δὲ τοῦτο καὶ ὅτι οἱ βόθυνοι τὴν

parts, the air is driven out of the skin together with its contents, so that the space previously occupied by air becomes empty ; hence the jar has room both for the skins and for more liquid. This is even more true in the case of wine, because there is more air in wine than in water. Similar to this is the fact that the same vessel can contain as much ashes and water together as it can of each when poured in separately. For there seem to be many empty spaces in ashes. Hence the water being lighter sinks into them and fills them up completely, so that the mass grows dense, and because the filling has taken place with each of the parts (for everything which is filled by degrees becomes more full than if it is done all at once), when this happens the ashes subside ; at the same time the ashes admit the liquid because they have interstices. But ashes which are cast into the water when hot, cleave the water and cause evaporation. When the water is poured in before, and the ashes are introduced afterwards, the same thing happens, so that the water also would have interstices and empty spaces in it. Or is it not the water which absorbs the ashes, but the ashes the water ? For it seems natural that it should be the substance with the lighter parts which penetrates. This also is proved by experiment. For when the ashes are sprinkled over, on whatever part they are sprinkled the rest of the water flows into it ; the opposite ought to happen, if it were the water which admits the ashes. Or does this not occur, if the water is poured in first and fills the vessel up ? If anything further is put in, it overflows. But if once the ashes are poured over and fall into the water, the effect takes place at once, for the ashes are actually the recipient. An illustration of

939 a

ἐκβληθεῖσαν ἐξ αὐτῶν γῆν οὐ δέχονται· ἔοικεν γὰρ
δὴ ἀήρ τις προκαταλαμβάνων τὸν τόπον καὶ διὰ
τοῦτο μὴ δέχεσθαι.

10 Διὰ τί ὁ ἀὴρ παχύτερος ὢν τοῦ φωτὸς διέρχεται 9
διὰ τῶν στερεῶν; ἢ διότι τὸ μὲν φῶς κατ᾽
εὐθεῖαν φέρεται μόνον, διὸ καὶ διὰ τῶν ἀραιῶν οὐ
διορᾷ ἡ ὄψις, οἷον κισήριδος; ἐπαλλάττουσιν γὰρ
οἱ πόροι· ἀλλ᾽ οὐκ ἐν τῇ ὑάλῳ, ὁ δὲ ἀὴρ οὐ κωλύεται
15 διὰ τὸ μὴ εὐθυπορεῖν οὗ διέρχεται.

Διὰ τί ὁ ἀὴρ ψυχρὸς μὲν γίνεται διὰ τὸ ἅπτεσθαι 10
τοῦ ὕδατος, δίυγρος δὲ οὔ, κἂν σφόδρα τις φυσᾷ εἰς
τὸ ὕδωρ ὥστε κυμαίνειν, ὅτι δὲ ψυχρός, δηλοῖ μεθ-
ιστάμενος· ψύχει γὰρ ⟨ὁ⟩[1] ἀπὸ τῶν ὑδάτων; ἢ ὅτι
20 ψυχρὸς μὲν πέφυκεν εἶναι καὶ θερμός, ὥστε μεταβάλλει τῇ ἁφῇ οὗ ἂν τινος ἅπτηται, ὑγρὸς δὲ
οὐκέτι διὰ τὸ κουφότερος εἶναι; καὶ οὐδέποτε εἰς
τὸ βάθος τοῦ ὕδατος ἔρχεται, ἀλλ᾽ ἀεὶ τοῦ ἐπιπέδου
ἅπτεται, κἂν βιάζηται κάτω· καὶ τὸ ὕδωρ ἔτι
κατωτέρω φέρεται, ὥστε μήποτε εἰς βάθος ἰέναι.

25 Διὰ τί ὁ ἐκ τῶν πομφολύγων καὶ κάτωθεν ἀνιὼν 11
οὐ διερὸς ἐξέρχεται; ἢ διότι οὐκ ἐπιμένει τὸ
ὑγρόν, ἀλλ᾽ ὀλισθαίνει τὸ ὕδωρ; τὸ δ᾽ ἐπὶ τῇ
πομφόλυγι καὶ ἔλαττόν ἐστιν ἢ ὥστε διερεῖν.

Διὰ τί ὁ ἀὴρ οὐκ ἀναπίμπλησι, τὸ δὲ ὕδωρ; καὶ 12
30 εἰς τὸν ἀέρα γὰρ μετατιθέμενον διερόν. ἢ ὅτι
ὥσπερ οὐδὲ ὁ λίθος; οὐ γὰρ πᾶν ἐστιν ἀνα-
πληστικόν, ἀλλὰ τὸ γλίσχρον ἢ ὑγρόν.

---

[1] ⟨ὁ⟩ added by Bonitz.

ᵃ This Problem is not very clear, but it seems to mean
that if a substance containing air spaces (*e.g.* ashes) is put
into a vessel and water poured in afterwards, the water will
replace the air and thus ashes + water will take up no more
room than ashes alone. If the water is put in first, and then
ashes, the water will overflow because the ashes will carry

62

the same fact appears in that trenches will not hold all the earth that is thrown out of them, for some air seems to occupy the space and hence the trench will not hold all the earth.[a]

Why does air, which is denser than light, penetrate 9 through solid bodies ? Is it because light only travels in straight lines, so that vision cannot see through porous substances, such as pumice-stone ? For the channels change direction ; but this is not the case with glass, but the air is not obstructed because it does not travel straight through what it penetrates.

Why does air become chilled through contact with 10 water, but not saturated with moisture, even if one blows it into the water violently enough to make waves, but it shows by its change that it becomes cold, for air from water causes cold ? Is it because air by nature is both cold and hot, so that it changes by contact with whatever it touches, but it does not become moist because it is too light ? It never penetrates into the depth of the water, but only touches the surface, even if it is forced downwards ; the water always recedes lower still, so that the air never reaches the depths.

Why is it that the air from bubbles even when it 11 rises from below never comes out wet ? Is it because the liquid does not remain in it but the water slides off ? The water on a bubble is too little to wet it.

Why does not air soak into another substance, 12 while water does ? Water soaks even when transformed into air. Is it for the same reason that a stone does not ? For not every substance soaks, but only what is viscous or liquid.

air down with them, but afterwards the air will escape and the whole subside

939 a

* * * ἢ ὅτι ὁ ἀὴρ ἄνω φέρεται; ὁ γὰρ ἀσκὸς ¹
ὅταν μὲν κενὸς ᾖ κάτω φέρεται, ὅταν δὲ φυσηθῇ,
35 ἄνω ἐπιμένει διὰ τὸ τοῦτον ἀναφέρειν. εἰ δὲ ὁ
ἀὴρ ἀνακουφίζει καὶ κωλύει κάτω φέρεσθαι, διὰ
τί βαρύτεροι γίνονται φυσηθέντες; καὶ πῶς, ὅτε
μὲν βαρύτερός ἐστιν, ἐπιμένει, κουφότερος δὲ γενόμενος καταφέρεται;

Διὰ τί ὁ ἀὴρ * * * οὐκ ἄνω φέρεται; εἰ γὰρ ¹
939 b τὰ πνεύματα τούτου κινουμένου ὑπὸ τοῦ θερμοῦ
γίνεται, πέφυκεν δὲ τὸ πῦρ ἄνω φέρεσθαι, καὶ τὸ
πνεῦμα εἰς τὸ ἄνω ἐβάδιζεν, εἴπερ τό τε κινοῦν
εἰς τὸ ἄνω θεῖ καὶ τὸ κινούμενον οὕτω πέφυκε
φέρεσθαι. νῦν δὲ φαίνεται λοξὴν τὴν φορὰν
ποιούμενος.

5 Διὰ τί τὸ ἀφ' ἕω ψυχρότερον ἢ τὸ ἀφ' ἑσπέρας; ¹
ἢ ὅτι τὸ μὲν ἐγγύτερον μέσων νυκτῶν, τὸ δὲ
μεσημβρίας; ἔστι δὲ ἡ μεσημβρία θερμότατον διὰ
τὸ εἶναι ἐγγύτατον ἡλίου, αἱ δὲ μέσαι νύκτες
ψυχρότεραι διὰ τὸ ἐναντίον.

Διὰ τί αἱ νύκτες τῶν ἡμερῶν ἐν ταῖς ἀλέαις ¹
10 πνιγηρότεραι; ἢ διὰ τὴν ἄπνοιαν; οἱ γὰρ ἐτησίαι
καὶ πρόδρομοι τὰς νύκτας ἧττον πνέουσιν.

Διὰ τί τὰ ἐν τοῖς ἀσκοῖς ἄσηπτα φυσηθεῖσιν,
καὶ ἐν τοῖς περιπωματιζομένοις; ἢ διότι σήπεται
μὲν κινούμενα, ἅπαντα δὲ τὰ πλήρη ἀκίνητα,
ταῦτα δὲ πλήρη.

15 Διὰ τί τῆς αἰθρίας μᾶλλον ψῦχος γίνεται ἢ ἐπι- ¹
νεφέλων ὄντων; τὰ δὲ ἄστρα καὶ ὁ οὐρανὸς θερμός.
ἢ ὅτι οὐθὲν ἀποστέγει ἐν τῇ αἰθρίᾳ τὴν ἀτμίδα,

ᵃ This question is supplied from Th. G.

(Why do inflated skins float ?) [a] Is it because air 13 travels upwards ? For the skin when empty travels downwards, but when it is blown up, it remains on the surface, because the air carries it upwards. If, then, the air makes the skin lighter and prevents it from being carried downwards, why are skins heavier when they are blown up ? And how do they remain on the surface when they are heavier, and sink when they are lighter ?

Why does the air not travel upwards ? For if the 14 winds occur when the air is moved by heat, and it is the nature of fire to travel upwards, the wind also should also travel upwards, since the motive power rushes upwards and that which is moved is naturally carried in the same direction. But as it is the air clearly travels sideways.

Why is it colder at dawn than in the evening ? 15 Is it because the former is nearer to midnight, the latter to midday ? But midday is the warmest time because it is nearest to the sun, while midnight is colder for the contrary reason.

Why are the nights more stifling than the days in 16 hot weather ? Is it owing to the absence of breeze ? For the Etesian and the northerly winds blow less strongly at night.

Why do not substances decompose in inflated 17 wineskins and in jars which are closed ? Is it because decomposition takes place when things are moving, but there is no movement when the container is full, and inflated wineskins are full ?

Why is the cold more severe under a clear sky than 18 when it is overcast ? For the stars and heavens are hot. Is it because under a clear sky there is nothing to restrict evaporation, which permeates through ;

939 b

ἀλλὰ διαχεῖται· ἐν δὲ τοῖς ἐπινεφέλοις ἀποστέγεται;
καὶ βορείων γε ἢ νοτίων διὰ τὸ αὐτό· ὁ μὲν γὰρ
20 νότος ἄγει τὸ τοιοῦτον, ὁ δὲ ἀπωθεῖ. καὶ ἀτμίζειν
δὲ φαίνεται βορείοις μᾶλλον ἢ νοτίοις, καὶ χειμῶνος
ἢ θέρους. ἢ παρὰ τὸ ἀνόμοιον; ἢ ὅτι θερμοῦ
ψυχομένου ἐστὶν ἡ ἀτμίς;

Διὰ τί ἀὴρ ὁ ἐλάττων θερμότερος τοῦ πλείονος; 1
αἱ γὰρ στενοχωρίαι ἀλεεινότεραι. ἢ διότι κινεῖται
25 μᾶλλον ὁ πολύς, ἡ δὲ κίνησις ποιεῖ ψυχρόν;
σημεῖον δὲ τούτου, ὅτι κινούμενα ψύχεται τὰ
θερμά.

Διὰ τί ὕδωρ μὲν καὶ γῆ σήπεται, ἀὴρ δὲ καὶ πῦρ 2
οὐ σήπεται; ἢ ὅτι θερμότατον γίνεται τὸ σηπόμενον ἅπαν, πυρὸς δὲ οὐδὲν θερμότερον; ἢ ὅτι
30 ψυχθῆναι δεῖ πρότερον, τὸ δὲ πῦρ ἀεὶ θερμόν, ὁ δὲ
ἀὴρ πυρὸς πλήρης; σήπεται δὲ οὐδὲν θερμόν, ἀλλὰ
ψυχθέν· γῆ δὲ καὶ ὕδωρ[1] καὶ θερμὰ καὶ ψυχρὰ
γίνεται.

Διὰ τί τὰ ἐπινέφελα ἀλεεινότερα τῶν αἰθρίων; 2
πότερον ὡς οἱ ἀρχαῖοι ἔλεγον ὅτι τὰ ἄστρα ψυχρά;
35 ἢ λίαν τοῦτό γε ἄτοπον, ἀλλὰ διότι ἀτμίζει;
ἐπισημαντέον δὲ ὅτι ἐν νηνεμίᾳ ἡ δρόσος καὶ ἡ
πάχνη γίνεται. ὅταν μὲν οὖν αἰθρία ᾖ, διαπνεῖ τὸ
θερμόν, ὑφ' οὗ ἀνάγεται τὸ ὑγρόν, ὥστε ψυχρὸς ὁ
ἀήρ· διὸ καὶ δροσίζει ἀφιέμενον τὸ ὑγρὸν ἀπὸ τοῦ
θερμοῦ. ὅταν δὲ ἐπινέφελον ᾖ, ἀποστέγεται, διὸ
940 a οὐ γίνεται δρόσος οὐδὲ πάχνη ὄντων ἐπινεφέλων.
περὶ οὖν τὴν γῆν ὑπομένον τὸ θερμὸν ποιεῖ τὴν
ἀλέαν.

[1] ὕδωρ καὶ ἀὴρ Ruelle.

but under a cloudy sky it is restricted? For the same reason it is colder with a north than with a south wind. For the south wind attracts, but the north wind repels clouds. There also seems to be more evaporation with a north wind than with a south wind, and also more in winter than in summer. Or is it due to the difference in conditions? Or is it because evaporation takes place when the warm is cooling?

Why is a small quantity of air warmer than a larger 19 quantity? For closely confined places are warmer. Is it because the large quantity moves more, and movement produces cold? This is proved by the fact that hot things cool when they are moved about.

Why do water and earth decompose, but air and 20 fire do not? Is it because everything which decomposes becomes very hot, and there is nothing hotter than fire? Or is it because it must be cooled before it decomposes, and fire is permanently hot, and air is full of fire? So nothing hot decomposes, but only when it has been cooled; now earth and water become both hot and cold.

Why is an overcast sky warmer than a clear one? 21 Is it, as the ancients said, because the stars are cold? Or is this quite an absurd suggestion, and is it due to evaporation? That this takes place is proved by the fact that dew and frost form in calm weather. When, then, the sky is clear, the heat, by which the moisture is taken up, is dispersed so that the air becomes cold; so the moisture given off from the heat causes dew. But when the sky is overcast, the moisture is restricted, so that there is neither dew nor hoar-frost when it is cloudy. So the heat remaining near the earth produces warmth.

Διὰ τί ἐν τοῖς ὑψηλοῖς τῶν οἴκων ὁ ἀὴρ δι- 22
ευριπίζει, καὶ μάλιστα ταῖς εὐδίαις; ἢ διότι ὁ ἀὴρ
5 πολύκενός τίς ἐστι τὴν σύγκρισιν. ὅταν οὖν
ἄρξηται εἴσω ῥεῖν, συγχωρεῖ ὁ ἐν τῷ οἰκήματι
ἀὴρ καὶ συστέλλεται. τούτου δὲ συμπίπτοντος
τῷ χρόνῳ πολυκενώτερος γίνεται ὁ ἔξωθεν, καὶ
χώραν πολλὴν ἴσχει. εἰς ταύτην οὖν τὴν χώραν
πίπτει ὁ ἐκ τοῦ οἰκήματος ἀήρ, ὢν πλησίον, καὶ
10 φέρεται εἰς ταύτην τὴν χώραν διὰ τὸ κρέμασθαι
καὶ τὴν τοῦ κενοῦ φύσιν μὴ δύνασθαι ἀντιστηρίζειν.
κατὰ πολλὰ δὲ αὐτοῦ μέρη τούτου συμβαίνοντος,
ἕπεται αὐτῷ ὁ πλησίον διὰ τὴν πρόωσιν[1]· εἶτα
πολλοῦ ἔξωθεν φερομένου ὁ μὲν ἔσω τόπος πολύ-
κενος γίνεται, ὁ δὲ ἔξω πυκνότερος, καὶ πάλιν
15 ἔξωθεν εἴσω φέρεται. καὶ ταῦτα ἀλλάσσονται.

[1] πρόωσιν Sylb. : πρόσοψιν Ruelle.

Why is it that in lofty rooms the air is constantly 22 ebbing and flowing, and particularly in calm weather? Is it because the air is made up of many empty spaces? So when air begins to flow inwards, the air already in the room contracts and is compressed. When it collects, after a time the outside air becomes more empty and has much space in it. So the air out of the room, being near by, makes for this space and it travels into it because it is in suspense and it is the nature of the void to be unable to resist it. Now when this happens in many different parts, the air near by follows because of the thrust ; so, as much air is travelling from outside, the part inside becomes full of empty spaces but the outside becomes denser, and it rushes again from the outside to the inside. And this change repeats itself.

ΟΣΑ ΠΕΡΙ ΤΟΥΣ ΑΝΕΜΟΥΣ

Διὰ τί ὁ καικίας μόνος τῶν ἀνέμων ἐφ᾽ ἑαυτὸν 1
ἄγει τὰ νέφη; ἢ ὅτι ἀφ᾽ ὑψηλοτέρων τόπων πνεῖ;
20 ἔστι γὰρ τὰ πρὸς ἔω ὑψηλότερα τῶν πρὸς ἑσπέραν.
σημεῖον δὲ τὸ τῆς πρὸς ἑσπέραν θαλάττης μέγεθος
καὶ βάθος. πνέων δὲ ἄνωθεν εἰς τοὐναντίον
γραμμὴν ποιεῖ τῇ φορᾷ τὰ κοῖλα πρὸς τὴν γῆν
ἔχουσαν. προσπίπτων δέ, ὡς εἴρηται, τοῖς πρὸς
ἑσπέραν τῆς γῆς τόποις, καὶ συστέλλων τὰ νέφη
25 διὰ τὸ τῆς γραμμῆς σχῆμα, τῇ ἐκεῖθεν ἀνακλάσει
ἐφ᾽ αὑτὸν[1] ὠθεῖ αὐτά. ποιεῖ δὲ μόνος τοῦτο τῶν
λοιπῶν τῷ τοὺς μὲν ὑψηλοτέρους, τοὺς δ᾽ ἐναντίους
εἶναι τόπους, πρὸς οὓς τοῦ κάτωθεν ἢ ἐπ᾽ εὐθείας
τὴν φορὰν γίνεσθαι συμβαίνει, τὰ κυρτὰ πρὸς τὴν
γῆν ἐχούσης, ὥστε ἀνάκλασιν μὴ γίνεσθαι τοῦ
30 πνεύματος τῷ μὴ πρὸς τὴν γῆν [ἐχούσης] ἀέρα
ἔχειν τὴν τελευτὴν τῆς φορᾶς, ἐν ᾧ οὐδὲ νέφη ἐστὶ
περὶ τὴν γῆν· τοῖς δὲ ἧττον κοίλοις καὶ τῷ ἀπ-
ηλιώτῃ τῷ μὴ εἶναι ὑγρόν. ὥστε οὐ συνιστὰς

[1] ἐφ᾽ ἑαυτὸν Forster : ἐπ᾽ αὐτὸν Ruelle.

---

[a] Caecias is really more easterly than the N.E. wind. The
whole of this Problem is obscure in meaning and the text more

70

BOOK XXVI

Problems connected with the Winds

Why does Caecias[a] alone of the winds attract 1
clouds towards itself? Is it because it blows from
higher districts? For the eastern parts of the world
are higher than the western. The size and depth
of the sea towards the west prove this. This wind,
then, blowing from higher ground to the lower
describes a line in its course which is curved towards
the earth. Falling then, as has been said, upon regions
of the earth which are towards the west, and collecting the clouds because of the shape of its path, on its
return journey it thrusts the clouds towards itself.
It is the only one of the winds which does this, because some places are higher and some lower, against
which the course of the wind either comes from below
or in a straight line, this line being convex in relation
to the earth, so that no refraction of the wind takes
place because the air does not end its course in
relation to the earth at a place where there are no
clouds near the earth. The winds which travel on a
less curved course such as the east wind collect no
clouds because they carry no moisture. So in failing

than doubtful. Considerable use has been made of the Latin
translation, but even so the problem is hardly satisfactory.

940 a

ἧττον καταφανής ἐστιν αὐτοῦ ποιῶν τοῦτο ὃ
ποιεῖ.

35 Διὰ τί βορέαι μὲν ἐτήσιοι γίνονται, νότοι δὲ οὔ;
ἢ γίνονται μὲν καὶ νότοι, ἀλλ᾽ οὐ συνεχεῖς, ὅτι
πόρρω ἡμῶν ἡ ἀρχὴ τοῦ νότου ἐστίν, ὑπὸ δὲ τῷ
βορέᾳ οἰκοῦμεν; ἔτι οἱ μὲν ἐτησίαι βορέαι καθ-
940 b εστηκότος τοῦ ἀέρος πνέουσιν (θέρους γὰρ πνέουσιν), οἱ δὲ νότοι ἦρος, ὅθ᾽ ἧττον ἕστηκεν τὰ περὶ
τὸν ἀέρα. πρὸς δὲ τούτοις ὁ μὲν νότος ὑγρός, τῷ
δ᾽ ὑγρῷ ὁ ἄνω τόπος ἀλλότριός ἐστι· διὸ ταχὺ
διαλύεται τὰ ἐν αὐτῷ συνιστάμενα ὑγρά. καὶ τὰ
5 ὑγρὰ πλανητικά ἐστιν, ὥστε οὐ μένων ἐν ταὐτῷ
τόπῳ συμμεθίστησι καὶ τὴν τοῦ ἀέρος κίνησιν.
κινουμένου δὲ μὴ ἐν ταὐτῷ πνεύματα ἄλλα συμβαίνει γίνεσθαι· ἔστι γὰρ πνεῦμα ἀέρος κίνησις.

Διὰ τί νότος πνεῖ μετὰ πάχνην; ἢ διότι ἡ μὲν
πάχνη γίνεται πέψεως γινομένης, μετὰ δὲ τὴν
10 πέψιν καὶ τὴν ἀποκάθαρσιν ἡ μεταβολὴ εἰς τοὐναντίον γίνεται; ἐναντίον δὲ τῷ βορρᾷ νότος ἐστίν.
διὰ ταὐτὸ δὲ καὶ μετὰ τὴν χιόνα πνεῖ νότος. ὅλως
δὲ καὶ ἡ χιὼν καὶ ἡ χάλαζα καὶ τὸ ὕδωρ καὶ πᾶσα
ἡ τοιαύτη ἀποκάθαρσις πέψεως σημεῖόν ἐστιν.
15 διὸ καὶ μετὰ τὸν ὑετὸν καὶ τὰς τοιαύτας χειμασίας
πίπτει τὰ πνεύματα.

Διὰ τί αἱ τροπαὶ πνέουσιν; ἢ διὰ τὸ αὐτὸ ὃ καὶ
οἱ εὔριποι ῥέουσιν; μέχρι γὰρ τοῦ ῥεῖν καὶ ἡ
θάλαττα φέρεται καὶ ὁ ἀήρ· εἶθ᾽ ὅταν ἀντιπέσῃ
καὶ μηκέτι δύνηται τὰ ἀπόγεια προάγειν διὰ τὸ
20 μὴ ἰσχυρὰν ἔχειν τὴν ἀρχὴν τῆς κινήσεως καὶ
φορᾶς, πάλιν ἀνταποδίδωσιν.

Διὰ τί αἱ τροπαὶ ἐκ τῆς θαλάττης εἰσίν; ἢ ὅτι

to collect clouds the east wind is less obvious in doing what it does than the north-east wind.

Why are the north winds periodic, whereas the 2 south winds are not ? Or are the south winds also periodic, but not continuous, because the origin of the south wind is far away from us, but we live under the north wind ? Again, the periodic north winds blow when the air is still (for they blow in summer), but the south winds blow in the spring, when the atmospheric conditions are less stable. In addition to this, the south wind is wet, but the upper district is unfavourable to the wet ; so the moisture which collects there is most rapidly dispersed. But moisture wanders about and so the south wind not remaining in the same place produces movement of the air. As the air when it moves changes its position, other winds arise ; for wind is a movement of the air.

Why does the south wind blow after a frost ? Is it 3 because frost occurs after concoction has taken place, and after absorption and concoction a change to the contrary occurs ? And the south wind is contrary to the north. For the same reason the south wind also blows after snow. Speaking generally, snow and hail and rain and all such purgation are proof of concoction. So after rain and storms of a like nature the winds blow.

Why do variable winds blow ? Is it for the same 4 reason as that which makes narrow channels ebb and flow ? For both sea and air are set in motion until they flow ; then, when opposition occurs and the offshore wind can no longer drive them because the origin of the movement and impetus is not sufficiently strong, they flow back again.

Why do these variable winds come from the sea ? 5

940 b

ἡ θάλαττα πλησίον; ἢ ὅτι ἐναντίον ἐστὶ τῇ ἀπο-
γείᾳ ἡ τροπαία, καὶ ἔστιν ἡ τροπαία οἷον ἀναστροφὴ
ἀπογείας; ἡ δὲ ἀπογεία τὸ ἐκ τῆς γῆς πρὸς τὴν
25 θάλατταν πνεῦμα γινόμενον, ἡ δὲ τροπαία ἡ τούτου
παλίρροια. ὥστε ἀνάγκη ἐκ θαλάττης εἶναι. ἢ[1]
διὰ τὸ εἰς τὴν θάλατταν ἀθροισθῆναι τὸν ῥυέντα
ἀέρα; τοῦ δὲ μὴ εἰς τὴν γῆν τοῦτο συνίστασθαι
καὶ τοῦ ἀνακάμπτειν ἀπιὸν αἴτιον ὅτι ἡ θάλαττα
ἐν κοίλῳ ἐστίν· ὁ δὲ ἀήρ, ὥσπερ τὸ ὕδωρ, ῥεῖ ἀεὶ
εἰς τὸ κοιλότατον.

30 Διὰ τί οἱ ἐκνεφίαι ὕδατος γενομένου θᾶττον 6
παύονται; ἢ ὅτι αἱ κοιλίαι συμπίπτουσιν τοῦ
νέφους, ὕδατος γενομένου, ἐν αἷς ἡ ἀρχὴ τοῦ
πνεύματος συνίσταται;

Διὰ τί οὐχ οἱ αὐτοὶ ἄνεμοι πανταχοῦ ὑέτιοί 7
εἰσιν; ἢ ὅτι οὐχ οἱ αὐτοὶ πανταχοῦ πρὸς ὄρη ἀντι-
35 πνέουσιν, ἀλλ' ἕτεροι κεῖνται πρὸς ἕτερα ὄρη; οἷον
γὰρ πρὸς ἄναντη μόλις ῥεόντων, ἐνταῦθα ὑφίσταται
μᾶλλον τὰ νέφη, οὗ ἀδυνατεῖ ἔτι προωθεῖν αὐτὰ
ἄνεμος. ὑφιστάμενα δὲ καὶ πιεζόμενα ῥήγνυται.

941 a Διὰ τί αἱ μὲν καθαραὶ δύσεις εὐδιεινὸν σημεῖον, 8
αἱ δὲ τεταραγμέναι χειμερινόν; ἢ ὅτι χειμὼν
γίνεται συνισταμένου καὶ πυκνουμένου τοῦ ἀέρος;
ὅταν μὲν οὖν κρατῇ ὁ ἥλιος, διακρίνει καὶ αἰθριάζει
5 αὐτόν, ὅταν δὲ κρατῆται, ἐπινεφῇ ποιεῖ. ἐὰν μὲν
οὖν ἰσχυρὰ ᾖ ἡ σύστασις, εὐθὺς ἡμέρας γίνεται
χειμών· ἐὰν δὲ ἀσθενεστέρα, μὴ παντάπασιν δὲ
κρατουμένη, τὸ συνιστάμενον ἐξωθεῖται πρὸς τὰς
δύσεις. ἐνταῦθα δὲ μένει διὰ τὸ παχύτερον[2] εἶναι
τὸν περὶ τὴν γῆν ἀέρα τοῦ χειμῶνος. ταχὺ δὲ
10 συνίσταται καὶ ὁ ἄλλος διὰ τὸ ἔχειν ἀρχὴν καὶ

---

[1] ἢ Forster : ἡ θάλαττά ἐστι Ruelle.
[2] παχύτερον Forster : παχύτατον Ruelle.

Is it because the sea is near by ? Or is it because the changing wind is contrary to the offshore wind, and because it is, so to speak, a reversal of the offshore wind ? The land wind is a breeze which blows from the land towards the sea, and the changing wind is the reversal of this, so that it must come from the sea. Or is it because the flowing air has collected on the sea ? The reason why it does not collect on the land and of its curving back as it retreats is that the sea is in a hollow ; and the air, like water, always flows into the deepest hollow.

Why do hurricanes cease more quickly after the 6 rain falls ? Is it because, when the rain falls, the hollow spaces in the cloud in which the wind takes its rise, collapse ?

Why are not the same winds rainy everywhere ? 7 Is it because the same winds do not everywhere blow towards the mountains, but different winds blow against different mountains ? For instance, when winds blow with difficulty against steep mountains, there clouds are more likely to form, where the wind cannot push them further. When they have formed and are subject to pressure, they break.

Why is a clear sunset a sign of fine weather, but a 8 confused sunset a sign of stormy weather ? Is it because a storm occurs when the air is compressed and thick ? So when the sun is in control, it disperses and clears it, but when it is overpowered, it makes it cloudy. If, then, the compression is powerful, a storm arises as soon as it is day ; if the pressure is weaker, but not completely overpowered, the compressed part is driven towards the setting sun. And there it remains, because the air near the earth is denser than the storm. The rest of the air gathers quickly, because it has a place of origin and support

941 a

ἔρεισμα, ὃ δέξεται καὶ ἀθροίσει τὸ προσιόν¹·
ὥσπερ γὰρ ἐν τροπῇ ἑνὸς ἀντιστάντος καὶ οἱ ἄλλοι
μενοῦσιν, οὕτω καὶ ἐπὶ τοῦ ἀέρος. διὸ ταχὺ καὶ
ἐξαίφνης ἐνίοτε γίνεται καὶ ἐπινέφελα. ὅταν οὖν
15 αἱ δύσεις τεταραγμέναι ὦσι, σημεῖόν ἐστιν ἰσχυρὸν
ὅτι οὐ κεκράτηκεν ὁ ἥλιος τῆς συστάσεως, πολὺν
χρόνον ἐναντιούμενος αὐτῇ, ὥστε εἰκότως ἔστι
συστῆναι πλέον. καὶ ἧττον δέ ἐστι φοβερόν, ὅταν
προχειμάσαντος ἢ ὅταν ἐξ εὐδίας τοῦτο συμβῇ.
ἐκείνως μὲν γὰρ ἔοικεν ὥσπερ ὑπόλειμμά τι εἶναι,
οὕτω δὲ ἀρχὴ συστάσεως.

20 Διὰ τί λέγεται " οὔ ποτε νυκτερινὸς βορέας 9
τρίτον ἵκετο φέγγος "; ἢ διότι ἀσθενῆ τὰ πνεύματα τὰ ἀπὸ τῆς ἄρκτου, ὅταν ᾖ νυκτερινά;
σημεῖον γὰρ ὅτι οὐ πολὺς ὁ κινηθεὶς ἀήρ, τὸ
τηνικαῦτα πνεῦσαι, ὅτε ὀλίγη θερμότης ὑπῆρχεν·
ἡ δὲ ὀλίγη ὀλίγον ἐκίνει ἀέρα. τελευτᾷ δὲ ἐν
25 τρισὶ πάντα, καὶ τὰ ἐλάχιστα ἐν τῇ πρώτῃ τριάδι,
ὥστε καὶ τοῦτο τὸ πνεῦμα.

Διὰ τί ὁ βορέας πυκνότερον πνεῖ ἢ ὁ νότος; ἢ 10
ὅτι ὁ μὲν βορέας γειτνιῶν τῇ οἰκουμένῃ οὐ λανθάνει ὀλιγοχρόνιος ὤν (ἅμα γὰρ πνεῖ καὶ πάρεστιν),
30 ὁ δὲ νότος οὐκ ἀφικνεῖται διὰ τὸ πόρρωθεν πνεῖν;

Διὰ τί ὁ νότος ἧττον μετὰ χειμερινὰς νύκτας 11
πνεῖ ἢ μεθ' ἡμέρας; ἢ ὅτι καὶ τῆς νυκτὸς ὁ ἥλιος
ἐγγύς ἐστι τῇ πρὸς νότον χώρᾳ, καὶ ἀλεεινότεραι
αἱ νύκτες ἐκεῖ ἢ πρὸς ἄρκτον αἱ ἡμέραι; ὥστε
35 πολὺς κινεῖται ὁ ἀήρ, καὶ οὐθὲν ἐλάττων ἢ μεθ'
ἡμέραν· ἀλλ' αἱ θερμότεραι ἡμέραι κωλύουσι
μᾶλλον πνεῖν, ξηραίνουσαι τὰς ὑγρότητας.

¹ Omitting, with Forster, the meaningless καθάπερ ὄρθρος
add. Ruelle.

ᵃ Theophrastus, *De Ventis*, § 9.

which will receive and collect all that reaches it ; for just as in a rout if one man resists the rest will also stand firm, so also with the air. Consequently, it sometimes becomes cloudy quite quickly and suddenly. When, therefore, the sunset is disturbed, it is strong evidence that the sun is not in control of the mass, though opposing it for a considerable time, so that naturally the mass becomes greater. It is less alarming when this occurs after a storm than when it arises out of a calm. For in the former case it seems to be only the remainder of the storm, but in the latter it is the beginning of a massing of cloud.

Why is there a saying " Boreas at night does not 9 survive the third day " ? [a] Is it because the winds blowing from the north are weak when they occur at night ? The proof that the quantity of air moved is not great is the fact that the wind blows from that quarter when there was but little heat ; and a small amount of heat moves a small quantity of air. Now all things end in threes and the weakest in the first triad, and that is what this wind does also.

Why is the north wind more frequent than the 10 south wind ? Is it because the north wind being near the earth is noticed though it lasts only a short time (for it blows and appears at the same moment), but the south wind does not reach us because it blows from a great way off ?

Why does the south wind blow less after stormy 11 nights than after stormy days ? Is it because in the night the sun is near to the south region and the nights there are warmer than days in the north ? So that much air is moved, and no less than in the day-time ; but the warmer days prevent more blowing because they dry the moisture.

941 a

Διὰ τί ἐπὶ κυνὶ ὁ νότος πνεῖ, καὶ τοῦτο ὥσπερ 12
τι ἄλλο γίνεται τεταγμένως; ἢ διότι θερμὰ τὰ
κάτω, τοῦ ἡλίου ⟨οὐ⟩¹ πόρρω ὄντος, ὥστε πολλὴ ἡ
ἀτμὶς γίνεται; καὶ πολλοὶ δὴ ⟨ἂν⟩² ἔπνεον, εἰ μὴ
941 b διὰ τοὺς ἐτησίας. νῦν δὲ οὗτοι κωλύουσιν, ἢ ὅτι
ἐπὶ πᾶσι μὲν σημαίνει τοῖς ἄστροις δυομένοις ἢ
ἐπιτέλλουσιν, οὐχ ἥκιστα δὲ ἐπὶ τούτῳ; δῆλον
δὲ ὅτι πνεύματα μάλιστα ἐπὶ τούτῳ καὶ μετ᾽
5 αὐτόν. ἐπεὶ δὲ πνίγει, καὶ πνεύματα εἰκότως
ἐπ᾽ αὐτῷ τὰ θερμότατα κινεῖται· ὁ δὲ νότος θερμός
ἐστιν. ἐπεὶ δὲ εἴθισται μάλιστα ἐκ τῶν ἐναντίων
εἰς τὰ ἐναντία μεταβάλλειν, πρὸ κυνὸς δὲ οἱ πρόδρομοι πνέουσιν ὄντες βορέαι, εἰκότως μετὰ κύνα
νότος πνεῖ, ἐπειδὴ ἐπισημαίνει μέν, ἐπιτέλλουσι
10 δὲ τοῖς ἄστροις τὸ [δὲ] ἐπισημαίνειν ἐστὶν μετα-
βολὴν τοῦ ἀέρος ποιεῖν· μεταβάλλει δὲ πάντα εἰς
τοὺς ἐναντίους ἢ τοὺς ἐπὶ δεξιὰ ἀνέμους τὰ πνεύματα. ἐπεὶ δὲ βορέας εἰς τοὺς ἐπιδεξίους ⟨οὐ⟩³
μεταβάλλει, εἴη ἂν αὐτῷ λοιπὸν εἰς νότον μεταβάλλειν. ἔστιν δὲ καὶ ἡ μετὰ τὰς χειμερινὰς
15 τροπὰς πεντεκαιδεκάτη νότιος, διὰ τὸ τὰς μὲν
τροπὰς ἀρχήν τινα εἶναι, κινεῖν δὲ τὸν κατ᾽ αὐτὴν
μάλιστα ἀέρα τὸν ἥλιον, εἶναι δὲ ἐν ταύταις ταῖς
τροπαῖς πρὸς νότον. καθάπερ οὖν καὶ τὰ ἀπ᾽
ἀνατολῆς κινῶν ἀπηλιώτας ἀνέμους ἤγειρεν, οὕτω
καὶ τὰ ἀπὸ μεσημβρίας κινῶν νότους ἐγείρει. οὐκ
20 εὐθὺ δὲ ἀπὸ τροπῶν ποιεῖ τοῦτο διὰ τὸ βραχυτάτας
ποιεῖσθαι τὰς μεταστάσεις τότε, ἀλλ᾽ ἐν τῇ πεντε-
καιδεκάτῃ διὰ τὸ τὸν χρόνον τοῦτον συμμέτρως
ἔχειν τῇ κατὰ τὴν μετάστασιν πρώτῃ φαντασίᾳ·

---

¹ οὐ added by Forster.   ² ἂν added by Forster.
³ οὐ added by Forster from Th. G.

Why does the south wind blow at the time of the 12 Dog-star, and that too just like any other periodic occurrence ? Is it because the lower region is hot as the sun is not far away, so that there is considerable evaporation ? They would blow often if it were not for the Etesian winds, but, as it is, these prevent them. Or is it because some sign accompanies the setting and rising of all stars, and of the Dog-star as much as any ? For it is clear that the winds occur at the time of its rising and after it. But when the weather is stifling, naturally the hottest winds occur at this time ; and the south wind is hot. But as it is usual for change to take place between opposites, and as the " precursors," which are northerly winds, blow before the Dog-star, naturally the south wind blows after it, since it is a sign, and at the rising of the stars the sign in question means a change in the air. Now all winds change either to their opposites or to those on their right.[a] Now since the north wind does not change to the winds on the right, its only possible change is to a south wind. Now on the fifteenth day after the winter solstice the wind is in the south, because the solstice marks the beginning of a change, and the sun sets in motion the air which is nearest to it, and at the time of the winter solstice the sun is in the south. Just as it rouses the east winds when it affects the eastern regions, so it rouses the south winds when it affects the southern regions. It does not produce this effect immediately after the solstice, because at the time the change affects a very small area, but it does so on the fifteenth day, because this is the moment which coincides with the first impression produced by the change ; for that

[a] Right, *i.e.* according to the compass points : here, therefore, the East.

ὅλου γάρ ἐστι μέρος εὐσημότατον ὁ εἰρημένος χρόνος.

Διὰ τί ἐπὶ Ὠρίωνι γίνονται αἰόλοι μάλιστα αἱ
25 ἡμέραι καὶ ἀκαιρίαι τῶν πνευμάτων; ἢ ὅτι ἐν
μεταβολῇ ἀεὶ πάντα ἀοριστεῖ μάλιστα, ὁ δ᾽ Ὠρίων
ἀνατέλλει μὲν ἐν ἀρχῇ ὀπώρας, δύνει δὲ χειμῶνος,
ὥστε διὰ τὸ μήπω καθεστάναι μίαν ὥραν, ἀλλὰ
τὴν μὲν γίνεσθαι, τὴν δὲ παύεσθαι, διὰ ταῦτα
30 ἀνάγκη καὶ τὰ πνεύματα ἀκατάστατα εἶναι διὰ
τὸ ἐπαμφοτερίζειν τὰ ἐξ ἑκατέρας. καὶ χαλεπὸς
δὴ λέγεται καὶ δύνων καὶ ἀνατέλλων ὁ Ὠρίων διὰ
τὴν ἀοριστίαν τῆς ὥρας· ἀνάγκη γὰρ ταραχώδη
εἶναι καὶ ἀνώμαλον.

Διὰ τί ὁ νυκτερινὸς βορέας τριταῖος λήγει;
35 πότερον ὅτι ἀπὸ μικρᾶς καὶ ἀσθενοῦς ἀρχῆς, ἡ
τρίτη δὲ κρίσιμος; ἢ ὅτι ἀθρόος ἡ ἔκρυσις, ὥσπερ
τῶν ἐκνεφιῶν; ταχεῖα οὖν ἡ παῦλα.

Διὰ τί βορέαι πλεῖστοι πνέουσι τῶν ἀνέμων;
ἢ διὰ τὸ πρὸς τούτῳ τὴν οἰκουμένην τῷ τόπῳ
942 a ὑποκεῖσθαι ὄντι ὑψηλῷ καὶ ἔξω τροπῶν καὶ
πλήρει χιόνος, ἢ οὐδέποτε ἔνια ὄρη λείπει; τὸ
πολὺ οὖν ὑγραινομένων τῶν πεπηγότων πολλάκις
πνεῦμα γίνεται. τοῦτο δέ ἐστι βορέας, τὸ ἐκ τῶν
ἀπὸ τῆς ἄρκτου τόπων πνεῦμα.

5 Διὰ τί οἱ νότοι πνέουσι μὲν χειμῶνος καὶ ἔαρος
ἀρχομένου καὶ μετοπώρου λήγοντος, εἰσὶ δὲ
κυματοειδεῖς καὶ συνεστραμμένοι, καὶ τοῖς ἐν
Λιβύῃ ὁμοίως ψυχροὶ ὡς οἱ βορέαι ἐνταῦθα; ἢ
διότι πλησίον τοῦ ἡλίου ὄντος ἀνάγκη κινεῖσθαι
τὰ πνεύματα; ὁ δὲ ἥλιος τοῦ χειμῶνος πρὸς
10 νότον φέρεται, καὶ τοῦ μὲν ἔαρος ἀρχομένου, τοῦ
δὲ μετοπώρου τελευτῶντος ἤδη θερμαίνει, τὸ δὲ

date is the most significant moment in the whole process.

Why is there more variety in the day and more 13 frequent change of wind at the rising of Orion than at other times ? Is it because everything is less fixed in time at the moment of change, and Orion rises at the beginning of autumn, and sets in the winter, so that as one season is not yet established, but one is arriving and another dying, for this reason the winds also must be unsettled because the conditions are intermedial between the two seasons ? In fact, Orion is described as an unpleasant season both rising and setting because of the lack of fixity of the season ; it must necessarily be a time of confusion and inconsistency.

Why does the nightly north wind cease on the third 14 day ? Is it because it arises from a small and weak beginning, and the third day is its critical moment ? Or is it because it rushes on all at once, like the hurricane winds ? So its cessation is equally swift.

Why are the north winds the commonest of all 15 winds ? Is it because the inhabited world lies nearest to the north which is high, outside the range of the solstice and full of snow, which never leaves some mountains ? So the mass of frozen matter as it liquefies often produces wind. And this is the north wind, the wind, that is, which comes from the region of the North Pole.

Why do the south winds blow at the beginning of 16 winter and spring and at the end of autumn, and are gusty and move in circles, and are as cold in Libya as the north wind in this country ? Is it because the sun being near the winds must be set in motion? Now in winter the sun travels towards the south, and at the beginning of spring and at the end of autumn it is already giving out heat, whereas throughout the

942 a

θέρος πρὸς βορέαν φέρεται, ἐκείνους δὲ ἀπολείπει
τοὺς τόπους. θερμὸς δέ ἐστι διὰ τὸ μίγνυσθαι
τὸ πνεῦμα τῷ κατὰ Λιβύην ἀέρι θερμῷ ὄντι· καὶ
διὰ τοῦτο μεγαλοκύμων νοτίζειν ποιεῖ τὸ θέρος,
15 ἐμπίπτων εἰς τὴν θάλατταν.

Διὰ τί ὁ νότος δυσώδης; ἢ ὅτι ὑγρὰ καὶ θερμὰ 17
ποιεῖ τὰ σώματα, ταῦτα δὲ σήπεται μάλιστα; οἱ
δὲ ἐκ τῆς θαλάττης νότοι ἀγαθοὶ φυτοῖς· ἐκ
θαλάττης γὰρ αὐτοῖς προσπίπτει. καὶ τῆς Ἀτ-
20 τικῆς τῷ Θριασίῳ πεδίῳ αἴτιον, διότι ἀπεψυγμένος
ἀφικνεῖται. αἱ δ᾽ ἐρυσῖβαι γίνονται ὑπὸ ὑγρότητος
θερμῆς μέν, ἀλλοτρίας δέ.

Διὰ τί ἄνεμος γίνεται πρὸ τῶν ἐκλείψεων ὡς 18
τὰ πολλά, ἀκρόνυχον μὲν πρὸ τῶν μεσονυκτίων
ἐκλείψεων, μεσονύκτιον δὲ πρὸ τῶν ἑώων; ἢ
25 διότι ἀμαυροῦται τὸ θερμὸν τὸ ἀπὸ τῆς σελήνης
διὰ τὸ πλησίον ἤδη φορὰν εἶναι, ἐν ᾧ γενομένῳ
ἔσται ἡ ἔκλειψις; ἀνιεμένου οὖν ᾧ κατείχετο ὁ
ἀὴρ καὶ ἠρέμει, πάλιν κινεῖται καὶ γίνεται πνεῦμα
τῆς ὀψιαίτερον ἐκλείψεως ὀψιαίτερον.

Διὰ τί ὁ νότος οὐκ ἀρχόμενος, ἀλλὰ λήγων 19
30 ὑέτιος; πότερον ὅτι πόρρωθεν συνάγει τὸν ἀέρα;
γίνεται δὲ συνιστάντος τὸ ὕδωρ, συνίσταται δὲ
ὕστερον ἢ ἄρχεται. ἢ ὅτι ἀρχομένου θερμός
ἐστιν ὁ ἀὴρ ἔτι διὰ τὸ ἐκ τοιούτου ἐληλυθέναι,
ἐπιχρονιζόμενος δὲ ψυχθεὶς συνίσταται μᾶλλον εἰς
ὕδωρ;

Διὰ τί ὁ νότος, ὅταν μὲν ἐλάττων ᾖ, αἴθριός 20
35 ἐστιν, ὅταν δὲ μέγας, νεφώδης καὶ χρονιώτερος;
πότερον, ὥσπερ τινὲς λέγουσιν, διὰ τὴν ἀρχήν;
ἐὰν μὲν γὰρ ἀπ᾽ ἐλάττονος, αἴθριος, ἐὰν δὲ ἀπὸ

summer it is travelling towards the north, and deserting those quarters. It is hot because the wind mingles with the air in Libya which is hot ; so it is gusty and, by falling on the sea, makes the summer wet.

Why does the south wind produce an unpleasant 17 smell ? Is it because it makes bodies moist and hot, and in this condition they are most liable to decomposition ? But south winds from the sea are good for plants ; for they fall upon them from the sea. This is the case in Attica on the Thriasian Plain, for the south wind arrives cool. Now red blight is due to moisture which is hot, but comes from elsewhere.

Why does wind arise as a rule before an eclipse, at 18 nightfall before an eclipse at midnight, and at midnight before an eclipse at dawn ? Is it because the heat from the moon lessens as its direction is near the earth, which is the condition of an eclipse ? So when that by which the air is controlled and kept at rest slackens off, the wind moves again and comes later when the eclipse is later.

Why does the south wind bring rain, not at the 19 beginning but when it is dying down ? Is it because it collects the air from far off ? Now the rains come when the air collects, and it collects more later on than at the beginning. Or is it because when the wind first rises the air is still hot, having just come from a hot region, but as time goes on it grows cool and collects more into rain ?

Why does the south wind, when it is slight, come 20 with a clear sky, but when it is strong, brings cloud and lasts for a longer time ? Is it due, as some say, to its source ? For if it arises from a weaker source the

942 a
πλείονος ὁρμήσῃ, νεφελώδης. ἢ ὅτι ἐλάττων
ἀρχόμενός ἐστιν, ὥστε οὐ πολὺν ἀέρα ὠθεῖ, ἐπὶ
942 b τέλει δὲ εἴωθεν γίνεσθαι μέγας; διὸ καὶ παροιμιά-
ζονται '' ἀρχομένου γε νότου καὶ λήγοντος βορέαο.''

Διὰ τί προΐεται τοῦ χειμῶνος ἀπὸ τῆς ἔω τὰ 21
πνεύματα, τοῦ θέρους δὲ καὶ ἀφ' ἑσπέρας; ἢ ὅτι
5 ὅταν μηκέτι κρατῇ ὁ ἥλιος, ἀφιέμενος ὁ ἀὴρ ῥεῖ;
δύνων τε οὖν καταλείπει νέφη, ἀφ' ὧν οἱ ζέφυροι·
καὶ ὅσον ἂν ἐπαγάγῃ ἐκείνοις τοῖς ἐν τῷ κάτω
ἡμισφαιρίῳ οἰκοῦσιν, ἑωθινὸν πνεῦμα γίνεται.
τἀναντία δέ, ὅταν δύνῃ ἐν τῷ κάτω μέρει, ἐκείνοις
10 τε ζεφύρους ποιήσει καὶ ἐνταῦθα ἑωθινὸν πνεῦμα
ἀπὸ τοῦ ἑπομένου ἀέρος αὐτῷ. διὰ τοῦτο κἂν
καταλάβῃ ἄλλον ἄνεμον, μείζων γίνεται αἱρομένου,
ὅτι προσέθηκεν.

Διὰ τί οἱ κύνες τὰ ἴχνη ἥκιστα εὑρίσκουσιν 22
ζεφύρου πνέοντος; ἢ διότι μάλιστα συγχεῖ διὰ
15 τὸ συνεχέστατος εἶναι τῶν ἀνέμων καὶ μάλιστα
ὑπὸ τὴν γῆν πνεῖν;

Διὰ τί, ὅταν ἀστέρες διάττωσιν, ἀνέμου σημεῖον; 23
ἢ ὅτι ὑπὸ τοῦ πνεύματος φέρονται, καὶ πρότερον
ἐκεῖ γίνεται πνεῦμα ἢ παρ' ἡμῖν; διὸ καὶ ἀφ' οὗ
ἂν τόπου φέρωνται οἱ ἀστέρες, ἐν τούτῳ καὶ τὸ
πνεῦμα γίνεται.

20 Διὰ τί μεγίστας νεφέλας τῶν ἀνέμων ὁ ζέφυρος 24
ἄγει; ἢ διότι ἐκ πελάγους πνεῖ καὶ κατὰ τὴν
θάλατταν; ἐκ πολλοῦ οὖν καὶ συνάγει.

Διὰ τί οἱ ἐπὶ τέλει ἄνεμοι μέγιστοι; ἢ ὅτι ὅταν 25
ἀθρόοι ἐκπνεύσωσιν, ὀλίγον τὸ θερμόν;

ᵃ For the whole proverb cf. 945 a 29.

sky is clear, but if from a larger source the sky is cloudy. Or is it smaller to begin with, so that it does not drive along much air, but it usually becomes strong at the end ? Hence they quote the proverb " When the south wind begins and the north wind dies down." [a]

Why do the winds come from the east in the 21 winter, and from the west also in the summer ? Is it because, when the sun can no longer exercise control, the air flows free ? So, when the sun sets, it leaves clouds behind, from which the west winds blow ; and all that the sun takes with it to those who live in the southern hemisphere, produces an east wind with them. On the contrary, when the sun sets in the southern hemisphere, it will produce a west wind for those who dwell there and an east wind here from the air which follows it. For this reason also if it finds another wind blowing it will blow stronger as the sun rises, because it adds to it.

Why are dogs least able to follow scent when the 22 west wind blows ? Is it because the scent is most confused because the west is the most constant of all the winds and blows most upon the land ?

Why is it a sign of wind when there are shooting 23 stars ? Is it because they are carried by the wind, and the wind reaches them before us ? So also the wind rises in the quarter from which the stars are travelling.

Why of all the winds does the south wind collect 24 the largest clouds ? Is it because it blows from the open sea and over the sea ? So it collects clouds over a large range.

Why are winds strongest at the end ? Is it be- 25 cause when they expend themselves all at once, the quantity of heat is small ?

25 Διὰ τί, ἐὰν περὶ ἰσημερίαν λὶψ πνεύσῃ, ὕδωρ 26
γίνεται; ἢ ὅτι καθ᾽ ὃν ἂν ᾖ ὁ ἥλιος τόπον τοῦ
κόσμου, τὰ ἐντεῦθεν πνεύματα κινεῖ; διὸ καὶ ἡ
τῶν πνευμάτων περίστασις κατὰ τὴν τοῦ ἡλίου
φορὰν γίνεται. ἐπεὶ δ᾽ ἡ ἰσημερία μεθόριόν ἐστι
30 χειμῶνος καὶ θέρους, ὅταν συμβῇ τὸν ἥλιον κατὰ
τὴν ἡμῖν φαινομένην ἰσημερίαν ὑπερβεβληκέναι ἢ
ἐκλείπειν τοῦ ἀκριβοῦς ὅρου καὶ εἶναι μᾶλλον ἐν
τοῖς χειμερίοις, συμβαίνει τοὺς ἐκ τούτου τοῦ
μέρους ἀνέμους πνεῖν, ὧν ἐστι πρῶτος λίψ, ὧν
ὑγρὸς φύσει. ὄντος δὲ τοῦ ἡλίου μᾶλλον ἐν τῷ
χειμερίῳ μέρει τοῦ κόσμου, καὶ κινοῦντος τὰ ἐν
35 αὐτῷ πνεύματα, τὰ χειμῶνος ἔργα συμβαίνει
γίνεσθαι· τούτων δέ ἐστιν ὁ ὄμβρος. ἔτι δὲ
ἐπειδὴ ἡ ἰσημερία ἐστὶν καθάπερ χειμὼν καὶ θέρος
ἰσοκρατές, ἐὰν ὁποτερωοῦν αὐτῶν τι προστεθῇ,
943 a εὔσημον τὴν ῥοπὴν ποιεῖ, καθάπερ ἐπὶ τῶν ἰσα-
ζόντων ζυγῶν. ἐπεὶ δὲ ὁ λὶψ ἔκ τε τῆς χειμερίου
τάξεώς ἐστιν καὶ ὑγρὸς φύσει, προστεθεὶς ἐν τῇ
ἰσημερίᾳ ῥοπὴν χειμῶνος ἐποίησεν καὶ ὄμβρον· ὁ
γὰρ ὄμβρος χειμών ἐστιν οἰκειότατος τῷ πνεύματι.

5 Διὰ τί ὁ νότος καὶ ὁ εὖρος θερμότεροι ὄντες τῶν 27
ἐναντίων, ὁ μὲν τοῦ βορέου, ὁ δὲ τοῦ ζεφύρου,
ὑδατωδέστεροί εἰσιν; καίτοι διὰ ψυχρότητα ὕδωρ
ἐξ ἀέρος γίνεται. οὐ γὰρ διὰ τὸ ἀπωθεῖν τὸν
βορέαν ἐντεῦθεν γίνεται τὰ νέφη· ὁ γὰρ ζέφυρος
10 καὶ ὁ εὖρος ἀπάγουσιν ἄμφω (ὁμοίως γὰρ πλάγιοι),
καὶ οἱ ἄλλοι δὲ πάντες, ὅθεν πνέουσιν. πότερον
ὅτι ἀντιπεριίσταται τὸ ψυχρὸν εἴσω μᾶλλον, ὅταν

Why is it that, if the south-west wind blows at the 26 time of the equinox, rain follows ? Is it because the sun drives the wind in that part of the world in which it is ? So the veering of the winds depends upon the course of the sun. But since the time of the equinox is the boundary between winter and summer, when the sun has passed beyond what appears to us the equinox or is short of the precise boundary and is more in the wintry quarter, the winds are those which blow from that quarter, of which the south-west is the first, being naturally a wet wind. But when the sun is rather in the wintry quarter of the world, and drives the winds in that quarter, wintry conditions naturally occur, and one of these is rain. Again, since the equinox is a time at which winter and summer are equally powerful, if any addition is made to either of them, the balance in that direction becomes marked, as we also see happens with balanced scales. But since the south-west wind arises from wintry conditions and is naturally wet, when it is added at the time of the equinox it produces a balance in favour of winter and rain, for rain is the wintry condition most closely related to this wind.

Why is it that the south and the south-east wind, 27 which are warmer than the opposite winds—the north and west winds—are more rainy ? And yet rain comes from the atmosphere owing to cold. For it is not due to the north wind thrusting them away from our part of the world that the clouds form ; for the west and south-east winds both drive away the clouds (for they equally blow sideways) and so do all the other winds drive the clouds from the quarters from which they blow. Is it because the cold is compressed more within, when the heat without is

943 a

ἢ ἔξω τὸ θερμὸν μᾶλλον; ἢ ἔστι μέν τι καὶ διὰ
τὸ ὅθεν πνέουσιν, αἰθρίους εἶναι; καὶ γὰρ εὖρος
ἀπ᾽ ἠοῦς ἐστίν. πρὸς δὲ ἑσπέραν κεῖται ζέφυρος.[1]
15 ἀλλὰ καὶ διότι πρότερον θερμαινόμενος ὁ ἀήρ,
ὥσπερ καὶ τὰ ὕδατα, τάχιστα καὶ μάλιστα ψύχεται.
φέρεται οὖν ὁ μὲν ἀπὸ τοῦ εὔρου ἀπ᾽ ἀνατολῆς
ἀὴρ θερμός, ὁ δὲ ἀπὸ τοῦ νότου ἀπὸ μεσημβρίας.
ὅταν οὖν ἔλθωσιν εἰς τὸν ψυχρότερον τόπον, ταχὺ
20 πήγνυνται καὶ συνίστανται εἰς ὕδωρ. καὶ μᾶλλον
ὁ εὖρος ποιεῖ ὕδωρ, ὅτι ἀπὸ τοῦ ἡλίου μᾶλλον
φέρει τὸν ἀέρα, καὶ ὁμοίως θερμόν. ὁ δὲ νότος
λήγων ὑδατώδης, ὅτι ψυχρὸς ὁ πρῶτος φερόμενος
ἀὴρ ἀπὸ τῆς θαλάττης, ὁ δὲ τελευταῖος διάθερμος
ὢν ἀπὸ τῆς γῆς κομίζει. ἢ οὐ μόνον τοῦτ᾽ αἴτιον,
25 ἀλλ᾽ ὅτι καὶ μείζων λήγων ὁ νότος γίνεται; διὸ
καὶ ἡ παροιμία εἰς αὐτὸν " ἀρχομένου τε νότου."
οἱ δὲ μείζους ψυχρότεροι. ὥστε πηγνύει ὕστερον
τὰ νέφη. ἢ διὰ τοῦτο ὑδατωδέστερος ἢ ἀρχόμενος;

Διὰ τί οἱ ἄνεμοι ξηραίνουσι ψυχροὶ ὄντες; ἢ
διότι ἀτμίζειν ποιοῦσιν οἱ ψυχρότεροι; διὰ τί
30 δὲ μᾶλλον ἢ ὁ ἥλιος; ἢ διότι ἀπάγουσι τὴν
ἀτμίδα, ὁ δὲ ἥλιος καταλείπει; ὑγραίνει μὲν οὖν
μᾶλλον, ξηραίνει δὲ ἧττον.

Διὰ τί ὁ καικίας μόνος τῶν ἀνέμων ἐφ᾽ ἑαυτὸν
ἄγει τὰ νέφη, ὥσπερ καὶ ἡ παροιμία λέγει " ἕλκων
ἐφ᾽ αὑτὸν ὥσπερ καικίας νέφος." οἱ γὰρ ἄλλοι,

---

[1] ἥδε δὲ ἡ χώρα πρὸς ἑσπέραν κεῖται καὶ ζέφυρος ms. The
text has been revised according to Th. G.

[a] 945 a 29 for complete proverb.

greater ? Or is it due to the direction from which they blow, that they cause clear skies ? For the south-east wind blows from an easterly direction ; but the west wind lies towards the west. But it is also because air which is previously heated also cools very quickly, just as water does. Now the air which is carried by the south-east wind from the east is warm, and so is the air carried by the south-west from the south. So when they reach a colder district, they quickly condense and form rain. The south-east wind produces rain even more, because it brings the air more from the direction of the sun and this is equally warm. But the south wind is a rainy wind when it is dying down, because the air, when it first comes off the sea, is cold, but that which comes last, when it is warmed through, comes from the land. Perhaps this is not the only reason but it is also due to the fact that the south wind becomes stronger when it is dying down. Hence the proverb, " When the south wind begins." [a] But the stronger winds are colder. So that the south wind masses the clouds later on. Is it for this reason that it is more rainy than at the beginning ?

Why do winds which are cold have a drying effect ? 28 Is it because the colder winds produce evaporation ? Why do they cause more evaporation than the sun ? Is it because they drive off the vapour, but the sun leaves it ? So it produces more moisture and less dryness.

Why is the north-easter the only wind which at- 29 tracts clouds to itself, as the proverb says, " Drawing clouds to itself like the north-easter " ? For the other winds drive (the clouds) from the quarter

943 a

35 ὅθεν ἂν πνέωσιν, ἐνταῦθα ἀναστέλλουσιν. πότερον
αἴτιον ὅτι ἅμα ὁ ἐναντίος πνεῖ; ἢ οὐκ ἂν ἐλάν-
θανεν, ἀλλὰ πέφυκεν τὸ πνεῦμα κύκλου γραμμὴν
φέρεσθαι; οἱ μὲν οὖν ἄλλοι περὶ τὴν γῆν πνέουσιν·
943 b τοῦτο δὲ τὸ κοῖλον τῆς γραμμῆς πρὸς τὸν οὐρανὸν
καὶ οὐκ ἐπὶ τὴν γῆν ἐστιν, ὥστε ἐπὶ τὴν ἀρχὴν
πνέων ἐφ᾽ αὑτὸν τὰ νέφη ἄγει.

Διὰ τί ἀπὸ μὲν τῆς θαλάττης οὐκ ἀποπνεῖ ἕωθεν 3
5 ψυχρόν, ἀπὸ δὲ τῶν ποταμῶν; ἢ ὅτι ἡ μὲν
θάλαττά ἐστιν ἐν ἀναπεπταμένοις τόποις, οἱ δὲ
ποταμοὶ ἐν στενοῖς; ἡ οὖν ἀπὸ τῆς θαλάττης αὔρα
εἰς πολὺν τόπον σκίδναται, ὥστε εἶναι ἀσθενής, ἡ
δὲ ἀπὸ τῶν ποταμῶν ἀθρόως φέρεται καὶ μᾶλλον
10 ἰσχύει· διὸ μᾶλλον εἰκότως φαίνεται ψυχρά. ἢ οὐ
τοῦτ᾽ ἐστὶν αἴτιον, ἀλλ᾽ οἱ μὲν ποταμοὶ ψυχροί
εἰσιν, ἡ δὲ θάλαττα οὔτε θερμὴ οὔτε ψυχρά;
γίνεται δὲ ἡ αὔρα καὶ ἀποπνοὴ θερμαινομένων
ἢ ψυχομένων· ὁπότερον γὰρ ἂν τούτων πάσχῃ,
ἐξαεροῦται, ἐξαερουμένου δὲ τοῦ ὕδατος ὁ ἀὴρ
γινόμενος φέρεται, ὅ ἐστιν αὔρα. τὸ μὲν οὖν ἀπὸ
15 τῶν ψυχρῶν ψυχρὸν εἰκότως ἀποπνεῖ, τὰ δὲ ἀπὸ
τῶν σφόδρα θερμῶν ἀποπνέοντα ψύχεται καὶ
γίνεται ψυχρά. τοὺς μὲν οὖν ποταμοὺς ψυχροὺς
ἅπαντας εὕροι τις ἄν, ἡ δὲ θάλαττα οὔτε ψυχρὰ
οὔτε θερμὴ σφόδρα ἐστίν. οὔτε οὖν τὸ ἀποπνέον
ψυχρὸν ἀπ᾽ αὐτῆς ἐστιν, διὰ τὸ μὴ ψυχρὰν εἶναι
20 σφόδρα, οὔτε ψύχεται ταχύ, διὰ τὸ μὴ θερμὴν
εἶναι σφόδρα.

Διὰ τί ὁ ζέφυρος εὐδιεινὸς καὶ ἥδιστος δοκεῖ εἶναι 3
τῶν ἀνέμων, καὶ οἷον καὶ Ὅμηρος ἐν τῷ Ἠλυσίῳ
πεδίῳ, '' ἀλλ᾽ αἰεὶ ζεφύροιο διαπνείουσιν ἀῆται '';
ἢ πρῶτον μὲν ὅτι ἔχει τὴν τοῦ ἀέρος κρᾶσιν; οὔτε

from which they blow. Is the reason that the contrary wind blows at the same time ? Or would this be obvious, but does the wind naturally travel along the circumference of a circle ? The other winds all blow round the earth ; but the concave side of this circle faces the heavens and not the earth, so that it blows back in the direction of its starting-point, and it draws the clouds towards itself.

Why does it not blow cold in the morning off the sea, whereas it does off rivers ? Is it because the sea lies in wide expanses, but rivers in confined areas ? Thus the breeze which blows off the sea is scattered over a wide area, so that it is feeble, but that from the rivers travels in concentrated form and is stronger, so that it naturally seems colder. Or is this not the reason, but are rivers cold, whereas the sea is neither hot nor cold ? Now a breeze and an exhalation occur when things are becoming either warm or cold : whichever of these conditions is present, there is evaporation, and when water evaporates the resultant air begins to move and this is a breeze. What, then, blows from cold liquids naturally blows cold, and what blows from very hot liquids cools and grows cold. So one would find that all rivers are cold, but the sea is neither very cold nor very hot. So that which blows from it is not cold, because the sea is not very cold nor does it cool quickly, because it is not very hot.

Why does the south-west wind seem to be calm and the gentlest of all the winds, as Homer describes it in the Elysian Plain,[a] " The winds there ever blow from the south-west " ? Is it because in the first place it contains a mixture of air ? For it is

---

[a] *Od.* iv. 567, but it is not the accepted reading.

943 b

25 γὰρ θερμὸς ὥσπερ οἱ ἀπὸ μεσημβρίας καὶ ἔω, οὔτε
ψυχρὸς ὥσπερ οἱ ἀπὸ τῆς ἄρκτου, ἀλλ' ἐν μεθορίῳ
ἐπὶ τῶν ψυχρῶν καὶ θερμῶν πνευμάτων· γειτνιῶν
δὲ ἀμφοῖν τῆς δυνάμεως αὐτῶν κοινωνεῖ, διὸ καὶ
εὔκρατός ἐστι καὶ πνεῖ ἔαρος μάλιστα. ἔτι τὰ
πνεύματα περιίσταται ἢ εἰς τἀναντία ἢ ἐπὶ τὰ
30 δεξιά. μετὰ οὖν τὸν βορέαν πνέων (ἐπὶ δεξιὰ γὰρ
ὁ τόπος) εὐδοκιμεῖ, ὥσπερ παρὰ χαλεπὸν πρᾶος.
καὶ ἅμα ὅταν ἀποχειμάσῃ, εὐδία εἴωθεν γίνεσθαι
ὡς ἐπὶ τὸ πολύ. ὁ δὲ βορέας χειμέριος ἄνεμος.
[καὶ ὁ ἀπηλιώτης δὲ ἐν τῷ μέσῳ ὢν τῶν θερμῶν
καὶ τῶν ψυχρῶν πνευμάτων ἧττον αὐτοῖς κοινωνεῖ.
35 ἀπηλιώτης μὲν γὰρ πνέων τὰ πρὸς νότου πνεύματα
κινεῖ (ἐνταῦθα γὰρ ἡ μετάστασις αὐτοῦ ἐστιν),
κινῶν δὲ οὐ μίγνυται αὐτοῖς. ὁ δὲ ζέφυρος καὶ
944 a κινεῖται ὑπὸ τῶν νοτίων, καὶ πνέων κινεῖ τὰ βόρεια·
τελευτᾷ γὰρ ἐνταῦθα ἡ περίοδος τῶν πνευμάτων.
διὸ τῶν μὲν τὴν τελευτὴν τῶν δὲ τὴν ἀρχὴν ἔχων
ἐν αὐτῷ δικαίως ἡδύς ἐστι καὶ δοκεῖ εἶναι.]

Διὰ τί ἐπὶ κυνὶ νότος πνεῖ; ἢ ὅτι ἐπὶ πᾶσι μὲν 3?
5 σημαίνει τοῖς ἄστροις δυομένοις ἢ ἐπιτέλλουσιν,
οὐχ ἥκιστα δὲ ἐπὶ τούτῳ; δῆλον ὅτι πνεύματα
μάλιστα ἐπὶ τούτῳ καὶ μετ' αὐτόν. ἐπεὶ δὲ πνίγει,
καὶ πνεύματα εἰκότως ἐπ' αὐτῷ τὰ θερμότατα
κινεῖται· ὁ δὲ νότος θερμός ἐστιν.

10 Διὰ τί ὁ ζέφυρος πρὸς τὴν δείλην πνεῖ, πρωῒ δὲ 3?

---

[a] *Cf.* Problem 12, note.
[b] This contradicts Problem 12.

neither hot like the wind that blows from the south and east, nor cold like the wind that blows from the north, but it is on the border-line between the cold and the hot winds : being near both these it shares the power of both, so that it is well mixed and blows most in springtime. Winds, moreover, change either to a contrary direction or to their right.[a] As, then, the south-west wind blows after the north (for it is on the right), it is held in good repute and is mild in contrast with the bitter north.[b] And when the wind drops, the weather is usually calm. But the north wind is a wintry wind. [The east wind though it lies between hot and cold winds shares their nature less. For the east wind as it blows stirs the southerly winds (for that is the direction into which it changes), but though it stirs them it does not mingle with them. For the south-west wind is stirred by the south wind, and when it blows it stirs the northerly winds ; for the circuit of the winds ends here. So, as it contains the ends of some winds and the beginning of others, it justly is and is regarded as a pleasant wind.][c]

Why does the south wind blow at the time of the **32** Dog-star ? Is it because there are significant signs at the time of the rising and setting of all the stars and this is no less true of the Dog-star ? It is clear that winds blow most at this time and after it. But since it is stifling, the hottest winds naturally blow at this time, and the south wind is hot.[d]

Why does the south-west wind blow towards even- **33**

[c] This passage, which seems inappropriate here, is omitted from at least one ms. It is, however, translated by Th. G. It recurs in Problem 55, to which it seems more applicable.

[d] The remainder of this problem is here omitted, being identical with the last part of Problem 12, from ἐπεὶ δέ (941 b 6) to the end.

944 a

οὔ; ἢ αἴτιος μέν ἐστιν ὡς ἐπὶ τὸ πολὺ τῶν πνευμάτων ὁ ἥλιος ἀνατέλλων καὶ δύνων; ὅταν γὰρ
ὑγρὸν ὄντα τὸν ἀέρα διαθερμαίνων πέττῃ καὶ
διακρίνῃ, εἰς πνεῦμα διακρίνει· ἐὰν δὲ ᾖ πνευματώδης ὁ ἀήρ, ἔτι μᾶλλον ἐκπνευματοῦται ὑπὸ
15 τοῦ ἡλίου. ὅταν μὲν οὖν ἐπ’ ἀνατολῇ ᾖ ὁ ἥλιος,
πόρρω ἐστὶ τοῦ ζεφύρου· ἀπὸ γὰρ δυσμῶν πνεῖ.
ὅταν δὲ περὶ τὸ δύνειν ἤδη, τότε διακεκριμένον ἐστὶ
τὸ πνεῦμα τελέως. ἀπὸ δὲ μέσου ἡμέρας καὶ πρὸς
τὴν δείλην συμμετρότατα ἔχει πρὸς τὸ διαθερμᾶναι
καὶ διακρῖναι. διὰ ταῦτα δὲ καὶ ὁ ἀπηλιώτης πρωῒ
ἄρχεται πνεῖν· τοῦ γὰρ ὑπὲρ γῆς ἀέρος τῆς νυκτὸς
ἐξυγραινομένου καὶ τῇ γῇ πλησιάσαντος διὰ βάρος,
ἕωθεν διακρίνων αὐτὸν ὁ ἥλιος τὸν καθ’ αὑτὸν κινεῖ
πρῶτον. τὸ δὲ ἀπὸ τοῦ ἡλίου πνεῦμα ἀνατέλλοντος
ἐντεῦθεν ἀπηλιώτης καλεῖται.

25 Διὰ τί αἰρομένου τοῦ ἡλίου καὶ αὐξάνεται καὶ 34
πίπτει τὰ πνεύματα; ἢ ὅτι τὸ πνεῦμά ἐστιν ἤτοι
τοῦ ἀέρος ἢ τοῦ ἀναχθέντος ὑγροῦ κίνησις; αὕτη
δὲ ὅταν μὲν ἐλάττων ᾖ, ταχὺ καταναλίσκεται ὑπὸ
τοῦ ἡλίου, ὥστε οὐ γίνεται πνεῦμα· ὅταν δὲ πλείων,
30 κινεῖται μᾶλλον τοῦ ἡλίου ἀνατείλαντος· ὁ γὰρ
ἥλιος ἀρχὴ τῶν κινήσεών ἐστιν.

Διὰ τί ὁ ζέφυρος τῆς δείλης πνεῖ; ἢ ἅπαντα τὰ 35
πνεύματα τοῦ ἡλίου διαχέοντος τὸ ὑγρὸν γίνεται;
πρότερον γὰρ συνεστηκός, ὅταν ἡ τοῦ θερμοῦ
δύναμις πλησιάζῃ, ἐξάπτει. ὁ δὲ ζέφυρος ἀφ’
35 ἑσπέρας πνεῖ. εἰκότως οὖν τῆς δείλης γίνεται· τότε
γὰρ ὁ ἥλιος εἰς τὸν τόπον αὐτοῦ ἀφικνεῖται. καὶ
ὁ βορέας καὶ ὁ νότος διὰ τοῦτο πλειστάκις πνέουσιν,

ing and not in the morning ? Is the rising and the
setting of the sun usually the cause of winds ? For
when the sun, warming the air which is damp, concocts and dissolves it, it dissolves it into wind : if,
then, the air is full of breath, it is still further turned
into breath by the sun. Now when the sun is in the
east, it is far away from the south-west ; for this wind
blows from the direction of the setting sun. But
when the sun is near to setting, then the breath is completely dissolved. During the period from midday to
evening the conditions are best suited for warming
and dissolving the air. This is also why the east wind
begins to blow in the early morning, for the air over
the earth has grown damp during the night and owing
to its weight is close to the ground ; then in the early
morning the sun dissolves it and sets in motion first
the air which is near to it. The breeze, then, that
comes from the rising sun is called Apeliotes.[a]

Why as the sun is rising do the winds rise and fall ? 34
Is it because wind is a movement either of air or of
rising moisture ? When this movement is slight, it is
quickly exhausted by the sun, so that there is no
wind ; but when the movement is greater, it is
increased by the rising sun ; for the sun is the origin
of all such movements.

Why does the south-west wind blow in the evening ? 35
Do all winds occur when the sun is dispersing the
moisture ? For the moisture having been previously
collected is dissolved [b] when the power of the heat gets
near to it. Now the south-west wind blows from
a westerly direction. So it naturally rises in the
evening ; for at that time the sun is reaching that
quarter. The reason why the north and south winds

[a] *i.e.* its name is derived from ἀπὸ ἡλίου.
[b] The Greek word ἐξάπτει means nothing ; but Th. G. has
tabescit, which is here translated.

95

944 a

ὅτι τὸ ἐναντίον ὑπὸ τοῦ ἐναντίου κρατούμενον κατ᾽
εὐθυωρίαν ἥκιστα δύναται διαμένειν, ἀλλὰ μᾶλλον ἐκ
944 b τοῦ πλαγίου. ὁ μὲν οὖν νότος καὶ βορέας ἐκ τῶν
ἐφ᾽ ἑκάτερα τόπων τῆς τοῦ ἡλίου φορᾶς πνέουσιν,
οἱ δὲ ἄλλοι μᾶλλον ἐκ τοῦ κατ᾽ ἀντικρύ.

Πότερον τὸ πνεῦμα ἀπὸ πηγῆς τινος φέρεται
5 ὥσπερ τὸ ὕδωρ, καὶ ταύτης οὐκ ἔστιν ἀνωτέρω
αὐτὸ ἐνεχθῆναι, ἢ οὔ; καὶ πότερον ἀπὸ ἑνὸς
σημείου ἢ ἀπὸ πλείονος τόπου; ἔνια μὲν οὖν ἐστιν
ὅμοια, ἃ καὶ ἐπὶ τῶν ὑδάτων φαίνεται συμβαίνειν·
τό τε γὰρ ὕδωρ, ὅταν εἰς τὸ κάταντες φέρηται,
θᾶττον ῥεῖ ἢ ὅταν ἐν τῷ ἐπιπέδῳ καὶ ὁμαλοῦ
10 λιμνάζῃ. ὁμοίως δὲ καὶ τὰ πνεύματα· ἐπὶ μὲν γὰρ
τοῖς ἄκροις καὶ τοῖς ὑψηλοῖς ἀεὶ ἐν κινήσει ὁ ἀήρ,
ἐν δὲ τοῖς κοίλοις πολλάκις ἠρεμεῖ καὶ ἄπνοια
γίνεται. ἔτι ἐπὶ τοῖς σφόδρα ὑψηλοῖς ὄρεσιν οὐ
γίνεται τὰ πνεύματα, οἷον ἐπὶ τῷ Ἄθῳ καὶ τοῖς
ἄλλοις τοῖς τοιούτοις. σημεῖον δέ· ἃ γὰρ ἂν κατα-
15 λείπωσιν οἱ τῷ προτέρῳ ἔτει θύοντες, εὑρίσκεσθαί
φασι διαμένοντα τῷ ὑστέρῳ. δῆλον οὖν ὅτι ὥσπερ
ἀπὸ πηγῆς τινος καὶ ἡ τοῦ πνεύματος φορὰ γίνεται.
εἰς τὸ ἄνω οὖν οὐκέτι δύναται δικνεῖσθαι. διὰ
τοῦτο οὖν ἐπὶ τοῖς ὑψηλοῖς τοῦτο συμβαίνει. ὁμοίως
δ᾽ ἂν καὶ ἐπὶ τοῦ ὕδατος εἴη· οὔτε γὰρ ὕδωρ λάβρον
20 οὔτε πνεῦμα ἐξαίσιον ἐν τοῖς ὑψηλοῖς φαίνεται
γίνεσθαι.

Διὰ τί ποτε τοῦ μὲν νότου πνέοντος ἡ θάλαττα 3
κυανέα γίνεται, τοῦ δὲ βορέου ζοφώδης; ἢ ὅτι ὁ
βορέας ἧττον τὴν θάλατταν ταράττει, τὸ δὲ ἀτάρα-
κτότερον ἅπαν μέλαν φαίνεται;

25 Διὰ τί οἱ νότοι μικρὰ μὲν πνέοντες οὐ ποιοῦσιν 3
ἐπίνεψιν [ἤτοι συνέφειαν], μεγάλοι δὲ γενόμενοι ἐπι-

are the commonest is that, when one contrary is over-powered by another, it is least able to continue in a straight line, but it is better able to resist a wind blowing across it. So the south and north winds blow from districts which are on either side of the course of the sun, but the others blow in the exactly contrary direction.

Does the wind travel from a source as water does, 36 and can it not travel higher than its source, or is this not so ? Again, does the wind arise from a single point, or from a more extended area ? There are indeed some similarities to that which appears to happen in the case of water ; for water when it is travelling down a steep slope flows more quickly than when it is stagnant in a plain and on the level, and it is somewhat similar with winds ; for on peaks and in high places the air is always in motion, but in hollow places it is often calm and there is no wind. Again, on some very high mountains there is no wind—for instance on Mount Athos and in other similar places. We have proof of this ; for whatever is left behind by those who sacrifice in one year, is said to be found still remaining the year after. So it is clear that the course of the wind also is derived as it were from some source. So it can never penetrate upwards. This accounts for what happens on high places. It would be similar in the case of water ; for water does not seem to flow strongly, nor wind to blow violently in high places.

Why is the sea blue when the south wind blows, 37 but black when the north wind blows ? Is it because the north wind disturbs the sea less, and everything which is less disturbed appears black ?

Why do the south winds not make the sky overcast, 38 when they blow gently, but when they are violent

97

944 b

νεφοῦσιν; ἢ διότι μικροὶ μὲν πνέοντες οὐ δύνανται
πολλὰ νέφη ποιεῖν; ὀλίγον οὖν τόπον κατίσχουσιν.
ὅταν δὲ μεγάλοι γένωνται, πολλὰ ἀπωθοῦσι, διὸ
καὶ δοκοῦσι μᾶλλον ἐπινεφεῖν.

30 Διὰ τί ὁ μὲν βορέας ἀρχόμενος μέγας, λήγων δὲ 3
μικρός, ὁ δὲ νότος ἀρχόμενος μὲν μικρός, λήγων δὲ
μέγας; ἢ ὅτι ὁ μὲν βορέας ἐγγὺς ἡμῶν, ὁ δὲ νότος
πόρρω; ὁ μὲν οὖν ὅταν ἄρξηται, εὐθὺς παρ' ἡμῖν,
τοῦ δὲ ἅτε διὰ πολλοῦ χρόνου ἡ ἀρχὴ διασκεδάν-
35 νυται, καὶ πρὸς ἡμᾶς μικρὸν ἐξικνεῖται αὐτῆς τὸ
πρῶτον· τῆς δὲ τελευτῆς τοῦ μὲν αἰσθανόμεθα, τοῦ
δὲ ὅλως οὐκ αἰσθανόμεθα. ὥστε εἰκότως ὁ μὲν
ἀσθενὴς παυόμενος (ἀσθενὴς γὰρ ἡ τελευτὴ πάντων), ὁ δὲ οὔ· τῆς γὰρ τελευτῆς οὐκέτι αἰσθανόμεθα
αὐτοῦ.

945 a

Διὰ τί οἱ μὲν κόλποι εἰσί, τροπαῖαι γίνονται, οὗ 4
δὲ ἀναπεπταμένα πελάγη, οὐ γίνονται; ἢ διότι εἰς
μὲν τοὺς κόλπους ῥέον οὐ διασπᾶται τὸ πνεῦμα
μᾶλλον, ἀλλ' ἀθρόον ἐπὶ τὸ πολὺ φέρεται, ἐν δὲ
5 τοῖς ἀναπεπταμένοις ἐξ ἀρχῆς τε αἱ ἀπογέαι εὐθὺς
διασπῶνται μᾶλλον, καὶ ὅταν ῥέωσι, ταῦτο πάσχουσι διὰ τὸ πολλαχῇ ἐξεῖναι ὁρμῆσαι· ἔστι γὰρ
ἡ τροπαία ἀπογέας[1] ἀνάκλασις;

Διὰ τί λέγεται " ἀρχομένου τε νότου καὶ λή- 4
γοντος βορέαο "; ἢ διότι ὁ μὲν βορέας, διὰ τὸ
10 ὑποικεῖν ἡμᾶς αὐτῷ καὶ εἶναι τὴν οἴκησιν πρὸς
ἄρκτον, εὐθὺς μέγα πνεῖ; ἅμα γὰρ ἄρχεται καὶ
πάρεστι. διὸ παυόμενος ἡδὺ πνεῖ· τότε γὰρ
ἀσθενὴς πνεῖ. ὁ δὲ νότος διὰ τὸ πόρρωθεν ὕστερον
μείζων ἀφικνεῖται.

---

[1] ἀπογέας Ross : ἀπόγεος ms.

98

they do? Is it because when they blow gently they cannot produce many clouds? So they only affect a small area. But when they grow strong, they drive many clouds before them, and so they seem to make the sky more overcast.

Why is the north wind strong when it begins to 39 blow, but gentle when it is ceasing, whereas the south wind blows gently at first but becomes strong at the end? Is it because the north wind is near to us, but the south wind far away? So the former when it begins is upon us at once, but the beginning of the latter is scattered owing to the long time it takes to reach us, and little of it reaches us at first; so we notice the end of the north wind, but not that of the south wind. So naturally the north wind is weak as it ceases (for the end of everything is weak), but the south wind is not; for we never feel its end at all.

Why do variable winds arise where there are bays, 40 but not where there is open sea? Is it because the wind when it blows into bays is not scattered, but generally travels in a mass, but in open seas land breezes are more quickly scattered from the first, and when they blow, suffer the same effect, because it is possible for them to move in many directions; for the changeable wind is the refraction of the land wind?

What is the origin of the saying " When the south 41 wind begins and the north wind dies " ? [a] Is it that the north wind, because we live near it and have our habitation towards the north, blows strongly at once? For no sooner does it begin than it is with us. So it blows gently as it ceases; for then it is weak. But the south wind reaches us with more violence late because it comes from a distance.

[a] For the complete proverb cf. 945 a 29.

945 a

Διὰ τί ἐν τοῖς νοτίοις βαρύτερον ἔχουσι καὶ 42
15 ἀδυνατώτερον οἱ ἄνθρωποι; ἢ διότι ἐξ ὀλίγου πολὺ
ὑγρὸν γίνεται, διατηκόμενον διὰ τὴν ἀλέαν, καὶ
ἐκ πνεύματος κούφου ὑγρὸν βαρύ· εἶτα ἡ δύναμις
ἀτονεῖ.

Διὰ τί ἐν τοῖς βορείοις βρωτικώτεροι ἢ ἐν τοῖς 43
νοτίοις; ἢ διότι ψυχρότερα τὰ βόρεια;

20 Διὰ τί ὁ νότος οὐ πνεῖ κατ' αὐτὴν τὴν Αἴγυπτον 44
τὰ πρὸς θάλατταν, οὐδ' ὅσον ἡμέρας δρόμον καὶ
νυκτός· τὰ δὲ ὑπὲρ Μέμφεως καὶ ἀποσχόντι δρόμον
ἡμέρας καὶ νυκτὸς λαμπρός· καὶ πρὸς ἑσπέραν οὐ
πνεῖ, ὅσον δύο ἡμερῶν καὶ νυκτῶν δρόμον, τὰ δὲ
25 πρὸς ἔω λίβες πνέουσιν; ἢ διότι κοίλη τὰ κάτω ἡ
Αἴγυπτός ἐστιν· διὸ ὑπερπίπτει αὐτῆς, ἄνω δὲ καὶ
πόρρω ὑψηλότεροι οἱ τόποι.

Διὰ τί ὁ νότος ἀρχόμενος μὲν μικρός ἐστι, λήγων 45
δὲ μείζων γίνεται, ὁ δὲ βορέας ἀνάπαλιν, διὸ καὶ ἡ
παροιμία λέγεται " εὖ πλεῖν ἀρχομένου τε νότου
30 καὶ λήγοντος βορέαο "; ἢ διότι πρὸς ἄρκτον μᾶλλον
ἢ πρὸς μεσημβρίαν οἰκοῦμεν, πνεῖ δὲ ὁ μὲν βορέας
ἀπὸ τῆς ἄρκτου, ὁ δὲ νότος ἀπὸ τῆς μεσημβρίας;
εἰκότως οὖν ὁ μὲν ἀρχόμενος εὐθὺς σφοδρὸς πρόσ-
κειται τοῖς πλησίον τόποις μᾶλλον, καὶ μετὰ ταῦτα
μεταλλάττει τὸ σφοδρὸν πρὸς ἐκείνους. ὁ δὲ νότος
35 τοὐναντίον ἀρχόμενος μὲν τοῖς πρὸς μεσημβρίαν
οἰκοῦσιν ἔγκειται, ἐπειδὰν δὲ παραλλάξῃ, τοῖς πρὸς
ἄρκτον λαμπρὸς καταπνεῖ.

Διὰ τί λέγεται " εἰ δ' ὁ νότος βορέαν προκαλέσ- 46
σεται, αὐτίκα χειμών "; ἢ διότι ὁ νότος τοιοῦτός

Why are men heavier and more feeble when the 42 wind is in the south ? Is it because moisture becomes abundant instead of scanty, permeating through the warmth, and heavy moisture replaces light air ? So men's strength is relaxed.

Why are men more inclined to eat when the wind 43 is in the north than when it is in the south ? Is it because the north winds are colder ?

Why does not the south wind blow in Egypt itself, 44 in the sea districts, nor for a march of a night and a day from the coast ? But above Memphis and for a march of a night and a day, it is fresh. It does not blow towards the west for a march of two days and two nights, but towards the east the south-west wind blows. Is it because in its lower parts Egypt is hollow ? So it blows over it, but higher up and farther off the district is higher.

Why is the south wind slight when it begins, but 45 grows stronger when it is dying down, whereas the north wind is just the reverse ? Hence the proverb says that " it is good for sailing when the south wind is rising and the north wind is dying down." Is it because we live towards the north rather than towards the south, and the north wind blows from the north, but the south wind from the south ? Naturally therefore the north wind when it begins falls more violently upon the district nearer to it, and afterwards transfers its violence to the other parts. But the south wind on the contrary, when it begins, attacks those who live in the south, and when it has passed over them blows freshly upon those who live towards the north.

Why is it said that " if the south wind summons the 46 north wind, winter is upon us " ? Is it because it is

945 a
ἐστιν οἷος νεφέλας καὶ ὕδωρ πολὺ συναίρειν; ὅταν
945 b οὖν τοιαύτης τῆς καταστάσεως οὔσης ἐπιπνεύσῃ ὁ
βορέας, πολλῆς αὐτῷ ὕλης ὑπαρχούσης πήγνυσι καὶ
χειμῶνα ποιεῖ. διὸ λέγεται " εἰ βορρᾶς πηλὸν
καταλήψεται, αὐτίκα χειμών." ὁ δὲ πηλὸς καὶ
ὅλως τὰ ὕδατα ὑπὸ τοῦ νότου ἢ μάλιστα ἢ πλειστάκις γίνεται.

5   Διὰ τί ἐπὶ μὲν τῷ νότῳ ταχὺς ὁ βορέας, ἐπὶ δὲ 47
τούτῳ ὁ νότος οὐ ταχὺς ἐπιπίπτει; ἢ ὅτι τῷ μὲν
ἐγγύθεν, τῷ δὲ πόρρωθεν ἡ ἄφιξις; ἡ γὰρ οἴκησις
πρὸς βορέαν ἡμῶν.

Διὰ τί τὰ πνεύματα ψυχρά ἐστιν, ὄντα ἀπὸ τῆς 48
τοῦ θερμοῦ συγκινήσεως; ἢ οὐ πάντως ἡ ὑπὸ τοῦ
10 θερμοῦ κίνησις θερμὴ γίνεται, ἐὰν μὴ τρόπον τινὰ
γίνηται; ἀλλ' ἐὰν μὲν ἀθρόως ἐμπίπτῃ, καίει αὐτὸ
τὸ ἀφιὲν θέρμῃ. ἐὰν δὲ διὰ στενοῦ καὶ κατὰ
μικρόν, αὐτὴ μὲν θερμή, ὁ δὲ ὑπὸ τούτου κινούμενος
ἀήρ, οἷος ἄν ποτε τυγχάνῃ προϋπάρχων, τοιαύτην
καὶ τὴν κίνησιν ἀπετέλεσεν, ὥσπερ καὶ ἐπὶ τοῦ
15 σώματος. φασὶ γὰρ ἐκ τοῦ αὐτοῦ θερμὸν καὶ
ψυχρὸν ἡμᾶς πνεῖν, τοῦτο δὲ οὐκ ἀληθές, ἀλλὰ τὸ
μὲν ἐξιὸν θερμὸν ἀεί. σημεῖον δὲ τὸ ἐγγὺς προσ-
αγαγόντι τοιοῦτον φαίνεσθαι. διαφέρει δὲ ἡ
ἔκπτωσις αὐτοῦ. ἐὰν μὲν γὰρ διὰ πολλοῦ ἀφίωμεν
χανόντες, θερμὸν φαίνεται διὰ τὸ αὐτοῦ αἰσθάνε-
20 σθαι, ἐὰν δὲ διὰ στενοῦ, σφοδρότερον γινόμενον
ὠθεῖ τὸν πλησίον ἀέρα, κἀκεῖνος τὸν ἐχόμενον.
ψυχροῦ δὲ ὄντος τοῦ ἀέρος καὶ ἡ κίνησις αὐτοῦ
ψυχρὰ γίνεται. μήποτε δὲ καὶ ἐπὶ τῶν πνευμάτων
τὸ αὐτὸ συμβαίνει, καὶ διὰ στενοῦ ἡ πρώτη κίνησις·

the nature of the south wind to collect clouds and
heavy rain ? So when in these conditions the north
wind blows as well, as it carries much matter with it,
it freezes and produces winter. This is the origin of
the saying " If the north wind finds mud winter is
upon us." But mud and water generally are produced
usually or most commonly by the south wind.

Why does the north wind follow swifly on the 47
south, but the south wind does not follow swiftly on
the north ? Is it because the arrival of the former is
from near by, but of the latter from a distance ? For
we live near the north.

Why are winds cold, although they are due to a 48
movement of heat ? Or is movement produced by
heat not invariably hot, only if it arises in a particular
way ? If it falls in a concentrated state, it burns by
its heat the very thing which sends it forth. But if it
passes through a narrow passage and arrives a little
at a time, then it is itself hot, but the air which is
moved by it accomplishes its movement in the same
condition as it was to start with, as is also true in the
case of the human body. For they say that we breathe
both hot and cold from the same source, but this is
untrue, as the breath which comes out is always hot.
This is proved by the fact that the breath appears
hot to that which is applied to it. The difference
lies in the manner of its emission. If we emit the
breath from a wide opening as when we yawn, it
seems to be hot because we feel it ; but if we emit it
through a narrow gap, as it travels more violently it
pushes on the air near to it, and this again pushes
the air next to it. If the air is cold its movement is
also cold. Perhaps the same thing happens with the
winds, and their initial movement is through a narrow

245 b

εἶτ' ἐκεῖνον μὲν διήνεγκεν, ἕτερος δὲ ἀὴρ ἐπιρρεῖ.
25 διὸ καὶ τοῦ μὲν θέρους θερμά, τοῦ δὲ χειμῶνος
ψυχρὰ τὰ πνεύματα, ὅτι ἐν ἑκατέρῳ τοιοῦτος ὁ ἀὴρ
ὁ προϋπάρχων· ἐπεὶ ὅτι γε οὔτε αὐτὸς ὑφ' ἑαυτοῦ
κινούμενος ὁ ἀὴρ οὔτε ὑπὸ τοῦ θερμοῦ κρατούμενος
φέρεται ταύτην τὴν φοράν, δῆλον οὐ μόνον τούτῳ
ὅτι θερμαίνει τὰ πνεύματα πλείονος τοῦ θερμοῦ
30 ἐνόντος, ἀλλὰ καὶ ἄνω ἐφέρετο. τὸ γὰρ πῦρ
τοιοῦτον, τὸ δὲ ψυχρὸν κάτω πέφυκεν φέρεσθαι. τὰ
δὲ πνεύματα πλάγια εἰκότως· ἐπεὶ γὰρ τὸ μὲν ἄνω,
τὸ δὲ κάτω βιάζεται, καὶ οὐδέτερον κρατεῖ, μένειν
δὲ οὐχ οἷόν τε, λοξὴν τὴν φορὰν εἰκότως γίνεσθαι.

35   Διὰ τί οἱ νότοι ἐν τῇ Λιβύῃ ψυχροί, ὥσπερ παρ' 4
ἡμῖν οἱ βορέαι; ἢ πρῶτον μὲν διὰ τὸ ἐγγυτέρω
εἶναι ἡμῖν τε κἀκείνοις τὰς ἀρχὰς τῶν πνευμάτων;
εἰ γάρ, ὥσπερ εἴπομεν, διὰ στενοῦ γίνεται τὰ
πνεύματα, τοῖς ἐγγυτέρω ψυχρότερα ἔσται διὰ τὴν
946 a σφοδρότητα τῆς κινήσεως· εἰς γὰρ τὸ πόρρω
προϊούσης διαχεῖται. διὸ καὶ παρ' ἡμῖν οἱ βορέαι
ψυχροί, ὅτι ἐγγυτέρω καὶ παντελῶς πρὸς τῇ ἄρκτῳ
οἰκοῦμεν.

Διὰ τί οἱ νότοι οἱ ξηροὶ καὶ μὴ ὑδατώδεις 5
5 πυρετώδεις. ἢ ὅτι ὑγρότητα θερμὴν ἀλλοτρίαν
ἐμποιοῦσι τοῖς σώμασιν; εἰσὶ γὰρ ὑγροὶ καὶ θερμοὶ
φύσει, τοῦτο δ' ἐστὶ πυρετῶδες· ὁ γὰρ πυρετὸς ὑπ'
ἀμφοτέρων τούτων ἐστὶν ὑπερβολῆς. ὅταν μὲν οὖν
ὑπὸ τοῦ ἡλίου ἄνευ ὕδατος πνέωσιν, ταύτην τὴν
διάθεσιν[1] ποιοῦσιν, ὅταν δὲ ἅμα τῷ ὕδατι, τὸ ὕδωρ
καταψύχει.

10   Διὰ τί οἱ ἐτησίαι ταύτην δὴ τὴν ὥραν ἀεὶ καὶ 5

---

[1] MS. τὴν τάξιν. The reading in the text is supplied by
Forster from 862 a 21.

104

channel; then it tosses the air aside, and other air flows in. So in the summer the winds are hot and in the winter cold, because in each case the air which was there beforehand was of this character. For, that the air does not follow this path because it is self-moved or overpowered by heat is clear not merely from the fact that it heats the winds when it contains more heat, but also because it was originally travelling upwards. This is the characteristic of fire, but cold is inclined to travel downwards. Naturally the winds move sideways; for since the one is forced upwards and the other downwards, and neither can achieve the mastery, and yet they cannot remain stationary, the direction must naturally be sideways.

Why are the south winds cold in Libya, as the 49 north winds are with us? Is it in the first place because the origins of the two winds are respectively nearer to us and to them? For if, as we have said, the winds blow first through a narrow channel, they will be colder to those nearer to them owing to the violence of the movement. For as the movement proceeds farther the wind is dispersed. So the north winds are cold with us, because we live nearer to them and, speaking generally, near to the north pole.

Why are the south winds which are dry and not 50 rainy liable to produce fever? Is it because they produce in the body an unnatural warm moisture? For these winds are naturally moist and warm, and this produces fever. For fever is due to an excess of these two things. So when the winds blow under the influence of the sun without bringing rain they produce this condition in us, but when they come in conjunction with rain, the water cools us.

Why do the Etesian winds always blow in their 51

τοσοῦτοι πνέουσιν; καὶ διὰ τί ληγούσης τῆς
ἡμέρας λήγουσι καὶ τῆς νυκτὸς οὐ πνέουσιν; ἢ
τοῦτο μὲν διὰ τὸ τὴν χιόνα τηκομένην παύεσθαι
ὑπὸ τοῦ ἡλίου πρὸς ἑσπέραν καὶ τὴν νύκτα; ὅλως
δὲ πνέουσιν, ὅταν ὁ ἥλιος κρατεῖν καὶ λύειν ἄρξηται
15 τὸν πρὸς βορέαν πάγον. ἀρχομένου μὲν οὖν οἱ
πρόδρομοι, ἤδη δὲ λυομένου οἱ ἐτησίαι.

Διὰ τί ὁ ζέφυρος λειότατός τε τῶν ἀνέμων καὶ 52
ψυχρός, καὶ δύο ὥρας πνεῖ μάλιστα, ἔαρ τε καὶ
μετόπωρον, καὶ πρὸς ἑσπέραν τῆς ἡμέρας, καὶ ἐπὶ
20 τὴν γῆν μάλιστα; ἢ ψυχρὸς μὲν διὰ τὸ πνεῖν ἀπὸ
τῆς θαλάττης καὶ πεδίων ἀναπεπταμένων; ἧττον
μὲν οὖν ψυχρὸς τοῦ βορέου διὰ τὸ ἀφ' ὕδατος
πνευματουμένου καὶ μὴ χιόνος πνεῖν· ψυχρὸς δὲ διὰ
τὸ μετὰ χειμῶνα, ἄρτι τοῦ ἡλίου κρατοῦντος, πνεῖν
καὶ μετοπώρου, ὅτε οὐκέτι κρατεῖ ὁ ἥλιος. οὐ γὰρ
25 ὥσπερ ἐν γῇ ὑπομένει τὴν εἴλην, ἀλλὰ πλανᾶται
διὰ τὸ ἐφ' ὑγροῦ βεβηκέναι. καὶ ὁμαλὸς διὰ τὸ
αὐτό· οὐ γὰρ ἀπὸ ὀρέων πνεῖ, οὐδὲ βίᾳ τηκομένου,
ἀλλὰ ῥᾳδίως ὥσπερ δι' αὐλῶνος ῥέων. τὰ μὲν γὰρ
πρὸς βορέαν καὶ νότον ὀρεινά· πρὸς ἑσπέραν δὲ
οὔτε ὄρος οὔτε γῆ ἐστίν, ἀλλὰ τὸ Ἀτλαντικὸν
30 πέλαγος, ὥστε ἐπὶ τῆς γῆς φέρεται. καὶ πρὸς
ἑσπέραν δὲ τῆς ἡμέρας πνεῖ διὰ τὸν τόπον· τότε γὰρ
ὁ ἥλιος πλησιάζει τῷ τόπῳ. καὶ τῆς νυκτὸς
παύεται διὰ τὸ ἐκλείπειν τὴν τοῦ ἡλίου κίνησιν.

Διὰ τί, ὅταν ὁ εὖρος πνεῖ, μείζω φαίνεται τὰ 53
πάντα; ἢ ὅτι ζοφωδέστατον τὸν ἀέρα ποιεῖ;

35 Διὰ τί τὸν μὲν χειμῶνα πρωῒ ἀπὸ τῆς ἕω τὰ 54
106

season and with such strength ? And why do they cease at close of day and do not blow at night ? Is this because the melting of the snow by the sun ceases at eventide and the beginning of night ? As a rule they blow when the sun begins to master and dissolve the ice in the north. When this begins, the " precursor " winds blow, and when it is melting, the Etesian.

Why is the south-west wind the gentlest of the 52 winds and yet cold, and why does it blow most often at two seasons, spring and late autumn, and towards the evening of the day, and mostly towards the land ? Is it cold because it blows off the sea and the wide open plains ? It is less cold than the north wind because it blows from evaporated water and not from snow ; but it is cold because it blows after the winter, when the sun is only just becoming powerful, and in late autumn, when the sun is powerful no longer. For it does not wait for the sun's heat, as it would if it were a land wind, but it wanders freely because it has come over the water. For the same reason it is a steady wind; for it does not blow from the mountains, nor from what is forcibly melted, but flows easily as through a pipe. For the districts to the north and south are both mountainous ; but to the west there is neither mountain nor land, but only the Atlantic Ocean, so that it travels towards the land. It blows towards evening owing to its position ; for at that time the sun is approaching its quarter. It ceases during the night because the movement caused by the sun fails.

Why, when the east wind blows, do all the things 53 seem larger ? Is it because it makes the air very gloomy ?

Why is it that during the winter the winds blow early 54

946 a

πνεύματα πνεῖ, τὸ δὲ θέρος δείλης καὶ ἀπὸ δυσμῶν
ἡλίου; ἢ ὅτι ἃ ἡμῖν συμβαίνει τοῦ θέρους, ταῦτα
τοῦ χειμῶνος τοῖς τὸ ἐναντίον τῆς γῆς ἡμισφαίριον
οἰκοῦσιν, ἡμῖν δὲ τοῦ χειμῶνος πρωῒ καὶ ἀφ' ἕω

946 b τὰ πνεύματα πνεῖ διὰ τὸ τὸν ἀέρα κάθυγρον ἐν τῇ
νυκτὶ διακρίνεσθαι καὶ κινεῖσθαι τὸ πρωῒ ὑπὸ τοῦ
ἡλίου, καὶ πρῶτον τὸν ἔγγιστα τοῦ ἡλίου; ποιεῖ
δὲ τοῦτο ὁ ἥλιος καὶ πρὸ ἀνατολῆς· διὸ αὖραι οὐχ
ἧττον πρὸ ἀνατολῆς πνέουσιν. ἐπειδὴ οὖν καὶ ἐφ'
5 ἑαυτὸν ἕλκει ὁ ἥλιος τὰ ὑγρὰ καὶ κινεῖ πρὸ ἀνατολῆς
τοῦ χειμῶνος ὑγρὸν ὄντα τὸν παρ' ἡμῖν ἀέρα, δῆλον
ὡς καὶ ἐφ' αὑτὸν ἂν ἕλκοι, ὢν ἐν τῷ κάτω ἡμισφαιρίῳ, καὶ δείλῃ ἐκείνοις ὃ ἡμῖν ἐστιν ὄρθρος.
ὥστε συμβαίνοι ἂν τὸν ὑπὸ τοῦ ἡλίου πρὸ ἀνατολῆς
παρ' ἡμῶν ἐφ' αὑτὸν ἑλκόμενον ἀέρα, τοῦτον τοῖς
10 κάτω γενέσθαι ζέφυρον καὶ δείλης πνεῖν. ὃ δὲ ἐν
τῷ παρ' ἡμῖν χειμῶνι, τῆς ἕω ἐκείνοις συμβαίνει,
ὃ δὲ ἐν τῷ θέρει, τῆς δείλης ἡμῖν. ὅτε γὰρ παρ'
ἡμῖν θέρος, ἐκεῖ χειμών ἐστι, καὶ ἡ ἡμετέρα δείλη
ἐκείνοις ὄρθρος, καθ' ἣν ἐκείνοις μὲν αὔρας ἐξ
ἑώας συμβαίνει πνεῖν, ἡμῖν δὲ ζεφύρους διὰ ταῦτα
15 τοῖς προειρημένοις. τοῦ δὲ θέρους καὶ ἑῷαι μὲν
οὐ πνέουσιν, ὅτι εἰς ξηρότερον ἔτι τὸν παρ' ἡμῖν
ἀέρα ὁ ἥλιος ἀνατέλλει διὰ τὸ ὀλίγον αὐτοῦ χρόνον
ἀπογεγονέναι· ζέφυροι δὲ οὐ πνέουσιν δείλης τοῦ
χειμῶνος, ὅτι οὐδ' ἐν τῷ κάτω ἡμισφαιρίῳ ἑῷοι
ταύτην τὴν ὥραν διὰ τὰ προειρημένα, ὅθεν ὁ
20 ἥλιος ἐφ' ἑαυτὸν ἕλκων τὰ ὑγρὰ τὸν παρ' ἡμῖν
ζέφυρον ποιεῖ.

Διὰ τί ὁ ζέφυρος εὐδιεινὸς καὶ ἥδιστος δοκεῖ εἶναι 5

in the morning and from the east, while in summer they blow in the evening and from the setting sun ? Is it because the conditions which obtain with us in the summer are present in the winter to those who live in the opposite hemisphere ? With us in the winter the winds blow early in the morning and from the east because the moist night air is dissolved and set in motion at dawn by the sun, and first of all the air nearest to the sun. The sun produces this effect even before it rises, so the breezes blow just as much before sunrise. Since then the sun draws the moisture to itself and before sunrise during the winter moves the air near to us which is damp, it would also obviously draw it towards itself in the southern hemisphere, and their evening would be our morning. So it would happen that the air drawn towards itself by the sun before dawn with us would become a west wind with them and blow in the evening. But what happens in our winter, happens with them at dawn, and what happens in our summer happens to them in the evening. For when it is summer with us it is winter there, and our evening is their dawn, at which time the breezes blow with them from the east and with us from the west for the reasons that we have already stated. But in the summer the winds do not blow from the east, because the sun when it rises finds the air with us too dry, because it has only been away for a short time ; but west winds do not blow in the evening during the winter, because east winds do not blow in the southern hemisphere at this season for the reasons we have given, for which reasons the sun, drawing the moisture to itself, produces a west wind with us.

Why does the west wind seem to bring fine weather 55

946 b

τῶν ἀνέμων; ἢ ὅτι ἐν μεθορίῳ ἐστὶ τῶν θερμῶν
καὶ ψυχρῶν πνευμάτων, γειτνιῶν δὲ ἀμφοῖν τῆς
δυνάμεως αὐτῶν κοινωνεῖ· διὸ εὔκρατός ἐστιν. ὁ
25 δὲ ἀπηλιώτης ἧττον κοινωνεῖ, ὢν ἐν τῷ μέσῳ τῶν
αὐτῶν. ἀπηλιώτης μὲν γὰρ πνέων τὰ πρὸς νότον
πνεύματα κινεῖ (ἐνταῦθα γὰρ ἡ μετάστασις αὐτοῦ
ἐστίν), κινῶν δὲ οὐ μίγνυται αὐτοῖς. ὁ δὲ ζέφυρος
καὶ κινεῖται ὑπὸ τῶν νότων καὶ πνέων κινεῖ τὰ
βόρεια· τελευτᾷ γὰρ ἐνταῦθα ἡ περίοδος τῶν
30 πνευμάτων. διὸ τῶν μὲν τὴν τελευτήν, τῶν δὲ
τὴν ἀρχὴν ἔχων ἐν ἑαυτῷ δικαίως ἡδύς ἐστι καὶ
δοκεῖ εἶναι.

Διὰ τί ἄλλοις ἄλλοι τῶν ἀνέμων ὑέτιοι, οἷον ἐν 56
μὲν τῇ Ἀττικῇ καὶ ταῖς νήσοις ὁ Ἑλλησποντίας, ἐν
Ἑλλησπόντῳ δὲ ὁ βορέας καὶ ἐν Κυρήνῃ, περὶ
35 Λέσβον δὲ νότος; ἢ ὅπου ἂν ἄθροισις νεφῶν,
ἐνταῦθα ὕδωρ; ἐνταῦθα γὰρ ἡ πύκνωσις ἀθροίζεται, ὅπου ἂν προκαθίζεσθαι ἔχῃ. διὸ καὶ ἐν τοῖς
ὄρεσι μᾶλλον ὕει ἢ ὅπου ἂν τὸ πλῆθος ὑπεξάγειν
δύνηται· περικαταλαμβανόμενον γὰρ πυκνοῦται· δεῖ
δὲ τοῦτο γενέσθαι. καὶ ἐν ταῖς εὐδίαις μᾶλλον ὕει.
947 a ἐν Ἑλλησπόντῳ μὲν οὖν ἄνωθεν ὁ βορέας πολλὰ
συνωθεῖ νέφη, πρὸς δὲ τὴν Ἀττικὴν καὶ τὰς νήσους
ὁ Ἑλλησποντίας, ὥσπερ ὕλην ἔχων· καὶ γὰρ περιίσταται τὰ πολλὰ ἐκ τοῦ βορέου. περὶ δὲ Λέσβον
5 ὁ εὖρος καὶ ὁ νότος ἐκ τοῦ πελάγους φέροντες
πολλὰ νέφη προσβάλλει τῇ χώρᾳ. τὸν αὐτὸν
τρόπον καὶ ἐπὶ τῶν ἄλλων.

Διὰ τί λέγεται " μή ποτ᾽ ἀπ᾽ ἠπείρου δείσῃς 57

and to be the pleasantest of all the winds ? Is it because it is on the border-line between the hot and the cold winds, and being a neighbour to both shares their characteristics : so it is a good mixture ? The east wind shares these dual characteristics less, though it is also between the same extremes. For the east wind when it blows sets in motion the winds towards the south (for that is the direction in which it changes), but though it sets them in motion it does not mingle with them. But the west wind is set in motion by the south winds, and when it blows it sets in motion the north winds ; for at this point the succession of the winds ceases. So, containing in itself the end of some winds and the beginning of others, it justly is and is generally regarded as a pleasant wind.

Why do different winds bring rain in different 56 places ? For instance, in Attica and the islands the east wind is rainy, in the Hellespont and in Cyrene it is the north wind, and round Lesbos the south wind. Is it because rain occurs wherever there is a concentration of clouds ? For a density collects at any place where it is able to settle. So it rains more in the mountains than where the mass of clouds can move along ; for it condenses if it is confined ; and this must be the case. Also there is more rain in calm weather. So in the Hellespont the north wind coming from above collects many clouds, and the east winds drive them towards Attica and the islands, being thus provided with material ; for most of the clouds come round from the north. But near Lesbos the south-east and south winds bring many clouds from the sea and drive them up against the land. And conditions are similar with the other winds.

What is the meaning of the saying " Never fear 57 the cloud which comes from mainland in winter,

947 a

νέφος ἀλλ' ἀπὸ πόντου χειμῶνος, θέρεος δὲ ἀπ'
ἠπείροιο μελαίνης''; ἢ διότι τοῦ μὲν χειμῶνος ἡ
10 θάλαττα θερμοτέρα, ὥστε εἴ τι συνέστη, δῆλον ὅτι
ἀπ' ἀρχῆς ἰσχυρᾶς συνέστηκεν· ἐλύθη γὰρ ἂν διὰ
τὸ ἀλεεινὸν εἶναι τὸν τόπον. τοῦ δὲ θέρους ἡ μὲν
θάλαττα ψυχρά, καὶ τὰ πόντια πνεύματα, ἡ δὲ γῆ
θερμή, ὥστε εἴ τι ἀπὸ τῆς γῆς φέρεται, διὰ μείζονος ἀρχῆς συνέστη· διελύθη γὰρ ἄν, εἰ ἀσθενὲς ἦν.

Διὰ τί ἐν τῇ Ἀρκαδίᾳ ὑψηλῇ οὔσῃ τὰ μὲν πνεύ- 58
ματα οὐθὲν ψυχρότερα τῶν παρὰ τοῖς ἄλλοις, ὅταν
δὲ νηνεμία ᾖ καὶ ἐπινέφελα, ψυχρά, ὥσπερ ἐν τοῖς
ὁμαλέσιν τοῖς ἑλώδεσιν; ἢ ὅτι καὶ ἡ Ἀρκαδία
ὁμοία γίνεται τοῖς ἑλώδεσιν· οὐ γὰρ ἔχει ἐξόδους
20 τοῖς ὕδασιν εἰς θάλατταν, διὸ καὶ βάραθρα πολλὰ
αὐτόθι ἐστίν. ὅταν μὲν οὖν ᾖ ἄνεμος, ἀπορριπίζει
τὴν ἐκ τῆς γῆς ἀναθυμίασιν, οὖσαν ψυχράν, αὐτὰ
δὲ τὰ πνεύματα οὐ ψυχρὰ διὰ τὸ ἀπὸ τῆς θαλάττης
προσβάλλειν· ἐν δὲ ταῖς νηνεμίαις ἀνιοῦσα ἡ ἀτμὶς
ἀπὸ τοῦ ἐμμένοντος ὕδατος ποιεῖ τὸ ψῦχος.

25 Διὰ τί, ἂν ἕωθεν πνεῖν ἄρξηται, διημερεύει 59
μᾶλλον; ἢ διότι ἀρχομένου τοῦ ἡλίου σφοδροτάτη
ἡ φορά, διὸ ἐκτείνεται τοιαύτη οὖσα; σημεῖον δὲ
ὅτι ἰσχυρὰ ἡ σύστασις.

Διὰ τί βορέας τὴν ἡμέραν μὲν λαμπρός, τὴν δὲ 60
νύκτα πίπτει; ἢ διότι γίνεται ἀπὸ πεπηγότος
30 ὑετοῦ, ὅταν ἀναθυμιᾶται διὰ τὸν ἥλιον; πίπτει δὲ
νυκτός, ὅτι οὐχ ἡ αὐτὴ γένεσις, ἀλλὰ τοὐναντίον
ποιεῖ· τὰς γὰρ νύκτας ἐκπνεῖ, τὰς δὲ ἡμέρας ἧττον.

Διὰ τί τὰ ἀράχνια τὰ πολλὰ ὅταν φέρηται, πνεύ- 6

but beware of the cloud from the sea ; and in the summer from the dark mainland " ? Is it due to the fact that in winter the sea is warmer, so that if any cloud gathers, it has evidently gathered from a strong source ? For otherwise it would have dispersed because the region is warm. But in summer the sea is cold, and so are winds from the sea, while the land is warm, so that if any cloud travels from the land, it has gathered from a more powerful source ; for if it were weak, it would have dispersed.

Why is it that in Arcadia, which is high, the winds 58 are not at all cooler than in other districts, but when it is calm and cloudy, the winds are cold, just as they are in flat marshy districts ? Is it because Arcadia resembles the marshy districts ? For there are no exits for the water to the sea, so that there are many chasms there. When, then, there is a wind, it blows away the evaporation from the land, which is cold, but the winds themselves are not cold because they approach from the sea ; but in calm weather the vapour rising from the stationary water makes it cold.

Why, if the wind begins at dawn, is it more likely 59 to last through the day ? Is it because, when the sun begins, the wind travels with considerable force, and so continues in the same character ? This is proved by the fact that the mass it forms is strong.

Why is the north wind fresh during the day, but 60 subsides at night ? Is it because it springs from frozen rain, when it is evaporated by the sun ? It subsides at night because its origin is not the same, but is produced by a contrary cause. For during the night the wind blows itself out, but it is less apt to do so during the day.

Why is it that when many spiders' webs blow about 61

947 a

ματός ἐστι σημεῖα; πότερον ὅτι ἐργάζεται ὁ
35 ἀράχνης ἐν ταῖς εὐδίαις, φέρεται δὲ διὰ τὸ ψυχό-
μενον τὸν ἀέρα συνιέναι πρὸς τὴν γῆν, τὸ δὲ
ψύχεσθαι ἀρχὴ χειμῶνος; σημεῖον οὖν ἡ φορὰ
τῶν ἀραχνίων. ἢ ὅτι μετὰ τὰ ὕδατα καὶ τοὺς
χειμῶνας γίνεται τῶν ἀραχνῶν¹ ἀθρόα ἡ φορά, ἐν
ταῖς εὐδίαις ἐργαζομένων, διὰ τὸ ἐν τῷ χειμῶνι μὴ
947 b φαίνεσθαι; δύσριγον γὰρ τόδε. καὶ φερόμενοι ὑπὸ
τοῦ πνεύματος πολὺ ἐκπηνίζονται. μετὰ δὲ
τὰ ὕδατα εἴωθεν πνεύματα γίνεσθαι ὡς τὰ πολλά.

Διὰ τί οἱ βορέαι μεγάλοι τοῦ χειμῶνος ἐν τοῖς 6
5 ψυχροῖς τόποις ἐπινέφελοι, ἔξω δὲ αἴθριοι; ἢ ὅτι
ἅμα ψυχροί εἰσι καὶ μεγάλοι, ἐγγὺς δὲ μᾶλλον
ψυχροί, ὥστε φθάνουσι πηγνύντες πρὶν ἀπῶσαι τὰ
νέφη; ὅταν δὲ παγῇ, μένουσι διὰ βάρος. ἔξω
δὲ τῷ μεγέθει ἐργάζονται μᾶλλον ἢ τῷ ψυχρῷ.

¹ ἀραχνῶν Forster : ἀραχνιῶν MS.

114

it is a sign of wind ? Is it because the spider works in the calm weather, but the webs travel because the air as it cools collects on the ground, and this cooling is the beginning of winter ? So the blowing about of the spiders' webs is a sign of winter. Or is it because after the rain and storm the movement of spiders is considerable, as they work in the calm weather because they do not appear in winter ? For this (insect) cannot bear the cold. So when they are blown about by the wind they spin a long thread. And it is after rain that winds generally come.

Why do strong north winds in winter bring clouds 62 in cold places, but a clear sky in others ? Is it because they are both cold and strong, and colder when they are nearer, so that they freeze the clouds before they can drive them away ? But once they are frozen, they remain stationary because of their weight. But in other places their effect is due rather to their size than to their coldness.

ΚΖ

ΟΣΑ ΠΕΡΙ ΦΟΒΟΝ ΚΑΙ ΑΝΔΡΕΙΑΝ

Διὰ τί οἱ φοβούμενοι τρέμουσιν; ἢ διὰ τὴν 1
κατάψυξιν; ἐκλείπει γὰρ τὸ θερμὸν καὶ συστέλλεται· διὸ καὶ αἱ κοιλίαι λύονται τοῖς πολλοῖς.

15 Διὰ τί οὖν καὶ διψῶσιν ἔνιοι, καθάπερ οἱ μέλ- 2
λοντες κολάζεσθαι; οὐ γὰρ ἔδει καταψυχομένων.
ἢ οὐκ ἐν ταὐτῷ τόπῳ ἡ κατάψυξις καὶ ἡ θερμότης,
ἀλλ' ἡ μὲν ἐν τῷ ἐπιπολῆς, ἔνθεν ἐκλείπει τὸ
θερμόν, ἡ δὲ ἐν τῷ ἐντός, ὥστε ἐκθερμαίνει;
20 σημεῖον δὲ καὶ τὸ λύεσθαι τὰς κοιλίας. ἀναξηραινομένου δὴ τοῦ κυρίου τόπου τὸ δίψος. ὅμοιον δὲ
ἔοικεν ὥσπερ τοῖς ἠπιαλοῦσιν, οἳ ἅμα τῷ ῥιγοῦν
διψῶσιν· οὐδὲ γὰρ ὁ αὐτὸς οὐδ' ἐκεῖ τόπος ψύχεται
καὶ θερμαίνεται.

Διὰ τί ἐν μὲν τοῖς θυμοῖς εἰς τὸ ἐντὸς ἀθροιζο- 3
μένου τοῦ θερμοῦ διάθερμοι καὶ θαρραλέοι, ἐν δὲ
25 τοῖς φόβοις ἀνάπαλιν; ἢ οὐκ εἰς τὸν αὐτὸν τόπον,
ἀλλὰ τοῖς μὲν ὀργιζομένοις περὶ τὴν καρδίαν, διὸ
καὶ θαρρητικοὶ καὶ ἐν ἐρυθήματι καὶ πνεύματος
πλήρεις, ἄνω τῆς φορᾶς οὔσης, τοῖς δὲ φοβουμένοις
κάτω συμφευγόντων τοῦ αἵματος καὶ τοῦ θερμοῦ,

BOOK XXVII

PROBLEMS CONNECTED WITH FEAR AND COURAGE

WHY do the frightened tremble ? Is it owing to 1
their being chilled ? For the heat leaves them and
is contracted ; this is also why the bowels become
loose with many people.

Why are the frightened sometimes thirsty, as, for 2
instance, those who are about to be punished ? They
ought not to be, seeing that they are being chilled.
Or are the chilling and warmth in different parts, the
former being on the surface, which the heat has left,
while the latter is inside, so that it warms this part ?
The loosening of the bowels is evidence of this.
But when the controlling part becomes dry, thirst
follows. It is the same with those with ague, who are
thirsty and shiver at the same time ; for in that case
also it is not the same part which is both chilled and
warmed.

Why is it that in a state of anger, when the heat 3
collects within, men become heated and bold, but in
a state of fear they are in the opposite condition ?
Or is not the same part affected ? In the case of the
angry it is the heart which is affected, which is the
reason why they are courageous, flushed and full of
breath, as the direction of the heat is upwards, but in
the case of the frightened the blood and the heat

117

947 b

30 διὸ καὶ ἡ λύσις τῶν κοιλιῶν· ἐπεὶ καὶ ἡ τῆς καρδίας
πήδησις οὐχ ὁμοία, ἀλλὰ τοῖς μὲν ὡς ἂν διὰ τὴν
ἔκλειψιν πυκνὴ καὶ νυγματώδης, τοῖς δὲ ὡς ἂν
ἀθροιζομένου πλείονος θερμοῦ· διὸ καὶ τὸ ἀναζεῖν
καὶ τὸ ὀρίνεσθαι τὸν θυμὸν καὶ ταράττεσθαι, καὶ
ὅσα τοιαῦτα λέγουσιν οὐ κακῶς, ἀλλ᾽ οἰκείως. ἆρ᾽
35 οὖν καὶ διὰ τοῦτο τὸ δίψος, ἐπεὶ τό γε ξηρὸν πτύειν
καὶ ὁ σαυσαρισμὸς καὶ τὰ τοιαῦτα γίνεται διὰ τὴν
ἀναφορὰν τοῦ πνεύματος ἅμα καὶ θερμοῦ; καὶ τὸ
δίψος δὲ δῆλον ὡς ἐκθερμαινομένου τοῦ σώματος.
πῶς οὖν ὁ αὐτὸς τόπος ἀναξηραίνεται ἀμφοῖν, ᾧ
διψῶμεν, καὶ τῷ φοβουμένῳ καὶ τῷ ὀργιζομένῳ·
948 a ὁ δὲ φόβος ὅτι διψητικόν, καὶ οἱ ἐν ταῖς τροπαῖς
δηλοῦσιν· οὐδαμοῦ γὰρ οὕτω διψῶσιν. καὶ οἱ
ἀγωνιῶντες δὲ σφόδρα· διὸ καὶ διακλύζονται καὶ
ἐπιρροφοῦσιν, καθάπερ Παρμένων ὁ ὑποκριτής. ἢ
5 τούτοις μὲν οὐκ ἔστιν δίψος, ἀλλὰ ξηρότης πεφευ-
γότος τοῦ αἵματος, ὅθεν καὶ ὠχροί; σημεῖον δὲ
τὸ μὴ πίνειν πολύ, ἀλλὰ καὶ βροχθίσαι. οἱ δ᾽
ἐν ταῖς τροπαῖς μετὰ πόνου. διὸ διψῶσι καὶ οἱ
μέλλοντες κολάζεσθαι· καὶ οὐθὲν ἄτοπον. ἐν δὲ
τοῖς πολεμικοῖς ἔνιοι καὶ τῶν ἀνδρείων, ὅταν δια-
σκευασθῶσιν, καὶ τρέμουσιν οὐκ ἐξεστηκότες, ἀλλὰ
10 θαρροῦντες· ὧν εἰώθασιν μαστιγοῦν τὸ σῶμα πλατεῖ
νάρθηκι, εἰ δὲ μή, ταῖς χερσὶν ἀναθερμανθέντες.
ἔοικεν δὴ διὰ τὴν ὀξύτητα καὶ τὴν φορὰν τοῦ
θερμοῦ ἀνωμαλία τις εἶναι περὶ τὸ σῶμα ταρα-
χώδης.

Διὰ τί οἱ ἀνδρεῖοι ὡς ἐπὶ τὸ πολὺ φίλοινοι;   ἢ 4

118

escape downwards, whence comes the loosening of the bowels. The beating of the heart is also different (in the two cases), since with the frightened it is rapid and strongly punctuated as would naturally occur from a failure of heat, whereas in the case of the angry it functions as one would expect if more heat was collecting there ; so the phrases " boil up," " rise," " be disturbed " and similar expressions are not wrongly but quite naturally used of the temper. Is it also for this reason that thirst results, and the drying of saliva, and a paralysis of the tongue and similar symptoms owing to the upward passage of the breath and heat ? The thirst is evidently due to the heating of the body. How is it, then, that the same part of us, that with which we thirst, dries both in fear and in anger ? That fear produces thirst is shown by men in a rout ; for in no other circumstances is thirst so intense. So also those who are under great strain are thirsty ; that is why they wash out their mouths and swallow greedily, as Parmeno the actor used to do. Or is this not really thirst, but is it a dryness due to the draining of blood, which is also why they become pale ? A proof of this is that they do not drink a large quantity but gulp it down. Those who are in a rout combine their fear with exertion. So those also who are expecting punishment are thirsty ; and this is in no way surprising. In war even some brave men, when they are equipped for the fray, tremble, not because they are distraught, but because they are full of courage ; these are accustomed to beat their body with a broad stick, or otherwise to warm it with their hands. It seems that owing to the sharpness and rush of the heat a disturbing inequality of temperature is set up in the body.

Why are brave men usually fond of wine ? Is it 4

948 a

ὅτι οἱ ἀνδρεῖοι θερμοί, ἡ δὲ θερμότης περὶ τὰ
15 στήθη. ἐνταῦθα γὰρ καὶ ὁ φόβος φαίνεται, γινόμενος κατάψυξίς τις. ὥστε[1] περὶ τὴν καρδίαν
ἧττον μὲν μένει, τοῖς δὲ πηδᾷ ψυχομένη. ὅσοι
οὖν τὸν πνεύμονα ἔχουσιν ἔναιμον, θερμὸν ἔχουσι
τοῦτον ὥσπερ οἰνωμένοι, ὥστε οὐ ψύχει ἡ φαν-
τασία τοῦ δεινοῦ. οἱ δὲ τοιοῦτοι καὶ φιλοπόται·
20 ἥ τε γὰρ τοῦ ποτοῦ ἐπιθυμία διὰ τὴν τούτου τοῦ
μορίου θερμότητά ἐστιν (εἴρηται δὲ περὶ αὐτοῦ ἐν
ἄλλοις) καὶ τοῦ παυστικοῦ ἡ ἐπιθυμία. ὁ δὲ οἶνος
θερμὸς μὲν τὴν φύσιν, παύει δὲ τὴν δίψαν μᾶλλον
τοῦ ὕδατος, καὶ μάλιστα τῶν τοιούτων[2]· δι' ἣν
αἰτίαν, εἴρηται ἐν ἄλλοις. διὸ καὶ οἱ ἐν τῇ περι-
25 πνευμονίᾳ καὶ οἱ μαινόμενοι ἀμφότεροι ἐπιθυμοῦσιν
οἴνου· καίτοι τῶν μὲν διὰ τὴν θερμασίαν θερμὸς ὁ
πνεύμων, τῶν δὲ διὰ τὴν ταραχήν. ἐπεὶ οὖν οἱ
αὐτοὶ ὡς ἐπὶ τὸ πολὺ τῷ γένει διψητικοὶ καὶ
ἀνδρεῖοι, οἴνου δὲ οἱ διψητικοὶ ἐπιθυμητικοί, οἱ δὲ
τοιοῦτοι φιλοπόται, ἀναγκαῖον ὡς ἐπὶ τὸ πολὺ
παρακολουθεῖν ἀλλήλοις τὰς φύσεις· διὸ καὶ οἱ
30 οἰνωμένοι ἀνδρειότεροι τῶν μή.

Διὰ τί μάλιστα τὴν ἀνδρείαν τιμῶσιν αἱ πόλεις,
οὐ βελτίστην οὖσαν τῶν ἀρετῶν; ἢ ὅτι διατελοῦσιν ἢ πολεμοῦντες ἢ πολεμούμενοι, αὕτη δὲ
ἐν ἀμφοῖν χρησιμωτάτη ἐστίν· τιμῶσι δὲ οὐ τὰ
βέλτιστα, ἀλλὰ τὰ αὑτοῖς βέλτιστα.

35 Διὰ τί οἱ φοβούμενοι μάλιστα τρέμουσι τὴν
φωνὴν καὶ τὰς χεῖρας καὶ τὸ κάτω χεῖλος; ἢ διότι
ἔκλειψίς ἐστι τὸ πάθος θερμοῦ ἐκ τῶν ἄνω τόπων·
διὸ καὶ ὠχριῶσιν. διὰ μὲν οὖν τὸ ἐκ τοῦ στήθους

---

[1] Ruelle inserts τοῖς μὲν after ὥστε without ms. authority.
[2] τῶν τοιούτων Forster : τῶν αὐτῶν ms.

because brave men are warm, and the warmth lies about the chest ? For it is there that fear makes itself felt, in the form of chilling. So that less heat remains about the heart, and with some people the heart palpitates as it cools. Those whose lungs contain much blood have hot lungs like those under the influence of wine, so that the presentiment of fear does not cool them. Men of this character are fond of drink ; for the desire of drink is due to the heat of this part (this subject has been discussed elsewhere) and it is a desire for what will stop the heat. But wine is naturally hot, and quenches thirst more than water does, especially with the brave ; why this is so has been explained elsewhere. So those who are suffering from pneumonia and the insane both crave for wine ; yet the lungs of the former are hot as the result of inflammation, those of the latter owing to their disturbed state. Since, then, the same men are generally thirsty and courageous, the thirsty desiring to drink wine and therefore fond of drinking, it follows that these characteristics generally accompany each other. This is why those who drink wine are more courageous than those who do not.

Why do cities give most honour to courage, which 5 is not the greatest of the virtues ? Is it because brave men hold out, whether in aggression or in defence, and in either case courage is most useful to the city ? So they honour not what is absolutely best, but what is best for themselves.

Why do the frightened tremble most in voice and 6 in the hands and the lower lip ? Is it because this condition involves a draining of heat from the upper parts ? This is why they grow pale. It is due to the draining of heat from the breast that the voice

ἡ φωνὴ τρέμει, ψυχομένου ᾧ κινεῖται. ὁμοίως δὲ
καὶ αἱ χεῖρες· ἐκ τοῦ στήθους γὰρ ἤρτηνται. τὸ δὲ
948 b κάτω χεῖλος, ἀλλ' οὐ τὸ ἄνωθεν ⟨τρέμει, διότι τὸ
ἄνωθεν⟩[1] κάτω κρέμαται ᾗ ῥέπει· τὸ δὲ κάτωθεν
ἄνω παρὰ φύσιν, ἀλλ' ὑπὸ τοῦ θερμοῦ ἄνω ἠρεμεῖ·
οὗ ὑφαιρουμένου διὰ τὸ ψύχεσθαι τρέμει. καὶ ἐν
5 τοῖς θυμοῖς δὲ διὰ τὸ αὐτὸ ἀποκρεμάννυται τὸ
χεῖλος. δῆλον δὲ ἐπὶ τῶν παιδίων· συνθεῖ γὰρ εἰς
τὴν καρδίαν τὸ θερμόν.

Διὰ τί οἱ φοβούμενοι τρέμουσι, καὶ μάλιστα τὴν
φωνὴν καὶ τοῦ σώματος τὰς χεῖρας καὶ τὸ κάτω
χεῖλος; ἢ διότι ἐκ τούτου τοῦ τόπου ἐκλείπει τὸ
θερμὸν ἐν ᾧ ἡ φωνή; τὸ δὲ χεῖλος καὶ τὰς χεῖρας,
10 ὅτι εὐκινητότατα καὶ ἥκιστα ἔναιμα. καὶ προΐενται μὲν τὴν χολήν, συσπῶσι δὲ τὰ αἰδοῖα,
προΐενται μὲν διὰ τὸ συντήκειν τὸ καταβαῖνον
θερμόν, ἀνασπῶσι δέ, ὅτι ἔξωθεν φόβος· εἰς
τοὐναντίον οὖν ἡ φυγή.

Διὰ τί οἱ φοβούμενοι καὶ διψοῦσιν καὶ ῥιγοῦσιν;
ταῦτα δὲ ἐναντία τὰ πάθη. ἢ ῥιγοῦσι μὲν ψυχό-
15 μενοι, διψῶσι δὲ θερμαινόμενοι. διότι ἐν τῷ
φοβεῖσθαι τὸ θερμὸν ἐκλείπει καὶ τὸ ὑγρὸν ἐκ τῶν
ἄνω τόπων. δηλοῖ δὲ τὸ χρῶμα καὶ αἱ κοιλίαι· τὸ
μὲν γὰρ πρόσωπον ὠχρόν, αἱ δὲ κοιλίαι ἐνίοτε
λύονται. διὰ μὲν οὖν τὸ ἐκλείπειν τὸ θερμὸν ἐκ
τῶν ἄνωθεν τὸ ῥῖγος γίνεται, διὰ δὲ τὸ ὑγρὸν
ἡ δίψα.

20 Διὰ τί τοῦ τε φόβου λύπης τινὸς ὄντος καὶ τῆς
ἀλγηδόνος, οἱ μὲν ἀλγοῦντες ἀναβοῶσιν, οἱ δὲ
φοβούμενοι σιωπῶσιν; ἢ οἱ μὲν ἀλγοῦντες κατ-

---

[1] Forster adds τρέμει . . . ἄνωθεν from Th. G.'s trans-

trembles, as the part cools by which both the tongue
and the hands are moved ; for they depend on the
breast. It is the lower lip which trembles not the
upper, because the latter hangs down in the direction
of its weight ; the lower lip points upwards in an
unnatural direction, and remains in this position
because of the heat ; so, as the heat is withdrawn, it
trembles because it is cooling. In temper the lip
hangs down for the same reason. This is clear in the
case of children ; for the heat rushes to the heart.

Why do the frightened tremble especially in voice, 7
in the hands and in the lower lip ? Is it because the
heat fails from that part in which the voice resides ?
In the case of the lip and the hands it is because these
parts are most easily moved and contain least blood.
Men in this condition emit bile, and suffer contraction
of the privates ; the emission is due to the melting
caused by the descending heat, and the contraction
takes place because fear comes from the outside ; so
the flight is in the opposite direction.

Why do the frightened feel thirsty and shiver ? 8
For these are contrary affections. Do men shiver
when they are getting chilled, and are they thirsty
when growing hot ? It is because in fear heat and
moisture leave the upper parts of the body. The
colour of the skin and the bowels prove this. For the
face grows pale, and the bowels are sometimes loose ;
so the shivering is due to the draining of the heat
from the upper parts, while the thirst is due to the
departure of moisture.

Why is it, seeing that fear is a form of pain and 9
grief, that those in pain cry out, but the frightened
are silent ? Is it because those in pain hold the

lation " non superius labrum quatitur quia superius . . . pen-
det."

ἔχουσι τὸ πνεῦμα (διὸ ἀθρόον ἐξιὸν μετὰ βοῆς
ἐξέρχεται), τῶν δὲ φοβουμένων κατέψυκται τὸ
σῶμα καὶ τὸ θερμὸν κάτω ἐνήνεκται, ὃ ποιεῖ
25 πνεύματα; ἢ οὖν ἐνήνεκται μάλιστα, ἐνταῦθα καὶ
ποιεῖ αὐτά. διὸ καὶ ἀποψοφοῦσιν οἱ φοβούμενοι.
ἡ δὲ φωνή ἐστι φορὰ πνεύματος ἄνω πως καὶ διά
τινων γινομένη. τοῦ δὲ τοὺς ἀλγοῦντας κατέχειν
τὸ πνεῦμα αἴτιον, ὅτι ταῖς ἐνυπαρχούσαις ἡμῖν
30 βοηθείαις φύσει εὐθὺς πάντες παθόντες ἄνευ λογισμοῦ χρώμεθα, καθάπερ καὶ τὰ ἄλλα ζῷα· τὰ μὲν
γὰρ κέρασι, τὰ δὲ ὀδοῦσι, τὰ δὲ ὄνυξιν ἀμύνεται.
πρὸς δὲ τὰ ἀλγήματα πάντα ἢ τὰ πλεῖστα βοηθεῖ
ἡ θερμότης. ὃ ποιεῖ ὁ κατέχων τὸ πνεῦμα· θερμαίνει γὰρ καὶ ἐκπέττει τὸ ἄλγημα, συστέλλων
ἐντὸς τὸ θερμὸν τῷ πνεύματι.

35 Διὰ τί τοῖς φοβουμένοις αἱ κοιλίαι λύονται καὶ
οὐρητιῶσιν; ἢ τὸ θερμὸν τὸ ἐν ἡμῖν ἐστιν ὥσπερ
ζῷον; τοῦτ' οὖν φεύγει ὅ τι ἂν φοβηθῇ. ἔξωθεν
οὖν γινομένων τῶν τε ὑπὸ τῆς ἀγωνίας φόβων καὶ
τῶν τοιούτων, καὶ ἐκ τῶν ἄνωθεν εἰς τὰ κάτω καὶ
949 a ἐκ τῶν ἐπιπολῆς εἰς τὰ ἐντός, ἐκθερμαινόμενοι δὲ
οἱ περὶ τὴν κοιλίαν τόποι καὶ τὴν κύστιν δια-
λύονται, καὶ ποιοῦσιν αὐτὰς εὐτρεπεῖς. καὶ γὰρ τὰ
ἄνηθα καὶ τὰ ἀψίνθια, καὶ ὅσα οὐρητικά, θερ-
μαντικά. ὁμοίως δὲ καὶ τὰ πρὸς τὴν κοιλίαν
5 φάρμακα τῶν¹ κάτω θερμαντικά· καὶ τὰ μὲν τῶν
εἰσενεχθέντων μόνον² λυτικά, τὰ δὲ καὶ ἑτέραν
σύντηξιν ποιεῖ, οἷον τὸ σκόροδον εἰς τὸ οὖρον.
τὸ αὐτὸ δὲ τοῖς τοιούτοις ἡ ἐκ τῶν ἐπιπολῆς
θερμασία εἰς τούτους τοὺς τόπους συνιοῦσα δρᾷ.

Διὰ τί οἱ φοβούμενοι συσπῶσιν τὰ αἰδοῖα; εἰκὸς
10 γὰρ ἦν τοὐναντίον, τοῦ θερμοῦ εἰς τοῦτον τὸν τόπον

breath (so when it escapes in a mass it escapes with a cry), but in the case of the frightened the body is chilled and the heat travels downwards, and creates breath ? It creates most wind in the region to which it is carried. So the frightened break wind. Now voice is due to the rush of the breath upwards in some way and by certain channels. But the reason why those in pain hold the breath is that all men when suffering make use of the natural aids we possess without thinking, just as the other animals do ; some defend themselves with their horns, others with their teeth, and others again with their claws. Now in all pains, or most of them, warmth assists. This is what occurs when a man holds his breath ; for he heats and concocts the pain, by collecting the heat within by means of the breath.

Why should the frightened have relaxed bowels 10 and desire to pass urine ? Is it because the heat within us behaves as if it were alive ? This, therefore, flees from what it fears. So, as the causes of fears due to nervousness and the like are external and pass downwards from above and from the surface to the inside, the parts near the stomach and bladder growing hot relax and make the organs ready to function. For aniseed and wormwood, and all other diuretic drugs are heating. In the same way drugs which affect the stomach heat the lower parts : some drugs when introduced only relax, but others produce further melting, as garlic does with the urine. The heat which passes into these regions from the surface has the same effect as these drugs.

Why do the privates of the frightened contract ? 11 The opposite effect would be expected, seeing that

<hr />

¹ τῶν Foster : τὰ MS.　　² μόνων Ruelle : μόνον several MSS.

949 a

ἀθροιζομένου τῶν φοβουμένων, ἀνίεσθαι αὐτά. ἢ
οἱ φοβούμενοι σχεδὸν ἅπαντες ὥσπερ ῥιγοῦντές
εἰσιν; ἐκλελοιπότος οὖν ἐκ τῶν ἐπιπολῆς τοῦ
θερμοῦ συσπῶσιν. διὸ καὶ βομβυλίζουσιν οἱ δεινῶς
δεδιότες. δοκεῖ δὲ συσπᾶν τὸ ἐπιπολῆς καὶ τὸ
15 δέρμα τῶν ῥιγούντων, ἅτε τοῦ θερμοῦ ἐκκεκρι-
μένου· διὸ καὶ φρίττουσιν. συσπᾶται δὲ καὶ ἡ
ὀσχέα τοῦ αἰδοίου ἄνω, καὶ συνεφέλκονται καὶ οἱ
ὄρχεις αὐτῇ συστελλομένῃ.[1] θᾶττον δὲ φαίνεται
ἐπὶ τῶν ἀφροδισίων· ὁ γὰρ φόβος ἐκκρίνει, καὶ
πολλοῖς τῶν ἀγωνιώντων καὶ τῶν περιφόβων
20 συμβαίνει[2] τῆς γονῆς πρόεσις.

[1] αὐτοῖς συστελλομένων Ruelle. The reading in the text is
taken by Forster from Th. G.
[2] συμβαίνει Platt : συγκινεῖ ἡ Ruelle.

the heat collects in this region when men are frightened—namely that they should relax. Are the frightened almost always in the same condition as the cold ? So when the heat has left the surface the privates contract. This is why, when men are very frightened, they have rumblings in the bowels. The surface and skin of the cold seem to contract, because the heat is driven from them ; hence they shiver. The scrotum contracts upwards and the testicles are drawn with it as it contracts. This is more obvious at the time of sexual intercourse ; for fear causes excretion, and an emission of semen often occurs with the nervous and the very frightened.

949 a ΟΣΑ ΠΕΡΙ ΣΩΦΡΟΣΥΝΗΝ ΚΑΙ ΑΚΟΛΑ-
ΣΙΑΝ, ΚΑΙ ΕΓΚΡΑΤΕΙΑΝ ΚΑΙ ΑΚΡΑΣΙΑΝ

Διὰ τί ἔνιοι κάμνουσιν, ὅταν ἐθισθέντες ἀκο- 1
25 λάστως ζῆν μὴ ἀκολάστως διαιτῶνται, οἷον Διο-
νύσιος ὁ τύραννος, ἐπεὶ ἐν τῇ πολιορκίᾳ ἐπαύσατο
πίνων ὀλίγον τινὰ χρόνον, εὐθὺς ἐφθισίασεν, ἕως
πάλιν εἰς τὴν μέθην μετέβαλεν; ἢ μέγα μέν τι
καὶ τὸ ἔθος ἐστὶν ἑκάστοις· φύσις γὰρ ἤδη γίνεται.
30 καθάπερ ἂν ἰχθὺς ἐν ἀέρι ἢ ἄνθρωπος ἐν ὕδατι
διατελῶν φαύλως ἂν ἴσχοι, οὕτω καὶ οἱ τὰ ἔθη
μεταβάλλοντες χαλεπῶς ἀπαλλάττουσιν, καὶ τὸ
πάλιν εἰς τὰ εἰωθότα ἐλθεῖν σωτηρία γίνεται αὐτοῖς
ὥσπερ εἰς φύσεως κατάστασιν. ἔτι δὲ καὶ συν-
τηκτικοὶ γίνονται, εἰωθότες τροφῇ χρῆσθαι δαψιλεῖ
τῇ ἰδίᾳ· μὴ λαμβάνοντες γὰρ τὴν εἰωθυῖαν ὥσπερ
35 ὅλως μὴ λαμβάνοντες διατίθενται. οὐ μὴν ἀλλὰ
καὶ τὰ περιττώματα τροφῇ μεμιγμένα πολλῇ ἀ-
φανίζεται, αὐτὰ δὲ ἐπιπολάζει μόνα ὄντα, καὶ φέρεται εἰς ὄμματα ἢ πνεύμονα· προσενεγκαμένοις
949 b δὲ τροφὴν κατακεραννύμενα ὑδαρῆ γίνεται καὶ
ἀβλαβῆ. γίνεται δὲ τοῖς ἀκολάστως ζῶσιν πλείω τὰ
περιττώματα ἄχρι τινὸς λήξασι τοῦ εἰωθότος βίου,

BOOK XXVIII

Problems connected with Self-Control and Lack of Control, with Continence and Incontinence

Why is it that some men become ill, when, being 1 accustomed to live an intemperate life, they no longer live thus ; for instance, Dionysius the tyrant, when in the siege he ceased drinking wine for a time, immediately became consumptive, until he reverted to his drinking ? Is habit a large factor in every man's life, since it soon becomes second nature ? Just as a fish in air or a man in water would suffer after a time, so those who alter their mode of life suffer from the change, and their only safety lies in returning to their usual life, like a return to nature. Moreover, they waste away, if they are accustomed to enjoy an abundant supply of a special diet ; for if they fail to receive their usual diet their condition is the same as if they received no food at all. In addition to this, when the waste products are mixed with a large quantity of food they disappear, but when undiluted they rise to the surface, and travel to the eyes and the lungs ; but when men are receiving food, being mixed with it these waste products become diluted and so innocuous. Now when those who live intemperate lives abandon their usual manner of living, the waste products grow greater up to a

949 b

διὰ τὸ πολλὴν ἀκαταχώριστον ἐν αὐτοῖς ὕλην
ὑπάρχειν ἐκ τοῦ προτέρου βίου, ἧς τηκομένης ὑπὸ
5 τοῦ συμφύτου θερμοῦ, καθάπερ χιόνος πολλῆς,
ῥεύματα ἁδρὰ συμβαίνει γίνεσθαι.

Διὰ τί κατὰ δύο μόνας αἰσθήσεις ἀκρατεῖς 2
λέγομεν, οἷον ἁφὴν καὶ γεῦσιν; ἢ διὰ τὰς ἀπὸ
τούτων γινομένας ἡδονὰς ἡμῖν καὶ τοῖς ἄλλοις
ζῴοις; ἅτε οὖν κοιναὶ οὖσαι ἀτιμόταταί εἰσι, διὸ
καὶ μάλιστα ἢ μόναι ἐπονείδιστοί εἰσιν. ὥστε
10 τὸν ὑπὸ τούτων ἡττώμενον ψέγομεν καὶ ἀκρατῆ
καὶ ἀκόλαστον εἶναι φαμέν, διὰ τὸ ὑπὸ τῶν χειρίστων ἡδονῶν ἡττᾶσθαι.

Διὰ τί ἀκρατεῖς λέγονται κατὰ τὰς ἐπιθυμίας 3
μόνον, οὔσης τῆς ἀκρασίας καὶ περὶ τὴν ὀργήν;
15 ἢ ὅτι ἀκρατὴς μέν ἐστιν ὁ παρὰ τὸν λόγον τι πράτ-
των καὶ ἀκρασία ἡ παρὰ τὸν λόγον ἀγωγή, εἰσὶ
δὲ αἱ μὲν ἐπιθυμίαι ὡς ἐπίπαν εἰπεῖν παρὰ τὸν
λόγον, αἱ δὲ ὀργαὶ μετὰ λόγου, οὐχ ὡς κελεύσαντος
τοῦ λόγου, ἀλλ' ὡς δηλώσαντος τὸν προπηλακισμὸν
ἢ τὴν αἰτίαν;

20 Διὰ τί τὴν μὲν ἐγκράτειαν καὶ σωφροσύνην ἐπὶ 4
τῶν νέων καὶ πλουσίων μάλιστα ἐξετάζομεν, τὴν
δὲ δικαιοσύνην ἐπὶ τῶν πενήτων; ἢ ὅτι οὗ
μάλιστα δεῖταί τις, εἰ τούτου ἀπέχεται, μᾶλλον
θαυμάζοιτ' ἂν ἢ τῶν ἐναντίων; ὁ μὲν οὖν πένης
εὐπορίας δεῖται, ὁ δὲ νέος καὶ πλούσιος ἀπο-
25 λαύσεως.

Διὰ τί ἧττον ἀνέχονται διψῶντες ἢ πεινῶντες; 5
πότερον ὅτι λυπηρότερον; σημεῖον δὲ τοῦ λυπηρο-
τέρου, ὅτι ἥδιον τὸ διψῶντα πιεῖν ἢ πεινῶντα φαγεῖν.

point, because there is much unseparated matter in them left from their previous mode of living, and when this is dissolved by the natural heat, like a quantity of melted snow, violent fluxes take place.

Why do we describe men as incontinent in respect 2 of two senses only, touch and taste ? Is it because the pleasures derived from these two senses are common to us and to the other animals ? Because they are common to them they are the least honoured senses, and so they are the only pleasures open to reproach or at any rate more so than others. So we blame the man who is a slave to them and call him incontinent and intemperate, because he is a slave to the worst pleasures.

Why do we call men incontinent only in respect of 3 their desires, although they can also be incontinent in anger ? Is it because the incontinent man is he who acts contrary to reason, and incontinence is a way of living which is contrary to reason ? Now desires are, speaking generally, contrary to reason, but feelings of anger are combined with reason, not because reason prompts them, but because it is reason which indicates the insult or accusation.

Why are continence and self-control the virtues we 4 most admire among the young and rich, but justice among the poor ? Is it because more admiration is given to one who abstains from what he wants most than when he abstains from the opposite ? Now the poor man feels the need of well-being, but the young and rich of enjoyment.

Why can men bear thirst less easily than hunger ? 5 Is it because it is more painful ? The proof of its being more painful lies in the fact that the thirsty man finds more pleasure in drinking than the hungry man

949 b

τὸ δὲ ἐναντίον τῷ ἡδεῖ λυπηρότερον. ἢ διότι
30 μᾶλλον δεῖται τοῦ ὑγροῦ τὸ θερμὸν ᾧ ζῶμεν[1]; ἢ
ὅτι δυοῖν ἡ δίψα ἐπιθυμία, ποτοῦ καὶ τροφῆς, ἡ
δὲ πεῖνα ἑνὸς μόνου, τροφῆς;

Διὰ τί ἧττον καρτεροῦμεν διψῶντες ἢ πεινῶντες;
ἢ διότι λυπούμεθα μᾶλλον; σημεῖον δὲ τῆς λύπης·
ἡ ἡδονὴ σφοδροτέρα. εἶτα ὁ μὲν διψῶν δυοῖν
35 ἐνδεής, τροφῆς καὶ καταψύξεως (ἄμφω γὰρ ἔχει
τὸ ποτόν), ὁ δὲ πεινῶν θατέρου μόνον.

Διὰ τί οἱ κατὰ τὴν τῆς ἁφῆς ἢ γεύσεως ἡδονήν,
οὗ ἂν ὑπερβάλλωσιν, ἀκρατεῖς λέγονται; οἵ τε
950 a γὰρ περὶ τὰ ἀφροδίσια ἀκόλαστοι, οἵ τε περὶ τὰς
τῆς τροφῆς ἀπολαύσεις. τῶν δὲ κατὰ τὴν τροφὴν
ἀπ᾽ ἐνίων μὲν ἐν τῇ γλώττῃ τὸ ἡδύ, ἀπ᾽ ἐνίων δὲ
ἐν τῷ λάρυγγι, διὸ καὶ Φιλόξενος γεράνου φάρυγγα
5 εὔχετο ἔχειν. οἱ δὲ κατὰ τὴν ὄψιν καὶ τὴν ἀκοὴν
οὐκέτι. ἢ διὰ τὸ τὰς ἀπὸ τούτων γινομένας
ἡδονὰς κοινὰς εἶναι ἡμῖν καὶ τοῖς ἄλλοις ζῴοις;
ἅτε οὖν οὖσαι κοιναὶ ἀτιμόταταί εἰσι καὶ μάλιστα
ἢ μόναι ἐπονείδιστοι, ὥστε τὸν ὑπὸ τούτων
ἡττώμενον ψέγομεν καὶ ἀκρατῆ καὶ ἀκόλαστον
λέγομεν διὰ τὸ ὑπὸ τῶν χειρίστων ἡδονῶν ἡτ-
10 τᾶσθαι. οὐσῶν δὲ τῶν αἰσθήσεων πέντε, τά τε
ἄλλα ζῷα ἀπὸ δύο μόνων τῶν προειρημένων
ἥδεται, κατὰ δὲ τὰς ἄλλας ἢ ὅλως οὐχ ἥδεται ἢ
κατὰ συμβεβηκὸς τοῦτο πάσχει. ὁρῶν μὲν γὰρ ὁ
λέων[2] ἢ ὀσφραινόμενος χαίρει ὅτι ἀπολαύσει[3] καὶ

---

[1] Text Ross : δεῖται τὸ θερμὸν τοῦ ὑγροῦ ἢ τὸ ξηρὸν ᾧ ζῶμεν,
Ruelle.
[2] λέων Richards (from *Eth. Nic.* 1118 a 18 ff.): ὁρῶν Ruelle.
[3] ἀπολαύσει Bonitz : ἀπολαύει Ruelle.

---

[a] Obviously a quotation from *Eudemian Ethics*, 1231,

in eating. But the opposite to the pleasant is the more painful. Or is it because the warmth by which we live has more need of moisture? Or is it because thirst is a desire for two things, drink and nourishment, but hunger of one only, namely nourishment?

Why do we bear thirst less well than hunger? Is 6 it because we are more distressed by it? The proof of our pain is that the pleasure is greater. Again the thirsty man lacks two things, food and cooling (for drink contains both), but the hungry only one.

Why are men called incontinent whenever they 7 exceed in the pleasures of touch and taste? For those are called undisciplined who exceed in sexual lusts and in the enjoyment of food. Now the enjoyment connected with food is in some cases a pleasure in the tongue, in others in the throat, wherefore Philoxenus *a* prayed to have the throat of a crane. But those whose pleasures lie in sight and hearing are not so described. Is it because we share the pleasures from these (*i.e.* touch and taste) with the other animals? So as they are thus shared they are held in less honour and generally or alone are regarded as subjects of reproach, so that we censure the man who is overcome by them, and call him incontinent and intemperate because he is a slave to the lowest pleasures. Now, though there are five senses, the other animals only derive pleasure from the two we have mentioned, and in respect of the others they either derive no pleasure at all, or are only affected incidentally. For the lion who sees or scents his victim rejoices because he is going to enjoy it; and when he has had his fill, such things

where Polyxenus is called " Son of Eryxis " (?). Possibly the same as in Aristophanes, *Frogs*, 934, but otherwise unknown.

950 a

ὅταν πληρωθῇ, οὐδὲ τὰ τοιαῦτα ἡδέα αὐτῷ,
15 ὥσπερ οὐδὲ ἡμῖν ἡ τοῦ ταρίχου ὀδμή, ὅταν ἅδην
ἔχωμεν τοῦ φαγεῖν· ὅταν δὲ ἐνδεεῖς ὦμεν, ἡδέα.
ἡ δὲ τοῦ ῥόδου ἀεὶ ἡδεῖα.

Διὰ τί ἧττον κατέχουσι τὸν γέλωτα παρόντων 8
τῶν γνωρίμων; ἢ ὅταν σφόδρα ἐξηρμένον ᾖ τι,
20 εὐκίνητόν ἐστιν; ἡ δ᾽ εὔνοια ἐξαίρει, ὥστε κινεῖ
μᾶλλον τὸ γελοῖον.[1]

[1] Text Forster : ἡ δ᾽ εὔνοια εἰπεῖν μᾶλλον γελοῖον, ὥστε κινεῖ MS.

are pleasant to him no longer, just as the smell of smoked fish no longer pleases us when we have eaten sufficient of it ; but when we need the fish, the smell is pleasant. But the scent of the rose is always pleasant.

Why do men restrain laughter less, when their acquaintances are present ? Is it because when anything is violently excited it is easily set in motion, and goodwill excites, so that laughter moves us more ?

ΟΣΑ ΠΕΡΙ ΔΙΚΑΙΟΣΥΝΗΝ ΚΑΙ ΑΔΙΚΙΑΝ

Διὰ τί μείζονος ὄντος ἀδικήματος, ἐάν τις
βλάπτῃ εἰς τὸ μεῖζον ἀγαθόν, τῆς δὲ τιμῆς οὔσης
μείζονος ἀγαθοῦ, ἡ τῶν χρημάτων ἀδικία μᾶλλον
25 δοκεῖ, καὶ οἱ ἄδικοι μᾶλλον εἶναι δοκοῦσι περὶ τὰ
χρήματα; ἢ διότι αἱροῦνται τὰ χρήματα μᾶλλον
τῆς τιμῆς, καὶ πᾶσίν ἐστι κοινότατον, ἡ δὲ τιμὴ
ὀλίγοις, καὶ ὀλιγάκις συμβαίνει ἡ χρῆσις αὐτῆς;

Διὰ τί παρακαταθήκην δεινότερον ἀποστερεῖν ἢ
δάνειον; ἢ ὅτι αἰσχρὸν ἀδικεῖν φίλον; ὁ μὲν
30 οὖν τὴν παρακαταθήκην ἀποστερῶν φίλον ἀδικεῖ·
οὐδεὶς γὰρ παρακατατίθεται μὴ πιστεύων. οὗ δὲ
τὸ χρέος, οὐ φίλος· οὐ γὰρ δανείζει, ἐὰν ᾖ φίλος,
ἀλλὰ δίδωσιν. ἢ ὅτι μεῖζον τὸ ἀδίκημα; πρὸς
γὰρ τῇ ζημίᾳ καὶ τὴν πίστιν παραβαίνει, δι' ἣν, εἰ
καὶ μηδὲν ἕτερον, δεῖ ἀπέχεσθαι τοῦ ἀδικεῖν. ἔτι
35 τὸ μὴ τοῖς ἴσοις ἀμύνεσθαι φαῦλον· ὁ μὲν οὖν
ἔδωκεν ὡς φίλῳ, ὁ δὲ ἀπεστέρησεν ὡς ἐχθρόν· ὁ
δὲ δανείζων οὐχ ὡς φίλος ἔδωκεν. ἔτι τῶν μὲν ἡ
δόσις φυλακῆς καὶ ἀποδόσεως χάριν, τῶν δὲ καὶ
ὠφελείας· ἧττον δὲ ἀγανακτοῦμεν ἀποβάλλοντες,

136

BOOK XXIX

Problems connected with Justice and Injustice

Why is it that, although injustice is greater if one 1
wrongs the greater good, and honour is a greater
good, yet injustice in money matters is thought worse,
and the unjust in money matters are thought to be
more unjust ? Is it because they prefer money to
honour, as money is common to all, but honour belongs to the few and the chance of enjoying it does
not often occur ?

Why is it more serious to make away with a deposit 2
than with a loan ? Is it because it is disgraceful to
commit an act of injustice against a friend ? Now
the man who makes away with a deposit robs a
friend ; for no one makes a deposit except with a
man whom he trusts. But where a debt is involved,
there is no friend ; for if a man is a friend he does not
lend but gives. Or is it because the wrong done is
really greater ? For, in addition to the loss involved,
he has betrayed a trust, for which reason, if for
no other, he should abstain from the wrongdoing.
Besides, it is mean not to return like for like ; for the
depositor gave it as to a friend, but the other took it
away as from an enemy ; but the lender did not give
the money as a friend. Moreover, in the former
case the gift was made for safe-guarding and return,
but in the latter for profit. We are less indignant at

950 b εἰ κέρδος θηρεύομεν, οἷον οἱ ἁλιεῖς τὰ δελέατα·
προφανὴς γὰρ ὁ κίνδυνος. ἔτι παρακατατίθενται
μὲν ὡς ἐπὶ τὸ πολὺ οἱ ἐπιβουλευόμενοι καὶ ἀ-
τυχοῦντες, δανείζουσι δὲ οἱ εὐποροῦντες· δεινότερον
δέ ἐστι τὸν ἀτυχοῦντα ἢ τὸν εὐτυχοῦντα ἀδικεῖν.
5 Διὰ τί ἐνίοις δικαστηρίοις τοῖς γένεσι μᾶλλον ἢ 3
ταῖς διαθήκαις ψηφίζονται[1]; ἢ ὅτι γένους μὲν οὐκ
ἔστι καταψεύσασθαι, ἀλλὰ τὸ ὂν ἀποφαίνειν·
διαθῆκαι δὲ πολλαὶ ψευδεῖς ἤδη ἐξηλέγχθησαν
οὖσαι.

Διὰ τί ἡ πενία παρὰ τοῖς χρηστοῖς τῶν ἀνθρώπων 4
10 μᾶλλον ἢ παρὰ τοῖς φαύλοις ἐστίν; ἢ διὰ τὸ ὑπὸ
πάντων μισεῖσθαι καὶ ἐξελαύνεσθαι πρὸς τοὺς
ἐπιεικεῖς καταφεύγει, οἰομένη μάλιστα παρὰ τούτοις σωτηρίας τυχεῖν καὶ διαμεῖναι; εἰ δὲ πρὸς
πονηροὺς ἔλθοι, οὐκ ἂν διαμεῖναι ἐν τῇ αὐτῇ
δυνάμει αὐτούς, ἀλλ' ἢ κλέπτειν ἢ λῄζεσθαι, ὧν
15 γινομένων οὐκ ἂν ἔτι εἶναι αὐτὴν παρ' αὐτοῖς. ἢ
ὅτι τοὺς ἐπιεικεῖς οἴεται τῶν ἀνθρώπων ἄριστα
ἂν αὐτῇ χρῆσθαι, καὶ ἥκιστα ἂν ὑβρισθῆναι ὑπ'
αὐτῶν; καθάπερ οὖν τὰς τῶν χρημάτων παρα-
καταθήκας πρὸς τοὺς ἐπιεικεῖς τιθέμεθα, οὕτω καὶ
αὐτὴ[2] διατάττεται. ἢ ὅτι θήλεια οὖσα ἀπορωτέρα
20 ἐστίν, ὥστε τῶν ἐπιεικῶν δεῖται; ἢ ὅτι αὐτὴ
κακὸν οὖσα πρὸς τὸ κακὸν οὐκ ἂν ἔλθοι; εἰ γὰρ
τὸ κακὸν ἕλοιτο, παντάπασιν ἂν δυσίατον εἴη.

Διὰ τί οὐχ ὁμοίως αἱ ἀδικίαι μείζους περὶ τὰ 5
χρήματα[3] καὶ τὰ ἄλλα, οἷον ὁ μικρὸν εἰπὼν οὐκ ἂν
25 καὶ τὸ ἀπόρρητον εἴποι, οὐδ'[4] ὁ ἕνα προδοὺς καὶ

---

[1] ψηφίζονται Bekker : ψηφιοῦνται Ruelle.
[2] αὐτὴ ὑπὲρ αὑτῆς Ruelle.   [3] χρήματα γ[a] : ῥήματα Ruelle.
[4] οὐδ' Forster from Th. G. : ἀλλ' Ruelle.

losing, if we are in pursuit of gain, like fishermen when they lose their bait ; for the risk is an obvious one. Once more, men make a deposit mostly when they are intrigued against and unfortunate, but it is the well-to-do who lend ; and it is more terrible to wrong the unfortunate than the fortunate.

Why in some law-courts do the jury give their votes 3 rather in accordance with family connexion than with the terms of the will ? Is it because there is no possibility of falsehood about family connexions, but the true facts can be shown ? But many wills before now have been proved to be forgeries.

Why is it that poverty exists more among the good 4 men than among the bad ? Does poverty, because she is hated and driven away by all men, seek refuge with the good, because she thinks that among them she is most likely to find safety and an abiding place ? If she were to go to the wicked, they would not remain in the same condition, but they would steal or rob, and when this took place she could no longer remain with them. Or is it because she thinks that good men would treat her best, and that she would be least insulted by them ? So just as we place deposits of money with the good, so also poverty of her own accord ranges herself with them. Or is it because, being feminine, she is more helpless, so that she needs the support of good men ? Or is it because, being herself an evil, she cannot go to the evil ? For if she were to choose the evil, her state would be quite beyond cure.

Why is it that wrongs are not so liable to be com- 5 mitted on a large scale as they are in respect of money ? For instance, the man who divulges something of small moment would not necessarily divulge a great secret ; nor would the man who has betrayed one person also betray a whole city, as the man who

950 b

πόλιν, ὥσπερ ὁ ὀβολὸν ἀποστερήσας καὶ τάλαντον;
ἢ ὅτι [ἀπὸ] μείζονος ἀδικίας ἔνια ἐλάττω ἐστὶ δι᾿
ἀδυναμίαν;

Διὰ τί παρακαταθήκην αἴσχιον[1] ἀποστερῆσαι 6
μικρὰν ἢ πολὺ δανεισάμενον; ἢ ὅτι ὁ τὴν παρα-
30 καταθήκην ἀποστερῶν τὸν ὑπολαβόντα εἶναι αὐτὸν
ἐπιεικῆ ἐξαπατᾶται; ἢ ὅτι ὁ τοῦτο κἂν ἐκεῖνο
ποιήσειεν;

Διὰ τί ἄνθρωπος μάλιστα παιδείας μετέχων 7
ζῴων ἁπάντων ἀδικώτατόν ἐστιν; ἢ ὅτι πλείστου
λογισμοῦ κεκοινώνηκεν; μάλιστα οὖν τὰς ἡδονὰς
35 καὶ τὴν εὐδαιμονίαν ἐξήτακεν· ταῦτα δ᾿ ἄνευ
ἀδικίας οὐκ ἔστιν.

Διὰ τί ὁ πλοῦτος ὡς ἐπὶ τὸ πολὺ παρὰ τοῖς 8
φαύλοις μᾶλλον ἢ τοῖς ἐπιεικέσιν ἐστίν; ἢ διότι,
τυφλὸς ὤν, τὴν διάνοιαν οὐ δύναται κρίνειν οὐδὲ
αἱρεῖσθαι τὸ βέλτιστον;

951 a   Διὰ τί δικαιότερον εἶναι νενόμισται τοῖς τετελευ- 9
τηκόσιν ἢ τοῖς ζῶσιν ἐπαμύνειν; ἢ ὅτι οἱ μὲν
ζῶντες δύναιντ᾿ ἂν ἑαυτοῖς ἐπαρκέσαι, ὁ δὲ
τετελευτηκὼς οὐκέτι;

Διὰ τί ὑγιαίνοντι μὲν ὁ συνὼν οὐδὲν ὑγιέστερος 10
5 γίνεται, οὐδὲ ἰσχυρῷ ἢ καλῷ εἰς τὰς ἕξεις ἐπι-
δίδωσιν οὐθέν, δικαίῳ δὲ καὶ σώφρονι καὶ ἀγαθῷ;
ἢ διότι τὰ μὲν ἀμίμητα, τὰ δὲ μιμητὰ τῇ ψυχῇ;
ἀγαθὸς δὲ τῇ ψυχῇ, ὑγιὴς δὲ τῷ σώματι· ἐθίζεται
οὖν χαίρειν ὀρθῶς καὶ λυπεῖσθαι. ὁ δὲ ὑγιεῖ συνὼν
οὐκέτι· οὐ γὰρ ἐν τῷ τισὶ χαίρειν ἢ μὴ ὁ ὑγιής·
10 οὐθὲν γὰρ τούτων ποιεῖ ὑγίειαν.

Διὰ τί δεινότερον γυναῖκα ἀποκτεῖναι ἢ ἄνδρα; 11

[1] αἴσχιον Bonitz : αἰσχρὸν Ruelle.

140

has stolen an obol would also steal a talent. Is it because some offences fall short of a greater injustice through lack of power ?

Why is it more discreditable to steal a small deposit 6 than a large loan ? Is it because the man who steals a deposit is deceiving one who believed him to be honest ? Or is it because the man who does the one would do the other also ?

Why is it that man in spite of his education is the 7 most unjust of all creatures ? Is it because he has the largest share of reasoning power ? Hence he has most carefully examined pleasures and happiness, and these are impossible without injustice.

Why does wealth generally exist more often among 8 the bad than among the good ? Is it because wealth being blind can neither judge character nor choose the best ?

Why is it considered more just to defend the dead 9 than the living ? Is it because the living can protect themselves, but the dead can no longer do so ?

Why is it that the man who associates with one who 10 is healthy becomes no healthier, nor does one who associates with the strong and beautiful acquire anything, but he who associates with the just, the temperate and the good does so ? Is it because the former qualities cannot be imitated, but the latter can be imitated by the soul ? For a man's goodness lies in his soul, but his health lies in his body ; so he is accustomed to feel both joy and pain on the right occasions. But he who associates with the healthy man becomes no more healthy ; for health does not consist in enjoying or not enjoying certain things ; for none of these produces health.

Why is it a more terrible thing to kill a woman than 11

951 a

καίτοι βέλτιον τὸ ἄρρεν τοῦ θήλεος φύσει. ἢ
διότι ἀσθενέστερον, ὥστε ἐλάττω ἀδικεῖ; ἢ ὅτι οὐ
νεανικὸν τὸ ἰσχυρίζεσθαι πρὸς τὸ πολὺ ἧττον;

15 Διὰ τί ποτε τῷ φεύγοντι ἐν τῷ δικαστηρίῳ τὴν 12
δεξιὰν στάσιν διδόασιν; ἢ ὅτι ἐπανισοῦν βούλονται; πλεονεκτοῦντος οὖν τοῦ διώκοντος τὴν
στάσιν τῷ φεύγοντι διδόασιν. εἶθ' ὡς ἐπὶ τὸ πολὺ οἱ
φεύγοντες παραφυλάττονται· ἐπὶ δεξιὰ δὲ ἡ φυλακὴ
γίνεται, ἐὰν ὁ φεύγων ἔχῃ τὴν ἐν δεξιᾷ στάσιν.

20 Διὰ τί ποτε, ὅταν καὶ τῷ φεύγοντι καὶ τῷ 13
διώκοντι φαίνωνται αἱ ψῆφοι ἴσαι, ὁ φεύγων νικᾷ;
ἢ ὅτι ὁ μὲν φεύγων ἐν τῷ ἀγῶνι μόνον ἀκήκοεν
αὐτοῦ πρὸς ἃ δεῖ αὐτὸν ἀπηγορεῖσθαι, καὶ τοὺς
μάρτυρας παρασχέσθαι πρὸς [τὸ] τὰ κατηγορημένα
25 [ἔχεσθαι],¹ εἴ τι μέλλουσιν ὠφελήσειν; οὐ ῥᾴδιον
δὲ τὸ μαντεύσασθαί τινα ὧν δεῖ αὐτὸν παρα-
σκευάσασθαι ἢ μάρτυρας ἢ ἄλλο τεκμήριον ὅτι
οὐθὲν ἀδικεῖ. τῷ δὲ διώκοντι ἔστιν ὅπως βούλεται,
καὶ πρὸ τοῦ τὴν δίκην κλητεύσασθαι, ἐνστήσασθαι
τὸ πρᾶγμα, καὶ ἤδη κεκληκότα, πλασάμενον ὅ τι
βούλεται πιθανόν, κατηγορεῖν αὐτοῦ. ὁρῶν δὴ
30 κατὰ πάντα ταῦτα ἐλαττούμενον ὁ νομοθέτης τὸν
φεύγοντα, προσέθετο τῷ φεύγοντι ὅ τι ἂν οἱ δικασταὶ
ἀμφιδοξήσωσιν. ἀλλὰ μὴν καὶ τοῦτ' ἄν τις ἴδοι. ἐν
γὰρ τοῖς φόβοις ὄντες πολλὰ παραλιμπάνουσιν ὧν
αὐτοὺς ἔδει εἰπεῖν ἢ πρᾶξαι, οἱ δὲ φεύγοντες ἀεὶ
35 ἐν μείζοσι κινδύνοις ὡς ἐπὶ τὸ πολὺ τυγχάνουσιν
ὄντες, ὥστ' εἰ παραλιμπάνουσιν ὧν δεῖ αὐτούς,
εἴπερ ἐξισοῦνται τοῖς δικαίοις, δῆλον ὅτι εἰ μὴ

¹ Omitting τὸ (inserted by Ruelle) and ἔχεσθαι, which is
probably due to the preceding παρασχέσθαι.

142

a man ? And yet the male sex is naturally better than the female. Is it because she is weaker, so that she does less injustice ? Or is it because it is unmanly to use force against what is much weaker ?

Why do they give the defendant in the law-court a 12 position on the right (of the judge) ? Is it because they want to equalize matters ? So as the prosecutor has the advantage they give this position to the defendant. Again, defendants are usually guarded ; and the guard is on the right, if the defendant has the position on the right.

Why is it that when the votes for the defendant and 13 the prosecutor are shown to be equal, the defendant wins ? Is it because during the action the defendant has heard the charges which he must answer only in court and can only provide witnesses on the points on which he is accused, if they are to help his case ? And it is not easy to predict the purposes for which he will require witnesses, or any other form of proof that he has done nothing wrong. But the prosecutor can, just as he pleases, both initiate action before getting the summons issued and, even after he has summoned his opponent, he can invent any plausible charge he likes and accuse him of it. So the legislator, recognizing that the defendant is in the weaker position in all these ways, has given the advantage to the defendant in any case in which the jury are divided in opinion. One should also consider another point. When men are in a state of fear they omit many things which they ought to have said or done, and the defendant is generally speaking always liable to the greater risk, so that if they leave something necessary out and still their claims are equal, it is obvious that if they had not left anything out they

951 a

παρελίμπανον, ἐκράτουν ἄν. ἔτι δὲ ἕκαστος ἡμῶν
951 b μᾶλλον ἂν προέλοιτο τοῦ ἀδικοῦντος ἀποψηφίσασθαι ὡς οὐκ ἀδικεῖ ἢ τοῦ μὴ ἀδικοῦντος καταψηφίσασθαι ὡς ἀδικεῖ, οἷον εἴ τις φεύγει δουλείας
ἢ ἀνδροφονίας. τούτων γὰρ ἑκάστου ὄντων ἃ κατ-
ηγορεῖ αὐτῶν, μᾶλλον ἂν ἀποψηφίσασθαι ἑλοί-
5 μεθα ἢ μὴ ὄντων καταψηφίσασθαι. ἔστι γάρ,
ὅταν τις ἀμφιδοξῇ, τὰ ἐλάττω τῶν ἁμαρτημάτων
αἱρετέον. δεινὸν γὰρ καὶ τὸ τοῦ δούλου ὡς
ἐλεύθερός ἐστι καταγνῶναι· πολὺ δὲ δεινότερον,
ὅταν τις τοῦ ἐλευθέρου ὡς δούλου καταψηφίσηται.
ἔτι δὲ ἐὰν ὁ μὲν τύχῃ ἐγκαλῶν, ὁ δὲ ἀμφισβητῶν
10 ὑπὲρ ὁτουοῦν, οὐκ εὐθὺς οἰόμεθα δεῖν ἀποδοῦναι
τῷ ἐγκαλοῦντι, ἀλλὰ νέμεσθαι τὸν κεκτημένον,
ἕως ἂν κριθῇ. τὸν αὐτὸν δὲ τρόπον καὶ ἐπὶ τῶν
πλειόνων, ὅταν ἰσάζῃ τὸ πλῆθος τῶν τε φασκόντων
ἀδικεῖν καὶ τῶν μὴ ὁμολογούντων, ὥσπερ ὅτε ἐξ
ἀρχῆς ὁ μὲν ἐνεκάλει, ὁ δὲ ἀπηρνεῖτο, οὐκ οἰόμεθα
15 δεῖν τὸν νομοθέτην προστιθέναι τῷ ἐγκαλοῦντι,
ἀλλὰ τὸν φεύγοντα κύριον εἶναι, ἕως ἂν ὑπεροχήν
τινα ἔχῃ ὁ διώκων.[1] ὁμοίως δὲ καὶ ἐπὶ τῶν κριτῶν,
ἐπειδὴ οὐδεμίαν ὑπεροχὴν ἰσασθεισῶν τῶν ψήφων,
κατὰ χώραν εἴασεν ὁ νομοθέτης ἔχειν· ἔτι δὲ τῶν
μὲν ἀξιολόγων ἁμαρτημάτων μεγάλαι καὶ αἱ
20 κολάσεις εἰσίν, ὥστε ἀδίκως μὲν καταψηφισαμένοις
καὶ μεταγνοῦσιν[2] οὐκ ἔστιν ἐπανορθοῦσθαι καιρὸν
λαβόντας· ἀπολύσασι δὲ παρὰ τὸ προσῆκον, εἰ μὲν
οὕτως εὐλαβῶς ⟨ζῴη⟩[3] ὥστε μηθὲν ἔτι ποτὲ ἁμαρ-

---

[1] διώκων Bonitz : ἀδικῶν Ruelle.
[2] μεταγνοῦσιν Richards : μὴ γνοῦσιν Ruelle.
[3] ζῴη added by Forster.

would have won. Again, every one of us would rather
acquit a guilty man as innocent than condemn an
innocent man as guilty, in a case where a man
was accused of enslaving or murder. For in each
of these cases if the charges were true we should
prefer to vote for their acquittal on the charges
against them, rather than to vote for their condemnation, if the charges were untrue. For when
there is any doubt one should choose the lesser of two
errors. For it is a serious matter to decide in the case
of a slave that he is free ; but it is much more serious
to condemn a free man as a slave. Moreover, if one
happens to be bringing a charge, and the other to be
disputing his claim to something, we do not think it
right to hand it over immediately to the prosecutor,
but that it should remain in the hands of the pos-
sessor until the case is settled. In the same way, in
a case involving several persons, when the number of
those who say that the accused is wrong and of those
who deny it is equal (as when one lays the accusation
and the other denies it from the start), we do not
consider that the lawgiver should give it to the
accuser, but that the defendant should remain in
possession, until the prosecutor has established a
superiority. Similarly in the case of judges, when
the prosecutor has established no superiority because
the votes on the two sides are equal, the lawgiver
has allowed matters to remain as they are. Again,
the penalties for serious offences are heavy, so that
if the jury vote unjustly for condemnation and afterwards change their minds, they cannot wait for
a suitable opportunity and put matters right ; but
supposing they vote for acquittal when they should
not, if the defendant afterwards lives so circum-
spectly as never to commit an offence again, how could

τεῖν, τί ἂν καὶ μέγα ἡμαρτηκότες οἱ κριταὶ εἴησαν,
τοιοῦτον ἄνθρωπον ἀπολύσαντες θανάτου; εἰ δέ
25 τι ἐξ ὑστέρου ἁμαρτάνοι, δι᾽ ἀμφότερα [ἂν] αὐτὸν
νῦν κολάζεσθαι ἀξιοῖ. ἢ ὅτι ἀδικωτέρου μέν ἐστιν
ἀνδρὸς ταῦτα ἀδικεῖν ἃ ἧττον εἰκός ἐστιν ἀδίκως
ἐγκαλεῖσθαι; τὸ μὲν γὰρ ἀδικεῖν καὶ δι᾽ ὀργὴν
καὶ διὰ φόβον καὶ δι᾽ ἐπιθυμίαν καὶ δι᾽ ἄλλα πολλὰ
γίνεται, καὶ οὐ μόνον ἐκ προνοίας· τὸ δὲ ἀδίκως
30 ἐγκαλεῖν ὡς τὸ πολὺ ἐκ προνοίας ἐστίν. ὥστε
ἐπεὶ ἴσαι αἱ ψῆφοι γεγόνασιν, τὸ δὲ ἀδίκως τὸν
ἐγκαλοῦντα ἐγκαλεῖν καὶ τὸν φεύγοντα ἀδικεῖν,
φαύλου κριθέντος τοῦ ἀδίκως ἐγκαλοῦντος τὸ
νικᾶν τῷ φεύγοντι ὁ νομοθέτης ἀπένειμεν. ἔτι δὲ
καὶ αὐτοὶ οὕτως ἔχομεν πρὸς τοὺς θεράποντας,
35 ὥστε ὅταν ὑποπτεύσωμέν τι αὐτοὺς ἡμαρτηκέναι
καὶ μηθὲν ἀκριβὲς ἔχωμεν, ἀλλ᾽ ὅμως αὐτοὺς
ὑπολαμβάνωμεν πεπραχέναι, οὐκ εὐθὺς ἐπὶ τὸ
952 a κολάζειν ἐρχόμεθα· καὶ ἐὰν μηθὲν μᾶλλον δυνώμεθα
ἐξετάσαι, ἀφίεμεν ταύτης τῆς αἰτίας. ἔτι μείζω
μὲν ἀδικεῖ ὁ ἐκ προνοίας ἀδικῶν ἢ ὁ μὴ ἐκ προνοίας. ὁ μὲν δὴ συκοφαντῶν ἀεὶ ἐκ προνοίας
ἀδικεῖ, ὁ δὲ ἕτερόν τι ἀδικῶν τὰ μὲν δι᾽ ἀνάγκην,
5 τὰ δὲ δι᾽ ἄγνοιαν, τὰ δὲ ὅπως ἔτυχεν ἀδικεῖν αὐτῷ
συμπίπτει. ὅταν δὲ ἴσαι γένωνται αἱ ψῆφοι, ὁ μὲν
διώκων κέκριται ὑπὸ τῶν ἡμίσεων ἐκ προνοίας
ἀδικεῖν, ὁ δὲ φεύγων ὑπὸ τῶν λοιπῶν αὖ ἀδικεῖν
μέν, οὐ μέντοι γε ἐκ προνοίας, ὥστε ἐπεὶ ἀδικεῖν

---

[a] Some subject must be supplied for the verb ἀξιοῖ, and ὁ νομοθέτης seems the most probable.

[b] This sentence means little and the Greek text is probably wrong.

the judges be regarded as having erred grievously in acquitting the prisoner of a capital crime ? But if he does commit a crime again at a later date, the lawgiver ^{a} thinks it right that he should be punished on this occasion for both offences. Or is our reason that it is the mark of the greater criminal to commit offences for which he is not likely to be unjustly accused ? ^{b} For offences are committed from anger, fear, desire and many other causes, and not only of malice aforethought, but an unjust accusation is usually due to malice aforethought. So when the votes on the two sides are equally divided between those who think that the accuser has brought an unjust charge and those who think that the defendant has committed an offence, because the unjust accuser is judged to be an inferior person the legislator has given the verdict to the defendant. This is how we ourselves deal with our servants, so that when we suspect them of having committed some offence and have no certain evidence to act upon, but we nevertheless suspect them of having done it, we do not immediately proceed to their punishment ; and if we cannot discover any further evidence, we acquit them of the charge. Now the man who does wrong from malice aforethought is more guilty than he who does not. But the informer always does wrong from malice aforethought, whereas he who commits any other offence acts sometimes under compulsion, sometimes through ignorance and sometimes his evil deed is a matter of chance. But when the votes on the two sides are equal, the prosecutor is judged by half the jury to offend by malice aforethought, whereas the defendant is judged by the rest to offend but not of malice aforethought, so that since the prosecutor

μείζω κέκριται ὁ διώκων τοῦ φεύγοντος, εἰκότως
10 ὁ νομοθέτης νικᾶν ἔκρινε τὸν τὰ ἐλάττω ἀδικοῦντα.
ἔτι δὲ ἀεὶ μὲν ἀδικώτερός ἐστιν ὁ μὴ οἰόμενος
λανθάνειν ὃν ἀδικεῖ καὶ ὅμως ἀδικῶν, ἢ ὁ οἰόμενος
λανθάνειν. ὁ μὲν γὰρ ἀδίκως τινὶ ἐγκαλῶν οὐκ
οἴεται λανθάνειν τοῦτον ὃν συκοφαντεῖ, οἱ δ' ἄλλο
15 τι ἀδικοῦντες ὡς ἐπὶ τὸ πολὺ οἰόμενοι λανθάνειν
ὃν ἀδικοῦσιν ἐπιχειροῦσιν ἀδικεῖν, ὥστε ἀδικώ-
τεροι καὶ ἂν κρίνοιντο οἱ διώκοντες ἢ οἱ φεύγοντες.

Διὰ τί ποτε, ἐὰν μέν τις ἐκ βαλανείου κλέψῃ ἢ 1
ἐκ παλαίστρας ἢ ἐξ ἀγορᾶς ἢ τῶν τοιούτων τινός,
θανάτῳ ζημιοῦται, ἐὰν δέ τις ἐξ οἰκίας, διπλοῦν
20 τῆς ἀξίας τοῦ κλέμματος ἀποτίνει; ἢ ὅτι ἐν μὲν
ταῖς οἰκίαις φυλάξαι ὁπωσοῦν ἔστιν· καὶ γὰρ ὁ
τοῖχος ἰσχυρὸς καὶ κλεῖς ἐστιν, καὶ οἰκέταις τοῖς
ἐν τῇ οἰκίᾳ πᾶσιν ἐπιμελές ἐστιν ὅπως σώζηται
τὰ ἐνόντα; ἐν δὲ τῷ βαλανείῳ, καὶ ἐν τοῖς οὕτω
κοινοῖς οὖσιν ὥσπερ τὸ βαλανεῖον, ῥᾴδιον τῷ
25 βουλομένῳ κακουργεῖν· οὐδὲν γὰρ ἰσχυρὸν ἔχουσι
πρὸς τὴν φυλακὴν οἱ τιθέντες ἀλλ' ἢ τὸ αὑτῶν
ὄμμα, ὥστε ἂν μόνον τις παραβλέψῃ, ἐπὶ τῷ
κλέπτοντι ἤδη γίνεται. διὸ ὁ νομοθέτης οὐχ
ἱκανοὺς ὄντας ἡγησάμενος εἶναι φύλακας, τὸν
νόμον αὐτοῖς ἐπέστησεν ἀπειλοῦντα σφοδρῶς ὡς
30 οὐ βιωσομένοις ἐάν τι σφετερίζωνται τῶν ἀλλο-
τρίων. ἔτι δὲ εἰς μὲν τὴν οἰκίαν ἐπὶ τῷ κεκτη-
μένῳ ἐστὶν ὅν τινα ἂν βούληται εἰσδέχεσθαι, καὶ
ᾧ μὴ πιστεύει εἰσφέρεσθαι· τῷ δὲ ἐν τῷ βαλανείῳ

has been judged more guilty than the defendant, naturally the legislator has decided that the man who has committed the lesser offence should win. Again, the man who does not expect to be undetected by the man whom he wrongs and yet does the wrong, is more guilty than the man who expects to be undetected. For the man who brings an unjust accusation against another does not expect to be undetected by the man against whom he gives information, but other wrongdoers, as they usually expect to escape detection by the man whom they wrong, deliberately plan an act of injustice, so that the prosecutor in such a case should be judged more guilty than the defendant.

Why is it that, if a man steals from a public bath or 14 a wrestling school or a market or any such place, he is punished by death, but if he steals from a private house his penalty is double the value of the thing stolen ? Is it because in private houses it is possible to set a guard of some sort ; for the wall is strong and there is a key, and it is the duty of all the servants in the house to safeguard what is in it ? But in a public bath, and places which like the bath are open to the general public, it is easy for anyone who wishes to do evil ; for those who put down their property have no sure means of protection, except their own eye, so that if one merely looks away, everything is in the power of the thief. So, as the lawgiver has not considered the safeguards adequate, he has established a law with a violent threat that men shall no longer live if they annex the property of others. Again, in a private house it rests with the owner to admit whomsoever he chooses and to allow anyone to enter whom he does not trust ; but the

952 a

θεμένῳ τι οὐκ ἔξεστιν οὐθένα κωλῦσαι οὔτε
εἰσιέναι, οὔτε εἰσελθόντα μὴ παρὰ κλέπτην τὸ
αὑτοῦ ἱμάτιον θέσθαι ἀποδύντα [ἄν]· ἀλλ' ὡς οὐ
35 βούλεται, ἐν τῷ αὐτῷ ᾗ τε τοῦ κλέπτου ἐσθὴς καὶ
ἡ τοῦ μέλλοντος ἀπολλύναι ἀναμεμιγμέναι κεῖνται.
διὸ ὁ νομοθέτης τῷ μὲν ἑκόντι εἰσδεξαμένῳ τὸν
952 b κλέπτην καὶ αὐτῷ ἡμαρτηκότι οὐ λίαν μεγάλαις
τιμωρίαις βεβοήθηκεν, τοῖς δὲ ἐξ ἀνάγκης κοινωνοῦσιν τῆς εἰς τὸ βαλανεῖον εἰσόδου καὶ τῆς
ἀναμίξεως μεγάλας τιμωρίας φανερός ἐστι καθ-
ιστὰς τοῖς κλέπτουσιν. ἔτι δὲ οἱ μὲν ἐν τοῖς οὕτω
5 κοινοῖς οὖσι τῷ βουλομένῳ εἰσιέναι κλέπτοντες
καταφανεῖς ἅπασι γίνονται ὅτι πονηροί[1] εἰσιν, ὥστε
περιγενόμενοι οὐδὲ καρπισμοῦ ἔτι χάριν ἐπιεικεῖς
εἶναι δοκεῖν βούλονται, ὡς μάτην αὐτοῖς ὂν πρὸς
τοὺς γνόντας πλάττεσθαι ὅτι ἐπιεικεῖς εἰσιν· κατα-
φανῶς οὖν ἤδη πονηροὶ διατελοῦσιν ὄντες. οἱ δὲ
10 ἑνὶ μόνῳ φανεροὶ γενόμενοι πρὸς τοὺς ἄλλους
ἐπιχειροῦσι πείθειν, ἀποτίσαντές τι, ὅπως μὴ
καταφανεῖς αὐτοὺς ποιήσῃ· διὸ οὐ παντελῶς ἂν
εἶεν πονηροὶ διὰ τέλους, ἀνθ' ὧν ὁ νομοθέτης
ἐλάττω αὐτοῖς τὰ ἐπιζήμια ἐποίησεν. ἔτι δὲ τῶν
ἁμαρτιῶν μάλιστα αἰσχύνουσιν τὴν πόλιν αἱ ἐν
τοῖς κοινοτάτοις συλλόγοις τε καὶ συνόδοις γινό-
15 μεναι, ὥσπερ καὶ τιμὴν φέρουσι πολὺ μάλιστα αἱ
ἐν τῷ κοινῷ εὐταξίαι· καταφανεῖς γὰρ μάλιστα
διὰ τῶν τοιούτων καὶ αὐτοῖς καὶ τοῖς ἄλλοις.
συμβαίνει οὖν οὐ μόνον ἰδίᾳ τὸν ἀπολέσαντα
βλάπτεσθαι ἐκ τῶν τοιούτων τινός, ἀλλὰ καὶ πρὸς
τὴν πόλιν λοιδορίας γίνεσθαι. διὸ καὶ τὸν κλέψαντα
20 ταῖς μείζοσι ζημίαις ἐκόλασεν τῶν ἐξ οἰκίας τινὸς

---

[1] πονηροί Forster : φανεροί Ruelle.

man who puts his property in a public bath has no authority either to prevent anyone from entering, nor when he has entered can he avoid putting his clothes, when he has taken them off, alongside a thief ; but contrary to his wishes the clothes of the thief and of the man who is destined to be robbed lie mixed up in the same place. So the lawgiver has not given assistance by extremely heavy penalties to the man who has voluntarily admitted the thief and by his own mistake, but in the case of those who necessarily share the entrance to the bath and the mixing of clothes he has evidently set heavy penalties on thieves. Again, those who steal in places such as these which are open to anyone who wishes to enter are evidently bad men, so that even if they continue to live they do not wish to appear respectable for the advantage they would gain from it, as it is quite useless for them to pose as respectable before those who know the facts ; so they will evidently continue to live as bad men. But those whose character is known to one alone try to persuade him by returning what they have stolen not to make them known to the rest of the world ; so they are not likely to be utterly bad to the end, as a result of which the lawgiver has set less heavy penalties on them. Again, offences committed in the most public gatherings and places of meeting discredit the city most, just as orderly behaviour in public brings the city greatest credit ; for it is by such actions that citizens show their character both among themselves and to others. The result is that from thefts of the kind described not only does the actual loser suffer privately, but also abuse is heaped on the city. For this reason (the lawgiver) has punished the man who thieves (from the public) more heavily than him

952 b

ἀφελομένων. ἔτι δὲ καὶ ὁ ἐξ οἰκίας τι ἀπολέσας
ἐν τοιούτῳ τόπῳ τυγχάνει ὤν, ὅθεν ῥᾴδιον μήτε
παθόντα μήτε χλευασθέντα ὑπό τινων, οἴκοι ὄντα
τὸ ἀτύχημα φέρειν. τῷ δ' ἤ τε ἀποχώρησις
25 ἐργώδης γεγυμνωμένῳ, προσέτι δὲ χλευάζεσθαι
ὑπό τινων ὑπάρχει τοῖς πολλοῖς, ὃ πολὺ δυσχερέ-
στερόν ἐστι τῆς ἀπωλείας. διὸ καὶ ὁ νομοθέτης
μείζους αὐτοῖς ζημίας ἐνέγραψεν. ἔτι δὲ παραπλήσια τούτοις πολλὰ φαίνονται νενομοθετηκότες,
30 οἷον καὶ ἐὰν μέν τις ἄρχοντα κακῶς εἴπῃ, μεγάλα
τὰ ἐπιτίμια, ἐὰν δέ τις ἰδιώτην, οὐδέν. καὶ καλῶς·
οἴεται γὰρ τότε οὐ μόνον εἰς τὸν ἄρχοντα ἐξαμαρτάνειν τὸν κακηγοροῦντα, ἀλλὰ καὶ εἰς τὴν
πόλιν ὑβρίζειν. τὸν αὐτὸν δὲ τρόπον καὶ τὸν ἐν
τῷ λιμένι κλέπτοντα οὐ μόνον τὸν ἰδιώτην βλάπτειν, ἀλλὰ καὶ τὴν πόλιν αἰσχύνειν. ὁμοίως δὲ καὶ
35 ἐν τοῖς ἄλλοις, οὗ κοινῇ που συνερχόμεθα.

Διὰ τί ἐν τοῖς δικαστηρίοις ἐὰν ἴσαι γένωνται 1
ψῆφοι τοῖς ἀντιδίκοις, ὁ φεύγων νικᾷ; ἢ ὅτι ὁ
953 a φεύγων ὑπὸ τοῦ διώκοντος οὐθὲν πέπονθεν, ἀλλ'
ἐν τοῖς ἴσοις αὐτῷ ἤδη ἔμελλε νικᾶν;

Διὰ τί ἐπὶ μὲν κλοπῇ θάνατος ἡ ζημία, ἐπὶ δὲ 1
ὕβρει, μείζονι οὔσῃ ἀδικίᾳ, τίμησις τί χρὴ παθεῖν
5 ἢ ἀποτῖσαι; ἢ διότι τὸ μὲν ὑβρίζειν ἀνθρώπινόν
ἐστι πάθος, καὶ πάντες πλέον ἢ ἔλαττον αὐτοῦ
μετέχουσι, τὸ δὲ κλέπτειν οὐ τῶν ἀναγκαίων;
καὶ ὅτι ὁ κλέπτειν ἐπιχειρῶν καὶ ὑβρίζειν ἂν
προέλοιτο.

who steals from a private house. Again, a man who loses anything from a private house is in a place where it is easy to avoid suffering and being mocked by anyone, as he can bear his misfortune at home. But it is troublesome to retire (from the bath) without any clothes, and besides in most cases he will be laughed at by some, which is much more unpleasant than the actual loss. So for such cases the lawgiver has allotted heavier penalties. Moreover, similar laws to these have been laid down in many cases ; for instance, if a man reviles a magistrate the penalties are heavy, but if he reviles a private individual there is no penalty. And this is right ; for (the law) considers that the reviler is not merely offending against the magistrate, but is insulting the city as well. In the same way the man who steals in the harbour not only harms the individual, but discredits the city as well. And it is just the same in other places, where we congregate in public.

Why is it that in the courts if an equal number of votes are cast for the two litigants, the defendant wins ? Is it because the defendant has not been affected by the prosecutor's action, and would have won if the positions had been equal ?

Why is it that in the case of theft the penalty is death, but in one of assault, which is a greater offence, an assessment is made of what the guilty should suffer or pay ? Is it because violence is a natural human failing, and all share in it to a greater or lesser degree, but stealing is not a necessary characteristic of man ? Also because the man who undertakes to steal would be quite ready also to commit an assault.

Λ

ΟΣΑ ΠΕΡΙ ΦΡΟΝΗΣΙΝ ΚΑΙ ΝΟΥΝ ΚΑΙ ΣΟΦΙΑΝ

10 Διὰ τί πάντες ὅσοι περιττοὶ γεγόνασιν ἄνδρες [1]
ἢ κατὰ φιλοσοφίαν ἢ πολιτικὴν ἢ ποίησιν ἢ τέχνας
φαίνονται μελαγχολικοὶ ὄντες, καὶ οἱ μὲν οὕτως
ὥστε καὶ λαμβάνεσθαι τοῖς ἀπὸ μελαίνης χολῆς
ἀρρωστήμασιν, οἷον λέγεται τῶν τε ἡρωϊκῶν τὰ
15 περὶ τὸν Ἡρακλέα; καὶ γὰρ ἐκεῖνος ἔοικε γενέσθαι
ταύτης τῆς φύσεως, διὸ καὶ τὰ ἀρρωστήματα τῶν
ἐπιληπτικῶν ἀπ' ἐκείνου προσηγόρευον οἱ ἀρχαῖοι
ἱερὰν νόσον. καὶ ἡ περὶ τοὺς παῖδας ἔκστασις καὶ
ἡ πρὸ τῆς ἀφανίσεως ἐν Οἴτῃ τῶν ἑλκῶν ἔκφυσις
γενομένη τοῦτο δηλοῖ· καὶ γὰρ τοῦτο γίνεται
πολλοῖς ἀπὸ μελαίνης χολῆς. συνέβη δὲ καὶ
20 Λυσάνδρῳ τῷ Λάκωνι πρὸ τῆς τελευτῆς γενέσθαι
τὰ ἕλκη ταῦτα. ἔτι δὲ τὰ περὶ Αἴαντα καὶ Βελ-
λεροφόντην, ὧν ὁ μὲν ἐκστατικὸς ἐγένετο παντελῶς, ὁ δὲ τὰς ἐρημίας ἐδίωκεν, διὸ οὕτως
ἐποίησεν Ὅμηρος

αὐτὰρ ἐπεὶ καὶ κεῖνος ἀπήχθετο πᾶσι θεοῖσιν,
ἤτοι ὁ καππεδίον τὸ Ἀλήϊον οἶος ἀλᾶτο,
25 ὃν θυμὸν κατέδων, πάτον ἀνθρώπων ἀλεείνων.

154

BOOK XXX

Problems connected with Thought, Intelligence and Wisdom

Why is it that all men who have become outstanding 1
in philosophy, statesmanship, poetry or the arts are
melancholic,[a] and some to such an extent that they
are infected by the diseases arising from black bile,
as the story of Heracles among the heroes tells ? For
Heracles seems to have been of this character, so that
the ancients called the disease of epilepsy the " Sacred
disease " after him. This is proved by his frenzy
towards his children and the eruption of sores which
occurred before his disappearance on Mount Oeta ;
for this is a common affection among those who suffer
from black bile. Similar sores also appeared on
Lysander the Spartan before his death. The same is
true of Ajax and Bellerophontes ; the former went
completely insane,[b] and the latter craved for desert
places, so that Homer wrote of him :

But when he was hated of all the gods, then he wandered
alone on the plain of Aleïum, eating out his heart, and avoiding the track of men.[c]

---

[a] *i.e.* those in whose temperament there is too much black
bile.   [b] Sophocles, *Ajax*.   [c] Homer, *Iliad*, vi. 200.

953 a

καὶ ἄλλοι δὲ πολλοὶ τῶν ἡρώων ὁμοιοπαθεῖς
φαίνονται τούτοις. τῶν δὲ ὕστερον Ἐμπεδοκλῆς
καὶ Πλάτων καὶ Σωκράτης καὶ ἕτεροι συχνοὶ τῶν
γνωρίμων. ἔτι δὲ τῶν περὶ τὴν ποίησιν οἱ
πλεῖστοι. πολλοῖς μὲν γὰρ τῶν τοιούτων γίνεται
30 νοσήματα ἀπὸ τῆς τοιαύτης κράσεως τῷ σώματι,
τοῖς δὲ ἡ φύσις δήλη ῥέπουσα πρὸς τὰ πάθη.
πάντες δ᾿ οὖν ὡς εἰπεῖν ἁπλῶς εἰσί, καθάπερ
ἐλέχθη, τοιοῦτοι τὴν φύσιν. δεῖ δὴ λαβεῖν τὴν
αἰτίαν πρῶτον ἐπὶ παραδείγματος οὐκ ἀτόπου
ἐκ τοῦ οἴνου[1] προχειρισαμένους. ὁ γὰρ οἶνος ὁ
πολὺς μάλιστα φαίνεται παρασκευάζειν τοιούτους
35 οἵους λέγομεν τοὺς μελαγχολικοὺς εἶναι, καὶ
πλεῖστα ἤθη ποιεῖν πινόμενος, οἷον ὀργίλους,
φιλανθρώπους, ἐλεήμονας, ἰταμούς· ἀλλ᾿ οὐχὶ τὸ
μέλι οὐδὲ τὸ γάλα οὐδὲ τὸ ὕδωρ οὐδ᾿ ἄλλο τῶν
τοιούτων οὐδέν. ἴδοι δ᾿ ἄν τις ὅτι παντοδαποὺς
ἀπεργάζεται, θεωρῶν ὡς μεταβάλλει τοὺς πίνοντας
953 b ἐκ προσαγωγῆς· παραλαβὼν γὰρ ἀπεψυγμένους ἐν
τῷ νήφειν καὶ σιωπηλοὺς μικρῷ μὲν πλείων ποθεὶς
λαλιστέρους ποιεῖ, ἔτι δὲ πλείων ῥητορικοὺς καὶ
θαρραλέους, προϊόντας δὲ πρὸς τὸ πράττειν ἰταμούς,
ἔτι δὲ μᾶλλον πινόμενος ὑβριστάς, ἔπειτα μανικούς,
5 λίαν δὲ πολὺς ἐκλύει καὶ ποιεῖ μωρούς, ὥσπερ τοὺς
ἐκ παίδων ἐπιλήπτους ἢ καὶ ἐχομένους τοῖς μελαγ-
χολικοῖς ἄγαν. ὥσπερ οὖν ὁ εἷς ἄνθρωπος μεταβάλλει τὸ ἦθος πίνων καὶ χρώμενος τῷ οἴνῳ ποσῷ
τινί, οὕτω καθ᾿ ἕκαστον τὸ ἦθος εἰσί τινες ἄνθρωποι. οἷος γὰρ οὗτος μεθύων νῦν ἐστιν, ἄλλος
10 τις τοιοῦτος φύσει ἐστίν, ὁ μὲν λάλος, ὁ δὲ κεκινη-

---

[1] The words οὐκ ἀτόπου ἐκ τοῦ οἴνου are missing in the ms.
and supplied from Th. G.

156

And many other heroes seem to have suffered in the same way as these. In later times also there have been Empedocles, Plato, Socrates and many other well-known men. The same is true of most of those who have handled poetry. For many such men have suffered from diseases which arise from this mixture in the body, and in others their nature evidently inclines to troubles of this sort. In any case they are all, as has been said, naturally of this character. First of all, we must consider the cause of this, using wine as a natural example. For wine in large quantities seems to produce the characteristics which we ascribe to the melancholic, and when it is drunk produces a variety of qualities, making men ill-tempered, kindly, merciful or reckless ; but neither honey nor milk nor water nor any such thing produces these effects. One can see that wine produces every sort of character, by watching how it gradually changes those who drink it ; for finding them chilled when they are sober and inclined to be silent, when a slightly too great quantity has been drunk it makes them talkative, a still larger quantity makes them eloquent and bold, and as they go on they become reckless ; when still more is drunk, it makes them first arrogant and then mad ; a very large quantity relaxes them and makes them stupid, like those who are epileptic from childhood, and are very near the melancholic. So, just as a single individual changes his character by drinking and using a certain quantity of wine, so there are men corresponding to each character. For just as the one man is for the moment when he is drunk, so is another by nature ; one is talkative, one is emotional, and another prone

953 b

μένος, ὁ δὲ ἀρίδακρυς· ποιεῖ γάρ τινας καὶ τοιούτους, διὸ καὶ Ὅμηρος ἐποίησε

καί μέ φησι δακρυπλώειν βεβαρημένον οἴνῳ.

καὶ γὰρ ἐλεήμονές ποτε γίνονται καὶ ἄγριοι καὶ
σιωπηλοί· ἔνιοι γὰρ αὖ ἀποσιωπῶσι, καὶ μάλιστα
15 τῶν μελαγχολικῶν ὅσοι ἐκστατικοί. ποιεῖ δὲ καὶ
φιλητικοὺς ὁ οἶνος· σημεῖον δὲ ὅτι προάγεται ὁ
πίνων καὶ τῷ στόματι φιλεῖν, οὓς νήφων οὐδ' ἂν
εἷς φιλήσειεν ἢ διὰ τὸ εἶδος ἢ διὰ τὴν ἡλικίαν. ὁ
μὲν οὖν οἶνος οὐ πολὺν χρόνον ποιεῖ περιττόν, ἀλλ'
20 ὀλίγον, ἡ δὲ φύσις ἀεί, ἕως τις ἂν ᾖ· οἱ μὲν γὰρ
θρασεῖς, οἱ δὲ σιωπηλοί, οἱ δὲ ἐλεήμονες, οἱ δὲ
δειλοὶ γίνονται φύσει. ὥστε δῆλον ὅτι διὰ τὸ αὐτὸ
ποιεῖ ὅ τε οἶνος καὶ ἡ φύσις ἑκάστου τὸ ἦθος·
πάντα γὰρ κατεργάζεται τῇ θερμότητι ταμιευό-
μενα. ὅ τε δὴ χυμὸς καὶ ἡ κρᾶσις ἡ τῆς μελαίνης
χολῆς πνευματικά ἐστιν· διὸ καὶ τὰ πνευματώδη
25 πάθη καὶ τὰ ὑποχονδριακὰ μελαγχολικὰ οἱ ἰατροί
φασιν εἶναι. καὶ ὁ οἶνος δὲ πνευματώδης τὴν
δύναμιν. διὸ δή ἐστι τὴν φύσιν ὅμοια ὅ τε οἶνος
καὶ ἡ κρᾶσις. δηλοῖ δὲ ὅτι πνευματώδης ὁ οἶνός
ἐστιν ὁ ἀφρός· τὸ μὲν γὰρ ἔλαιον θερμὸν ὂν οὐ
ποιεῖ ἀφρόν, ὁ δὲ οἶνος πολύν, καὶ μᾶλλον ὁ μέλας
30 τοῦ λευκοῦ, ὅτι θερμότερος καὶ σωματωδέστερος.
καὶ διὰ τοῦτο ὅ τε οἶνος ἀφροδισιαστικοὺς ἀπεργάζεται, καὶ ὀρθῶς Διόνυσος καὶ Ἀφροδίτη
λέγονται μετ' ἀλλήλων εἶναι, καὶ οἱ μελαγχολικοὶ
οἱ πλεῖστοι λάγνοι εἰσίν. ὅ τε γὰρ ἀφροδισιασμὸς
πνευματώδης. σημεῖον δὲ τὸ αἰδοῖον, ὡς ἐκ
35 μικροῦ ταχεῖαν ποιεῖται τὴν αὔξησιν διὰ τὸ ἐμ-

to tears ; for wine produces these characteristics in some, which is the reason why Homer writes :

And he says that my tears flow because I am heavy with wine.[a]

For men sometimes become merciful and savage and silent ; for some maintain complete silence, especially those melancholic persons who are mad. Wine also makes men affectionate ; this is proved by the fact that under the influence of wine a man is induced to kiss one whom no one would kiss, if he were sober, either because of their appearance or their age. Wine endows man with extraordinary qualities, not for long but only for a short time, but nature makes them permanent for so long as the man lives ; for some men are bold, others silent, others merciful and others cowardly by nature. So that it is evident that wine and nature produce each man's characteristic by the same means ; for every function works under the control of heat. Now both the juice of the grape and the atrabilious temperament are full of breath ; this is why physicians say that diseases of the lungs and the chest are due to black bile. And the power of wine is due to air. So wine and the atrabilious temperament are similar in nature. Froth shows the wine contains air ; for oil though it is hot does not produce froth, but wine produces a large quantity, and red wine more than white because it is hotter and more full of body. And for this reason wine makes men inclined to love, and Dionysus and Aphrodite are rightly associated with each other ; and the melancholic are usually lustful. For sexual excitement is due to breath. The penis proves this, as it quickly increases from small to large by inflation.

[a] *Od.* xix. 122. The quotation is not exact.

953 b

φυσᾶσθαι. καὶ ἔτι πρὶν δύνασθαι προΐεσθαι σπέρμα,
γίνεταί τις ἡδονὴ ἔτι παισὶν οὖσιν, ὅταν ἐγγὺς
ὄντες τοῦ ἡβᾶν ξύωνται τὰ αἰδοῖα δι' ἀκολασίαν·
γίνεται δὲ δῆλον διὰ τὸ πνεῦμα διεξιέναι διὰ τῶν
πόρων, δι' ὧν ὕστερον τὸ ὑγρὸν φέρεται. ἥ τε
954 a ἔκχυσις τοῦ σπέρματος ἐν ταῖς ὁμιλίαις καὶ ἡ
ῥῖψις ὑπὸ τοῦ πνεύματος ὠθοῦντος φανερὸν
γίνεσθαι. ὥστε καὶ τῶν ἐδεσμάτων καὶ ποτῶν
εὐλόγως ταῦτ' ἐστὶν ἀφροδισιαστικά, ὅσα πνευματώδη τὸν περὶ τὰ αἰδοῖα ποιεῖ τόπον. διὸ καὶ
5 ὁ μέλας οἶνος οὐδενὸς ἧττον τοιούτους ἀπεργάζεται, οἷοι καὶ οἱ μελαγχολικοί. δῆλοι δ' εἰσὶν
ἐπ' ἐνίων· σκληροὶ γὰρ οἱ πλείους τῶν μελαγχολικῶν, καὶ αἱ φλέβες ἐξέχουσιν· τούτου δ' αἴτιον
οὐ τὸ τοῦ αἵματος πλῆθος, ἀλλὰ τοῦ πνεύματος,
10 διότι δὲ οὐδὲ πάντες οἱ μελαγχολικοὶ σκληροὶ
οὐδὲ μέλανες, ἀλλ' οἱ μᾶλλον κακόχυμοι, ἄλλος
λόγος· περὶ οὗ δὲ ἐξ ἀρχῆς προειλόμεθα διελθεῖν,
ὅτι ἐν τῇ φύσει εὐθὺς ὁ τοιοῦτος χυμὸς ὁ μελαγ-
χολικὸς κεράννυται· θερμοῦ γὰρ καὶ ψυχροῦ κρᾶσίς
ἐστιν· ἐκ τούτων γὰρ τῶν δυοῖν ἡ φύσις συνέστηκεν.
15 διὸ καὶ ἡ μέλαινα χολὴ καὶ θερμότατον καὶ ψυχρό-
τατον γίνεται. τὸ γὰρ αὐτὸ πάσχειν πέφυκε ταῦτ'
ἄμφω, οἷον καὶ τὸ ὕδωρ ὂν ψυχρόν, ὅμως ἐὰν
ἱκανῶς θερμανθῇ, οἷον τὸ ζέον, τῆς φλογὸς αὐτῆς
θερμότερόν ἐστι, καὶ λίθος καὶ σίδηρος διάπυρα
γενόμενα μᾶλλον θερμὰ γίνεται ἄνθρακος, ψυχρὰ
20 ὄντα φύσει. εἴρηται δὲ σαφέστερον περὶ τούτων
ἐν τοῖς περὶ πυρός. καὶ ἡ χολὴ δὲ ἡ μέλαινα
φύσει ψυχρὰ καὶ οὐκ ἐπιπολαίως οὖσα, ὅταν μὲν
οὕτως ἔχῃ ὡς εἴρηται, ἐὰν ὑπερβάλλῃ ἐν τῷ
σώματι, ἀποπληξίας ἢ νάρκας ἢ ἀθυμίας ποιεῖ ἢ

Even before they can emit semen boys, when they are near to the age of puberty, derive pleasure through lust by rubbing the privates ; this pleasure is clearly due to the breath passing through the channels through which the moisture is afterwards conveyed. The emission and ejection of semen in intercourse must be due to the impulse of the breath. So those solid and liquid foods are rightly considered stimulating to sex which produce breath in the region of the private parts. So red wine above all things produces the characteristics found in the melancholic. This is obvious in some cases ; for most melancholic persons are hard and their veins stand out ; the reason for this is the quantity not of blood, but of air ; the reason why not all melancholic persons are hard nor dark, but only those who are full of evil humours, is another question. But to revert to our former discussion, that such melancholic humour is already mixed in nature ; for it is a mixture of hot and cold ; for nature consists of these two elements. So black bile becomes both very hot and very cold. For the same thing can be naturally affected by both these conditions, as for instance water which is cold, but if it is sufficiently heated so as to reach boiling-point it is hotter than the flame itself, and stone and steel when heated in the flame become hotter than the coal, though by nature they are cold. There is a clearer discussion of this subject in the work on *Fire*.[a] Now black bile, which is naturally cold and does not reside on the surface when it is in the condition described, if it is in excessive quantity in the body, produces apoplexy or torpor, or despondency or fear ; but if it becomes

[a] The reference is unknown.

954 a

25 φόβους, ἐὰν δὲ ὑπερθερμανθῇ, τὰς μετ᾽ ᾠδῆς
εὐθυμίας καὶ ἐκστάσεις καὶ ἐκζέσεις ἑλκῶν καὶ
ἄλλα τοιαῦτα. τοῖς μὲν οὖν πολλοῖς ἀπὸ τῆς καθ᾽
ἡμέραν τροφῆς ἐγγινομένη οὐδὲν τὸ ἦθος ποιεῖ
διαφόρους, ἀλλὰ μόνον νόσημά τι μελαγχολικὸν
ἀπειργάσατο. ὅσοις δὲ ἐν τῇ φύσει συνέστη
κρᾶσις τοιαύτη, εὐθὺς οὗτοι τὰ ἤθη γίνονται
30 παντοδαποί, ἄλλος κατ᾽ ἄλλην κρᾶσιν· οἷον ὅσοις
μὲν πολλὴ καὶ ψυχρὰ ἐνυπάρχει, νωθροὶ καὶ μωροί,
ὅσοις δὲ λίαν πολλὴ καὶ θερμή, μανικοὶ καὶ
εὐφυεῖς καὶ ἐρωτικοὶ καὶ εὐκίνητοι πρὸς τοὺς
θυμοὺς καὶ τὰς ἐπιθυμίας, ἔνιοι δὲ καὶ λάλοι
μᾶλλον. πολλοὶ δὲ καὶ διὰ τὸ ἐγγὺς εἶναι τοῦ
35 νοεροῦ τόπου τὴν θερμότητα ταύτην νοσήμασιν
ἁλίσκονται μανικοῖς ἢ ἐνθουσιαστικοῖς, ὅθεν Σίβυλ-
λαι καὶ Βάκιδες καὶ οἱ ἔνθεοι γίνονται πάντες, ὅταν
μὴ νοσήματι γένωνται ἀλλὰ φυσικῇ κράσει.
Μαρακὸς δὲ ὁ Συρακούσιος καὶ ἀμείνων ἦν ποιητής,
ὅτ᾽ ἐκσταίη. ὅσοις δ᾽ ἂν ἐπανεθῇ ἡ ἄγαν θερμό-
954 b της[1] πρὸς τὸ μέσον, οὗτοι μελαγχολικοὶ μέν εἰσι,
φρονιμώτεροι δέ, καὶ ἧττον μὲν ἔκτοποι, πρὸς
πολλὰ δὲ διαφέροντες τῶν ἄλλων, οἱ μὲν πρὸς
παιδείαν, οἱ δὲ πρὸς τέχνας, οἱ δὲ πρὸς πολιτείαν.
5 πολλὴν δὲ καὶ εἰς τοὺς κινδύνους ποιεῖ διαφορὰν
ἡ τοιαύτη ἕξις τοῦ ἐνίοτε ἀνωμάλους εἶναι μὲν
τοῖς φόβοις πολλοὺς τῶν ἀνδρῶν. ὡς γὰρ ἂν
τύχωσι τὸ σῶμα ἔχοντες πρὸς τὴν τοιαύτην
κρᾶσιν, διαφέρουσιν αὐτοὶ αὐτῶν. ἡ δὲ μελαγ-
χολικὴ κρᾶσις, ὥσπερ καὶ ἐν ταῖς νόσοις ἀνω-
10 μάλους ποιεῖ, οὕτω καὶ αὐτὴ ἀνώμαλός ἐστιν· ὁτὲ
μὲν γὰρ ψυχρά ἐστιν ὥσπερ ὕδωρ, ὁτὲ δὲ θερμή.
ὥστε φοβερόν τι ὅταν εἰσαγγελθῇ, ἐὰν μὲν ψυχρο-

overheated, it produces cheerfulness with song, and madness, and the breaking out of sores and so forth. In most cases, arising as it does from the daily food, it does not make men any different in character, but only produces a melancholic disease. But those with whom this temperament exists by nature, at once develop various types of character, differing according to their different temperaments ; those for instance in whom the bile is considerable and cold become sluggish and stupid, while those with whom it is excessive and hot become mad, clever or amorous and easily moved to passion and desire, and some become more talkative. But many, because this heat is near to the seat of the mind, are affected by the diseases of madness or frenzy, which accounts for the Sibyls, soothsayers, and all inspired persons, when their condition is due not to disease but to a natural mixture. Maracus, the Syracusan, was an even better poet when he was mad. But those with whom the excessive heat has sunk to a moderate amount are melancholic, though more intelligent and less eccentric, but they are superior to the rest of the world in many ways, some in education, some in the arts and others again in statesmanship. This state produces considerable variations in the face of danger because many men are sometimes inconsistent in the face of fear. For they differ at different times according to the relation of their body to this mixture. The melancholic temperament is in itself variable, just as it has different effects on those who suffer from the diseases which it causes ; for, like water, sometimes it is cold and sometimes hot. So that when some alarming news is brought, if it happens at a time when the

---

[1] Text Bywater : ms. has ἐπανθῇ τὴν ἄγαν θερμότητα.

τέρας οὔσης τῆς κράσεως τύχῃ, δειλὸν ποιεῖ·
προωδοπεποίηκε γὰρ τῷ φόβῳ, καὶ ὁ φόβος
καταψύχει. δηλοῦσι δὲ οἱ περίφοβοι· τρέμουσι
15 γάρ. ἐὰν δὲ μᾶλλον θερμή, εἰς τὸ μέτριον κατ-
έστησεν ὁ φόβος, καὶ ἐν αὑτῷ καὶ ἀπαθῆ. ὁμοίως
δὲ καὶ πρὸς τὰς καθ' ἡμέραν ἀθυμίας· πολλάκις
γὰρ οὕτως ἔχομεν ὥστε λυπεῖσθαι, ἐφ' ὅτῳ δέ, οὐκ
ἂν ἔχοιμεν εἰπεῖν· ὁτὲ δὲ εὐθύμως, ἐφ' ᾧ δ' οὐ
20 δῆλον. τὰ δὴ τοιαῦτα πάθη καὶ τὰ ἐπιπόλαια¹ λε-
χθέντα κατὰ μέν τι μικρὸν πᾶσι γίνεται· πᾶσι γὰρ
μέμικταί τι τῆς δυνάμεως· ὅσοις δ' εἰς βάθος,
οὗτοι δ' ἤδη ποιοί τινές εἰσι τὰ ἤθη. ὥσπερ γὰρ
τὸ εἶδος ἕτεροι γίνονται οὐ τῷ πρόσωπον ἔχειν,
ἀλλὰ τῷ ποιόν τι τὸ πρόσωπον, οἱ μὲν καλόν, οἱ
25 δὲ αἰσχρόν, οἱ δὲ μηθὲν ἔχοντες περιττόν, οὗτοι
δὲ μέσοι τὴν φύσιν, οὕτω καὶ οἱ μὲν μικρὰ μετ-
έχοντες τῆς τοιαύτης κράσεως μέσοι εἰσίν, οἱ δὲ
πλήθους ἤδη ἀνόμοιοι τοῖς πολλοῖς. ἐὰν μὲν γὰρ
σφόδρα κατακορὴς ᾖ ἡ ἕξις, μελαγχολικοί εἰσι
λίαν, ἐὰν δέ πως κραθῶσι, περιττοί. ῥέπουσι δ',
ἂν ἀμελῶσιν, ἐπὶ τὰ μελαγχολικὰ νοσήματα, ἄλλοι
30 περὶ ἄλλο μέρος τοῦ σώματος· καὶ τοῖς μὲν ἐπι-
ληπτικὰ ἀποσημαίνει, τοῖς δὲ ἀποπληκτικά, ἄλλοις
δὲ ἀθυμίαι ἰσχυραὶ ἢ φόβοι, τοῖς δὲ θάρρη λίαν,
οἷον καὶ Ἀρχελάῳ συνέβαινε τῷ Μακεδονίας
βασιλεῖ. αἴτιον δὲ τῆς τοιαύτης δυνάμεως ἡ
κρᾶσις, ὅπως ἂν ἔχῃ ψύξεώς τε καὶ θερμότητος.
35 ψυχροτέρα μὲν γὰρ οὖσα τοῦ καιροῦ δυσθυμίας
ποιεῖ ἀλόγους· διὸ αἵ τ' ἀγχόναι μάλιστα τοῖς
νέοις, ἐνίοτε δὲ καὶ πρεσβυτέροις. πολλοὶ δὲ
καὶ μετὰ τὰς μέθας διαφθείρουσιν ἑαυτούς. ἔνιοι

---

¹ ἐπιπόλαια Forster : παλαιά Ruelle.

mixture is cooler, it makes a man cowardly ; for it has shown the way to fear, and fear has a chilling effect. Those who are terrified prove this ; for they tremble. But if the bile is hot, fear reduces it to the normal and makes a man self-controlled and unmoved. So it is also with daily despondencies ; for often we are in a condition of feeling grief, but we cannot say what we grieve about ; and sometimes we are feeling cheerful, but it is not clear why. Such affections which are called superficial come to everyone to some extent, for some of the force which produces them is mingled in everyone ; but those with whom they go deep are already of this character. For just as men differ in appearance not because they have faces, but because they have a certain type of face, some handsome, some ugly and some again having no outstanding characteristics (these are of normal character), so those who have a small share of this temperament are normal, but those who have much are unlike the majority. If the characteristic is very intense, such men are very melancholic, and if the mixture is of a certain kind, they are abnormal. But if they neglect it, they incline towards melancholic diseases, different people in different parts of the body ; with some the symptoms are epileptic, with others apoplectic, others again are given to deep despondency or to fear, others are over-confident, as was the case with Archelaus, king of Macedonia. The cause of such force is the mixture, how it is related to cold and heat. For when it is colder than the occasion demands it produces unreasonable despondency ; this accounts for the prevalence of suicide by hanging amongst the young and sometimes amongst older men too. But many commit suicide after a bout of drinking. Some

954 b

δὲ τῶν μελαγχολικῶν ἐκ τῶν πότων ἀθύμως δι-
άγουσιν· σβέννυσ γὰρ ἡ τοῦ οἴνου θερμότης τὴν
955 a φυσικὴν θερμότητα. τὸ δὲ θερμὸν τὸ περὶ τὸν
τόπον ᾧ φρονοῦμεν καὶ ἐλπίζομεν ποιεῖ εὐθύμους.
καὶ διὰ τοῦτο πρὸς τὸ πίνειν εἰς μέθην πάντες
ἔχουσι προθύμως, ὅτι πάντας ὁ οἶνος ὁ πολὺς
εὐέλπιδας ποιεῖ, καθάπερ ἡ νεότης τοὺς παῖδας·
5 τὸ μὲν γὰρ γῆρας δύσελπί ἐστιν, ἡ δὲ νεότης
ἐλπίδος πλήρης. εἰσὶ δέ τινες ὀλίγοι οὓς πίνοντας
δυσθυμίαι λαμβάνουσι, διὰ τὴν αὐτὴν αἰτίαν δι'
ἣν καὶ μετὰ τοὺς πότους ἐνίους. ὅσοις μὲν οὖν
μαραινομένου τοῦ θερμοῦ αἱ ἀθυμίαι γίνονται,
μᾶλλον ἀπάγχονται. διὸ καὶ οἱ νέοι [ἢ]¹ καὶ οἱ
10 πρεσβῦται μᾶλλον ἀπάγχονται· τὸ μὲν γὰρ γῆρας
μαραίνει τὸ θερμόν, τῶν δὲ τὸ πάθος φυσικὸν ὄν.²
ὅσοις δὲ σβέννυται³ ἐξαίφνης, οἱ πλεῖστοι δια-
χρῶνται ἑαυτούς, ὥστε θαυμάζειν πάντας διὰ τὸ
μηθὲν ποιῆσαι σημεῖον πρότερον. ψυχροτέρα μὲν
οὖν γινομένη ἡ κρᾶσις ἡ ἀπὸ τῆς μελαίνης χολῆς,
15 ὥσπερ εἴρηται, ποιεῖ ἀθυμίας παντοδαπάς, θερμοτέρα δὲ οὖσα εὐθυμίας. διὸ καὶ οἱ μὲν παῖδες
εὐθυμότεροι, οἱ δὲ γέροντες δυσθυμότεροι. οἱ μὲν
γὰρ θερμοί, οἱ δὲ ψυχροί· τὸ γὰρ γῆρας κατάψυξίς
τις. συμβαίνει δὲ σβέννυσθαι ἐξαίφνης ὑπό τε
20 τῶν ἐκτὸς αἰτιῶν, ὡς καὶ παρὰ φύσιν τὰ πυρω-
θέντα, οἷον ἄνθρακα ὕδατος ἐπιχυθέντος. διὸ καὶ
ἐκ μέθης ἔνιοι ἑαυτοὺς διαχρῶνται· ἡ γὰρ ἀπὸ τοῦ
οἴνου θερμότης ἐπείσακτός ἐστιν, ἧς σβεννυμένης
συμβαίνει τὸ πάθος. καὶ μετὰ τὰ ἀφροδίσια οἱ
πλεῖστοι ἀθυμότεροι γίνονται, ὅσοι δὲ περίττωμα
25 πολὺ προΐενται μετὰ τοῦ σπέρματος, οὗτοι εὐ-

¹ Omitting ἢ with Richards.
² Omitting ms. καὶ αὐτὸ τὸ μαραινόμενον θερμόν.

melancholic persons continue to be despondent after drinking ; for the heat of the wine quenches the natural heat. But heat in the region with which we think and hope makes us cheerful. This is why all are eager to drink up to the point of drunkenness, because much wine makes all men confident, just as youth does boys ; for old age is despondent, but youth is full of hope. There are some few persons who are seized with despondency while drinking, for the same reason that some are so after drinking. Those upon whom despondency falls as the heat dies away are more inclined to hang themselves. This is why young men and old men are more liable to hang themselves ; for old age causes the heat to die away, but in the young the cause is their condition which is natural. But when the heat is suddenly quenched is the time at which most men make away with themselves, so that everyone is amazed as they have given no sign of it before. Now when the mixture due to black bile becomes colder, it gives rise, as has been said, to all kinds of despair, but when it is hotter, to cheerfulness. This is why the young are more cheerful, and the old less so. For the former are hot and the latter cold ; for old age is a form of chilling. But it may happen that the heat is suddenly quenched by extraneous causes, just as objects which are heated in the fire and cooled unnaturally, like coals when water is poured over them. This is why some men commit suicide after drinking ; for the heat from the wine is a foreign element, and when it is quenched the affection occurs. After sexual intercourse most men are rather depressed, but those who emit much waste product with the semen are more cheerful ; for they are

---

955 a

θυμότεροι· κουφίζονται γὰρ περιττώματός τε καὶ
πνεύματος καὶ θερμοῦ ὑπερβολῆς. ἐκεῖνοι δὲ
ἀθυμότεροι πολλάκις· καταψύχονται γὰρ ἀφρο-
δισιάσαντες διὰ τὸ τῶν ἱκανῶν τι ἀφαιρεθῆναι·
δηλοῖ δὲ τοῦτο τὸ μὴ πολλὴν τὴν ἀπορροὴν γε-
γονέναι. ὡς οὖν ἐν κεφαλαίῳ εἰπεῖν, διὰ μὲν τὸ
30 ἀνώμαλον εἶναι τὴν δύναμιν τῆς μελαίνης χολῆς
ἀνώμαλοί εἰσιν οἱ μελαγχολικοί· καὶ γὰρ ψυχρὰ
σφόδρα γίνεται καὶ θερμή. διὰ δὲ τὸ ἠθοποιὸς
εἶναι (ἠθοποιὸν γὰρ τὸ θερμὸν καὶ ψυχρὸν μάλιστα
τῶν ἐν ἡμῖν ἐστιν) ὥσπερ ὁ οἶνος πλείων καὶ
ἐλάττων κεραννύμενος τῷ σώματι ποιεῖ τὸ ἦθος
35 ποιούς τινας ἡμᾶς. ἄμφω δὲ πνευματικά, καὶ ὁ
οἶνος καὶ ἡ μέλαινα χολή. ἐπεὶ δ᾽ ἔστι καὶ
εὔκρατον εἶναι τὴν ἀνωμαλίαν καὶ καλῶς πως
ἔχειν, καὶ ὅπου δεῖ θερμοτέραν εἶναι τὴν διάθεσιν
καὶ πάλιν ψυχράν, ἢ τοὐναντίον διὰ τὸ ὑπερβολὴν
ἔχειν, περιττοὶ μέν εἰσι πάντες οἱ μελαγχολικοί,
40 οὐ διὰ νόσον, ἀλλὰ διὰ φύσιν.

955 b   Διὰ τί κατ᾽ ἐνίας μὲν τῶν ἐπιστημῶν ἕξιν ἔχειν 2
λέγομεν, κατ᾽ ἐνίας δὲ οὔ; ἢ καθ᾽ ὅσας εὑρετικοί
ἐσμεν, ἕξιν ἔχειν λεγόμεθα; τὸ γὰρ εὑρίσκειν
ἀπὸ ἕξεως.

Διὰ τί τῶν ζῴων ὁ ἄνθρωπος φρονιμώτατον; 3
5 πότερον ὅτι μικροκεφαλώτατον κατὰ λόγον τοῦ
σώματος; ἢ ὅτι ἀνωμάλως ἐλάχιστον; διὰ γὰρ
τοῦτο καὶ μικροκέφαλον, καὶ αὐτῶν οἱ τοιοῦτοι
μᾶλλον τῶν μεγαλοκεφάλων φρονιμώτεροι.

Διὰ τί δοκεῖ ἡμῖν πλείων εἶναι ἡ ὁδός, ὅταν μὴ 4
10 εἰδότες πόση τίς ἐστι βαδίζωμεν, μᾶλλον ἢ ὅταν
εἰδότες, ἐὰν τὰ ἄλλα ὁμοίως τύχωμεν ἔχοντες; ἢ

relieved of waste product and of breath and of excessive heat. But the others are usually rather depressed; for they are chilled by sexual intercourse, because they are deprived of something important. This is proved by the fact that the quantity of semen emitted is small. To sum up what we have said, the melancholic are not equable in behaviour, because the power of the black bile is not even; for it is both very cold and very hot. But because it has an affect on character (for heat and cold are the greatest agents in our lives for the making of character), just like wine according as it is mixed in our body in greater or less quantity it makes our dispositions of a particular kind. Both wine and black bile are full of air. But since it is possible that even varying state may be well attempered, and in a sense be a good condition, and since the condition may be warmer when necessary and then again cold, or conversely, owing to the presence of excess, all melancholic persons are abnormal, not owing to disease but by nature.

Why is it that in some branches of knowledge we 2 say that we have a habit, and in others not? Are we said to have a habit in respect of those branches of knowledge in which we make discoveries? For discovery depends on habit.

Why is man the most sensible of all living creatures? 3 Is it because he has the smallest head in proportion to his body? Or is it because some parts are disproportionately small? This is why he has a small head, and such persons are more sensible than those with large heads.

Why is it that the road seems to us longer when we 4 walk along it without knowing how long it is, than when we do know it, if our conditions are equal in other respects? Is it because knowing how long it is

ὅτι τὸ εἰδέναι πόση, ἐστὶν εἰδέναι ἀριθμόν; τὸ
γὰρ ἄπειρον καὶ ἀναρίθμητον ταυτόν, καὶ πλέον
ἀεὶ τὸ ἄπειρον τοῦ ὡρισμένου. ὥσπερ οὖν εἰ
ᾔδει ὅτι τοσήδε ἐστί, πεπερασμένην αὐτὴν ἀνάγκη
15 εἶναι, οὕτως εἰ μὴ οἶδε πόση τίς ἐστιν, ὡς ἀντι-
στρέφοντος παραλογίζεται ἡ ψυχή, καὶ φαίνεται
αὕτη εἶναι ἄπειρος, ἐπεὶ τὸ ποσὸν ὡρισμένον ἐστὶ
καὶ τὸ ὡρισμένον ποσόν. ὅταν τοίνυν μὴ φαίνηται
ὡρισμένον, ὥσπερ ἄπειρον δόξει εἶναι, διὰ τὸ τὸ
πεφυκὸς ὡρίσθαι, ἂν μὴ ᾖ ὡρισμένον, ἄπειρον
20 εἶναι, καὶ τὸ φαινόμενον μὴ ὡρίσθαι φαίνεσθαι
ἀνάγκη πως ἀπέραντον.

Διὰ τί πρεσβύτεροι μὲν γινόμενοι μᾶλλον νοῦν 5
ἔχομεν, νεώτεροι δὲ ὄντες θᾶττον μανθάνομεν;
ἢ ὅτι ὁ θεὸς ὄργανα ἐν ἑαυτοῖς ἡμῖν δέδωκε δύο,
25 ἐν οἷς χρησόμεθα τοῖς ἐκτὸς ὀργάνοις, σώματι μὲν
χεῖρα, ψυχῇ δὲ νοῦν; ἔστι γὰρ καὶ ὁ νοῦς τῶν
φύσει ἐν ἡμῖν ὥσπερ ὄργανον ὑπάρχων· αἱ δὲ
ἄλλαι ἐπιστῆμαι καὶ τέχναι τῶν ὑφ' ἡμῶν ποιητῶν
εἰσίν, ὁ δὲ νοῦς τῶν φύσει. καθάπερ οὖν τῇ χειρὶ
οὐκ εὐθὺς γενόμενοι χρώμεθα βέλτιστα, ἀλλ' ὅταν
30 ἡ φύσις αὐτὴν ἐπιτελέσῃ (προϊούσης γὰρ τῆς
ἡλικίας ἡ χεὶρ μάλιστα δύναται ἀποτελεῖν τὸ
ἑαυτῆς ἔργον), τὸν αὐτὸν τρόπον καὶ ὁ νοῦς τῶν
φύσει οὐκ εὐθὺς ἀλλ' ἐπὶ γήρως ἡμῖν μάλιστα
παραγίνεται καὶ τότε ἀποτελεῖται μάλιστα, ἢν μὴ
ὑπό τινος πηρωθῇ, καθάπερ καὶ τὰ ἄλλα τὰ φύσει
35 ὑπάρχοντα. ὕστερον δὲ τῆς τῶν χειρῶν δυνάμεως
ὁ νοῦς παραγίνεται ἡμῖν, ὅτι καὶ τὰ τοῦ νοῦ
ὄργανά ἐστι τῶν τῆς χειρός. ἔστι γὰρ νοῦ μὲν
ὄργανον ἐπιστήμη (τούτῳ γάρ ἐστι χρήσιμος,
καθάπερ αὐλοὶ αὐλητῇ), χειρῶν δὲ πολλὰ τῶν

implies knowing a number ? For the infinite and the unnumbered are the same thing, and the infinite is always larger than the finite. If one knows that it is so long, it must be limited ; in the same way if one does not know how long it is, then the mind miscalculates as though one were reversing it, and the journey seems to be infinite, since a definite quantity is limited and what is limited is a definite quantity. So when it does not seem to be limited, it will appear infinite, because what is naturally limited is infinite, if the limit is not laid down, and what appears not to be limited must appear in a sense infinite.

Why have we more sense when we grow older, but 5 learn more quickly when we are young ? Is it because God has endowed us with two instruments within ourselves by means of which we employ outside instruments, the hand for the body and the mind for the soul ? For the mind exists within us among our natural functions as an instrument ; other branches of knowledge and the crafts are among the things created by us, but the mind is one of the gifts of nature. So, just as we do not use the hand in the best way as soon as we are born, but only when nature has brought it to perfection (for as our age advances the hand gains power to achieve its function), in the same way also the mind, which is a natural function, does not assist us in the best way at once, but in old age, and then reaches its highest perfection if it is not crippled by any agent, just like all the other things which belong to us by nature. But the mind comes to us at a later date than the power of the hands, because the instruments of the mind develop later than those of the hand. For the instrument of the mind is knowledge (for this is useful to the mind, just as flutes are useful to the flute-player), and there are many useful

171

955 b

φύσει ὄντων· ἡ δὲ φύσις αὐτή γε ἐπιστήμης πρό-
40 τερον, καὶ τὰ ὑπ' αὐτῆς γινόμενα. ὧν δὲ τὰ
ὄργανα πρότερα, καὶ τὰς δυνάμεις πρότερον εἰκὸς
956 a ἐγγίνεσθαι ἡμῖν· τούτοις γὰρ χρώμενοι ἕξιν λαμ-
βάνομεν, καὶ ἔχει ὁμοίως τὸ ἑκάστου ὄργανον πρὸς
αὐτό· καὶ ἀνάπαλιν, ὡς τὰ ὄργανα πρὸς ἄλληλα,
οὕτω ⟨ὧν⟩[1] τὰ ὄργανα πρὸς αὐτά. ὁ μὲν οὖν νοῦς
5 διὰ ταύτην τὴν αἰτίαν πρεσβυτέροις οὖσιν ἡμῖν
μᾶλλον ἐγγίνεται. μανθάνομεν δὲ θᾶττον νεώτεροι
ὄντες διὰ τὸ μηδέν πω ἐπίστασθαι. ὅταν δὲ ἐπιστώμεθα, οὐκέτι ὁμοίως δυνάμεθα δέχεσθαι,[2] καθάπερ καὶ μνημονεύομεν μᾶλλον οἷς ἂν ἔωθεν πρῶτον
10 ἐντυγχάνωμεν, ἔπειτα προϊούσης τῆς ἡμέρας οὐκέτι
ὁμοίως διὰ τὸ πολλοῖς ἐντετυχηκέναι.

Διὰ τί ἀνθρώπῳ πειστέον μᾶλλον ἢ ἄλλῳ ζῴῳ; 6
πότερον ὥσπερ Πλάτων Νεοκλεῖ ἀπεκρίνατο, ὅτι
ἀριθμεῖν μόνον ἐπίσταται τῶν ἄλλων ζῴων; ἢ
ὅτι θεοὺς νομίζει μόνον; ἢ ὅτι μιμητικώτατον·
μανθάνειν γὰρ δύναται διὰ τοῦτο.

15 Διὰ τί οὐ χαίρομεν θεώμενοι οὐδὲ ἐλπίζοντες 7
ὅτι τὸ τρίγωνον δύο ὀρθαῖς ἴσας ἔχει τὰς ἐντὸς
γωνίας, οὐδὲ τῶν ἄλλων τῶν τοιούτων οὐθέν, εἰ
μὴ τῇ θεωρίᾳ, αὕτη δὲ ὁμοίως ἐστὶν ἡδεῖα κἂν
εἰ τρισὶν ὀρθαῖς ἢ πλείοσιν ἴσας ἔσχεν· ἀλλ' ὅτι
Ὀλυμπίᾳ ἐνικῶμεν, καὶ περὶ τῆς ναυμαχίας τῆς
20 ἐν Σαλαμῖνι, χαίρομεν καὶ μεμνημένοι καὶ ἐλπίζοντες τοιαῦτα, ἀλλ' οὐ τἀναντία τοῖς τοιούτοις.
ἢ ὅτι ἐπὶ μὲν τοῖς τοιούτοις χαίρομεν ὡς γενομένοις

---

[1] ὧν added by Richards.
[2] δυνάμεθα δέχεσθαι Richards: δυνάμεθα. δυνάμεθα δὲ ἔχεσθαι Ruelle.

functions for the hands ; but nature itself is prior to knowledge, and so also are the things produced by it. It is natural that, where the instruments are prior, the functions should also appear earlier in us ; for it is by using these that we acquire a habit, and the instrument of each function bears the same relation to it ; conversely, as the instruments are related to each other, so are the functions of which they are the instruments. So it is for this reason that the mind is more developed in us when we are older. But we learn more quickly when we are younger, because we know nothing yet. But when we possess knowledge, we are no longer equally able to admit more. Just as we remember better those whom we first meet with in the morning ; then as the day goes on we have not the same capacity, because we have met with many people.

Why should more obedience be paid to man than 6 to any other animal ? Is it, as Plato replied to Neocles, because he alone of all animals can count ? Or because he alone believes in gods ? Or because he is the most imitative animal ? For this is the reason why he can learn.

Why do we feel no pleasure when we see or even 7 expect that a triangle has its interior angles together equal to two right angles, nor in any such facts, except for the pleasure derived from speculation, and this would be equally pleasant if the angles were equal to three right angles or more ? But we do feel pleasure, either that of memory or of anticipation, in such facts as our victory at Olympia or our sea-fight at Salamis, and no pleasure in facts the opposite to these. Is it because we rejoice in such things as either past or present events, but in the case of happenings

956 a

ἢ οὖσιν, ἐπὶ δὲ τοῖς κατὰ φύσιν ὡς κατὰ ἀλήθειαν
θεωρίας ἡδονήν, ὡς ἔχει, μόνην ἡμῖν ποιεῖν, τὰς
25 δὲ πράξεις τὴν ἀπὸ τῶν συμβαινόντων ἀπ᾽ αὐτῶν;
ἀνομοίων οὖν οὐσῶν τῶν πράξεων, καὶ τὰ ἀπο-
βαίνοντα ἀπ᾽ αὐτῶν γίνεται τὰ μὲν λυπηρά, τὰ
δὲ ἡδέα· φεύγομεν δὲ καὶ διώκομεν καθ᾽ ἡδονὴν
καὶ λύπην ἅπαντα.

Διὰ τί μέχρι ὑγιείας πραγματεύονται οἱ ἰατροί; 8
ἰσχναίνει γάρ, εἶτα ἐκ τούτου ξηραίνει, εἶτα
30 ὑγείαν ἐποίησεν, εἶτα ἐνταῦθα ἔστη. πότερον
οὐκ ἔστι δυνατὸν ἐκ τούτου γενέσθαι ἄλλο; ἢ εἰ
δυνατόν, ἄλλης ἐπιστήμης, καὶ ἔσται ὅ τις ἐξ
ὑγείας ποιήσει ἄλλο τι; εἰ δὴ γίνεται ἐκ τῶν
ἐναντίων καὶ τῶν μεταξύ, δῆλον ὅτι ἀρρωστεῖ ἢ
ξηρότερος ἢ ὑγρότερος ἤ τι τοιοῦτον. ποιεῖ δὴ
35 ἐκ ψύχους ἧττον σφόδρα, καὶ τέλος[1] ὡδὶ θερμὸν
καὶ ὡδὶ ξηρὸν ἢ ὑγρὸν μεταβαῖνον ἐκ τῶν ἐναντίων ἢ μεταξύ, ἕως ἂν ἔλθῃ εἰς τὸ οὕτως ἔχειν,
ὃ ἦν τοῦ ὑγιαίνειν· ἔκ τε τούτου οὐ πέφυκεν ἄλλο
τι ὂν ἢ τὸ μεταξύ. δύναται μὲν οὖν ποιῆσαι ὁ
ἔχων. ὡς γὰρ ἦλθεν, ἀναλῦσαι δύναται καὶ
40 ἀπελθεῖν. οὐ μὴν ἥ γε τέχνη τούτου ἐστίν. ἀεὶ
γὰρ βέλτιον. ὥστε οὐδὲ ἄλλη, οὔτε αὐτὴ ποιήσει
956 b ἐξ ὑγείας ἄλλο τι· οὐθὲν γὰρ ἐγίνετο ἢ τὸ ἐναντίον
τούτου, εἴπερ ἡ αὐτὴ ἐπιστήμη. οὕτω καὶ ἐπὶ
οἰκίας οὐδὲν ποιήσειεν ἂν τοὐναντίον· οὐκ ἔστιν
ἄλλη τέχνη[2] ἐκ τούτου ποιήσουσα, πλὴν ὡς μέρους,
οἷον ἡ σκυτικὴ ὑπόδημα ἐκ προσχίσματος. ἐξ

---

[1] τέλος Forster from Th. G. : τέλεον Ruelle.
[2] ἄλλη τέχνη Forster from Th. G. : ἐν ἄλλῃ τέχνῃ Ruelle.

in nature they really only give us the pleasure of contemplation, but actions give us the pleasure which arises from their results ? So, as actions are unlike, the results also differ : some are painful and some are pleasant ; for we avoid and pursue everything according to the pleasure or pain it gives.

Why do doctors exercise their craft only as far 8 as health is concerned ? For the doctor thins the patient down, then dries him ; then he has produced health and there he stops. Is it not possible for some other condition to be produced from health ? Or if it is possible does it belong to another science, and will it be another condition which a man will produce from health ? Now if health is produced from an opposite or intermediate condition, evidently a man is ill because he is too dry or too moist, or something of the kind. Now the doctor produces a less violent state from cold, and at the end makes his patient so hot and so dry or so moist from an opposite or intermediate condition, until he reaches a condition which is that of health ; and from this condition no state is possible except an intermediate one. Now the man who possesses an art can produce this condition. For just as he has reached his point, he can undo his work and leave it, but the doctor's art is not like this ; for he always aims at a better condition ; so neither any other art nor the art of medicine itself will produce anything else from health ; for, if the art remains the same, nothing comes from it except its opposite. So, too, with a house, nothing could make the opposite. Nor can any other art make anything out of health, except in the sense of making the whole from a part, as the shoemaker's art can make a complete shoe from the forepart of a shoe. For one thing can

5 ἑκατέρου γὰρ γίνεται διττῶς, ἢ συντιθεμένου ἢ φθειρομένου.

Διὰ τί τὸν φιλόσοφον τοῦ ῥήτορος οἴονται δια- 9 φέρειν; ἢ ὅτι ὁ μὲν φιλόσοφος περὶ αὐτὰ τὰ εἴδη τῶν πραγμάτων διατρίβει, ὁ δὲ περὶ τὰ μετέχοντα, οἷον ὁ μὲν τί ἐστιν ἀδικία, ὁ δὲ ὡς 10 ἄδικος ὁ δεῖνα, καὶ ὁ μὲν τί ἡ τυραννίς, ὁ δὲ οἷόν τι ὁ τύραννος;

Διὰ τί οἱ Διονυσιακοὶ τεχνῖται ὡς ἐπὶ τὸ πολὺ 1 πονηροί εἰσιν; ἢ ὅτι ἥκιστα λόγου ⟨καὶ⟩[1] σοφίας κοινωνοῦσι διὰ τὸ περὶ τὰς ἀναγκαίας τέχνας τὸ πολὺ μέρος τοῦ βίου εἶναι, καὶ ὅτι ἐν ἀκρασίαις τὸ 15 πολὺ τοῦ βίου εἰσίν, τὰ δὲ καὶ ἐν ἀπορίαις; ἀμφό- τερα δὲ φαυλότητος παρασκευαστικά.

Διὰ τί οἱ ἐξ ἀρχῆς τῆς μὲν κατὰ τὸ σῶμα 1 ἀγωνίας ἆθλόν τι προὔταξαν, σοφίας δὲ οὐθὲν ἔθηκαν; ἢ ὅτι ἐπιεικῶς δεῖ τοὺς κριτάς, ἃ περὶ διάνοιάν ἐστιν, ἢ μηθὲν χείρους τῶν ἀγωνιστῶν εἶναι ἢ κρείττους; εἰ δὲ ἔδει σοφίᾳ τοὺς πρω- 20 τεύοντας ἀγωνίζεσθαι καὶ ἆθλον προυτέτακτο, κριτῶν ἂν ἠπόρουν αὐτοῖς. ἐπὶ δὲ τῶν γυμνικῶν ἀγώνων ἅπαντός ἐστι κρῖναι, τῇ ὄψει μόνῃ θεα- σάμενον. ἔτι δὲ ὁ ἐξ ἀρχῆς κατασκευάζων οὐκ ἐβούλετο τοιαύτην ἀγωνίαν προθεῖναι τοῖς Ἕλλησιν, 25 ἐξ ὧν ἔμελλον στάσεις καὶ ἔχθραι μεγάλαι ἔσεσθαι· οἷον οἱ ἄνθρωποι, ὅταν τις ἢ ἐκκριθῇ ἢ προσδεχθῇ εἴς τι τῶν κατὰ τὸ σῶμα ἀθλημάτων, οὐ πάντῃ χαλεπῶς φέρουσιν οὐδὲ εἰς ἔχθραν καθίστανται τοῖς κρίνουσιν, ὑπὲρ δὲ τοῦ φρονιμωτέρους ἢ μοχθηροτέρους εἶναι τοῖς κρίνουσι μάλιστα ὀργί-

---

[1] καὶ added by Forster from Aulus Gellius (xx. 4), who quotes this Problem.

be made from another in two ways, either by adding to or destroying the original.[a]

Why do men consider the philosopher better than 9 the orator ? Is it because the philosopher's interest is in the actual form of things, but the orator only with things which partake of these forms ? For instance the philosopher asks what is injustice, the orator states that so-and-so is an unjust man : the former inquires into the nature of despotism, the latter what is a despot.

Why are Dionysiac artists [b] generally bad char- 10 acters ? Is it because they partake very little of reason and wisdom since most of their life is spent in arts which they practise for a living, and because much of their life is spent in incontinence and some in dire straits ? Both these conditions are productive of baseness.

Why did men originally institute a prize for com- 11 petitions of the body, but none for wisdom ? Is it because the judges in matters of the intellect must properly be no worse than the competitors or even superior to them ? But if those in the foremost rank had to compete in wisdom and a prize were instituted for it, they would lack judges. But in the case of an athletic competition anyone can judge, merely by watching it. Again, the first lawgiver did not want to institute a competition among the Greeks from which great quarrels and hatreds would arise ; now men, when anyone is ruled out or accepted for a bodily competition, are not in any way angry nor do they conceive hatred against the judges, but on the question whether they are more intelligent or inferior they

---

[a] This Problem is unsatisfactory in its text and apparently pointless.   [b] *i.e.* actors at the Dionysiac Festivals.

956 b

ζονται καὶ ἀγανακτοῦσιν. στασιῶδες δὲ καὶ
30 μοχθηρὸν τὸ τοιοῦτόν ἐστιν. ἔτι δὲ δεῖ τῆς
ἀγωνίας τὸ ἆθλον κρεῖττον εἶναι. ἐπὶ μὲν γὰρ
τῶν γυμνικῶν ἀθλημάτων τὸ ἆθλον αἱρετώτερον
καὶ βέλτιον τῆς ἀγωνίας· σοφίας δὲ τί ἂν ἆθλον
βέλτιον γένοιτο;

Διὰ τί ἄλλο νοεῖ καὶ ποιεῖ ἄνθρωπος μάλιστα; 12
ἢ ὅτι τῶν ἐναντίων ἡ αὐτὴ ἐπιστήμη; ἢ ὅτι ὁ
35 μὲν νοῦς πολλῶν ἐστίν, ἡ δὲ ὄρεξις ἑνός; ὁ μὲν
οὖν ἄνθρωπος τῷ νῷ τὰ πλεῖστα ζῇ, τὰ δὲ θηρία
ὀρέξει καὶ θυμῷ καὶ ἐπιθυμίᾳ.

Διὰ τί φρόνιμοί τινες κτώμενοι οὐ χρώμενοι 13
διατελοῦσιν; πότερον ὅτι τῷ ἔθει χρῶνται; ἢ
διὰ τὸ ἐν ἐλπίδι ἡδύ;

* * * ὅτι ἡ αἴσθησις καὶ ἡ διάνοια τῷ ἠρεμεῖν 14
40 τὴν ψυχὴν ἐνεργεῖ; ὃ καὶ ἡ ἐπιστήμη δοκεῖ εἶναι,
937 a ὅτι τὴν ψυχὴν ἵστησιν· κινουμένης γὰρ καὶ φερο-
μένης οὔτε αἰσθέσθαι οὔτε διανοηθῆναι δυνατόν.
διὸ καὶ τὰ παιδία καὶ οἱ μεθύοντες καὶ οἱ μαινόμενοι ἀνόητοι· διὰ γὰρ τὸ πλῆθος τοῦ θερμοῦ τοῦ
ἐνυπάρχοντος πλείστη κίνησις αὐτοῖς καὶ σφοδρο-
5 τάτη συμβαίνει, ληγούσης δὲ ταύτης ἐμφρονέστεροι
γίνονται· ἀταράχου γὰρ οὔσης τῆς διανοίας μᾶλλον
ἐφιστάναι δύνανται αὐτήν. οἵ τ᾽ ἐν τῷ καθεύδειν
ἐνυπνιαζόμενοι ἱσταμένης τῆς διανοίας, καὶ καθ᾽
ὅσον ἠρεμεῖ, ὀνειρώττουσιν. μάλιστα γὰρ ἐν τοῖς
ὕπνοις ἡ ψυχὴ κινεῖται. περισταμένου γὰρ τοῦ
10 θερμοῦ ἐκ τοῦ ἄλλου σώματος εἰς τὸν ἐντὸς τόπον,
τότε πλείστη καὶ σφοδροτάτη κίνησις ὑπάρχει,
οὐχ ὥσπερ οἱ πολλοὶ ὑπολαμβάνουσι τότε ἠρεμεῖν
καὶ καθ᾽ αὑτὴν εἶναι, καὶ μάλιστα ὅταν μηδὲν

are irritated and become very angry with the judges. So this question produces quarrels and troubles. Again, the prize must be more desirable than the competition. For in the case of athletic contests the prize is more desirable and better than the competition ; but what prize could be better than wisdom ?

Why is man specially apt to think one thing and 12 do another ? Is it because the same knowledge is concerned with opposites ? Or is it because the mind thinks of many things, but appetite only aims at one ? Now man lives for the most part by the intelligence, but beasts live by appetite, temper and desire.

Why do some wise men continue to acquire and 13 not to use ? Is it because they are slaves of habit, or because of the pleasure they find in anticipation ?

(Why is it that those who sleep most heavily and 14 pleasantly see no dreams ? Is it) [a] because sensation and thought perform their functions when the soul is at rest ? Knowledge—ἐπιστήμη—seems to be that which checks—ἴστησι—the soul ; for, when the soul is moved and travelling, it is not possible either to feel or to think. This is why children, the intoxicated and madmen cannot think; for owing to the quantity of heat within them the movement is very great and violent, but when this ceases they become more sensible ; for as the mind is untroubled they can control it more. Those who dream while they are asleep dream while the mind is steady and in so far as it is at rest. For the soul moves most in sleep. For when the heat collects from the rest of the body in the region within, then the movement is greatest and most violent, and does not at that time remain quiet and steady, as most people suppose, and especially when

[a] From Th. G.

179

ARISTOTLE

ἴδωσιν ἐνύπνιον. συμβαίνει δὲ τοὐναντίον· διὰ γὰρ
τὸ ἐν πλείστῃ κινήσει εἶναι καὶ μηδὲ κατὰ μικρὸν
15 ἠρεμεῖν, οὐδὲ διανοεῖσθαι δύναται. ἐν πλείστῃ δὲ
κινήσει, ὅταν ἥδιστα καθεύδῃ, εἰκότως ἐστίν, ὅτι
τότε μάλιστα καὶ πλεῖστον θερμὸν ἀθροίζεται εἰς
τὸν εἴσω τόπον. ὅτι δὲ ἐν τῇ κινήσει οὖσα ἡ
ψυχὴ οὐ μόνον ὕπαρ ἀλλ᾽ οὐδ᾽ ἐν τοῖς ὕπνοις
δύναται διανοεῖσθαι, κἀκεῖνο σημεῖον· ἐν γὰρ τοῖς
20 μετὰ τὴν πρόσεσιν τῶν σιτίων ὕπνοις ἥκιστα ἔστιν
ἐνύπνια ὁρᾶν. τότε δὲ μάλιστα συμβαίνει κινεῖσθαι
αὐτὴν διὰ τὴν ἐπεισαχθεῖσαν τροφήν. τό τε
ἐνύπνιόν ἐστιν, ὅταν διανοουμένοις καὶ πρὸ ὀμμάτων τιθεμένοις ὕπνος ἐπέλθῃ. διὸ καὶ ταῦτα
μάλιστα ὁρῶμεν ἃ πράττομεν ἢ μέλλομεν ἢ βου-
25 λόμεθα· περὶ γὰρ τούτων μάλιστα πλειστάκις
λογισμοὶ καὶ φαντασίαι ἐπιγίνονται. καὶ οἱ βελτίους βελτίω τὰ ἐνύπνια ὁρῶσι διὰ ταῦτα, ὅτι καὶ
ἐγρηγορότες περὶ βελτιόνων διανοοῦνται, οἱ δὲ
χεῖρον ἢ τὴν διάνοιαν ἢ τὸ σῶμα διακείμενοι χείρω.
καὶ γὰρ ἡ τοῦ σώματος διάθεσις πρὸς τὴν τῶν
30 ἐνυπνίων φαντασίαν συμβλητικόν· τοῦ γὰρ νοσοῦν-
τος καὶ αἱ τῆς διανοίας προθέσεις φαῦλαι, καὶ ἔτι
διὰ τὴν ἐν τῷ σώματι ταραχὴν ἐνοῦσαν ἡ ψυχὴ οὐ
δύναται ἠρεμεῖν. οἱ δὲ μελαγχολικοὶ διὰ τοῦτο
ἐξάττουσιν ἐν τοῖς ὕπνοις, ὅτι πλείονος τῆς θερμασίας οὔσης, μᾶλλον τοῦ μετρίου ἡ ψυχὴ ἐν
35 κινήσει, σφοδροτέρας δὲ τῆς κινήσεως οὔσης οὐ
δύνανται καθεύδειν.

no dream is seen. The truth is the exact opposite ; for because it is subject to the greatest movement and cannot even keep still for a short time, it cannot even think. So naturally the time of greatest movement is when sleep is pleasantest, because it is then most of all that the greatest quantity of heat is collected in the region within. There is a further proof, that when the soul is in motion it cannot have a waking vision nor even think in sleep ; for in the sleep which comes after the taking of food it is least possible to see dreams ; and then is the time when the soul is most disturbed owing to the introduction of food. Now, a dream comes when sleep overtakes men while they are thinking and have something before their eyes. This is why we most often see what we are doing or intending to do or wishing to do ; for it is in connexion with these things that calculations and fantasies most often occur. Better men have better dreams for this reason, that they think of better things when they are awake, but those who are inferior either in mind or in body think of inferior things. For the condition of the body does contribute to the appearance of dreams ; the projections of a sick man's thought are inferior, and also his soul cannot rest because of the disturbance which exists in his body. This is why the melancholic start in their sleep, because, as the heat is excessive, the soul has more movement than the normal, and as the movement is more violent they cannot sleep.

ΟΣΑ ΠΕΡΙ ΟΦΘΑΛΜΟΥΣ

957 a   Διὰ τί τρίψαντες τὸν ὀφθαλμὸν παυόμεθα τῶν 1
πταρμῶν; ἢ ὅτι ἀναπνοὴ ταύτῃ γίνεται τῷ ὑγρῷ;
40 δακρύει γὰρ ὁ ὀφθαλμὸς μετὰ τὴν τρῖψιν· ὁ δὲ
957 b πταρμὸς διὰ πλῆθος ὑγροῦ. ἢ ὅτι τὸ ἔλαττον
θερμὸν φθείρεται ὑπὸ τοῦ πλείονος; ὁ δὲ ὀφθαλμὸς
τριφθεὶς πλείω λαμβάνει θερμότητα τῆς ἐν τῇ
ῥινί. διὰ τοῦτο δὲ κἄν τις αὐτὴν τὴν ῥῖνα τρίψῃ,
παύεται ὁ πταρμός.

5   Διὰ τί τῷ ἑνὶ ὀφθαλμῷ ἀκριβέστερον ὁρῶσιν ἢ 2
τοῖν δυοῖν; ἢ ὅτι πλείους οὖσαι κινήσεις τοῖν
δυοῖν γίνονται, οἷον τοῖς διεστραμμένοις; οὔκουν
μία ἡ κίνησις, τοῦ δὲ ἑνὸς ἁπλῆ. ἧττον οὖν
ὁρῶσιν ἀκριβέστερον.

    Διὰ τί ὀργιζόμενοι μὲν τοὺς ὀφθαλμοὺς μάλιστα 3
10 ἐπιδιδόασι πρὸς τὸ ἐρυθριᾶν, αἰσχυνόμενοι δὲ τὰ
ὦτα; ἢ διότι οἱ μὲν καταψύχονται ἐν τῇ αἰδοῖ (ἐν
ὀφθαλμοῖς γὰρ αἰδώς) ⟨ὥστε⟩[1] ἀντιβλέπειν οὐ δύ-
νανται· καὶ ἡ δειλία κατάψυξίς τίς ἐστιν ἐνταῦθα.
μεθίσταται δὲ εἰς τοὐναντίον τῷ ἔμπροσθεν τὸ θερμόν.[2] τὰ δὲ ὦτα ἀντίκειται· διὸ καὶ μάλιστα ἐρυ-
15 θριῶσιν αἰσχυνόμενοι. ἐν δὲ τῷ κνήθεσθαι ἐπὶ τὸ
αἰσθητικώτερον καὶ κινητικώτερον ἡ βοήθεια ὡς

----
[1] ὥστε added by Forster.

BOOK XXXI

Problems connected with the Eyes

Why do we stop sneezing if we rub our eyes ? Is 1
it because by this means there is an evaporation of
moisture ? For the eye weeps after rubbing ; and
sneezing is due to a quantity of moisture. Or is it
because the lesser heat is destroyed by the greater ?
The eye when rubbed has greater heat than the heat
in the nostril. For this reason, if one rubs the
nostril itself, the sneezing stops.

Why can men see more clearly with one eye than 2
with two ? Is it because the two eyes can have more
than one movement, as happens with those who
squint ? So their movement is not one, but the
movement of the single eye is simple. So the two
see less clearly.

Why when men grow angry do their eyes tend very 3
much to redden, but when they are ashamed their
ears ? Is it because in shame the eyes are chilled (for
shame resides in the eyes), so that they cannot face
one ? Cowardice also involves a chilling in that part.
Now the heat travels in a direction away from the
forepart of the head, and the ears are situated in the
opposite part of it ; so they grow red when men are
ashamed. But in a state of irritation help is sent
to the more sensitive and emotional part, as though

---

² θερμὸν Forster from Th. G. : ὄπισθεν Ruelle.

957 b

ἀδικουμένου· φοβουμένοις γὰρ ἐνταῦθα ἐκλείπει μάλιστα.

Διὰ τί θατέρου καταληφθέντος ὀφθαλμοῦ ὁ 4 ἕτερος ἀτενίζει μᾶλλον; ἢ διότι ἐκ ταὐτοῦ 20 ἤρτηνται αἱ ἀρχαὶ τῶν ὀφθαλμῶν; θατέρου οὖν κινουμένου καὶ ἡ κοινὴ ἀρχὴ κινεῖται, ἐκείνης δὲ κινουμένης καὶ ὁ ἕτερος. ληφθέντος οὖν θατέρου ἡ κίνησις κινήσει αὐτόν, ὥστε δύναται ἀτενίζειν μᾶλλον.

Διὰ τί οἱ ἐκ γενετῆς τυφλοὶ οὐ γίνονται φαλα- 5 κροί; ἢ ὅτι πημαίνει τὰ ὄμματα ὑγρότης οὖσα 25 πολλὴ ἐν τῷ περὶ τὴν κεφαλὴν τόπῳ; διὸ τῶν ῥευματικῶν εἰς τοὺς ὀφθαλμοὺς τάς τε περὶ τοὺς κροτάφους φλέβας κάουσι, πυκνοῦντες τοὺς τῶν ὑγρῶν πόρους, καὶ ξύουσι τὴν κεφαλήν, δια-τέμνοντες τὸ ἐν αὐτῇ δέρμα. ἐπεὶ οὖν πημαίνει τοὺς ὀφθαλμοὺς τὸ ἐν αὐτῇ περίττωμα γινόμενον, 30 κωλύοι ἂν αὐτοὺς ταὐτὸ τοῦτο ἐξ ἀρχῆς γίνεσθαι, πλέον συνιστάμενον ἐν αὐτῇ. ἐπεὶ δὲ ἐκ περιτ-τωμάτων θρὶξ φύεται, τοῦτο δὲ ἐν τῇ τῶν τυφλῶν κεφαλῇ ἐκ γενετῆς ἐστι πολύ, εἰκότως οὐκ εἰσὶ φαλακροί.

Διὰ τί οἱ ἐξόφθαλμοι καπνίζονται μᾶλλον; ἢ 6 ὅτι τάχιστα προσπίπτει προέχοντα;

35 Διὰ τί εἰς μὲν τὰ δεξιὰ ἀμφοτέρας τὰς ὄψεις ἅμα 7 διαστρέφειν δυνάμεθα, καὶ εἰς τὰ ἀριστερὰ καὶ πρὸς τὴν ῥῖνα, καὶ εἰς τὸ ἀριστερὸν δὲ ἢ τὸ δεξιὸν τὴν ἑτέραν, ἅμα δὲ εἰς τὸ δεξιὸν καὶ ἀριστερὸν ἀδυνατοῦμεν; ὁμοίως δὲ καὶ εἰς τὸ κάτω καὶ εἰς 40 τὸ ἄνω· ἅμα μὲν γὰρ ἐπὶ ταὐτὸ δυνάμεθα, χωρὶς

it were being ill-treated; for in the frightened it fails most there.

Why is it that if one eye is covered, the other 4 stares harder? Is it because the origins of the eye are connected at one point? So when one is moved, the common origin of the two eyes is also moved, and when that is moved, so is the other eye. So when one eye is covered, the movement of the other eye will move this eye also, so that it can stare more.

Why do those who are blind from birth never 5 become bald? Is it because a large quantity of moisture in the region of the head does harm to the eyes? So when men have running at the eyes, they burn the veins about the eyebrows, thus thickening the channels of the liquids, and scrape the head, cutting the skin upon it. So since the waste product in it does harm to the eyes, this same waste product by collecting in the head in large quantity might prevent the eyes from forming at the beginning. But since hair grows from waste product, and this is abundant in the head of those who are blind from birth, they are naturally not bald.

Why do those with prominent eyes suffer more 6 from smoke? Is it that the smoke attacks such eyes quickly because they protrude?

Why is it that we can turn both eyes to the right at 7 the same time and to the left and towards the nose, and also one eye either to the left or to the right, but we cannot turn one to the left and one to the right at the same time? [a] The same thing applies to up and down; for we can turn them simultaneously in the same direction, but not separately. Is it because the

[a] Aristotle of course means simultaneous movement outwards.

δὲ οὔ. ἢ ὅτι αἱ ὄψεις δύο οὖσαι ὅμως ἐξ ἑνὸς
συνήρτηνται; ὅσα δὲ τοιαῦτα, ἄκρου θατέρου
κινουμένου ἀνάγκη θάτερον ἀκολουθεῖν ἐπὶ ταὐτό.
τῷ γὰρ ἑτέρῳ ἄκρῳ ἡ ἀρχὴ θάτερον ἄκρον. εἰ
οὖν τὸ ἓν ἀδύνατον ἅμα εἰς τἀναντία κινεῖσθαι,
ἀδύνατον καὶ τὰς ὄψεις. τὰ μὲν γὰρ ἄκρα εἰς
5 τἀναντία ἂν κινοῖτο, εἰ τὸ μὲν ἄνω τὸ δὲ κάτω
κινοῖτο, ἡ δὲ ἀρχὴ ἀμφοῖν ἂν ἀκολουθοίη, ὅπερ
ἀδύνατον.   ἡ δὲ διαστροφή ἐστι τῶν ὀμμάτων
διὰ τὸ ἀρχὴν ἔχειν τὰς σφαίρας, καὶ μέχρι του[1]
στρέφεσθαι εἰς τὰ ἄνω καὶ κάτω καὶ εἰς πλάγιον.
10 ὅταν οὖν ἔχουσαι ὡς ἂν ὁμοίως ἔχοιεν τῇ θέσει
ἀλλήλαις, καὶ ἐν μέσῳ τοῦ ἐπὶ τὸ ἄνω καὶ κάτω
κινεῖσθαι, καὶ εἰς πλάγιον ἐπὶ τοῦ αὐτοῦ σημείου
ἑαυτῶν λάβωσιν τὴν ὄψιν, αὗται μὲν ἀδιάστροφοί
τε καὶ μάλιστα ἀκίνητοι τῇ θέσει· ὅσαι δὲ ἐπὶ
ταὐτοῦ σημείου λάβωσι τὰς ὄψεις, ἀδιάστροφοι
15 μέν εἰσι, διαφέρουσι δὲ ἀλλήλων. καίτοι κρύπτεται
τοῦ μέλανός τι καὶ τοῖς ἄνω βάλλουσι τὰ λευκά,
οἷον μελλέπταρμοι· ἕτεροι δὲ εἰς τὸ πλάγιον,
ὥσπερ οἱ μανικοί, οἱ δὲ εἰς τοὺς μυκτῆρας, ὥσπερ
τὰ τραγικὰ πρόσωπα καὶ οἱ στρυφνοί· σύννουν γὰρ
τὸ βλέμμα.   ὅσοι δὲ μήθ' ὁμοίως κειμένων τῶν
σφαιρῶν ἐπὶ ταὐτῷ σημείῳ ἔχουσι τὰς ὄψεις, ἢ
20 ὁμοίως μὲν κειμένων, μὴ ἐπὶ τῷ αὐτῷ δέ, οὗτοι
διεστραμμένοι εἰσίν· διὸ ὑποβλέπουσι καὶ συνάγουσι τὰ ὄμματα. πειρῶνται γὰρ ἐπὶ ταὐτὸν
καταστῆσαι σχῆμα τὴν σφαῖραν. ὥστε τὸν μὲν
ἐῶσι, τὸν δὲ σχηματίζουσι τῶν ὀφθαλμῶν. ἐὰν
γὰρ μὴ κατὰ ταὐτὸ[2] σημεῖον τεθῶσιν αἱ ὄψεις,
25 ἀνάγκη διεστράφθαι. ὥσπερ γὰρ τοῖς ὑποβάλ-

---

[1] του Forster : τοῦ Ruelle.
[2] κατὰ ταὐτὸ Bussemaker : κατ' αὐτὸ Ruelle.

eyes, although they are two, are connected at one point ? In such cases when one extreme moves the other must follow in the same direction. For the one extreme causes movement to the other extreme. If, then, it is impossible to move one thing in contrary directions at the same time, it is equally impossible to do it with the eyes. For the extremes would be moving in opposite directions, if one moved upwards and one downwards, and the source of both would make corresponding movements, which is impossible. Squinting with the eyes is due to the fact that the eyeballs have a source and can move upwards, downwards, and sideways to a certain extent. When, then, they are so placed as to be in a similar position to one another and between an upward and a downward movement, and they receive a light ray at a slant on the same spot, then they do not squint and remain quite immobile ; those which receive the rays on the same point never squint, although they differ from each other. Yet when the whites of the eyes are turned up part of the black is hidden, as happens when men are about to sneeze ; others, for instance madmen, turn their eyes sideways, and others again towards the nostrils, as one sees in tragic masks and in those who have an austere expression ; for their look is thoughtful. But those who do not receive the light ray on the same point because the eyeballs are not similarly placed, or who do not receive it on the same point, even though the eyes are similarly placed, such men squint ; this is why they blink and contract the eyes. For they try to force the eyeballs into the same position. So they neglect the one and arrange the other eye. For if the eyes are not set on the same point, squinting is inevitable. For just as when

958 a
λουσιν ὑπὸ τὸν ὀφθαλμὸν [τὸ ἓν] δύο φαίνεται (καὶ
γὰρ ἐκείνοις κεκίνηται ἡ ἀρχή), καὶ τούτοις ὁμοίως.
ἐὰν μὲν οὖν ἄνω κινηθῇ ὁ ὀφθαλμός, τὸ πέρας
κάτω τῆς ὄψεως γίνεται, ἐὰν δὲ κάτω, ἄνω τὸ
πέρας. ἐν ἑνὶ δὲ ὀφθαλμῷ μεθισταμένῳ κινεῖσθαι
30 μὲν τὸ ὁρώμενον δοκεῖ διὰ ταῦτα ἄνω ἢ κάτω, ὅτι
καὶ ἡ ὄψις, δύο δὲ οὐ φαίνεται, ἂν μὴ δύο αἱ ὄψεις
ὦσιν, καὶ διαστρέφει. τοιαύτη μὲν τῷ ἑτεροφθάλμῳ
γίνεται, ὥστε δύο φαίνεσθαι· κατὰ τὴν θέσιν δὲ
γίνεται τῷ μὴ κατὰ μέσον τοῦ ὄμματος κεῖσθαι.

35 Διὰ τί οἱ μύωπες μικρὰ γράμματα γράφουσιν; 8
ἄτοπον γὰρ τὸ μὴ ὀξὺ ὁρῶντας ποιεῖν ἔργον ὀξὺ
ὁρώντων. πότερον ὅτι μεγάλα φαίνεται τὰ μικρά,
ἐὰν ᾖ ἐγγύς, οἱ δὲ προσάγοντες γράφουσιν; ἢ διὰ
τὸ συνάγοντας τὰ βλέφαρα γράφειν; δι᾽ ἀσθένειαν
958 b γὰρ τῆς ὄψεως, ἂν μὲν ἀναπεπταμένοις γράφωσι
τοῖς ὄμμασι, διασπωμένη ἡ ὄψις ἀμβλὺ ὁρᾷ, οὕτω
δὲ ἀθρόως προσπίπτει· γωνίαν δὲ μικρὰν ποιοῦσα
ἐξ ἀνάγκης ποιεῖ μικρὰ γράφειν.

Διὰ τί ὀφθαλμιάσαντες ἔνιοι ὀξύτερον ὁρῶσιν; 9
5 ἢ διὰ τὸ ἀποκεκαθάρθαι τὰ ὄμματα; πολλάκις
γὰρ ἡ ἔξω πυκνότης ἀποστέγει τὴν ὄψιν, ἀπο-
δακρύσαντι δὲ λύεται. διὸ καὶ τὸ ἀποδάκνεσθαι
συμφέρει, οἷον κρόμμυον· θάτερον δὲ πολέμιον,
οἷον ὀρίγανον.

Διὰ τί τῇ μιᾷ ὄψει ἀπαθέστεροι; ἢ διότι
10 ἔλαττον ἡ ψυχὴ πάσχει, ὥστε ἔλαττον τὸ πάθος;

Διὰ τί τοῖς διισταμένοις δύο φαίνεται; ἢ διότι

men put a finger under the eye a single image appears double (for the source is shifted), so it is in the other case. If, then, the eye is moved upwards, the terminus of the vision is lowered, and if downwards, it is raised. In shifting the position of one eye the object seen seems on this account to move up or down, because the sight has moved in the same direction, but the image does not appear double, unless the sight is double and there is a squint. The same thing happens to a man with different eyes, so that the image appears double ; but this is due to the position because it does not lie in the centre of the eye.

Why do the short-sighted write small letters ? 8 For it seems strange that those who have not keen vision should do the work of the sharp-sighted. Is it because small letters appear large, if they are close, and they bring their eyes close to write ? Or is it because they contract the eyelids to write ? For owing to their weakness of sight, if they write with the eyes wide open, the sight is scattered and only sees dimly, but when the eyelids are contracted it is made to strike in a concentrated way ; for as it makes a narrow angle it must produce small writing.

Why do men after suffering from ophthalmia some- 9 times have clearer vision ? Is it because the eyes are cleaned ? For sometimes a thickness outside covers the vision, but this is cleared if the eye discharges. So what bites the tongue, such as onion, is beneficial ; but the opposite, such as marjoram, does harm.

Why are men with one eye less easily affected ? Is 10 it because the soul suffers less, and so the effect is less ?

Why do images appear double, if the eyes are wide 11 apart ? Is it because the movement does not affect

οὐκ ἀφικνεῖται ἐπὶ τὸ αὐτὸ σημεῖον ἑκατέρου τῶν
ὀμμάτων ἡ κίνησις; ὥσπερ οὖν δύο ὁρᾶν τὸ δὶς
ὁρᾶν οἴεται ἡ ψυχή. ὅμοιον καὶ ἐπὶ τῶν δακτύλων
15 τῆς ἐπαλλάξεως· δύο γὰρ τὸ ἓν δοκεῖ τῷ δὶς
ἁπτομένῳ¹ ἑνί.

Διὰ τί οὐ διαφέρουσιν αἱ αἰσθήσεις αἱ ἐν τοῖς 12
δεξιοῖς τῶν ἀριστερῶν, ἐν δὲ τοῖς ἄλλοις πᾶσι
κρείττω τὰ δεξιά; πότερον διὰ τὸ ἔθος, ὅτι εὐθὺς
ὁμοίως ἀμφοῖν ἐθιζόμεθα αἰσθάνεσθαι; τὰ δὲ
20 δεξιὰ τῷ ἔθει δοκεῖ διαφέρειν, ἐπεὶ ἐθισθεῖσιν
ἀμφιδέξιοι γίνονται. ἢ ὅτι τὸ μὲν αἰσθάνεσθαι
πάσχειν τί ἐστι, τὰ δὲ δεξιὰ διαφέρει τῷ ποιητι-
κώτερα εἶναι καὶ ἀπαθέστερα τῶν ἀριστερῶν;

Διὰ τί ἐν μὲν τοῖς ἄλλοις κρείττω τὰ δεξιά, ἐν 13
δὲ ταῖς αἰσθήσεσιν ὅμοια; ἢ διότι ταῦτα μὲν
25 ὁμοίως ἐθιζόμεθα κατ᾽ ἀμφότερα τῷ ἔθει; ἔτι τὸ
μὲν αἰσθάνεσθαι πάσχειν τί ἐστιν, ἡ δὲ τῶν δεξιῶν
διαφορὰ τῷ εἰς τὸ ποιεῖν καὶ οὐκ εἰς τὸ πάσχειν.

Διὰ τί τὸ γυμνάζεσθαι ἀσύμφορον πρὸς ὀξυωπίαν; 14
ἢ ὅτι ξηρὸν ποιεῖ τὸ ὄμμα ἡ γυμνασία, ὥσπερ καὶ
30 τὸ ἄλλο σῶμα; ἡ δὲ ξηρότης σκληρύνει τὸ δέρμα
πᾶν, ὥστε καὶ τὸ ἐπὶ τῇ κόρῃ. διὸ καὶ οἱ πρεσβῦται οὐκ ὀξὺ ὁρῶσιν· καὶ γὰρ τῶν γερόντων
σκληρόδερμα, ἅμα δὲ καὶ ῥυσά, ὥστε ἐπικα-
λύπτεται ἡ ὄψις.

Διὰ τί οἱ μύωπες βλέπουσι μὲν οὐκ ὀξύ, γράφουσι 15
35 δὲ μικρά; καίτοι τὸ μικρὸν ὀξὺ βλέποντος καθ-
ορᾶν ἐστιν. ἢ διότι ἀσθενῆ ἔχοντες τὴν ὄψιν
συνάγουσι τὰ βλέφαρα εἰς μικρόν; ἀθρόα γὰρ
ἐξιοῦσα ἡ ὄψις μᾶλλον ὁρᾷ, ἀναπεπταμένου δὲ τοῦ
ὄμματος διασπᾶται. διὰ μὲν οὖν τὴν ἀσθένειαν

---

¹ τῷ δὶς ἁπτομένῳ Forster : ὡς δὶς ἁπτομένη Ruelle.

ᵃ Cf. De Somniis, 460 b 20.

the same point in each of the two eyes? So the soul thinks that in seeing one object twice, it sees two objects. The same thing occurs when the fingers are crossed; for the one thing feels like two to the finger which touches it twice.[a]

Why are the senses on the right not superior to 12 those on the left, whereas in all other respects the right is stronger? Is it due to habit, because we soon accustom ourselves to perceive equally well with the senses on both sides? It is by habit also that the right seems superior, since men grow ambidextrous by habit. Is it because to feel sensation is to be passive, but the right is superior because it is accustomed to be more active and less passive than the left?

Why are the right parts superior to the left in other 13 respects but the two are equal in sensation? Is it because in both cases we are influenced by habit? Moreover, sensation is a form of passivity, and the superiority of the right parts lies in activity, not in passivity.

Why does athletic exercise do harm to keen 14 vision? Is it because exercise makes the eye dry, as it does the rest of the body? Now dryness hardens the whole skin, as it also hardens the skin over the pupil. This is why old men have not keen vision; for it is characteristic of old men to have hard and wrinkled skin, so that the vision is obscured.

Why is it that the short-sighted have not keen vi- 15 sion, and yet write in small characters? And yet to see what is small is characteristic of the keen-sighted. Is it because having weak sight they contract the eyelids? For when the vision is projected in a concentrated form it sees better, but when the eye is wide open the sight is dissipated. So it is owing to weak-

958 b

συνάγουσιν εἰς μικρὸν τὸ βλέφαρον, διὰ δὲ τὸ ἐκ
959 a μικροῦ ὁρᾶν μικρὸν μέγεθος ὁρῶσιν. ὅσον δὲ
ὁρῶσι μέγεθος, τοσοῦτον καὶ γράφουσιν.

Διὰ τί οἱ μύωπες συνάγοντες τὰ βλέφαρα ὁρῶσιν; 1
ἢ δι' ἀσθένειαν τῆς ὄψεως, ὥσπερ καὶ οἱ πρὸς
5 τὰ πόρρω τὴν χεῖρα προσάγοντες, οὕτω καὶ τὰ βλέφαρα πρὸς τὰ ἐγγὺς προστίθενται [ὥσπερ χεῖρα];
τοῦτο δὲ ποιοῦσιν, ἵνα ἁθρωτέρα ἡ ὄψις ἐξίῃ, δι'
ἐλάττονος ἐξιοῦσα, καὶ μὴ εὐθὺς ἐξ ἀναπεπταμένου ἐξιοῦσα διασπασθῇ, ὁρᾷ δὲ ἡ πλείων μεῖζον.

Διὰ τί εἰς τὸ πλάγιον κινοῦσι τὸν ὀφθαλμὸν οὐ 1
10 φαίνεται δύο τὸ ἕν; ἢ ὅτι ἐπὶ τῆς αὐτῆς γίνεται
γραμμῆς ἡ ἀρχή; δύο δὲ φαίνεται ταύτης μετα-
βαλλούσης ἄνω ἢ κάτω, εἰς δὲ πλάγιον οὐδὲν
διαφέρει, ἐὰν μὴ ἅμα καὶ ἄνω. τί δὴ ἐπὶ μὲν
τῆς ὄψεώς ἐστιν ὥστε φαίνεσθαι τὸ ἕν δύο, ἄν
πως τεθῶσιν οἱ ὀφθαλμοὶ πρὸς ἀλλήλους, ἐπὶ
15 δὲ τῶν ἄλλων αἰσθήσεων οὐκ ἔστιν; ἢ καὶ ἐπὶ τῆς
ἁφῆς γίνεται τῇ ἐπαλλάξει τῶν δακτύλων τὸ ἕν
δύο; ἐπὶ δὲ τῶν ἄλλων οὐ γίνεται, ὅτι οὔτε ἔξω
ἀποτεινομένων αἰσθάνεται, οὐδὲ δύο. γίνεται δὲ
[διὰ] τοῦτο διόπερ καὶ ἐπὶ τῶν δακτύλων· μιμεῖται
γὰρ τὴν ὄψιν.

20 Διὰ τί τοῦ μὲν ἄλλου σώματος τὰ ἀριστερὰ 1
ἀσθενέστερα, τῶν δὲ ὀφθαλμῶν οὔ, ἀλλ' ὁμοίως
ὀξύ; ἢ ὅτι τὰ μὲν δεξιὰ τῷ ποιητικὰ εἶναι διαφέρουσιν, τῷ δὲ παθητικὰ οὐ διαφέρουσιν; αἱ δὲ
ὄψεις παθητικαί.

Διὰ τί τῇ ὄψει πρὸς μὲν τὰ ἄλλα ἀτενίζοντες 1
25 χεῖρον διατιθέμεθα, πρὸς δὲ τὰ χλωρὰ καὶ ποώδη,
οἷον λάχανα καὶ τὰ τούτοις ὅμοια, βέλτιον; ἢ ὅτι

192

ness that they contract the eyelid, and because they are looking at a small thing from a short distance they see it large. So they write the same size as they see.

Why do the short-sighted contract the eyelids when 16 they look at something? Is it due to their weakness of sight, like those who put up their hand to their eyes when looking at a distant object, so they contract their eyelids to look at near objects? They do this in order that the vision may be more concentrated by passing out through a narrower space, and that it may not be dispersed by passing straight from a wide-open eye, but the wider-open eye sees more.

Why, when one moves the eye sideways, does not 17 the one image appear as two? Is it because the source is in the same line? When this shifts up or down, two objects are seen, but a sideways movement makes no difference, unless it is also upwards. Why, then, in the case of sight does one object appear as two, if the eyes are in a certain relation to each other, but this is not the case with the other senses? Does it happen in the case of touch by crossing the fingers that one feels like two? But it does not happen with the other senses because they are not conscious of what stretches away from them, and they are not double. This is why it happens in the case of the fingers; for they imitate vision.

Why is it that in the rest of the body the left side 18 is the weaker, but it is not so with the eyes, which are equally keen? Are the right parts superior in their activity, but not in their passivity? And vision is passive.

Why does our vision deteriorate if we stare at other 19 things, but improve if we look at green and grassy things such as vegetables, and the like? Is it because

959 a

πρὸς μὲν τὸ λευκὸν καὶ μέλαν ἥκιστα δυνάμεθα
ἀτενίζειν (ἄμφω γὰρ λυμαίνεται τὴν ὄψιν), τὰ δὲ
τοιαῦτα τῶν χρωμάτων μέσον ἔχει τούτων· διὸ
μετρίως τῆς ὄψεως διατιθεμένης οὐδὲ ἐξαδυνα-
30 τοῦμεν αὐτῇ, βέλτιον δὲ διατιθέμεθα. τάχα δὲ
ἴσως καθάπερ ἐπὶ τῶν σωμάτων σφοδρότερον
πονοῦντες χεῖρον ἔχομεν, τὸ μέσον δὲ βέλτιστα
διατίθησιν, τὸν αὐτὸν τρόπον καὶ τὴν ὄψιν. πρὸς
μὲν γὰρ στερεὰ ἀτενίζοντες πονοῦμεν αὐτήν, πρὸς
δὲ τὰ ὑγρὰ μηδενὸς ἀντιφράττοντος οὐ διαπονοῦμεν.
35 τὰ δὲ χλωρὰ στερεά τε μετρίως, καὶ ὑγρὸν ἐν
αὐτοῖς ἱκανόν. διὸ βλάπτει τε οὐθέν, καὶ δι-
αναγκάζει τὴν ὄψιν πρὸς τούτοις εἶναι διὰ τὸ τὴν
τοῦ χρώματος κρᾶσιν σύμμετρον ἔχειν πρὸς τὴν
ὄψιν.

Διὰ τί τὰ μὲν ἄλλα ἀμφοτέροις τοῖς ὀφθαλμοῖς 2
μᾶλλον ὁρῶμεν, τὰ δὲ εὐθὺ τὸ ἐπὶ τῶν στίχων
40 τῷ ἑνὶ προσάγοντες πρὸς τὰ γράμματα μᾶλλον
959 b καθορῶμεν; ἢ ἀμφότεραι μὲν αἱ ὄψεις συμ-
πίπτουσαι, καθάπερ λέγουσιν οἱ περὶ τὰ ὀπτικά,
ταραχὴν παρέχουσιν, ἐπειδὰν δὲ τῇ μιᾷ θεωρῶμεν,
πρὸς εὐθεῖαν τὴν ὄψιν, ὥσπερ πρὸς κανόνα, μᾶλλον
φαίνεται τὸ εὐθύ.

5 Διὰ τί ὁ καπνὸς τοὺς ὀφθαλμοὺς μᾶλλον δάκνει; 3
ἢ ὅτι μόνοι ἀσθενέστατοι; ἀεὶ γὰρ τὰ ἔσω τοῦ
σώματος ἀσθενέστατα. σημεῖον δὲ ὅτι καὶ τὸ
ὄξος καὶ ἕκαστον τῶν δριμέων τὴν μὲν ἔξω σάρκα
οὐ δάκνει, τὴν δὲ ἐντός, ὅτι ἀραιότατον τοῦ σώ-
10 ματος καὶ μάλιστ' ἔχει πόρους· αἱ γὰρ ὄψεις διά
τινων πόρων ἐκπίπτουσιν, ὥστε τὸ ἔσω δηκτικώ-
τατον ἀπὸ τῆς σαρκὸς ἀποπίπτει. ὁμοίως δὲ καὶ
τὸ κρόμμυον, καὶ ὅσα ἄλλα δάκνει τοὺς ὀφθαλμούς.

194

we can stare least at white and black (for both harm the sight), but such colours are intermediate between these ; so that, our vision being now intermediate, we are not rendered impotent by it, but rather improved ? Perhaps, as is the case with bodies, we suffer because of too violent exercise, but the mean puts us in the best position, and similarly with sight. For when we stare at solid objects we strain the sight, but when we look at liquid objects we do not strain it, because there is nothing to interrupt the vision. Now green objects are only moderately solid and there is sufficient moisture in them. So they do no harm and they encourage the sight to rest on them, because the mixture of colour is well adjusted to the vision.

Why do we look at other things with both eyes, but 20 we can see the straightness of lines better by looking at the letters with one eye ? When both eyes act together do they produce a confusion, as writers on optics say, but when we look with one eye with direct vision, as if along a rod, we can see the straight line more clearly ?

Why does smoke make the eyes smart more than 21 other parts ? Is it because they alone are very weak ? For parts within the body are always the weakest. This is proved by the fact that vinegar and all astringent things never make the flesh outside smart, but they do the flesh inside because it is the rarest part of the body and contains most pores ; for the sight travels outwards through pores so that what produces most smart within passes away *a* from the flesh. The same is true of the onion and all other things which make the eyes smart. Of liquids, olive-

a The Greek word is almost certainly wrong.

959 b

τὸ δὲ ἔλαιον μάλιστα τῶν ὑγρῶν, ὅτι λεπτομερέστατον· τοιοῦτον δ᾽ ὂν εἰσδύνει διὰ τῶν πόρων· τὸ δ᾽ ὄξος ἐν φαρμάκῳ τῇ ἄλλῃ σαρκί.

15 Διὰ τί ὁ ὀφθαλμὸς μόνον τοῦ σώματος, ἀσθενέ- 21 στατος ὤν, οὐ ῥιγοῖ; ἢ ὅτι πίων ἐστὶν ὁ ὀφθαλμός, σαρκὸς δὲ οὐθέν; τὰ δὲ τοιαῦτα ἄριγά ἐστιν. οὐ γὰρ δὴ ὅτι γε πῦρ ἐστιν ἡ ὄψις, διὰ τοῦτο οὐ ῥιγοῖ· οὐ γὰρ τοιοῦτόν γέ ἐστι τὸ πῦρ ὥστε θερμαίνειν.

20 Διὰ τί δάκρυα, ἐὰν μὲν κλαίοντες ἀφίωμεν, 2 θερμά ἐστιν, ἐὰν δὲ πονοῦντες τοὺς ὀφθαλμοὺς δακρύωμεν, ψυχρά; ἢ ὅτι τὸ μὲν ἄπεπτον ψυχρόν, τὸ δὲ πεπεμμένον θερμόν; ἡ δὲ μαλακία ὅλως πᾶσά ἐστιν ἐξ ἀπεψίας, καὶ τῶν τοὺς ὀφθαλμοὺς πονούντων ἄπεπτόν ἐστι τὸ δάκρυον· διὸ ψυχρόν.

25 διὰ τοῦτο καὶ οἱ ἰατροὶ οἴονται σημεῖον εἶναι μεγάλης νόσου τοὺς ψυχροὺς ἱδρῶτας, τοὺς δὲ θερμοὺς τοὐναντίον ἀπαλλακτικούς. ὅταν μὲν γὰρ ᾖ τὸ περίττωμα πολύ, οὐ δύναται τὸ ἐντὸς θερμὸν πέττειν, ὥστε ἀνάγκη ψυχρὸν εἶναι· ὅταν δὲ ὀλίγον, κρατεῖ. γίνονται δὲ ἐκ τῶν περιττωμάτων αἱ 30 ἀρρωστίαι.

Διὰ τί ποτε εὐκινήτων ὄντων τῶν δεξιῶν μερῶν 2 ὁ ὀφθαλμὸς ὁ ἀριστερὸς μᾶλλον τοῦ δεξιοῦ συνάγεται; ἢ ὅτι τὰ ἀριστερὰ πάντα ὑγρότερα τῶν δεξιῶν ἐστιν, τὰ δὲ ὑγρότερα μᾶλλον συνάγεσθαι 35 πέφυκεν· εἶτα εἰς τὸ δεξιὸν μᾶλλον ἀποτελεῖν δύναται, τοῦ ἀριστεροῦ δυναμένου καὶ καθ᾽ αὑτό.

Διὰ τί ἀμφότεροι κατὰ ἀσθένειάν τινα τῶν 2 ὀφθαλμῶν διακείμενοι, ὅ τε μύωψ καὶ ὁ πρεσβύτης,

196

oil has this effect most because its parts are lightest; being of this nature it sinks in through the pores, but vinegar acts as medicine for the rest of the flesh.

Why is it that the eye alone, which is the weakest 22 part of the body, does not shiver? Is it because the eye is fat but not fleshy? Such substances do not shiver. It is not because the vision is fire that it does not shiver; for its fire is not such as to heat it.

Why is it that tears, if we shed them while crying, 23 are hot, but if the weeping is due to trouble in the eye, the tears are cold? Is it because what is unconcocted is cold but what is concocted is hot? Every weakness arises from lack of concoction, and the tears of those who have a pain in the eye are unconcocted; hence they are cold. For this reason doctors consider that cold sweats are a symptom of serious disease, but that hot ones on the contrary remove disease. For when the waste product is considerable the internal heat cannot concoct it, so that it must be cold; but when there is little of it, the internal heat gains the mastery. But diseases all arise from waste products.

Why is it that, although parts on the right are most 24 easily moved, the left eye closes more easily than the right? Is it because all the left parts are moister than the right, and the moister parts naturally close more readily? [*The concluding sentence of this problem is untranslatable.*] [a]

Why is it that though both the short-sighted and 25 the old man suffer from weakness of the eyes, the

[a] Th. G. seems to translate a different text: " The right eye could act more efficiently; the left, being moister, would be more likely to follow a lead."

959 b
ὁ μὲν ἐγγὺς προσάγει, ἄν τι βούληται ἰδεῖν, ὁ δὲ
40 πόρρω ἀπάγει; ἢ ὅτι οὐχ ὁμοία ἡ ἀσθένεια
960 a παρέπεται αὐτοῖς; ὁ μὲν γὰρ πρεσβύτης αὐτὸ
ἰδεῖν ἀδύνατός ἐστιν· οὗ δὴ συμπίπτει ἡ ὄψις αὐτῷ,
ἀπάγει τὸ θεώμενον, ἅτε καὶ μάλιστα μέλλων
ὄψεσθαι· πόρρω δὲ συμπίπτει. ὁ δὲ αὐτὸ μὲν
ὁρᾷ, ποῖα δὲ κοῖλα ἢ ποῖα ἐξέχοντα τοῦ ὁρωμένου
5 οὐκέτι δύναται κρίνειν, ἀλλὰ περὶ ταῦτα ἀπατᾶται.
τὰ δὲ κοῖλα ἢ τὰ ἐξέχοντα μάλιστα τῇ αὐγῇ
κρίνεται. πόρρωθεν μὲν οὖν οὐ δύναται τῇ αὐγῇ
καταμαθεῖν πῶς ἐπιβάλλει ἐπὶ τὸ ὁρατόν· ἐγγύθεν
δὲ μᾶλλον καταφανής ἐστιν.

Διὰ τί τῶν ζῴων ἄνθρωπος ἢ μόνον ἢ μάλιστα 26
10 διαστρέφεται; ἢ ὅτι ἢ μόνον ἢ μάλιστα ἐπίληπτον
ἐν τῇ νεότητι γίνεται, ὅτε καὶ διαστρέφεσθαι
συμβαίνει πᾶσιν;

Διὰ τί οἱ ἄνθρωποι μόνοι τῶν ἄλλων ζῴων τὰ 27
ὄμματα διαστρέφονται; πότερον διὰ τὸ ἐλάχιστον
διάστημα εἶναι τῶν ὀμμάτων, καὶ ἐπ' εὐθείας,
15 ὥστε εὔδηλον σφόδρα γίνεται τὸ μὴ κατωρθωμένον.
ἢ διότι τῶν ἄλλων μονόχροα τὰ ὄμματά ἐστι
μᾶλλον; εἰ δ' ἦν ἐν χρώματι τοῦ ὄμματος, οὐκ
ἦν διαστροφή. ἢ διότι μόνοι ἐν τῷ γένει ἐπίληπτοι
γίνονται τῶν ζῴων, ἡ δ' ἐπίληψις διαστροφὴν
ποιεῖ, ὅταν γένηται, ὥσπερ καὶ τῶν ἄλλων μορίων·
20 ἀλλ' ἐνίοις ὀψὲ παντελῶς γίνεται ἡ διαστροφή,
ὅσοις τὸ ἀρρώστημα;

Διὰ τί πρὸς τὸν λύχνον καὶ πρὸς τὸν ἥλιον 28
προστησάμενοι τὴν χεῖρα πρὸ τοῦ φωτὸς μᾶλλον
ὁρῶμεν; ἢ ὅτι τὸ ἀπὸ τοῦ ἡλίου καὶ λύχνου φῶς
προσπῖπτον μὲν ἡμῶν πρὸς τὴν ὄψιν ἀσθενεστέραν
25 ποιεῖ δι' ὑπερβολήν; φθείρει γὰρ αὐτὰ καὶ τὰ
198

former brings the object he wishes to see near, while the latter holds it at a distance ? Is it because their inherent weaknesses are not similar ? For the old man is unable to see the object ; so he holds the object far away at the point on which his vision falls, as he will then see it best ; and his vision falls at a distance. The short-sighted man can see it, but he cannot distinguish which parts of the object have an inward curve and which have an outward curve, but he is deceived on these points. Now these inward and outward curves are most easily judged by a ray of light. So from a distance he cannot tell by the light how it falls on the object seen ; but this is more distinct when close by.

Why is man alone or more than any other animal 26 most liable to squint ? Is it because he alone or more than other animals suffers from epilepsy in his youth, when it happens that all squint ?

Why do men alone among animals squint ? Is it 27 because of the very small distance between the eyes, and, their eyes being in a straight line, what is not straight becomes very obvious ? Or is it because the eyes of the other animals tend to be of one colour only ? But if there were only one colour in the eye, there would be no squinting. Or is it because in the animal world men alone suffer from epilepsy, and epilepsy produces squinting, when it occurs, just as it produces distortion in other parts of the body ? But to some squinting comes quite late in life, if they have a disease.

Why is it that if we stretch out our hand towards a 28 lamp or the sun in front of the light we can see better ? Is it because the light from the sun or the lamp falling on our vision makes it weaker because it is excessive ? For kindred things themselves cause destruction by

960 a

συγγενῆ τῇ ὑπερβολῇ. εἰρχθέντα δὲ ὑπὸ τῆς χειρὸς τὴν μὲν ὄψιν οὐ πημαίνει, τὸ δὲ ὁρώμενον ὁμοίως ἐστὶν ἐν φωτί. διὸ ἡ μὲν μᾶλλον ὁρᾷ,[1] τὸ δὲ ὁρώμενον οὐδὲν ἧττον ὁρᾶται.

Διὰ τί χεὶρ μὲν καὶ ποὺς διαφορὰν ἔχει πρὸς [τὰ] 2
30 δεξιὰ ⟨καὶ⟩ τὰ ἀριστερά, ὄμμα δὲ καὶ ἀκοὴ οὔ; ἢ ὅτι τὰ στοιχεῖα τὰ εἰλικρινῆ ἀδιάφορα, ἐν δὲ τοῖς ἐκ τῶν στοιχείων ἡ διαφορά; αὗται δὲ αἱ αἰσθήσεις εἰσὶν ἐξ εἰλικρινῶν, ἡ μὲν ὄψις πυρός, ἡ δ' ἀκοὴ ἀέρος.

---

[1] ὁρᾷ Richards : δρᾷ Ruelle.

excess. When the light is shut off by the hand it does not harm the vision, but the object seen is just as much in the light (as before). So the sight sees better and the object is equally visible.

Why are the hand and the foot different on the 29 right- and the left-hand sides, but the eye and the hearing are not? Is it because the pure elements exhibit no differences, but there is difference in what is made out of the elements? These senses are made from the pure elements, sight from fire and hearing from air.

ΛΒ

ΟΣΑ ΠΕΡΙ ΩΤΑ

Διὰ τί τὰ ὦτα ὄντα ἀναιμότατα τοῦ προσώπου, 1
ὅταν αἰσχύνωνται, ἐρυθριᾷ μάλιστα; πότερον ὅτι
εἰς τὸ κενὸν μάλιστα πορεύεσθαι πέφυκεν τὸ ἀλλότριον ὑγρόν, ὥστε ὅταν διαλυθῇ ὑπὸ τῆς θερ-
40 μότητος, ἣ γίνεται αἰσχυνομένοις, συνέρχεται εἰς
ταῦτα; ἢ διότι ἐπὶ τοῖς κροτάφοις ἐπίκεινται,
960 b εἰς οὓς τὸ ὑγρὸν ἀθροίζεται μάλιστα; αἰσχυ-
νομένων δὲ εἰς τὸ πρόσωπον ἔρχεται ἡ ὑγρότης·
διὸ καὶ ἐρυθριῶσιν. τοῦ δὲ προσώπου ἥκιστα
βάθος ἔχει τὰ ὦτα· καὶ φύσει θερμότατα καὶ
εὔχροα, ἐὰν μὴ ἀπηρτημένα πόρρωθεν ᾖ τῷ ψύχει.
5 διὸ καὶ εὐχρούστατον τῶν ἐν τῷ προσώπῳ μορίων.
ὥστε ὅταν σκεδασθῇ ἡ θερμότης, μάλιστα ἐπιπολῆς οὖσα ἐν τούτοις ποιεῖ ἐρυθρά.

Διὰ τί τὰ ὦτα ἐν τῇ θαλάττῃ ῥήγνυται τοῖς 2
κολυμβῶσιν; πότερον διὰ τὸ κατέχειν τὸ πνεῦμα
10 πληρούμενον βιάζεται; ἢ εἰ τοῦτ᾽ αἴτιον, ἔδει καὶ
ἐν τῷ ἀέρι. ἢ ὅτι μὴ ὑπεῖκον διακόπτεται θᾶττον,
καὶ ὑπὸ σκληροτέρου ἢ μαλακοῦ; τὸ οὖν πεφυ-
σημένον ἧττον ὑπείκει. τὰ δὲ ὦτα, ὥσπερ εἴρηται,
ὑπὸ τοῦ κατέχεσθαι τὸ πνεῦμα ἐμφυσᾶται, ὥστε

BOOK XXXII

Problems connected with the Ears

Why do the ears, which are the most bloodless part 1 of the face, grow most red when men are ashamed ? Is it because the alien liquid naturally travels most into the empty space, so that when it is released by the heat, which happens when men are ashamed, it collects in the ears ? Or is it because the ears are close to the temples into which the liquid most readily collects ? Now when men are ashamed, the moisture goes to the face ; hence they blush. Now of all parts of the face the ears have the smallest depth ; and are naturally hottest and most coloured, unless they have been long affected by the cold. So this is the reason why of all parts of the face this has the most colour. So that when the heat is scattered, being mostly on the surface it makes them red.

Why do the ear-drums of divers burst in the sea ? Is 2 it because the ear becoming full owing to the holding of the breath is subject to violent pressure ? If this is the cause, it ought to happen in the air also. Or is it because, if a thing cannot yield, it is more easily broken, and more so under a hard than under a soft blow ? Now what is inflated yields less. But the ears, as has been said, are inflated because the air is held in

960 b

τὸ ὕδωρ σκληρότερον ὂν τοῦ ἀέρος, προσπῖπτον διακόπτει.

15 Διὰ τί οἱ κολυμβηταὶ σπόγγους περὶ τὰ ὦτα 3 καταδοῦνται; ἢ ἵνα ἡ θάλαττα βίᾳ ἰοῦσα μὴ ῥηγνύῃ τὰ ὦτα; οὕτω μὲν γὰρ οὐ γίνεται, ὥσπερ ἀφῃρημένων, πλήρη.

Διὰ τί ὁ ἐν τοῖς ὠσὶ ῥύπος πικρός ἐστιν; ἢ 4 διότι ὁ ἱδρώς ἐστι σαπρός; ἔστιν οὖν ἁλμυρὸν
20 σαπρόν. τὸ δὲ σαπρὸν ἁλμυρὸν πικρόν.

Διὰ τί οἱ σπογγεῖς διατέμνονται τὰ ὦτα καὶ τοὺς 5 μυκτῆρας; ἢ ὅπως εὐπνούστεροι ὦσι; ταύτῃ γὰρ ἐξιέναι δοκεῖ τὸ πνεῦμα.[1] πονεῖν γὰρ δή φασι
25 μᾶλλον αὐτοὺς ἐν τῇ δυσπνοίᾳ τῷ μὴ δύνασθαι προΐεσθαι θύραζε· ὅταν δὲ ὥσπερ ἐξεράσωσι, κουφίζονται. ἄτοπον οὖν εἰ μὴ δύνανται τυγχά- νειν ἀναπνοῆς καταψύξεως χάριν· ἀλλ' ἔοικε τοῦτο ἀναγκαιότερον εἶναι. ἢ εὐλόγως ὁ πόνος πλείων κατέχουσιν, ὀγκουμένων καὶ διατεινομένων; φαί-
30 νεται δὲ καὶ αὐτόματός τις εἶναι φορὰ τοῦ πνεύ- ματος ἔξω· εἰ δὲ καὶ εἴσω, σκεπτέον. ἔοικεν δέ. ὁμοίως γὰρ ἀναπνοὴν ποιοῦσι τοῖς κολυμβηταῖς λέβητα καταφέντες. οὐ πίμπλαται γὰρ οὗτος τοῦ ὕδατος, ἀλλὰ τηρεῖ τὸν ἀέρα. μετὰ βίας γὰρ ἡ κάθεσις. ὀρθὸν γὰρ ὁτιοῦν παρεγκλιθὲν εἰσρεῖ.

35 Διὰ τί ἔνιοι τὰ ὦτα σκαλεύοντες βήττουσιν; ἢ 6 ὅτι ἐπὶ τοῦ αὐτοῦ πόρου τῷ πνεύμονι καὶ τῇ ἀρτη- ρίᾳ ἡ ἀκοή; σημεῖον δέ, ὅτι ἀναπληροῦνται ⟨ἂν⟩ [καὶ]² γίνονται ἐνεοί. θερμαινομένου οὖν τῇ τρίψει

---

[1] The ms. has ἀνατέμνουσι δὲ καὶ τὸν τόπον καὶ πρὸς εὐπνοιαν here, but the words are omitted by Th. G. and seem out of place.

[2] ἂν added and καὶ bracketed by Ross.

them, so that, the water being harder than air, it presses on them and bursts them.

Why do divers fasten sponges round their ears 3 when they dive ? Is it to prevent the sea breaking the ear-drums, when it enters them violently ? For in this case the ears do not become filled as they do when the sponges are taken away.

Why is dirt in the ears bitter ? Is it because 4 sweat is rotten ? And what is rotten is salt ; and what is salt and rotten is bitter.

Why do divers for sponges slit their ears and 5 nostrils ? Is it that they may more easily admit the air ? For in this way the air seems to escape. For they say that they suffer more in the difficulty of breathing because they cannot expel the breath ; but when they have as it were vomited forth the air they are relieved. It is therefore strange that they cannot manage to breathe for the purpose of cooling ; this seems to be even more necessary. Or is the strain naturally greater if they hold the breath, and they are therefore swollen and distended ? But there seems to be a spontaneous passage of the breath outwards ; but we must consider whether a movement inwards is also automatic. It seems to be so. For they can give respiration to divers equally by letting down a cauldron. For this does not fill with water, but retains its air. Its lowering has to be done by force. For any vessel which is upright admits the water if it is tilted.

Why do some men cough when they scratch their 6 ears ? Is it because the hearing is connected with the same passage as the lung and the windpipe ? This is proved by the fact that if the lung and the windpipe are filled up, a man becomes deaf. So, when

960 b
συντήκεται ἐπὶ τὴν ἀρτηρίαν ἀπὸ τοῦ πόνου
κάτωθεν ὑγρόν, ὃ ποιεῖ τὴν βῆχα.

40 Διὰ τί τὸ ἀριστερὸν οὖς θᾶττον συμφύεται ὡς 7
961 a ἐπὶ τὸ πολύ, ὅταν τρυπηθῇ; διὸ καὶ αἱ γυναῖκες
τὸ μὲν ἄρρεν, τὸ δὲ θῆλυ καλοῦσι τῶν ὤτων. ἢ
ὅτι τὰ ἀριστερὰ ὑγρὰ καὶ θερμὰ μᾶλλον, συμφύεται δὲ τὰ τοιαῦτα μάλιστα; διὸ καὶ ἐν φυτο-
5 τοῖς χλωροῖς ἡ σύμφυσις· καὶ τὰ τῶν νέων δὲ
ἕλκη μᾶλλον συμφύεται ἢ τὰ τῶν πρεσβυτέρων.
σημεῖον δὲ ὅτι ὑγρὰ μᾶλλον καὶ ὅλως θηλυκώτερα
τὰ ἀριστερά.

Διὰ τί τοῖς μὲν αἰσχυνομένοις ἄκρα τὰ ὦτα 8
ἐπιφοινίσσεται, τοῖς δὲ ὀργιζομένοις οἱ ὀφθαλμοί;
10 ἢ ὅτι ἡ μὲν αἰδὼς ἐν ὀφθαλμοῖς κατάψυξίς τις
μετὰ φόβου, ὥστε εἰκότως ἀπολείπει τὸ θερμὸν
τοὺς ὀφθαλμούς; χωριζόμενον δὲ εἰς τὸν δεκτι-
κώτατον φέρεται τόπον. τοιοῦτος δὲ ὁ ἐν τοῖς
ἄκροις τῶν ὤτων· ὁ γὰρ ἄλλος ὀστώδης. ὀργιζομένοις δ᾽ ἐπανέρχεται τὸ θερμόν. μάλιστα δὲ
15 γίνεται φανερὸν ἐν τοῖς ὀφθαλμοῖς διὰ τὴν χρόαν
οὖσαν λευκήν.

Διὰ τί ὁ ἦχος ὁ ἐν τοῖς ὠσίν, ἐάν τις ψοφήσῃ, 9
παύεται; ἢ διότι ὁ μείζων ψόφος τὸν ἐλάττω
ἐκκρούεται;

Διὰ τί, ἐὰν εἰς τὸ οὖς ὕδωρ ἐγχυθῇ, ἔλαιον 10
προσεγχέονται, οὐ δυναμένου τοῦ ἐνόντος ὑγροῦ
20 ἐξελθεῖν δι᾽ ἄλλου ὑγροῦ; πότερον διὰ τὸ ἐπιπολῆς
γίνεσθαι τὸ ἔλαιον τοῦ ὕδατος, καὶ διὰ γλισχρότητα
αὐτοῦ ἔχεσθαι τὸ ὕδωρ ἐξιόντος τοῦ ἐλαίου, ἵνα
συνεξίῃ τὸ ὕδωρ; ἢ ἵνα ὀλισθηροῦ τοῦ ὠτὸς

the ear is heated by rubbing, moisture is caused by melting from the seat of the irritation to the wind-pipe, which produces a cough.

Why does the left ear heal more quickly, as a 7 general rule, when it has been pierced ? This is why women call the right ear male and the left ear female. Is it because the parts on the left are moister and hotter, and such things heal most quickly ? This is why healing takes place in green plants ; and the scars of the young heal more quickly than those of older people. This proves that the parts on the left are moister and generally speaking more akin to the female.

Why is it that when men are ashamed the tips 8 of their ears grow red, but when they are angry their eyes ? Is it because shame is a certain chilling in the eyes coupled with fear, so that the heat naturally leaves the eyes ; when it drains from there, it passes into the region best able to receive it ? And the region of the ear-tips is such a place ; for the rest of the region is bony. When men are angry, the heat rises. It appears most noticeably in the eyes because the colour there is light.

Why does humming in the ears cease if one makes 9 a noise ? Is it because the greater sound drives out the less ?

Why do they pour oil on top, if water has been 10 poured into the ear, seeing that the moisture in-side cannot escape through other moisture ? Is it because the oil is on the surface of the water and because of its viscosity the water adheres to it when the oil comes out, so that the water comes out with it ? Or is it that the water may come out when the

γενομένου ἐξέλθῃ τὸ ὕδωρ; τὸ γὰρ ἔλαιον λεῖον
ὂν ποιεῖ ὀλισθαίνειν.

25 Διὰ τί ἧττον ὦτα ῥήγνυται τοῖς κολυμβῶσιν, 11
ἐὰν προεγχέωσιν εἰς τὰ ὦτα τὸ ἔλαιον; ἢ τοῦ
μὲν ῥήγνυσθαι τὰ ὦτα εἴρηται πρότερον ἡ αἰτία,
τὸ δὲ ἔλαιον ἐγχυθὲν εἰς τὰ ὦτα τὴν ὕστερον
θάλατταν ἀπολισθαίνειν ποιεῖ, καθάπερ ἐπὶ τῶν
ἔξω τοῦ σώματος συμβαίνει τοῖς ἀληλιμμένοις.
ὀλισθαίνουσα δὲ πληγὴν οὐ ποιεῖ εἰς τὸ ἐντὸς τοῦ
30 ὠτός, διόπερ οὐ ῥήγνυσιν.

Διὰ τί τῶν ὤτων ἀναίμων ὄντων μάλιστα οἱ 12
αἰσχυνόμενοι ἐρυθριῶσιν; ἢ ἕκαστον εἰς τὸ κενὸν
ἑκάστου μάλιστα φέρεται; δοκεῖ δὲ τοῦ αἰσχυνο-
μένου ἄνω θερμὸν φέρεσθαι τὸ αἷμα. εἰς οὖν τὸ
κενώτατον ἐρυθριᾶν ποιεῖ. τὸ δ' αὐτὸ τοῦτο
35 καὶ ἐπὶ τῶν γνάθων. ἔτι δὲ καὶ ὅτι λεπτότατον
τὸ δέρμα τὸ περιτεταμένον, μάλιστα δὴ φαίνεται
δι' αὐτά.

Διὰ τί οὐδεὶς χασμώμενος τὸ οὖς σκαλεύει; ἢ 1.
ὅτι ὅτε χασμᾶται, ἐμφυσᾶται καὶ ἡ μῆνιγξ, δι'
ἧς ἀκούει; σημεῖον δέ· ἥκιστα γὰρ ἀκούουσι
40 χασμώμενοι. τὸ γὰρ πνεῦμα, ὥσπερ καὶ κατὰ
τὸ στόμα, καὶ εἰς τὰ ὦτα ἐντὸς πορευόμενον, ἐξ-
961 b ωθεῖται τὸν ὑμένα καὶ κωλύει τὸν ψόφον εἰσιέναι.
ἐὰν οὖν οὕτως ἔχοντος ἅψηται τῆς ἀκοῆς ὡς
σκαλεύειν, μάλιστ' ἂν βλάψειε· πρὸς ἀντιπῖπτον
γὰρ ἡ πληγὴ γίνεται, καὶ οὐ πρὸς ὑπεῖκον τὸ τοῦ
5 πνεύματος. τὸ δὲ δέρμα καὶ τὴν μήνιγγα ἀφ-
εστάναι τῶν στερεῶν δῆλον. ὥστε πόνον μάλιστα
οὕτω ποιεῖ, καὶ τραυματίζοι ἄν.

ear has become slimy ? For oil being smooth makes it slimy.

Why are divers less apt to break their ear-drums, if 11 they pour oil beforehand into the ears ? The reason why the ear-drums break has been stated before,[a] but oil poured into the ears makes the sea-water which comes in later slip along, just as happens with the outer parts of the body, when men are smeared with oil. As it slips along, it does not strike a blow on the inside of the ear and so does not break it.

Why is it, seeing that the ears are the most blood-12 less part of the face, that men grow red in the ears when they are ashamed ? Does each substance travel most readily to that part which is most empty of it ? When a man is ashamed, the blood seems to travel upwards in a heated condition. So it causes that part which contains least blood to grow red. The same thing is true of the cheeks. It is also due to the fact that the skin is stretched tight and very thin, and hence the blood shows more through them.

Why does no one scratch his ear while yawning ? 13 Is it because, when he yawns, the ear-drum through which he hears is inflated ? There is proof of this ; for men can hear least well while they are yawning. For, just as with the mouth, the air entering within the ear pushes out the membrane and prevents the sound from entering. If in this condition one touches the hearing organ to scratch it, one would do great harm ; for the blow meets with a resisting, not a yielding surface. For it is clear that the skin and the ear-drum are far from solid. So that this produces great pain and might cause a wound.

[a] Cf. 2 supra.

ΛΓ

ΟΣΑ ΠΕΡΙ ΜΥΚΤΗΡΑ

Διὰ τί ὁ πταρμὸς λυγμὸν μὲν παύει, ἐρυγμὸν δὲ 1
10 οὐ παύει; ἢ διότι οὐ τοῦ αὐτοῦ τόπου τὸ πάθος
ἑκάτερον, ἀλλ' ὁ μὲν ἐρυγμὸς κοιλίας, ὁ δὲ λυγμὸς
τοῦ περὶ τὸν πνεύμονα κατάψυξις καὶ ἀπεψία
πνεύματος καὶ ὑγροῦ; κοινωνοῦσιν δ' οἱ περὶ τὸν
ἐγκέφαλον τόποι τῷ πνεύμονι, οἷον τοῖς ὠσίν.
φανερὸν δέ· ἅμα γὰρ ἐνεοὶ καὶ κωφοὶ γίνονται,
15 καὶ αἱ νόσοι ἀντιπεριίστανται αἱ τοῦ ὠτὸς εἰς τὰ
τοῦ πνεύμονος πάθη. ἐν τοῖς¹ δὲ σκαλεύουσι τὸ
οὖς βῆχες ἐγγίνονται. τὸ δὲ περὶ τὸν πταρνύμενον
τόπον εἶναι τῆς ῥινὸς κοινωνίαν τῷ πνεύμονι δηλοῖ
ἡ ἀναπνοὴ κοινὴ οὖσα. ὥστε πτάρνυται μὲν θερμαινομένου αὐτοῦ· τῷ δὲ συμπάσχειν ὁ κάτω
20 τόπος, ἐν ᾧ ἐστὶν ὁ λυγμός. ἡ δὲ θερμασία πέττει.
διὸ ὄξος τε παύει λυγμὸν καὶ ἡ ἀπνευστία, ἐὰν
ἠρεμαία ᾖ ἡ λύγξ. ἐκθερμαίνει γὰρ τὸ πνεῦμα
κατεχόμενον, ὥστε καὶ ἐν τῷ πταρμῷ ἡ ἀντι-
κατάσχεσις γενομένη τοῦ πνεύματος τοῦτο ποιεῖ,
καὶ οἰκείως ἡ ἔκπνευσις γίνεται, καὶ ἐκ τοῦ ἄνω
25 τόπου· ἀδύνατον γὰρ πτάρειν μὴ ἐκπνέοντα. ἡ
οὖν ὁρμὴ ῥήγνυσι τὸ ἐγκατειλημμένον πνεῦμα, ὃ
ποιεῖ τὸν λυγμόν.

¹ ἐν τοῖς Forster : ἐνίοις Ruelle.

BOOK XXXIII

Problems connected with the Nostrils

Why does sneezing stop hiccough, but not eructa- 1 tion ? Is it because the two affections do not belong to the same region, but eructation is a cooling and lack of concoction in the stomach, whereas hiccough is due to a similar condition in the region of the lungs ? Now the parts about the brain are connected with the lung, as they are with the ears. This is obvious ; for men become deaf and dumb at the same time, and diseases of the ear change into diseases of the lung. So when men scratch the ear, they cough at the same time. That there is a connexion between the nose, where the sneezing occurs, and the lung, is shown by the fact that breathing is common to both. So a man sneezes when this part grows hot ; but the lower region, in which the hiccough takes place, acts in sympathy. Now heating causes concoction. So vinegar and holding the breath both stop hiccoughs, if they are slight. For it heats the air which is constrained, so that in the case of a sneeze also the restraining of the breath produces the same result, and the expiration takes place naturally and from the upper region ; for it is impossible to sneeze without expiration. The violence of the sneeze thus breaks up the enclosed air, which is the cause of hiccough.

Διὰ τί, ἐάν τις μέλλων πτάρνυσθαι τρίψῃ τὸν 2
ὀφθαλμόν, ἧττον πτάρνυται; ἢ διότι τὸ ποιοῦν
τὸν πταρμὸν θερμότης τίς ἐστιν, ἡ δὲ τρῖψις
30 θερμότητα ποιεῖ, ἢ διὰ τὸ πλησίον εἶναι τῶν
ὀφθαλμῶν τὸν τόπον ᾧ πτάρνυται, ἀφανίζει τὴν
ἑτέραν, ὥσπερ τὸ ἔλαττον πῦρ ὑπὸ τοῦ πλείονος
μαραινόμενον;

Διὰ τί δὶς πτάρνυται ὡς ἐπὶ τὸ πολύ, καὶ οὐχ 3
ἅπαξ ἢ πλεονάκις; ἢ διότι δύο εἰσὶ μυκτῆρες;
35 ἑκάτερον οὖν διέσχισται τὸ φλέβιον, δι' οὗ πνεῦμα
ῥεῖ.

Διὰ τί πρὸς τὸν ἥλιον βλέψαντες πτάρνυνται 4
μᾶλλον; ἢ διότι κινεῖ θερμαίνων; καθάπερ οὖν
πτεροῖς θιγγάνοντες. ἀμφότεροι γὰρ τὸ αὐτὸ
ποιοῦσιν· τῇ γὰρ κινήσει θερμαίνοντες ἐκ τοῦ
ὑγροῦ θᾶττον πνεῦμα ποιοῦσιν. τούτου δὲ ἡ
40 ἔξοδος πταρμός.

Διὰ τί λύγγα παύει πταρμὸς καὶ πνεύματος 5
ἐπίσχεσις καὶ ὄξος; ἢ ὁ μὲν πταρμός, ὅτι ἀντι-
περίστασίς ἐστι τοῦ κάτω πνεύματος, ὥσπερ αἱ
ἄνω φαρμακεῖαι πρὸς τὴν κάτω κοιλίαν; ἡ δὲ
5 ἀπνευστία τὰς ἀσθενεῖς λύγγας, ὅτι ἡ μικρὰ ὁρμὴ
τοῦ πνεύματος ἡ ἀνιοῦσα, ὥσπερ περὶ τὴν βῆχα,
⟨ἢ,⟩[1] ἐάν τις κατάσχῃ, παύεται, οὕτω καὶ ἐνταῦθα
καὶ κατέσπασε καὶ κατέπνιξε καὶ συναπεβιάσατο.
τὸ δὲ ὄξος παύει, ὅτι τὸ περιεστὸς ὑγρὸν καὶ
κωλῦον ἀπερυγεῖν ἐπνευμάτωσεν τῇ θερμασίᾳ.
10 ἔστι γὰρ ἐρυγμὸς μέν, ὅταν πνευματωθῇ τὸ ἐν
τῇ ἄνω κοιλίᾳ ὑγρὸν καὶ πεφθῇ, ἡ δὲ λύγξ, ὅταν
ὑπὸ ὑγροῦ κατέχηται πνεῦμα περιττὸν περὶ τὸν
πνευματικὸν τόπον. τοῦτο γὰρ ὁρμῶν καὶ μὴ
δυνάμενον διακόψαι σπασμὸν ποιεῖ, ὁ δὲ σπασμὸς

Why is it that, if one rubs the eye when about to **2** sneeze, one is less liable to sneeze ? Is it because the cause of a sneeze is a form of heat, but friction produces heat which, because the eyes are near the region of the sneeze, causes the other heat to disappear, just as the lesser fire is extinguished by the greater ?

Why does one generally sneeze twice and neither **3** once nor a large number of times ? Is it because we have two nostrils ? So the channel through which the air passes is divided into two.

Why is one more apt to sneeze after looking at the **4** sun ? Is it because the sun heats us and produces a disturbance ? So it is the same thing as tickling with feathers. For both produce the same effect ; for producing movement by heat they create breath faster from the moisture. The exit of this breath is a sneeze.

Why is it that a sneeze, holding the breath, and **5** vinegar all check a hiccough ? In the case of the sneeze, is it because it causes a change in the position of the breath below, just as medicines administered above affect the stomach below ? Stopping the breath checks slight hiccough because the small assault of air which rises (just as with a cough which stops if one controls it) checks, stifles, and forces back the hiccough. Vinegar stops hiccough because by its heat it aerates the surrounding moisture and prevents eructation. For eructation occurs when the moisture in the upper stomach is aerated and concocted, but hiccough occurs when excessive moisture is retained in the region of the lung. This breath rising and unable to escape causes a spasm, and this spasm

---

[1] ἡ added by Forster.

οὗτος καλεῖται λύγξ. καὶ διὰ τοῦτο ῥιγώσαντας
15 λὺγξ λαμβάνει, ὅτι τὸ ψῦχος τὸ ὑγρὸν ποιεῖ συστὰν
ἐκ τοῦ πνεύματος ἔτι· περιλαμβανόμενον δὲ τὸ
ἄλλο πηδᾷ· οὗ ἡ κίνησις λυγμός ἐστιν.

Διὰ τί ἐνίοις ὕδωρ ψυχρὸν προσχέομεν καὶ πρὸς 6
τὸ πρόσωπον, ἡνίκα αἷμα ῥεῖ ἐκ τῶν μυκτήρων; ἢ
ἀντιπεριίσταται εἴσω τὸ θερμόν; ἂν οὖν ἐπιπολῆς
20 τύχῃ αἷμα, ἐξυγραίνει μᾶλλον.

Διὰ τί τὸν μὲν πταρμὸν θεῖον[1] ἡγούμεθα εἶναι, 7
τὴν δὲ βῆχα ἢ τὴν κόρυζαν οὔ; ἢ διότι ἐκ τοῦ
θειοτάτου τῶν περὶ ἡμᾶς τῆς κεφαλῆς, ὅθεν ὁ
λογισμός ἐστι, γίνεται; ἢ ὅτι τὰ μὲν ἄλλα ἀπὸ
νοσούντων γίνεται, τοῦτο δὲ οὔ;

25 Διὰ τί τρίψαντες τὸν ὀφθαλμὸν παυόμεθα τῶν 8
πταρμῶν; ἢ ὅτι ἀνάπνοια ταύτῃ γίνεται τῷ
ὑγρῷ; δακρύει γὰρ ὁ ὀφθαλμὸς μετὰ τρῖψιν, ὁ
δὲ πταρμὸς διὰ πλῆθος ὑγρότητος. ἢ ὅτι τὸ
ἔλαττον θερμὸν φθείρεται ὑπὸ τοῦ πλείονος, ὁ δὲ
ὀφθαλμὸς τριφθεὶς πλείω λαμβάνει θερμότητα τῆς
30 ἐν τῇ ῥινί; διὰ ταῦτα δὴ κἄν τις αὐτὴν τὴν ῥῖνα
τρίψῃ, παύεται ὁ πταρμός.

Διὰ τί τῶν μὲν ἄλλων πνευμάτων αἱ ἔξοδοι, οἷον 9
φύσης καὶ ἐρυγμοῦ, οὐχ ἱεραί, ἡ δὲ τοῦ πταρμοῦ
ἱερά; πότερον ὅτι τριῶν τόπων ὄντων, κεφαλῆς
35 καὶ θώρακος καὶ τῆς κάτω κοιλίας, ἡ κεφαλὴ
θειότατον; ἔστι δὲ φῦσα μὲν ἀπὸ τῆς κάτω
κοιλίας πνεῦμα, ἐρυγμὸς δὲ τῆς ἄνω, ὁ δὲ πταρμὸς
τῆς κεφαλῆς. διὰ τὸ ἱερώτατον οὖν εἶναι τὸν
τόπον καὶ τὸ πνεῦμα τὸ ἐντεῦθεν ὡς ἱερὸν προσκυνοῦσιν. ἢ ὅτι ἅπαντα τὰ πνεύματα σημαίνει

is called a hiccough. This is why hiccough seizes men after they have had a fit of shivering, because the cold makes the moisture from the breath set ; but the rest being still enclosed causes a jerk, and this movement is a hiccough.

Why do we sometimes pour water on people's 6 faces when blood flows from their nostrils? Is the heat thus compressed within? So if the blood chances to be on the surface it tends to liquefy it.

Why do we consider that sneezing is of divine ori- 7 gin, but not coughing or running at the nose? Is it because it arises from the most divine part of us — the head, whence reasoning comes? Or is it because the other symptoms arise from disease, but this does not?

Why do we stop sneezing if we rub our eye? Is it 8 because by this means air is brought to the moisture? For the eye weeps after rubbing, but sneezing is due to the quantity of moisture. Or is it because the lesser heat is destroyed by the greater, and the eye when rubbed acquires more heat than is present in the nose? For this reason, if one rubs the nose itself, the sneezing stops.

Why is it that other emissions of breath such as 9 wind and eructation are not regarded as sacred, but that sneezing is? Is it because of the three regions, the head, the chest, and the stomach, the head is the most divine? Wind is breath from the lower part of the stomach, eructation from the upper part, and sneezing from the head. From the fact, then, that this region is the most divine, they also worship as divine the breath which is there. Or is it that all discharges of breath show that the parts we have men-

---

[1] θεῖον Richards : θεὸν Ruelle.

ARISTOTLE

40 τοὺς εἰρημένους τόπους βέλτιον ἔχειν ὡς ἐπὶ τὸ
πολύ; μὴ διαχωρούντων γὰρ κουφίζει τὸ πνεῦμα
962 b διεξιόν, ὥστε καὶ ὁ πταρμὸς τὸν περὶ τὴν κεφαλὴν
τόπον, ὅτι ὑγιαίνει καὶ δύναται πέττειν. ὅταν
γὰρ κρατήσῃ ἡ ἐν τῇ κεφαλῇ θερμότης τὴν ὑγρότητα, τὸ πνεῦμα τότε γίνεται πταρμός. διὸ καὶ
5 τοὺς ἐκθνήσκοντας κρίνουσιν πταρμικῷ, ὡς ἐὰν
μὴ τοῦτο δύνωνται πάσχειν, ἀσώτους ὄντας.
ὥστε ὡς σημεῖον ὑγείας τοῦ ἀρίστου καὶ ἱερωτάτου
τόπου προσκυνοῦσιν ὡς ἱερόν, καὶ φήμην ἀγαθὴν
ποιοῦνται.

Διὰ τί ἄνθρωπος πτάρνυται μάλιστα τῶν ἄλλων
ζῴων; πότερον ὅτι τοὺς πόρους εὐρεῖς ἔχει, δι'
10 ὧν τὸ πνεῦμα καὶ ἡ ὀσμὴ[1] εἰσέρχεται; τούτοις
γὰρ πληρουμένοις πνεύματος πτάρνυται. ὅτι δ'
εὐρεῖς, σημεῖον ὅτι ἥκιστα ὀσφραντικὸν τῶν ζῴων.
ἀκριβέστεροι δὲ οἱ λεπτοὶ πόροι. εἰ οὖν εἰς μὲν
τοὺς εὐρεῖς πλεῖον καὶ πλεονάκις εἰσέρχεται τὸ
ὑγρόν, οὗ πνευματουμένου ὁ πταρμὸς γίνεται,
15 τοιούτους δὲ μάλιστα τῶν ζῴων οἱ ἄνθρωποι
ἔχουσι, πλειστάκις ἂν πταρνύοιντο[2] εἰκότως, ὅσοις
ἐλάχιστοι οἱ μυκτῆρες, ὥστε τὸ θερμανθὲν ὑγρὸν
ταχὺ ἐξιέναι δύναται πνεῦμα γενόμενον· ἐν δὲ τοῖς
ἄλλοις διὰ μῆκος καταψύχεται πρότερον.

Διὰ τί οἱ μὲν ἀπὸ μέσων νυκτῶν ἄχρι μέσης
20 ἡμέρας οὐκ ἀγαθοὶ πταρμοί, οἱ δὲ ἀπὸ μέσης
ἡμέρας ἄχρι μέσων νυκτῶν; ἢ ὅτι ὁ μὲν πταρμὸς
μᾶλλον δοκεῖ ἐπισχεῖν τοὺς ἀρχομένους καὶ ἐν τῇ
ἀρχῇ; διὸ ὅταν μέλλωσιν ἀρχομένοις συμβῆναι,
μάλιστα ἀποτρεπόμεθα τοῦ πράττειν. ἡ μὲν οὖν

---

[1] ὀσμὴ Bussemaker : ῥύμη Ruelle.
[2] πταρνύοιντο Forster : πτάρνυντο Ruelle.

tioned are generally speaking in better condition ? For without anything else passing out the breath as it escapes lightens the body, and so the sneeze lightens the region about the head, because it is healthy and capable of concoction. For when the heat in the head gains mastery over the moisture, then the breath becomes a sneeze. So they test the dying by their capacity to sneeze, and, if they cannot do this, they are past saving. So men regard sneezing as sacred because it is a sign of the health of the best and most divine region, and they consider it a good omen.

Why does man sneeze more than any other animal ? 10 Is it because he has wide channels, through which breath and smell enter ? When these are full of air, he sneezes. That they are wide is proved by the fact that man has less power of smell than other animals, but narrow channels are more discriminating. If, then, the moisture whose evaporation involves sneezing, flows in larger quantity and more often into wide channels, and man has these to a greater extent than animals, those would naturally sneeze most often whose nostrils are smallest, so that the hot moisture when it evaporates could escape most quickly ; in other animals owing to the length of their nostrils it is cooled earlier.

Why is it that sneezing between midnight and 11 midday is not a good thing, but between midday and midnight it is ? Is it because sneezing seems inclined to check those who are starting anything and are at the beginning ? So when sneezing occurs, when we are about to do something and are at the beginning,[a] we are diverted from our action. Now dawn and the

---

[a] The Greek text is untranslatable and the present translation is from Th. G.

962 b

[καὶ] ἠὼς καὶ τὸ ἀπὸ μέσων νυκτῶν οἷον ἀρχή τις·
25 διὸ εὐλαβούμεθα πτάρειν, μὴ κωλύσωμεν ὡρμη-
μένον. πρὸς δείλης δὲ καὶ ἐπὶ μέσας νύκτας οἷον
τελευτή τις καὶ ἐναντίον ἐκείνῳ, ὥστε ἐν τῷ
ἐναντίῳ ταὐτὸν αἱρετέον.

Διὰ τί οἱ πρεσβῦται χαλεπῶς πτάρνυνται;
πότερον οἱ πόροι συμπεπτώκασιν δι' ὧν τὸ πνεῦμα;
30 ἢ ὅτι αἴρειν τὰ ἄνω οὐκέτι δυνάμενοι ῥαδίως εἶτα
βίᾳ ἀφιᾶσι κάτω;

Διὰ τί, ἐάν τις ἀπνευστιάζῃ, ἡ λὺγξ παύεται;
ἢ διότι ἡ μὲν ὑπὸ καταψύξεως γίνεται (διὸ καὶ
οἱ φοβούμενοι καὶ οἱ ῥιγοῦντες λύζουσιν), κατεχόμενον δὲ τὸ πνεῦμα ἐκθερμαίνει τὸν ἐντὸς
τόπον;

35 Διὰ τί οἱ κωφοὶ ἐκ τῶν μυκτήρων διαλέγονται
ὡς ἐπὶ τὸ πολύ; ἢ ὅτι ὁ πνεύμων ἐστὶ τούτοις
πεπονηκώς; τοῦτο γάρ ἐστιν ἡ κωφότης, πλή-
ρωσις τοῦ τόπου τοῦ πνευμονικοῦ. οὔκουν ῥαδίως
ἡ φωνὴ φέρεται, ἀλλ' ὥσπερ τὸ πνεῦμα τῶν
40 πνευστιώντων ἢ ἀσθμαινόντων δι' ἀδυναμίαν
ἀθρόον, οὕτως ἐκείνοις ἡ φωνή. βιάζεται οὖν καὶ
963 a διὰ τῶν μυκτήρων. βιαζομένη δὲ τῇ τρίψει
ποιεῖ τὸν ἦχον. ἔστι γὰρ ἡ διὰ τῶν ῥινῶν διά-
λεκτος γινομένη, ὅταν τὸ ἄνω τῆς ῥινὸς εἰς τὸν
οὐρανόν, ᾗ συντέτρηται, κοῖλον γένηται· ὥσπερ
κώδων γὰρ ὑπηχεῖ, τοῦ κάτωθεν στενοῦ ὄντος.

5 Διὰ τί μόνον ὁ πταρμὸς ἡμῖν καθεύδουσιν οὐ
γίνεται, ἀλλ' ὡς εἰπεῖν ἅπαντα ἐγρηγορόσιν; ἢ
ὅτι ὁ μὲν πταρμὸς γίνεται καὶ ὑπὸ θερμοῦ τινος
κινήσαντος τὸν τόπον τοῦτον ἀφ' οὗ γίνεται· διὸ
καὶ ἀνακύπτομεν πρὸς τὸν ἥλιον, ὅταν βουλώμεθα
πτάρειν· ⟨ἢ⟩ ὅτι καθευδόντων ἡμῶν ἀντιπερι-
218

time after midnight is, so to speak, a time of beginning ; so we carefully avoid sneezing, lest we
should check what has been begun. But the evening
and up to midnight is a kind of finishing time and
opposite to the other, so that in contrary conditions
the same thing becomes desirable.

Why do the old sneeze with difficulty ? Have the 12
channels through which the breath passes become
closed ? Or is it because they can no longer raise the
breath upwards easily, and so they need an effort to
expel it downwards ?

Why does a hiccough cease, if one holds the breath ? 13
Is it because a hiccough is due to chilling (this is
why the frightened and shivering hiccough), but when
the breath is held it heats the region within ?

Why do the deaf usually talk through their noses ? 14
Is it because with them the lung has been affected ?
For deafness is really a congestion in the region of
the lungs. So the voice does not travel easily, but as
the breathing of those who puff and pant accumulates
because of their lack of strength, so is the voice with
the deaf. So it is forced out through the nostrils.
As it is forced out it makes a noise due to the
friction. For talking through the nose occurs when
the upper part of the nose, where the holes are
leading to the roof of the mouth, becomes hollow ;
then it echoes like a bell because the lower part is
narrow.

Why does not a sneeze occur when we are asleep, 15
but practically always when we are awake ? Is it
because a sneeze is due to some hot agent disturbing
the region from which it comes ? This is why we turn
towards the sun, when we want to sneeze. Or is it
because when we are asleep the heat is compressed

963 a

10 ἵσταται τὸ θερμὸν ἐντός; διὸ καὶ γίνεται τὰ κάτω
θερμὰ τῶν καθευδόντων, καὶ τὸ πνεῦμα τὸ πολὺ
αἴτιόν ἐστιν τοῦ ἐξονειρώττειν ἡμᾶς. εἰκότως οὖν
οὐ πταρνύμεθα· ἀπαλλαγέντος γὰρ τοῦ θερμοῦ τοῦ
ἐκ τῆς κεφαλῆς, ὃ κινεῖν πέφυκεν τὸ ἐνταῦθα
ὑγρόν, οὗ ἐξαιρουμένου γίνεται ὁ πταρμός, καὶ τὸ
15 συμβαῖνον πάθος εἰκὸς μὴ γίνεσθαι. ἀποψοφοῦσι
δὲ μᾶλλον ἢ πτάρνυνται καὶ ἐρεύγονται καθ-
εύδοντες,[1] ὅτι ἐκθερμαινομένου τοῦ περὶ τὴν
κοιλίαν τόπου ἐν τοῖς ὕπνοις μᾶλλον ἐκπνευμα-
τοῦσθαι συμβαίνει τὰ περὶ αὐτὴν ὑγρά, πνευ-
ματούμενα δὲ εἰς τοὺς ἔγγιστα τόπους φέρεσθαι.
20 ἐνταῦθα γὰρ καὶ συναπωθεῖται ὑπὸ τοῦ ἐν τῷ
ὕπνῳ γινομένου πνεύματος, καθεκτικώτερος γάρ
ἐστιν ἢ προετικώτερος ὁ καθεύδων τοῦ πνεύματος,
διὸ καὶ συστέλλει τὸ θερμὸν ἐντός. ὁ δὲ κατέχων
τὸ πνεῦμα ὠθεῖ κάτω αὐτό· παρὰ φύσιν γάρ ἐστι
τῷ πνεύματι ἡ κάτω φορά, διὸ καὶ χαλεπόν ἐστι
25 κατέχειν τὸ πνεῦμα. τὸ δ' αὐτὸ αἴτιον καὶ τοῦ
καθεύδειν ἡμῖν ἐστιν. οὔσης γὰρ τῆς ἐγρηγόρσεως
κινήσεως, ταύτης δ' ἐν τοῖς αἰσθητηρίοις ἡμῶν
γινομένης μάλιστα ἐν τῷ ἐγρηγορέναι ἡμᾶς, δῆλον
ὡς καὶ ἠρεμούντων ἡμῶν καθεύδοιμεν ἄν. ἐπεὶ
δὲ τὸ μὲν πῦρ κινητικόν ἐστι τῶν ἐν ἡμῖν μορίων,
30 τοῦτο δ' ἐν τῷ ὕπνῳ ἐντὸς περιίσταται, λιπὸν τὸν
περὶ τὴν κεφαλὴν τόπον οὗ ἐστι τὸ αἰσθητήριον,
ἠρεμοίη ἂν μάλιστα ἡμῶν τότε τὰ αἰσθητήρια· ὃ
εἴη ἂν αἴτιον τοῦ καθεύδειν.

Διὰ τί πτάραντες καὶ οὐρήσαντες φρίττουσιν;
ἢ ὅτι κενοῦνται αἱ φλέβες ἀμφοτέροις τούτοις τοῦ
35 πρότερον ἐνυπάρχοντος ἀέρος θερμοῦ, κενωθέντων
δὲ ἄλλος ἀὴρ ἔξωθεν εἰσέρχεται ψυχρότερος τοῦ

within ? For this reason the lower parts grow warm when we are asleep, and the large quantity of breath is the cause of the emission of semen during sleep. So naturally we do not sneeze ; for when the heat (which naturally moves the moisture there, the withdrawal of which causes a sneeze) is expelled from the head, the affection which accompanies it is not likely to occur. Wind is more common when men are asleep than sneezing and eructation, because as the region about the stomach grows hot in sleep the moisture round it becomes more vaporized, and as it does so it travels to the nearest parts. There it is collected by the breath which forms in sleep, for the sleeper is more prone to hold the breath than to expel it, so that it collects the internal heat. But the man who holds his breath drives it downwards ; for a downward course is unnatural to the breath, so that it is difficult to hold the breath. The reason of our sleeping is the same. For being awake implies movement, and movement in our sense-organs takes place for the most part while we are awake, so it is obvious that when we are quite at rest we should sleep. But since fire produces movement in our parts, and this is confined within during sleep, leaving the region about the head where the sense-organ is, our sense-organs would naturally be most quiet at that time ; and this would be a cause of sleep.

Why do those who sneeze or make water shiver 16 afterwards ? Is it because in both cases the veins are emptied of the hot air which was in them before, and, when they are empty, other air enters from the

---

[1] ἢ ἐργηγορότες incl. Ruelle.

963 a

προϋπάρχοντος ἐν ταῖς φλεψίν· τοιοῦτος δ' εἰσιὼν
ποιεῖ φρίττειν;

Διὰ τί τοὺς λυγμοὺς οἱ πταρμοὶ παύουσιν; ἢ ὅτι [1]
ὁ λυγμὸς οὐχ ὥσπερ οἱ ἐρυγμοὶ ἀπὸ τῆς τὰ σιτία
40 δεχομένης κοιλίας ἐστίν, ἀλλ' ἀπὸ τοῦ πνεύματος,
963 b συμβαίνει δὲ μάλιστα ἀπὸ καταψύξεως ἐκ ῥίγους
καὶ λύπης καὶ φαρμακείας τῆς ἄνω μάλιστα
γίνεσθαι; θερμὸς γὰρ ὢν φύσει ὁ τόπος, ὅταν
καταψυχθῇ, οὐ προίεται τὸ πνεῦμα πᾶν, ἀλλ'
ὥσπερ πομφόλυγας ποιεῖ· διὸ καὶ τὸ πνεῦμα
5 κατασχοῦσι παύεται (ἐκθερμαίνεται γὰρ ὁ τόπος),
καὶ τὸ ὄξος, θερμαντικὸν ὄν, προσφερόμενον. τοῦ
δὴ θερμοῦ συμβαίνοντος ἀπὸ θερμασίας καὶ τοῦ
ἐγκεφάλου, τῶν ἄνω τόπων εἰς τὸν πνεύμονα
συντετρημένων, θερμοῦ τοῦ πνεύμονος ὄντος, ἥ
τε πρὸ τοῦ πταρμοῦ κατοχὴ καὶ ἡ ἄνωθεν κατά-
κρουσις λύει τὸ πάθος.

10 Διὰ τί οἱ οὐλότριχες, καὶ οἷς ἐπέστραπται τὸ [1]
τρίχιον, ὡς ἐπὶ τὸ πολὺ σιμότεροι; ἢ εἴπερ ἡ
οὐλότης ἐν παχύτητι, ἡ δὲ παχύτης μετὰ σκλη-
ρότητος, σκληρὸν δ' ὂν τὸ αἷμα θερμόν, ἡ δὲ
θερμότης οὐ ποιεῖ περίττωσιν, τὸ δὲ ὀστοῦν ἐκ
περιττώματος, ὁ δὲ χόνδρος ὀστοῦν, εὐλόγως ἂν
15 ἔκλειψις εἴη τοῦ μορίου; σημεῖον δὲ τὸ τὰ παιδία
πάντα εἶναι σιμά.

outside which is colder than what was in the veins before ; the entry of this produces sneezing ?

Why does sneezing check hiccough ? Is it because 17 hiccough, unlike eructation which comes from the stomach when it receives food, arises from breath, and occurs mostly after chill due to shivering and pain and medicine administered above ? For the region being naturally hot does not emit all the breath when it is cooled, but makes bubbles as it were ; so when men hold the breath the hiccough stops (for the region is warmed through), and vinegar also which is a heating agent produces the same effect when applied. Then as heat also collects from the heat of the brain, as the upper parts have aperture into the lungs and the lungs are also hot, the holding of the breath before the sneeze and the downward pressure from above stops the hiccough.

Why are those with woolly or curly hair generally 18 snub-nosed ? Is it because woolliness is due to fat, fat is accompanied by hardness, and blood when hard is hot, and heat does not produce waste product ? New bone arises from waste product and the cartilage of the nose is bony, so naturally there would be a scantiness in that part ? This is proved by the fact that all young children are snub-nosed.

ΛΔ

ΟΣΑ ΠΕΡΙ ΤΟ ΣΤΟΜΑ ΚΑΙ ΤΑ ΕΝ ΑΥΤΩΙ

Διὰ τί οἱ μανοὺς ἔχοντες τοὺς ὀδόντας οὐ μακρό-
βιοι; ἢ ὅτι τὰ μακρόβια πλείους ἔχουσιν, οἷον τὰ
20 ἄρσενα τῶν θηλειῶν, ἄνδρες γυναικῶν, πρόβατα
προβάτων. οἱ οὖν ἀραιόδοντες ὥσπερ ἂν ἐλάττονας
ἔχουσιν ὀδόντας ἐοίκασιν.

Διὰ τί οἱ ὀδόντες ἰσχυρότεροι τῶν σαρκῶν ὄντες
ὅμως τοῦ ψυχροῦ αἰσθάνονται μᾶλλον; ἢ ὅτι ἐπὶ
τοὺς πόρους προσπεφύκασιν, ἐν οἷς ὀλίγον ὂν τὸ
25 θερμὸν ταχὺ ὑπὸ τοῦ ψυχροῦ κρατούμενον ποιεῖ
τὴν ἀλγηδόνα;

Διὰ τί τοῦ ψυχροῦ μᾶλλον αἰσθάνονται οἱ ὀδόντες
ἢ τοῦ θερμοῦ, ἡ δὲ σὰρξ τοὐναντίον; πότερον ὅτι
ἡ μὲν σὰρξ τοῦ μέσου καὶ εὔκρατος, οἱ δὲ ὀδόντες
ψυχροί, ὥστε τοῦ ἐναντίου μᾶλλον αἰσθητικοί; ἢ
30 διότι λεπτῶν πόρων εἰσίν, ἐν οἷς μικρὸν τὸ θερμόν,
ὥστε ταχὺ πάσχουσιν ὑπὸ τοῦ ἐναντίου; ἡ δὲ
σὰρξ θερμή, ὥστε οὐδὲν πάσχει ὑπὸ τοῦ ψυχροῦ,
τοῦ δὲ θερμοῦ ταχὺ αἰσθάνεται· ὥσπερ γὰρ πῦρ
ἐπὶ πυρὶ γίνεται.

Διὰ τί ἡ γλῶττα σημαντικὸν πολλῶν; καὶ γὰρ
τῶν πυρετῶν ἐν τοῖς ὀξέσι νοσήμασιν, καὶ ἐὰν

224

BOOK XXXIV

PROBLEMS CONNECTED WITH THE MOUTH AND WHAT IS IN THE MOUTH

WHY are men with porous teeth not long-lived[a] ? 1
Is it because all long-lived creatures have more teeth ?
For instance, the male has more than the female, men
more than women, and rams more than ewes. So
those with porous teeth would seem to resemble those
with a smaller number.

Why is it that teeth, though stronger than flesh, are 2
yet more sensitive to cold ? Is it because they are
attached to channels in which the heat, being small,
is quickly mastered by the cold and causes pain ?

Why are the teeth more sensitive to cold than to 3
heat, while it is just the opposite with the flesh ? Is
it because flesh partakes of the mean and is luke-
warm, whereas the teeth are cold, so that they are
more sensitive to their opposite ? Or is it because
they consist of narrow pores in which there is little
heat, so that they are quickly affected by the opposite ?
But the flesh is warm, so that it does not suffer from
the cold, but is quickly affected by heat ; for it is as
if fire were added to fire.

Why does the tongue indicate many things ? For 4
in acute diseases it is a sign of fever, especially if it

[a] *Cf.* Book X. 48.

963 b

35 χάλαζαι ἐνῶσιν· καὶ τῶν ποικίλων προβάτων
ποικίλαι. ἢ ὅτι ὑγρότητος δεκτικόν, καὶ ἐπὶ τῷ
πνεύμονι ἐπίκειται, οὗ ἡ ἀρχὴ ἐπὶ τῶν πυρετῶν;
πολύχροα δὲ πάντα διὰ τὴν πολύχροιαν τῶν
ὑγρῶν· βάπτεται δὲ πρῶτον δι' οὗ πρῶτον ἠθεῖται·
ἡ δὲ γλῶττα τοιοῦτον. αἵ τε χάλαζαι διὰ τὸ
40 σομφὴν εἶναι συλλέγονται· ἔστι γὰρ ἡ χάλαζα
οἰονεὶ ἴονθος ἄπεπτος ἐν τοῖς ἐντός.

964 a

Διὰ τί ἡ γλῶττα γλυκεῖα μὲν οὐ γίνεται, πικρὰ
δὲ καὶ ἁλμυρὰ καὶ ὀξεῖα; ἢ ὅτι διαφθοραὶ ταῦτ'
ἐστίν, τῆς δὲ φύσεως οὐκ αἰσθάνεται;

Διὰ τί ὅσας ἂν χρόας ἔχῃ τὸ δέρμα, τοσαύτας
5 ἔχει καὶ ἡ γλῶττα; πότερον ὅτι ἓν μέρος ἐστὶν
ὥσπερ ἄλλο τι τῶν ἔξωθεν, ἀλλ' ἐντὸς περιείληπται·
διὰ δὲ τὸ λεπτὸν εἶναι ταύτῃ τὸ δέρμα καὶ ἡ μικρὰ
ποικιλία ἐμφαίνεται. ἢ διότι τὸ ὕδωρ ἐστὶν ὃ
ποιεῖ μεταβάλλειν τὰς χρόας; ἡ δὲ γλῶττα
μάλιστα πάσχει ὑπὸ τοῦ πόματος.

10 Διὰ τί ἐκ τοῦ στόματος καὶ θερμὸν καὶ ψυχρὸν
πνέουσιν; φυσῶσι μὲν γὰρ ψυχρόν, ἀάζουσι δὲ
θερμόν. σημεῖον δὲ ὅτι θερμαίνει, ἐὰν πλησίον
προσαγάγῃ τις τοῦ στόματος τὴν χεῖρα. ἢ ἀμφο-
τέρως ὁ ἀὴρ κινούμενος θερμός;[1] ὁ δὲ φυσῶν
κινεῖ τὸν ἀέρα οὐκ ἀθρόως, ἀλλὰ διὰ στενοῦ τοῦ
15 στόματος· ὀλίγον οὖν ἐκπνέων πολὺν κινεῖ τὸν
θύραθεν, ἐν ᾧ τὸ θερμὸν ὂν τὸ ἐκ τοῦ στόματος
οὐ φαίνεται δι' ὀλιγότητα. ὁ δὲ ἀάζων ἀθρόον
ἐκπνεῖ· διὸ θερμόν. ἔστι γὰρ φυσασμοῦ τὸ[2] διὰ-

---

[1] θερμός suggested by Ruelle from Th. G. : ψυχρός Ruelle's
text.

has pustules on it ; and the tongues of piebald sheep are also piebald. Is it because it is receptive of moisture and lies near to the region of the lung, which is the origin of fevers ? Things are many-coloured because liquids are many-coloured. For that through which liquids first percolate is coloured by them; and the tongue has this characteristic. Pustules collect on the tongue because it is porous ; for the pustule is a kind of pimple which is not internally concocted.

Why does the tongue never become sweet, but 5 bitter, salt, and acrid ? Is it because such qualities are corruptions and the tongue cannot perceive its own nature ?

Why does the tongue have as many colours as the 6 skin has ? Is it because it is the one part which is like any other outside part, though it is enclosed in the mouth ? But because the skin in this part is thin, even a small variation in colour becomes apparent. Or is it because it is water which is responsible for a change of colour ? And the tongue is most affected by drink.

Why do men breathe both hot and cold from the 7 mouth ? For they blow out cold but breathe out hot breath. There is proof that the breath causes heat, if one puts the hand near to the mouth. Or is the air moved hot in both cases ? But the man who blows hard does not move the air in a mass, but through a narrow mouth ; so, although he only blows out a little breath, he moves the air over a long range, in which case the heat coming from the mouth is not noticeable, because there is little of it. But the man who breathes out emits the breath all at once ; hence it is hot. For it is the characteristic of hard blowing to

---

² τὸ Forster : τῷ Ruelle.

964 a

φέρειν τῇ συστροφῇ· ὁ δ' ἀασμὸς ἀθρόου ἔκπνευσις.

Διὰ τί, ἐὰν σφόδρα καὶ ἀθρόον ἐκπνεύσωσιν, 8
20 ἀδυνατοῦσι πάλιν ἐκπνεῦσαι; ὁμοίως δὲ ἔχει καὶ ἐπὶ τοῦ ἀναπνεῦσαι· ἀδυνατοῦσι γὰρ δὶς ἐφεξῆς ποιεῖν αὐτό. ἢ ὅτι τὸ μὲν δίωσίς τίς ἐστι, τὸ δὲ συναγωγὴ τόπου; ἃ ἄχρι τινός ἐστι δυνατὰ γίνεσθαι. φανερὸν οὖν ὅτι ἐναλλὰξ ἀνάγκη ἄμφω γίνεσθαι, καὶ ἀδύνατον δὶς ἐφεξῆς.

25 Διὰ τί ἑτέρου τόπου ὄντος ᾗ τὰ σῖτα καὶ τὸ 9
ποτὸν διεξέρχεται καὶ ᾗ ἀναπνέομεν, ἐὰν μείζω ψωμὸν καταπίωμεν, πνιγόμεθα; οὐδὲν δὴ ἄτοπον· οὐ γὰρ μόνον ἐάν τι ἐμπέσῃ εἰς τὸν τόπον τοῦτον, ἀλλὰ κἂν ἔτι φραχθῇ, οὕτως μᾶλλον πνιγόμεθα.
30 ταῦτα δὲ παράλληλά ἐστιν, καθ' ὅ τε τὰ σιτία δεχόμεθα καὶ καθ' ὃ ἀναπνέομεν. ὅταν οὖν ἐμπέσῃ μείζων ψωμός, καὶ ἡ ἀναπνοὴ συμφράττει, ὥστε μὴ εἶναι τῷ πνεύματι ἔξοδον.

Διὰ τί, ὅσοι τὴν διὰ χειρὸς τομὴν ἔχουσι δι' 10
ὅλης, μακροβιώτατοι; ἢ διότι τὰ ἄναρθρα βραχύ-
35 βια καὶ ἀσθενῆ; σημεῖον δὲ τῆς μὲν ἀσθενείας τὰ νέα, τῆς δὲ βραχυβιότητος τὰ ἔνυγρα. δῆλον ἄρα ὅτι τὰ ἠρθρωμένα τοὐναντίον. τοιαῦτα δέ, ὧν καὶ τὰ φύσει ἄναρθρα μάλιστα ἤρθρωται. τῆς δὲ χειρὸς τὸ ἔσω ἀναρθρότατον.

Διὰ τί ἐν τῷ μακρὸν ἀναπνεῖν ἑλκόντων μὲν 11
964 b εἴσω τὸ πνεῦμα συμπίπτει ἡ κοιλία, ἐκπνεόντων δὲ πληροῦται; πιθανὸν δ' ἐστὶ τοὐναντίον συμβαίνειν. ἢ ὅτι τῶν μὲν ἀναπνεόντων συμπιεζου-

228

drive along the air in puffs ; but gentle breathing is an expulsion of the air all at once.

Why is it that, if a man exhales violently and 8 all at once, he cannot exhale again ? A similar thing is true of inhaling ; for men cannot do it twice in succession. Is it because the former is a sort of dilatation, and the latter is a contraction of the region ? Both these can only be carried to a certain limit. So it is evident that the two processes must alternate, and cannot be done twice in succession.

Why is it that although the channels by which food 9 and drink pass and that by which we breathe are different, yet if we swallow too large a piece of food, we choke ? This is not surprising, for not only do we choke if anything falls into this region, but if it is closed we choke all the more. Now the channels (that by which we absorb food and that by which we breathe) lie side by side. So when too large a piece of food goes down, the breath passage also is closed, so that there is no exit for the breath.

Why is it that those with whom the life-line tra- 10 verses the whole hand are long-lived ? Is it because all unarticulated creatures are short-lived and weak ? The young are instances of weakness, and water-animals of short life. So obviously the articulated creatures must be the opposite ; that is such creatures, as those whose naturally unarticulated parts are best articulated. And the inside of the hand has least articulation.

Why is it that in taking a long breath, when one 11 draws in the breath the stomach contracts, but when one exhales the stomach inflates ? The opposite might be expected to happen. Is it because when men

964 b

μένη ταῖς πλευραῖς κάτω, καθάπερ αἱ φῦσαι,
προσογκεῖν φαίνεται;

5 Διὰ τί ἀναπνέομεν; ἢ καθάπερ τὸ ὑγρὸν εἰς 12
πνεῦμα διαλύεται, οὕτως καὶ τὸ πνεῦμα εἰς τὸ
πῦρ; τὸ τῆς φύσεως οὖν θερμὸν ὅταν τὸ πολὺ τοῦ
πνεύματος πῦρ ποιήσῃ, ἀλγηδόνα ἐμποιεῖ, τοῖς
δὲ πόροις καὶ ὄγκον· διόπερ ἐξωθοῦμεν τὸ πῦρ
μετὰ τοῦ πνεύματος. ὅταν δ' ἐξέλθῃ τὸ πνεῦμα
10 καὶ τὸ πῦρ,[1] συμπιπτόντων τῶν πόρων καὶ καταψυχομένων ἀλγηδόνες γίνονται· ἕλκομεν οὖν τὸ
πνεῦμα πάλιν. εἶτα ἀνοίξαντες τοῦ σώματος τοὺς
πόρους καὶ βοηθήσαντες, πάλιν γίνεται τὸ πῦρ, καὶ
πάλιν ἀλγοῦντες ἐκπέμπομεν, καὶ διὰ τέλους τοῦτο
πράττομεν, καθάπερ καὶ σκαρδαμύσσομεν κατὰ τὸ
15 καταψύχεσθαι τὸ περὶ τὸν ὀφθαλμὸν σῶμα καὶ
ξηραίνεσθαι. καὶ βαδίζομεν οὖν προσέχοντες τῇ
βαδίσει τὸν νοῦν, κυβερνωμένης δὲ τῆς διανοίας
αὐτοῖς * * * τοῦτον οὖν τὸν τρόπον καὶ τὰ περὶ
τὴν ἀναπνοὴν ποιοῦμεν· μηχανώμενοι γὰρ τὸν ἀέρα
20 ἕλκειν ἀναπνέομεν, καὶ πάλιν ἕλκομεν.

[1] μετὰ . . . τὸ πῦρ: Ruelle's text omits this line.

inhale the stomach is compressed by the ribs below and then like bellows seems to expand ?

Why do we inhale ? Does breath dissolve into 12 fire, just as moisture does into air ? So the natural heat, when the greater part of the breath produces fire, causes pain and pressure on the channels ; consequently we expel the fire with the breath. Now when the breath and the fire have gone forth, as the channels contract and cool, there are pains ; so we draw in the breath again. Then when we have re-opened the channels of the body and reinforced them, fire forms again, and as we are again in discomfort we expel the breath, and go on doing so indefinitely, just as we blink because of the chilling and drying of the region in the neighbourhood of the eye. Just, then, as we walk without paying attention to our walking but with just the intellect to guide . . .[a] We act in the same way in breathing ; for we breathe by contriving to draw in the breath, and then we draw it in again.

[a] There is a lacuna in the ms. here. Th. G. has an adverb " conveniently," which would suit the context.

ΛΕ

ΟΣΑ ΠΕΡΙ ΤΑ ΥΠΟ ΤΗΝ ΑΦΗΝ

Διὰ τί μᾶλλον φρίττομεν ἑτέρου θιγόντος πως 1
ἢ αὐτοὶ ἡμῶν; ἢ ὅτι αἰσθητικωτέρα ἡ ἁφὴ τοῦ
ἀλλοτρίου ἢ ἡ τοῦ οἰκείου; τὸ γὰρ συμφυὲς
25 ἀναίσθητον. καὶ φοβερώτερον τὸ λάθρα καὶ ἐξ-
απιναίως γινόμενον, ὁ δὲ φόβος κατάψυξις· ἡ δὲ
ἀλλοτρία ἁφὴ πρὸς τὴν οἰκείαν ἄμφω ταῦτα ἔχει.
καὶ ὅλως δὲ παθητικὸν ἕκαστον πέφυκεν ἢ μᾶλλον
ἢ μόνον ὑπ' ἄλλου ἢ ὑφ' αὑτοῦ, οἷον καὶ ἐπὶ τοῦ
γαργαλίζεσθαι συμβαίνει.

30 Διὰ τί γαργαλίζονται τὰς μασχάλας καὶ τὰ ἐντὸς 2
τῶν ποδῶν; ἢ διὰ τὴν λεπτότητα τοῦ δέρματος;
καὶ ὧν ἀσυνήθης ἡ ἁφή, οἷον τούτων καὶ τοῦ
ὠτός;

Διὰ τί φρίττομεν οὐκ ἐπὶ τοῖς αὐτοῖς πάντες; 3
ἢ ὅτι οὐδ' ἐπὶ τοῖς αὐτοῖς πάντες ἡδόμεθα, ὥσπερ
35 οὐδὲ λυπούμεθα ἐπὶ τοῖς αὐτοῖς πάντες; ὁμοίως
δὴ οὐ φρίττομεν ἐπὶ τοῖς αὐτοῖς· ἔστι γὰρ ἡ αὐτὴ
κατάψυξίς τις. διὸ οἱ μὲν τοῦ ἱματίου δακνομένου
φρίττουσιν, οἱ δὲ πρίονος ἀκονουμένου ἢ ἑλκομένου,
οἱ δὲ κισήρεως τεμνομένης, οἱ δὲ ὄνου λίθον
ἀλοῦντος.

232

BOOK XXXV

Problems connected with Touch

Why do we shudder more readily when someone 1 else touches us anywhere than when we touch ourselves? Is it because another's touch provokes sensation more readily than our own? For what is an organic part of us is not readily perceived. Also what is done to us covertly and unexpectedly is more alarming, and alarm involves chilling. Now the touch of another has both these qualities in comparison with our own touch. Speaking generally, every passive sensation is either produced solely by someone else or to a greater degree than by oneself, as happens with tickling.

Why is one ticklish under the arms and on the 2 soles of the feet? Is it due to the thinness of the skin and because some parts are not accustomed to touch, such as these and the ear?

Why do we not all shudder at the same things? Is 3 it because we do not all enjoy the same things, just as we are not all pained by the same things? Similarly we do not all shudder at the same things. In all cases it is the same chilling process. So some of us shudder when a cloak is torn, some when a saw is sharpened or drawn across, others at the cutting of pumice-stone, and others again when the millstone is grinding on stone.

Διὰ τί τοῦ μὲν θέρους ὄντος θερμοῦ, τοῦ δὲ 4
935 a χειμῶνος ψυχροῦ, τὰ σώματα θιγγανόντων ψυχει-
νότερά ἐστι τοῦ θέρους ἢ τοῦ χειμῶνος; πότερον
ὅτι ὁ ἱδρὼς καὶ ἡ ἴδισις καταψύχει τὰ σώματα,
τοῦτο δ᾽ ἐν μὲν τῷ θέρει γίνεται, ἐν δὲ τῷ χειμῶνι
οὔ; ἢ ὅτι ἀντιπεριίσταται ἐναντίως τὸ ψυχρὸν καὶ
5 τὸ θερμὸν τῇ ὥρᾳ, καὶ ἔσω φεύγει ἐν τῷ θέρει,
διὸ καὶ ἱδρῶτα ἀνίησιν· ἐν δὲ τῷ χειμῶνι ἀποστέγει
τὸ ψῦχος καὶ ἀτμίζει τὸ σῶμα ὥσπερ ἡ γῆ;

Διὰ τί φρίττουσιν αἱ τρίχες ἐν τῷ δέρματι; ἢ 5
ὅταν σπάσωσιν τὸ δέρμα, εἰκότως ἐξανέστησαν;
10 συσπῶσι δὲ καὶ ὑπὸ ῥίγους καὶ ὑπ᾽ ἄλλων παθῶν.

Διὰ τί αὐτὸς αὑτὸν οὐθεὶς γαργαλίζει; ἢ ὅτι 6
καὶ ὑπ᾽ ἄλλου ἧττον, ἐὰν προαίσθηται, μᾶλλον δ᾽,
ἂν μὴ ὁρᾷ; ὥσθ᾽ ἥκιστα γαργαλισθήσεται, ὅταν
μὴ λανθάνῃ τοῦτο πάσχων. ἔστιν δὲ ὁ γέλως
15 παρακοπή τις καὶ ἀπάτη. διὸ καὶ τυπτόμενοι εἰς
τὰς φρένας γελῶσιν· οὐ γὰρ ὁ τυχὼν τόπος ἐστὶν
ᾧ γελῶσιν. τὸ δὲ λαθραῖον ἀπατητικόν. διὰ
τοῦτο καὶ γίνεται ὁ γέλως καὶ οὐ γίνεται ὑφ᾽
αὑτοῦ.

Διὰ τί ποτε τὰ χείλη μάλιστα γαργαλιζόμεθα; 7
ἢ διότι δεῖ τὸ γαργαλιζόμενον μὴ πρόσω τοῦ
20 αἰσθητικοῦ εἶναι; ἔστι δὲ τὰ χείλη περὶ τὸν τόπον
τοῦτον μάλιστα. διὰ τοῦτο δὲ γαργαλίζεται τὰ
χείλη τῶν περὶ τὴν κεφαλὴν τόπων, ἅ ἐστιν
εὔσαρκα, εὐκινητότατα οὖν μάλιστά ἐστιν.

Διὰ τί, ἐάν τις τὸν περὶ τὰς μασχάλας τόπον 8
κνήσῃ, ἐκγελῶσιν, ἐὰν δέ τινα ἄλλον, οὔ; ἢ διὰ
25 τί πτερῷ τὰς ῥῖνας κνήσαντες πτάρνυνται; ἢ

---

[a] The midriff is the muscle separating the heart and lungs

Why is it that, although summer is hot and winter **4** cold, bodies are colder to the touch in summer than in winter ? Is it because sweat and perspiration chill the body, and this occurs in summer but not in winter ? Is it because the compression of cold and heat takes place inversely to the season of the year, and in the summer the cold escapes inwards, so that it drives out the sweat, whereas in the winter the cold keeps the sweat inside and the body (like the earth) causes it to evaporate ?

Why do the hairs bristle on the skin ? Is it natural **5** that they should stand on end when one contracts the skin ? And the skin contracts through cold and other affections.

Why can no one tickle himself ? Is it for the same **6** reason that one feels another's tickling less if one anticipates it, and more if one does not see it coming ? So that one will be least ticklish when one is aware that it is happening. Now laughter is a form of derangement and deception. This is why men laugh when struck in the midriff [a] ; for it is not a chance part with which we laugh. Now what happens un- awares deceives us. This is why laughter occurs and is not produced by oneself.

Why are we most ticklish on the lips ? Is it be- **7** cause the tickled part must not be far from the sense- organ ? And the lips are particularly near this region. For this reason also the lips are the most ticklish part in the region of the head, because they are fleshy and so are easily moved.

Why is it that men laugh, if they are tickled about **8** the armpits, but not in any other place ? Or why do men sneeze when their nose is tickled with a feather ?

from the stomach and was in Greek theory the seat of the mind.

965 a

τόποι εἰσὶ τῶν φλεβίων, ὧν ἢ καταψυχομένων ἢ
τοὐναντίον πασχόντων ὑγραίνεται, ἢ εἰς πνεῦμα
ἐκ τοῦ ὑγροῦ διαλύεται; ὥσπερ ἐὰν τὰς ἐπὶ τοῦ
τραχήλου πιέσῃ τις φλέβας καθεύδουσιν ἡμῖν,
ἡδονὴ θαυμασία[1] τίς ἐστιν· τοῦτο δέ, ὅταν πλέον τὸ
30 πνεῦμα ἐγγένηται, ἀθρόον ἔξω ἀφίεμεν. ὡσαύτως
καὶ ἐπὶ πταρμῷ τῷ πτερῷ διαθερμάναντες καὶ
κνήσαντες διελύσαμεν εἰς πνεῦμα· πλέονος δὲ γενομένου ἐξεώσαμεν.

Διὰ τί μετὰ τὰ σιτία φρίττομεν πολλάκις; ἢ 9
ὅτι ψυχρὰ εἰσπορευόμενα ἀπὸ πρώτης κρατεῖ
35 μᾶλλον τοῦ φυσικοῦ θερμοῦ ἢ κρατεῖται;

Διὰ τί τὸ περιαγόμενον ἐναλλὰξ τοῖς δακτύλοις 1
δύο φαίνεται; ἢ διότι δυσὶν αἰσθητηρίοις ἁπτό-
μεθα; τοῖς γὰρ ἐκτὸς[2] τῶν δακτύλων, κατὰ φύσιν
ἔχοντες τὴν χεῖρα, ἀμφοτέροις οὐ δυνατὸν θιγεῖν.[3]

---

[1] καθεύδουσιν ἡμῖν, ἡδονὴ θαυμασία Ross : καθεύδουσιν. ἡ
μὲν ἡδονὴ θερμασία Ruelle.
[2] ἐκτὸς Forster : ἐντὸς Ruelle.
[3] θιγεῖν Ross : εἰπεῖν Ruelle.

236

Is it because these are in the neighbourhood of small veins, and when these are either chilled or suffering the opposite effect they grow moist, and from the moisture there is dissolution into breath ? So if some-one compresses the veins on the neck when we are asleep a wonderfully pleasant sensation is caused. And when the breath becomes considerable we emit it all at once. Just in the same way, in sneezing by warming with a feather and tickling, we dissolve the moisture into breath ; and when it becomes excessive we expel it.

Why do we often shiver after food ? Is it because the cold introduced from the first rather exercises control over the natural heat than suffers control ?

Why does one object feel as if it were two if it is grasped in the crossed fingers ? Is it because we are touching it with two sensitive parts ? For when we hold our hand naturally, we cannot touch an object with the outside of two fingers at once.

ΟΣΑ ΠΕΡΙ ΠΡΟΣΩΠΟΝ

Διὰ τί τοῦ προσώπου τὰς εἰκόνας ποιοῦνται; 1
πότερον ὅτι τοῦτο δηλοῖ ποῖοί τινες; ἢ ὅτι μάλιστα
γινώσκεται;

Διὰ τί τὸ πρόσωπον ἰδίουσι μάλιστα, ἀσαρκό- 2
5 τατον ὄν; ἢ διότι εὐΐδρωτα μὲν ὅσα ὕφυγρα καὶ
ἀραιά, ἡ δὲ κεφαλὴ τοιαύτη; ὑγρότητα γὰρ
οἰκείαν ἔχει πλείστην. δηλοῦσι δ' αἱ φλέβες
τείνουσαι ἐντεῦθεν, καὶ οἱ κατάρροι γινόμενοι ἐξ
αὐτῆς, καὶ ὁ ἐγκέφαλος ὑγρός, καὶ οἱ πόροι πολλοί·
σημεῖον δ' αἱ τρίχες, ὅτι πολλοὶ πόροι εἰσὶ πε-
10 ραίνοντες ἔξω. οὔκουν ἐκ τῶν κάτω ὁ ἱδρώς,
ἀλλ' ἐκ τῆς κεφαλῆς γίνεται. διὸ ἰδίουσιν καὶ
πρῶτον μάλιστα τὸ μέτωπον· ὑπόκειται γὰρ τὸ
πρῶτον. τὸ δ' ὑγρὸν κάτω ῥεῖ, ἀλλ' οὐκ ἄνω.

Διὰ τί ἐν τῷ προσώπῳ μάλιστα οἱ ἴονθοι; ἢ 3
15 διότι μανὸς ὁ τόπος καὶ ὑγρότητα ἔχει; σημεῖον
δὲ ἥ τε τῶν τριχῶν ἔκφυσις καὶ ἡ τῶν αἰσθήσεων
δύναμις· ὁ δὲ ἴονθος ὥσπερ ἐξάνθημα ὑγρότητός
τινος ἀπέπτου.

BOOK XXXVI

Problems connected with the Face

Why do men make likenesses of the face ? Is it 1 because this shows men's characters ? Or because the face is the part most easily recognized ?

Why does one sweat most in the face, which has 2 least flesh ? Is it because all parts which are moist and rare are most liable to sweat, and the head is of this nature ? For it contains the greatest quantity of natural moisture. This is proved by the fact that the veins stretch from the head, that catarrh comes from it, that the brain is moist, and that there are many pores in it ; the hair proves that there are many pores extending outwards. So sweat comes not from the lower parts, but from the head. So the forehead sweats first and most ; for it lies in the first place. And moisture flows downwards, not upwards.

Why do pimples appear most on the face ? Is it 3 because that region is porous and contains moisture ? The growth of hair and the power of sensation proves this ; and a pimple is a kind of florescence of un-concocted moisture.

ΟΣΑ ΠΕΡΙ ΟΛΟΝ ΤΟ ΣΩΜΑ

20 Διὰ τί ἀεὶ τοῦ σώματος ῥέοντος, καὶ τῆς ἀπ- 1
ορροῆς γινομένης ἐκ τῶν περιττωμάτων, οὐ κου-
φίζεται τὸ σῶμα, ἐὰν μὴ ἰδίῃ; ἢ διότι ἐλάττων
ἡ ἔκκρισις γίνεται; ὅταν γὰρ ἐξ ὑγροῦ μεταβάλῃ
εἰς ἀέρα, πλέον γίνεται ἐξ ἐλάττονος· τὸ γὰρ
25 διακρινόμενον πλέον, ὥστε ἐν πλείονι χρόνῳ ἡ
ἔκκρισις.

Διὰ τί δὲ τοῦτο; ἢ διότι δι' ἐλαττόνων πόρων 2
ἡ ἔξοδός ἐστιν; τὸ γὰρ γλίσχρον καὶ τὸ κολλῶδες
μετὰ μὲν τοῦ ὑγροῦ ἐκκρίνεται διὰ τὴν κατάμιξιν,
μετὰ δὲ τοῦ πνεύματος ἀδυνατεῖ. μάλιστα δὲ
30 τοῦτ' ἐστὶ τὸ λυποῦν. διὸ καὶ οἱ ἔμετοι τῶν
ἱδρώτων κουφίζουσι μᾶλλον, ὅτι συνεξάγουσι
τοῦτο, ἅτε παχύτεροι καὶ σωματωδέστεροι ὄντες.
ἢ καὶ ὅτι τῇ μὲν σαρκὶ πόρρω οὗτος ὁ τόπος, ἐν
ᾧ τὸ γλίσχρον καὶ τὸ κολλῶδες, ὥστε ἔργον μετα-
στῆσαι, τῇ δὲ κοιλίᾳ ἐγγύς; ἢ γὰρ ἐν ταύτῃ
35 γίνεται ἢ πλησίον· διὸ καὶ δυσεξάγωγος ἄλλως.

Διὰ τί αἱ τρίψεις σαρκοῦσιν; ἢ ὅτι αὐξητικώ- 3
τατον τῶν ἐν τῷ σώματι τὸ θερμόν ἐστιν; τοῦ
μὲν γὰρ ἐνυπάρχοντος μείζους οἱ ὄγκοι γίνονται
διὰ τὸ ἀεὶ αὐτὸ ἐν κινήσει εἶναι καὶ εἰς τὸ ἄνω
240

BOOK XXXVII

Problems connected with the Body Generally

Why is it that, although there is always a flow in 1
the body as well as the emission from waste products,
the body does not grow light, unless it sweats ? Is it
because the excretion is too little ? For when there
is a change from liquid to air, more is formed from
less ; for what separates out is more, so that the secre-
tion takes longer to act.

But why does this happen ? Is it because the 2
efflux is through fewer channels ? For the viscous and
sticky element is excreted with the liquid owing to
their being mixed, but cannot be excreted with the
breath. This is especially what causes discomfort.
So vomiting causes more lightening than sweat,
because it carries this viscous matter with it, being
thicker and more corporeal. Or is it also because the
region in which the viscous and sticky element lies is
far away from the flesh, so that it is hard to change its
position, but it is near to the stomach ? For it is
formed in the stomach or near to it ; so it is hard to
remove in any other way.

Why does massage make flesh ? Is it because heat 3
is most powerful in causing growth in the body ? For
the bulk grows greater than before because the body
is always in motion, and the moisture in us is travelling

241

966 a φέρεσθαι καὶ πνευματοῦν τὰ ἐν ἡμῖν ὑγρά, ὃ ἐν
τῇ τρίψει γίνεται· ἐκλείποντος δὲ φθίνει καὶ
ἐλαττοῦται τὸ σῶμα. ἢ ὅτι ὀγκοτέρα τῆς τροφῆς
γίνεται ἡ σὰρξ διὰ τὴν θερμασίαν; ἅπαν γὰρ τὸ
θερμὸν ἐπισπαστικὸν τοῦ ὑγροῦ ἐστίν, ἡ δ' εἰς
5 τὴν σάρκα διαδιδομένη τροφὴ ὑγρά ἐστι, καὶ
ἐπιδέχεται τὴν τροφὴν μᾶλλον διὰ τὴν ἀραίωσιν·
ἀραιοτέρα γὰρ γινομένη μᾶλλον δύναται δέχεσθαι
ὥσπερ σπογγιά. ἡ δὲ τρῖψις εὔπνουν καὶ ἀραιὰν
ποιεῖ τὴν σάρκα, καὶ κωλύει συστάσεις γίνεσθαι
κατὰ τὸ σῶμα. τούτου δὲ μὴ ὄντος οὐδὲ συντήξεις
10 γίνονται· αἱ γὰρ ἀτροφίαι καὶ αἱ συντήξεις ἐκ τῶν
ἀθροισθέντων εἰσίν. εὐπνούστερα δὲ καὶ ἀραιότερα
καὶ ὁμαλέστερα γινόμενα εἰκὸς μᾶλλον ὀγκοῦσθαι·
τῆς τε γὰρ τροφῆς δεκτικώτερα καὶ τῶν ἐκκρίσεων
προετικώτερα γίνεται, ὅτι οὐ δεῖ πυκνοῦν τὴν
15 σάρκα πρὸς ὑγίειαν, ἀλλ' ἀραιοῦν· ὥσπερ γὰρ
πόλις ὑγιεινή ἐστι καὶ τόπος εὔπνους (διὸ καὶ ἡ
θάλαττα ὑγιεινή), οὕτω καὶ σῶμα τὸ εὔπνουν
μᾶλλον ὑγιεινόν ἐστι τοῦ ἐναντίως ἔχοντος. δεῖ
γὰρ ἢ μὴ ὑπάρχειν μηδέν, ἢ τούτου ὡς τάχιστα
ἀπαλλάττεσθαι· καὶ δεῖ οὕτως ἔχειν τὸ σῶμα
20 ὥστε λαμβάνον εὐθὺς ἐκκρίνειν τὴν περίττωσιν,
καὶ εἶναι ἐν κινήσει ἀεὶ καὶ μηδέποτε ἠρεμεῖν.
τὸ μὲν γὰρ μένον σήπεται, ὥσπερ καὶ ὕδωρ τὸ
μὴ κινούμενον· σηπόμενον δὲ νόσον ποιεῖ· τὸ δὲ
ἐκκρινόμενον πρὸ τοῦ διαφθαρῆναι χωρίζεται.
τοῦτο οὖν πυκνουμένης μὲν τῆς σαρκὸς οὐ γίνεται
(ὡσπερεὶ γὰρ ἐμφράττονται οἱ πόροι), ἀραιουμένης
25 δὲ συμβαίνει. διὸ καὶ οὐ δεῖ ἐν τῷ ἡλίῳ γυμνὸν
βαδίζειν (συνίσταται γὰρ ἡ σὰρξ καὶ κομιδῇ

upwards and becoming vaporized, which occurs as the result of massage ; when this fails, the body withers and grows smaller. Or does the flesh become more bulky owing to the heating effect of food ? For all that is hot attracts liquid, and the food which is continually being distributed into the flesh is moist, and the flesh admits food more readily because of its rarity ; for when it becomes rare it can admit it more easily, as a sponge does. Now massage makes the flesh airy and fine, and prevents accumulations from forming in the body. When there is no such condition, no wastage takes place ; for atrophy and wasting arise from accumulations. It is quite natural that what is more airy, rarer and more consistent should also become more bulky ; for such things are more capable of accepting food and more able to eject secretions, because for health one does not need to thicken the flesh but to refine it ; for just as a city or a place is healthy if well-ventilated (this is why the sea is healthy), so also a well-ventilated body is in a healthier condition than one in an opposite condition. For either there should be no waste product from the first or the body should get rid of it as quickly as possible ; the body, then, should be in such a condition that on receiving the waste product it immediately excretes it, and it should be in motion and never still. For what is stagnant decays, just as water does which does not move, and decay produces disease ; but what is excreted is passed away before it decays. So this excretion does not take place when the body is densified (for the channels are, so to speak, obstructed), but it does when it is rarefied. This is why it is not wise to walk naked in the sun (for the flesh grows dense and acquires a completely

966 a

ἀποσαρκοῦται· τὸ μὲν γὰρ ἐντὸς ὑγρὸν διαμένει,
τὸ δ' ἐπιπολῆς ἀπαλλάττεται ἐξατμιζόμενον,
ὥσπερ καὶ τὰ κρέα τὰ ὀπτὰ τῶν ἐφθῶν μᾶλλον
τὰ ἐντὸς ὑγρά ἐστιν) οὐδὲ τὰ στήθη γυμνὰ ἔχοντα
80 βαδίζειν ἐν ἡλίῳ (ἀπὸ γὰρ τῶν ἄριστα ᾠκοδομη-
μένων τοῦ σώματος ὁ ἥλιος ἀφαιρεῖ, ὃ ἥκιστα
δεῖται ἀφαιρέσεως), ἀλλὰ μᾶλλον τὰ ἐντὸς ξηραν-
τέον. ἐκεῖθεν μὲν οὖν διὰ τὸ πόρρω εἶναι, ἐὰν
μὴ μετὰ πόνου, οὐκ ἔστιν ἱδρῶτα ἄγειν· ἀπὸ
τούτων δὲ διὰ τὸ πρόχειρα εἶναι ῥᾴδιον ἀναλῶσαι
τὸ ὑγρόν.

85 Διὰ τί ψυχθέντες ἀπὸ τῆς αὐτῆς θερμασίας καιό- 4
μεθα μᾶλλον καὶ ἀλγοῦμεν; πότερον διὰ τὴν
πυκνότητα στέγει ἡ σὰρξ τὸ προσπῖπτον θερμόν;
διὸ μόλυβδος ἐρίου θερμότερος. ἢ βίαιος γίνεται
τοῦ θερμοῦ ἡ δίοδος διὰ τὸ πεπηγέναι ὑπὸ ψυχροῦ
τὸ σῶμα;

966 b Διὰ τί αἱ ξηροτριβίαι στερεὰν τὴν σάρκα παρα- 5
σκευάζουσιν; ἢ ὅτι διὰ τὴν τρῖψιν τῆς θερμασίας
ἐπιγινομένης τὸ ὑγρὸν καταναλίσκεται; πρὸς δὲ
τούτοις ἡ σὰρξ τριβομένη πυκνοῦται· ἅπαντα δὲ
5 ὅσα πλείονος τρίψεως τυγχάνει πυκνοῦται καὶ
στερεὰ γίνεται. θεωρῆσαι δὲ τὸ τοιοῦτον ἔστιν
ἐπὶ πολλῶν· τὸ γὰρ σταῖς ἢ πηλὸς ἢ ἄλλο τι τῶν
τοιούτων, ἐὰν μὲν ὕδωρ ἐπιχέας ἕλκῃς, ὑγρὰ καὶ
κλυδῶντα διαμένει, ἐὰν δὲ πλείω τρῖψιν προσ-
αγάγῃς, πυκνοῦταί τε καὶ στερεοῦται ταχέως καὶ
γλίσχρα γίνεται.

10 Διὰ τί αἱ τρίψεις μᾶλλον σαρκοῦσι τῶν δρόμων; 6
ἢ ὅτι οἱ μὲν δρόμοι περιψύχουσιν τὴν σάρκα καὶ
οὐ δεκτικὴν τροφῆς παρασκευάζουσιν, ἀλλὰ τὰ
μὲν συσσείεται κάτω, τὰ δ' ἐπιπολῆς[1] πολλοῦ τοῦ
244

fleshy consistency ; for the internal moisture remains there, but that on the surface evaporates and disappears, just as in baked meat the inside is moister than in boiled). Nor should one walk in the sun with a bare chest (for the sun is then drawing from the best constructed part of the body, which least needs any drawing off), but the internal parts rather require drying. From these parts, because they are far away, it is not possible to drive the sweat without great difficulty ; but from the external parts it is easy to expend the moisture, because they are near at hand.

^a Why is it that from a given heat we burn and suffer 4 more if we are cold ? Does the flesh enclose the heat striking it because of its density ? This is why lead grows hotter than wool. Or is the passage of the heat violent because the body has become set by cold ?

Why does dry massage make the flesh hard ? Is it 5 because owing to the heat engendered by the massage the moisture is expended ? But in addition to this the flesh thickens when it is rubbed ; everything which is vigorously rubbed becomes thick and hard. This can be observed in many instances ; for with dough or clay or any similar substance, if you pour water on them before you pull them out, they remain wet and watery, but if you apply more rubbing, they rapidly become dense and hard and grow viscous.

Why does massage produce more flesh than running ? 6 Is it because running chills the flesh and makes it unable to receive food, but part of the food is shaken downwards and part remains on the surface, and, when

^a Cf. Book VIII. 19.

¹ ἐπιπολῆς Bussemaker : ἐπὶ mss.

966 b

φυσικοῦ θερμοῦ ἐπιτελουμένου παντελῶς λεπτυ-
νόμενα εἰς πνεῦμα διακρίνεται; ἡ δὲ παλάμη τῇ
15 τρίψει τὴν σάρκα ἀραιὰν καὶ δεκτικὴν αὐτῆς παρασκευάζει. καὶ ἡ ἔξωθεν δὴ ἀφὴ ἐναντιουμένη διὰ
τῆς πιλήσεως τῇ φορᾷ αὐτὸν συνέχει μᾶλλον, καὶ
ἀνάκλασιν τῆς σαρκὸς ποιεῖται.

the considerable natural heat is completely exhausted, grows thin and evaporates into air ? But the palm of the hand by massage makes the flesh thin and able to receive food. Also the external contact, because it opposes the natural movement of the flesh by its pressure, contracts it and drives it back upon itself.

ΛΗ

ΟΣΑ ΠΕΡΙ ΧΡΟΑΝ

Διὰ τί τὸν μὲν κηρὸν καὶ τοὔλαιον λευκαίνει ὁ 1
ἥλιος, τὴν δὲ σάρκα μελαίνει; ἢ ὅτι τὰ μὲν λευκαίνει ἀπάγων τὸ ὕδωρ; φύσει γὰρ τὸ ὑγρὸν
μέλαν διὰ τὴν μῖξιν τοῦ γεώδους [ὕδατος], τὴν δὲ
σάρκα ἐπικαίει.

25 Διὰ τί οἱ ἁλιεῖς καὶ πορφυρεῖς καὶ ἁπλῶς οἱ τὴν 2
θάλατταν ἐργαζόμενοι πυρροί εἰσιν; πότερον ὅτι
ἡ θάλαττα θερμὴ καὶ αὐχμώδης ἐστὶ διὰ τὴν
ἅλμην; τὸ δὲ τοιοῦτον πυρρὰς ποιεῖ τὰς τρίχας,
καθάπερ ἥ τε κονία καὶ τὸ ἀρσενικόν. ἢ τὰ μὲν
30 ἐκτὸς γίνονται θερμότεροι, τὰ δ' ἐντὸς περιψύχονται
διὰ τὸ βρεχομένων αὐτῶν ἀεὶ ξηραίνεσθαι ὑπὸ τοῦ
ἡλίου τὰ πέριξ; τούτων δὲ τοῦτο πασχόντων αἱ
τρίχες ξηραινόμεναι λεπτύνονται καὶ πυρροῦνται.
καὶ πάντες δὲ οἱ πρὸς ἄρκτον πυρρότριχες καὶ
λεπτότριχές εἰσιν.

Διὰ τί οἱ μὲν ἐν ἱματίῳ δρόμοι καὶ ἡ τοῦ ἐλαίου 3
35 εἰς ἱμάτιον χρῖσις ἄχρους ποιεῖ, οἱ δὲ γυμνοὶ
δρόμοι εὔχρους; ἢ ὅτι ἡ μὲν εὔπνοια εὔχροιαν
ποιεῖ, ἡ δὲ κατάπνιξις τοὐναντίον; διὰ δὴ τὸ
συνθερμαινόμενον τὸ ἐπιπολῆς ὑγρὸν μὴ διαψύχε-
σθαι ἄχροιαν ποιεῖ. ἄμφω δὲ ταὐτὸν ποιεῖ, ἡ

248

BOOK XXXVIII

Why is it that the sun bleaches wax and oil, but 1 blackens flesh ? Is it because the sun bleaches the former by abstracting the moisture, for the moisture is black in its natural state because it is mixed with earthy matter, but it burns the flesh ?

Why do fishermen, divers for murex, and generally 2 those whose work is on the sea have red hair ? Is it because the sea is hot and a drying agent because it is salty ? Such things make hair red, just as lye and yellow orpiment do. Or do the outside parts become hotter, while the internal parts are chilled, because, when they are wet, the surrounding parts are continually being dried by the sun ? When this occurs the hair as it dries becomes thin and red. All those also who live in the north are red and thin-haired.

Why does running in a cloak and the smearing with 3 oil inside the cloak make men pale, while running naked gives them a good colour ? Is it because good ventilation produces good colour, and stifling the opposite ? The cause of the pallor is that the surface moisture which grows hot does not cool. Both these

966 b
ἐν τῷ ἱματίῳ ἴδισις καὶ ἡ εἰς τὸ ἱμάτιον ἄλειψις·
967 a ἐγκατακλείεται γὰρ ἡ θερμότης. οἱ δὲ γυμνοὶ
δρόμοι εὔχρουν ποιοῦσιν διὰ τοὐναντίον, ὅτι καταψύχει ὁ ἀὴρ τὰς συνισταμένας ἐκκρίσεις καὶ
διαπνεῖ τὸ σῶμα. ἔτι τὸ ἔλαιον ὑγρὸν ὂν καὶ
λεπτόν, ὑπαλειφθὲν καὶ τοὺς πόρους ἐμφράττον,
5 οὔτε τὸ ἐκ τοῦ σώματος ὑγρὸν καὶ πνεῦμα ἔξω
ῥεῖν ἐᾷ, οὔτε τὸ ἐκτὸς πνεῦμα ἐντός. διὸ κατα-
πνιγόμενα ἐν τῷ σώματι ὑγρὰ περιττώματα σηπό-
μενα ἄχροιαν ποιεῖ.

Διὰ τί ἡ εὔπνοια εὐχρους ποιεῖ; ἢ ὅτι ἄχροια 4
ἔοικεν εἶναι οἷον σῆψίς τις χρωτός; ὅταν οὖν τὸ
10 ἐπιπολῆς ὑγρὸν καὶ θερμὸν ᾖ, τοῦτο συμβαίνει
καὶ χλωρὸν γίνεσθαι, ἐὰν μὴ ψυχθῇ καὶ ἀποπνεύσῃ
τὸ θερμόν.

Διὰ τί οἱ μὲν ἱδρώσαντες ἐκ τῶν γυμνασίων 5
εὔχροοί εἰσιν εὐθύς, οἱ δὲ ἀθληταὶ ἄχροοι; ἢ διότι
ὑπὸ μὲν τοῦ μετρίου πόνου τὸ θερμὸν ἐκκάεται
15 καὶ ἐπιπολάζει, ὑπὸ δὲ τῶν πολλῶν ἐξηθεῖται μετὰ
τοῦ ἱδρῶτος καὶ τοῦ πνεύματος, ἀραιουμένου τοῦ
σώματος ἐν τῷ πονεῖν; ὅταν μὲν οὖν ἐπιπολάσῃ
τὸ θερμόν, εὔχροοι γίνονται, καθάπερ οἵ τε θερμαινόμενοι καὶ αἰσχυνόμενοι· ὅταν δὲ ἐκλίπῃ,
ἄχροοι. οἱ μὲν οὖν ἰδιῶται μέτρια γυμνάζονται,
οἱ δὲ ἀθληταὶ πολλά.

20 Διὰ τί μᾶλλον καίονται ὑπὸ τοῦ ἡλίου οἱ καθ- 6
εζόμενοι τῶν γυμναζομένων; ἢ ὅτι οἱ ἐν κινήσει
ὄντες ὥσπερ ῥιπίζονται ὑπὸ τοῦ πνεύματος διὰ τὸ
κινεῖν τὸν ἀέρα, οἱ δὲ καθήμενοι οὐ πάσχουσι
τοῦτο;

Διὰ τί ὁ μὲν ἥλιος ἐπικάει, τὸ δὲ πῦρ οὔ; ἢ 7

conditions, sweating in a cloak and the oiling beneath the cloak, produce the same result; for in both cases the heat is confined. Naked running produces a good colour for exactly the opposite reason, namely that the air cools the collection of secretions and ventilates the body. Moreover, oil being liquid and light, when it is smeared on and obstructs the pores, does not allow the body's moisture and breath to escape outside, nor air from outside to pass in. So the wet waste products being stifled in the body decompose and cause pallor.

Why does plenty of air give men a good colour? 4 Is it because pallor seems to be, as it were, a decay of the skin? So when the surface is wet and warm, it tends to become pale, unless it is cooled and gives off the heat.

Why do those who sweat after gymnastic exercise 5 immediately develop a good colour, whereas athletes are pale? Is it because as a result of moderate exercise the heat burns out and comes to the surface, but with constant training the heat percolates through with the sweat and the breath, as the body becomes rarefied with the exercise? When, then, the heat is on the surface, men have a good colour, just as they have when heated or ashamed; but when the heat leaves them they are pale. Now the amateur takes moderate exercise, but the professional athlete takes much.

Why are those who sit still more burned by the 6 sun than those who take exercise? Is it because those who are in motion are, so to speak, fanned by the wind because they are moving the air, but those who are sitting still do not experience this?

Why does the sun scorch the skin, while fire does 7

967 a
25 διότι λεπτότερός ἐστιν ὁ ἥλιος, καὶ μᾶλλον δύναται
διαδύεσθαι εἰς τὴν σάρκα; τὸ δὲ πῦρ, ἐὰν καὶ
ἐπικαύσῃ, ἄνω μόνον ποιεῖ τὸ χρῶμα, τὰς φῳδὰς
καλουμένας· εἴσω δὲ οὐκ εἰσδύεται.

967 b Διὰ τί τὸ πῦρ οὐ ποιεῖ μέλανας, ὁ δὲ ἥλιος
ποιεῖ· τὸν δὲ κέραμον ποιεῖ, ὁ δὲ ἥλιος οὔ; ἢ οὐχ
ὁμοίως ἑκάτερον ποιεῖ, ἀλλ' ὁ μὲν ἐπικάων τὴν
χρόαν μελαίνει, τὸ δὲ πῦρ τὸν κέραμον ἀναπίμπλᾷ
5 ἢ ἀναφέρει ἀσβόλῳ; τοῦτο δ' ἔστι λεπτῆς μαρίλης,
ἀποθραυομένων ἅμα καὶ καομένων τῶν ἀνθράκων.
τοὺς δὲ ἀνθρώπους ὁ μὲν ἥλιος μελαίνει, τὸ δὲ
πῦρ οὔ, ὅτι τοῦ μὲν μαλθακὴ ἡ θερμότης, καὶ διὰ
μικρομέρειαν δύναται τὸ δέρμα αὐτὸ κάειν· ὥστε
διὰ μὲν τὸ τῆς σαρκὸς μὴ ἅπτεσθαι οὐκ ἀλγεινόν,
10 διὰ δὲ τὸ κάειν μέλαν ποιεῖ. τὸ δὲ πῦρ ἢ οὐχ
ἅπτεται ἢ εἴσω διέρχεται, ἐπεὶ μέλανα καὶ τὰ
πυρίκαυστα γίνεται, ἀλλ' οὐ μόνον ἐκεῖνον τὸν
τόπον κάει οὗ ἡ χροιά.

Διὰ τί οἱ γηράσκοντες μελάντεροι γίνονται; ἢ
ὅτι πᾶν σηπόμενον μελάντερον γίνεται, πλὴν
15 εὐρῶτος; ταὐτὸ[1] δ' ἐστὶ γῆρας καὶ σαπρότης. ἔτι
ἐπειδὴ τὸ αἷμα ξηραινόμενον μελάντερον γίνεται,
εἰκότως ἂν μελάντεροι εἶεν οἱ πρεσβύτεροι· τοῦτο
γάρ ἐστι τὸ χρῷζον ἡμῶν τὰ σώματα φυσικῶς.

Διὰ τί περὶ τὴν τῶν σίτων ἐργασίαν, οἱ μὲν περὶ
20 τὰς κριθὰς ἄχροοι γίνονται καὶ καταρροϊκοί, οἱ
δὲ περὶ τοὺς πυροὺς εὐεκτικοί; ἢ διότι εὐπεπτό-
τερος ὁ πυρὸς τῆς κριθῆς, ὥστε καὶ αἱ ἀπόρροιαι;

---

[1] ταὐτὸ Forster : τοῦτο Ruelle.

not ? Is it because the sun is lighter and so can penetrate the flesh more ? But the fire, even if it does burn, only affects the skin on top, producing what are called blisters ; but it does not penetrate within.

Why does the fire not make us black, whereas the 8 sun does, and why does the fire blacken potter's clay, but the sun does not ? Or are the two effects produced in different ways, the sun blackening the skin by burning it, while the fire permeates potter's clay with the soot which it throws up ? Soot consists of light charcoal, which forms when the coal simultaneously breaks up and burns. The sun blackens human beings and the fire does not, because the sun's heat is mild and can burn the actual skin because it consists of small particles ; as it is not in contact with the flesh it is not painful, but because it burns it makes it black. But fire either does not touch the flesh at all or penetrates within it, since what is burned in fire also becomes black, but it does not burn merely that part where the colour of the body lies.

Why do those who are getting older grow darker ? 9 Is it because everything which is decaying grows darker, except mildew ? And old age and decay are the same thing. Moreover, since blood as it dries grows darker, naturally old men would be darker. For it is the blood which gives the natural colour to the body.

Why in connexion with work on grain do those 10 who deal with barley become pale and subject to catarrh, while those who deal with wheat are in good condition ? Is it because wheat is more digestible than barley, and so also are the emanations from it ?

Διὰ τί ὁ μὲν ἥλιος τὸ μὲν ἔλαιον λευκαίνει, τὴν 1
δὲ σάρκα μελαίνει; ἢ ὅτι τοῦ μὲν ἐλαίου ἀπάγει
25 τὸ γεῶδες; τοῦτο δὲ ἦν τὸ μέλαν, ὥσπερ τὸ
γεῶδες τοῦ οἴνου. τὴν δὲ σάρκα μελαίνει, ὅτι
κάει· τὸ γὰρ γεῶδες καόμενον ἅπαν γίνεται μέλαν.

Why does the sun bleach oil but blacken flesh ? 11 Is it because it abstracts the earthy element from the oil ? This like the earthy element in wine is the black part of it. But the sun blackens the flesh because it burns it ; for the earthy element when burned always becomes black.

ARISTOTLE'S
RHETORIC TO ALEXANDER

INTRODUCTION

THE *Treatise on Rhetoric dedicated to Alexander* that has come down to us among the works of Aristotle is a practical handbook for public speakers. It merely considers the problem of how to carry conviction with an audience, and gives none of the warnings against the abuse of oratory nor any of the background of logic, psychology and ethics that render Aristotle's *Rhetoric* a philosophical work. In fact, it represents the sophistic school of rhetoric that Aristotle opposed.

Some scholars have, indeed, maintained that it is an earlier work of the master himself, later replaced by the other treatise as his authoritative treatment of the subject. But more probably it was written during the generation after his death, at the beginning of the third century B.C.,[a] the author basing his work on that of Aristotle, whose classificatory method he adopts with modifications, but keeping on the plane of practical utility.

It is probable that the author was also guided by the work of Isocrates, although he nowhere mentions him. Of Isocrates' *Techne Rhetorike* some fragments

[a] The latest event referred to is the expedition of the Corinthians under Timoleon to aid Syracuse against the Carthaginians in 341 B.C. There is no reference that supplements this *terminus a quo* with a *terminus ad quem*.

survive (see the Teubner *Isocrates*, pp. 275 ff.), and these are partly echoed in our treatise.

The name of the book and its ascription to Aristotle are due to the preface ; this is in the form of a letter from Aristotle to Alexander during the period of his campaign of conquest in the East. The writer presents to his former pupil a work (or works) on rhetoric, and lectures him like a schoolboy on the importance of the study ! This effusion has been rejected as spurious by most scholars from Erasmus onwards ; it reads like a particularly unconvincing forgery, ignoring as it does the change of relation that had taken place between professor and pupil. However, an attempt has been made by Wendland [a] to retain it as genuinely the work of Anaximenes (whom he regards as the author of the treatise)—a preface clumsily modified later to add value to the work by ascribing it to Aristotle !

' As to the treatise itself,' writes Cope,[b] ' though there is *some* general correspondence, in the treatment and topics selected and illustrated, between this author and Aristotle, yet the numerous and important differences in detail, as well as the marked inferiority in subtlety and spirit, power and interest, the entire absence of the logical element in this work, the striking contrast of *style* between them—here often obscure from its vagueness and indefiniteness though otherwise clear and simple, but feeble and inexpressive ; there, also often obscure and elliptical, but characterized by a terse and pregnant brevity—the more scientific exactness, and the much higher moral tone that appear in Aristotle's work, all unite to prove

[a] *Hermes*, xxxix. 499.
[b] *Introduction to Aristotle's Rhetoric*, pp. 401 ff.

beyond the possibility of doubt that the two arts of
Rhetoric could not have proceeded from the same
intellect, taste, judgement and moral standard. The
Rhet. ad Alex. is a work proceeding from an entirely
different and inferior order of mind and character.'

The ascription of the authorship to Anaximenes is
based on a passage in Quintilian (III. iv. 9, Spalding
vol. i. p. 455) :

*Anaximenes iudicialem et concionalem generales partes
esse uoluit ; septem autem species hortandi, dehortandi,
laudandi, uituperandi, accusandi, defendendi, exquirendi
(quod* ἐξεταστικόν *dicit) : quarum duae primae de-
liberatiui, duae sequentes demonstratiui, tres ultimae
iudiciales generis sunt partes.'*

This analysis of rhetoric does not, it is true, tally
exactly with our treatise, where the bipartite division
with which Quintilian begins does not occur ; but
even in Quintilian this clashes with the tripartite
division that follows—in fact his scheme looks like
a careless conflation of two distinct schemes. The
bipartite division follows Dionysius of Halicarnassus,
De Oratoribus Antiquis (Reiske vol. v. p. 626), who
says that Anaximenes ' has also handled deliberative
and forensic debates,' ἧπται δὲ καὶ συμβουλευτικῶν
καὶ διανοητικῶν ἀγώνων. But Quintilian's arrangement of seven species in three genera tallies with
our book, except that it classes *exquirendi species* as
a third division of *iudiciale genus,* whereas in the
Greek work *Exetastikon* stands alone as an independent
form of oratory, though it can also be introduced into
speeches of any of the other kinds.

The identification of the book before us with the
one described by Quintilian was first made by Publius

RHETORIC TO ALEXANDER

Victorius in his preface to the *Rhetoric* of Aristotle ; it is accepted as probable by Spalding in his edition of Quintilian and by Spengel, Hammer, and Grenfell and Hunt on the present work. Professor Forster thinks this was in any case written shortly before 300 B.C. by a Peripatetic, contemporary with Theophrastus.

Anaximenes of Lampsacus is said to have been a tutor of Alexander ; he went with him on his Asiatic expedition. He wrote histories of Philip and of Alexander, and a history of Greece from the mythical age down to the battle of Mantinea ; of each of these works a few fragments have been preserved. He was also an orator, and a teacher of rhetoric, and he composed speeches for others to deliver. As a specimen of his work he published (under another man's name) an oration decrying Sparta, Athens and Thebes.

The text of the present edition is based on that of Bekker in the Berlin Aristotle published in 1831, where it occupies pp. 1420-1447 in the second volume. References to the page, column (*a* and *b*) and line of that edition are printed in the margin of the text. Use has also been made of the text of Spengel as revised by Hammer in 1894 (Teubner, *Rhetores Graeci*, I. ii. pp. 8 ff.) and of valuable textual notes added by Professor E. S. Forster to his translation of the book in the Oxford *Works of Aristotle Translated*, vol. xi. The Teubner text was based on a collation of eleven MSS., which the editors divide into two groups, one of five copies of superior value (which they subdivide into groups of three and two), the other a group of six inferior copies. Since then the MS. evidence has been supplemented by a

261

papyrus found in Egypt and published by Grenfell and Hunt in 1906 (*Hibeh Papyrus*, Part I. No. 26, pp. 114-138) ; this contains eight fragments of the book, covering in all about 180 lines or 2½ pages of the Berlin edition. Grenfell and Hunt date the writing in the first half of the third century B.C., which puts this copy within about two generations of the authorship and seventeen centuries before the oldest of the MSS. previously extant ; these belong to the fifteenth and sixteenth centuries.

In the textual notes of this edition the readings of the papyrus are occasionally quoted under the title II. Only a few other variants of special interest are added, indicated merely as v.ll.

As to the translation, it is necessary to explain that no attempt has been made to render it either as literal or as idiomatic as possible ; it is designed to assist the reader of the Greek, and not to substitute an English book for it. The rendering of technical terms is always a difficulty ; in this book, as the Greek is to hand, they are Englished as far as possible : for instance the Ecclesia, being the Commons of Athens in Parliament assembled, figures as 'parliament' and the oratory addressed to it as 'parliamentary.' The kaleidoscopic term λόγος must always evade the translator; he may be pardoned if he varies his version with the context, and uses 'word,' 'spoken word,' 'speech,' 'rational speech,' 'argument,' 'reason,' etc., as the spirit moves him. Some variation of the rendering of other terms is desirable, either to indicate the varieties of meaning in different contexts or merely to warn the reader that no English word is an exact equivalent of the Greek.

RHETORIC TO ALEXANDER

OUTLINE OF THE TREATISE

The essay begins with a scientific classification of ^{c. i.} the kinds of oratory. It is divided into three Genera —demegoric or Parliamentary, epideictic or Ceremonial, and dicanic or Forensic (viz. speeches delivered in the ecclesia, at festivals and other public gatherings, and in the law-courts) ; and into seven Species—Exhortation and Dissuasion, Eulogy and Vituperation, Prosecution and Defence (each of these pairs falling under one of the Genera), and lastly Investigation, which may either stand alone or (as is more usual, c. xxxvii. *init.*), be introduced into an oration of any genus.

Common topics used in orations of the first genus are justice, legality, expediency, honour, facility, practicability and necessity. Illustrations are given of the first three.

Next the subjects of oratory are reviewed. Parlia- ^{c. ii.} mentary speeches support or oppose proposals as to matters of religious ritual, legislation and constitutional reform, foreign policy (alliances, and peace and war), finance. Materials are suggested for enlarging on these subjects.

Ceremonial orations of eulogy or vituperation deal ^{c. iii.} with a person's character and fortunes, and with his conduct in youth and manhood, amplifying the creditable and minimizing the discreditable points, or *vice versa.*

Forensic speeches advance or refute charges of ^{c. iv.} error and crime. Various modes of accusation are described, and three methods of defence.

Investigation exposes inconsistencies in a man's ^{c. v.} conduct or statements.

c. vi.   Elements common to all species—in addition to
(1) the common topics enumerated with special
reference to political oratory in c. i., and (2) the
methods of amplification and minimization that in
c. iii. were specially attached to the ceremonial genus
—are (3) proofs, and (4) anticipation, postulation,
recapitulation, length of speech, explanation.

cc. vii.-xiii.   Proofs are either (1) direct, employing probabilities, examples, tokens (infallible), ' enthymemes '
or considerations, maxims, signs (fallible) and refuta-
c. xiv. tions—the distinctions between which are explained ;
cc. xv.-xvii. or (2) supplementary, based on the opinion of the
speaker, evidence given voluntarily by witnesses or
extracted under torture, and unproved affirmations
made on oath.

cc. xviii.-   Next are discussed Anticipation of the probable
xxviii. arguments of the other side, Appeals to the court
for attention, justice and sympathy, Repetition to
drive home one's case, Irony, Elegancies of style,
Length of speech appropriate to different cases,
Choice and Arrangement of words, and Forms of
Sentence—viz. Antithesis, Parisosis or parallelism
of construction, and Paromoeosis or parallelism of
sound.

c. xxix.   Structure of a Parliamentary speech of Exhortation or Dissuasion : (1) Introduction—preliminary
statement of the case, request for attention, and
conciliation of the audience when friendly, or neutral,
or hostile either owing to misrepresentation of the
past or the present, or owing to one's personality, or
to the circumstances.

cc. xxx -   (2) Exposition, stating past facts or the present
xxx situation or anticipating the future, must be clear in
style, brief and convincing. Arrangement of material.

Confirmation by proof, or if the facts are obvious by general considerations.

(3) Anticipation of the arguments of the other side. c. xxxiii.

(4) Appeal to feelings of friendship, gratitude and pity in Exhortation, of envy and hatred in Dissuasion. c. xxxiv.

Structure of Ceremonial orations of Eulogy or Vituperation, praising or criticizing the subjects, character, pedigree, fortune, and past conduct in youth and manhood. c. xxxv.

Structure of Forensic speeches—(*a*) in Prosecution : (1) Introduction : conciliation of goodwill of the court for one's client ; refutation of misrepresentations. (2) Proof of the charge. (3) Anticipation of defendant's arguments. (4) Recapitulation. (*b*) In Defence : refutation of prosecutor's proof of his charge, or (admitting the action charged) justification or palliation ; reply to prosecutor's anticipation of your case ; rhetorical questions ; means to gain the goodwill of the court and to cause dislike of your opponent. c. xxxvi.

Structure of Investigational oratory (when used in a separate speech) : the introduction must create a favourable impression ; heads of criticism ; gentle tone and conciliatory bearing. c. xxxvii.

Miscellaneous : modes of making a political proposal ; modes of proof ; perorations ; personality of the speaker. c. xxxviii.

The book ends with a passage, unquestionably a spurious addition, in which various disconnected subjects are glanced at—sacrificial ritual, friendships and alliances, defence, revenue, foreign policy, good citizenship, generosity, means to victory, rupture of alliances, righteous conduct, goods of body and of mind.

ΑΡΙΣΤΟΤΕΛΟΥΣ
ΡΗΤΟΡΙΚΗ ΠΡΟΣ ΑΛΕΞΑΝΔΡΟΝ

ΑΡΙΣΤΟΤΕΛΗΣ ΑΛΕΞΑΝΔΡΩΙ ΕΥ ΠΡΑΤΤΕΙΝ

1420 a   'Επέστειλάς μοι ὅτι πολλάκις πολλοὺς πέπομφας
πρὸς ἡμᾶς τοὺς διαλεξομένους ὑπὲρ τοῦ γραφῆναί
σοι τὰς μεθόδους τῶν πολιτικῶν λόγων. ἐγὼ δὲ
οὐ διὰ ῥᾳθυμίαν ὑπερεβαλλόμην ἐν τούτοις τοῖς
10 χρόνοις, ἀλλὰ διὰ τὸ ζητεῖν οὕτως ὑπὲρ αὐτῶν
γραφῆναί σοι διηκριβωμένων ὡς οὐδεὶς ἄλλος γέ-
γραφε τῶν περὶ ταῦτα πραγματευομένων. ταύτην
δὲ εἰκότως τὴν διάνοιαν εἶχον· ὥσπερ γὰρ ἐσθῆτα
σπουδάζεις τὴν εὐπρεπεστάτην τῶν λοιπῶν ἀνθρώπων ἔχειν, οὕτω δύναμιν λόγων λαβεῖν ἐστί σοι
15 πειρατέον τὴν εὐδοξοτάτην· πολὺ γὰρ κάλλιόν ἐστι
καὶ βασιλικώτερον τὴν ψυχὴν ἔχειν εὐγνωμονοῦσαν
ἢ τὴν ἕξιν τοῦ σώματος ὁρᾶν εὐειματοῦσαν. καὶ
γὰρ ἄτοπόν ἐστι τὸν τοῖς ἔργοις πρωτεύοντα φαίνεσθαι τῶν τυχόντων τοῖς λόγοις ὑστερίζοντα, καὶ
ταῦτα εἰδότα ὅτι τοῖς μὲν ἐν δημοκρατίᾳ πολιτευο-
20 μένοις ἡ ἀναφορὰ περὶ πάντων τῶν πραγμάτων εἰς
τὸν νόμον[1] ἐστί, τοῖς δ' ὑπὸ τὴν τῆς βασιλείας

[1] C. F. Hermann: δῆμον codd.

ARISTOTLE'S
RHETORIC TO ALEXANDER

Aristotle to Alexander.   Salutations.[a]

You write to me that you have again and again sent *Preface.*
people to me to speak about my composing for you a
treatise on the principles of political oratory.   It is
not indolence on my part that has caused me to keep
putting it off all this time, but the endeavour to have
a treatise on the subject written for you with a degree 10
of accuracy that has not yet been attained by any
other of the authors dealing with it.   And there was
a good reason for my having this intention ; for just
as it is your desire to wear the most splendid attire of
all mankind, so it is proper that you should attempt
to attain the most distinguished ability in rational 15
discourse,[b] since it is much nobler and more kingly
to possess wisdom of mind than to see one's bodily
form finely apparelled.   Indeed it would be strange
that he who holds the first place in action should be
seen to lag behind ordinary people in discourse, and
this when he knows that whereas under democratic
government all matters of public business are referred 20
to the law, with nations ranged under royal leader-

[a] On this introductory letter, probably spurious, see
Introduction, pp. 258 ff.   [b] On λόγος see p. 262.

1420 a

ἡγεμονίαν τεταγμένοις πρὸς λόγον. ὥσπερ οὖν
τὰς αὐτονόμους τῶν πόλεων διορθοῦν εἴωθεν ἐπὶ
τὸ κάλλιστον ἄγων ὁ κοινὸς νόμος, οὕτω τοὺς ὑπὸ
25 τὴν σὴν βασιλείαν καθεστῶτας ἄγειν δύναιτ' ἂν ἐπὶ
τὸ συμφέρον ὁ σὸς λόγος. καὶ γὰρ ὁ νόμος ἐστὶν
ὡς ἁπλῶς εἰπεῖν λόγος ὡρισμένος καθ' ὁμολογίαν
κοινὴν πόλεως, μηνύων πῶς δεῖ πράττειν ἕκαστα.

Πρὸς δὲ τούτοις οὐκ ἄδηλον οἶμαί σοι τοῦτ' ἐστίν,
ὅτι τοὺς μὲν λόγῳ χρωμένους καὶ μετὰ τούτου
30 πάντα πράττειν προαιρουμένους ὡς ὄντας καλούς
τε καὶ ἀγαθοὺς ἐπαινοῦμεν, τοὺς δὲ ἄνευ λόγου τι
1420 b
5 ποιοῦντας ὡς ὄντας ὠμοὺς καὶ θηριώδεις μισοῦμεν.
διὰ τούτου¹ καὶ τοὺς² κακοὺς αὐτῶν τὴν³ κακίαν
ἐμφανίσαντας ἐκολάσαμεν, καὶ τοὺς ἀγαθοὺς δηλώ-
σαντας αὐτῶν τὴν ἀρετὴν ἐζηλώσαμεν. τούτῳ⁴ καὶ
τῶν μελλόντων κακῶν ἀποτροπὴν εὑρήκαμεν καὶ
τῶν ὑπαρχόντων ἀγαθῶν ὄνησιν ἐσχήκαμεν,⁵ καὶ
10 διὰ τούτου καὶ τὰς ἐπιούσας δυσχερείας ἐφύγομεν
καὶ τὰς μὴ προσούσας ἡμῖν ὠφελείας ἐπορισάμεθα·
ὥσπερ γὰρ βίος ἄλυπος αἱρετός, οὕτω λόγος συ-
νετὸς ἀγαπητός. εἰδέναι δέ σε δεήσει ὅτι παρα-
δείγματά ἐστι τοῖς πλείστοις τῶν ἀνθρώπων τοῖς
15 μὲν ὁ νόμος τοῖς δὲ ὁ σὸς βίος καὶ λόγος· ὅπως
οὖν διαφέρων ᾖς πάντων Ἑλλήνων καὶ βαρβάρων
πᾶσάν ἐστί σοι σπουδὴν ποιητέον, ἵνα τὴν ἐκ
τούτου ἀπομίμησιν οἱ περὶ ταῦτα διατρίβοντες τοῖς
τῆς ἀρετῆς στοιχείοις καλλιγραφούμενοι μὴ πρὸς
τὰ φαῦλα σφᾶς αὐτοὺς ἄγωσιν ἀλλὰ καὶ⁶ τῆς
αὐτῆς ἀρετῆς μετέχειν ἐπιθυμῶσιν.

20 Ἔτι δὲ τὸ βουλεύεσθαι τῶν περὶ τὸν ἄνθρωπον

---

¹ v.l. τοῦτο.   ² τοὺς add. Sp. (Spengel).
³ Sp.: τὴν αὐτῶν codd.   ⁴ Sp.: οὕτω codd.

ship the reference is to reason. As, therefore, self-governing states are customarily guided to the noblest course by the common law, so the capacity to lead those who are under your royal government to an advantageous policy will rest with your reason. In 25 fact, to put it simply, law is reason defined in accordance with a common agreement of the state, setting forth how men are to act in each matter.

Moreover, I think it must be manifest to you that we praise as noble and good those persons who employ 30 reason and who make a principle of carrying on all their affairs with its aid, whereas we hate those who act without reason as being savage and bestial. By 1420 b means of reason[a] we are wont to punish the bad when 5 they display their badness and to applaud the good when they manifest their goodness. By it we have discovered means to avert impending evils, and have 10 had the benefit of existing goods, and by its aid we are wont to escape approaching annoyances and to procure advantages that we do not possess. For just as life without pain is desirable, so is wise reason acceptable. And it will be proper for you to know that the greatest part of mankind regulate their conduct either by the law or by your life and principle ; 15 therefore you must make every effort to excel all Greeks and foreigners, in order that those who occupy themselves in these pursuits may by means of the elements of virtue draw a fair copy therefrom, and so may not guide themselves to what is evil but may aspire to participate even in the same goodness.

Moreover, of all human things counsel is the most 20

[a] Or, reading δια τοῦτο, ' For this cause . . .'

[5] Rac. (Rackham): ἔσχομεν codd.   [6] και om. v.l.

1420 b
θειότατόν ἐστιν, ὥστε οὐκ εἰς τὰ πάρεργα καὶ
μηδενὸς ἄξια τὴν σπουδήν ἐστί σοι καταναλωτέον,
ἀλλὰ τὴν μητρόπολιν αὐτὴν τοῦ καλῶς βουλεύεσθαι
μαθεῖν βουλητέον. τίς γὰρ δή ποτ' ἂν ἀμφισβη-
τήσειε τῶν νοῦν ἐχόντων ὅτι τὸ μὲν πράττειν μὴ
25 βουλευσάμενον σημεῖόν ἐστιν ἀνοίας, τὸ δὲ κατὰ
τὴν ὑφήγησιν τοῦ λόγου συντελεῖν τι τῶν ὑπ'
ἐκείνου παραγγελθέντων παιδείας; ἰδεῖν δὲ ἔστι
πάντας τοὺς ἄριστα τῶν Ἑλλήνων πολιτευομένους
λόγῳ πρῶτον ἢ τοῖς ἔργοις συγγινομένους, πρὸς δὲ
τούτοις καὶ τοὺς μέγιστον ἀξίωμα τῶν βαρβάρων
30 ἔχοντας τούτῳ πρὸ τῶν πραγμάτων χρωμένους,
1421 a εἰδότας καλῶς ὡς ἀκρόπολίς ἐστι σωτηρίας ἡ διὰ
τοῦ λόγου γινομένη τοῦ συμφέροντος θεωρία.
ταύτην ἀπόρθητον οἰητέον, οὐ τὴν ἐκ τῶν οἰκο-
δομημάτων ἀσφαλῆ πρὸς σωτηρίαν εἶναι νομιστέον.
   Ἀλλὰ γὰρ ὀκνῶ ἔτι πλείω γράφειν, μή ποτε
5 καλλωπίζεσθαι δόξω περὶ τῶν ἀκριβῶς γνωριζο-
μένων ὡς οὐχ ὁμολογουμένων πίστεις ἐπιφέρων.
διόπερ ἀφήσω, ἐκεῖνα μόνον εἰπὼν περὶ ὧν ἔστι[1]
λέγειν εἰς ἅπαντα τὸν βίον, ὅτι τοῦτό ἐστιν ᾧ
διαφέρομεν τῶν λοιπῶν ζῴων [τοῦτο οὖν καὶ ἡμεῖς
διαφέρον τῶν λοιπῶν ἔξομεν ἀνθρώπων][2] οἱ μεγίστης
10 τιμῆς ὑπὸ τοῦ δαιμονίου τετυχηκότες· ἐπιθυμίᾳ μὲν
γὰρ καὶ θυμῷ καὶ τοῖς τοιούτοις χρῆται καὶ τὰ
λοιπὰ ζῷα πάντα, λόγῳ δὲ οὐδὲν τῶν λοιπῶν χωρὶς
ἀνθρώπων. ἀτοπώτατον οὖν ἂν[3] εἴη πάντων, εἰ
τούτῳ μόνῳ τῶν λοιπῶν ζῴων εὐδαιμονέστερον
15 βιοῦντες τὸ αἴτιον τοῦ καλῶς εἶναι διὰ ῥᾳθυμίαν
ἀφεῖμεν[4] κατολιγωρήσαντες. διακελεύομαι δή σοι

---

[1] v.l. ἔνεστι.　　　　　　　　　[2] secl. edd.
[3] v.ll. ἂν οὖν, ἂν, δ' ἂν.　　　　[4] Sp.: ἀφῶμεν codd.

divine, so that you must not waste your zeal on ^{1420 b} secondary or worthless matters but resolve to gain a knowledge of the very mother-city of wise counsel. For what person possessing intelligence could ever 25 question that it is a sign of folly to act without deliberation, and a mark of education to accomplish by the guidance of reason something that reason commands ? It may be seen that all the peoples of Greece possessing the best governments engage in discussion before embarking on action, and in addition to these, those foreigners also that have the highest repute employ discussion before action, well know- 30 ing that the consideration of what is expedient by 1421 a means of discussion is the citadel of safety. That is the citadel which should be deemed impregnable—no fortress that consists of buildings should be thought safe and secure.

However, I am reluctant to continue writing more, lest perchance, if I bring forward proofs about 5 matters of precise knowledge as if they were not admitted truths, I may be thought to be showing off. I will therefore desist, only stating what may be asserted as regards the whole of life, that it is in this that we are superior to the other living creatures—we upon whom divine power has be- stowed the greatest honour ; for appetite and 10 passion and the like are experienced by all the other living creatures also, but none of them except man employs reason. So it would be the strangest of all things if, while it is by means of reason only that we live more happily than the other animals, owing to slackness of spirit we were to despise and to relinquish that which is the cause of our well-being. I therefore 15

1421 a

πάλαι παρακεκλημένῳ τῆς τῶν λόγων ἀντέχεσθαι
φιλοσοφίας. καθάπερ γάρ ἐστι φυλακτικὸν σώματος ὑγίεια, οὕτω ψυχῆς φυλακτικὸν καθέστηκε
παιδεία. ταύτης γὰρ προηγουμένης οὐ πταίειν
συμβήσεταί σοι περὶ τὰς πράξεις, ἀλλὰ σῴζειν
20 ἁπάσας ὡς ἔπος εἰπεῖν τὰς ὑπαρχούσας σοι τῶν
ἀγαθῶν κτήσεις. χωρὶς δὲ τῶν εἰρημένων, εἰ τὸ
τοῖς ὀφθαλμοῖς βλέπειν ἡδύ, τὸ[1] τοῖς τῆς ψυχῆς
ὄμμασιν ὀξυδορκεῖν ἐστὶ θαυμαστόν. ἔτι δὲ ὥσπερ
ὁ στρατηγός ἐστι σωτὴρ στρατοπέδου, οὕτω[2] λόγος
μετὰ παιδείας ἡγεμών ἐστι βίου.
25 Ταυτὶ μὲν οὖν καὶ τὰ τούτοις ὅμοια παραλιπεῖν
νομίζω καλῶς ἡμῖν ἔχειν κατὰ τὸν ὑπάρχοντα
καιρόν.

Ἔγραψας δέ μοι διακελευόμενος ὅπως μηδεὶς
τῶν λοιπῶν ἀνθρώπων λήψεται τὸ βιβλίον τοῦτο,
καὶ ταῦτα εἰδὼς ὅτι καθάπερ τοὺς ἐξ αὐτῶν
γεννηθέντας οἱ γεννήσαντες τῶν ὑποβαλλομένων
30 μᾶλλον φιλοῦσιν, οὕτω καὶ οἱ εὑρόντες τι τῶν
μετεχόντων· ὥσπερ γὰρ ὑπὲρ τέκνων, οὕτω[3] τῶν
λόγων ὑπεραποτεθνήκασιν.[4] οἱ μὲν γὰρ Πάριοι
λεγόμενοι σοφισταὶ διὰ τὸ μὴ τεκεῖν αὐτοὶ διὰ
ῥᾳθυμίαν ἄμουσον οὐ στέργουσιν, ἀλλὰ χρήματα
λαβόντες ἀποκηρύττουσιν. διὰ τοῦτο οὖν ἐγώ σοι
35 παρακελεύομαι διαφυλάττειν οὕτω τοὺς λόγους
τούτους ὅπως νέοι καθεστῶτες ὑπὸ μηδενὸς[5] δια-
φθαρήσονται, κοσμίως δὲ μετὰ σοῦ συμβιώσαντες,
εἰς ἡλικίαν ἐλθόντες δόξης ἀκηράτου[6] τεύξονται.

----

[1] τὸ om. v.l.   [2] v.l. οὕτω καὶ.
[3] Sp.: τούτων codd.
[4] v.l. ὑπεραποθνήσκουσι.
[5] v.l. μηδενὸς χρήμασι.
[6] ἀγηράτου Ipfelkofer.

unceasingly exhort you to hold fast to the study of reasoned speech, to which you have long been urged. For education constitutes the safeguard of the mind, in the same way as health is the safeguard of the body ; since when education guides it will not befall you to stumble in the path of conduct, but to preserve 20 almost all the good possessions that are your property. And apart from what has been said, if to see with the bodily eyes is pleasant, the penetrating vision of the eyes of the mind is marvellous. And again, as the general is the preserver of the army, so reason coupled with education is the guide of life.

These particular matters, then, and those similar to 25 them I think we may well at the present season leave on one side.

You command me in your letter not to allow this book to come into the possession of anyone else whatever, and this when you know that those who have made some discovery love it more than those to whom 30 it is imparted, just as parents love their own offspring more than changelings ; for discoverers have given their lives on behalf of their theories, as on behalf of children. For the Parian sophists, as they are called, because owing to their uncultured slackness of mind they did not themselves give birth to their doctrines, have no affection for them, but hawk them about on sale for money. On that account I exhort you to 35 guard these discourses in such a manner that while they are still young they may not be corrupted by anyone, but may pass their lives with you in orderly wise, and when they arrive at adult years they may attain unsullied *a* glory.

a It seems unnecessary to change the ms. reading to ἀγηράτου, ' unaging ' (Forster).

Παρειλήφαμεν δέ, καθάπερ ἡμῖν ἐδήλωσε Νι-
κάνωρ, καὶ τῶν λοιπῶν τεχνογράφων εἴ τίς τι
40 γλαφυρὸν ὑπὲρ τῶν αὐτῶν τούτων γέγραφεν ἐν ταῖς
1421 b τέχναις. περιτεύξῃ δὲ δυσὶ τούτοις¹ βιβλίοις, ὧν
τὸ μέν ἐστιν ἐμόν, ἐν ταῖς ὑπ᾽ ἐμοῦ τέχναις Θεο-
δέκτῃ γραφείσαις, τὸ δὲ ἕτερον Κόρακος. τὰ δὲ
λοιπὰ τούτοις ἰδίᾳ πάντα γέγραπται περί τε τῶν
πολιτικῶν καὶ τῶν δικανικῶν παραγγελμάτων· ὅθεν
5 πρὸς ἑκάτερον αὐτῶν εὐπορήσεις ἐκ τῶνδε τῶν
ὑπομνημάτων σοι γεγραμμένων. ἔρρωσο.

I. Τρία² γένη τῶν πολιτικῶν εἰσὶ λόγων, τὸ μὲν
δημηγορικόν, τὸ δ᾽ ἐπιδεικτικόν, τὸ δὲ δικανικόν.
εἴδη δὲ τούτων ἑπτά, προτρεπτικόν, ἀποτρεπτικόν,
10 ἐγκωμιαστικόν, ψεκτικόν, κατηγορικόν,³ ἀπολογητικὸν καὶ ἐξεταστικόν, ἢ αὐτὸ καθ᾽ αὑτὸ ἢ πρὸς
ἄλλο. τὰ μὲν οὖν εἴδη τῶν λόγων τοσαῦτα ἀριθμῷ
ἐστίν, χρησόμεθα δὲ αὐτοῖς ἔν τε ταῖς κοιναῖς
δημηγορίαις καὶ ταῖς περὶ τὰ συμβόλαια δικαιολογίαις καὶ ταῖς ἰδίαις ὁμιλίαις. οὕτω δ᾽ ἂν ἑτοι-
15 μότατον λέγειν περὶ αὐτῶν δυνηθείημεν εἰ καθ᾽⁴ ἓν
ἕκαστον εἶδος ἀπολαβόντες ἀπαριθμησαίμεθα τὰς
δυνάμεις αὐτῶν καὶ τὰς χρήσεις καὶ τὰς τάξεις.⁵

---

¹ τοιούτοις? (sed cf. τοῦτο l. 37) Forster.
² δύο Sp. (et [τὸ δ᾽ ἐπιδεικτικόν] l. 8).
³ Sp. (cf. 1426 b 22, 25): κατηγορητικόν.
⁴ v.l. εἰ καὶ καθ᾽.   ⁵ Sp.: πράξεις.

ᵃ *i.e.* ' you will be able to correct and amplify both from
my essay ' (Wendland).
ᵇ According to Quintilian III. iv. 9 Anaximenes specified
only two kinds of oratory, deliberative and forensic ; and it

1421 a

Following the lesson taught us by Nicanor, we have
adopted from other writers anything that has been 40
well expressed by anybody writing on the same
subjects. You will find two books of this class ; one 1421 b
of them is my own—I refer to the treatise that I
wrote for Theodectes, the other is the work of Corax.
The remaining points in regard to the rules of political and forensic oratory have all been dealt with
separately in those treatises. So from the present
memoranda, written specially for you, you will be 5
well supplied with regard to each of them.[a] Farewell.

I. Public speeches are of three kinds,[b] parliament- *Oratory: its*
ary,[c] ceremonial and forensic. Of these there are *varieties classified.*
seven species,[d] exhortation, dissuasion, eulogy, vitu- 10
peration, accusation, defence, and investigation—
either by itself or in relation to another species. This
list enumerates the species to which public speeches
belong ; and we shall employ them in parliamentary
debates, in arguing legal cases about contracts, and
in private intercourse.[e] We may be able to discuss
them most readily if we take the species seriatim 15
and enumerate their qualities,[f] their uses [g] and their *Procedure of the treatise.*
arrangement.[h]

is noticeable that the order of the three here given is varied
just below, ll. 12 ff. But *cf.* 1432 b 8.
  [c] Addressed to the *Demos* in the *Ecclesia*, the Commons
in Parliament assembled.
  [d] It must be remembered that the Greek word is a technical
term of natural history, in which it denotes the smaller groups
into which each genus or kind is subdivided.
  [e] *i.e.* the first, third and second kinds of speech enumerated
at the start.
  [f] These follow here.
  [g] 1427 b 39 ff.   [h] 1436 a 28 ff.

1421 b

Καὶ πρῶτον μὲν τὰς προτροπὰς καὶ ἀποτροπάς,
ἐπείπερ ἐν ταῖς ἰδίαις ὁμιλίαις καὶ ταῖς κοιναῖς
δημηγορίαις ἐν τοῖς μάλιστα αὐτῶν χρῆσίς ἐστι,
20 διέλθωμεν.[1]

Καθόλου μὲν οὖν εἰπεῖν, προτροπὴ μέν ἐστιν ἐπὶ
προαιρέσεις ἢ λόγους ἢ πράξεις παράκλησις,
ἀποτροπὴ δὲ ἀπὸ προαιρέσεων ἢ λόγων ἢ πράξεων
διακώλυσις. οὕτω δὲ τούτων διωρισμένων, τὸν μὲν
προτρέποντα χρὴ δεικνύειν ταῦτα ἐφ᾽ ἃ παρακαλεῖ
25 δίκαια ὄντα καὶ νόμιμα καὶ συμφέροντα καὶ καλὰ
καὶ ἡδέα καὶ ῥάδια πραχθῆναι· εἰ δὲ μή, δυνατά τε
δεικτέον, ὅταν ἐπὶ δυσχερῆ παρακαλῇ, καὶ ὡς
ἀναγκαῖα ταῦτα ποιεῖν ἐστιν. τὸν δὲ ἀποτρέποντα
δεῖ διὰ τῶν ἐναντίων κώλυσιν ἐπιφέρειν, ὡς οὐ
δίκαιον οὐδὲ νόμιμόν ἐστιν οὐδὲ συμφέρον οὐδὲ
30 καλὸν οὐδὲ ἡδὺ οὐδὲ δυνατὸν πράττειν τοῦτο, εἰ δὲ
μή, ὡς ἐργῶδες καὶ οὐκ ἀναγκαῖον. ἅπασαι δ᾽ αἱ
πράξεις μετέχουσι τούτων ἀμφοτέρων, ὥστε μηδένα
τὴν ἑτέραν[2] τῶν ὑποθέσεων ἔχοντα[3] λόγων ἀπορεῖν.

Ὧν μὲν οὖν ὀρέγεσθαι δεῖ τοὺς προτρέποντας καὶ
ἀποτρέποντας, ταῦτά ἐστιν· ὁρίσασθαι δὲ πειρά-
35 σομαι τούτων ἕκαστον τί ἐστιν, καὶ δεῖξαι πόθεν
αὐτῶν εἰς τοὺς λόγους εὐπορήσομεν.

Δίκαιον μὲν οὖν ἐστι τὸ τῶν ἁπάντων ἢ τὸ τῶν
πλείστων ἔθος ἄγραφον, διορίζον τὰ καλὰ καὶ τὰ
αἰσχρά. ταῦτα[4] δ᾽ ἐστὶ τὸ γονέας τιμᾶν καὶ φίλους
εὖ ποιεῖν καὶ τοῖς εὐεργέταις χάριν ἀποδιδόναι·
40 ταῦτα γὰρ καὶ τὰ τούτοις ὅμοια οὐκ ἐπιτάττουσι[5]
τοῖς ἀνθρώποις οἱ γεγραμμένοι νόμοι ποιεῖν, ἀλλ᾽

---

[1] Sp.: διέλθοιμεν ἄν.
[2] Kayser: ὥστε μηδετέραν.   [3] [ἔχοντα] Sp.
[4] Rac.: τοῦτο.   [5] v.l. οὐ προστάττουσι.

1421 b
*Parliament-
ary oratory.*
20

First let us discuss exhortation and dissuasion, as these are among the forms most employed in private conversation and in public deliberation.

Speaking generally, exhortation is an attempt to urge people to some line of speech or action, and dissuasion is an attempt to hinder people from some line of speech or action. These being their definitions, one delivering an exhortation must prove that *its common* the courses to which he exhorts are just, lawful, *topics.* expedient, honourable, pleasant and easily practicable ; or failing this, in case the courses he is urging are disagreeable, he must show that they are feasible, and also that their adoption is unavoidable. One dissuading must apply hindrance by the opposite means : he must show that the action proposed is not just, not lawful, not expedient, not honourable, not pleasant and not practicable ; or failing this, that it is laborious and not necessary. All courses of action admit of both these descriptions, so that no one having one or other of these sets of fundamental qualities available need be at a loss for something to say.

These, then, are the lines of argument at which those exhorting or dissuading ought to aim. I will try to define the nature of each, and to show from what sources we can obtain a good supply of them for our speeches.

What is just is the unwritten custom of the whole or the greatest part of mankind, distinguishing honourable actions from base ones. The former are to honour one's parents, do good to one's friends and repay favours to one's benefactors ; for these and similar rules are not enjoined on men by written

1422 a ἔθει[1] ἀγράφῳ καὶ κοινῷ νόμῳ νομίζεται. τὰ μὲν
οὖν δίκαια ταῦτά ἐστι.

Νόμος δ' ἐστὶν ὁμολόγημα πόλεως κοινόν, διὰ
γραμμάτων προστάττον πῶς χρὴ πράττειν ἕκαστα.

Συμφέρον δ' ἐστὶ τῶν ὑπαρχόντων ἀγαθῶν φυ-
5 λακὴ ἢ τῶν μὴ προσόντων κτῆσις ἢ τῶν ὑπαρχόντων κακῶν ἀποβολὴ ἢ τῶν προσδοκωμένων
γενήσεσθαι βλαβερῶν διακώλυσις. διαιρήσεις δὲ
τοῦτο τοῖς μὲν ἰδιώταις εἰς σῶμα καὶ ψυχὴν καὶ τὰ
ἐπίκτητα. σώματι μὲν οὖν ἐστὶ συμφέρον ῥώμη
10 κάλλος ὑγίεια, ψυχῇ δὲ ἀνδρεία σοφία δικαιοσύνη,
τὰ δ' ἐπίκτητα φίλοι χρήματα κτήματα· τὰ δ'
ἐναντία τούτοις ἀσύμφορα. πόλει δὲ συμφέροντα
τὰ τοιαῦτά ἐστιν, ὁμόνοια, δύναμις πρὸς πόλεμον,
χρήματα καὶ προσόδων εὐπορία, συμμάχων ἀρετὴ
καὶ πλῆθος. καὶ συλλήβδην ἅπαντα τὰ τούτοις
15 ὁμοιότροπα συμφέροντα νομίζομεν, τὰ δὲ τούτοις
ἐναντία ἀσύμφορα.

Καλὰ δ' ἐστὶν ἀφ' ὧν εὐδοξία τις καὶ τιμή τις
ἔνδοξος γενήσεται τοῖς πράξασιν, ἡδέα δὲ τὰ χαρὰν
ἐργαζόμενα, ῥᾴδια δὲ τὰ μετ' ἐλαχίστου χρόνου καὶ
πόνου καὶ δαπάνης ἐπιτελούμενα, δυνατὰ δὲ πάντα
20 τὰ ἐνδεχόμενα γενέσθαι, ἀναγκαῖα δὲ τὰ μὴ ἐφ'
ἡμῖν ὄντα πράττειν, ἀλλ' ὡς[2] ἐξ ἀνάγκης θείας ἢ
ἀνθρωπίνης οὕτως[3] ὄντα.

Τὰ μὲν οὖν δίκαια καὶ τὰ νόμιμα καὶ τὰ συμφέροντα καὶ τὰ καλὰ καὶ τὰ ἡδέα καὶ τὰ ῥᾴδια
καὶ τὰ δυνατὰ καὶ τὰ ἀναγκαῖα τοιαῦτά[4] ἐστιν.
εὐπορήσομεν δὲ περὶ τούτων λέγειν ἐξ αὐτῶν τε
25 τῶν προειρημένων καὶ τῶν ὁμοίων τούτοις καὶ τῶν

---

[1] ἔθει: v.l. εὐθύς.
[2] ὡς v.l. om.　　　[3] v.l. ὄντως.　　　[4] Rac.: ταῦτα.

laws but are observed by unwritten custom and _{1422 a}
universal practice.   These then are the just things.

Law is the common agreement of the state en-
joining in writing how men are to act in various
matters.

What is expedient is the preservation of existing ₅
good things, or the acquisition of goods that we do
not possess, or the rejection of existing evils, or the
prevention of harmful things expected to occur.
Things expedient for individuals you will classify
under body, mind and external possessions.   Expedient for the body are strength, beauty, health ; for
the mind, courage, wisdom, justice ; expedient ex- ₁₀
ternal possessions are friends, wealth, property ; and
their opposites are inexpedient.   Expedient for a
state are such things as concord, military strength,
property and a plentiful revenue, good and numerous
allies.   And briefly, we consider all things that ₁₅
resemble these expedient, and things opposite to
these inexpedient.

Honourable things are those from which some
distinction or some distinguished honour will accrue
to the agents, pleasant things are those that cause
delight, easy ones those accomplished with very little
time and labour and expense, practicable all those
that are able to be done, necessary those the per- ₂₀
formance of which does not rest with ourselves but
which are as they are in consequence, as it were, of
divine or human compulsion.

Such is the nature of the just, the lawful, the
expedient, the honourable, the pleasant, the easy, the
practicable and the necessary.   We shall find plenty
to say about them by using these conceptions in
themselves as stated above, and also their analogies ₂₅

279

1422 a

ἐναντίων αὐτοῖς καὶ τῶν ἤδη κεκριμένων ὑπὸ θεῶν
ἢ ἀνθρώπων ἐνδόξων[1] ἢ ὑπ᾽ κριτῶν ἢ ὑπὸ τῶν
ἀνταγωνιστῶν ἡμῖν.

Τὸ μὲν οὖν δίκαιον οἷον αὐτό[2] ἐστιν[3] πρότερον[4]
ἡμῖν δεδήλωται. τὸ δὲ ὅμοιον τῷ δικαίῳ τοιόνδ᾽
30 ἐστίν· " ὥσπερ γὰρ δίκαιον νομίζομεν τοῖς γονεῦσι
πείθεσθαι, τὸν αὐτὸν τρόπον προσήκει τοὺς υἱεῖς
μιμεῖσθαι τὰς τῶν πατέρων πράξεις"· καὶ " καθάπερ τοὺς εὖ ποιήσαντας ἀντευεργετεῖν δίκαιόν
ἐστιν, οὕτω τοὺς μηδὲν ἡμᾶς κακὸν ἐργασαμένους
δικαιόν ἐστι μὴ βλάπτειν." τὸ μὲν οὖν ὅμοιον τῷ
δικαίῳ τὸν τρόπον τοῦτον δεῖ λαμβάνειν, ἐκ δὲ
35 τῶν ἐναντίων χρὴ καταφανὲς ποιεῖν αὐτὸ τὸ[5]
παράδειγμα· " καθάπερ γὰρ τοὺς κακόν τι ποιήσαντας δίκαιόν ἐστι τιμωρεῖσθαι, οὕτω[6] καὶ τοὺς
εὐεργετήσαντας προσήκει ἀντευεργετεῖν." τὸ δὲ
κεκριμένον ὑπό τινων ἐνδόξων δίκαιον οὕτω λήψῃ·
" ἀλλ᾽ οὐχ ἡμεῖς μόνοι μισοῦμεν καὶ κακῶς ποιοῦ-
40 μεν τοὺς ἐχθρούς, ἀλλὰ καὶ Ἀθηναῖοι καὶ Λακε-
δαιμόνιοι δίκαιον εἶναι κρίνουσι τοὺς ἐχθροὺς
τιμωρεῖσθαι." τὸ μὲν οὖν δίκαιον οὕτω μετιὼν[7]
1422 b πολλαχῶς[8] λήψῃ.

Τὸ δὲ νόμιμον αὐτὸ μὲν οἷόν ἐστιν ὥρισται ἡμῖν
πρότερον, δεῖ δέ, ὅπου ἂν ᾖ χρήσιμον, αὐτόν τε τὸν
ἀγορεύοντα καὶ τὸν νόμον λαμβάνειν, εἶτα τὸ ὅμοιον
τῷ γεγραμμένῳ νόμῳ. εἴη δ᾽ ἂν τοιόνδε· " ὥσπερ
5 γὰρ ὁ νομοθέτης μεγίσταις ζημίαις τοὺς κλέπτας
ἐκόλασεν, οὕτω δεῖ καὶ τοὺς ἐξαπατῶντας μάλιστα
τιμωρεῖσθαι· καὶ γὰρ οὗτοι κλέπτουσι τὴν διάνοιαν"· καὶ " καθάπερ ὁ νομοθέτης κληρονόμους
πεποίηκε τοὺς ἐγγυτάτω γένους ὄντας τοῖς ἄπαισιν

_____
¹ v.l. ἐνδόξων post ἢ ὑπό.

and their opposites and the previous judgements of them made by the gods or by men of repute or by judges or by our opponents.

The nature of justice we have, then, already explained. The argument from analogy to the just is as follows : ' As we deem it just to obey our parents, 30 in the same way it behoves our sons to copy the conduct of their fathers,' and ' As it is just to do good in return to those who do us good, so it is just not to do harm to those who do us no evil.' This is the way in which we must take the analogous to the just ; and we must illustrate the actual example given from its 35 opposites : ' As it is just to punish those who do us harm, so it is also proper to do good in return to those who do us good.' The judgement of men of repute as to what is just you will take thus : ' We are not alone in hating and doing harm to our enemies, but Athens and Sparta also judge it to be just to punish 40 one's enemies.' This is how you will pursue the topic of the just, taking it in several forms. 1422 b

The nature of legality we have previously defined ; but when it serves our purpose we must bring in the person of the legislator and the terms of the law, and next the argument from analogy to the written law. This may be as follows : ' As the lawgiver has 5 punished thieves with the severest penalties, so also deceivers ought to be severely punished, because they are thieves who steal our minds ' ; and ' Even as the lawgiver has made the next of kin the heirs of those

---

ἀποθνήσκουσιν, οὕτω καὶ τῶν τοῦ ἀπελευθέρου
10 χρημάτων ἐμὲ νῦν προσήκει κύριον γενέσθαι· τῶν
γὰρ ἀπελευθερωσάντων αὐτὸν τετελευτηκότων ἐγγυτάτω γένους αὐτὸς ὢν καὶ τῶν ἀπελευθέρων[1]
δίκαιος ἂν εἴην ἄρχειν.'' τὸ μὲν οὖν ὅμοιον τῷ
νομίμῳ τοῦτον τὸν τρόπον λαμβάνεται, τὸ δ'
ἐναντίον ὧδε· '' εἰ γὰρ ὁ νόμος ἀπαγορεύει τὰ
15 δημόσια διανέμεσθαι, δῆλον ὅτι τοὺς διαιρουμένους
αὐτὰ πάντας ἀδικεῖν ὁ νομοθέτης ἔκρινεν.'' '' εἰ
γὰρ τιμᾶσθαι οἱ νόμοι προστάττουσι τοὺς καλῶς
καὶ δικαίως τῶν κοινῶν ἐπιστατήσαντας, δῆλον
ὡς καὶ τοὺς τὰ δημόσια διαφθείροντας τιμωρίας
ἀξίους νομίζουσιν.'' ἐκ μὲν οὖν τῶν ἐναντίων
20 καταφανὲς οὕτω γίνεται τὸ νόμιμον, ἐκ δὲ τῶν
κεκριμένων ὧδε· '' καὶ οὐ μόνον ἐγὼ τὸν νόμον
τοῦτον εἵνεκα τούτων φημὶ τὸν νομοθέτην θεῖναι,
ἀλλὰ καὶ πρότερον οἱ δικασταὶ διεξιόντος Λυσιθείδου
παραπλήσια τοῖς νῦν ὑπ' ἐμοῦ λεγομένοις ἐψηφί-
σαντο ταῦτα περὶ τοῦ νόμου τούτου.'' τὸ μὲν οὖν
25 νόμιμον οὕτω μετιόντες πολλαχῶς[2] δείξομεν.

Τὸ δὲ συμφέρον αὐτὸ μὲν οἷόν ἐστιν ἐν τοῖς πρότερον ὥρισται, δεῖ δὲ λαμβάνειν εἰς τοὺς λόγους
μετὰ[3] τῶν προειρημένων καὶ ἐκ τοῦ συμφέροντος
ἂν ὑπάρχῃ τι, καὶ μετιόντας τὸν αὐτὸν τρόπον
ὅνπερ ὑπὲρ τοῦ νομίμου καὶ τοῦ δικαίου διήλθομεν,
30 οὕτω καὶ τὸ συμφέρον πολλαχῶς ἐμφανίζειν. εἴη δ'
ἂν τὸ μὲν ὅμοιον τῷ συμφέροντι τοιόνδε· '' ὥσπερ
γὰρ ἐν τοῖς πολέμοις συμφέρει τοὺς εὐψυχοτάτους
πρώτους τάττειν, οὕτως ἐν ταῖς πολιτείαις λυσι-

---

[1] τοῦ ἐλευθέρου (ut videtur) Forster.
[2] πολλάκις (ut videtur) Forster.
[3] μετὰ add. Kroll.

who die childless, so in the present case I ought to 10
have the disposal of the freedman's estate, because as
those who gave him his freedom are dead and gone,
it is just that I myself being their next of kin should
have control of their freedman.' This is how the
topic of analogy to the legal is taken. That of its
opposite is taken as follows : ' If the law prohibits the
distribution of public property, it is clear that the 15
lawgiver judged all persons who take a share in it to
be guilty of an offence.' ' If the laws enjoin that
those who direct the affairs of the community honourably and justly are to be honoured, it is clear that they
deem those who destroy public property deserving
of punishment.' This is the way in which what is
legal is illustrated from its opposites. It is illustrated 20
from previous judgements thus : ' Not only do I
myself assert that this was the intention of the lawgiver in enacting this law, but also on a former
occasion when Lysitheides put forward considerations
very similar to those now advanced by me the court
voted in favour of this interpretation of the law.'
This is how we shall pursue the topic of legality,
exhibiting it in several forms. 25

The nature of expediency has been defined in what
came before ; and we must include in our speeches
with the topics previously mentioned any argument
from expediency also that may be available, and
pursue the same method as that which we followed
in dealing with legality and justice, displaying the
expedient also in many forms. The argument from 30
analogy to the expedient may be as follows : ' As it is
expedient in war to post the bravest men in the front
line, so it is profitable in the constitution of states for

1422 b

τελεῖ τοὺς φρονιμωτάτους καὶ δικαιοτάτους προ-
εστάναι τοῦ πλήθους ''· καὶ '' καθάπερ τοῖς ἀνθρώποις
ὑγιαίνουσι συμφέρει φυλάττεσθαι μὴ νοσήσωσιν,
35 οὕτω καὶ ταῖς πόλεσιν ὁμονοούσαις συμφέρον ἐστὶ
προσκοπεῖν μὴ στασιάσωσιν.'' τὰ μὲν οὖν ὅμοια
τῷ συμφέροντι τοῦτον τὸν τρόπον μετιὼν πολλὰ
ποιήσεις· ἐκ δὲ τῶν ἐναντίων ὧδέ σοι τὸ συμφέρον
ἔσται καταφανές· '' εἰ γὰρ λυσιτελεῖ τοὺς ἐπιεικεῖς
40 τῶν πολιτῶν τιμᾶν, συμφέρον ἂν εἴη καὶ τοὺς
πονηροὺς κολάζειν ''· '' εἰ γὰρ οἴεσθε ἀσύμφορον τὸ
μόνους ἡμᾶς πρὸς Θηβαίους πολεμεῖν, συμφέρον
1423 a ἂν εἴη τὸ Λακεδαιμονίους συμμάχους ποιησαμένους
ἡμᾶς οὕτω Θηβαίοις πολεμεῖν.'' ἐκ μὲν δὴ τῶν
ἐναντίων οὕτω τὸ συμφέρον καταφανὲς ποιήσεις, τὸ
δὲ κεκριμένον ὑπ' ἐνδόξων κριτῶν[1] συμφέρον ὧδε
5 χρὴ λαμβάνειν· '' Λακεδαιμόνιοί τε γὰρ 'Αθηναίους
καταπολεμήσαντες συμφέρειν αὑτοῖς ᾠήθησαν μὴ
τὴν πόλιν αὐτῶν ἀνδραποδίσασθαι, καὶ πάλιν 'Αθη-
ναῖοι, μετὰ Θηβαίων,[2] ἐξὸν αὐτοῖς ἀνοικίσαι τὴν
Σπάρτην, συμφέρειν σφίσιν ᾠήθησαν περιποιῆσαι
Λακεδαιμονίους.''

Περὶ μὲν οὖν τοῦ δικαίου καὶ τοῦ νομίμου καὶ
10 τοῦ συμφέροντος οὕτω μετιὼν εὐπορήσεις· τὸ δὲ
καλὸν καὶ τὸ ῥάδιον καὶ τὸ ἡδὺ καὶ τὸ δυνατὸν
καὶ τὸ ἀναγκαῖον ὁμοιοτρόπως τούτοις μέτιθι. καὶ
περὶ μὲν τούτων ἐντεῦθεν εὑρήσομεν.

II. Πάλιν δὲ διορισώμεθα καὶ περὶ πόσων καὶ
ποίων καὶ ἐκ[3] τίνων ἔν τε τοῖς βουλευτηρίοις καὶ
15 ταῖς ἐκκλησίαις συμβουλεύομεν· ἂν γὰρ τούτων
ἕκαστα σαφῶς ἐπιστώμεθα, τοὺς μὲν ἰδίους λόγους
αὐτὰ τὰ πράγματα καθ' ἑκάστην ἡμῖν συμβουλίαν

---

[1] κριτῶν Π: om. cet.   [2] μετὰ Θηβαίων Π: om. cet.

284

the wisest and most just to rank above the multitude ;
and ' As it is expedient for people in health to be
on their guard against contracting disease, so also it
is expedient for states enjoying a period of concord **35**
to take precautions against the rise of faction.' This
is the mode of treatment which you will pursue in
multiplying cases of analogy to the expedient. You
will demonstrate the expedient from cases of the
opposite thus : ' If it is profitable to honour virtuous
citizens, it would be expedient to punish vicious ones '; **40**
' If you think it inexpedient for us to go to war with
Thebes single-handed, it would be expedient for us **1423 a**
to make an alliance with Sparta before going to war
with Thebes.' This is how you will demonstrate the
expedient from cases of the opposite. The proper
way to take the opinion of judges of repute is as
follows : ' When Sparta had defeated Athens in war **5**
she decided that it would be expedient for herself not
to enslave the city ; and again when Athens in co-
operation with Thebes had it in her power to destroy
Sparta, she decided that it would be expedient for her
to let it survive.'

You will have plenty to say on the topics of justice,
legality and expediency by pursuing them in this
manner. Develop those of honour, facility, pleasure, **10**
practicability and necessity in a similar way. These
rules will give us plenty to say on these topics.

II. Next let us determine the number and nature *Subjects of*
of the subjects about which and the considerations *Parliament-*
on which we deliberate in council-chambers and in **15** *ary oratory.*
parliaments. If we clearly understand the various
classes of these, the business in hand at each debate
will itself supply us with arguments specially adapted

---

³ ἐκ add. Usener.

1423 a

παραδώσει, τὰς δὲ κοινὰς ἰδέας ἐκ πολλοῦ προ-
ειδότες ἐπιφέρειν ἐφ' ἑκάσταις τῶν πράξεων ῥαδίως δυνησόμεθα. τούτων οὖν ἕνεκα διαιρετέον ἡμῖν
20 περὶ ὧν κοινῇ βουλεύονται πάντες.

Ἐν κεφαλαίῳ μὲν οὖν εἰπεῖν εἰσὶν ἑπτὰ τὸν ἀρι-
θμὸν προθέσεις περὶ ὧν δημηγορήσομεν. ἀνάγκη
γάρ ἐστι καὶ βουλεύεσθαι καὶ λέγειν ἡμᾶς ἐν βουλῇ
καὶ δήμῳ ἢ περὶ ἱερῶν ἢ περὶ νόμων ἢ περὶ τῆς
πολιτικῆς κατασκευῆς ἢ περὶ τῶν πρὸς ἄλλας
25 πόλεις συμμαχιῶν καὶ συμβολαίων ἢ περὶ πολέμων
ἢ περὶ εἰρήνης ἢ περὶ πόρου χρημάτων. αἱ μὲν
οὖν προθέσεις αὗται τυγχάνουσιν οὖσαι περὶ ὧν
βουλευσόμεθα καὶ δημηγορήσομεν· ἑκάστην δὲ
πρόθεσιν διελώμεθα, καὶ σκοπῶμεν ἐν οἷς τρόποις
ἐνδέχεται περὶ τούτων λόγῳ χρήσασθαι.

30 Περὶ μὲν οὖν ἱερῶν τριττῶς[1] ἀναγκαῖον λέγειν·
ἢ γὰρ ἐροῦμεν ὡς τὰ καθεστῶτα διαφυλακτέον ἢ
ὡς ἐπὶ τὸ μεγαλοπρεπέστερον μεταστατέον[2] ἢ ὡς
ἐπὶ τὸ ταπεινότερον. ὅταν μὲν οὖν λέγωμεν ὡς δεῖ
τὰ καθεστῶτα διαφυλάττειν, εὑρήσομεν ἀφορμὰς ἐκ
μὲν τοῦ δικαίου λέγοντες ὅτι τὰ πάτρια ἔθη παρὰ
35 πᾶσι παραβαίνειν ἄδικόν ἐστι, καὶ ὅτι τὰ μαντεῖα
πάντα τοῖς ἀνθρώποις προστάττει κατὰ τὰ πάτρια
ποιεῖσθαι τὰς θυσίας, καὶ ὅτι τῶν πρώτων οἰκι-
σάντων[3] τὰς πόλεις καὶ τοῖς θεοῖς ἱδρυσαμένων τὰ
ἱερὰ μάλιστα δεῖ διαμένειν τὰς περὶ τοὺς θεοὺς
ἐπιμελείας· ἐκ δὲ τοῦ συμφέροντος, ὅτι πρὸς χρη-
1423 b μάτων συντέλειαν ἢ τοῖς ἰδιώταις ἢ τῷ κοινῷ τῆς
πόλεως συμφέρον ἔσται κατὰ τὰ πάτρια τῶν ἱερῶν

---

[1] Bekker: περιττῶς.
[2] μεταστατέον Π: πως cet.
[3] Rac.: οἰκιζόντων aut οἰκίζοντας.

1423 a

to it, while we shall readily be able to produce general
ideas applicable to the particular matter in hand if we
have been familiar with them long before. For these
reasons, therefore, we must classify the matters that
universally form the subject of our deliberations in 20
common.

To speak summarily therefore, the subjects about
which we shall make public speeches are seven in
number : our deliberations and speeches in council
and in parliament must necessarily deal with either
religious ritual, or legislation, or the form of the constitution, or alliances and treaties with other states, 25
or war, or peace, or finance. These, then, being
the subjects of our deliberations in council and of our
speeches in parliament, let us examine each of them,
and consider the ways in which we can deal with them
when making a speech.

In speaking about rites of religion, three lines can 30
be taken : either we shall say that we ought to maintain the established ritual as it is, or that we ought to
alter it to a more splendid form, or alter it to a more
modest form. When we are saying that the established ritual ought to be maintained, we shall draw
arguments from considerations of right by saying that
in all countries it is deemed wrong to depart from
the ancestral customs, that all the oracles enjoin on 35
mankind the performance of their sacrifices in the
ancestral manner, and that it is the religious observances of the original founders of cities and builders of
the gods' temples that it behoves us most to conserve.
Arguing from expediency, we shall say that the performance of the sacrifices in the ancestral manner 1423 b
will be advantageous either for individual citizens or
for the community on the ground of economy, and

1423 b

θυομένων, καὶ ὅτι πρὸς εὐτολμίαν λυσιτελήσει[1] τοῖς
πολίταις, ἐπεὶ συμπομπευόντων ὁπλιτῶν ἱππέων
5 ψιλῶν εὐτολμότεροι γένοιντ' ἂν οἱ πολῖται φιλο-
τιμούμενοι περὶ ταῦτα· ἐκ δὲ τοῦ καλοῦ, εἰ οὕτω
λαμπρὰς τὰς ἑορτὰς ποιεῖσθαι[2] συμβέβηκεν· ἐκ δὲ
τῆς ἡδονῆς, εἰ καὶ πρὸς τὸ θεωρεῖσθαι ποικιλία τις
περὶ τὰς τῶν θεῶν θυσίας· ἐκ δὲ τοῦ δυνατοῦ, εἰ
μήτε ἔνδεια γεγένηται μήτε ὑπερβολὴ περὶ ταύτας.
10 ὅταν μὲν οὖν τοῖς καθεστῶσι συνηγορῶμεν, οὕτω
μετιοῦσι σκεπτέον ἐκ[3] τῶν προειρημένων ἢ τῶν
τούτοις ὁμοιοτρόπων, καὶ ὡς ἐνδέχεται διδάσκειν
περὶ τῶν λεγομένων.

Ὅταν δὲ ἐπὶ τὸ μεγαλοπρεπέστερον συμ-
βουλεύωμεν μεθιστάναι τὰς ἱεροποιίας, περὶ μὲν
τοῦ τὰ πάτρια κινεῖν ἀφορμὰς ἕξομεν εὐπρεπεῖς
15 λέγοντες ὅτι τὸ προστιθέναι τοῖς ὑπάρχουσιν οὐ
καταλύειν ἐστὶν ἀλλ' αὔξειν τὰ καθεστῶτα, ἔπειθ'
ὡς καὶ τοὺς θεοὺς εἰκὸς εὐνουστέρους εἶναι τοῖς
μᾶλλον αὐτοὺς τιμῶσιν, ἔπειθ' ὡς οὐδὲ οἱ πατέρες
ἀεὶ κατὰ τὰ αὐτὰ τὰς θυσίας ἦγον, ἀλλὰ πρὸς τοὺς
καιροὺς καὶ τὰς εὐπραγίας ὁρῶντες καὶ ἰδίᾳ καὶ
20 κοινῇ τὴν πρὸς τοὺς θεοὺς θεραπείαν ἐνομοθέτουν,
ἔπειθ' ὡς καὶ ἐπὶ τῶν λοιπῶν ἁπάντων οὕτω καὶ
τὰς πόλεις καὶ τοὺς ἰδίους οἴκους διοικοῦμεν· λέγε
δὲ καὶ εἰ τούτων κατασκευασθέντων ὠφέλειά τις
ἔσται τῇ πόλει ἢ λαμπρότης ἢ ἡδονή, μετιὼν ὥσπερ
ἐπὶ τῶν προτέρων εἴρηται. ὅταν δὲ ἐπὶ τὸ ταπεινό-

---

[1] Rac.: λυσιτελεῖ.
[2] Rac.: πρὸς τὸ θεωρεῖσθαι (ex seq.) aut θεωρῆσαι.
[3] Kayser: ἐπὶ

that it will profit the citizens in respect of courage
because if they are escorted in religious processions
by heavy infantry, cavalry and light-armed troops
the pride that they will take in this will make them
more courageous. We can urge it on the ground of 5
honour if it has resulted in the festivals being cele-
brated with so much splendour ; on the ground of
pleasure if a certain elaboration has been introduced
into the sacrifices of the gods merely as a spectacle ;
on the ground of practicability if there has been
neither deficiency nor extravagance in the celebra-
tions. These are the lines we must pursue when we 10
are advocating the established order, basing our considerations on the arguments already stated or arguments similar to them, and on such explanation of
our case as is feasible.

When we are advocating the alteration of the
sacrificial rites in the direction of greater splendour,
we shall find plausible arguments for changing the
ancestral institutions in saying (1) that to add to what 15
exists already is not to destroy but to amplify the
established order ; (2) that in all probability even the
gods show more benevolence towards those who pay
them more honour; (3) that even our forefathers used
not to conduct the sacrifices always on the same lines,
but regulated their religious observances both private
and public with an eye to the occasions and to the
prosperity of their circumstances ; (4) that this is the 20
manner in which we administer both our states and
our private households in all the rest of our affairs as
well ; (5) and also specify any benefit or distinction or
pleasure that will accrue to the state if these recom-
mendations are carried out, developing the subject
in the manner explained in the former cases. When,

289

1423 b

25 τερον συστέλλωμεν, πρῶτον μὲν ἐπὶ τοὺς καιροὺς
τὸν λόγον ἀνακτέον, τί πράττοντες χεῖρον οἱ πολῖται
τυγχάνουσι νῦν ἢ πρότερον· ἔπειθ' ὡς οὐκ εἰκὸς
τοὺς θεοὺς χαίρειν ταῖς δαπάναις τῶν θυομένων
ἀλλὰ ταῖς εὐσεβείαις τῶν θυόντων· εἶθ' ὡς πολλὴν
ἄνοιαν τούτων καὶ οἱ θεοὶ καὶ οἱ ἄνθρωποι κατα-
30 κρίνουσιν ὅσοι παρὰ δύναμίν τι ποιοῦσιν· ἔπειθ' ὅτι
οὐκ ἐπὶ τοῖς ἀνθρώποις μόνον ἀλλὰ καὶ ἐπὶ ταῖς
εὐπραγίαις καὶ κακοπραγίαις ἐστὶ τὰ περὶ τὰς
πολιτικὰς δαπάνας. ἀφορμὰς μὲν οὖν ταύτας καὶ
τὰς ὁμοιοτρόπους ταύταις ὑπὲρ τῶν περὶ τὰς
θυσίας προθέσεων ἕξομεν· ἵνα δὲ καὶ τὰ κατὰ τὴν
35 κρατίστην θυσίαν εἰδῶμεν εἰσηγεῖσθαι καὶ νομοθετεῖν, ὁρισώμεθα καὶ ταύτην. ἔστι γὰρ κρατίστη
θυσία πασῶν ἥτις ἂν ἔχοι πρὸς μὲν τοὺς θεοὺς
ὁσίως,[1] πρὸς δὲ τὰς δαπάνας μετρίως, πρὸς δὲ
πόλεμον ὠφελίμως, πρὸς δὲ τὰς θεωρίας λαμπρῶς.
ἕξει δὲ πρὸς μὲν τοὺς θεοὺς ὁσίως ἐὰν τὰ πάτρια
1424 a μὴ καταλύηται, πρὸς δὲ τὰς δαπάνας μετρίως ἐὰν
μὴ πάντα τὰ πεμπόμενα καταναλίσκηται, πρὸς δὲ
τὰς θεωρίας λαμπρῶς ἐὰν χρυσῷ καὶ τοῖς τοιούτοις
ἃ μὴ συναναλίσκεται δαψιλῶς τις χρήσηται, πρὸς
5 δὲ τοὺς πολέμους ὠφελίμως ἐὰν ἱππεῖς καὶ ὁπλῖται
διεσκευασμένοι συμπομπεύωσιν.

Τὰ μὲν δὴ περὶ τοὺς θεοὺς ἐκ τούτων κάλλιστα
κατασκευάσομεν, ἐκ δὲ τῶν πρότερον εἰρημένων
καθ' οὓς ἐνδέχεται τρόπους δημηγορεῖν περὶ
ἑκάστης ἱεροποιίας εἰσόμεθα.

Περὶ δὲ νόμων πάλιν καὶ τῆς πολιτικῆς κατα-
10 σκευῆς ὁμοιοτρόπως διέλθωμεν. εἰσὶ δὲ νόμοι συλ-

---

[1] Bekker: ὁσίως καὶ θείως.

1423 b

on the other hand, we are advocating a reduction to a
more modest form, we must first (1) direct our remarks ₂₅
to the condition of the times and show how the public
are less prosperous now than they were previously ;
then argue (2) that probably it is not the cost of the
sacrifices but the piety of those who offer them that
give pleasure to the gods ; (3) that people who do a
thing that is beyond their capacity are judged by both ₃₀
gods and men to be guilty of great folly ; (4) that
questions of public expenditure turn not only on the
human factor but also on the good or bad state of
finance. These, then, and similar lines of argument
will be available to support our proposals with regard
to sacrifices. Let us now define what is the best form
of sacrifice, in order that we may know how to frame ₃₅
proposals and pass laws for its regulation. The best
of all sacrificial ceremonies is one organized in a
manner that is pious towards the gods, moderate in
expense, of military benefit, and brilliant as a spectacle. It will show piety to the gods if the ancestral
ritual is preserved ; it will be moderate in expense **1424 a**
if not all the offerings carried in procession are
used up ; brilliant as a spectacle if lavish use is
made of gold and things of that sort which are not
used up in the celebration ; of military advantage
if cavalry and infantry in full array march in the ₅
procession.

These considerations will provide us with the finest
ways of organizing the ceremonies of religion ; and
what has been said before will inform us of the lines
that may be followed in public speeches about the
various forms of religious celebration.

Let us next in a similar manner discuss the subject
of law and the constitution of the state. Laws may ₁₀

1424 a

λήβδην μὲν εἰπεῖν ὁμολογήματα κοινὰ πόλεως, ἃ
διὰ γραμμάτων ὁρίζει καὶ προστάττει πῶς χρὴ
ἕκαστα πράττειν.

Δεῖ δὲ αὐτῶν τὴν θέσιν ἐν μὲν ταῖς δημοκρατίαις
τὰς μικρὰς ἀρχὰς καὶ τὰς πολλὰς κληρωτὰς ποιεῖν
(ἀστασίαστον γὰρ τοῦτο), τὰς δὲ μεγίστας χειρο-
15 τονητὰς ὑπὸ[1] τοῦ πλήθους· οὕτω γὰρ ὁ μὲν δῆμος
κύριος ὢν διδόναι τὰς τιμὰς οἷς ἂν ἐθέλῃ τοῖς
λαμβάνουσιν αὐτὰς οὐ φθονήσει, οἱ δ' ἐπιφανέ-
στεροι μᾶλλον τὴν καλοκἀγαθίαν ἀσκήσουσιν, εἰδότες
ὅτι τὸ παρὰ τοῖς πολίταις εὐδοκιμεῖν οὐκ ἀλυσι-
τελὲς αὐτοῖς ἔσται. περὶ μὲν οὖν τὰς ἀρχαιρεσίας
20 ἐν τῇ δημοκρατίᾳ οὕτω δεῖ νομοθετεῖν· περὶ δὲ τὴν
ἄλλην διοίκησιν καθ' ἓν μὲν ἕκαστον διελθεῖν πολὺ
ἂν ἔργον εἴη, συλλήβδην δὲ δεῖ παραφυλάττειν
ὅπως οἱ νόμοι τὸ μὲν πλῆθος ἀποτρέψωσι τοῖς τὰς
οὐσίας ἔχουσιν ἐπιβουλεύειν, τοῖς δὲ πλουτοῦσιν
25 εἰς τὰς κοινὰς λειτουργίας δαπανᾶν[2] φιλοτιμίαν ἐμ-
ποιήσωσιν. τοῦτο δὲ οὕτως ἂν κατασκευάσαιεν,
εἰ τοῖς μὲν τὰς οὐσίας ἔχουσιν ἀντὶ τῶν εἰς τὸ
κοινὸν δαπανωμένων τιμαί τινες [ἀπὸ τῶν νόμων][3]
ἀφωρισμέναι τυγχάνοιεν, τῶν δὲ πενομένων τοὺς τὴν
χώραν ἐργαζομένους καὶ τοὺς[4] ναυτικοὺς[5] τῶν ἀγο-
30 ραίων μᾶλλον προτιμῷεν, ὅπως οἱ μὲν πλουτοῦντες
ἑκόντες τῇ πόλει λειτουργήσωσι, τὸ δὲ πλῆθος οὐ
συκοφαντίας ἀλλ' ἐργασίας ἐπιθυμήσῃ. δεῖ δὲ πρὸς
τούτοις καὶ περὶ τοῦ μήτε χώραν ποιεῖν ἀνάδαστον
μήτε δημεύειν τὰς οὐσίας τῶν τελευτώντων[6]
ἰσχυροὺς κεῖσθαι νόμους, καὶ μεγάλας ἐπικεῖσθαι
35 τιμωρίας τοῖς παραβαίνουσι ταῦτα. χρὴ δὲ τοῖς ἐν

---

[1] Sp.: ἀπό.   [2] δαπανᾶν Π: ἑκουσίαν ἅπασαν cet.
[3] ἀπὸ τῶν νόμων om. M.   [4] τοὺς add. Rac.

292

be briefly described as common agreements of a state, defining and prescribing in writing various rules of conduct.

In democracies legislation should make the general run of minor offices elected by lot (for that prevents party faction) but the most important offices elected by the vote of the community ; under this system the people having sovereign power to bestow the honours on whom they choose will not be jealous of those who obtain them, while the men of distinction will the more cultivate nobility of character, knowing that it will be advantageous for them to stand in good repute with their fellow-citizens. This is how the election of officials should be regulated by law in a democracy. A detailed discussion of the rest of the administration would be a laborious task ; but to speak summarily, precautions must be taken to make the laws deter the multitude from plotting against the owners of landed estates and engender in the wealthy an ambition to spend money on the public services. This the law might effect if some offices were reserved for the propertied classes, as a return for what they spent on public objects, and if among the poorer people the laws paid more respect to the tillers of the soil and the sailor class than to the city rabble, in order that the wealthy may be willing to undertake public services and the multitude may devote itself to industry and not to cadging. In addition to this there should be strict laws laid down prohibiting the distribution of public lands and the confiscation of property on the decease of the owners, and severe penalties should be imposed on those who transgress these

---

⁵ ναυτικοὺς Π corr. Blass : ναυκληροῦντας cet.
⁶ τῶν ἰδιωτῶν Usener.

293

1424 a

πολέμῳ τελευτῶσιν εἰς ταφήν τι χωρίον δημόσιον
ἐν καλῷ πρὸ τῆς πόλεως ἀφωρίσθαι, καὶ τοῖς
παισὶν αὐτῶν ἕως ἥβης δημοσίαν τροφὴν δίδοσθαι.
τῶν μὲν οὖν ἐν τῇ δημοκρατίᾳ νόμων τὴν θέσιν
τοιαύτην δεῖ ποιεῖσθαι.

Περὶ δὲ τὰς ὀλιγαρχίας, τὰς μὲν ἀρχὰς δεῖ τοὺς
40 νόμους ἀπονέμειν ἐξ ἴσου πᾶσι τοῖς τῆς πολιτείας
1424 b μετέχουσι, τούτων δὲ εἶναι τὰς μὲν πλείστας κλη-
ρωτάς, τὰς δὲ μεγίστας κρυπτῇ ψήφῳ μεθ᾽ ὅρκων
καὶ πλείστης ἀκριβείας διαψηφιστάς. δεῖ δὲ τὰς
ζημίας ἐν τῇ ὀλιγαρχίᾳ μεγίστας ἐπικεῖσθαι τοῖς
ὑβρίζειν τινὰς τῶν πολιτῶν ἐπιχειροῦσιν· τὸ γὰρ
5 πλῆθος οὐχ οὕτω τῶν ἀρχῶν ἀγανακτεῖ στερού-
μενον ὡς ἔχει βαρέως ὑβριζόμενον. χρὴ δὲ καὶ τὰς
διαφορὰς τῶν πολιτῶν ὅτι τάχιστα διαλύειν καὶ μὴ
χρονίζεσθαι· μηδὲ συνάγειν ἐκ τῆς χώρας ἐπὶ τὴν
πόλιν τὸν ὄχλον, ἐκ γὰρ τῶν τοιούτων συνόδων
συστρέφεται τὰ πλήθη καὶ καταλύει τὰς ὀλιγ-
10 αρχίας.

Καθόλου δὲ εἰπεῖν, δεῖ τοὺς νόμους ἐν μὲν
ταῖς δημοκρατίαις κωλύειν τοὺς πολλοὺς ταῖς τῶν
πλουσίων οὐσίαις ἐπιβουλεύειν, ἐν δὲ ταῖς ὀλιγαρ-
χίαις ἀποτρέπειν τοὺς τῆς πολιτείας μετέχοντας
ὑβρίζειν τοὺς ἀσθενεστέρους καὶ συκοφαντεῖν τοὺς
πολίτας. ὧν μὲν οὖν ὀρέγεσθαι δεῖ τοὺς νόμους
15 καὶ τὴν πολιτικὴν κατασκευήν, ἐκ τούτων οὐκ
ἀγνοήσεις.

Δεῖ δὲ τὸν συναγορεύειν ἐθέλοντα νόμῳ δεικνύειν
τοῦτον ἴσον ὄντα τοῖς πολίταις ὁμολογούμενόν τε
τοῖς ἄλλοις νόμοις, καὶ συμφέροντα τῇ πόλει
μάλιστα μὲν πρὸς ὁμόνοιαν, εἰ δὲ μή, πρὸς τὴν τῶν

enactments. A public burial-ground in a fine situation outside the city should be assigned to those who
fall in war, and their sons should receive public
maintenance till they come of age. Such should
be the nature of the legal system enacted in a
democracy.

In the case of oligarchies, the laws should assign the
offices on an equal footing to all those sharing in
citizenship. Election to most of the offices should be 40
by lot, but for the most important it should be by **1424 b**
vote, under oath, with a secret ballot and very strict
regulations. The penalties enacted for those attempting to insult any of the citizens should in an oligarchy 5
be very heavy, as the multitude resents insolent treatment more than it is annoyed by exclusion from office.
Also differences between the citizens should be
settled as quickly as possible and not allowed to drag
on ; and the mob should not be brought together
from the country to the city, because such gatherings
lead to the masses making common cause and over-
throwing the oligarchies. 10

And, speaking generally, the laws in a democracy
should hinder the many from plotting designs upon
the property of the wealthy, and in an oligarchy
they should deter those who have a share in the
government from treating the weaker men with
insolence and toadying to their fellow-citizens.
These considerations will inform you of the objects
at which the laws and framework of the constitution
of the state should aim.

One who wishes to advocate a law has to prove that
it will be equal for the citizens, consistent with the
other laws, and advantageous for the state, best of all
as promoting concord, or failing that, as contributing

20 πολιτῶν καλοκἀγαθίαν ἢ πρὸς τὰς κοινὰς προσ-
όδους ἢ πρὸς εὐδοξίαν τῷ κοινῷ τῆς πόλεως ἢ
πρὸς τὴν πολιτικὴν δύναμιν ἢ πρὸς ἄλλο τι τῶν
τοιούτων. ἀντιλέγοντα δὲ δεῖ[1] σκοπεῖν πρῶτον μὲν
εἰ μὴ κοινὸς ὁ νόμος, ἔπειτα εἰ μὴ τοῖς ἄλλοις
ὁμολογῶν ἀλλ' ὑπεναντίος ἔσται, ἐπὶ τούτοις εἰ μὴ
25 πρὸς μηδὲν τῶν εἰρημένων συμφέρων ἀλλὰ τοὐναντίον βλαβερός.

Περὶ μὲν οὖν νόμων καὶ τῆς κοινῆς κατασκευῆς
ἐντεῦθεν καὶ τιθέναι καὶ λέγειν εὐπορήσομεν.

Περὶ δὲ συμμαχιῶν[2] καὶ τῶν πρὸς τὰς ἄλλας
πόλεις συμβολαίων διελθεῖν ἐπιχειρήσομεν. τὰ μὲν
οὖν συμβόλαια κατὰ[3] τάξεις ἀναγκαῖον καὶ[4] συνθήκας
30 κοινὰς γίνεσθαι, συμμάχους δὲ ποιεῖσθαι κατὰ τοὺς
καιροὺς τούτους ὅταν τινὲς καθ' ἑαυτοὺς ὦσιν
ἀσθενεῖς ἢ πόλεμός τις ᾖ προσδόκιμος, ἢ διὰ τοῦτο
ποιήσασθαι συμμαχίαν πρός τινας[5] ὅτι πολέμου
ἀποστήσειν τινὰς νομίζουσιν. αἰτίαι μὲν οὖν αὗται
καὶ παραπλήσιαι ταύταις ἄλλαι πλείους τοῦ ποιεῖ-
35 σθαι συμμάχους εἰσίν· δεῖ δέ, ὅταν συναγορεύειν
βούλῃ τῇ γινομένῃ συμμαχίᾳ, τὸν καιρὸν τοιοῦτον
ὑπάρχοντα ἐμφανίζειν, καὶ δεικνύναι τοὺς τὴν
συμμαχίαν ποιουμένους μάλιστα μὲν δικαίους ὄντας
καὶ πρότερόν τι τῇ πόλει ἀγαθὸν πεποιηκότας καὶ
40 δύναμιν μεγάλην ἔχοντας καὶ πλησίον τοῖς τόποις
κατοικοῦντας, εἰ δὲ μή, τούτων ἅπερ ἂν ὑπάρχῃ,
1425 a ταῦτα συνάγειν. ὅταν δὲ διακωλύῃς τὴν συμμαχίαν, ἐμφανίζειν ἐνδέχεται πρῶτον μὲν ὡς οὐκ
ἀνάγκη ποιεῖσθαι νῦν αὐτήν, ἔπειθ' ὡς οὐ δίκαιοι
τυγχάνουσιν ὄντες, εἶθ' ὡς πρότερον ἡμᾶς κακῶς

---

[1] δὲ δεῖ Rac.: δὲ aut δεῖ (in uno cod. δεῖ cum δὲ supra-
scripto).   [2] Sp.: συμμάχων.

to the noble qualities of the citizens or to the public 20
revenues or to the good repute of the commonwealth
or the power of the state or something else of the
kind. In speaking against a proposal the points to
consider are, first, is the law not impartial ? next,
will it be really at variance with the other laws and
not in agreement with them ? and in addition, instead
of promoting any of the objects stated, will it on the
contrary be detrimental to them ?   25

This will supply us with plenty of material for
making proposals and speeches about laws and the
constitution of the commonwealth.

We will proceed to the consideration of alliances
and covenants with other states. Covenants must
necessarily be framed in accordance with regulations
and common agreements ; and it is necessary to
secure allies on occasions when people by themselves 30
are weak or when a war is expected, or to make an
alliance with one nation because it is thought that
this will deter another nation from war. These and a
number of additional similar reasons are the grounds
for making allies ; and when one wishes to support
the formation of an alliance it is necessary to show 35
that the situation is of this nature, and to prove if
possible that the contracting nation is reliable in
character, and has done the state some service previously, and is very powerful and a near neighbour, or 40
failing this, you must collect together whichever of 1425 a
these advantages do exist. When you are opposing
the alliance you can show first that it is not necessary to make it now, secondly that the proposed allies
are not really reliable, thirdly that they have treated

---

³ κατὰ Sp.: καὶ τά.   ⁴ καὶ τὰ Sp.: κατὰ.
⁵ [ποιήσασθαι . . . πρός τινας] Usener.

πεποιηκότες, εἰ δὲ μή, ὡς μακρὰν τοῖς τόποις
5 ἀπέχοντες καὶ οὐχ ὑπάρχοντες δυνατοὶ κατὰ τοὺς
προσήκοντας παραγενέσθαι καιρούς. ταῖς μὲν οὖν
ἀντιλογίαις καὶ ταῖς συνηγορίαις ταῖς περὶ τῶν
συμμαχιῶν¹ ἐκ τούτων καὶ τῶν τούτοις ὁμοιοτρόπων εὐπορήσομεν χρῆσθαι.

Περὶ εἰρήνης δὲ πάλιν καὶ πολέμου τὸν αὐτὸν
10 τρόπον τὰς μεγίστας ἰδέας ἐκλάβωμεν. προφάσεις
μὲν οὖν εἰσὶ τοῦ πόλεμον ἐκφέρειν πρός τινας
αὗται· δεῖ πρότερον ἀδικηθέντας νῦν καιρῶν παρα-
πεπτωκότων ἀμύνασθαι τοὺς ἀδικήσαντας, ἢ νῦν
ἀδικουμένους ὑπὲρ ἑαυτῶν πολεμεῖν ἢ ὑπὲρ συγ-
γενῶν ἢ ὑπὲρ εὐεργετῶν, ἢ συμμάχοις ἀδικουμένοις
15 βοηθεῖν, ἢ τοῦ τῇ πόλει συμφέροντος ἕνεκεν ἢ εἰς
εὐδοξίαν ἢ εἰς εὐπορίαν ἢ εἰς δύναμιν ἢ εἰς ἄλλο τι
τῶν τοιούτων. ὅταν μὲν οὖν ἐπὶ τὸ πολεμεῖν
παρακαλῶμεν, τούτων τε τῶν προφάσεων ὅτι
πλείστας συνακτέον, καὶ μετὰ ταῦτα δεικτέον, ἐξ
ὧν ἔστι περιγενέσθαι τῷ πολέμῳ, ὅτι τὰ πλεῖστα
20 τούτων τοῖς παρακαλουμένοις ὑπάρχοντά ἐστιν.
περιγίνονται δὲ πάντες ἢ διὰ τὴν τῶν θεῶν εὔνοιαν,
ἣν εὐτυχίαν² προσαγορεύομεν, ἢ διὰ σωμάτων
πλῆθος καὶ ῥώμην, ἢ διὰ χρημάτων εὐπορίαν, ἢ διὰ
στρατηγοῦ φρόνησιν, ἢ διὰ συμμάχων ἀρετήν, ἢ
διὰ τόπων εὐφυΐαν. τούτων οὖν καὶ τῶν τοιούτων
25 τὰ τοῖς πράγμασιν οἰκειότατα³ λαμβάνοντες ἐμ-
φανιοῦμεν ὅταν ἐπὶ τὸ πολεμεῖν παρακαλῶμεν, τὰ
μὲν τῶν ἐναντίων ταπεινοῦντες, τὰ δ' ἡμέτερα ταῖς⁴
αὐξήσεσι μεγάλα καθιστῶντες.

---

¹ Rac.: συμμάχων.
² v.l. εὐψυχίαν (Usener add. ἢ δι' εὐψυχίαν post προσαγορεύομεν).

us badly before, or if not, that they are remote in locality and not really able to come to our assistance on the suitable occasions. From these and similar considerations we shall be well supplied with arguments to use in opposing and in advocating alliances.

Again, let us in the same manner pick out the most important considerations on the question of peace and war. The following are the arguments for making war on somebody: that we have been wronged in the past, and now that opportunity offers ought to punish the wrongdoers; or, that we are being wronged now, and ought to go to war in our own defence—or in defence of our kinsmen or of our benefactors; or, that our allies are being wronged and we ought to go to their help; or, that it is to the advantage of the state in respect of glory or wealth or power or the like. When we are exhorting people to go to war we should bring together as many of these arguments as possible, and afterwards show that most of the factors on which success in war depends are on the side of those whom we are addressing. Success is always due either to the favour of the gods which we call good fortune, or to man-power and efficiency, or financial resources, or wise generalship, or to having good allies, or to natural advantages of locality. When exhorting people to war we shall select and put forward those among these and similar topics that are most relevant to the situation, belittling the resources of the adversaries and magnifying and amplifying our own.

---

³ Sp.: οἰκεῖα aut οἰκειότερα.　　⁴ ταῖς om. v.l.

1425 a

Ἐὰν δὲ πόλεμον μέλλοντα γίνεσθαι διακωλύειν
ἐπιχειρῶμεν, πρῶτον μὲν διὰ[1] προφάσεων δεικτέον
30 ἢ παντελῶς οὐδεμίαν ὑπάρχουσαν ἢ μικρὰς καὶ
ταπεινὰς οὔσας τὰς δυσχερείας, ἔπειθ' ὡς οὐ
συμφέρει πολεμεῖν, διεξιόντας[2] τὰ κατὰ τὸν πόλεμον
ἀτυχήματα τοῖς ἀνθρώποις, πρὸς δὲ τούτοις τὰ πρὸς
νίκας συντείνοντα τοῦ πολέμου τοῖς ἐναντίοις ὑπάρχοντα μᾶλλον δεικτέον (ταῦτα δ' ἐστὶν ἅπερ ἀρτίως
35 κατηρίθμηται). γίνεσθαι μὲν οὖν μέλλοντα πόλεμον
ἐκ τούτων ἀποτρεπτέον· ἤδη δ' ἐνεστῶτα παύειν
ἐπιχειροῦντας, ἐὰν μὲν κρατῶσιν οἱ συμβουλευό-
μενοι, αὐτὸ τοῦτο πρῶτον λεκτέον, ὅτι δεῖ τοὺς
νοῦν ἔχοντας μὴ περιμένειν ἕως ἂν πέσωσιν[3] ἀλλ'
ἐν τῷ κρατεῖν ποιεῖσθαι τὴν εἰρήνην, ἔπειτα διότι
40 πέφυκεν ὁ πόλεμος καὶ τῶν εὐτυχούντων ἐν αὐτῷ
1425 b πολλοὺς ἀπολλύναι, ἡ δ' εἰρήνη τοὺς μὲν ἡτ-
τωμένους σῴζειν, τοὺς δὲ νικῶντας ὧν ἕνεκεν
ἐπολέμησαν παρέχειν ἀπολαύειν· διεξιτέον δὲ τὰς
μεταβολὰς τὰς ἐν τῷ πολέμῳ, ὡς πολλαὶ καὶ
παράλογοι γίνονται. τοὺς μὲν οὖν ἐν τῷ πολέμῳ
5 κρατοῦντας ἐκ τῶν τοιούτων ἐπὶ τὴν εἰρήνην
παρακλητέον, τοὺς δ' ἐπταικότας ἐξ αὐτῶν τε τῶν
συμβάντων, καὶ ἐκ τοῦ μὴ παροξύνεσθαι τοῖς προ-
αδικήσασι ταῖς συμφοραῖς πειθομένους, καὶ ἐκ τῶν
κινδύνων τῶν γεγενημένων ἐκ τοῦ[4] μὴ ποιήσασθαι
τὴν εἰρήνην, καὶ ἐκ τοῦ κρεῖττον εἶναι τοῖς κρείτ-
10 τοσι μέρος τι τῶν ὑπαρχόντων προέσθαι ἢ πολέμῳ
κρατηθέντας αὐτοὺς αὐτοῖς κτήμασιν ἀπολέσθαι.

---

[1] διὰ: τῶν Sp.
[2] Sp.· διεξιόντα.   [3] πταίσωσιν Finckh.
[4] ἐκ τοῦ Halm: τοῦ (τῷ Kayser).

1425 a

If, on the other hand, we are trying to prevent a war that is impending, we must first employ arguments to prove either that no grievance exists at all or that the 30 grievances are small and negligible; next we must prove that it is not expedient to go to war, by enumerating the misfortunes that befall mankind in war, and in addition we must show that the factors conducive to victory in war (which are those that were enumerated just above) are more to be found on the side of the enemy. These are the considerations to be employed to avert a war that is impending. 35 When we are trying to stop a war that has already begun, if those whom we are advising are getting the upper hand, the first thing to say is that sensible people should not wait till they have a fall but should make peace while they have the upper hand, and next that it is the nature of war to ruin 40 many even of those who are successful in it, whereas it is the nature of peace to save the vanquished while 1425 b allowing the victors to enjoy the prizes for which they went to war ; and we must point out how many and how incalculable are the changes of fortune that occur in war. Such are the considerations to be employed in exhorting to peace those who are gaining 5 the upper hand in a war. Those who have encountered a reverse we must urge to make peace on the ground of what has actually happened to them, and on the ground that they ought to learn from their misfortunes not to be exasperated with their wrongful aggressors, and because of the dangers that have already resulted from not making peace, and because it would be better to sacrifice a portion of their pos- 10 sessions to the stronger power than to be vanquished in war and lose their lives as well as their property.

ARISTOTLE

**1425 b**

συλλήβδην δὲ τοῦθ᾽ ἡμᾶς εἰδέναι δεῖ, ὅτι τότε
πάντες ἄνθρωποι τοὺς πολέμους εἰώθασι διαλύεσθαι
πρὸς ἀλλήλους ὅταν ἢ τὰ[1] δίκαια ἀξιοῦν τοὺς ἐναντίους ὑπολαμβάνωσιν ἢ διενεχθῶσι τοῖς συμμάχοις
15 ἢ τῷ πολέμῳ κάμωσιν[2] ἢ φοβηθῶσι τοὺς ἐναντίους
ἢ στασιάσωσι πρὸς σφᾶς αὐτούς.

Ὥστε τούτων τε πάντων καὶ τῶν τούτοις ὁμοιοτρόπων τὰ τοῖς πράγμασιν οἰκειότατα συνάγων οὐκ
ἀπορήσεις ὅθεν χρὴ περὶ πολέμου δημηγορεῖν καὶ
εἰρήνης.

Λείπεται δ᾽ ἡμᾶς ἔτι περὶ πόρου χρημάτων
20 διελθεῖν. πρῶτον μὲν οὖν σκεπτέον εἴ τι τῶν τῆς
πόλεως κτημάτων ἠμελημένον ἐστὶ καὶ μήτε πρόσ-
οδον ποιεῖ μήτε τοῖς θεοῖς ἐξαίρετόν ἐστιν. λέγω
δ᾽ οἷον τόπους τινὰς δημοσίους ἠμελημένους ἐξ ὧν
τοῖς ἰδιώταις ἢ πραθέντων ἢ μισθωθέντων πρόσοδος
ἂν τις τῇ πόλει γίγνοιτο· κοινότατος γὰρ ὁ τοιοῦτος
25 πόρος ἐστίν. ἂν δὲ μηδὲν ᾖ τοιοῦτον, ἀπὸ τιμημάτων ἀναγκαῖον ποιήσασθαι τὰς εἰσφοράς, ἢ τοῖς
μὲν πένησι τὰ σώματα παρέχειν εἶναι προστεταγ-
μένον εἰς τοὺς κινδύνους, τοῖς δὲ πλουτοῦσι τὰ
χρήματα, τοῖς δὲ τεχνίταις ὅπλα. συλλήβδην δὲ
δεῖ[3] περὶ πόρων εἰσηγούμενον[4] φάναι[5] αὐτοὺς ἴσους
30 τοῖς πολίταις καὶ πολυχρονίους καὶ μεγάλους[6]
ὄντας, τοὺς δὲ τῶν ἐναντίων τὰ ἐναντία τούτοις
ἔχοντας.

Τὰς μὲν οὖν προθέσεις περὶ ὧν δημηγορήσομεν,
καὶ τὰ μέρη τούτων ἐξ ὧν τοὺς λόγους συστήσομεν
καὶ προτρέποντες καὶ ἀποτρέποντες, ἐκ τῶν εἰρη-

---

[1] ἢ τὰ Sp.: ἤτοι. [2] Rac.: κάμνωσιν.
[3] δεῖ add. Sp. [4] v.l. εἰσηγούμενος.
[5] ἀποφῆναι Wurm. [6] ⟨μὴ⟩ μεγάλους Sp.

302

And briefly, we have to realize that it is the way of all mankind to bring their wars with one another to an end either when they think that their adversaries' claims are just, or when they quarrel with their allies or grow tired of the war or afraid of the enemy, or when internal faction breaks out among them.

Consequently if you collect those among all of these and similar points that are most closely related to the facts, you will not be at a loss for appropriate matter for a speech about war and peace.

It still remains for us to discuss finance. The first thing to be considered is whether any part of the national property has been neglected, and is neither producing revenue nor set apart for the service of religion. I refer, for example, to neglect of some public places the sale or lease of which to private citizens might bring revenue to the state ; for that is a very common source of income. If nothing of this sort is available, it is necessary to have a system of taxation based on property qualifications, or for the poor to be under the duty of rendering bodily service in emergencies while the rich furnish money and the craftsmen arms. To put it briefly, when introducing financial proposals one must say that they are fair to the citizens, permanent and productive, and that the plans of the opposition have the opposite qualities.

What has been said has shown us the subjects that we shall employ in parliamentary speeches, and the portions of those subjects that we shall use in composing speeches of exhortation and of dissuasion. Next

1425 b

μένων ἴσμεν· προθέμενοι δὲ πάλιν ἐφεξῆς τό τε
35 ἐγκωμιαστικὸν εἶδος καὶ τὸ ψεκτικὸν περιλάβωμεν.
III. Συλλήβδην μὲν οὖν ἐστὶ τὸ[1] ἐγκωμιαστικὸν
εἶδος προαιρέσεων καὶ πράξεων καὶ λόγων ἐνδόξων
αὔξησις καὶ μὴ προσόντων συνοικείωσις, ψεκτικὸν
δὲ τὸ ἐναντίον τούτῳ, τῶν μὲν ἐνδόξων ταπείνωσις,
40 τῶν δὲ ἀδόξων αὔξησις. ἐπαινετὰ μὲν οὖν ἐστι πράγ-
1426 a ματα[2] τὰ δίκαια καὶ τὰ νόμιμα καὶ τὰ συμφέροντα
καὶ τὰ καλὰ καὶ τὰ ἡδέα καὶ τὰ[3] ῥάδια πραχθῆναι
(ταῦτα δὲ αὐτά τε οἷά ἐστι καὶ ὅθεν αὐτὰ[4] πολλὰ
ποιήσομεν ἐν τοῖς πρὸ τούτων εἴρηται). δεῖ δὲ
5 τὸν εὐλογοῦντα δεικνύειν τοῖς λόγοις ὡς τούτῳ τῷ
ἀνθρώπῳ ἢ τοῖς πράγμασιν ὑπάρχει τι τούτων ὑπ'
αὐτοῦ κατεργασθὲν ἢ δι' αὐτοῦ πορισθὲν ἢ ἐκ
τούτου ἐπισυμβαῖνον[5] ἢ ἕνεκα τούτου γινόμενον ἢ
οὐκ ἄνευ τούτου ἐπιτελούμενον· ὁμοιοτρόπως δὲ καὶ
τῷ ψέγοντι τὰ ἐναντία τούτοις δεικτέον προσόντα
τῷ ψεγομένῳ. τὸ μὲν ἐκ τούτου, οἷον ἐκ τοῦ
10 φιλογυμναστεῖν τὸ σῶμα ὑγιαίνειν,[6] καὶ ἐκ τοῦ μὴ
φιλοπονεῖν ἐπ' ἀρρωστίαν ἐμπίπτειν, καὶ ἐκ τοῦ
φιλοσοφεῖν δεινότερον εἶναι περὶ φρόνησιν, καὶ ἐκ
τοῦ ἀμελεῖν ἐνδεᾶ τῶν ἀναγκαίων εἶναι· τὸ δ' ἕνεκα
τούτου, οἷον ἕνεκα τοῦ στεφανωθῆναι ὑπὸ τῶν
πολιτῶν πολλοὺς πόνους καὶ κινδύνους ὑπομένουσιν,
15 καὶ ἕνεκα τοῦ χαρίσασθαι τοῖς ἐρωμένοις τῶν ἄλλων οὐδὲν φροντίζουσιν· τὸ δὲ μὴ ἄνευ τούτου, οἷον
οὐκ ἄνευ τῶν ναυτῶν ναυμαχιῶν νῖκαι, καὶ οὐκ
ἄνευ τοῦ πίνειν αἱ παροινίαι. τὰ τοιαῦτα δὲ τοῖς

---

[1] ἐστὶ τὸ Sp.: ἐστίν.   [2] [πράγματα] ? Rac.
[3] τὰ οὐ ed. Basil.   [4] Sp.: αὐτοί.
[5] συμβαῖνον Sp.   [6] ὑγιαίνειν Halm: αἱ νῖκαι.

[a] Perhaps we should read ' not easy.'

1425 b

let us put forward for our consideration the eulogistic 35
and vituperative species of oratory.

III. The eulogistic species of oratory consists, to *Ceremonial* put it briefly, in the amplification of creditable pur- *oratory: its* poses and actions and speeches and the attribution of *subjects.* qualities that do not exist, while the vituperative species is the opposite, the minimization of creditable qualities and the amplification of discreditable ones. Praiseworthy things are those that are just, lawful, 40 expedient, noble, pleasant and easy *a* to accomplish **1426 a** (the exact nature of these qualities and where to find materials for enlarging on them has been stated in an earlier passage *b*). When eulogizing one must show in one's speech that one of these things belongs to the person in question or to his actions, as directly effected by him or produced through his agency or incidentally resulting from his action or done as a means to it or involving it as an indispensable condition of its performance ; and similarly in vituperating one must show that the qualities opposite to these belong to the person vituperated. Instances of incidental result are bodily health resulting from devotion to athletics, 10 loss of health as a result of a neglect of exercise, increased intellectual ability resulting from the pursuit of philosophy, destitution resulting from neglect of one's affairs. Examples of things done as a means are when men endure many toils and dangers for the sake of receiving a wreath of honour from their compatriots, or neglect everyone else for the sake of gratifying the persons they are in love with. 15 Examples of indispensable conditions are a supply of sailors as indispensable for a naval victory and the act of drinking as indispensable for intoxication. By

b See 1421 b 35 ff.

προειρημένοις ὁμοιοτρόπως μετιὼν ἐγκωμίων καὶ
ψόγων πολλῶν εὐπορήσεις.

20 Αὐξήσεις δὲ καὶ ταπεινώσεις συλλήβδην ἅπαντα
τὰ τοιαῦτα τόνδε τὸν τρόπον μετιών, πρῶτον μὲν
ἀποφαίνων,[1] ὥσπερ ἀρτίως μετῆλθον, ὑπὸ τουτουῒ
πολλὰ γεγενῆσθαι ἢ κακὰ ἢ ἀγαθά. εἰς μὲν οὖν
τρόπος τῆς αὐξήσεως οὗτος, δεύτερος δὲ κεκριμένον
μεταφέρειν,[2] ἂν μὲν ἐπαινῇς, ἀγαθόν, ἂν δὲ ψέγῃς,
25 κακόν, εἶτα παριστάναι τὸ ὑπὸ σοῦ λεγόμενον, καὶ
παραβάλλειν πρὸς ἄλληλα, τοῦ μὲν ὑπὸ σαυτοῦ
λεγομένου τὰ μέγιστα διεξιὼν[3] τοῦ δ' ἑτέρου τὰ
ἐλάχιστα, καὶ οὕτω μέγα φανῆναι.[4] τρίτος δὲ[5]
πρὸς τὸ ὑπὸ σαυτοῦ λεγόμενον ἀντιπαραβάλλειν
τοὐλάχιστον τῶν ὑπὸ τὴν αὐτὴν ἰδέαν πιπτόντων·
30 φανεῖται γὰρ οὕτω τὸ ὑπὸ σοῦ λεγόμενον μεῖζον,
ὥσπερ οἱ μέτριοι τὰ μεγέθη φαίνονται μείζους ὅταν
πρὸς βραχυτέρους παραστῶσιν. ἔσται δὲ καὶ ὧδε
πάντως αὔξειν· εἰ κέκριται μέγα ἀγαθὸν τοῦτο,
τούτῳ τι[6] ἐναντίον ἐὰν λέγῃς, μέγα κακὸν φανεῖται·
ὡσαύτως δὲ εἰ νομίζεται μέγα κακόν, ἐὰν τὸ[7]
35 τούτῳ ἐναντίον λέγῃς, μέγα ἀγαθὸν φανεῖται. ἔστι
δὲ καὶ ὧδε μεγάλα ποιεῖν τἀγαθὰ ἢ τὰ κακά, ἐὰν
ἀποφαίνῃς αὐτὸν[8] ἐκ διανοίας, συμβιβάζων ὡς ἐκ
πολλοῦ προενόησεν, ὡς πολλάκις[9] πράττειν ἐπ-
εβάλετο, ὡς πολὺν χρόνον ἔπραττεν, ὡς οὐδεὶς
ἄλλος πρότερον τούτοις ἐνεχείρησεν, ὡς μετὰ τού-
40 των ἔπραξε μεθ' ὧν οὐδεὶς ἄλλος, ὡς ἐπὶ τούτοις

---

[1] [ἀποφαίνων] Sp.   [2] μέγα φέρειν Finckh.
[3] διεξιόντα Sp.   [4] φανεῖται Sp.
[5] δὲ om. codd. pl.   [6] τὸ Sp.
[7] τὸ add. Rac.   [8] αἴτιον Usener.
[9] Rac.: πολλά.

pursuing such topics in the same manner as those discussed before you will have a good supply of matter for eulogy and vituperation.

To put it briefly, you will be able to amplify and minimize all such topics by pursuing the following method. First you must show, as I lately explained, that the actions of the person in question have produced many bad, or good, results. This is one method of amplification. A second method is to introduce a previous judgement—a favourable one if you are praising, an unfavourable one if you are blaming— and then set your own statement beside it and com-25 pare them with one another, enlarging on the strongest points of your own case and the weakest ones of the other and so making your own case appear a strong one. A third way is to set in comparison with the thing you are saying the smallest of the things that fall into the same class, for thus your case will appear 30 magnified, just as men of medium height appear taller when standing by the side of men shorter than themselves. Also the following way of amplifying will be available in all cases. Supposing a given thing has been judged a great good, if you mention some-thing that is its opposite, it will appear a great evil ; and similarly supposing something is considered a great evil, if you mention its opposite, it will appear a 35 great good. Another possible way of magnifying good or bad actions is if you prove that the agent acted intentionally, arguing that he had long premeditated doing the acts, that he repeatedly set about doing them, that he went on doing them a long time, that no one else had attempted them before, that he did them in conjunction with persons whom no one else 40 had acted with or in succession to persons whom no

1426 b μεθ' οὓς οὐδεὶς ἕτερος, ὡς ἑκών, ὡς ἐκ προνοίας, ὡς
εἰ πάντες τούτῳ ἴσως ποιοῖμεν, εὐδαιμονοῖμεν ἂν
ἢ φαύλως πράττοιμεν. χρὴ δὲ καὶ εἰκάζοντα συμβιβάζειν, καὶ ἐποικοδομοῦντα τὸ ἕτερον ὡς[1] ἐπὶ τὸ
ἕτερον αὔξειν τρόπῳ τοιῷδε· '' ὅστις δὲ τῶν φίλων
5 κήδεται, τοῦτον εἰκὸς καὶ τοὺς αὑτοῦ γονεῖς τιμᾶν·
ὃς δὲ τοὺς γονέας τιμᾷ, οὗτος καὶ τὴν πατρίδα τὴν
ἑαυτοῦ εὖ ποιεῖν βουλήσεται.'' συλλήβδην δέ, ἐὰν
πολλῶν αἴτιον ἀποφαίνῃς, ἐάν τε ἀγαθῶν ἐάν τε
κακῶν, μεγάλα[2] φανεῖται. σκοπεῖν δὲ καὶ πότερον
μεῖζον φαίνεται τὸ πρᾶγμα[3] κατὰ μέρη[4] διαιρού-
10 μενον ἢ καθόλου λεγόμενον, καὶ ὁποτέρως ἂν μεῖζον
ᾖ, τόνδε τὸν τρόπον αὐτὸ λέγειν. τὰς μὲν οὖν
αὐξήσεις οὕτω μετιὼν πλείστας ποιήσεις καὶ
μεγίστας.

Ταπεινώσεις δὲ τοῖς λόγοις καὶ τὰ ἀγαθὰ καὶ τὰ
κακὰ τὸν ἐναντίον τρόπον μετιὼν ἢ[5] ὡς εἰρήκαμεν
15 ἐπὶ τῶν μεγάλων, καὶ μάλιστα μὲν ἂν μηδενὸς
αἴτιον ἐπιδεικνύῃς, εἰ δὲ μή, ὡς ἐλαχίστων καὶ
σμικροτάτων.

Ὡς μὲν οὖν ἐγκωμιάζοντες καὶ ψέγοντες αὐξήσομεν καὶ ταπεινώσομεν ἅπερ ἂν ἐκφέρωμεν,[6] ἐκ
τούτων ἴσμεν· χρήσιμοι δὲ αἱ τῶν αὐξήσεων ἀφορ-
20 μαί εἰσι καὶ ἐν τοῖς ἄλλοις εἴδεσιν, ἀλλ' ἡ πλείστη
δύναμις αὐτῶν ἐστιν ἐν τοῖς ἐγκωμίοις καὶ ἐν
τοῖς ψόγοις. περὶ μὲν οὖν τούτων ἐντεῦθεν
εὐπορήσομεν.

IV. Διέλωμεν[7] δὲ πάλιν ὁμοιοτρόπως τούτοις τό
τε κατηγορικὸν καὶ τὸ ἀπολογητικὸν εἶδος, ὃ περὶ

---

[1] [ὡς] Sp.   [2] μέγα Sp.
[3] πότερον . . . πρᾶγμα Π : τὸ πρᾶγμα ὁποῖον φανεῖται cet.
[4] κατὰ μέρη om. Π.

one else had followed, that he was acting willingly, 1426 b
that he was acting deliberately, that we should all be
happy, or unfortunate, if we all acted like him.   One
must also argue one's case by employing comparison,
and amplify it by building up one point on another, as
follows : ' It is probable that anybody who looks after 5
his friends, also honours his own parents ; and anybody who honours his parents will also wish to benefit
his own country.'   And in brief, if you prove a man
responsible for many things, whether good or bad,
they will bulk large in appearance.   You must also
consider whether the matter bulks larger when
divided up into parts or when stated as a whole, and 10
state it in whichever way it makes a bigger show.
By pursuing these methods in amplifications you will
be able to make them most numerous and most
effective.

To minimize either good points or bad ones by your
speeches you will pursue the opposite method to that
which we have described in the case of magnifying—
best of all, if you prove the person not to be respon- 15
sible at all, or failing that, only responsible for the
fewest and smallest things possible.

These rules instruct us how we are to amplify or
minimize whatever matters we are bringing forward
for eulogy or vituperation.   The materials for amplification are useful in the other species of oratory as
well, but it is in eulogy and vituperation that they are 20
most efficacious.   The above remarks will make us
adequately equipped in regard to them.

IV. Let us next in a similar manner define the *Forensic*
elements composing and the proper mode of employ-   *oratory.*

---

⁵ ἤ add. Rac. (vel οἷς pro ὡς).   ⁶ Π: ἐθέλωμεν cet.
          ⁷ διέλθωμεν Sp

1426 b

τὴν δικανικήν ἐστι πραγματείαν,[1] αὐτά τε ἐξ ὧν
25 συνέστηκε, καὶ ὡς δεῖ αὐτοῖς χρῆσθαι. ἔστι δὲ τὸ
μὲν κατηγορικὸν συλλήβδην εἰπεῖν ἁμαρτημάτων
καὶ ἀδικημάτων ἐξάγγελσις, τὸ δ' ἀπολογητικὸν
ἁμαρτημάτων καὶ ἀδικημάτων κατηγορηθέντων ἢ
καθυποπτευθέντων διάλυσις. ἑκατέρου δὲ τῶν
εἰδῶν τὰς δυνάμεις ταύτας[2] ἔχοντος, κατηγοροῦντα
30 μὲν ἀναγκαῖον λέγειν, ὅταν μὲν εἰς πονηρίαν κατ-
ηγορῇς,[3] ὡς αἱ τῶν ἐναντίων πράξεις ἄδικοι καὶ
παράνομοι καὶ τῷ πλήθει τῶν πολιτῶν ἀσύμφοροι
τυγχάνουσιν οὖσαι, ὅταν δὲ εἰς ἀβελτερίαν, ὡς αὐτῷ
τε τῷ πράττοντι ἀσύμφοροι καὶ αἰσχραὶ καὶ ἀηδεῖς
35 καὶ ἀδύνατοι ἐπιτελεσθῆναι. ταῦτα μὲν καὶ τὰ
τούτοις ὅμοια κατά τε τῶν πονηρῶν καὶ τῶν
ἀβελτέρων ἐπιχειρήματά ἐστιν. δεῖ δὲ καὶ τοῦτο
παρατηρεῖν τοὺς κατηγοροῦντας, ἐπὶ ποίοις τῶν
ἀδικημάτων οἱ νόμοι τὰς τιμωρίας τάττουσιν, καὶ
περὶ ἃ τῶν ἀδικημάτων οἱ δικασταὶ τὰς ζημίας
40 ὁρίζουσιν. ὅταν μὲν οὖν ᾖ νόμος διωρικώς, τοῦτο
δεῖ μόνον σκοπεῖν τὸν κατήγορον, ὅπως ἂν ἐπιδείξῃ
1427 a τὸ πρᾶγμα γεγενημένον. ὅταν δὲ οἱ δικασταὶ
τιμῶσι, πρῶτον μὲν ἀνάγκη ἐπιδεῖξαι τὰ κατηγορούμενα,[4] ἔπειτα[5] αὐξητέον ἐστὶ τὰ ἀδικήματα
καὶ τὰ τῶν ἐναντίων ἁμαρτήματα,[6] καὶ μάλιστα μὲν
δεικτέον ὡς ἑκὼν καὶ ἐκ προνοίας οὐ τῆς τυχούσης
5 ἀλλὰ μετὰ παρασκευῆς πλείστης ἠδίκησεν· ἐὰν δὲ
μὴ δυνατὸν ᾖ τοῦτο ποιεῖν, ἀλλὰ νομίζῃς δείξειν[7]
τὸν ἐναντίον ὡς ἥμαρτε τρόπον τινὰ ἢ ὅτι ταῦτα

---

[1] ὃ . . . πραγματείαν om. Π.   [2] v.l. τὰς αὐτὰς.
[3] Rac.: κατηγορῇ aut κατηγορῶ.
[4] τιμῶσι . . . κατηγορούμενα Π: τὸ κατηγορούμενον
εἰδῶσι cet.

ing the species of oratory used in accusation and
defence—the oratory connected with forensic practice. 25
To put it briefly, the oratory of accusation is the
recital of errors and offences, and that of defence the
refutation of errors and offences of which a man is
accused or suspected. These being the functions of
each of these species, the line to take in accusing is to 30
say, in a case where your accusation refers to wickedness, that the actions of your adversaries are actually
dishonest and illegal and detrimental to the mass of
the citizens, and when it refers to folly, that they are
detrimental to the agent himself, disgraceful, unpleasant and impracticable. These and similar 35
accusations are the line of attack against persons
guilty of wickedness or folly. But accusers must also
be careful to notice what are the kinds of offences for
which there are punishments fixed by law and which
are the offences in regard to which the penalties are
decided by the jury. In cases where the law has
determined the penalty, the accuser must direct his 40
attention solely to proving that the act has been
committed. When the jury assess, he must amplify 1427 a
the offences and the errors of his opponents, and if possible prove that the defendant committed the offence
of his own free will, and not from a merely casual intention, but with a very great amount of preparation; 5
or if it is not possible to prove this, but you think the
other side will try to prove that the accused made
a mistake in some way, or that although intending

---

⁵ ἔπειτα add. Forster.
⁶ [καὶ τὰ . . . ἁμαρτήματα] Sauppe.
⁷ v.l. δεῖξαι.

1427 a

πρᾶξαι διανοηθεὶς καλῶς ἠτύχησε, περιαιρετέον τὴν
συγγνώμην λέγοντα τοῖς ἀκούουσιν ὡς οὐ δεῖ πρά-
ξαντας ἡμαρτηκέναι φάσκειν ἀλλὰ πρὶν πράττειν
10 εὐλαβεῖσθαι, ἔπειθ᾽ ὡς εἰ καὶ ἐξήμαρτεν ἢ ἠτύχησεν
ἐκεῖνος, δεῖ διὰ τὰς ἀτυχίας καὶ τὰς ἁμαρτίας
ζημιωθῆναι μᾶλλον αὐτὸν ἢ τὸν μηδέτερον τούτων
ποιήσαντα· πρὸς δὲ τούτοις καὶ ὁ νομοθέτης
οὐκ ἀφῆκε τοὺς ἐξαμαρτάνοντας ἀλλ᾽ ὑποδίκους
ἐποίησεν, ἵνα μὴ πάντες¹ ἐξαμαρτάνωσιν. λέγε δὲ
15 καὶ ὡς εἰ τὸν τὰ τοιαῦτα ἀπολογούμενον ἀποδέξονται, πολλοὺς τοὺς ἀδικεῖν προαιρουμένους
ἕξουσιν· κατορθώσαντες μὲν γὰρ ἅπερ ἂν ἐθέλωσι
πράξουσιν, ἀποτυχόντες δὲ φάσκοντες ἠτυχηκέναι
τιμωρίαν οὐχ ὑφέξουσιν. τοῖς μὲν οὖν κατηγοροῦ-
σιν ἐκ τῶν τοιούτων ἡ συγγνώμη περιαιρετέα· καὶ
20 ὡς πρότερον εἴρηται, διὰ τῶν αὐξήσεων πολλῶν
αἴτια κακῶν τὰ τῶν ἐναντίων ἔργα δεικτέον.

Τὸ μὲν οὖν κατηγορικὸν εἶδος διὰ τῶν μερῶν
ἀποτελεῖται τούτων.

Τὸ δὲ ἀπολογητικὸν διὰ τριῶν μεθόδων συν-
ίσταται.² ἢ γὰρ ἀποδεικτέον τῷ ἀπολογουμένῳ ὡς
25 οὐδὲν τῶν κατηγορουμένων ἔπραξεν· ἢ ἐὰν ἀναγκά-
ζηται ὁμολογεῖν, πειρατέον δεικνύναι ἔννομον καὶ
δίκαιον καὶ καλὸν καὶ συμφέρον τῇ πόλει τὸ πε-
πραγμένον· ἐὰν δὲ μὴ τοῦτο δύνηται ἀποδεῖξαι, εἰς
ἁμάρτημα ἢ εἰς ἀτύχημα ἄγοντα τὰς πράξεις καὶ
μικρὰς βλάβας³ ἀπ᾽ αὐτῶν γεγενημένας⁴ ἀποφαί-
30 νοντα συγγνώμης τυχεῖν πειρατέον. ἀδικίαν δὲ

---

¹ v.l. πᾶσιν: πάλιν Sauppe.
² v.l. συνίσταται πόθεν ἄν τις ἀπολογήσαιτο (οἶμαι τοῦτο
εἶναι σχόλιον Victorius).
³ v.l. τὰς βλάβας: τὰς βλάβας ⟨τὰς⟩ ? Rac.

to act honourably in the matter he failed by bad
luck, you must dissipate compassion by telling your
audience that men have no business to act first
and afterwards say they have made a mistake,
but that they ought to look before they leap ;
and next, that even if the defendant really did
make a mistake or have bad luck, it is more proper
for him to be punished for his failures and mistakes
than a person who has committed neither ; moreover, the lawgiver did not let off people who make
mistakes but made them liable to justice, or else
everybody would be making mistakes. Also say
that. if they listen to a man who puts up a defence of that sort, they will have many people doing
wrong on purpose, as if they bring it off they will be
able to do whatever they like, and if they fail they
will escape being punished by saying that it was an
accident. This is the sort of argument which accusers
must employ to dissipate compassion ; and, as has
been said before, they must employ amplification to
show that their opponents' actions have been attended
by many bad consequences.

These, then, are the divisions composing the species
of oratory used in accusation.

The defensive species comprises three methods. A
defendant must either prove that he did none of the
things he is charged with ; or if he is forced to admit
them, he must try to show that what he did was lawful
and just and noble and to the public advantage ; or if
he cannot prove this, he must attempt to gain forgiveness by representing his acts as an error or misfortune,
and by showing that only small mischief has resulted
from them. You must distinguish between injustice,

ᵃ v.l. γενομένας.

1427 a

καὶ ἁμάρτημα καὶ ἀτυχίαν ὧδε διόριζε[1]· τὸ μὲν ἐκ
προνοίας κακόν τι ποιεῖν ἀδικίαν τίθει, καὶ φάθι
δεῖν τιμωρίαν ἐπὶ τοῖς τοιούτοις τὴν μεγίστην
λαμβάνειν· τὸ δὲ δι᾿ ἄγνοιαν βλαβερόν τι πράττειν
35 ἁμαρτίαν εἶναι φατέον· τὸ δὲ μὴ δι᾿ ἑαυτὸν ἀλλὰ δι᾿
ἑτέρους τινὰς ἢ διὰ τύχην μηδὲν ἐπιτελεῖν τῶν
βουλευθέντων καλῶς ἀτυχίαν τίθει. καὶ φάθι τὸ
μὲν ἀδικεῖν εἶναι τῶν πονηρῶν ἀνθρώπων ἴδιον, τὸ
δ᾿ ἐξαμαρτεῖν καὶ περὶ τὰς πράξεις ἀτυχεῖν οὐ
μόνου[2] εἶναι σεαυτοῦ[3] ἴδιον, ἀλλὰ καὶ κοινὸν καὶ τῶν
40 δικαζόντων καὶ τῶν ἄλλων ἀνθρώπων· ἀξίου δὲ
συγγνώμην ἔχειν ἀναγκασθείς τι ὁμολογεῖν · τῶν
τοιούτων αἰτιῶν, κοινὸν τοῖς ἀκούουσι ποιῶν τὸ
1427 b ἁμαρτάνειν καὶ τὸ ἀτυχεῖν. δεῖ δὲ τὸν ἀπολογούμενον πάντα θεωρεῖν ἐφ᾿ οἷς τῶν ἀδικημάτων οἵ τε
νόμοι τὰς τιμωρίας ἔταξαν καὶ οἱ δικασταὶ τὰς[4]
ζημίας τιμῶσιν, καὶ ὅταν ὁ νόμος ὁρίζῃ τὰς τι-
5 μωρίας, δεικτέον ὡς οὐκ ἐποίησε τὸ παράπαν ἢ ὡς
ἔννομα καὶ δίκαια ἐποίησεν, ὅτε δὲ οἱ δικασταὶ
καθεστήκασι τιμηταὶ τῆς ζημίας, ὁμοίως πάλιν οὐ
φατέον ὅτι ταῦτα οὐκ ἐποίησεν, ἀλλὰ μικρὰ
βεβλαμμένον τὸν ἐναντίον καὶ ἀκούσια ἀποφαίνειν
πειρατέον.

Ἐκ τούτων μὲν οὖν καὶ τῶν τούτοις ὁμοιο-
10 τρόπων ἐν ταῖς κατηγορίαις καὶ ταῖς ἀπολογίαις
εὐπορήσομεν· λείπεται δ᾿ ἡμῖν ἔτι διεξελθεῖν τὸ
ἐξεταστικὸν εἶδος.

V. Ἐν κεφαλαίῳ μὲν οὖν εἰπεῖν, ἡ ἐξέτασίς ἐστι
προαιρέσεως ἢ πράξεως ἢ λόγων πρὸς ἄλληλα ἢ
πρὸς τὸν ἄλλον βίον ἐναντιουμένων ἐμφάνισις, δεῖ
15 δὲ τὸν ἐξετάζοντα ζητεῖν εἴ που ἢ ὁ λόγος ὂν

_____

[1] Sp.: ὁρίζεις aut -οις aut -ειν.   [2] Rac.: μόνον.

error, and misfortune : define injustice as the deliberate commission of evil, and say that for offences of that sort the severest penalties should be inflicted ; declare that a harmful action done unwittingly is an error ; and class a failure to carry out some honourable intention, if it is not due to oneself but to other people or to luck, as misfortune. Also say that unjust conduct is peculiar to wicked people, but that error and misfortune in one's actions is not peculiar to yourself alone but is common to all mankind, including the members of the jury. You must claim to receive compassion for being forced to plead guilty to a charge of that sort, making out that error and misfortune are shared by your hearers. A defendant must have in view all the offences for which the laws have fixed the punishments and for which the jury assesses the penalties ; and in a case where the law fixes the punishments he should show that he did not commit the act at all or that his conduct was lawful and right, whereas when the jury has been made the assessor of the penalty, he should not in the same way deny having committed the act, but try to show that he did his adversary little damage and that that was involuntary.

These and similar arguments will supply us with plenty of material in accusations and defences. It still remains for us to discuss the species of oratory employed in investigation.

V. Investigation may be summarily defined as the exhibition of certain intentions or actions or words as inconsistent with one another or with the rest of someone's conduct. The investigator must try to find some

Investigational oratory.

---

³ Rac. : ἑαυτῷ.   ⁴ τὰς add. Kayser.

ἐξετάζει ἢ αἱ πράξεις τοῦ ἐξεταζομένου ἢ αἱ προαιρέσεις ἐναντιοῦνται ἀλλήλαις. ἡ δὲ μέθοδος ἥδε, σκοπεῖν ἐν τῷ παροιχομένῳ χρόνῳ εἴ πως πρῶτόν τινος φίλος γενόμενος πάλιν ἐχθρὸς ἐγένετο καὶ πάλιν φίλος τῷ αὐτῷ τούτῳ, ἤ τι ἄλλο ἐναντίον εἰς
20 μοχθηρίαν φέρον ἔπραξεν, ἢ ἔτι πράξει, ἐὰν οἱ καιροὶ παραπέσοιεν αὐτῷ, ἐναντίον τοῖς πρότερον ὑπ' αὐτοῦ πεπραγμένοις. ὡσαύτως δὲ ὅρα καὶ εἴ τι εἰπὼν νῦν λέγει ἐναντίον τοῖς πρότερον αὐτῷ εἰρημένοις[1] [ἢ εἴ τι εἴποι ἐναντίον τοῖς λεγομένοις ἢ τοῖς πρότερον εἰρημένοις][2]. ὡσαύτως δὲ καὶ
25 εἴ τι προείλετο ἐναντίον τοῖς πρότερον εἰρημένοις ὑπ' αὐτοῦ, ἢ προέλοιτ' ἂν καιρῶν παραπεσόντων. ὁμοιοτρόπως δὲ τούτοις λαμβάνειν καὶ πρὸς τὰ ἄλλα ἔνδοξα ἐπιτηδεύματα τὰς ἐν τῷ τοῦ ἐξεταζομένου βίῳ ἐναντιώσεις. τὸ μὲν οὖν ἐξεταστικὸν εἶδος οὕτω μετιὼν οὐδένα παραλείψεις τρόπον τῆς
30 ἐξετάσεως.

Ἁπάντων δὲ τῶν εἰδῶν ἤδη διῃρημένων, δεῖ καὶ χωρὶς τούτων ἑκάστῳ, ὅταν ἁρμόττῃ, χρῆσθαι, καὶ κοινῇ, συμμιγνύντα τὰς δυνάμεις αὐτῶν. ταῦτα γὰρ ἔχει μὲν διαφορὰς εὐμεγέθεις, ἐπικοινωνοῦσι μέντοι κατὰ τὰς χρήσεις ἀλλήλοις, καὶ ταὐτὸ
35 πεπόνθασι τοῖς τῶν ἀνθρώπων εἴδεσιν· καὶ γὰρ οὗτοι τῇ μὲν ὅμοιοι τῇ δὲ ἀνόμοιοι τὰς ὄψεις καὶ τὰς αἰσθήσεις εἰσίν.

Οὕτω δὲ τῶν εἰδῶν διωρισμένων, καὶ ὧν προσδέονται κοινῇ πάλιν ἐξαριθμήσωμεν καὶ διεξέλθωμεν ὡς αὐτοῖς δεῖ χρῆσθαι.

VI. Πρῶτον μὲν οὖν καὶ τὸ δίκαιον καὶ τὸ νόμι-

_____

[1] προῃρημένοις Sp.
[2] [ἢ . . . εἰρημένοις] Buhl.

point in which either the speech that he is investigating is self-contradictory or the actions or the intentions of the person under investigation run counter to one another. This is the procedure—to consider whether perhaps in the past after having first been a friend of somebody he afterwards became his enemy and then became the same man's friend again; or committed 20 some other inconsistent action indicating depravity; or is likely in the future, should opportunities befall him, to act in a manner contrary to his previous conduct. Similarly observe also whether something that he says when speaking now is contrary to what he has said before; and likewise also whether he has 25 ever adopted a policy contrary to his previous professions, or would do so if opportunities offered. And on similar lines you should also take the features in the career of the person under investigation inconsistent with his other habits of conduct that are estimable. By thus pursuing the investigational species of oratory there is no method of investiga- 30 tion that you will leave out.

All the species of oratory have now been distinguished. They are to be employed both separately, when suitable, and jointly, with a combination of their qualities—for though they have very considerable differences, yet in their practical application they overlap. In fact the same is true of them as of the 35 various species of human beings; these also are partly alike and partly different in their appearance and in their perceptions. *Elements common to all species of oratory.*

Having thus defined the various species of oratory, let us next enumerate their common requirements, and discuss their proper mode of employment.

VI. In the first place, although the just, the lawful,

1427 b

40 μον καὶ τὸ συμφέρον καὶ τὸ καλὸν καὶ τὸ ἡδὺ καὶ
τὰ τούτοις ἀκόλουθα, καθάπερ ἐν ἀρχῇ διειλόμην,
1428 a κοινὰ πᾶσι τοῖς εἴδεσίν ἐστι, μάλιστα δ᾽ αὐτοῖς τὸ
προτρεπτικὸν[1] προσχρῆται. δεύτερον δὲ τὰς αὐξήσεις καὶ τὰς ταπεινώσεις χρησίμους ἀναγκαῖον
εἶναι παρὰ τὰ λοιπὰ[2] πάντα, μάλιστα δ᾽ αὐτῶν ἐν
τῷ ἐγκωμίῳ[3] καὶ τοῖς ψόγοις αἱ χρήσεις. τρίτον
5 δὲ πίστεις, αἷς ἀνάγκη μὲν πρὸς πάντα τὰ μέρη[4]
τῶν λόγων χρῆσθαι, χρησιμώταται δ᾽ εἰσὶν ἐν
ταῖς κατηγορίαις καὶ ταῖς ἀπολογίαις· αὗται[5] γὰρ
πλείστης ἀντιλογίας δέονται. πρὸς δὲ τούτοις
προκαταλήψεις καὶ αἰτήματα καὶ παλιλλογίαι καὶ
μῆκος λόγου καὶ μετριότης μήκους καὶ βραχυλογία
10 καὶ ἑρμηνεία· ταῦτα γὰρ καὶ τὰ τούτοις ὅμοια
κοινὰς ἔχει πᾶσι τοῖς εἴδεσι τὰς χρήσεις.

Περὶ μὲν οὖν τῶν δικαίων καὶ τῶν νομίμων καὶ
τῶν τούτοις ὁμοιοτρόπων πρότερον διωρισάμην καὶ
τὴν χρῆσιν αὐτῶν διεξῆλθον, καὶ περὶ[6] τῶν αὐ-
15 ξήσεων καὶ ταπεινώσεων εἶπον. νῦν δὲ περὶ τῶν
ἄλλων δηλώσω, πρῶτον ἀπὸ τῶν πίστεων ἀρξάμενος.

VII. Εἰσὶ δὲ δύο τρόποι τῶν πίστεων. γίνονται
γὰρ αἱ μὲν ἐξ αὐτῶν τῶν λόγων καὶ τῶν πράξεων
καὶ[7] τῶν ἀνθρώπων, αἱ δ᾽ ἐπίθετοι τοῖς λεγομένοις
καὶ τοῖς πραττομένοις· τὰ μὲν γὰρ εἰκότα καὶ
20 παραδείγματα καὶ τεκμήρια καὶ ἐνθυμήματα καὶ
αἱ[8] γνῶμαι καὶ τὰ σημεῖα καὶ οἱ ἔλεγχοι πίστεις
ἐξ αὐτῶν τῶν λόγων καὶ τῶν ἀνθρώπων καὶ τῶν

---

[1] προτρεπτικὸν ⟨καὶ ἀποτρεπτικὸν⟩ Sp.
[2] [τὰ λοιπὰ] Sp. (v.l. πάντα τὸν λόγον).
[3] τοῖς ἐγκωμίοις Sp.   [4] μέρη ⟨καὶ εἴδη⟩ Sp.
[5] αὗται Sp.: ταῦτα.   [6] Sp.: περὶ μὲν.
[7] [καὶ] Sp., sed cf. b 17.   [8] αἱ add. Sp.

318

1427 b
40

the expedient, the honourable, the pleasant and the
other topics in the list are, as I defined at the beginning,[a] common to all the species, they are specially 1428 a
employed by the oratory of exhortation. Secondly,
amplification and minimization, although bound to be
useful for all the rest of the species, are specially
employed in eulogy and vituperation. Thirdly, there
are proofs, which, though it is necessary to use them 5
for all the departments of oratory, are most useful
in accusations and defences, since these require the
most employment of refutation. In addition there
are anticipations of one's opponents' arguments,
postulation, recapitulation, prolixity, moderation in
length, brevity, interpretation ; the employment of 10
these and similar devices is common to all the species
of oratory.

I have previously defined the just, the lawful and
similar topics, and have explained the mode of employing them ; and I have discussed amplification and
minimization. I will now explain the other topics, 15
beginning with proofs.

VII. Of proofs there are two modes : some proofs *Modes of*
are drawn from words and actions and persons them- *proof:*
(a) direct:
selves, others are supplementary to what the persons
say and do. Probabilities, examples, tokens, enthymemes,[b] maxims, signs[c] and refutations are proofs 20
drawn from actual words and persons and actions ; the

[a] See 1421 b 24 ff.

[b] Or ' considerations,' syllogisms employing premises that
are probable but not certain.

[c] Σημεῖον in Aristotelian logic means a probable indica-
tion, τεκμήριον, ' token,' a certain proof.

πραγμάτων εἰσίν, ἐπίθετοι δὲ ⟨δόξα τοῦ λέγοντος,⟩[1]
μαρτυρίαι, βάσανοι, ὅρκοι.[2] δεῖ δὴ[3] τούτων ἑκάστην
αὐτήν τε συνιέναι ποία τίς ἐστι, καὶ πόθεν τῶν εἰς
25 αὐτὴν λόγων εὐπορήσομεν, καὶ τί ἀλλήλων διαφέρουσιν.

Εἰκὸς μὲν οὖν ἐστιν οὗ λεγομένου παραδείγματα
ἐν ταῖς διανοίαις ἔχουσιν οἱ ἀκούοντες· λέγω δ' οἷον
εἴ τις φαίη τὴν πατρίδα βούλεσθαι μεγάλην εἶναι
καὶ τοὺς οἰκείους εὖ πράττειν καὶ τοὺς ἐχθροὺς
ἀτυχεῖν καὶ τὰ τούτοις ὅμοια συλλήβδην, εἰκότα
30 δόξειεν ἄν[4]· ἕκαστος γὰρ τῶν ἀκουόντων σύνοιδεν
αὐτὸς αὑτῷ περὶ τούτων καὶ τῶν τούτοις ὁμοιοτρόπων ἔχοντι τοιαύτας ἐπιθυμίας. ὥστε τοῦτο δεῖ
παρατηρεῖν ἡμᾶς ἐν τοῖς λόγοις ἀεί, εἰ τοὺς ἀκούοντας συνειδότας ληψόμεθα περὶ τοῦ πράγματος οὗ[5]
λέγομεν· τούτοις γὰρ αὐτοὺς εἰκός ἐστι μάλιστα
πιστεύειν. τὸ μὲν οὖν εἰκὸς τοιαύτην ἔχει φύσιν,
διαιροῦμεν δὲ αὐτὸ εἰς τρεῖς ἰδέας. μία μὲν οὖν
ἐστι τὸ τὰ πάθη τὰ κατὰ φύσιν ἀκολουθοῦντα τοῖς
ἀνθρώποις τοῖς[6] λόγοις συμπαραλαμβάνειν ἐν τῷ
κατηγορεῖν ἢ ἀπολογεῖσθαι· οἷον ἐὰν τύχωσί τινες
καταφρονήσαντές τινα ἢ δείσαντες, ἢ καὶ αὐτοί[7]
τοῦτο τὸ πρᾶγμα πολλάκις πεποιηκότες,[8] ἢ πάλιν
1428 b ἠσθέντες ἢ λυπηθέντες, ἢ ἐπιθυμήσαντες[9] ἢ πεπαυ-
μένοι τῆς ἐπιθυμίας,[10] ἢ[11] τι τοιοῦτον ἕτερον πεπονθότες πάθος ταῖς ψυχαῖς ἢ τοῖς σώμασιν ἢ τινι
τῶν ἄλλων αἰσθήσεων οἷς συμπάσχομεν· ταῦτα γὰρ
5 καὶ τὰ τούτοις ὅμοια, κοινὰ τῆς ἀνθρωπείας φύσεως

---

[1] add. Sp., cf. 1431 b 9.
[2] Sp.: μάρτυρες, ὅρκοι, βάσανοι (aut καὶ βάσανοι).
[3] v.l. δέ. [4] Sp.: δόξειεν aut δόξειαν.
[5] ὃ vel περὶ οὗ ? Rac. [6] ⟨ἐν⟩ τοῖς] Finckh.

1428 a

opinion of the speaker, the evidence of witnesses, evidence given under torture, oaths are supplementary. We ought, then, to understand the exact nature of each of these, and the sources that will supply us with arguments for each, and the differences between 25 them.

A probability is a statement supported by examples (1) *Probabilities.* present in the minds of an audience. I mean, for instance, if a person said that he desired his country to be great, his friends prosperous and his enemies unfortunate, and things like these in general, the statements would seem probable, because each 30 member of the audience is personally conscious of having corresponding desires about these and similar matters himself. Consequently we must always pay attention in our speeches to the question whether we shall find our hearers possessed of a personal knowledge of the thing we are speaking of, as that is the sort of statement they are most likely to believe. Such being the nature of the probable, we divide it 35 into three classes. One is when in accusing or defending we call in to aid our argument those emotions that human beings naturally experience—if, for instance, it happens that certain persons despise or fear someone, or have often done the thing in question themselves, 40 or again feel a pleasure or a pain or a desire, or have 1428 b ceased to feel the desire, or have experienced in mind or body or any other field of sensation some other feeling of the sort that we jointly experience; for 5 these and similar feelings being common experiences

---

⁷ Rac.: αὐτό.

⁸ [ἢ καὶ αὐτὸ . . . πεποιηκότες] Finckh.

⁹ v.l. ἐπιθυμοῦντες.   ¹⁰ v.l. τῶν ἐπιθυμῶν.

¹¹ v.l. add. πλουτοῦντες ἢ (παροινοῦντες ἤ Usener, cf. 1429 a 19).

ὄντα πάθη, γνώριμα τοῖς ἀκούουσίν ἐστιν. τὰ μὲν
οὖν κατὰ φύσιν εἰθισμένα τοῖς ἀνθρώποις γίνεσθαι
τοιαῦτά ἐστιν· ἃ φαμεν δεῖν συμπαραλαμβάνειν τοῖς[1]
λόγοις. ἕτερον δὲ μέρος ἐστὶ τῶν εἰκότων ἔθος,[2] ὃ
κατὰ συνήθειαν ἕκαστοι ποιοῦμεν. τρίτον δὲ κέρδος·
10 πολλάκις γὰρ διὰ τούτου τὴν φύσιν βιασάμενοι καὶ
τὰ ἤθη προειλόμεθα πράττειν.[3]

Οὕτω δὲ τούτων διωρισμένων, ἐν μὲν ταῖς προτροπαῖς καὶ ταῖς ἀποτροπαῖς δεικτέον ὑπὲρ τῶν
ζητουμένων ὅτι τοῦτο τὸ πρᾶγμα ἐφ’ ὃ ἡμεῖς
παρακαλοῦμεν ἢ ᾧ ἀντιλέγομεν αὐτὸ ὡς ἡμεῖς
15 φαμὲν γίνεται, εἰ δὲ μή, ὅτι τὰ τούτῳ τῷ πράγματι
ὅμοια τοῦτον τὸν τρόπον γίνεται ὃν ἡμεῖς φαμὲν ἢ
τὰ πλεῖστα ἢ τὰ πάντα. κατὰ μὲν οὖν τῶν
πραγμάτων οὕτω τὸ εἰκὸς ληπτέον· κατὰ δὲ τῶν
ἀνθρώπων ἐν μὲν[4] ταῖς κατηγορίαις, ἐὰν ἔχῃς,
ἐπιδείκνυε τὸ αὐτὸ τοῦτο πρᾶγμα πολλάκις πε-
20 ποιηκότα πρότερον, εἰ δὲ μή, ὅμοια τούτῳ. πειρῶ
δὲ ἀποφαίνειν καὶ ὡς λυσιτελὲς ἦν αὐτῷ ταῦτα
ποιεῖν· οἱ γὰρ πλεῖστοι τῶν ἀνθρώπων αὐτοὶ τὸ
λυσιτελὲς μάλιστα προτιμῶντες καὶ τοὺς ἄλλους
νομίζουσιν ἕνεκα τούτου πάντα πράττειν. ἂν μὲν
οὖν ἔχῃς ἀπὸ τῶν ἀντιδίκων αὐτῶν τὸ εἰκὸς λαμ-
25 βάνειν, οὕτως αὐτὸ σύναγε,[5] εἰ δὲ μή, ἀπὸ τῶν
ὁμοίων τὰ εἰθισμένα φέρε. λέγω δ’ οἷον, εἰ[6] νέος
ἐστὶν οὗ κατηγορεῖς, εἰ οἷα περὶ τὴν ἡλικίαν ταύτην
ὄντες πράττουσιν ταῦτα λέγεις πεποιηκέναι αὐτόν·
πιστευθήσεται γὰρ κατὰ τὴν ὁμοιότητα καὶ[7] κατὰ
τούτου λεγόμενα. τὸν αὐτὸν δὲ τρόπον καὶ ἐὰν

---

[1] Rac. (cf. a 37): ἐν τοῖς.　　[2] [ἔθος] ? Rac.
[3] ⟨τι⟩ πράττειν Kayser.　　[4] [μὲν] Kayser.
[5] Halm: συνάγεται aut συνάγαγε.

of human nature are intelligible to the audience.
Such are the experiences customary to man by
nature; and these we say should be called in to
support our arguments. Another division of the
probable is custom—that which the various classes
among us are in the habit of doing. A third is profit,
for the sake of which we frequently choose to act in a
manner that does violence to our nature and our
character.

These definitions having been made, in exhortations
and dissuasions it has to be proved about the matter
under consideration that the line of action which we
are urging or opposing itself has the effect that we
assert it has; or if not, that actions resembling this 15
line of action generally or invariably turn out in the
way that we assert. This is how the argument from
probability is to be taken in regard to actions. With
regard to persons, in accusations prove if you can that
the party has often committed the same act before, or
if not, actions like it. Also try to show that it was 20
profitable to him to do it, because as most men set the
highest value on profit themselves they think that
everybody else too always acts from motives of profit.
This is how you must bring in the argument from
probability if you are able to derive it from your
opponents personally; failing that, infer what is 25
normally the case from people resembling them. I
mean, for example, if, supposing the person you are
accusing is a young man, you say that he has acted as
persons of that age usually do act, for the allegations
will be believed against him too on the ground of
similarity. In the same way also if you show his

---

[6] εἰ add. Rac.   [7] v.l. καὶ τὰ.

1428 b

30 τοὺς ἑταίρους αὐτοῦ δεικνύῃς τοιούτους ὄντας οἷον
σὺ τοῦτον φῄς· καὶ γὰρ διὰ τὴν πρὸς ἐκείνους
συνήθειαν δόξει τὰ αὐτὰ τοῖς φίλοις ἐπιτηδεύειν.
τοὺς μὲν οὖν κατηγοροῦντας οὕτω χρὴ μετιέναι τὸ
εἰκός.

Τοῖς δὲ ἀπολογουμένοις μάλιστα δεικτέον ὡς
οὐδεπώποτε τῶν κατηγορουμένων τι πρότερον οὔτε
35 αὐτοὶ οὔτε τῶν φίλων οὐδεὶς οὔτε τῶν ὁμοίων
αὐτοῖς ἔπραξέ τις, οὐδ’ ἐλυσιτέλησε[1] τοιαῦτα πράττειν. ἂν δὲ φανερὸς ᾖς ταὐτὸ τοῦτο πρότερον
πεποιηκώς, αἰτιατέον τὴν ἡλικίαν, ἤ τινα πρόφασιν
ἄλλην[2] οἰστέον[3] δι’ ἣν εἰκότως ἐξήμαρτες τότε,
λέγε δὲ καὶ ὡς οὔτε ταῦτα τότε σοι πράξαντι
40 συνήνεγκεν οὔτε νῦν ἐλυσιτέλησεν ἄν. ἂν δέ σοι
1429 a μηδὲν ᾖ πεπραγμένον τοιοῦτον, τῶν δὲ φίλων σού
τινες τυγχάνωσι τοιαῦτα πεποιηκότες, χρὴ λέγειν
ὡς οὐ δίκαιόν ἐστι δι’ ἐκείνους αὐτὸν[4] διαβάλλεσθαι,
καὶ δεικνύναι τῶν σαυτῷ[5] συνήθων ἑτέρους ἐπιεικεῖς ὄντας· οὕτω γὰρ ἀμφίβολον ποιήσεις τὸ κατ-
5 ηγορούμενον. ἂν δὲ τῶν ὁμοίων δεικνύωσί τινας
ταὐτὰ πεποιηκότας, ἄτοπον εἶναι φάσκε[6] διότι
ἕτεροί τινες ἐξαμαρτάνοντες φαίνονται πίστιν εἶναι[7]
ὅτι τῶν ἐγκαλουμένων τι καὶ σὺ πεποίηκας. ἂν
μὲν οὖν ἔξαρνος ᾖς μὴ πεποιηκέναι τὴν κατηγορου-
μένην πρᾶξιν, οὕτως ἐκ τῶν εἰκότων χρή σε ἀπο-
10 λογεῖσθαι· ἀπίθανον γὰρ ποιήσεις τὴν κατηγορίαν.
ἂν δὲ ὁμολογεῖν ἀναγκάζῃ, τοῖς τῶν πολλῶν ἤθεσιν[8]
ἀφομοίου τὰς σαυτοῦ πράξεις ὅτι μάλιστα, λέγων

---

[1] ἐλυσιτέλησεν ἄν ? Rac., cf. l. 40.
[2] v.l. ἄλλην τοιαύτην.
[3] εἰσοιστέον ? Rac., cf. l. 25.
[4] v.l. σαυτόν.   [5] v.l. αὐτῷ.
[6] Sp.: φάσκε εἰ.   [7] πιστεύεται Kayser

companions to be the same sort of persons that you 30
say that he is, since it will be supposed that he follows
the same pursuits as his friends on account of his
association with them. This is how the argument
from probability should be pursued by those accusing.

The best line for those on their defence is to show
that neither they themselves nor any of their friends
or their class have ever previously committed any of 35
the actions of which they are accused, and that it
would not have paid them to commit such actions.
If it is notorious that you have done the same thing
before, you must plead your youth, or bring forward
some other excuse that made it natural for you to go
astray at the time, and say that you gained nothing
by doing it then, nor would it have paid you to do it 40
now. If you have never done anything of the kind
but some of your friends happen to have done things 1429 a
like it, you must say that it is not fair that you yourself
should be discredited on their account, and must
prove that others of your associates are respectable
persons, as by these means you will make the
accusation seem doubtful. If they prove that some 5
people of your class have done the same things,
declare it to be absurd that the fact that certain others
are seen to do wrong is to be a proof that you too have
committed any of the offences of which you are
accused. That is how you must base your defence on
the argument from probability if your case is a flat
denial of having done the thing of which you are
accused, because this line will make the accusation
unconvincing. If you are obliged to admit the 10
charge, do your best to show that your own conduct
resembles the habits of the mass of mankind, by

---

[8] v.l. ἔθεσιν.

1429 a

ὡς οἱ πλεῖστοι καὶ¹ οἱ πάντες τοῦτο καὶ τὰ τοιαῦτα
πράττουσιν οὕτως ὡς σοὶ τυγχάνει πεποιημένον.
15 ἂν δὲ μὴ δυνατὸν ᾖ τοῦτο δεῖξαι, καταφευκτέον ἐπὶ
τὰς ἀτυχίας ἢ τὰς ἁμαρτίας, καὶ συγγνώμης πειρατέον τυγχάνειν παραλαμβάνοντα τὰ κοινὰ τῶν
ἀνθρώπων γινόμενα πάθη δι' ὧν ἐξιστάμεθα τοῦ
λογισμοῦ· ταῦτα δ' ἐστὶν ἔρως ὀργὴ μέθη φιλοτιμία
20 καὶ τὰ τούτοις ὁμοιότροπα. τὸ μὲν οὖν εἰκὸς διὰ
ταύτης τῆς μεθόδου τεχνικώτατα μέτιμεν.

VIII. Παράδειγματα δ' ἐστὶ πράξεις ὅμοιαι γε-
γενημέναι καὶ ἐναντίαι ταῖς νῦν ὑφ' ἡμῶν λεγο-
μέναις. τότε δὲ χρηστέον αὐταῖς ἐστὶν ὅτε ἄπιστον
25 ὂν τὸ ὑπὸ σοῦ λεγόμενον εἶναι² φανερὸν ποιῆσαι
θέλεις ἐὰν διὰ τοῦ εἰκότος μὴ πιστεύηται, ὅπως
πρᾶξιν ὁμοίαν ἑτέραν τῇ ὑπὸ σοῦ λεγομένῃ κατα-
μαθόντες³ οὕτω πεπραγμένην ὡς σὺ φῇς γεγενῆσθαι,⁴ μᾶλλον πιστεύσωσι τοῖς ὑπὸ σοῦ λεγομένοις.

Εἰσὶ δὲ τῶν παραδειγμάτων δύο τρόποι· τὰ μὲν
γὰρ τῶν πραγμάτων γίνεται κατὰ λόγον τὰ δὲ παρὰ
30 λόγον, ποιεῖ δὲ τὰ μὲν κατὰ λόγον γινόμενα πιστεύε-
σθαι, τὰ δὲ μὴ κατὰ λόγον ἀπιστεῖσθαι. λέγω δ'
οἷον εἴ τις φάσκει⁵ τοὺς πλουσίους δικαιοτέρους
εἶναι τῶν πενομένων, καὶ φέρει⁶ τινὰς πράξεις
πλουσίων ἀνδρῶν δικαίας· τὰ μὲν οὖν τοιαῦτα τῶν
παραδειγμάτων κατὰ λόγον εἶναι δοκεῖ· τοὺς γὰρ
35 πλείστους ἔστιν ἰδεῖν νομίζοντας τοὺς πλουτοῦντας
δικαιοτέρους εἶναι τῶν πενομένων. εἰ δέ τις πάλιν
ἀποφαίνοι τινὰς τῶν πλουσίων ἐπὶ χρήμασιν ἀδικήσαντας, τῷ παρὰ τὸ εἰκὸς γεγενημένῳ παρα-

---

¹ ἢ Finckh.　　　　　　　　² [εἶναι] Sp.
³ v.l. μαθόντες.　　　　　　⁴ v.l. πεπρᾶχθαι.
⁵ v.l. φάσκοι.　　　　　　　⁶ v.l. φέροι.

saying that most men, indeed all men, do the thing in question and things like it in the same manner in which it happens to have been done by you. If you are unable to prove this, you must take refuge in pleas of misfortune or error, and try to gain pardon by bringing in the passions to which all mankind are liable, that divert us from rational calculation—namely love, anger, intoxication, ambition and the like. This is the most skilful way of developing the argument from probability.

VIII. Examples are actions that have occurred (2) *Examples.* previously and are similar to, or the opposite of, those which we are now discussing. They should be employed on occasions when your statement of the case is unconvincing and you desire to illustrate it, if it cannot be proved by the argument from probability, in order that your audience may be more ready to believe your statements when they realize that another action resembling the one you allege has been committed in the way in which you say that it occurred.

There are two modes of examples. This is because some things happen according to reasonable expectation, others against reasonable expectation ; and those happening according to expectation cause credit, those not according to expectation incredulity. I mean, for instance, if somebody asserts that the rich are more honest than the poor, and produces cases of honest conduct on the part of rich men : examples of this sort appear to be in accordance with reasonable expectation, because most people obviously think that those who are rich are more honest than those who are poor. If, on the other hand, one were to produce instances of rich men acting dishonestly for money, by employing this example of something that

1429 a
δείγματι χρώμενος ἀπίστους ἂν ποιοῖ τοὺς πλου-
τοῦντας· ὡσαύτως δὲ καὶ εἴ τις φέρει παράδειγμα τῶν
1429 b κατὰ λόγον εἶναι δοκούντων, διότι¹ Λακεδαιμόνιοί
ποτε ἢ Ἀθηναῖοι πολλῷ πλήθει χρώμενοι συμμάχων
κατεπολέμησαν τοὺς ἐναντίους, καὶ προτρέπει² τοὺς
ἀκούοντας πολλοὺς συμμάχους ποιεῖσθαι. τὰ μὲν δὴ
τοιαῦτα παραδείγματα κατὰ λόγον ἐστίν· ἅπαντες
5 γὰρ νομίζουσιν ἐν τοῖς πολέμοις τὸ πλῆθος οὐ
μετρίαν ῥοπὴν ἔχειν πρὸς τὴν νίκην. εἰ δέ τις
ἀποφαίνειν ἐθέλοι μὴ τοῦτ' αἴτιον τοῦ νικᾶν, τοῖς
παρὰ τὸ εἰκὸς γεγενημένοις πράγμασι χρήσαιτ' ἂν
παραδείγμασι, λέγων ὡς οἱ μὲν Ἀθήνησι φυγάδες
10 τὸ πρῶτον μετὰ πεντήκοντα ἀνδρῶν Φυλήν τε
καταλαβόντες καὶ πρὸς τοὺς ἐν ἄστει πολλῷ
πλείους ὄντας καὶ συμμάχοις Λακεδαιμονίοις χρωμένους πολεμήσαντες κατῆλθον εἰς τὴν ἰδίαν πόλιν·
Θηβαῖοι δὲ Λακεδαιμονίων καὶ σχεδὸν ἁπάντων
Πελοποννησίων εἰς τὴν Βοιωτίαν ἐμβαλόντων
15 μόνοι περὶ τὰ Λεῦκτρα παραταξάμενοι τὴν Λακεδαιμονίων δύναμιν ἐνίκησαν· Δίων δὲ ὁ Συρακούσιος μετὰ τρισχιλίων ὁπλιτῶν εἰς Συρακούσας
πλεύσας Διονύσιον πολλαπλάσιον ἔχοντα δύναμιν
κατεπολέμησεν· ὡσαύτως δὲ Κορίνθιοι Συρακουσίοις ἐννέα τριήρεσι βοηθήσαντες Καρχηδονίους
20 ἑκατὸν καὶ πεντήκοντα ναυσὶν ἐπὶ τοῖς λιμέσι τῶν
Συρακουσίων ἐφορμοῦντας τὴν δὲ πόλιν ἅπασαν
πλὴν τῆς ἀκροπόλεως ἔχοντας οὐδὲν ἧττον κατεπολέμησαν. συλλήβδην δὲ ταῦτα καὶ τὰ τούτοις
ὅμοια παρὰ λόγον πραχθέντα τὰς κατὰ τὸ εἰκὸς
γινομένας συμβουλὰς ἀπίστους ποιεῖν εἴωθεν. τῶν
25 μὲν οὖν παραδειγμάτων τοιαύτη τις ἡ φύσις ἐστί.

---

¹ οἷον ὅτι ? Rac.   ² v.l. προτρέποι.

has happened contrary to probability he would cause
the rich to be discredited; and similarly if one produces an example of things that seem to be in accord- 1429 b
ance with general expectation, arguing that on one
occasion Sparta, or Athens, defeated its adversaries in war by employing a large number of allies,
and so disposes his hearers to secure many allies.
Examples of this sort are according to expectation,
because everybody thinks that numbers in war have 5
great importance for victory. But if one wanted to
prove that numbers are not the cause of victory, one
would use as examples events that have happened
contrary to probability : one would tell how the exiles
at Athens with fifty men to start with captured Phyle
and fought the far more numerous party in the city with 10
their Spartan allies, and so got back to their own city;
and how the Thebans, when Boeotia was invaded by the
Spartans and almost the whole of the Peloponnesians,
took the field at Leuctra single-handed and defeated 15
the Spartan forces ; and how the Syracusan Dion
with 3000 heavy infantry sailed to Syracuse and waged
a victorious war against Dionysius who had a force
many times as large ; and similarly how the Corinthians coming to the aid of the Syracusans with nine
triremes defeated the Carthaginians in spite of the
fact that they were blockading the harbours of Syracuse 20
with 150 vessels and held the whole of the city except
the citadel.[a] To sum up, these and similar instances
of actions accomplished against reasonable expectation usually succeed in discrediting counsels of policy
that are based on probability. Such is the nature of 25
examples.

[a] See Introd. p. 258 note a.

1429 b

Χρηστέον δ' αὐτῶν ἑκατέρῳ τρόπῳ, ὅταν μὲν
ἡμεῖς λέγωμεν τὰ κατὰ λόγον γινόμενα, δεικνύντας
ὡς ἐπὶ τὸ πολὺ τοῦτον τὸν τρόπον ἐπιτελουμένας
τὰς πράξεις, ὅταν δὲ τὰ παρὰ λόγον γινόμενα,
φέροντας ὅσα παρὰ λόγον δοκοῦντα γενέσθαι τῶν
30 πραγμάτων εὐλόγως ἀποβέβηκεν· ὅταν δ' οἱ ἐναντίοι λέγωσι τοῦτο, χρὴ δεικνύειν ὡς εὐτυχήματα
ταῦτα συνέβη, καὶ λέγειν ὅτι αἱ τοιαῦται πράξεις
ἐν τῷ σπανίῳ γεγόνασιν, οἵας δὲ σὺ λέγεις, πολλάκις. τοῖς μὲν οὖν παραδείγμασιν οὕτω χρηστέον·
35 ὅταν γε μὴν τὰ παρὰ λόγον γινόμενα φέρωμεν, χρὴ
συνάγειν αὐτῶν ὅτι πλεῖστα, καὶ καταλέγειν[1] ὡς
οὐδὲν μᾶλλον ἐκεῖνα τούτων εἴωθε γίνεσθαι. δεῖ
δὲ χρῆσθαι τοῖς παραδείγμασι μὴ μόνον ἐκ τούτων[2] ἀλλὰ καὶ ἐκ τῶν ἐναντίων· λέγω δ' οἷον
ἐὰν ἀποφαίνῃς τινὰς πλεονεκτικῶς τοῖς συμμάχοις
χρωμένους καὶ διὰ τοῦτο λυθεῖσαν αὐτῶν τὴν
1430 a φιλίαν, καὶ λέγῃς[3] " ἡμεῖς δέ, ἂν ἴσως καὶ κοινῶς
πρὸς αὐτοὺς προσφερώμεθα, πολὺν χρόνον τὴν
συμμαχίαν φυλάξομεν"· καὶ πάλιν, ἄν τινας ἑτέρους
ἀπαρασκευάστως[4] πολεμήσαντας καὶ διὰ τοῦτο
5 καταπολεμηθέντας ἀποφαίνῃς, εἶτα λέγῃς " ἂν
παρασκευασάμενοι πολεμῶμεν, βελτίους ἂν περὶ
τῆς νίκης τὰς ἐλπίδας ἔχοιμεν." πολλὰ δὲ λήψῃ
παραδείγματα διὰ τῶν προγεγενημένων πράξεων
καὶ διὰ τῶν νῦν γινομένων· τὰ γὰρ πλεῖστα τῶν
ἔργων τῇ μὲν ὅμοια τῇ δὲ ἀνόμοια ἀλλήλοις ἐστίν·
10 ὥστε διὰ τὴν αἰτίαν ταύτην καὶ παραδειγμάτων
εὐπορήσομεν καὶ τοῖς ὑπὸ τῶν ἄλλων λεγομένοις οὐ
χαλεπῶς ἀντεροῦμεν.

---

[1] [κατα]λέγειν Finckh. [2] τοιούτων ? Rac.
[3] λέγῃς v.l. om. [4] ἀπαρασκευάστους ? Rac.

1429 b

The way to employ either mode of example is—
when we are proposing what may reasonably be
expected to happen, to show that operations are
usually carried through successfully in this way ; but
when we are foretelling an unexpected result, to produce all the cases of things that have turned out
satisfactorily though seeming to have been contrary 30
to reasonable expectation. When your opponents
take this line, you must show that their instances
were lucky accidents, and say that such occurrences
are a rarity, whereas such as you specify have often
occurred. This is how to employ examples. Of
course when we are bringing forward things counter
to expectation, we must collect as many examples 35
of these as possible and go through them to show
that unexpected occurrences are just as common
as ones that were expected. And we must draw
examples not only from similar cases but also from the
opposite : I mean, for instance, if you produce a case
of people overreaching their allies and their friendship
consequently being dissolved, and say ' But for our 1430 a
part we shall keep their alliance for a long time if we
deal with them fairly and on terms of partnership ' ;
and again, if you produce an instance of other people
who went to war without preparation and who were
consequently defeated, and then say ' We should have 5
better hope of victory provided we are prepared for
war.' The events of the past and those occurring
now will supply you with many examples ; most
actions are partly like and partly unlike one another,
so that for this reason we shall be well supplied with
examples, and also shall have no difficulty in counter- 10
ing those put forward by the other side.

Τῶν μὲν οὖν παραδειγμάτων τούς τε τρόπους
ἴσμεν, καὶ ὡς αὐτοῖς χρησόμεθα, καὶ ὅθεν πολλὰ
ληψόμεθα.

IX. Τεκμήρια δ' ἐστὶν ὅσα ἂν ἐναντίως ᾖ πε-
15 πραγμένα τῷ περὶ οὗ ὁ λόγος καὶ[1] ὅσα ὁ λόγος
αὐτὸς ἑαυτῷ ἐναντιοῦται. τῶν γὰρ ἀκουόντων οἱ
πλεῖστοι τοῖς συμβαίνουσι περὶ τὸν λόγον ἢ τὴν
πρᾶξιν ἐναντιώμασι τεκμαίρονται μηδὲν ὑγιὲς εἶναι
μήτε τῶν λεγομένων μήτε τῶν πραττομένων.
πολλὰ δὲ λήψῃ τεκμήρια σκοπῶν εἴτε ὁ λόγος τοῦ
20 ἐναντίου αὐτὸς αὐτῷ[2] ἐναντιοῦται, εἴτε ἡ πρᾶξις
αὐτοῦ[3] ἐναντία τῷ λόγῳ ἐστίν.

Τὰ μὲν οὖν τεκμήρια τοιαῦτά ἐστι, καὶ οὕτως
αὐτὰ πλεῖστα ποιήσεις.

X. Ἐνθυμήματα δ' ἐστὶν οὐ μόνον τὰ τῷ λόγῳ
καὶ τῇ πράξει ἐναντιούμενα, ἀλλὰ καὶ τοῖς ἄλλοις
25 ἅπασιν. λήψῃ δὲ πολλὰ μετιὼν ὡς ἐν τῷ ἐξετα-
στικῷ εἴδει εἴρηται, καὶ σκοπῶν εἴ πῃ ὁ λόγος
ἑαυτῷ ἐναντιοῦται, ἢ τὰ πεπραγμένα τοῖς δικαίοις
ἢ τῷ νόμῳ ἢ τῷ συμφέροντι ἢ τῷ καλῷ ἢ τῷ
δυνατῷ ἢ τῷ ῥᾳδίῳ ἢ τῷ εἰκότι ἢ τῷ ἤθει τοῦ
λέγοντος ἢ τῷ ἔθει[4] τῶν πραγμάτων. τὰ μὲν οὖν
30 τοιαῦτα τῶν ἐνθυμημάτων κατὰ τῶν ἐναντίων
ἐκληπτέον, τὰ δ' ἐναντία τούτοις ὑπὲρ ἡμῶν αὐτῶν
δεῖ λέγειν, ἀποφαίνοντας τὰς πράξεις τὰς ἡμετέρας
καὶ τοὺς λόγους ἐναντιουμένους τοῖς ἀδίκοις καὶ
τοῖς ἀνόμοις καὶ τοῖς ἀσυμφόροις καὶ τοῖς τῶν

---

[1] καὶ ⟨καθ'⟩ Usener.   [2] Buhl: αὐτῷ τῷ πράγματι.
[3] Finckh: αὐτὴ.   [4] v.l. ἤθει.

---

[a] i.e. infallible signs, contrasted with mere signs, which are
fallible : cf. infra c. xii. The limitation of the term to
negative proofs is peculiar to this passage.

1430 a

We now know what kinds of examples there are, and how they are to be employed, and where we can obtain a good supply of them.

IX. Tokens [a] are previous facts running counter to the fact asserted in the speech, and points in which the speech contradicts itself. For most hearers infer from inconsistencies occurring in connexion with a speech or action that the line of argument or conduct taken is entirely unsound. You will obtain a good supply of tokens by considering whether your adversary's speech contradicts itself, or whether his conduct contradicts his words.

Such is the nature of tokens and the way in which you will make a very large supply of them.

X. Considerations [b] are (1) facts that run counter to the speech or action in question, and also (2) those that run counter to anything else. You will obtain a good supply of them by pursuing the method described under the investigatory species of oratory,[c] and by considering whether the speech contradicts itself in any way, or the actions committed run counter to the principles of justice, law, expediency, honour, feasibility, facility or probability, or to the character of the speaker or the usual course of events. This is the sort of consideration to be chosen as a point to use against our opponents. In support of our own case we must state the opposite ones, proving our actions and words to be exactly contrary to those that are unjust, unlawful and inexpedient, and to the usual

(3) Tokens.

(4) Considerations.

15

20

25

30

---

[b] As a technical term of Aristotelian logic an enthymeme is a syllogism drawing its conclusion from premisses that are statements of probabilities. In rhetoric it denotes any syllogism of which one premiss is not stated but left to be understood.

[c] See 1421 b 10, 1427 b 12.

333

1430 a

35 ἀνθρώπων τῶν πονηρῶν ἔθεσι[1] καὶ συλλήβδην τοῖς
μοχθηροῖς νομιζομένοις εἶναι. δεῖ δὲ τούτων
ἕκαστα[2] συναγαγεῖν[3] ὡς εἰς βραχύτατα,[4] καὶ φράζειν ὅτι μάλιστα ἐν ὀλίγοις τοῖς[5] ὀνόμασιν.

Τὰ μὲν οὖν ἐνθυμήματα τοῦτον τὸν τρόπον πολλὰ
ποιήσομεν, καὶ οὕτως αὐτοῖς ἄριστα χρησόμεθα.

40 XI. Γνώμη δ᾽ ἐστὶ μὲν ἐν κεφαλαίῳ καθ᾽ ὅλων
1430 b τῶν πραγμάτων δόγματος ἰδίου δήλωσις, δύο δὲ
τρόποι τῶν γνωμῶν εἰσίν, ὁ μὲν ἔνδοξος ὁ δὲ
παράδοξος. ὅταν μὲν οὖν ἔνδοξον λέγῃς, οὐδὲν δεῖ
τὰς αἰτίας φέρειν, οὔτε γὰρ ἀγνοεῖται τὸ λεγόμενον
5 οὔτ᾽ ἀπιστεῖται· ὅταν δὲ παράδοξον λέγῃς, χρὴ
φράζειν τὰς αἰτίας συντόμως, ἵνα τὴν ἀδολεσχίαν
καὶ τὴν ἀπιστίαν διαφύγῃς. δεῖ δὲ τὰς γνώμας
οἰκείας φέρειν τῶν πραγμάτων,[6] ἵνα μὴ σκαιὸν καὶ
ἀπηρτημένον φαίνηται τὸ λεγόμενον. πολλὰς δὲ
ποιήσομεν αὐτὰς ἢ ἐκ τῆς ἰδίας φύσεως ἢ ἐξ
10 ὑπερβολῆς ἢ ἐκ παρομοιώσεως. αἱ μὲν οὖν ἐκ
τῆς ἰδίας φύσεως τοιαίδε τινές εἰσιν· " οὐκ εἶναί
μοι δοκεῖ δεινὸν γενέσθαι στρατηγὸν[7] πραγμάτων
ἄπειρον ὄντα"· ἑτέρα δ᾽ ἐστὶν ἥδε· " νοῦν ἐχόντων
ἀνδρῶν ἐστι τοῖς τῶν προγεγενημένων παραδείγμασι χρωμένους πειρᾶσθαι διαφυγεῖν τὰς ἐκ τῆς
15 ἀβουλίας ἁμαρτίας." ἐκ μὲν οὖν τῆς ἰδίας φύσεως
τοιαύτας ποιήσομεν γνώμας, ἐξ ὑπερβολῆς δὲ
τοιάδε· " δεινότερά μοι δοκοῦσιν οἱ κλέπτοντες
τῶν ληϊζομένων ποιεῖν· οἱ μὲν γὰρ λαθραίως οἱ δὲ
φανερῶς τὰ χρήματα περιαιροῦνται." τὰς μὲν οὖν

---

[1] Rac.: ἤθεσι.
[2] v.l. ἑκάστοις. [3] Casaubon: συνηγορεῖν.
[4] v.l. βραχύτητα (fortasse ἑκάστοις συνηγορεῖν ὡς βραχύτατα Rac.). [5] ὀλιγίστοις Sp.
[6] τῷ πράγματι Sp. [7] στρατηγὸν ⟨τὸν⟩ ? Rac.

1430 a
35

conduct of bad men—in brief to the things deemed
to be evil. We must condense each of these topics
into the briefest possible shape, and express them
in as few words as we can.

This is the way in which we shall make a large
supply of considerations, and this is how we shall best
employ them.

XI. A maxim may be summarily defined as the 40
(5) *Maxims.*
1430 b
expression of an individual opinion about general
matters of conduct. Maxims have two modes, one
agreeing with accepted opinion and the other running
counter to it. When you say something that is
usually accepted, there is no need to produce
reasons because what you say is not unfamiliar and
does not meet with incredulity ; but when what you 5
say is paradoxical, you must specify the reasons briefly,
so as to avoid prolixity and not arouse incredulity.
The maxims that you produce should be related to the
matter in hand, in order that what you say may not
seem clumsy and irrelevant. We shall make a supply
of maxims either from the particular nature of the 10
case or by using hyperbole or by drawing a parallel.
Instances of maxims drawn from the particular nature
of the case are as follows : ' I do not think it possible
for a man to become an able general if he is without
experience of affairs ' ; and another : ' It is characteristic of sensible people to use the examples of their
predecessors and to endeavour so to escape the errors
arising out of imprudence.' Such are the maxims 15
that we shall construct from the particular nature of
the case. The following is a specimen of those based
on hyperbole : ' I think that thieves commit worse
outrages than highwaymen, because the former rob
us of our property by stealth, the latter openly.'

ἐξ ὑπερβολῆς γνώμας τὸν τρόπον τοῦτον πολλὰς
20 ποιήσομεν, αἱ δ' ἐκ παρομοιώσεως τοιαίδε εἰσίν·
" ὁμοιότατόν μοι δοκοῦσιν οἱ τὰ χρήματα ἀπο-
στεροῦντες τοῖς τὰς πόλεις προδιδοῦσι ποιεῖν·
πιστευθέντες γὰρ ἀμφότεροι τοὺς πιστεύσαντας
ἀδικοῦσιν"· ἑτέρα δέ " παραπλήσιόν μοι δοκοῦσι
ποιεῖν οἱ ἀντίδικοι¹ τοῖς τυράννοις· ἐκεῖνοί τε γὰρ
25 ὧν μὲν αὐτοὶ ἀδικοῦσιν οὐκ ἀξιοῦσι διδόναι δίκας,
ὧν δὲ τοῖς ἄλλοις ἐγκαλοῦσιν ἀνυπερβλήτως τι-
μωροῦνται· οὗτοί τε εἰ μέν τι αὐτοὶ τῶν ἐμῶν
ἔχουσιν οὐκ ἀποδιδόασιν, εἰ δέ τι ἐγὼ τούτων
ἔλαβον, καὶ αὐτὸ καὶ τοὺς τόκους οἴονται δεῖν
κομίσασθαι."

Γνώμας μὲν οὖν τὸν τρόπον τοῦτον μετιόντες
πολλὰς ποιήσομεν.

30 XII. Σημεῖον δ' ἐστὶν ἄλλο ἄλλου, οὐ τὸ τυχὸν
τοῦ τυχόντος οὐδ' ἅπαν ἅπαντος,² ἀλλὰ τό γ'
εἰθισμένον γίνεσθαι πρὸ τοῦ πράγματος ἢ ἅμα τῷ
πράγματι ἢ μετὰ τὸ πρᾶγμα. ἔστι δὲ σημεῖον τό
τε³ γενόμενον μὴ μόνον τοῦ γενομένου ἀλλὰ καὶ
35 τοῦ μὴ γενομένου, ὡσαύτως δὲ καὶ τὸ μὴ γεγονὸς
οὐ μόνον τοῦ μὴ ὄντος ἀλλὰ καὶ τοῦ ὄντος. ποιεῖ
δὲ τῶν σημείων τὸ μὲν οἴεσθαι τὸ δ' εἰδέναι·
κάλλιστον δὲ τὸ εἰδέναι ποιοῦν, δεύτερον δὲ τὸ
δόξαν πιθανωτάτην ἐργαζόμενον. πολλὰ δὲ ποιήσομεν σημεῖα συλλήβδην εἰπεῖν ἐξ ἑκάστου τῶν
40 πεπραγμένων καὶ λεγομένων καὶ ὁρωμένων, καθ'
ἓν ἕκαστον λαμβάνοντες, ἔκ τε τοῦ μεγέθους καὶ
1431 a τῆς σμικρότητος τῶν ἀποβαινόντων κακῶν ἢ
ἀγαθῶν· ἔτι δὲ ἐκ τῶν μαρτύρων⁴ καὶ ἐκ τῶν

---

¹ v.l. ἄδικοι. ² Sp.: παντός.
³ τό γε vel τὸ [τε] ? Sp. ⁴ Sp.: μαρτυριῶν.

This is how we shall make a large supply of maxims
based on hyperbole. Those made by drawing a 20
parallel are such as the following : ' I think that those
who cheat people out of money act exactly like those
who betray their country, because both of them after
being trusted rob those who have trusted them ' ;
and another : ' I think that my opponents are acting
very like tyrants, because the latter claim not to be 25
punished for the wrongs committed by themselves
but exact unequalled penalties for the offences of
which they accuse others, while the former, if they
themselves have something that belongs to me, do
not return it, but if I have taken something of theirs,
think that they ought to get it back and receive
interest into the bargain.'

By following this method we shall make a large
supply of maxims.

XII. One thing is a sign of another—not any 30
casual thing of any other casual thing, nor everything (6) *Signs.*
whatever of everything whatever, but only a thing
that normally precedes or accompanies or follows a
thing. Something happening may be a sign not only
of something happening but also of something not
happening, and something that has not happened 35
may be a sign not only that something is not a fact
but also that something is a fact. A sign may produce
either opinion or full knowledge ; the best kind of
sign is one that produces knowledge, but one that
causes an extremely probable opinion is the second
best kind. We shall construct a large supply of signs
from everything (to put it summarily) that has been
done or said or seen, taking each thing separately, and 40
also from the magnitude or smallness of the evil or 1431 a
good that results from them ; also from witnesses and

1431 a

μαρτυρουμένων, καὶ ἐκ τῶν συμπαρόντων ἡμῖν ἢ
τοῖς ἐναντίοις, καὶ ἐξ αὐτῶν ἐκείνων, καὶ ἐκ τῶν
5 προκλήσεων, καὶ ἐκ τῶν χρόνων, καὶ ἐξ ἄλλων
πολλῶν. τῶν μὲν οὖν σημείων ἐντεῦθεν εὐπορήσομεν.

XIII. Ἔλεγχος δ' ἐστὶ μὲν ὃ μὴ δυνατὸν ἄλλως
ἔχειν ἀλλ' οὕτως¹ ὡς ἡμεῖς λέγομεν· λαμβάνεται
δὲ ἐκ τῶν φύσει ἀναγκαίων ἢ ἀναγκαίων² ὡς ἡμεῖς
λέγομεν,³ καὶ ἐκ τῶν κατὰ φύσιν ἀδυνάτων⁴ ἢ
10 ἀδυνάτων ὡς οἱ ἐναντίοι λέγουσιν. κατὰ φύσιν
μὲν οὖν ἀναγκαῖόν ἐστιν οἷον τοὺς ζῶντας σιτίων
δεῖσθαι, καὶ τὰ τούτοις ὅμοια· ὡς δ' ἡμεῖς λέγομεν ἔστιν ἀναγκαῖον τοὺς μεμαστιγωμένους ὁμολογεῖν ἅπερ οἱ μαστιγοῦντες κελεύουσιν. κατὰ
φύσιν δὲ πάλιν ἀδύνατόν ἐστι παιδάριον μικρὸν
15 κλέψαι τοσοῦτον ἀργύριον ὅσον μὴ δυνατὸν φέρειν
καὶ οἴχεσθαι τοῦτο φέρον· ὡς δ' ἂν ὁ ἐναντίος
λέγοι ἔσται ἀδύνατον, ἂν φάσκῃ μὲν ἐν χρόνοις
τισὶν Ἀθήνησι ποιήσασθαι τὸ συμβόλαιον, ἡμεῖς
δ' ἔχωμεν ἐπιδεῖξαι τοῖς ἀκούουσιν ὡς κατὰ τοὺς
τότε καιροὺς ἀπεδημοῦμεν ἐν ἑτέρᾳ πόλει τινί.
20 τοὺς μὲν οὖν ἐλέγχους ἐκ τούτων καὶ ἐκ τῶν τούτοις ὁμοιοτρόπων ποιησόμεθα.

Συλλήβδην δὲ τὰς ἐξ αὐτοῦ τοῦ λόγου καὶ τῶν
πράξεων καὶ τῶν ἀνθρώπων πίστεις ἁπάσας
διεληλύθαμεν· σκεψώμεθα δὲ καὶ τί ἀλλήλων
διαφέρουσιν.

XIV. Τὸ μὲν τοίνυν εἰκὸς τοῦ παραδείγματος
25 ταύτῃ διαφέρει, διότι τοῦ μὲν εἰκότος ἔχουσιν

¹ [οὕτως]? Rac.   ² ἢ ἀναγκαίων add. Sp.
³ v.l. λέγομεν ἢ ὁ ἀντιλέγων.
⁴ Sp.: δυνατῶν.

338

1431 a

evidence, and from those who take our side or that
of our opponents, from our opponents themselves,
and from the challenges made by the parties, and from
dates, and from many other things. These will pro- 5
vide us with a plentiful supply of signs.

XIII. A refutation[a] is something that cannot be (7) *Refuta-
otherwise than as we say it is. It is based on some *tions.*
necessity in the nature of things, or something
necessary as alleged by us, or on something impossible in the nature of things, or impossible as
alleged by our opponents. Instances of things neces- 10
sary by nature are ' Living men require food,' and
propositions of that sort ; a thing necessary as alleged
by us is ' Men being scourged confess exactly what
the people scourging them tell them to.' Again, a
thing impossible by nature is ' A little boy stole a sum
of money larger than he could carry and went off with
it ' ; and it will be a thing impossible as alleged by 15
our opponent if he avers that at a certain date we
made the contract in question at Athens, whereas we
are able to prove that during the period indicated
we were away in some other city. We shall form 20
our refutations from these and similar materials.

We have summarily gone through all the forms of
proof derived from actual words and from deeds and
from persons. Let us consider how they differ from
one another.

XIV. The differences between a probability and an 25
example is that a probability is a thing of which the

*Differences
between these
varieties of
direct proof.*

---

[a] *Elenchus* in Aristotle's logic is ' the proof of the contra-
dictory of a given thesis,' *Soph. Elench.* 170 b 1 ; but
the technical sense is ignored or at all events not developed
here.

1431 a

αὐτοὶ οἱ ἀκούοντες ἔννοιαν, τὰ δὲ παραδείγματα
* * *[1] καὶ ἐκ τῶν ἐναντίων καὶ ἐκ τῶν ὁμοίων
φέρειν ἔστιν, τὰ δὲ τεκμήρια μόνον ἐκ τῶν περὶ τὸν
λόγον καὶ τὴν πρᾶξιν ἐναντίων συντίθεται. καὶ
μὴν ἐνθύμημα τεκμηρίου ταύτην τὴν διαφορὰν
30 ἔσχηκεν, ὅτι τὸ μὲν τεκμήριον περὶ τὸν λόγον καὶ
τὴν πρᾶξιν ἐναντίωσίς ἐστι, τὸ δ' ἐνθύμημα καὶ
τὰς περὶ τὰς ἄλλας ἰδέας ἐναντιώσεις ἐξείληφεν,
ἢ καὶ διότι τὸ μὲν τεκμήριον οὐκ ἐφ' ἡμῖν ἐστὶ
λαμβάνειν ἂν μὴ περὶ τὰ πράγματα καὶ τοὺς λόγους
ἐναντίωσίς τις ὑπάρχῃ, τὸ δ' ἐνθύμημα πολλαχό-
35 θεν οἷόν τε πορίζεσθαι τοῖς λέγουσιν. γνῶμαι δ'
ἐνθυμημάτων διαφέρουσιν ᾗ τὰ μὲν ἐνθυμήματα
μόνον ἐκ τῶν ἐναντιώσεων σύγκειται, τὰς δὲ
γνώμας καὶ μετὰ τῶν ἐναντιώσεων καὶ ἁπλῶς
αὐτὰς καθ' αὑτὰς δυνατόν ἐστιν ἐμφανίζειν. τὰ
δὲ σημεῖα τῶν γνωμῶν καὶ τῶν προειρημένων
40 ἁπάντων ταύτῃ διαφέρουσιν, ὅτι τὰ μὲν ἄλλα
πάντα οἴησιν ἐμποιεῖ τοῖς ἀκούουσιν, τῶν δὲ
σημείων ἔνια καὶ σαφῶς εἰδέναι ποιήσει τοὺς
κρίνοντας, καὶ διότ τῶν μὲν ἑτέρων[2] οὐκ ἔστιν
1431 b αὐτοὺς πορίσασθαι τὰ πλεῖστα, τῶν δὲ σημείων
πολλὰ ῥᾳδίως ἔστι ποιήσασθαι. καὶ μὴν ἔλεγχος
σημείου ταύτῃ διαφέρει, διότι τῶν μὲν σημείων
ἔνια μόνον οἴεσθαι ποιεῖ τοὺς ἀκούοντας, ἔλεγχος
δὲ πᾶς τὴν ἀλήθειαν διδάσκει τοὺς κρίνοντας.
5 Ὥστε τὰς μὲν ἐκ[3] τῶν λόγων καὶ τῶν πράξεων
πίστεις, οἷαί τ' εἰσὶ καὶ ὅθεν αὐτῶν εὐπορήσομεν
καὶ τίνι ἀλλήλων διαφέρουσιν, ἐκ τῶν προειρη-

---

[1] Lacunam Sauppe ⟨παρ' ἡμῶν εἰσφέρομεν. τὰ δὲ παραδείγματα διαφέρει τῶν τεκμηρίων ὅτι τὰ μὲν παραδείγματα⟩.
[2] Usener tr. τῶν μὲν ἑτέρων πολλὰ ῥᾳδίως ἔστι ποιήσα-

340

hearers themselves have some notion, but examples ⟨are produced from our own resources. Examples differ from tokens because examples⟩[a] can be drawn both from contrary and from similar things, whereas tokens are constructed only from contrarieties in word and deed. Moreover, a consideration possesses this difference from a token, that whereas a token is a contrariety in word or deed, a consideration also selects contrarieties in regard to other forms of things; that is to say, that whereas we cannot obtain tokens unless there exists some contrariety in regard to deeds or words, speakers can produce a consideration from many sources. Maxims differ from considerations, in that, whereas considerations can only be constructed from contrarieties, maxims can be exhibited both in connexion with contraries and simply by themselves. What distinguishes signs from maxims and all the other proofs already mentioned is that whereas all the others create in their hearers an opinion, certain of the signs will cause those who judge to have clear knowledge ; and that whereas it is impossible for us to supply most of the other proofs for ourselves, many signs can easily be constructed. Moreover, a refutation differs from a sign because some signs only cause the hearers to think, whereas every refutation teaches the judges the truth.

Thus what has been said before has informed us of the nature of the proofs derived from words and actions, the sources from which we shall obtain a supply of them, and the difference that exists between

[a] These words are a conjectural addition to the Greek.

σθαι, τῶν δὲ σημείων οὐκ ἔστιν αὐτοὺς πορίσασθαι τὰ πλεῖστα.

3 ἐκ add. Sp.

μένων ἴσμεν· τῶν δ᾽ ἐπιθέτων ἑκάστην πάλιν διέλθωμεν.

Ἡ μὲν οὖν δόξα τοῦ λέγοντός ἐστι τὸ τὴν αὑτοῦ
10 διάνοιαν ἐμφανίζειν κατὰ τῶν πραγμάτων. δεῖ δ᾽
ἔμπειρον ἀποφαίνειν ἑαυτὸν περὶ ὧν ἂν λέγῃ, καὶ
ἐπιδεικνύναι ὡς συμφέρει τἀληθῆ λέγειν περὶ
τούτων, τὸν δ᾽ ἀντιλέγοντα μάλιστα δεικνύναι
μηδεμίαν ἐμπειρίαν ἔχοντα τὸν ἐναντίον περὶ ὧν
15 ἀποφαίνεται τὴν δόξαν ὅμως.[1] ἂν δὲ τοῦτο μὴ
δυνατὸν ᾖ, δεικτέον ὡς καὶ οἱ ἔμπειροι πολλάκις
ἐξαμαρτάνουσιν· ἂν δὲ τοῦτο μὴ ἐνδέχηται, λέγειν
ὡς ἀσύμφορόν ἐστι τοῖς ἐναντίοις τἀληθῆ περὶ
τούτων εἰπεῖν. ταῖς μὲν οὖν δόξαις τοῦ λέγοντος
οὕτω χρησόμεθα, καὶ αὐτοὶ ἀποφαινόμενοι καὶ
ἑτέροις ἀντιλέγοντες.

20 XV. Μαρτυρία δ᾽ ἐστὶν ὁμολογία συνειδότος
ἑκόντος. ἀναγκαῖον δ᾽ εἶναι τὸ μαρτυρούμενον ἢ
πιθανὸν ἢ ἀπίθανον ἢ ἀμφίβολον πρὸς πίστιν,
ὡσαύτως δὲ καὶ τὸν μάρτυρα ἢ[2] πιστὸν ἢ ἄπιστον
ἢ ἀμφίδοξον. ὅταν μὲν οὖν τὸ μαρτυρούμενον ᾖ
πιθανὸν καὶ ὁ μάρτυς ἀληθινός, οὐδὲν δέονται αἱ
25 μαρτυρίαι ἐπιλόγων, ἐὰν μὴ βούλῃ γνώμην ἢ
ἐνθύμημα συντόμως εἰπεῖν τοῦ ἀστείου ἕνεκεν.
ὅταν δὲ ὑποπτεύηται ὁ μάρτυς, ἀποδεικνύειν δεῖ
ὡς οὔτε χάριτος ἕνεκεν οὔτε τιμωρίας ἢ κέρδους
ὁ τοιοῦτος ἂν τὰ ψευδῆ μαρτυρήσειεν· δεῖ δὲ καὶ
διδάσκειν ὅτι οὐ συμφέρει τὸ ψεῦδος μαρτυρεῖν·
30 αἱ μὲν γὰρ ὠφέλειαι μικραὶ τὸ δ᾽ ἐξελεγχθῆναι
χαλεπόν,[3] γνωσθέντα δ᾽ οὐ μόνον εἰς ἀργύριον
οἱ νόμοι ζημιοῦσιν ἀλλὰ καὶ εἰς δόξαν καὶ εἰς

---

[1] Forster: τήν τε δόξαν ὁμοίως.
[2] ἢ add. Sp.   [3] ⟨οὐ⟩ χαλεπόν Finckh.

them. Let us next discuss the various supplementary proofs.

The opinion of the speaker is the pronouncement
of his own view about things. He must show that he is experienced in the matters about which he is talking, and must further prove that it is to his interest to speak the truth about them ; and one who is contradicting must, if possible, prove that his adversary has no experience of the matters about which he is nevertheless pronouncing an opinion. If this is not 15 possible, he must show that even experts are often quite mistaken ; and should this not be feasible, he must say that it is against his opponents' interest to speak the truth about the matter in question. This is how we shall use the opinions expressed by the speaker, both when declaring our own and when contradicting other people.

XV. Evidence is an admission voluntarily made by
one who knows the facts. What is stated in evidence must necessarily be either probable or improbable or of doubtful credit, and similarly the witness must be either trustworthy or untrustworthy or questionable. When the thing stated is probable and the witness truthful, there is no need of further comment on the 25 evidence, unless for the sake of style you choose briefly to introduce a maxim or consideration. When the witness is suspected, you must declare that a man of that sort would not give false testimony either as a favour or for the sake of revenge or gain ; you must also explain that it does not pay to give false testimony, because the profits are small and it is a serious 30 matter to be found out, and when detected in it a man not only incurs a pecuniary penalty under the laws but also suffers in reputation and in loss of credit.

ἀπιστίαν. τοὺς μὲν οὖν μάρτυρας οὕτω πιστοὺς
ποιήσομεν.

Ἀντιλέγοντας δὲ μαρτυρίᾳ δεῖ τὸν τρόπον τοῦ
μάρτυρος διαβάλλειν ἂν ᾖ πονηρός, ἢ τὸ μαρ-
35 τυρούμενον ἐξετάζειν ἂν ἀπίθανον ὂν¹ τυγχάνῃ,
ἢ καὶ συναμφοτέροις τούτοις ἀντιλέγειν, συν-
άγοντας² τὰ φαυλότατα τῶν ἐναντίων εἰς ταὐτό.
σκεπτέον δὲ καὶ εἰ φίλος ἐστὶν ὁ μάρτυς ᾧ μαρτυρεῖ,
ἢ εἰ μέτεστί ποθεν αὐτῷ τοῦ πράγματος, ἢ ἐχθρός
ἐστιν οὗ καταμαρτυρεῖ, ἢ πένης· τούτων γὰρ οἱ
40 μὲν διὰ χάριν, οἱ δὲ διὰ τιμωρίαν, οἱ δὲ διὰ κέρδος
ὑποπτεύονται τὰ ψευδῆ μαρτυρεῖν. καὶ τὸν τῶν
ψευδομαρτυριῶν νόμον ἐπὶ τούτοις τεθεικέναι
φήσομεν τὸν νομοθέτην· ἄτοπον οὖν εἶναι τοῦ
1432 a νομοθέτου τοῖς μάρτυσι μὴ πιστεύσαντος τοὺς
κρίνοντας πιστεύειν αὐτοῖς τοὺς³ κατὰ τοὺς νόμους
κρινεῖν⁴ ὀμωμοκότας. τοὺς μὲν οὖν μάρτυρας
οὕτως ἀπιθάνους ποιήσομεν.

Ἔστι δὲ καὶ κλέπτειν τὴν μαρτυρίαν τρόπῳ
τοιῷδε· "Μαρτύρησόν μοι, ὦ Καλλίκλεις.⁵" "Μὰ
5 τοὺς θεοὺς οὔκουν ἔγωγε· κωλύοντος γὰρ ἐμοῦ
ταῦτ' ἔπραξεν οὗτος." καὶ διὰ τούτου ἐν ἀπο-
φάσει ψευδομαρτυρήσας ψευδομαρτυρίας⁶ δίκην
οὐχ ὑφέξει. τοιγαροῦν ὅταν μὲν ἡμῖν συμφέρῃ
κλέπτειν τὴν μαρτυρίαν, οὕτως αὐτῇ χρησόμεθα·
ἐὰν δὲ οἱ ἐναντίοι τοιοῦτόν τι ποιήσωσιν, ἐμ-

---

¹ ὂν add. Sp. (v.l. ἂν ᾖ πιθανὸν).
² Sp.: συνάγοντα.
³ τοὺς add. Sp.   ⁴ Sp.: κρίνειν.
⁵ v.l. Λυσικλῆς.   ⁶ Sp.: ψευδομάρτυρος.

ᵃ If a witness gave false evidence, the injured party could
sue him for damages; but it is here implied that proceedings

This is how we shall make out the witnesses to be trustworthy.

When contradicting evidence we must run down the character of the witness if he is a rascal, or subject his evidence to examination if it is improbable, or even speak against both the person and his evidence together, collecting under one head the worst points in our adversaries' case. Another thing to consider is whether the witness is a friend of the man for whom he is giving evidence, or in some way connected with his act, or whether he is an enemy of the person against whom he is giving evidence, or a poor man ; because witnesses in these circumstances are suspected of giving false testimony, from motives in the one case of favour, in the other of revenge, and in the other of gain. We shall say that it was to deal with these cases that the lawgiver has enacted the law as to false witness, so that it would be strange that those judging the case, who have sworn to give judgement according to the law, should trust the witnesses when the lawgiver did not trust them. This is how we shall throw discredit on the witnesses.

It is also possible to get evidence by a trick, in such a way as this : ' Callicles, bear me witness '— ' No, by heaven I will not, because the man did commit the crime in spite of my endeavour to prevent him.' By these means in the form of a refusal to give evidence he will have given false evidence without being liable to prosecution for that offence.[a] So this is the way in which we shall manage the evidence when it is to our advantage to procure it by a trick. If our opponents do something of the sort,

could not be taken if the false statement was thrown in incidentally, and not as part of the evidence.

ARISTOTLE

1432 a

10 φανιοῦμεν τὴν κακοποιίαν αὐτῶν καὶ συγγραψα-
μένους μαρτυρεῖν κελεύσομεν.

Μάρτυσι μὲν οὖν καὶ μαρτυρίαις ἐκ τούτων
ἴσμεν ὡς δεῖ χρήσασθαι.

XVI. Βάσανος δ' ἐστὶ μὲν ὁμολογία παρὰ
συνειδότος ἄκοντος δέ. ὅταν μὲν οὖν συμφέρῃ
ἡμῖν ποιεῖν αὐτὴν ἰσχυράν, λεκτέον ὡς οἵ τε[1]
15 ἰδιῶται περὶ τῶν σπουδαιοτάτων καὶ αἱ πόλεις
περὶ τῶν μεγίστων ἐκ βασάνων τὰς πίστεις
λαμβάνουσι, καὶ διότι πιστότερόν ἐστι βάσανος
μαρτύρων, τοῖς μὲν γὰρ μάρτυσι συμφέρει πολλάκις ψεύσασθαι, τοῖς δὲ βασανιζομένοις λυσιτελεῖ
τἀληθῆ λέγειν· οὕτω γὰρ παύσονται τάχιστα τῆς
20 κακοπαθείας. ὅταν δὲ βούλῃ τὰς βασάνους ἀ-
πίστους ποιεῖν, πρῶτον μὲν λεκτέον ὡς οἱ βασανιζόμενοι τοῖς ἐκδοῦσι πολέμιοι γίνονται καὶ διὰ
τοῦτο πολλοὶ τῶν δεσποτῶν καταψεύδονται, ἔπειθ'
ὅτι πολλάκις τοῖς βασανίζουσιν ὁμολογοῦσιν οὐ
τὰς ἀληθείας, ἵν' ὡς τάχιστα τῶν κακῶν παύσωνται·
25 δεικτέον δ' ὅτι καὶ τῶν ἐλευθέρων πολλοὶ ἤδη
βασανιζόμενοι καθ' ἑαυτῶν ἐψεύσαντο, βουλόμενοι
τὴν παραυτίκα κακοπάθειαν ἐκφυγεῖν, ὥστε πολὺ
μᾶλλον εὔλογον τοὺς δούλους ψευσαμένους κατὰ
τῶν δεσποτῶν βούλεσθαι τὴν αὐτῶν τιμωρίαν
30 ἐκφυγεῖν, ἢ πολλὰς κακοπαθείας τοῖς σώμασι καὶ
ταῖς ψυχαῖς ὑπομείναντας ἵν' ἕτεροι μηδὲν πάθωσιν
αὐτοὺς βούλεσθαι[2] μὴ ψεῦδος εἰπεῖν.

Τὰς μὲν οὖν βασάνους ἐκ τῶν τοιούτων καὶ τῶν
τούτοις ὁμοιοτρόπων πιθανὰς καὶ ἀπιθάνους καταστήσομεν.

---

[1] Sp. : γε.
[2] [αὐτοὺς βούλεσθαι] Sp.

we shall expose their malpractice, and call upon them
to produce written depositions.

These suggestions inform us of the proper way in
which to handle witnesses and evidence.

XVI. Evidence under torture is a confession of (3) *Evidence under torture.*
complicity unwillingly given. When it is to our
advantage to make it carry weight, we must say that
private individuals employ torture as a means to
obtain proofs about very important matters, and so
do governments about affairs of the greatest magni- 15
tude ; and that torture is more reliable than ordinary
evidence, because it is often to the interest of witnesses to lie, whereas it pays men being tortured to
tell the truth because in that way they will most
speedily obtain release from their suffering. When
you want to discredit torture, you must say in the first 20
place that persons under torture become hostile to
the people who handed them over for it, and on that
account in many cases make false statements against
their masters ; secondly that those under torture
often make confessions that are not true in order to
bring their sufferings to an end as quickly as possible ;
and you must point out that even free men before 25
now have often under torture made false statements
against themselves, in their desire to escape from the
agony of the moment, so that it is much more probable
that slaves should wish to escape being punished
themselves by telling lies against their masters, than
that when enduring great agony of body and mind
they should not be willing to tell a lie themselves in 30
order to save others from suffering.

By means of such arguments and similar ones we
shall secure credit or discredit for evidence given
under torture.

1432 a

XVII. Ὅρκος δ' ἐστὶ μετὰ θείας παραλήψεως
φάσις ἀναπόδεικτος. δεῖ δ' αὐτὸν¹ ὅταν μὲν αὔξειν
35 ἐθέλωμεν, λέγειν οὕτως " οὐδεὶς ἂν ἐπιορκεῖν
βούλοιτο, φοβούμενος τήν τε παρὰ τῶν θεῶν
τιμωρίαν καὶ τὴν παρὰ τοῖς ἀνθρώποις αἰσχύνην,"
καὶ διεξιέναι ὅτι τοὺς μὲν ἀνθρώπους λαθεῖν ἔστι,
τοὺς δὲ θεοὺς οὐκ ἔστιν. ὅταν δὲ οἱ ἐναντίοι κατα-
φύγωσιν εἰς ὅρκον καὶ βουλώμεθα ταπεινοῦν αὐτόν,
40 δεικτέον ὡς τῶν αὐτῶν ἐστιν ἀνθρώπων τὰ πονηρὰ
1432 b πράττειν καὶ μὴ φροντίζειν ἐπιορκοῦντας· ὅστις
γὰρ κακουργῶν οἴεται λανθάνειν τοὺς θεούς, οὗτος
οὐδὲ ἐπιορκῶν τιμωρίας οἴεται τεύξεσθαι. καὶ περὶ
μὲν τῶν ὅρκων ὁμοιοτρόπως τοῖς προειρημένοις
μετιόντες λέγειν εὐπορήσομεν ὑπὲρ² αὐτῶν.

5 Συλλήβδην δὲ τὰς πάσας πίστεις ἤδη, καθάπερ
ὑπεθέμεθα, διεξεληλύθαμεν, καὶ δεδηλώκαμεν³ οὐ
μόνον ἣν ἑκάστη αὐτῶν δύναμιν ἔσχηκεν ἀλλὰ
καὶ τί ἀλλήλων διαφέρουσι καὶ πῶς αὐταῖς
χρηστέον. νῦν δ' ὑπὲρ τῶν ὑπολοίπων, ἃ τῶν
τριῶν⁴ εἰδῶν ἐστι καὶ παρὰ πάντας τοὺς λόγους
10 χρήσιμα γίνεται, διδάσκειν ἐπιχειρήσομεν.

XVIII. Προκατάληψις μὲν οὖν ἐστι δι' ἧς τά
τε τῶν ἀκουόντων ἐπιτιμήματα καὶ τοὺς τῶν
ἀντιλέγειν μελλόντων λόγους προκαταλαμβάνοντες
ὑπεξαιρήσομεν τὰς ἐπιφερομένας δυσχερείας. καὶ
τὰς μὲν τῶν ἀκουόντων ἐπιτιμήσεις ὧδε χρὴ
15 προκαταλαμβάνειν· " ἴσως δέ τινες ὑμῶν θαυμά-
ζουσιν ὅτι νέος ὢν οὕτω περὶ μεγάλων πραγμάτων

---

¹ αὐτὸν post μὲν Sp.   ² v.l. περί.
³ Sylberg: δεδώκαμεν.   ⁴ τῶν ἑπτὰ Sylberg.

ᵃ At 1421 b 7 foll. oratory was divided into three genera
and seven species.

1432 a
(4) *Evidence*
on oath.

XVII. An oath is an unproved statement sup- ported by an appeal to the gods. When we desire to uphold its validity we must say ' Nobody would be 35 willing to commit perjury, as he would be afraid of punishment from the gods and discredit with men,' and we must enlarge on the point that although it is possible to escape being detected by men it is not possible to escape the notice of the gods. When our opponents have recourse to an oath and we want to depreciate it, we must point out that it belongs to the 40 same persons to do wicked actions and not to mind perjuring themselves, because one who thinks that 1432 b the gods do not notice his malpractices also thinks he will not meet with punishment if he commits perjury. We shall have plenty to say about oaths if we follow up the subject in a manner similar to what has been said already.

We have now carried out our intention of summarily 5 reviewing all the kinds of proof, and have shown not only the capacity of each kind but also the differences between them and the proper method of employing them. Now we will endeavour to explain the remaining expedients which belong to the three species [a] of oratory and can be used in the course 10 of speeches of all sorts.

XVIII. Anticipation is the device by which we shall *Anticipa-* remove ill-feeling that we encounter by anticipating *tion.* the criticisms of our audience and the arguments of those who are going to speak on the other side. The 15 way to anticipate the criticisms of the audience is this : ' But perhaps some of you will be surprised that a young man like me should have attempted to address the house on such important matters ' ; and

1432 b

ἐπεχείρησα δημηγορεῖν''· καὶ πάλιν '' μηδεὶς
ἀπαντήσῃ μοι δυσκόλως¹ ὅτι μέλλω συμβουλεύειν
ὑμῖν περὶ ὧν ὀκνοῦσί τινες ἄλλοι παρρησιάζεσθαι
πρὸς ὑμᾶς.'' περὶ μὲν οὖν τῶν μελλόντων δυσ-
20 χεραίνεσθαι τοῖς ἀκούουσιν οὕτω δεῖ προκαταλαμβάνοντα φέρειν αἰτίας παρ' ἃς ὀρθῶς ποιεῖν δόξεις
συμβουλεύων, δεικνύντα τὴν ἐρημίαν τῶν λεγόντων
ἢ² τὸ μέγεθος τῶν κινδύνων ἢ τὸ τῷ κοινῷ συμφέρον ἢ ἄλλην τινὰ³ τοιαύτην αἰτίαν δι' ἧς λύσεις
25 τὴν ἐπιφερομένην δυσχέρειαν. ἂν δὲ μηδὲν ἧττον
θορυβῶσιν οἱ ἀκούοντες, χρὴ λέγειν συντόμως ἢ
ὡς ἐν γνώμης ἢ ὡς ἐν⁴ ἐνθυμήματος σχήματι,
διότι⁵ πάντων ἀτοπώτατόν ἐστιν ἥκειν μὲν ὡς
περὶ τῶν πραγμάτων βουλευσομένους τὰ κράτιστα,
νῦν δὲ μὴ βουλομένους ἀκούειν τῶν λεγόντων
οἴεσθαι καλῶς ἂν βουλεύσασθαι, καὶ πάλιν ὅτι
30 καλόν ἐστιν ἢ αὐτοὺς ἀνισταμένους συμβουλεύειν
ἢ τῶν συμβουλευόντων ἀκούσαντας ἅπερ ἂν αὐτοῖς
δοκῇ χειροτονεῖν. ἐν μὲν οὖν ταῖς δημηγορίαις
οὕτω καὶ ταῖς προκαταλήψεσι χρηστέον καὶ τοῖς
θορύβοις ἀπαντητέον.

Ἐν δὲ ταῖς δικαιολογίαις προκαταληψόμεθα μὲν
35 ὁμοιοτρόπως τοῖς προειρημένοις, ἀπαντήσομεν δὲ
τοῖς θορύβοις, ἐὰν μὲν ἐν ἀρχαῖς γίνωνται τῶν
λόγων, ὧδέ· ''πῶς οὐκ⁶ ἄλογον οὖν⁷ ἐστὶ τὸν μὲν
νομοθέτην προστάξαι δύο λόγους ἑκάστῳ τῶν
ἀντιδίκων ἀποδοῦναι, τοὺς δὲ δικάζοντας ὑμᾶς
ὀμωμοκέναι κατὰ τὸν νόμον κρίνειν, εἶτα μηδὲ τὸν
40 ἕνα λόγον ἀκοῦσαι βούλεσθαι; κἀκεῖνον μὲν ὑμῶν

---

¹ Sylberg: δύσκολος.   ² ἢ add. Rac.   ³ v.l. om. τινὰ.
⁴ ἐν add. Finckh.   ⁵ διότι (uel ὅτι) Bekker: διό.
⁶ Sic Sp.: ὧδέ πως· οὐκ alii.   ⁷ [οὖν] ? Hammer.

again, ' Let no one meet me with resentment for
proposing to offer you advice upon matters about
which certain other persons are reluctant to speak
freely to you.' This is how you must employ anticipa- 20
tion about matters that are likely to annoy the
audience, by producing reasons that will make them
think that you are acting rightly in offering your
advice—you must point to the lack of speakers or the
magnitude of the dangers, or to considerations of
public interest, or to some other plea of that sort
which will enable you to dissipate the ill-feeling that
you encounter. If the audience still go on inter- 25
rupting none the less, you must make some brief
remark in the form of a maxim or a consideration,
to the effect that it is extremely odd of them to
have come there for the purpose of taking the
best counsel about the matter, and yet to fancy that
they can take wise counsel if they refuse to listen to
the speakers ; and again, that the proper course is 30
either to stand up and offer counsel themselves, or to
listen to those who do so and then to express their
own opinion by a show of hands. This is how to
use anticipation and to meet interruptions in parliamentary speeches.

In addressing a court of law we shall anticipate our
opponents' case by methods similar to those already
stated ; and we shall meet interruptions, if they 35
occur at the beginning of our speeches, as follows :
' Now surely it is unreasonable that when the lawgiver enjoined that every litigant should be allowed
two speeches, and when you of the jury have sworn to
try the case according to the law, you yet refuse to
listen even to a single speech ; and that whereas he 40

1433 a τοσαύτην πρόνοιαν ἔχειν ὅπως ἀκούσαντες πάντων
τῶν λεγομένων εὐόρκως θῆσθε[1] τὴν ψῆφον, ὑμᾶς δὲ
περὶ τούτων οὕτως ὀλιγώρως ἔχειν ὥστε μηδὲ τὰς
ἀρχὰς ὑπομείναντας αὐτὰς τῶν λόγων ἤδη νομίζειν
ἀκριβῶς ἅπαντα γινώσκειν;" καὶ ἄλλως "πῶς
5 οὐκ ἄλογόν ἐστι τὸν μὲν νομοθέτην τάξαι τῶν
ψήφων ἴσων γινομένων τὸν φεύγοντα νικᾶν, ὑμᾶς
δὲ οὕτως ἐναντίως γινώσκειν περὶ τούτων ὡς μηδὲ
ἀπολογουμένων τῶν διαβεβλημένων ἀκούειν; κἀκεῖνον μὲν διὰ τὸ μᾶλλον κινδυνεύειν τοὺς φεύγοντας
ἀπονεῖμαι ταύτην τὴν πλεονεξίαν αὐτοῖς ἐν ταῖς
10 ψήφοις, ὑμᾶς δὲ τοῖς μὲν ἀκινδύνως κατηγοροῦσι
μὴ φιλονεικεῖν, τοὺς δὲ μετὰ φόβων καὶ κινδύνων
περὶ τῶν κατηγορουμένων ἀπολογουμένους[2] θορυβοῦντας ἐκπλήττειν;" ἐὰν μὲν οὖν ἐν ἀρχαῖς οἱ
θόρυβοι γίνωνται, τοῦτον τὸν τρόπον αὐτοῖς[3] ἀπαν-
τητέον· ἐὰν δὲ προεληλυθότος τοῦ λόγου θορυ-
15 βῶσιν, ἐὰν μὲν ὀλίγοι τινὲς τοῦτο ποιῶσιν, ἐπι-
τιμητέον τοῖς θορυβοῦσι καὶ πρὸς αὐτοὺς λεκτέον
ὅτι δίκαιον νῦν μὲν αὐτοὺς ἀκούειν ἐστίν, ἵνα μὴ
κωλύσωσι τοὺς ἄλλους ὀρθῶς δικάζειν, ἐπὰν δὲ
ἀκούσωσι, τότε ποιεῖν ὅ τι ἂν ἐθέλωσιν. ἐὰν δὲ
20 τὸ πλῆθος θορυβῇ, μὴ τοῖς κρίνουσιν ἀλλὰ σαυτῷ
ἐπίπληξον· τὸ μὲν γὰρ ἐκείνοις ἐπιτιμᾶν ὀργὴν
ἐργάζεται, τὸ δὲ σαυτῷ ἐπιπλῆξαι καὶ λέγειν[4]
ἡμαρτηκέναι συγγνώμης ποιήσει τυχεῖν. δεῖ δὲ
καὶ δεῖσθαι τῶν κρινόντων[5] εὐμενῶς σαυτοῦ[6]
ἀκοῦσαι [τοῦ λόγου],[7] καὶ μὴ[8] περὶ ὧν μέλλουσι
κρύβδην τὴν ψῆφον φέρειν, ἤδη τὴν διάνοιαν

---

[1] v.l. θήσεσθε.   [2] v.l. ἀπολογουμένους ὡς.
[3] αὐτοῖς v.l. om.   [4] v.l. λέγειν ἐν τῷ λέγειν.
[5] v.l. τῶν κρειττόνων.   [6] Sauppe: αὑτούς.

made such careful provision for you so as to secure 1433 a
that you should give your vote according to your oath
after hearing all the speeches, you treat these regulations with such contempt that you think you know
the whole of the facts perfectly already, without so
much as waiting for even the opening sentences of the
speeches.'[7] And on another line : ' Surely it is unreasonable that whereas the lawgiver made the rule 5
that if the votes prove equal the defendant should
win the case, you take so opposite a view on these
matters that you will not even hear the defence of
persons who have been misrepresented ; and that
whereas he assigned the defendants this advantage
in the votes because their risk is the greater, you 10
raise no quarrel with the accusers who are running
no risk, but terrify with your uproar those who
in fear and peril are offering their defence on the
charges brought.' This is the way to meet interruptions if they occur at the start. If the audience
clamour when your speech has made some progress,
supposing the interrupters are few in number, you 15
must rebuke them and tell them that justice requires
them to give you a hearing now, so as not to prevent
the rest of the jury from forming a correct judgement,
but that when they have heard you they can do what
they please. If the uproar comes from the mass of
the audience, do not reproach the court but reproach
yourself, because to rebuke them would make them 20
angry but to reproach yourself and say you have
committed an error will bring you forgiveness. You
must also beg the judges to give you a gracious
hearing, and not to make public in advance their
opinion on the issue upon which they are about to give

---

[7] Rac.: v.l. τοὺς λόγους.   [8] μὴ add. Victorius.

1433 a

25 φανερὰν τίθεσθαι. συλλήβδην δὲ τοῖς θορύβοις
ἀπαντήσομεν κεφαλαιωδῶς ἢ γνώμαις ἢ ἐνθυμήμασι, δεικνύντες τοὺς θορυβοῦντας ἢ τοῖς δικαίοις
ἢ τοῖς νόμοις ἢ τῷ συμφέροντι τῆς πόλεως ἢ τῷ
καλῷ ἐναντιουμένους· ἐκ γὰρ τῶν τοιούτων ἔστιν
ὅτι μάλιστα παῦσαι τοὺς ἀκούοντας θορυβοῦντας.

30 Ταῖς μὲν οὖν πρὸς τοὺς ἀκροατὰς προκαταλήψεσιν ὡς δεῖ χρῆσθαι, καὶ ὅπως τοῖς θορύβοις
ἀπαντητέον, ἐκ τῶν προειρημένων ἴσμεν· τὰ δὲ
ὑπὸ τῶν ἀνταγωνιστῶν ἐπίδοξα λέγεσθαι πάλιν
ὡς δεῖ προκαταλαμβάνειν, ἀποδείξω.[1] "ἴσως οὖν
ὀδυρεῖται τὴν[2] αὑτοῦ πενίαν, ἧς οὐκ ἐγὼ ἀλλ' ὁ
35 τούτου τρόπος ὑπαίτιός ἐστι[3]." καὶ πάλιν "πυν-
θάνομαι αὐτὸν τὸ καὶ τὸ μέλλειν λέγειν." ἐν μὲν
οὖν τοῖς προτέροις[4] λόγοις οὕτω δεῖ τὰ ἐπίδοξα
λέγεσθαι ὑπὸ τῶν ἐναντίων προκαταλαμβάνοντας[5]
διαλύειν καὶ ἀσθενῆ ποιεῖν· καὶ γὰρ κἂν πάνυ
ἰσχυρὰ ᾖ τὰ προδιαβεβλημένα,[6] οὐχ ὁμοίως φαί-
40 νεται μεγάλα τοῖς ἤδη προακηκοόσιν. ἐὰν δὲ τοὺς
1433 b ὑστέρους λόγους λέγωμεν[7] καὶ οἱ ἐναντίοι προ-
κατειληφότες ὦσιν ἃ μέλλομεν λέγειν, ἀντιπρο-
καταληπτέον ἐστὶν αὐτὰ λύοντας[8] τόνδε τὸν τρόπον·
"οὗτος δ' οὐ μόνον μου κατέψευσται πολλὰ πρὸς
5 ὑμᾶς, ἀλλὰ καὶ σαφῶς εἰδὼς[9] ὅτι ἐξελέγξω αὐτόν,
προκατέλαβέ μου τὸν λόγον καὶ προδιέβαλεν,[10] ἵν'
ὑμεῖς μὴ ὁμοίως αὐτῷ προσέχητε ἢ ἐγὼ μὴ εἴπω
πρὸς ὑμᾶς αὐτὸν[11] διὰ τὸ διασεσύρθαι πρότερον ὑπὸ
τούτου. ἐγὼ δ' οἶμαι δεῖν τοὺς ἐμοὺς λόγους παρ'
ἐμοῦ πυνθάνεσθαι ὑμᾶς ἀλλὰ μὴ παρὰ τούτου, εἰ[12]

---

[1] Sp.: ὑποδείξω.　　[2] τὴν add. Sp.　　[3] Sp.: ἔσται.
[4] v.l. πρότερον.　　[5] Sp.: προκαταλαμβάνοντα.
[6] διαβεβλημένα Sp.　　[7] Sp.: ἔχωμεν.

a secret ballot. And in general, we shall meet inter- 25
ruptions summarily with maxims or with considerations, pointing out that those who clamour are running
counter to justice or law or public interest or morality;
such are the best means of stopping the audience
from interrupting.

The preceding remarks inform us how to employ 30
anticipation in relation to the audience and how to
meet interruptions. Next I will demonstrate how
we should anticipate the points that are likely to
be made by our opponents. ' Now perhaps he will
lament his poverty, the blame for which rests not with
me but with his own character '; and again, ' I am 35
told that he is going to say so and so.' This is how
when speaking first we must anticipate the things
that are probably going to be said by our opponents,
in order to discredit them and weaken their force ;
arguments misrepresented in advance, even though
quite strong ones really, do not appear so important
to an audience that has heard them already. If we are 40
speaking after the other side and they have antici- 1433 b
pated what we are going to say, we must counter their
anticipations by rebutting them in this way : ' My
opponent has not only told you a number of things
against me that are false, but also, as he knew quite
well that I should refute him, he anticipated my
argument and misrepresented it in advance, in order 5
that you may not pay the same attention to it, or that
I may not use it in my speech to you because it has
been discredited in advance by him. But my view is
that you ought to learn my arguments from me and

⁸ Sp.: λύοντα.   ⁹ v.l. ἀφειδῶς: σάφ᾽ εἰδὼς Sauppe.
   ¹⁰ Sp.: διέβαλεν.   ¹¹ αὐτὸς ? Hammer.
¹² v.l. εἰ δέ: ⟨ὥστ᾽⟩ εἰ καὶ . . . διέσυρε, λέξω Sauppe.

355

1433 b

καὶ ταῦθ' οὗτος προδιέσυρε λέγων ἅ φημι οὐ μικρὰ
10 σημεῖα εἶναι τοῦ μηδὲν ὑγιὲς τοῦτον λέγειν."
κέχρηται δὲ καὶ Εὐριπίδης ἐν Φιλοκτήτῃ τεχνικῶς
τούτῳ τῷ εἴδει διὰ τοῦδε·

λέξω δ' ἐγώ, κἄν μου διαφθεῖραι[1] δοκῇ
λόγους ὑποστὰς[2] αὐτὸς ἠδικηκέναι·
ἀλλ' ἐξ ἐμοῦ γὰρ πράγματ' αὖτ' εἴσῃ[3] κλύων,
ὁ δ' αὐτὸς αὑτὸν ἐμφανιζέτω[4] λέγων.

15 Ταῖς μὲν οὖν προκαταλήψεσιν ὡς δεῖ χρῆσθαι καὶ
πρὸς τοὺς κριτὰς[5] καὶ πρὸς τοὺς ἐναντίους, ἴσμεν
διὰ τούτων.

XIX. Αἰτήματα δ' ἐστὶν ἐν τοῖς λόγοις ἃ παρὰ
τῶν ἀκουόντων οἱ λέγοντες αἰτοῦνται. τούτων δ'
ἐστὶ τὰ μὲν ἄδικα τὰ δὲ δίκαια. δίκαιον μὲν οὖν
20 ἐστὶ τὸ[6] προσέχειν τοῖς λεγομένοις αἰτεῖσθαι καὶ
μετ' εὐνοίας ἀκούειν· δίκαιον δὲ καὶ τὸ κατὰ τοὺς
νόμους αὐτῷ βοηθῆσαι, καὶ τὸ μηδὲν παρὰ τοὺς
νόμους ψηφίσασθαι, καὶ τὸ τοῖς ἀτυχήμασι συγγνώμην ἔχειν· ἐὰν δὲ[7] ᾖ παρὰ τοὺς νόμους, ἄδικον
[ἐὰν δὲ μή, δίκαιον][8]. τὰ μὲν οὖν αἰτήματα ταῦτά
25 ἐστι, διειλόμεθα δ' αὐτῶν τὰς διαφοράς, ἵν' εἰδότες
τό τε δίκαιον καὶ τὸ ἄδικον χρώμεθα κατὰ τὸν
καιρόν, καὶ μὴ λανθάνωσιν ἡμᾶς οἱ ἐναντίοι ἄδικόν
τι αἰτοῦντες τοὺς δικάζοντας. καὶ περὶ μὲν τούτων
ἐκ τῶν εἰρημένων οὐκ ἀγνοήσομεν.

XX. Παλιλλογία δ' ἐστὶ[9] σύντομος ἀνάμνησις, δεῖ
30 δ' αὐτῇ χρῆσθαι καὶ παρὰ[10] τῶν μερῶν καὶ παρὰ[10]

---

[1] Rac.: διαφθείρας.   [2] ὑφιστὰς Ribbeck.
[3] Wecklein: γὰρ τἀμὰ μαθήσῃ.
Pflugk: ἐμφανιεῖ σοι (ἐμφανίζει σοι Finckh).
[5] ἀκροατὰς Sp.   [6] v.l. τό τε.   [7] v.l. μὲν.
[8] Secl. Sp.   [9] v.l. ἐστὶ μὲν.   [10] Sp.: περὶ bis.

not from him, even if he did try to discredit them by
saying things that I declare to be no small indications
that all that he says is unsound.' Also Euripides in 10
Philoctetes has made skilful use of this species of argument by means of the following passage [a] :

> I will speak, even though he think to have foiled
> My words by taking on himself the guilt.
> No, you shall learn from me the very facts—
> Let his own words show him for what he is.

These considerations show us how to employ antici- 15
pations both in regard to the court and in regard to
our opponents.

XIX. Postulates [b] in speeches are demands made by *Postulation.*
the speakers on the audience. Some are justifiable,
others not. It is just to demand that they shall attend
to what is said and give a favourable hearing. It is also 20
just to demand that they shall give one redress in
accordance with the law, and not give any verdict
that is contrary to law, and have compassion on
misfortune ; but it is unjust to demand anything that
is against the law. These then are postulates ; and
we have distinguished their varieties in order that we 25
may know which are justifiable and which not, and
employ them appropriately, and in order that we may
detect our opponents when they make a demand of
the court that is unjust. From what has been said
we shall not be ignorant on these matters.

XX. Recapitulation is a brief reminder. It should *Recapitula-*
be employed both at the end of a division of a *tion.* 30

---

[a] Euripides fr. 794 (Dindorf).

[b] In Aristotelian logic αἴτημα means a premiss assumed
without proof, without the consent of the opponent (a premiss
assumed with his consent being ὑπόθεσις); but the word is not
used in that technical sense here.

1433 b

τῶν ὅλων λόγων τὰς τελευτάς. παλιλλογήσομεν δὲ
ἐν κεφαλαίοις ἢ διαλογιζόμενοι ἢ προαιρούμενοι ἢ
ἐπερωτῶντες[1] ἢ ἀπολογιζόμενοι.[2] δείξω δ' αὐτῶν
οἷον ἕκαστόν ἐστιν. τὸ μὲν οὖν διαλογίζεσθαι
35 τοιόνδε τι ἐστίν· " ἀπορῶ δ' ἔγωγε τί ἂν ἐποίησαν
οὗτοι, εἰ μὴ[3] φανεροὶ μὲν ἦσαν ἡμᾶς πρότερον
ἐγκαταλελοιπότες, ἐξηλέγχοντο δὲ ἐπὶ τὴν πόλιν
ἡμῶν στρατεύσαντες, οὐδὲν δὲ πώποτε ὧν ὡμο-
λογήκασι ποιήσαντες." τὸ μὲν οὖν διαλογίζεσθαι
τοιοῦτόν ἐστι, τὸ δὲ ἀπολογίζεσθαι τοιόνδε[4]·
40 " ἀπέδειξα δ' αὐτοὺς διαλύσαντας προτέρους τὴν
συμμαχίαν, καὶ πρῶτον ἐπιθεμένους ἡμῖν ὅτε πρὸς
1434 a Λακεδαιμονίους ἐπολεμοῦμεν, καὶ μάλιστα σπου-
δάσαντας ἐξανδραποδίσασθαι τὴν πόλιν ἡμῶν." τὸ
μὲν οὖν ἀπολογίζεσθαι τοιοῦτο[5] ἐστί, τὸ δ' ἐκ
προαιρέσεως ἀναμιμνήσκειν τοιόνδε· " ἐνθυμεῖσθαι
5 δὲ δεῖ ὅτι συμβέβηκεν ἡμῖν, ἐξ ὅτου τὴν φιλίαν
πρὸς τούτους ἐποιησάμεθα, μηδέποτε κακὸν ὑπὸ
τῶν πολεμίων παθεῖν· βοηθήσαντες γὰρ ἡμῖν πολλάκις ἐκώλυσαν Λακεδαιμονίους τὴν χώραν ἡμῶν
διαφθεῖραι, χρήματα δὲ πολλὰ καὶ νῦν φέροντες
διατελοῦσιν." ἐκ προαιρέσεως μὲν οὖν[6] οὕτως
10 ἀναμνήσομεν, ἐξ ἐπερωτήσεως δὲ τόνδε τὸν τρόπον·
" ἡδέως δ' ἂν αὐτῶν πυθοίμην διὰ τί τὰς συντάξεις
ἡμῖν οὐκ ἀποδιδόασιν. οὐ γὰρ ὡς ἀποροῦσιν εἰπεῖν
ἂν τολμήσαιεν, οἳ τοσαῦτα χρήματα καθ' ἕκαστον
ἐνιαυτὸν ἐκ τῆς χώρας ἐπιδεικνύονται λαμβάνειν,[7]
οὐδ' αὖ φήσουσιν εἰς τὴν τῆς πόλεως διοίκησιν

---

[1] Rac.: προσερωτῶντες.
[2] v.l. add. ἢ ἐκ προαιρέσεως.
[3] μὴ ⟨φίλοι ἀλλ' ἐχθροὶ ἡμῖν ἐγένοντο, οἳ⟩ Sp.
[4] Sp.: τοιοῦτον.   [5] Sp.: τοιόνδε.

speech and at the end of the whole. In summing up
we shall recapitulate either in the form of a calculation or of a proposal of policy or of a question or of an
enumeration. I will show what is the nature of each
of these. The following is an example of calculation : ' For my part I am at a loss to know what these 35
men would have done, if it were not manifest that
they left us in the lurch on a former occasion, and if
they were not proved to have marched against our
city and to have never yet fulfilled a single one of their
agreements.' Such is the nature of calculation. The
following is an example of enumeration : ' I have
shown that they were the first to break the treaty of 40
alliance, and attacked us first when we were at war 1434 a
with Sparta, and displayed the greatest eagerness to
reduce our city to absolute slavery.' That is the
nature of enumeration. Reminder made by proposing
a line of action is as follows : ' You must bear in mind
that ever since we made friends with these people it 5
has never befallen us to suffer injury from our enemies,
because they have frequently come to our assistance
and prevented the Spartans from ravaging our
country, and they continue even now to make large
contributions to our funds.' That is how we shall
make a reminder by proposing a line of action. We
shall remind by interrogation as follows : ' I should 10
be glad if they would inform me why they do not pay
us their assessments. They cannot venture to say
they are short of funds, when it is proved that they
draw such a large annual revenue from their land ; nor
yet will they say they are spending a large amount on
the administration of their city, since it is clear that

---

⁶ οὖν add. Sp.　　　　⁷ v.l. λαμβάνοντες.

1434 a

15 πολλὰ δαπανᾶν, παντελῶς γὰρ ἐλάχιστα τῶν νη-
σιωτῶν ἀναλίσκοντες φαίνονται." ἐκ μὲν οὖν
ἐπερωτήσεως οὕτω παλιλλογήσομεν.

XXI. Εἰρωνεία δ᾽ ἐστὶ λέγειν τι προσποιούμενον
μὴ λέγειν ἢ¹ τοῖς ἐναντίοις ὀνόμασι τὰ πράγματα
προσαγορεύειν. εἴη δ᾽ ἂν αὐτῆς τὸ σχῆμα τοιοῦτον
20 ἐν τῷ περὶ τῶν εἰρημένων συντόμως ἀναμιμνή-
σκειν· " οὐδὲν δ᾽ οἶμαι δεῖν λέγειν ὅτι οὗτοι μὲν οἱ
φάσκοντες πολλὰ ἀγαθὰ πεποιηκέναι πλεῖστον φαίνονται τὴν πόλιν κεκακουργηκότες, ἡμεῖς δ᾽ οὓς
οὗτοί φασιν ἀχαρίστους εἶναι, τούτοις τε πολλάκις
βοηθήσαντες καὶ τοὺς ἄλλους οὐδὲν ἀδικοῦντες."
25 τὸ μὲν οὖν ἐν προσποιήσει παραλείψεως λέγοντα
συντόμως ἀναμιμνήσκειν τοιοῦτόν ἐστι, τὸ δὲ τοῖς
ἐναντίοις ὀνόμασι προσαγορεύειν τὰ πράγματα
πάλιν τοιόνδε²· " οὗτοι μὲν οἱ χρηστοὶ πολλὰ φαίνονται τοὺς συμμάχους κακὰ πεποιηκότες, ἡμεῖς
δ᾽ οἱ φαῦλοι πολλῶν³ ἀγαθῶν αὐτοῖς⁴ αἴτιοι κατα-
στάντες."

30 Διὰ τούτων μὲν οὖν συντόμως ἀναμιμνήσκοντες
ταῖς παλιλλογίαις χρησόμεθα καὶ παρὰ⁵ τῶν μερῶν
καὶ παρὰ⁵ τῶν ὅλων λόγων τὰς τελευτάς.

XXII. Ὅθεν δ᾽ ἔστιν ἀστεῖα λέγειν καὶ τὰ⁶ μήκη
τῶν λόγων ποιεῖν ὅπως ἄν τις θέλῃ, τοῦτο διέξιμεν
πάλιν.

35 Ἀστεῖα μὲν οὖν λέγειν ἐκ τούτου τοῦ τρόπου⁷
ἔστιν, οἷον τὰ ἐνθυμήματα λέγοντας ἡμίση,⁸ ὥστε
τὸ ἥμισυ αὐτοὺς ὑπολαμβάνειν τοὺς ἀκούοντας. δεῖ
δὲ καὶ γνώμας συμπαραλαμβάνειν. χρὴ δὲ τούτων

---

¹ ἢ Finckh: ἢ ἐν.
² τοιόνδε cj. Hammer: τοιοῦτον aut τοιοῦτόν ἐστι.
³ πολλῶν om. v.l. ⁴ αὐτοῖς om. v.l.

1434 a

they have absolutely the smallest expenditure of all 15
the islanders.' That is how we shall recapitulate by
means of interrogation.

XXI. Irony is saying something while pretending *Irony.*
not to say it, or calling things by the opposite of their
real names. It may take the form of briefly recalling 20
things said before, as follows : ' I do not think that
anything need be said to show that these men who
profess to have done the state many services are
seen to have done it a very great deal of harm, while
we, whom they charge with ingratitude, are seen to
have often given them assistance and to do no wrong
to other people.' Such is a brief reminder conveyed
under a pretence of passing the matter over. The 25
following illustrates the device of calling things by
the opposite names : ' It appears that whereas these
honourable gentlemen have done our allies a great
deal of harm we base creatures have caused them
many benefits.'

These are the means by which we shall employ 30
recapitulation in the form of a brief reminder, both at
the end of the divisions of a speech and at the conclusion of the whole.

XXII. We will next explain how to obtain an
agreeable style, and how to regulate the length of
one's speeches as one may wish.

An agreeable style may be achieved by the follow- 35
ing method,—by stating half of a consideration so that *Elegancies of style.*
the audience may understand the other half them-
selves. Also one must bring in maxims—one should

---

⁵ παρὰ bis Sp.: περί. v.l. om. τῶν μερῶν...l. 33 μήκη :
? om. καὶ περὶ τῶν μερῶν...τελευτάς (cf. 1433 b 30) Rac.
(v.l. καὶ περὶ τῶν λόγων καὶ τῶν μερῶν τελευτάς).

⁶ τὰ v.l. om.   ⁷ v.l. τόπου.

⁸ ὅλα ἢ ἡμίση (aut ἡμίσυ) codd.: om. ὅλα ἢ Sp.

1434 a

κατὰ πάντα τὰ μέρη συγκαταλέγειν,[1] διαλλάττοντα
τοὺς λόγους καὶ μηδέποτε ὅμοια εἰς τὸ αὐτὸ πολλὰ
τιθέντα. καὶ οὕτως ὁ λόγος ἀστεῖος φανεῖται.

1434 b Μηκύνειν δὲ τοὺς λόγους βουλόμενον δεῖ μερίζειν
τὸ πρᾶγμα καὶ ἐν ἑκάστῳ μέρει τὰ ἐνόντα οἷά τέ
ἐστιν τὴν φύσιν διδάσκειν καὶ τὴν χρῆσιν καὶ ἰδίᾳ
καὶ κοινῇ, καὶ τὰς προφάσεις αὐτῶν ἐκδιηγεῖσθαι.
ἂν δὲ καὶ ἔτι μακρότερον θελήσωμεν τὸν λόγον
5 ποιεῖν, δεῖ πολλοῖς ὀνόμασι περὶ ἑκάστου χρῆσθαι.
χρὴ δὲ παρὰ μέρος ἕκαστον τοῦ λόγου παλιλλογεῖν,
καὶ τὴν παλιλλογίαν σύντομον ποιεῖσθαι. ἐν δὲ τῇ
τελευτῇ τοῦ λόγου ταῦτα περὶ ὧν καθ᾽ ἓν ἕκαστον
εἴρηκας ἀθρόα συντιθέναι, καὶ περὶ ὅλων τῶν
10 πραγμάτων λέγειν. τοῦτον μὲν οὖν τὸν τρόπον
μῆκος ἕξουσιν οἱ λόγοι.

Βραχυλογεῖν δὲ βουλόμενος[2] ὅλον τὸ πρᾶγμα ἑνὶ
ὀνόματι περιλαμβάνειν, καὶ τούτῳ ὃ ἂν ὑπάρχῃ
βραχύτατον τῷ πράγματι· χρὴ δὲ καὶ συνδέσμους
ὀλίγους ποιεῖν, τὰ πλεῖστα δὲ ζευγνύναι. ὀνομάζειν
15 μὲν οὕτω, τῇ δὲ λέξει εἰς δύο χρῆσθαι·[3] καὶ παλιλλογίαν τὴν σύντομον ἐκ τῶν μερῶν ἀφαιρεῖν, ἐν δὲ
ταῖς τελευταῖς μόνον παλιλλογεῖν. καὶ τοῦτον μὲν
τὸν τρόπον βραχεῖς τοὺς λόγους ποιήσομεν.

Ἐὰν δὲ βούλῃ μέσως λέγειν, τὰ μέγιστα τῶν
μερῶν ἐκλέγων περὶ τούτων ποιεῖσθαι τοὺς λόγους.
20 χρὴ δὲ καὶ τοῖς ὀνόμασι τοῖς μέσοις χρῆσθαι, καὶ
μήτε τοῖς μακροτάτοις μήτε τοῖς βραχυτάτοις μήτε

---

[1] συχνὰ ἐκλέγειν Kayser.
[2] Usener (cf. infra 18 et 1425 b 29): βουλόμενον.
[3] ⟨μὴ⟩ χρῆσθαι Kayser.

1434 a

introduce a selection of these in all the divisions of a
speech, varying the words and never putting several
similar phrases in the same passage. In this way the 40
speech will have an agreeable effect.

If you want to lengthen a speech, you must divide 1434 b
the subject up, and in each division explain the nature *Length.*
of the points that it contains and their particular and
general application, and state fully the justifications
for them. If we wish to make the speech still longer, 5
we must employ a number of words about each topic.
At each division of the speech we should recapitulate,
and we should make the recapitulation concisely.
At the end of the speech you should gather together
the topics with which you have dealt separately, and
discuss the matter as a whole. This is the way in 10
which speeches will be given length.

If you wish to speak briefly, include the whole of an
idea in a single word, and that the shortest that is
appropriate to the idea ; and you must also use few
connecting particles, and couple up most of the words
into one clause.[a] That is how you must use words.
Also make a vocable serve two purposes[b] ; and do 15
away with the concise recapitulation from the divisions, and only recapitulate at the end. In this way
we shall make our speeches brief.

If you wish to speak at moderate length, pick out
the most important of the divisions of your subject
and make your speech about these. Also you must
employ words of medium length, neither the longest 20
nor the shortest, nor yet several words, albeit of

---

[a] Cf. *Rhet.* 1407 b 38 where the instance given is πορευθεὶς
διελέχθην (instead of ἐπορεύθην καὶ διελέχθην).

[b] Cf. *ibid.* 36 τῆς ἡμετέρας γυναικός (more concise than
τῆς γυναικὸς τῆς ἡμετέρας).

πολλοῖς περί γε ἑνὸς ἀλλὰ μετρίοις. χρὴ δὲ καὶ
τοὺς ἐπιλόγους ἐκ τῶν ἀνὰ μέσον μερῶν μήτε
παντελῶς ἐξαιρεῖν μήτε πᾶσι τοῖς μέρεσιν ἐπιφέρειν, ἀλλ᾽ ἅπερ ἂν μάλιστα βούλη κατανοῆσαι
25 τοὺς ἀκούοντας, ἐπὶ τούτων μάλιστα παλιλλογεῖν
ἐπὶ τῇ τελευτῇ.¹

Τὰ μὲν οὖν μήκη τῶν λόγων ἐκ τούτων ποιήσομεν, ἡνίκ᾽ ἂν θέλωμεν.

Ἂν δὲ ἀστεῖον γράφειν θέλῃς λόγον, παραφύλαττε
ὡς μάλιστα ὅπως τὰ ἤθη τῶν λόγων ὁμοιοῦν τοῖς
ἀνθρώποις δυνήσῃ. τοῦτο δὲ ποιήσεις, ἂν ἐπιθεωρῇς
30 τὰ μεγάλα τῶν ἠθῶν καὶ τὰ ἀκριβῆ καὶ τὰ μέτρια.

Περὶ μὲν οὖν τούτων ἐντεῦθεν οὐκ ἀγνοήσεις,
περὶ δὲ ὀνομάτων συνθέσεως² δηλώσωμεν· καὶ γὰρ
τοῦτο τῶν ἀναγκαίων ἐστίν.

XXIII. Πρῶτον μὲν οὖν τρόποι ὀνομάτων εἰσὶ
τρεῖς, ἁπλοῦς ἢ σύνθετος ἢ μεταφέρων. ὡσαύτως
35 καὶ συνθέσεις τρεῖς, μία μὲν εἰς φωνήεντα τελευτᾶν τὰς συμβολὰς³ καὶ ἀπὸ φωνήεντος ἄρχεσθαι,
δευτέρα δὲ ἀπὸ ἀφώνου ἀρχόμενον⁴ εἰς ἄφωνον
τελευτᾶν, τρίτη δὲ τὰ ἄφωνα πρὸς τὰ φωνήεντα
συνδεῖν. τάξεις δὲ τέσσαρες, μία μὲν τὰ ὅμοια τῶν
ὀνομάτων ἢ παράλληλα τιθέναι ἢ διασπείρειν, ἄλλη
40 δὲ ἢ⁵ τοῖς αὐτοῖς ὀνόμασι χρῆσθαι ἢ μεταβάλλειν εἰς
1435 a ἕτερα, τρίτη δὲ ἢ⁵ ἑνὶ ἢ πολλοῖς ὀνόμασι τὸ πρᾶγμα
προσαγορεύειν, τετάρτη δὲ ἢ⁵ ἑξῆς τὰ πραγματευ-
θέντα⁶ ὀνομάζειν ἢ ὑπερβιβάζειν.

---

¹ [ἐπὶ τῇ τελευτῇ] Kayser.
² περὶ δὲ ἑρμηνείας Usener.
³ Rac.: ταῖς συμβολαῖς (v.l. συλλαβαῖς).
⁴ Usener: ἀρξάμενον. ⁵ ἢ tris add. Rac.
⁶ v.ll. πράγματα θέντα, πραχθέντα.

1434 b

moderate length, to express one thing. You must not altogether omit the conclusions from all the intermediate divisions, nor yet append conclusions to all the divisions, but at the final conclusions devote your recapitulation particularly to the points to which you 25 most desire your audience to direct their attention.

These rules will guide us in regulating the length of our speeches, when we may desire to do so.

If you wish to write a pleasing speech, be careful as far as possible to adapt the character of your speech to that of your public. You will achieve this if you observe their character—noble, petty 30 or average.

These considerations will inform you on these matters. We will now explain the putting together of words, for that is also an essential topic.

XXIII. In the first place there are three kinds *Diction.* of words,—simple, compound and metaphorical. So also are there three ways of putting words together— one for the juxtaposed words to end with a vowel 35 and begin with a vowel, the second to end with a consonant when an initial consonant is to follow, the third to connect consonants with vowels. And there are four questions as to arrangement[a]—one, whether to put similar words side by side or to keep them separate ; another, whether to use the same words or to change to different ones ; third, whether to designate a thing by one word or by many ; 40 fourth, whether to mention the things treated of in 1435 a order or to transpose them.

---

[a] τάξις hardly describes the second and third of the questions that follow.

1435 a

Ὅπως δὲ καλλίστην ποιήσεις τὴν ἑρμηνείαν ιῦν δηλώσομεν.

XXIV. Πρῶτον μὲν οὖν ὅπως¹ εἰς δύο ἑρμηνεύειν, 5 εἶτα ὅπως¹ σαφῶς δεῖ λέγειν.

Σχήματα δ' ἐστὶ τοῦ εἰς δύο λέγειν τάδε, ἓν μὲν ὅτι αὐτὸς δύναται καὶ τοῦτο καὶ ἕτερον, δεύτερον δὲ ὅτι οὗτος² μὲν οὐ δύναται ἕτερος δὲ δύναται, τρίτον δὲ ὅτι οὗτος² καὶ τοῦτο καὶ ἕτερον δύναται, τέταρτον δὲ ὅτι οὔτ' αὐτὸς οὔθ' ἕτερος δύναται, 10 πέμπτον δὲ ὅτι αὐτὸς μὲν οὐ³ δύναται ἕτερος δὲ δύναται, ἕκτον δὲ ὅτι αὐτὸς μὲν ἕτερον δύναται, ἐκεῖνος δὲ οὐ δύναται ἕτερον. ἕκαστον δὲ τούτων ἐπὶ τῶνδε θεωρήσεις. ὅτι μὲν γὰρ αὐτὸς δύναται καὶ τοῦτο καὶ ἕτερον, τοιόνδε ἐστίν· "ἐγὼ δὲ οὐ μόνον τούτων αἴτιος ὑμῖν ἐγενόμην,⁴ ἀλλὰ 15 καὶ Τιμόθεον μέλλοντα στρατεύειν ἐφ' ὑμᾶς διεκώλυσα." ὅτι δὲ οὗτος⁵ μὲν οὐ δύναται ἕτερος δὲ δύναται, τοιόνδε· "αὐτὸς μὲν⁶ ἀδυνάτως ἔχει πρεσβεύειν ὑπὲρ ἡμῶν, οὗτος δὲ φίλος ἐστὶ τῇ πόλει τῶν Σπαρτιατῶν, καὶ μάλιστ' ἂν δυνηθείη πρᾶξαι ἃ βούλεσθε." τὸ δὲ ὅτι οὗτος⁷ καὶ τοῦτο καὶ ἕτερον δύναται, τοιόνδε· "οὐ μόνον δὲ ἐν τοῖς 20 πολέμοις εὔρωστον αὐτὸν παρέσχεν, ἀλλὰ καὶ βουλεύσασθαι τῶν πολιτῶν οὐχ ἥκιστα δύναται." τὸ δὲ ὅτι οὔτ' αὐτὸς οὔθ' ἕτερος δύναται, τοιόνδε· "οὔτ' ἂν αὐτὸς δυνηθείη⁸ ὀλίγην δύναμιν ἔχων καταπολεμῆσαι τοὺς ἐναντίους, οὔτ' ἄλλος οὐδεὶς τῶν πολιτῶν." τὸ δὲ ὅτι ἐκεῖνος μὲν δύναται 25 αὐτὸς δὲ οὐ δύναται, τοιόνδε· "οὗτος μὲν γὰρ

---

¹ ὅπως bis add. Usener.   ² αὐτὸς bis ? Rac.
³ οὐ hic Ross: post ἕτερος δὲ.   ⁴ v.l. κατέστην.
⁵ αὐτὸς ? Rac.   ⁶ v.l. μὲν οὖν.

1435 a

We will now show how you will make your state-ment most attractive.

XXIV. First then as to how to frame a statement with a twofold division, next how to express the meaning clearly.

The forms of a twofold statement are these : (1) to *Method of statement.* say that one can oneself do the thing in question and also something else, (2) that this man cannot do a thing but somebody else can, (3) that this man can do the thing in question and also something else, (4) that neither can one do a thing oneself nor can anyone else, (5) that one cannot do a thing oneself but someone else can, (6) that one can do one thing oneself but the other person cannot do something else. You will see each of these forms illustrated in the following examples : (1) An example of the statement that one can oneself do the thing and also something else is ‘ For my part I not only brought about these results for you, but also prevented Timotheus when he was going to lead his army against you.’ (2) An example of the statement that this man cannot do a thing but another man can is ‘ He himself is incapable of going on a mission on our behalf, but this man is a friend of the Spartan government and would be very able to do what you want.’ (3) That this man can do the thing in question and also something else is instanced by ‘ He not only showed himself a sturdy man in the wars, but is also not the least competent of our citi-zens to advise on policy.’ (4) That neither can one do a thing oneself nor can anyone else is instanced by ‘ I could not myself defeat our adversaries with a small force, nor yet could any other of our citizens.’ (5) That someone else can do it but one cannot oneself

---

⁷ αὐτὸς ? Rac.   ⁸ Sp.: δυνηθείη.

1435 a

ἔρρωται τῷ σώματι, ἐγὼ δ᾽ ἀρρωστῶν τυγχάνω."
τὸ δὲ ὅτι αὐτὸς μὲν ἕτερον δύναται, ἐκεῖνος δὲ οὐ
δύναται ἕτερον, τοιόνδε· " ἐγὼ μὲν γὰρ κυβερνῆσαι
δυνατός εἰμι, οὗτος δὲ οὐδὲ κωπηλατῆσαι δύναται."

Σχήματα μὲν οὖν τοῦ εἰς δύο ἑρμηνεύειν ὧδε
30 ποιήσεις ἐπὶ τῶν πραγμάτων ἁπάντων τὸν αὐτὸν[1]
τρόπον μετιών.

Σαφῶς δὲ ὅθεν δηλώσεις, τοῦτο πάλιν σκεπτέον.

XXV. Πρῶτον μὲν οὖν ὀνόμαζε τοῖς οἰκείοις
ὀνόμασιν ὅ τι ἂν λέγῃς, διαφεύγων τὸ ἀμφίβολον.
εὐλαβοῦ δὲ περὶ τὰ φωνήεντα τῶν γραμμάτων ὅπως
35 μὴ ἐξῆς τεθήσεται.[2] πρόσεχε δὲ καὶ τοῖς καλου-
μένοις ἄρθροις ὅπως ἐν τῷ δέοντι προστιθῆται.
σκόπει δὲ καὶ τὴν σύνθεσιν τῶν ὀνομάτων ὅπως
μήτε συγκεχυμένη μήθ᾽ ὑπερβατὴ ἔσται· τὰ γὰρ
οὕτω λεγόμενα δύσγνωστα συμβαίνει. μετὰ δὲ
συνδέσμους οὓς ἂν προείπῃς, ἀποδίδου τοὺς
40 ἀκολουθοῦντας. τὸ μὲν οὖν[3] συνδέσμους ἀποδιδόναι τοὺς ἀκολουθοῦντας τοιόνδε ἐστίν· " ἐγὼ
1435 b μὲν παρεγενόμην οὗ ἔφην, σὺ δὲ φάσκων ἥξειν
οὐκ ἦλθες." πάλιν ὅταν ὁ αὐτὸς σύνδεσμος
ἀκόλουθος[4] ᾖ, οἷον " σὺ γὰρ κἀκείνων αἴτιος
ἐγένου καὶ τούτων αἴτιος εἶ.[5]" περὶ μὲν οὖν τῶν
5 συνδέσμων εἴρηται, καὶ ἀπὸ τούτων τεκμαίρεσθαι
δεῖ καὶ περὶ τῶν ἄλλων.

Δεῖ δὲ καὶ τὴν σύνθεσιν τῶν ὀνομάτων μήτε
συγκεχυμένην μήτε ὑπερβατὴν εἶναι.[6] τὸ μὲν γὰρ
συγκεχυμένως τοιόνδε ἐστίν, ὡς ὅταν εἴπῃς

---

[1] τοῦτον τὸν Sp. [2] Funckhaenel: τεθήσονται.
[3] v.l. οὖν τοὺς. [4] v.l. αὐτὸς συνακόλουθος.
[5] v.l. σύ. [6] v.l. ποιεῖν.

by ' Yes, he is of strong physique, but I as a matter of
fact am not.' (6) That one can do the thing oneself
but the other man cannot do another thing by ' Yes,
I am a competent helmsman, but he cannot even
row.'

This is how you will construct the forms of a twofold
statement, pursuing the same method in all subjects. 30

Next we must consider how you will make your
meaning clear.

XXV. First, call everything you speak of by its *Clarity.*
proper name, avoiding ambiguity. Beware of putting
vowels in juxtaposition.[a] Be careful to add the
' articles ' where necessary. Study the construction 35
of the sentence, so as to avoid both confusion and
transposition of words, since these cause them to be
difficult to catch. After employing introductory connecting particles put in following particles. An
example of putting in a following particle to correspond 40
is : ' I on the one hand turned up where I said I 1435 b
would, but you *on the other hand*, though you declared
that you were going to be there, did not come.'
Again, when the same particle follows, as : ' For you
both were the cause of that *and* are the cause of this.'
That is an account of connecting particles ; from the
instances mentioned you must infer about the others 5
also.

The construction of words in the sentence must
be neither confused nor transposed. An example of
confused construction is : ' It is monstrous for this

---

[a] Perhaps the reference is to elisions that cause ambiguity,
e.g. Theognis 112 μνῆμα δὲ χοῦσι or μνῆμα δ' ἔχουσι (Rhys
Roberts quoted by Forster). *Cf.* Aristophanes, *Frogs* 1443
ὅταν τὰ νῦν ἄπιστα πίσθ' ἡγώμεθα, τὰ δ' ὄντα πίστ' ἄπιστα.

" δεινόν ἐστι τοῦτον τοῦτον τύπτειν "· ἄδηλον γὰρ[1]
ὁπότερος[2] ἦν ὁ τύπτων· ἐὰν δὲ εἴπῃς οὕτως,
10 δῆλον ποιήσεις· " δεινόν ἐστι τοῦτον ὑπὸ τούτου
τύπτεσθαι." τὸ μὲν οὖν συγχεῖν τὴν σύνθεσιν τῶν
ὀνομάτων τοιοῦτον[3] ἐστίν.

Τὸ δὲ προσέχειν τοῖς ἄρθροις, ὅπως ἐν τῷ δέοντι
προστιθῆται, ἐπὶ τῶνδε ὅρα· " οὗτος ὁ ἄνθρωπος
τοῦτον τὸν ἄνθρωπον ἀδικεῖ." νῦν μὲν οὖν ἐγγινό-
μενα τὰ ἄρθρα σαφῆ ποιεῖ τὴν λέξιν, ἐξαιρεθέντα
15 δὲ ἀσαφῆ ποιήσει. ἔσθ' ὅτε δὲ συμβαίνει καὶ τὸ
ἀνάπαλιν. τὰ μὲν οὖν ἐν τοῖς ἄρθροις τοιαῦτά
ἐστιν.

Τὰ δὲ φωνήεντα μὴ τίθει παράλληλα, ἂν μή
ποτε ἄλλως ἀδύνατον ᾖ δηλῶσαι, ἢ ἀνάπνευσις[4]
ᾖ τις ἢ ἄλλη διαίρεσις.

Τὸ δὲ τὰ ἀμφίβολα διαφεύγειν τοιόνδε ἐστίν·
20 ἔνια τῶν ὀνομάτων ταὐτὰ ἐπὶ πλείοσι πράγμασι
κεῖται, οἷον ὁδὸς τῶν θυρῶν καὶ ὁδὸς ἣν βαδίζουσιν·
δεῖ δὲ ἐπὶ τοῖς τοιούτοις τὸ ἴδιον ἀεὶ συμπαραλαμβάνειν.

Καὶ σαφῶς μὲν ἐν[5] τοῖς ὀνόμασιν, ἂν ταῦτα
ποιῶμεν, διαλεξόμεθα· εἰς δύο δ' ἑρμηνεύσομεν διὰ
τῆς προτέρας μεθόδου.

25 XXVI. Περὶ δὲ ἀντιθέτων καὶ παρισώσεων καὶ
ὁμοιοτήτων λέγωμεν ἤδη· δεησόμεθα γὰρ καὶ
τούτων.

Ἀντίθετον μὲν οὖν ἐστι τὸ ἐναντίαν τὴν ὀνο-

---

[1] Sp.: γὰρ ἦν. [2] v.l. ὁπότερος ἄν.
[3] Sp.: τοιόνδε. [4] Forster: ἀνάπτυξις.
[5] [ἐν] Finckh.

---

a The ambiguity caused by the Greek employment of an
accusative as subject of an infinitive cannot be reproduced in
370

man to strike this man ' [a]—as it is not clear which of
the two was the striker ; though you will make it
clear if you express it thus : ' It is monstrous for this
man to be struck by this man.' That is an example
of confused construction of words.

The following examples illustrate attention to the
insertion of the articles in the necessary places.
' The man there wrongs the man there ': in this
case the presence of the articles makes the meaning
clear ; to remove them will obscure it.[b] But in
some cases the result is the contrary. This is how
things stand in respect of the articles.

Do not juxtapose vowels, except in cases where it
is impossible to express the meaning otherwise, or
when a pause for breath or some other interval occurs.

The following is the method of avoiding ambiguities.
In some cases the same word denotes several things,
e.g. doorway and pathway.[c] In such cases you must
always add something denoting the proper sense.

If we keep these rules, our style will be clear in
its use of words. Sentences that fall into two divisions we shall construct by employing the method
described before.

XXVI. Let us now speak about antitheses, pari-
soses[d] and similarities,[e] as we shall also require these.

A sentence is antithetical when either terminology *Antithesis.*

English. *Cf.* Ennius, *Annals* vi. 5, quoted by Cicero, *De
Divinatione* ii. 116, Aio te, Aeacida, Romanos uincere posse
(Rhys Roberts, *Cl. Rev.* xxvi. 177).
    [b] The point of this is not clear.
    [c] The confusion caused in Greek by ignoring the presence
or absence of the aspirate might be paralleled in English by
' way ' and ' whey,' ' witch ' and ' which.'
    [d] *i.e.* parallelism of structure.
    [e] *i.e.* parallelism of sound : the more technical term is
παρομοίωσις c. xxviii. *init.*

1435 b

μασίαν ἅμα καὶ τὴν δύναμιν τοῖς ἀντικειμένοις
ἔχον, ἢ τὸ ἕτερον τούτων. τοῖς μὲν οὖν ὀνόμασιν
εἴη ἂν ἐναντίον ἅμα καὶ τῇ δυνάμει τόδε· " οὐ
30 γὰρ δίκαιον τοῦτον μὲν τὰ ἐμὰ ἔχοντα πλουτεῖν,
ἐμὲ δὲ τὰ ὄντα προέμενον¹ οὕτω πτωχεύειν." τοῖς
δ' ὀνόμασι μόνοις· " διδότω γὰρ ὁ πλούσιος καὶ
εὐδαίμων τῷ πένητι καὶ ἐνδεῖ." τῇ δὲ δυνάμει·
" ἐγὼ μὲν τοῦτον νοσοῦντα ἐθεράπευσα, οὗτος δ'
ἐμοὶ μεγίστων κακῶν αἴτιος γέγονεν "· ἐνταῦθα
35 μὲν γὰρ τὰ ὀνόματα οὐκ ἐναντία, αἱ δὲ πράξεις
ἐναντίαι. κάλλιστον μὲν οὖν εἴη ἂν τὸ κατ'
ἀμφότερα ἀντίθετον, καὶ κατὰ τὴν δύναμιν καὶ
κατὰ τὴν ὀνομασίαν· ἔστι δὲ καὶ τὰ λοιπὰ δύο
ἀντίθετα.

XXVII. Παρίσωσις δ' ἐστὶ μὲν ὅταν δύο ἴσα
40 λέγηται κῶλα, εἴη δ' ἂν ἴσα καὶ πολλὰ μικρὰ ὀλίγοις
1436 a μεγάλοις καὶ ἴσα τὸ μέγεθος καὶ ἴσα² τὸν ἀριθμόν.
ἔχει δὲ τοιόνδε τὸ σχῆμα ἡ παρίσωσις· " ἢ διὰ
χρημάτων ἀπορίαν ἢ διὰ πολέμου μέγεθος "·
ταῦτα γὰρ οὔτε ὅμοια οὔτε ἐναντία, ἀλλ' ἴσα
μόνον ἀλλήλοις.

5 XXVIII. Παρομοίωσις δ' ἐστὶν³ μείζων τῆς
παρισώσεως· οὐ γὰρ μόνον ἴσα τὰ κῶλα ποιεῖ,
ἀλλὰ καὶ ὅμοια ἐξ ὁμοίων ὀνομάτων, οἷον⁴ " εἰ⁵
δεῖ σοι⁶ λόγου μίμημα, φέρε πόθου⁷ τέχνημα."
μάλιστα δὲ ποιεῖν⁸ ὅμοια τὰ τελευταῖα τῶν ὀνομά-
των· ταῦτα γὰρ μάλιστα ποιεῖ τὴν παρομοίωσιν.⁹
10 ὅμοια δ' ἐστὶν ὀνόματα τὰ ἐξ ὁμοίων συλλαβῶν,

---

¹ v.l. προϊέμενον.
² καὶ ἴσα (uel καὶ) Rac.: ἴσα aut ἴσοις.
³ ἐστὶν Sp.: ἐστὶν ἡ.   ⁴ οἷον Sp.: ὅσον.
⁵ εἰ add. Rac.   ⁶ Rac.: σε (del. Usener).

1435 b

or meaning, or both at once, are opposite in the opposed clauses. The following would be an instance of opposition in terms and meaning at once : ' It is not fair for my opponent to have my money and be a 30 rich man while I from parting with[a] my substance am a mere beggar.' Opposition in terms only : ' Let the rich and prosperous give to the poor and needy.' In meaning : ' I nursed him when he was ill, but he has caused me a very great deal of harm '—here the terms are not opposed but the actions are. Antithesis 35 in both respects, in meaning and in terminology, would be most effective, but the two remaining forms are also antithetical.

XXVII. Parisosis occurs when a sentence has two *Parallelism of structure.* equal members. Equality may exist between many 40 small things and a few large things, and between an equal number of things of equal size. Parisosis has **1436 a** the following form : ' Either owing to lack of funds or owing to the magnitude of the war '—these clauses are neither like one another nor opposite, but only equal.

XXVIII. Paromoeosis[b] goes further than parisosis, 5 as it not only makes the members equal in length but *Parallelism of sound.* assimilates them by constructing them of similar words, for example : ' If you want an imitation of wording, produce a simulation of wishing.' Assimilate specially the terminations of words—this is the best way of producing paromoeosis. Similar words 10 are those formed of similar syllables, having most of

---

[a] προιεσθαι is colloquial for ' lending.' *N.E.* 1164 a 23, 35, b 26. Demosthenes xxxvii. 36.

[b] See note on ' Similarities,' c. xxvi. *init.*

---

[7] πόνον Usener.   [8] ποίει Buhl, δεῖ ποιεῖν ? Sp.
          [9] Rac.: ὁμοίωσιν.

1436 a

ἐν αἷς πλεῖστα γράμματα τὰ αὐτά ἐστιν, οἷον
" πλήθει μὲν ἐνδεῶς, δυνάμει δὲ ἐντελῶς." ὅσα
δὲ ἔξω τέχνης κεῖται, τὸ αὐτόματον αὐτὸ δείξει.

Περὶ μὲν οὖν τούτων ἀπόχρη. καὶ γὰρ τὸ
15 δίκαιον καὶ τὸ νόμιμον[1] καὶ τὸ καλὸν καὶ τὸ συμφέρον καὶ τὰ λοιπὰ αὐτά τε ἴσμεν οἷα[2] ἐστι καὶ
ὅθεν αὐτὰ πολλὰ ποιήσομεν. ὡσαύτως δὲ καὶ
τὰς αὐξήσεις καὶ τὰς ταπεινώσεις γινώσκομεν,
αἵ τινές τ᾽ εἰσὶ καὶ ὅθεν αὐτῶν εἰς τοὺς λόγους
εὐπορήσομεν. ὁμοιοτρόπως δὲ τούτοις τάς τε
20 προκαταλήψεις καὶ τὰ παρὰ τῶν ἀκουόντων
αἰτήματα καὶ τὰς παλιλλογίας καὶ τὰς ἀστειο-
λογίας καὶ τὰ μήκη τῶν λόγων καὶ τῆς ἑρμηνείας
τὴν σύνθεσιν ἅπασαν ἴσμεν, ὥστε τὰς κοινὰς
δυνάμεις ἁπάντων τῶν εἰδῶν καὶ[3] τὰς χρήσεις
αὐτῶν ἐκ τῶν προειρημένων εἰδότες, ἂν ἐθίσωμεν
25 ἡμᾶς αὐτοὺς καὶ γυμνάσωμεν ἀναλαμβάνειν αὐτὰς
κατὰ τὰ προγυμνάσματα,[4] πολλὴν εὐπορίαν καὶ
γράφοντες καὶ λέγοντες ἐξ αὐτῶν ἕξομεν.

Κατὰ μέρη μὲν οὖν οὕτως ἀκριβέστατα ἂν διέλοις
τὰς τῶν λόγων μεθόδους· ὡς δ᾽ ἐπὶ τοῖς εἴδεσι
χρὴ τάττειν τοὺς λόγους σωματοειδῶς, τίσι τε
30 πρώτοις τῶν μερῶν χρῆσθαι, καὶ πῶς τούτοις
αὐτοῖς, ταῦτα πάλιν δηλώσω.

Προοίμια[5] μὲν οὖν προτάττω· κοινὸν γὰρ[6] ἐστὶ
τῶν ἑπτὰ εἰδῶν, καὶ ἐπὶ πᾶσι τοῖς πράγμασιν
ἁρμόσει λεγόμενον.

XXIX. Ἔστι δὲ προοίμιον καθόλου μὲν εἰπεῖν

---

[1] καὶ τὸ νόμιμον add. Sp.
[2] οἷα Sp.: ἃ (ἅτινά τ᾽ ? Rac.).
[3] v.l. εἰδῶν καὶ τὰς διαφορὰς καί.
[4] προστάγματα Usener.   [5] προοίμιον Sp.   [6] Sp.: δέ.

their letters the same : for example, ' In number defectively but in capacity effectively.'—Automatic suggestion will supply details that lie outside the scope of science.

This is enough about these subjects. For we know the nature of justice, legality, honour, expediency and the rest of these topics, and the sources from which we shall produce them in abundance. And similarly we understand the meaning of amplifications and minimizations, and how to procure a good supply of them for our speeches. In like manner we know anticipations, postulates demanded of the audience, recapitulations and pleasantries, and the question of the length of speeches and the whole subject of composing a statement ; and consequently, the qualities common to all the species and the modes of employing them being known to us from what has been said previously, if we habituate and train ourselves to repeat them on the lines of our preparatory exercises, they will supply us with plenty of matter both in writing and in speaking.

You will, then, distinguish most accurately the methods of speaking by thus taking the parts separately. I will next explain the proper mode of arranging speeches organically in the various species of oratory—which of the parts should be dealt with first and how these parts are themselves to be dealt with.

I deal, therefore, first with introductions, as this is a matter common to the seven species, and the discussion of it will apply to all subjects.

XXIX. In general terms, the introduction is a pre-

1436 a

35 ἀκροατῶν παρασκευῇ καὶ τοῦ πράγματος ἐν κεφαλαίῳ μὴ εἰδόσι δήλωσις, ἵνα γινώσκωσι περὶ ὧν ὁ λόγος παρακολουθῶσί τε τῇ ὑποθέσει, καὶ ἐπὶ τὸ προσέχειν παρακαλέσαι, καὶ καθ' ὅσοι τῷ λόγῳ δυνατόν, εὔνους ἡμᾶς αὐτοὺς ποιῆσαι. τούτων μὲν οὖν εἶναι δεῖ τὸ προοίμιον παρασκευαστικόν.

40 Ὡς δὲ αὐτῷ χρησόμεθα, πρῶτον μὲν ἐπὶ τῶν δημηγοριῶν[1] καὶ προτρεπτικῶν καὶ ἀποτρεπτικῶν,[2] τοῦτο δείξω.

1436 b

Τὸ μὲν οὖν προεκτιθέναι τὸ πρᾶγμα τοῖς ἀκούουσι καὶ φανερὸν ποιεῖν τοιόνδε ἐστίν· '' ἀνέστην συμβουλεύσων ὡς χρὴ πολεμεῖν ἡμᾶς ὑπὲρ Συρακουσίων ''· '' ἀνέστην ἀποφανούμενος ὡς οὐ χρὴ βοηθεῖν ἡμᾶς Συρακουσίοις.'' τὸ μὲν οὖν φράζειν ἐν κεφαλαίῳ τὸ πρᾶγμα τοιοῦτον[3] ἐστίν.

5 Προσέχειν δὲ παρακαλεῖν ἐκ τούτων ἂν εἰδείημεν, εἰ κατανοήσαιμεν αὐτοὶ ποίοις μάλιστα καὶ λόγοις καὶ πράγμασι βουλευόμενοι προσέχομεν. ἆρ' οὖν οὐ τούτοις, ὅταν ἢ ὑπὲρ μεγάλων ἢ φοβερῶν ἢ τῶν ἡμῖν οἰκείων βουλευώμεθα, ἢ φάσκωσιν[4] οἱ 10 λέγοντες ὡς δίκαια καὶ καλὰ καὶ συμφέροντα καὶ ῥᾴδια καὶ ἀληθινὰ ἐπιδείξουσιν ἡμῖν ἐφ' ἃ πράττειν παρακαλοῦσιν, ἢ[5] δεηθῶσιν ἡμῶν ἀκοῦσαι αὐτῶν προσέχοντας τὸν νοῦν; ὥσπερ οὖν αὐτοὶ τοῖς ἄλλοις, οὕτω καὶ ἡμεῖς τὰ οἰκειότατα τῶν προειρημένων τοῖς ὑφ' ἡμῶν πράγμασι λεγομένοις 15 λαμβάνοντες καὶ τοῖς ἀκούουσιν ἐνδεικνύμενοι

---

[1] Sp.: δημηγορικῶν.
[2] καὶ ἀποτρεπτικῶν add. Sp.
[3] Hammer: τοιόνδε.
[4] Bekker: φάσκωσιν ἐπιδείξειν.   [5] ἢ: καὶ Kayser.

1436 a

Structure of Parliamentary oration :

35

(1) *Introduction.*

paration of the hearers and a summary explanation of the business to persons who are not acquainted with it, in order to inform them what the speech is about and to enable them to follow the line of argument, and to exhort them to attend, and to make them well-disposed towards us—so far as this can be done by means of a speech. These are the preparatory measures that the introduction must be designed to effect.

I will first explain our mode of employing the introduction in the case of parliamentary oratory and speeches of exhortation and dissuasion.

The following are examples of a preliminary exposition and explanation of one's case to the audience : ' I rise to recommend that we ought to go to war on behalf of Syracuse ' ; ' I rise to prove that we ought not to assist Syracuse.' These are examples of a summary statement of one's case.

We may learn how to appeal for attention by noticing what are the kinds of arguments and facts to which we ourselves pay most attention when in council. Is it not when we are deliberating about matters that are important or alarming or that closely concern ourselves, or when the speakers declare that they will prove that the course of action that they are exhorting us to adopt is just and honourable and expedient and easy and honest, or when they entreat us to give them an attentive hearing ? Therefore we shall make them attend to us in the same way as we ourselves are made attentive to others—by taking those of the points enumerated which are most applicable to the case that we are putting forward and

προσέχειν αὐτοὺς[1] ποιήσομεν. ἐπὶ μὲν οὖν τὸ προσέχειν διὰ τούτων παρακαλοῦμεν.

Τὴν εὔνοιαν δὲ παρασκευασόμεθα διασκεψάμενοι πρῶτον πῶς πρὸς ἡμᾶς αὐτοὶ τυγχάνουσιν ἔχοντες, εὐνοϊκῶς ἢ δυσμενῶς ἢ μήτε εὖ μήτε κακῶς. ἐὰν
20 μὲν οὖν εὖνοι τυγχάνωσιν ὄντες, περίεργον λέγειν περὶ εὐνοίας· ἐὰν δὲ πάντως βουλώμεθα, χρὴ συντόμως μετ' εἰρωνείας εἰπεῖν τοῦτον τὸν τρόπον· " ὅτι μὲν οὖν εὔνους εἰμὶ τῇ πόλει, καὶ πολλάκις μοι πεισθέντες συμφερόντως ἐπράξατε, καὶ διότι πρὸς τὰ κοινὰ δίκαιον ἐμαυτὸν παρέχω καὶ μᾶλλόν
25 τι τῶν ἰδίων προϊέμενον ἢ ἀπὸ τῶν δημοσίων ὠφελούμενον, περίεργον εἶναι νομίζω πρὸς ὑμᾶς τοῦτό γε σαφῶς εἰδότας λέγειν· ὡς δὲ ἦν[2] καὶ νῦν μοι πεισθῆτε καλῶς βουλεύσεσθε, τοῦτο πειράσομαι διδάσκειν." τοῦτον μὲν οὖν τὸν τρόπον τοῖς εὖ διακειμένοις ἐν ταῖς δημηγορίαις τῆς εὐμενείας ὑπομνηστέον.
30 Τοῖς δὲ μήτε διαβεβλημένοις μήτε εὖ διακειμένοις ῥητέον ὡς δίκαιόν ἐστι καὶ συμφέρον τοῖς μὴ πεῖραν δεδωκόσι τῶν πολιτῶν εὔνους ἀκροατὰς γενέσθαι· ἔπειτα τοὺς ἀκούοντας ἐπαίνῳ θεραπευτέον, δικαίως καὶ νουνεχῶς τοὺς λόγους ὡς εἰώθασι δοκιμάζειν· ἔτι δὲ τὰς ἐλαττώσεις οἰστέον,
35 λέγοντας[3] ὡς[4] " οὐ δεινότητι πιστεύων ἀνέστην, ἀλλὰ νομίζων τῷ κοινῷ τὸ συμφέρον εἰσηγήσεσθαι." καὶ τοῖς μὲν μήτε εὖ μήτε κακῶς διακειμένοις ἐκ τῶν τοιούτων τὴν εὔνοιαν ποριστέον.

Τοὺς δὲ διαβεβλημένους ἀναγκαῖον τὰς διαβολὰς

---

[1] Finckh: αὐτοῖς.　　　　　　　　　[2] Rac.: εἰ.
[3] λέγοντα Halm.　　　　[4] ὡς v.l. om.: οὕτως ? Rac.

1436 b
15

laying them before our hearers. These are the means
that we shall employ in appealing for attention.

We shall secure their goodwill by first considering
how they happen to be disposed towards us of themselves—whether they are friendly or hostile or merely
neutral. If they are friendly, to talk about goodwill
is superfluous, but if all the same we wish to do so, 20
we must speak briefly, in a tone of irony, thus : ' I
think it is superfluous for me to tell you that I am
a loyal citizen, that you have often been led by my
advice to take an advantageous line of action, and
that I show myself true to my public duties and more
ready to sacrifice part of my private interests than to
profit at the public expense—you know this perfectly 25
well ; but I shall try to prove to you that you will be
well advised if you take my advice on the present
occasion also.' This is the way in which in parliamentary speeches a friendly audience should be
reminded of its goodwill.

To an audience neither hostile nor friendly we must 30
say that it is proper and expedient to give a favourable
hearing to fellow-citizens who have not yet given
proof of themselves ; then we must flatter our
audience by complimenting them on their habit of
estimating the speeches in a fair and sensible manner;
furthermore we must employ self-depreciation, saying
' I have risen not owing to confidence in my own 35
ability, but in the belief that the proposal which I am
about to introduce is advantageous for the community.' Such are the methods by which we must
secure the goodwill of our audience when it is neither
well nor ill disposed towards us.

If there is prejudice against the speaker, it
must attach either to himself personally, or to

1436 b

ἢ αὐτοὺς ἔχειν ἢ τὰ πράγματα ὑπὲρ ὧν λέγουσιν
ἢ τὸν λόγον.

40   Αὐτῶν[1] δ' αἱ διαβολαὶ γίνονται ἢ ἐκ τοῦ παρόντος
1437 a ἢ ἐκ τοῦ παροιχομένου χρόνου.

Ἐκ μὲν οὖν τοῦ παροιχομένου χρόνου ἐάν τις ὑποπτεύηται εἰς πονηρίαν τινά, πρῶτον μὲν δεῖ[2] πρὸς
τοὺς ἀκροατὰς προκαταλήψει χρῆσθαι, καὶ λέγειν
ὡς[3] " οὐδ' αὐτὸς ἀγνοῶ διαβεβλημένος, ἀλλ' ἐπιδείξω
5 ψευδεῖς οὔσας τὰς διαβολάς." ἔπειτα κεφαλαιωδῶς ἐν τοῖς προοιμίοις ἀπολογητέον, ἂν ἔχῃς τι
λέγειν ὑπὲρ σαυτοῦ, καὶ[4] τὰς κρίσεις ψεκτέον·
ἀναγκαῖον γάρ, ἄν τε πρὸς τὸ δημόσιον ᾖ τις
διαβεβλημένος ἄν τε πρὸς τοὺς ἰδιώτας, ἢ γεγενη-
σθαι κρίσιν ἢ μέλλειν γενήσεσθαι ἢ μὴ βούλεσθαι
10 τοὺς τὴν αἰτίαν ἐπενεγκόντας λαβεῖν κρίσιν· καὶ[5]
ῥητέον ὡς ἀδίκως ἡ κρίσις ἐγένετο καὶ ὡς ὑπὸ τῶν
ἐχθρῶν κατεστασιάσθημεν· ἢ ἐὰν τοῦτο μὴ ἐνδέχηται, λέγε ὡς ἱκανὸν ἡμῖν ἀτυχήσασι τότε, καὶ ὡς
δίκαιόν ἐστι τῶν πραγμάτων ἤδη κεκριμένων μὴ
περὶ τῶν αὐτῶν ἔτι διαβολὴν ἔχειν. ἂν δ' ἐπίδοξος
5 ἡ κρίσις ᾖ γενέσθαι, λεκτέον ὡς ἕτοιμος εἶ περὶ
τῶν διαβολῶν ἐν τοῖς καθημένοις ἤδη κρίνεσθαι, κἂν
ἐλεγχθῇς τι τὴν πόλιν ἀδικῶν, ἀποθνήσκειν ὑποτιμᾷ.[6] ἐὰν δὲ οἱ ἐγκαλέσαντες μὴ ἐπεξίωσιν, αὐτὸ
τοῦτο χρὴ σημεῖον ποιεῖσθαι διότι τὴν διαβολὴν
20 ψευδῶς ἡμῶν κατήνεγκαν· οὐ γὰρ εἰκὸς εἶναι δόξει
τοὺς ἀληθῶς ἐγκαλοῦντας μὴ βούλεσθαι κρίσιν

---

[1] Sp.: αὗται.   [2] Halm: τῇ.   [3] οὗτως? Sp.
[4] καὶ: v.l. ἢ.   [5] καὶ ⟨εἰ ἐγένετο⟩ Kayser.
[6] Finckh: ὑποτιμᾷ aut ὑποτιμῶ.

the subject on which he is speaking, or the actual speech.

Prejudice against speakers themselves arises either 40 out of the present situation or out of something in the past.

If someone is under suspicion of some misconduct in the past, he must first employ anticipation to the audience, and say ' Even I myself am not unaware that there is a prejudice against me, but I will prove that the charges against me are false.' Then 5 in your introduction you must summarily state any argument you have to offer in your defence, and you must raise objections against the forms of trial, since, whether one has been depreciated publicly or in private company, it is bound to be the case either that a trial has been held, or is going to be held, or that those who have brought the charge do not want 10 to have a trial held; and we must say that the trial was conducted unjustly, and that our enemies got the better of us by methods of faction ; or if this is not possible, say that our misfortune on that occasion has been a sufficient punishment, and that when the matter has been already tried it is only fair that one should not lie under discredit any longer about the same affair. If the trial is expected to 15 be held, you must say that you are ready to be tried at once before the court in session on the charges made against you, and that, if you are proved guilty of any offence against the state, you assess your penalty at death. If the authors of the charge do not want to prosecute, we must use this fact itself as a proof that the accusation they have brought against us is false, 20 as it will be thought unlikely that persons making a true charge should not wish to obtain a trial. You

1437 a

λαβεῖν. ἀεὶ δὲ κατηγορεῖν χρὴ διαβολῆς, καὶ λέγειν
ὡς δεινὸν καὶ κοινὸν[1] καὶ πολλῶν κακῶν αἴτιον·
ἐμφανιστέον δ᾽ ὅτι καὶ πολλοὶ ἤδη διεφθάρησαν
ἀδίκως διαβληθέντες· χρὴ δὲ καὶ διδάσκειν ὡς
25 εὔηθές ἐστιν ὑπὲρ τῶν κοινῶν βουλευομένους μὴ
παρὰ πάντων τοὺς λόγους ἀκούοντας τὸ συμφέρον
σκοπεῖν, ἀλλὰ ταῖς ἐνίων διαβολαῖς δυσχεραίνειν.
δεῖ δὲ καὶ ἐπαγγέλλεσθαι[2] δίκαια καὶ συμφέροντα[3]
ἐπιδείξειν ἃ ὑπέσχου[4] συμβουλεύειν. τοὺς μὲν οὖν
30 ἐκ τοῦ παροιχομένου χρόνου διαβεβλημένους τοῦτον
τὸν τρόπον ἐν ταῖς δημηγορίαις τὰς διαβολὰς
λυτέον.

Ἐκ δὲ τοῦ παρόντος χρόνου διαβάλλει τοὺς
λέγοντας πρῶτον μὲν ἡλικία· ἐάν τε γὰρ νέος
παντελῶς ἐάν τε πρεσβύτης δημηγορῇ, δυσχεραί-
νεται, τῷ μὲν γὰρ οὔπω ἦρχθαι τῷ δὲ ἤδη πεπαῦ-
35 σθαι προσήκειν οἴονται. ἔπειτα ἐὰν συνεχῶς εἰώθῃ
λέγειν· πολυπράγμων γὰρ εἶναι δοκεῖ οὗτος. καὶ
ἐὰν μηδέποτε πρότερον εἰρήκῃ· καὶ γὰρ οὗτος ἕνεκά
τινος ἰδίου δοκεῖ παρὰ τὸ ἔθος δημηγορεῖν. ἐκ μὲν
οὖν τοῦ παρόντος χρόνου οὕτω τοι διαβολαὶ περὶ
τὸν δημηγοροῦντα γενήσονται· προφασίζεσθαι δὲ
40 ὑπὲρ αὐτῶν δεῖ τὸν μὲν νεώτερον ἐκ τῆς ἐρημίας
1437 b τῶν συμβουλευόντων, καὶ ἐκ τοῦ προσήκοντος
τούτῳ, λέγω δ᾽ οἷον ὑπὲρ λαμπαδαρχίας ἢ ὑπὲρ
γυμνασίου ἢ ὑπὲρ ὅπλων ἢ ἵππων ἢ πολέμου[5]·
τούτων γὰρ οὐκ ἐλάχιστον μέρος τῷ νέῳ μέτεστιν.

---

[1] κενὸν Kayser.
[2] v.l. ἐπαγγέλλεσθαι καὶ ὑπισχνεῖσθαι.
[3] v.ll. συμφέροντα καλά, συμφέροντα καὶ καλά, καλὰ καὶ
συμφέροντα.   [4] v.l. ὑπέσχοντο.
[5] v.l. περὶ πολέμου.

1437 a

must always accuse them of misrepresentation, and
say that it is a monstrous thing, and a matter of
general concern, and a cause of many evils : you
must declare that many men before now have been
ruined by unjust misrepresentation, and you must
also point out that it is foolish when deliberating 25
about a matter of public concern not to consider the
proper course in the light of what all the parties have
to say but to allow ill-feeling to be aroused by the
misrepresentations of some of them.   Also you must
declare that you will prove that the advice you have
undertaken to give is just and expedient.   This is
the method of refuting misrepresentations that should
be employed in parliamentary speeches by persons 30
lying under prejudice arising out of the past.

Arising out of the present, the first thing that discredits speakers is their age : if a man who is quite
young or quite old addresses the house, he causes
resentment, because people think that the former
ought not yet to have begun speaking and the latter
ought to have left off.   Next, a man encounters 35
prejudice who makes a constant practice of speaking,
as he is thought to be a busybody.   Also if he has
never spoken before, as in that case he is supposed to
have some special private reason for speaking contrary
to his custom.   These, then, may be said to be the
ways in which prejudices in regard to a speaker will
arise out of the present.   The defence against them
in the case of a comparatively young man must be 40
based on the plea of lack of advisers, and on his special 1437 b
interest in the matter—I mean for instance in a
case about the superintendence of a torch-race or
about a gymnasium, or about armour or horses, or in
regard to war, as those are for the most part a young

ῥητέον δὲ καὶ ὡς εἰ μήπω καθ᾽ ἡλικίαν τὸ φρονεῖν,
5 ἀλλὰ κατὰ φύσιν καὶ ἐπιμέλειαν. ἐμφανιστέον δὲ
καὶ ὡς ἁμαρτόντι μὲν ἴδιον τὸ ἀτύχημα, κατορθώ-
σαντι δὲ κοινὴ ἡ ὠφέλεια. τῷ μὲν οὖν νέῳ ἐκ τῶν
τοιούτων προφασιστέον, τῷ γέροντι δὲ προφασι-
στέον¹ ἔκ τε τῆς ἐρημίας τῶν συμβουλευόντων καὶ
ἐκ τῆς ἐμπειρίας αὐτοῦ, πρὸς δὲ τούτοις καὶ ἐκ τοῦ
10 μεγέθους καὶ ἐκ τῆς καινότητος τῶν κινδύνων καὶ
ἐκ τῶν ἄλλων τῶν τοιούτων. τῷ δὲ λίαν εἰθισμένῳ
ἐκ τῆς ἐμπειρίας² καὶ ἐκ τοῦ αἰσχρὸν εἶναι πρότερον
ἀεὶ³ λέγοντα νῦν μὴ ἀποφαίνεσθαι γνώμας. τῷ δὲ
μὴ εἰθισμένῳ ἔκ τε τοῦ μεγέθους τῶν κινδύνων καὶ
15 ἐκ τοῦ ἀναγκαῖον εἶναι πάντα τινὰ ᾧ τῆς πόλεως
μέτεστιν ὑπὲρ τῶν νῦν προκειμένων ἀποφαίνεσθαι
γνώμην.

Τὰς μὲν οὖν περὶ αὐτὸν τὸν ἄνθρωπον διαβολὰς
ἐν ταῖς δημηγορίαις ἐκ τῶν τοιούτων ἐπιχειρήσομεν λύειν.

Αἱ δὲ περὶ τὸ πρᾶγμα γίνονται μέν, ὅταν τις
ἡσυχίαν πρὸς τοὺς μηδὲν ἀδικοῦντας ἢ πρὸς τοὺς
20 κρείττονας συμβουλεύῃ λύειν,⁴ ἢ εἰρήνην ποιεῖσθαι αἰσχράν, ἢ παραινῇ περὶ τὰς θυσίας μικρὰ
συντελεῖν, ἤ τι τοιοῦτον εἰσηγῆται. δεῖ δὲ περὶ
τῶν τοιούτων πρότερον μὲν πρὸς τοὺς ἀκροατὰς
προκαταλήψει χρῆσθαι, ἔπειτα τὴν αἰτίαν εἰς τὴν
ἀνάγκην καὶ τὴν τύχην καὶ τοὺς καιροὺς καὶ τὸ
25 συμφέρον ἀναφέρειν, καὶ λέγειν ὡς οὐχ οἱ συμ-
βουλεύοντες τῶν τοιούτων ἀλλὰ τὰ πράγματά ἐστιν

---

¹ προφασιστέον v.l. om.: alii λέγοντι pro γέροντι δὲ
προφασιστέον.
² Kayser: εὐπορίας. ³ Sp.: δεῖ aut δὴ.
⁴ Roberts: συμβουλεύειν aut συμβουλεύῃ.

man's concern. Also he must say that, if he has
not yet the wisdom given by years, still he is wise
by nature and by training. He must also point out 5
that when a man fails the misfortune is his own, but
when he succeeds the benefit is shared by others.
Such are the considerations on which a young man
must base his defence. An old man must excuse
himself on the ground of lack of advisers, and also
because of his experience, and in addition to these
points on the ground of the magnitude and the un- 10
precedented nature of the dangers, and by means
of other similar pleas. One who is in the habit of
speaking too frequently must plead his experience,
and say that it would be discreditable not to declare
his opinion now when he has previously been a constant speaker. One not in the habit of speaking
must plead the magnitude of the dangers and the
absolute necessity for every member of the com- 15
munity to pronounce an opinion on the matter now
before the house.

Such are the arguments by which in parliamentary
speeches we shall attempt to dispel prejudices relating to oneself personally.

Prejudices in relation to the subject arise when one
advises taking action against unoffending persons
or against those who are in a stronger position, or 20
making a discreditable peace, or when in connexion
with festivals one recommends making a small
contribution, or introduces some proposal of that
nature. In addressing an audience on such subjects
one should begin by using anticipation, and then put
the blame on necessity, fortune, circumstances, considerations of expediency, and say that the responsi- 25
bility in such matters rests not with the advisers

1437 b

αἴτια. καὶ τὰς μὲν περὶ τὸ πρᾶγμα διαβολὰς ἐκ
τῶν τοιούτων ἀπὸ τῶν συμβουλευόντων ἀπάξομεν.

Ὁ δὲ λόγος ἐν ταῖς δημηγορίαις διαβάλλεται
ὅταν ἢ μακρὸς ἢ ἀρχαῖος ἢ ἄπιστος λέγηται. ἐὰν
30 μὲν οὖν μακρὸς ᾖ, τὸ πλῆθος αἰτιατέον τῶν πραγ-
μάτων· ἐὰν δὲ ἀρχαῖος, διδακτέον ὅτι νῦν καιρὸς
ἂν¹ αὐτοῦ² εἴη· εἰ δὲ ἀπίθανος, ὑπισχνεῖσθαι δεῖ ὡς
ἀληθῆ ἐπιδείξεις ἐπὶ τοῦ λόγου.

Τὰς μὲν οὖν δημηγορίας ἐκ τούτων καταστησό-
μεθα, τάξομεν δὲ πῶς³; ἐὰν μὲν μηδεμίαν δια-
35 βολὴν ἔχωμεν μήτε αὐτοὶ μήτε ὁ λόγος μήτε τὸ
πρᾶγμα, τὴν πρόθεσιν ἐν ἀρχῇ εὐθέως ἐκθήσομεν,
ἐπὶ δὲ τὸ προσέχειν καὶ τοῦ λόγου εὐμενῶς ἀκούειν
ὕστερον παρακαλέσομεν· ἐὰν δὲ διαβολή τις ᾖ τῶν
προειρημένων περὶ ἡμᾶς, προκαταλαβόντες τοὺς
ἀκροατάς, καὶ περὶ τῶν διαβολῶν τὰς ἀπολογίας
40 καὶ τὰς προφάσεις συντόμως ἐνεγκόντες, οὕτω
1438 a προθήσομεν καὶ τοὺς ἀκροατὰς ἐπὶ τὸ προσέχειν
παρακαλέσομεν.

Τοῦτον μὲν οὖν τὸν τρόπον τὰς καταστάσεις τῶν
δημηγοριῶν ποιητέον.

XXX. Μετὰ δὲ τοῦτο ἀνάγκη ἡμᾶς ἐστὶν ἢ τὰς
προγεγενημένας πράξεις ἀπαγγέλλειν ἢ ἀναμιμνή-
5 σκειν, ἢ τὰς νῦν οὔσας μερίζοντας⁴ δηλοῦν, ἢ τὰς
μελλούσας γενήσεσθαι προλέγειν. ὅταν μὲν οὖν
πρεσβείαν ἀπαγγέλλωμεν, πάντα δεῖ τὰ ῥηθέντα
καθαρῶς διεξελθεῖν, ἵνα πρῶτον μὲν μέγεθος ὁ
λόγος ἔχῃ (ἀπαγγελία γὰρ μόνον ἔσται ἡ τοιαύτη,
καὶ οὐδὲν ἄλλο λόγου σχῆμα παρεμπεσεῖται), ἔπειθ'

---

¹ ἂν add. Rac. (post αὐτοῦ Funckhaenel).
² v.l. αὐτῶ: αὐτῷ ? Rac.   ³ οὕτως Sp.
⁴ v.l. μερίζοντα: del. Sp.

1437 b

but with the facts of the case. This is the class of
arguments by which we shall divert from the advisers
of a policy prejudices relating to the subject.

The actual speech delivered in addressing parliament arouses prejudice when it is lengthy or old-
fashioned or unconvincing. If it is lengthy, you must 30
lay the blame on the multiplicity of the facts ; if old-
fashioned, you must explain that it may be appropriate in the circumstances ; if unconvincing, you must
promise that you will prove the truth of your statements in the course of your speech.

These being the materials out of which we shall
construct our parliamentary speeches, how shall we
arrange them ? If no prejudice attaches either to
ourselves or to our speech or to our subject, we shall 35
set out our proposal straight away at the beginning, making our appeal for attention and a favourable hearing afterwards. If there be any prejudice
arising from something already said about us, we
must anticipate the reaction of the audience, and
briefly produce our defences and excuses about the 40
prejudices thus caused before we put forward our 1438 a
proposal and appeal to the audience for attention.

This is the manner in which public speeches should
be constructed.

XXX. After this we must either report or remind (2) *Exposi-*
our hearers of events that have occurred before, or *tion of the*
arrange in groups and exhibit the facts of the present, 5 *case :*
or forecast what is going to occur. So when we are
reporting an embassy, we should give a clear account
of everything that was said, in order that in the first
place our speech may have due bulk (for a speech of
this sort will be merely narrative, and no other form
of oratory will be introduced), and secondly in order

387

1438 a

10 ὅπως, ἂν μὲν ἀποτετυχηκότες ὦμεν, μὴ διὰ τὴν
ἡμετέραν ῥᾳθυμίαν οἱ ἀκούοντες οἴωνται δια-
μαρτεῖν[1] τῆς πράξεως ἀλλὰ δι' ἄλλην τινὰ αἰτίαν,
ἂν δὲ ἐπιτύχωμεν, μὴ διὰ τύχην ὑπολάβωσι τοῦτο
γεγενῆσθαι ἀλλὰ διὰ τὴν ἡμετέραν προθυμίαν.
ταῦτα δὲ πιστεύσουσιν,[2] ἐπειδὴ τοῖς πράγμασιν οὐ

15 παρεγένοντο πραττομένοις, ἐὰν ἐπὶ τοῦ λόγου τὴν
προθυμίαν ἡμῶν θεωρῶσι μηδὲν παραλειπόντων
ἀλλ' ἀκριβῶς ἕκαστα ἀπαγγελλόντων. ὅταν μὲν
οὖν πρεσβείαν ἀπαγγέλλωμεν, διὰ τὰς αἰτίας ταύτας
ἕκαστα ὃν τρόπον ἐγένετο ἀπαγγελτέον. ὅταν δὲ

20 αὐτοὶ δημηγοροῦντες τῶν παρεληλυθότων τι δι-
εξίωμεν ἢ[3] τὰ παρόντα δηλῶμεν ἢ τὰ μέλλοντα
προλέγωμεν, δεῖ τούτων ἕκαστον ποιεῖν σαφῶς καὶ
βραχέως[4] καὶ μὴ ἀπίστως, σαφῶς μὲν ὅπως κατα-
μάθωσι τὰ λεγόμενα πράγματα, συντόμως δὲ ἵνα
μνημονεύσωσι τὰ ῥηθέντα, πιστῶς δὲ ὅπως μὴ πρὸ

25 τοῦ ταῖς πίστεσι καὶ ταῖς δικαιολογίαις βεβαιῶσαι
τὸν λόγον ἡμᾶς τὰς ἐξηγήσεις ἡμῶν οἱ ἀκούοντες
ἀποδοκιμάσωσιν. σαφῶς μὲν οὖν δηλώσομεν ἀπὸ
τῶν ὀνομάτων ἢ ἀπὸ τῶν πραγμάτων. ἀπὸ μὲν
οὖν τῶν πραγμάτων, ἐὰν μὴ ὑπερβατῶς αὐτὰ
δηλῶμεν, ἀλλὰ τὰ πρῶτα πραχθέντα ἢ πραττόμενα

30 ἢ πραχθησόμενα πρῶτα λέγωμεν, τὰ δὲ λοιπὰ
ἐφεξῆς τάττωμεν, καὶ ἐὰν μὴ προαπολιπόντες τὴν
πρᾶξιν[5] περὶ ἧς ἂν ἐγχειρήσωμεν λέγειν δι' ἑτέρων[6]
ἐξαγγείλωμεν. ἀπὸ μὲν οὖν τῶν πραγμάτων
σαφῶς οὕτως ἐροῦμεν, ἀπὸ δὲ τῶν ὀνομάτων, ἐὰν
ὅτι μάλιστα τοῖς οἰκείοις τῶν πραγμάτων ὀνόμασι

35 τὰς πράξεις προσαγορεύωμεν, καὶ ἐὰν τοῖς κοινοῖς,

---

[1] Rac.: διαμαρτάνειν. [2] Sp.: πιστεύουσιν.
[3] Sp.: ἢ καὶ aut καὶ. [4] Sp.: βραχέως καὶ σαφῶς.

that, if our mission was a failure, the audience may not 10
think the affair miscarried owing to negligence on our
part but from some other cause, and if we succeeded,
they may suppose this to have happened not by
accident but owing to our zeal. As they were 15
not present when the affair was actually in progress,
they will believe this if they see our keenness at
the time of our speech, in leaving nothing out but
narrating everything in detail. For these reasons,
therefore, when we are reporting an embassy we
should give a detailed account of everything that
happened. In making a speech of our own, when we
are narrating something that happened in the past, 20
or describing the present situation, or forecasting the *(a) style;*
future, we must do each of these things clearly,
briefly and convincingly : we must be clear in order
that the audience may grasp the facts we are stating,
concise in order that they may remember what we
say, convincing in order that our hearers may not 25
reject our narrative before we have supported our
statement with proofs and justifications. Clearness
of exposition will be obtained from the language or
from the facts. From the facts if we do not set them
out in a transposed order, but state first the things
that were done or are being done or are going to be 30
done first, and arrange the remaining ones in sequence,
and if we do not leave the matter about which we
have undertaken to speak and make a story out of
something else. This is how our speech will gain
clearness from the facts. We shall obtain it from the
language if we designate the facts as far as possible
by the words appropriate to the things, and by those 35
in common use, and if we do not arrange them in a

---

⁵ v.l. τάξιν. ⁶ v.ll. πάλιν ἑτέρων, πρᾶξιν ἑτέρων.

καὶ μὴ ὑπερβατῶς αὐτὰ τιθῶμεν ἀλλ' ἀεὶ τὰ ἐχό-
μενα ἑξῆς τάττωμεν. σαφῶς μὲν οὖν δηλώσομεν
ταῦτα διαφυλάττοντες, συντόμως δέ, ἐὰν ἀπὸ τῶν
πραγμάτων καὶ τῶν ὀνομάτων περιαιρῶμεν τὰ μὴ
40 ἀναγκαῖα ῥηθῆναι, ταῦτα μόνα καταλείποντες ὧν
1438 b ἀφαιρεθέντων ἀσαφὴς ἔσται ὁ λόγος. καὶ συντόμως
μὲν τοῦτον τὸν τρόπον δηλώσομεν, οὐκ ἀπίστως δέ,
ἂν περὶ τὰς ἀπιθάνους πράξεις αἰτίας φέρωμεν παρ'
ἃς εἰκότως τὰ λεγόμενα δόξει πραχθῆναι. ὅσα δ'
5 ἂν λίαν ἄπιστα συμβαίνοι, δεῖ παραλείπειν· ἐὰν
δὲ ἀναγκαῖον ᾖ λέγειν, εἰδότα δεῖ φαίνεσθαι, καὶ
ἐπιπλέξαντα αὐτὰ τῷ τῆς παραλείψεως σχήματι
ὑπερβάλλεσθαι, καὶ προϊόντος τοῦ λόγου ἐπιδείξειν
ἀληθῆ[1] ὑπισχνεῖσθαι, προφασισάμενον ὅτι τὰ προειρημένα πρῶτον βούλει ἀποδεῖξαι ἀληθῆ ὄντα ἢ
δίκαια ἤ τι τῶν τοιούτων. καὶ τοῦτον μὲν τὸν
10 τρόπον τὰς ἀπιστίας ἰασόμεθα· συλλήβδην δὲ τὰς
ἀπαγγελίας καὶ τὰς δηλώσεις καὶ τὰς προρρήσεις
ἐξ ἁπάντων τῶν εἰρημένων σαφεῖς καὶ βραχείας καὶ
οὐκ ἀπίστους ποιήσομεν.

XXXI. Τάξομεν δὲ αὐτὰς διὰ τριῶν τρόπων. ὅταν
15 μὲν γὰρ ὦσιν ὀλίγα τὰ πράγματα περὶ ὧν λέγομεν
καὶ γνώριμα τοῖς ἀκούουσι, τῷ προοιμίῳ συνάψομεν, ἵνα μὴ βραχὺ τοῦτο τὸ μέρος καθ' ἑαυτὸ
τεθὲν γένηται. ὅταν δὲ λίαν ὦσιν αἱ πράξεις
πολλαὶ καὶ μὴ γνώριμοι, παρ' ἕκαστον[2] συνάπτας
ποιήσομεν καὶ δικαίας καὶ συμφερούσας καὶ καλὰς
20 ἀποφανοῦμεν, ἵνα μὴ μόνον πραγματολογοῦντες
ἁπλοῦν τὸν λόγον καὶ μὴ ποικίλον ποιῶμεν ἀλλὰ
καὶ τῶν ἀκουόντων τὰς διανοίας ἀναλαμβάνωμεν.

---

[1] Sp.: ἀληθές.　　　　　　　　[2] ἑκάστην ? Rac.

1438 a

transposed order but always place the words that are connected next to one another. By taking these precautions we shall make our exposition clear. It will be concise if we discard from our facts and our words those that are not necessary to be said, leaving only those the omission of which would make our 40 meaning obscure. This being how our exposition 1438 b will be concise, it will be convincing if in regard to facts that are improbable we bring forward reasons that will make the events that we allege seem likely to have taken place. Any occurrences that would be too improbable had better be omitted; but if you are 5 compelled to introduce them, you must show that you know them as facts, and must pass them over lightly, working them in by means of the figure of omission,[a] and promise that you will demonstrate their truth in the course of your speech, pleading that you wish first to prove the statements you have made already to be true or just or the like. This is how we shall provide an antidote to incredulity. To sum up, the collection 10 of devices stated will enable us to make our reports and expositions and forecasts clear, brief and convincing.

XXXI. There are three methods by which we shall (b) arrangement. arrange them. When the actions about which we 15 are speaking are few in number and familiar to the audience, we shall include them in the introduction, so that this part standing by itself may not be too short. When the actions are too numerous and not familiar, we shall in each case put them in connexion and prove 20 them to be just, expedient and honourable, so as not to make our speech only a plain unvarnished statement of fact but to win the attention of our hearers. If the

---

[a] See 1434 a 17 ff.

ἂν δ' ὦσιν αἱ πράξεις μέτριαι καὶ ἀγνοούμεναι, τὴν
ἀπαγγελίαν ἢ τὴν δήλωσιν ἢ τὴν πρόρρησιν ἐπὶ τῷ
25 φροιμίῳ δεῖ σωματοειδῆ τάττειν· τοῦτο δὲ ποιήσομεν, ἐὰν ἀπὸ τῆς ἀρχῆς τῶν πραγμάτων ἐπὶ τὸ
τέλος διέλθωμεν, μηδὲν ἄλλο συμπαραλαμβάνοντες
ἀλλ' ἢ τὰς πράξεις αὐτὰς ψιλὰς φράζοντες. καὶ
τὰς μὲν διηγήσεις ἐπὶ τοῖς προοιμίοις ὡς δεῖ τάττειν, οὕτως εἰσόμεθα.

XXXII. Μετὰ δὲ ταῦτα ἐστὶ βεβαίωσις, δι' ἧς[1] τὰς
30 προειρημένας πράξεις ἐκ τῶν πίστεων καὶ τῶν
δικαίων καὶ τῶν συμφερόντων οἵας ὑπεθέμεθα δείξειν βεβαιώσομεν. ὅταν μὲν οὖν συναπτὰς ποιῇς,
οἰκειόταται ταῖς δημηγορίαις εἰσὶ πίστεις τά τε
τῶν πραγμάτων ἔθη καὶ τὰ παραδείγματα καὶ τὰ
35 ἐνθυμήματα[2] καὶ ἡ δόξα τοῦ λέγοντος· χρηστέον δὲ
καὶ ἄν τις τῶν ἄλλων πίστεων παρεμπέσῃ. τάττειν
δὲ αὐτὰς ὧδε δεῖ, πρῶτον μὲν τὴν τοῦ λέγοντος
δόξαν, εἰ δὲ μή, τὰ τῶν πραγμάτων ἔθη, δεικνύντας[3] ὅτι ταῦθ' ἃ λέγομεν ἢ τὰ τούτοις ὅμοια οὕτως
εἴθισται γίνεσθαι. ἐπὶ δὲ τούτοις παραδείγματα
40 οἰστέον, καὶ εἰ ὁμοιότης τις ἐστί, πρὸς τὰ ὑφ' ἡμῶν
1439 a λεγόμενα προσακτέον. λαμβάνειν δὲ δεῖ τὰ παραδείγματα τὰ[4] οἰκεῖα τῷ πράγματι καὶ τὰ ἐγγύτατα
τοῖς ἀκούουσι χρόνῳ ἢ τόπῳ, ἐὰν δὲ μὴ ὑπάρχῃ
τοιαῦτα, τῶν ἄλλων τὰ μέγιστα καὶ γνωριμώτατα.
μετὰ ταῦτα γνωμολογητέον. δεῖ δὲ καὶ περὶ τὰ
5 μέρη τῶν εἰκότων καὶ τῶν παραδειγμάτων ἐπὶ
τελευτῆς[5] ἐνθυμηματώδεις καὶ γνωμολογικὰς τὰς
τελευτὰς ποιεῖσθαι. καὶ τὰς μὲν πίστεις οὕτως ἐπὶ
ταῖς πράξεσι προσακτέον.

---

[4] v.l. ταῦτα ἐπιβεβαιώσεις δι' ὧν.
[5] Sp.: ἐπενθυμήματα.   [3] δεικνύντας v.l. om.

1438 b

facts are moderate in number and not familiar, we
ought to place the report or exposition or prediction of
them bodily as an addition to the introduction; and we 25
shall do this if we go right through from the beginning
of the facts to the end, not introducing any side issue
but merely stating the bare facts themselves. This
will inform us how to arrange narratives of facts in
our introductions.

XXXII. After this comes confirmation, the method
by which we shall confirm the facts already stated as 30
being of such a nature as we undertook to show them *(3) Confirma-*
to be, by means of proofs and considerations of justice *tion by proof*
and expediency. When, therefore, you are including *consi.lera-*
proofs, those most appropriate to public speeches are *tions.*
the customary course of events, examples, considerations, and the opinion of the speaker ; and any other 35
proof available must also be employed. They must
be arranged as follows : first, the speaker's opinion,
or else the usual nature of the facts, to prove
that the things we assert or things like them usually
take place in this way. Next we must adduce
examples, and employ any available similarity to 40
support the statements we are making. We must **1439 a**
take examples that are akin to the case and those that
are nearest in time or place to our hearers, and if such
are not available, such others as are most important
and best known. After these we must cite maxims.
Also at the end of the sections devoted to probabilities 5
and examples we must frame the conclusions in the
form of considerations and maxims. This, then, is how
we must introduce proofs as to matters of fact.

---

⁴ τὰ add. Halm.   ⁵ [ἐπὶ τελευτῆς] Kayser.

Ἐὰν δὲ πιστεύηται τὰ πράγματα εὐθέως ῥηθέντα,
τὰς μὲν πίστεις παραλειπτέον, τῷ δὲ δικαίῳ καὶ
10 τῷ νομίμῳ καὶ τῷ συμφέροντι καὶ τῷ καλῷ καὶ
τῷ ἡδεῖ καὶ τῷ ῥᾳδίῳ καὶ τῷ δυνατῷ καὶ τῷ
ἀναγκαίῳ τὰς προειρημένας πράξεις βεβαιωτέον.
καὶ εἰ μὲν ὑπάρχει, πρῶτον τὸ δίκαιον τακτέον,
διεξιόντας διὰ αὐτοῦ¹ τε τοῦ δικαίου καὶ τοῦ
ὁμοίου τῷ δικαίῳ καὶ τοῦ ἐναντίου καὶ τοῦ κεκρι-
μένου δικαίου. δεῖ δὲ καὶ τὰ παραδείγματα τὰ²
15 τοῖς ὑπὸ σοῦ λεγομένοις δικαίοις ὅμοια φέρειν.
πολλὰ δὲ ἕξεις λέγειν³ ἐκ τῶν⁴ ἰδίᾳ παρ᾽ ἑκάστοις
δικαίων ὑπολαμβανομένων, καὶ ἐκ τῶν ἐν αὐτῇ τῇ
πόλει ἐν ᾗ λέγεις καὶ ἐκ τῶν ἐν ταῖς ἄλλαις πόλεσιν.
ὅταν δὲ ἅπαντα τοῦτον τὸν τρόπον μετιόντες δι-
20 έλθωμεν, ἐπὶ τελευτῆς αὐτοῦ γνώμας καὶ ἐνθυμήματα μέτρια καὶ ἀλλήλοις ἀνόμοια ἐνεγκόντες, ἐὰν
μὲν μακρὸν ᾖ τὸ μέρος καὶ βουλώμεθα μνημονεύε-
σθαι, συντόμως παλιλλογήσομεν, ἐὰν δὲ μέτριον ᾖ
καὶ μνημονεύηται, αὐτὸ τὸ μέρος ὁρισάμενοι πάλιν
ἕτερον προθησόμεθα. ἔστι δὲ ὃ λέγω τοιόνδε·
25 "ὡς μὲν δίκαιόν ἐστιν ἡμᾶς βοηθεῖν Συρακοσίοις,
ἐκ τῶν εἰρημένων ἱκανῶς ἀποδεδεῖχθαι νομίζω·
ὡς δὲ καὶ συμφέρει ταῦτα πράττειν, ἐπιχειρήσω
διδάσκειν." πάλιν δὲ περὶ τοῦ συμφέροντος ὁμοιοτρόπως τοῖς προειρημένοις ἐπὶ τοῦ δικαίου μετιών,
καὶ ἐπὶ τῇ τελευτῇ τούτου⁵ τοῦ μέρους ἢ παλιλ-
30 λογίαν ἢ ὁρισμὸν ἐπιθείς, πάλιν ἕτερον ὅ τι ἂν
ὑπάρχῃ σοι προτίθει. τοῦτον δὲ δεῖ τὸν τρόπον
ἄλλο ἄλλῳ συνάπτειν μέρει καὶ συνυφαίνειν τὸν
λόγον. ὅταν δὲ πάντα διεξέλθῃς ἐξ ὧν ἐνδέχεται

---

¹ Finckh: τούτου.   ² τὰ add. Finckh.
³ λέγειν om. v.l.   ⁴ Rac.; ἔκ τε τῶν.

If the mere statement of the facts carries immediate
conviction, proofs should be omitted, and the policies
already stated should be confirmed on grounds of
justice, legality, expediency, honour, pleasantness,
facility, practicability and necessity. We should
place the plea of justice first, if it is available, going
through the topics of absolute justice, approximate
justice, the opposite of justice, and justice as decided
by a previous judgement. You must also produce
examples conforming with the principles of justice
that you assert. You will be able to produce many
examples of the special conceptions of justice held in
particular communities, both those obtaining in the
city where you are speaking and those in other states.
When by following this method we have gone through
the whole of what we have to say, producing at the
end of it a variety of maxims and considerations of
moderate length, if the division is a long one and we
wish to aid the memory, we shall briefly recapitulate,
but if it is of moderate length and easy to remember,
we shall round off the division itself and put forward
another in turn. This is the sort of thing I mean :
' I think that what has been said has given a
sufficient proof of the justice of sending help to Syracuse. I shall now attempt to show that policy to be
also expedient.' Then you must treat the subject
of expediency in a manner similar to what you have
said already in the case of justice, and at the end of
this division add either a recapitulation or a definition,
and then put forward any other subject that you have
available. This is the way in which you must join one
division to another, and link your speech together.
When you have gone through all the subjects available

---

⁵ τούτου add. Sp.

1439 a

σοι βεβαιῶσαι τὴν προτροπήν, ἐπὶ τούτοις ἅπασι
κεφαλαιωδῶς μετὰ ἐνθυμημάτων καὶ γνωμῶν ἢ
35 σχημάτων δείκνυε ὡς ἄδικον καὶ ἀσύμφορον καὶ
αἰσχρὸν καὶ ἀηδὲς μὴ ποιεῖν ταῦτα, καὶ ἀντιτίθει
κεφαλαιωδῶς ὡς δίκαιον καὶ συμφέρον καὶ καλὸν
καὶ ἡδὺ πράττειν ἐφ᾿ ἃ παρακαλεῖς. ὅταν δὲ
ἱκανῶς ἤδη ἦς ἐγνωμολογηκώς, τὴν προτροπὴν
πέρατι ὅρισαι.

Καὶ τοῦτον μὲν τὸν τρόπον βεβαιώσομεν τὰ
1439 b προτεθέντα, μετὰ δὲ τοῦτο τὸ μέρος λέξομεν τὴν
προκατάληψιν.

XXXIII. Αὕτη δ᾿ ἐστὶ δι᾿ ἧς τὰς ἐνδεχομένας
ἀντιλογίας ῥηθῆναι τοῖς ὑπὸ σοῦ εἰρημένοις προ-
5 καταλαμβάνων διασύρεις. δεῖ δὲ τὰ μὲν ἐκείνων
μικρὰ ποιεῖν, τὰ δὲ σαυτοῦ αὔξειν, ὡς ἐν ταῖς
αὐξήσεσι προακήκοας. χρὴ δὲ παρατιθέναι καὶ
ἓν πρὸς ἕν, ὅταν τὸ σὸν μεῖζον ᾖ, καὶ πρὸς πλείω
πλείω, καὶ ἓν πρὸς πολλά, καὶ πολλὰ πρὸς ἕν,
διαλλάττοντα κατὰ πάντας τοὺς τρόπους, τὰ μὲν
10 σαυτοῦ αὔξοντα, τὰ δὲ τῶν ἐναντίων ἀσθενῆ καὶ
μικρὰ ποιοῦντα. καὶ τοῦτον μὲν τὸν τρόπον ταῖς
προκαταλήψεσι χρησόμεθα.

Ταῦτα δὲ διελθόντες ἐπὶ τελευτῇ παλιλλογήσομεν
τὰ προειρημένα σχῆμα[1] διαλογισμοῦ λαβόντες ἢ
ἀπολογισμοῦ ἢ ἐκ[2] προαιρέσεως ἢ ἐξ ἐπερωτήσεως
ἢ εἰρωνείας.

15 XXXIV. Ἐὰν δὲ ἐπὶ τὸ βοηθεῖν τισι προ-
τρέπωμεν, ἢ ἰδιώταις ἢ πόλεσιν, ἁρμόσει συντόμως

---

[1] Sp.: σχήματα.　　　　　　　[2] ἐκ add. Sp.

---

[a] *i.e.* the four rhetorical figures προκατάληψις 1432 b 10,
αἰτήματα 1433 b 17, παλιλλογία *ib.* b 29, εἰρωνεία 1434 a 17.

1439 a

for you to employ in confirmation of your exhortation,
in addition to all these prove summarily, with the aid
of considerations and maxims or figures,[a] that it is 35
unjust and inexpedient and disgraceful and unpleasant
not to do this, and oppose a summary proof that the
course you advocate is just and expedient and honourable and pleasant. When you have now made
sufficient use of maxims, round off the exhortation
with a conclusion.

This is the way in which we shall confirm the pro- 1439 b
posals we put forward. In the following section we
shall deal with anticipation.

XXXIII. Anticipation is the method by which you
anticipate the objections that can be advanced
against your arguments and sweep them aside. You 5
must minimize the other party's arguments and
amplify your own in the manner which you have
heard already in the passage dealing with amplifications. You must set one argument against one
other when yours is the stronger, and several against
several, and one against many, and many against
one, contrasting them in all possible ways, amplify- 10
ing your own and making those of your opponents
weak and trifling. This is the way in which we shall
employ anticipations.

When we have gone through these passages, in
conclusion we shall recapitulate what has been said
already, adopting the form of argument or of refutation or employing a proposal of policy or interrogation
or irony.

XXXIV. If we are urging our audience to render 15
assistance to certain parties, whether individuals or (4) *Appeal*
states, it will also be suitable briefly to mention *to feelings.*

397

εἰπεῖν καὶ εἴ τις προϋπάρχει τούτοις πρὸς τοὺς
ἐκκλησιάζοντας φιλία ἢ χάρις ἢ ἔλεος. μάλιστα
γὰρ τοῖς οὕτω διακειμένοις ἐθέλουσιν ἐπαμύνειν·
φιλοῦσι μὲν οὖν πάντες ὑφ᾽ ὧν[1] οἴονται κατὰ τὸ
20 προσῆκον εὖ πεπονθέναι ἢ πάσχειν ἢ πείσεσθαι, ἢ
ὑπ᾽ αὐτῶν ἢ τῶν φίλων, ἢ αὐτοὶ ἢ ὧν κηδόμενοι
τυγχάνουσιν· χάριν δ᾽ ἔχουσι τούτοις ὑφ᾽ ὧν
οἴονται παρὰ τὸ προσῆκον ἀγαθόν τι πεπονθέναι
ἢ πάσχειν ἢ πείσεσθαι, ἢ ὑπ᾽ αὐτῶν ἢ τῶν φίλων,
ἢ αὐτοὶ ἢ ὧν κηδόμενοι τυγχάνουσιν. τούτων μὲν
25 οὖν ἄν τι ἐνῇ, χρὴ συντόμως διδάσκειν, καὶ ἐπὶ
τὸν ἔλεον ἄγειν. εὐπορήσομεν δὲ ἐλεεινὰ ποιεῖν
ἅπερ ἂν ἐθέλωμεν ἐὰν συνειδῶμεν ὅτι πάντες
ἐλεοῦσι τούτους οὓς οἰκείως ἔχειν αὐτοῖς ὑπ-
ειλήφασιν ἢ οἴονται ἀναξίους εἶναι δυστυχεῖν. δεῖ
δὴ[2] ταῦτα ἀποφαίνειν ἔχοντας οὓς ἐθέλεις ἐλεεινοὺς
30 ποιεῖν, καὶ ἐπιδεικνύειν αὐτοὺς ἢ κακῶς πεπονθότας
ἢ πάσχοντας, ἢ πεισομένους ἐὰν μὴ οἱ ἀκούοντες
αὐτοῖς βοηθῶσιν. ἐὰν δὲ ταῦτα μὴ ἐνῇ, δεικτέον,
ὑπὲρ ὧν λέγεις, ἀγαθῶν ἐστερημένους ὧν τοῖς
ἄλλοις ἅπασιν ἢ τοῖς πλείστοις μέτεστιν, ἢ ἀγαθοῦ
μηδέποτε τετυχηκότας ἢ μὴ τυγχάνοντας, ἢ μὴ
35 τευξομένους ἐὰν μὴ νῦν οἱ ἀκούοντες οἰκτείρωσιν.
ἐκ τούτων μὲν οὖν ἐπὶ τὸν ἔλεον ἄξομεν.

Τὰς δὲ ἀποτροπὰς ἐκ τῶν ἐναντίων τούτοις
ποιήσομεν, τὸν αὐτὸν τρόπον φροιμιαζόμενοι καὶ
τὰ πράγματα διεξιόντες, ταῖς τε πίστεσι χρώμενοι,
καὶ τοῖς ἀκούουσι δεικνύντες ὡς ἐστὶν ἃ πράττειν

---

[1] ⟨τούτους⟩ ὑφ᾽ ὧν Sp.　　　　　[2] v.l. δέ.

any friendly feeling or cause for gratitude or compassion that already exists between them and the
members of the assembly. For these are specially
willing to assist people standing in those relations to
them ; everybody, therefore, feels kindly towards
people from whom personally or from whose friends 20
they think that they themselves or those they happen
to care for have received or are receiving or are going
to receive some merited service ; and are grateful to
those from whom personally or from whose friends
they think that they themselves or those they happen
to care for have received or are receiving or are going
to receive some unmerited benefit. If any one of 25
these circumstances is present, we must concisely
explain it, and lead our hearers to compassion. We
shall find it easy to excite compassion for anything
we wish if we remember that all men pity those
whom they conceive to be closely related to them,
or think not to deserve misfortune. You must, therefore, prove that this is the condition of those for whom
you wish to excite compassion and must show that 30
they either have been or are in distress, or will be
if your hearers do not assist them. If these circumstances are not present, you must show that those for
whom you are speaking have been deprived of
advantages which all or most men share, or have
never had any luck, or have none now, or will have 5
none if your hearers do not pity them now. These
are the means by which we shall lead our audience
to feel compassion.

For dissuasion we shall use the opposite methods,
opening the case and going through the facts in the
same manner, by employing proofs and demonstrating to our hearers that the actions they are taking in

1440 a ἐπιχειροῦσιν ἄνομα καὶ ἄδικα καὶ ἀσύμφορα καὶ
αἰσχρὰ καὶ ἀηδῆ καὶ ἀδύνατα καὶ ἐργώδη καὶ οὐκ
ἀναγκαῖα. ἡ δὲ τάξις ὁμοιότροπος¹ ἔσται οἵα καὶ
τῷ προτρέποντι. τοῖς μὲν οὖν καθ' αὑτοὺς ἀπο-
τρέπουσιν οὕτω τὰς τάξεις ποιητέον.

5 Τοὺς δὲ πρὸς τὰς ὑφ' ἑτέρων εἰρημένας προτροπὰς ἀντιλέγοντας πρῶτον μὲν ἐν τῷ προοιμίῳ
δεῖ οἷς μέλλουσιν ἀντιλέγειν προθέσθαι, τὰ δ' ἄλλα
καθ' αὑτὰ προοιμιάζεσθαι, μετὰ δὲ τὰ προοίμια
μάλιστα μὲν ἕκαστα τῶν προειρημένων καθ' ἓν
ἕκαστον προτιθέμενος² ἐπιδεικνύειν ὡς οὐκ ἔστι
10 δίκαια οὐδὲ νόμιμα οὐδὲ συμφέροντα οὐδὲ τούτοις
ἀκόλουθα ἐφ' ἃ παρακαλεῖ ὁ ἐναντίος. τοῦτο δὲ
ποιήσεις ἀποφαίνων ἢ ἄδικα ὄντα ἃ λέγει ἢ ἀ-
σύμφορα, ἢ τούτοις ὅμοια, ἢ ἐναντία τοῖς δικαίοις
καὶ τοῖς συμφέρουσι καὶ τοῖς κεκριμένοις τοιούτοις.
ὁμοιοτρόπως δὲ καὶ τῶν ἄλλων τὰ ὑπάρχοντα
15 μέτιθι. κράτιστος μὲν οὖν ὁ τρόπος τῆς ἀπο-
τροπῆς οὗτος ἐστίν, ἐὰν δὲ μὴ ἐνδέχηται τοῦτο
ποιεῖν, ἐκ τοῦ παραλελειμμένου τόπου³ ἀπότρεπε
λέγων· οἷον ἐὰν ὁ ἐναντίος δίκαιον ἀποφήνῃ, σὺ
ἐπιχείρει δεικνύναι ὡς ἐστὶν αἰσχρὸν ἢ ἀσύμφορον
ἢ ἐργῶδες ἢ ἀδύνατον ἢ ὅ τι ἂν ἔχῃς τοιοῦτον·
20 ἐὰν δὲ ἐκεῖνος ἔχῃ τὸ συμφέρον, σὺ ἐπιδείκνυε
ὡς ἄδικον, κἄν τι ἄλλο ἔχῃς πρὸς τούτῳ. δεῖ
δὲ καὶ τὰ μὲν σαυτοῦ⁴ αὔξειν τὰ δὲ τοὐναν-
τίου ταπεινοῦν, ποιοῦντα ὡς ἐν τῷ προτρεπτικῷ
εἴρηται. χρὴ δὲ καὶ γνώμας φέρειν καὶ ἐνθυμήματα

---

¹ Sp.: ὁμοιοτρόπως.
² Rac. cf. 1434 b 12 n.: προτιθέμενον (προτιθεμένους Sp.).
³ Finckh: τρόπου.
⁴ Sp.: αὑτοῦ aut αὑτοῦ.

hand are illegal, unjust, inexpedient, disgraceful, 1440 a
unpleasant, impossible, laborious and unnecessary.
The arrangement will be similar to that used in
persuasion. This, then, is how those who use dissuasion on their own account should arrange their
speeches.

Those replying to exhortations spoken by others 5
must first set out in their introduction the position
they are going to oppose, and make a preliminary
statement of their other points seriatim. After the
introduction the best plan is to put forward one at a
time each of the statements made in the previous
speech, and prove that they are not just nor lawful nor 10
expedient nor consistent with the policy advocated
by the opponent. You will do this by showing that
what he says is either unjust or inexpedient, or ap-
proximately so, or the opposite of what is just and
expedient and what has been judged to be so. And
treat the other points that are available in a similar
way. This is the best method of dissuasion; but if this 15
is not feasible, base your dissuasion on any topic that
has been omitted; for instance, if your opponent
makes out a policy to be just, attempt on your side
to prove that it is dishonourable or inexpedient or
laborious or impossible or whatever else of the sort
you can; and if he has expediency on his side, you 20
must show that his policy is unjust and whatever else
you can in addition. And you must amplify your
own points and run down those of your opponent,
following the method already set out in the section
on the oratory of persuasion. You must also, as in
that section, produce maxims and considerations, and

1440 a

καθάπερ ἐκεῖ,[1] καὶ τὰς προκαταλήψεις λύειν, καὶ
25 ἐπὶ τελευτῇ παλιλλογεῖν.

Πρὸς δὲ τούτοις ἐν μὲν ταῖς προτροπαῖς ἀποφαίνειν φιλίαν ὑπάρχουσαν[2] οἷς βοηθεῖν προ-
τρέπομεν πρὸς τοὺς προτρεπομένους,[3] ἢ χάριν τοὺς
προτρεπομένους ὀφείλοντας τοῖς[4] δεομένοις· οἷς
δ' οὐκ ἐῶμεν βοηθεῖν, ἢ ὀργῆς ἢ φθόνου ἢ ἔχθρας
ἀξίους ὑπάρχοντας. ἔχθραν μὲν οὖν ἐμποιήσομεν
30 ὑπ' ἐκείνων οὐ προσηκόντως τοὺς ἀποτρεπομένους
ἀποφαίνοντες κακῶς πεπονθότας[5] ἢ τῶν φίλων ἢ
αὐτοὺς ἢ ὧν κηδόμενοι τυγχάνουσιν· ὀργὴν δέ,
ἐὰν ἐπιδεικνύωμεν παρὰ τὸ προσῆκον ὠλιγωρη-
μένους ἢ ἠδικημένους ὑπ' ἐκείνων[6] ἢ τῶν φίλων[7]
ἢ αὐτοὺς ἢ ὧν κηδόμενοι τυγχάνουσιν.[8] φθόνον δὲ
35 παρασκευάσομεν συλλήβδην πρὸς τούτους οὓς ἀπο-
φαίνομεν ἀναξίως εὖ πεπραχότας ἢ πράττοντας
ἢ πράξοντας, ἢ ἀγαθοῦ μηδέποτε ἐστερημένους
ἢ μὴ στερουμένους ἢ μὴ στερησομένους, ἢ κακοῦ
μηδέποτε τετυχηκότας ἢ μὴ τυγχάνοντας ἢ μὴ[9]
τευξομένους. φθόνον μὲν οὖν καὶ ἔχθραν καὶ
40 ὀργὴν τοῦτον τὸν τρόπον ἐμποιήσομεν, φιλίαν δὲ
1440 b καὶ χάριν καὶ ἔλεον ἐκ τῶν ἐν ταῖς προτροπαῖς.
συνθήσομεν δὲ καὶ τάξομεν ἐξ ἁπάντων τῶν
προειρημένων αὐτὰς τόνδε τὸν τρόπον.[10]

Τὸ μὲν οὖν προτρεπτικὸν[11] εἶδος αὐτό τε ἴσμεν
οἷόν ἐστι καὶ ἐξ ὧν συνέστηκε καὶ ὡς αὐτῷ
χρηστέον.

5 XXXV. Τὸ δὲ ἐγκωμιαστικὸν καὶ τὸ κακολο-

---

[1] Sp.: ἐκεῖσε.　　　　　[2] Sp.: ὑπάρχειν.
[3] πρὸς τοὺς προτρεπομένους v.l. om.
[4] ἢ . . . τοῖς: v.l. καὶ ὀφείλοντας χάριν ἔχειν τοῖς.
[5] πεπονθότας ⟨ἢ ὑπ' αὐτῶν⟩ Sp.
[6] ὑπ' ἐκείνων add. Hammer.

refute anticipations, and at the conclusion recapitu- 25
late.

In addition to this, in persuasions we must show
that those whose support we are recommending are
friendly to those to whom our recommendation is
addressed, or that the latter owe a favour to the
appellants ; and that those whose support we are
opposing are deserving of anger or envy or enmity.
We shall engender enmity by showing that those 30
whom we are dissuading themselves or those whom
they care for have been wrongfully ill-treated by the
other party or by their friends ; anger, if we prove
that they or those they care for have been wrongfully
despised or injured by the other party. We shall cause
envy against those (to put it briefly) whom we 35
show to have been or to be or to be going to be
undeservedly prosperous, or never to have suffered or
not to be suffering or going to suffer the loss of some
good, or never to have encountered or not to be
encountering or going to encounter some evil. This
is the manner in which we shall engender envy, 40
hatred and anger, whereas friendship, favour and
compassion we shall arouse by the means stated in 1440 b
the case of exhortations; and this is the way in which
we shall construct and arrange them out of all the
materials already stated.

We now know the nature and component parts of
the persuasive kind of oratory and the manner in
which it is to be employed.

XXXV. Next let us set before us for examination 5

---

⁷ Post φίλων add. ἐκείνων aut ἐκείνοις codd.
⁸ Sp. : τυγχάνουσιν αὐτοί.   ⁹ v.l. ἢ μηδὲ.
       ¹⁰ [αὐτὰς . . . τρόπον] Sp.
   ¹¹ προτρεπτικὸν ⟨καὶ ἀποτρεπτικὸν⟩ Sp.

1440 b

γικὸν πάλιν προθέμενοι σκοπῶμεν. φροιμιαστέον
οὖν καὶ περὶ τούτων πρῶτον προθεμένους τὰς
προθέσεις καὶ τὰς διαβολὰς ἀπολυομένους[1] ὁμοίως
ὥσπερ ἐν τοῖς προτρεπτικοῖς. ἐπὶ δὲ τὸ προσέχειν
παρακαλοῦμεν ἔκ τε τῶν ἄλλων τῶν ἐν ταῖς
10 δημηγορίαις εἰρημένων, καὶ ἐκ τοῦ θαυμαστὰ καὶ
περιφανῆ[2] φάσκειν εἶναι[3] καὶ αὐτοὺς[4] ἴσα καὶ τοὺς
ἐγκωμιαζομένους καὶ τοὺς ψεγομένους ἀποφανεῖν[5]
πεπραγότας. ὡς γὰρ ἐπὶ τὸ πολὺ ἐπὶ τούτων
τῶν[6] εἰδῶν οὐκ ἀγῶνος ἀλλ' ἐπιδείξεως ἕνεκα
λέγομεν.

Τάξομεν δὲ πρῶτον τὰ προοίμια τὸν αὐτὸν
15 τρόπον ὅνπερ ἐπὶ τῶν προτροπῶν καὶ ἀποτροπῶν.
μετὰ δὲ τὸ προοίμιον δεῖ διελόμενον τὰ ἔξω τῆς
ἀρετῆς ἀγαθὰ καὶ τὰ ἐν αὐτῇ τῇ ἀρετῇ ὄντα ποιεῖν
οὕτω· τὰ μὲν οὖν ἔξω τῆς ἀρετῆς εἰς εὐγένειαν
καὶ ῥώμην καὶ κάλλος καὶ πλοῦτον, τὴν δ' ἀρετὴν
εἰς σοφίαν καὶ δικαιοσύνην καὶ ἀνδρείαν καὶ ἐπι-
20 τηδεύματα ἔνδοξα. τούτων δὲ τὰ μὲν τῆς ἀρετῆς
δικαίως ἐγκωμιάζεται, τὰ δ' ἔξω κλέπτεται, τοὺς
γὰρ ἰσχυροὺς καὶ τοὺς καλοὺς καὶ τοὺς εὐγενεῖς
καὶ τοὺς πλουσίους οὐκ ἐπαινεῖν ἀλλὰ μακαρίζειν
προσήκει. ταῦτα δὴ διαλογισάμενοι[7] μετὰ τὰ
προοίμια πρώτην τὴν γενεαλογίαν τάξομεν. πρῶ-
25 τον γὰρ τοῖς ἀνθρώποις καὶ τοῖς ἄλλοις ζῴοις
τοῦθ' ὑπάρχει ἔνδοξον ἢ ἄδοξον· τοιγαροῦν τὸν
μὲν ἄνθρωπον ἤ τι ἄλλο τοιοῦτο ζῷον εὐλογοῦντες[8]

---

[1] Sp.: ἀπολύομεν.
[2] v.l. διαφανῇ.
[3] ⟨εἶναι⟩ add. Wurm.
[4] Sp.: αὐτόν.
[5] Kayser: ἀποφαίνειν.
[6] ἐπὶ τούτων τῶν Sp. (τῷ τοιούτῳ εἴδεε Finckh): τῶν τοιούτων.

1440 b
Structure of ceremonial oration.

the oratory of eulogy and vituperation. With these also we must first in the introduction state our propositions and refute misrepresentations in the same way as in speeches of exhortation. We call for attention by the means that have been specified in the case of parliamentary speeches, especially by asserting that the facts are surprising and remarkable and that we shall prove the parties to have done deeds equal to those that win men eulogy or vituperation. For as a rule in speeches of this class we are not speaking to contest a case but for display.

(1) *Topics of eulogy.*

We shall first arrange the introduction in the same way as in speeches of exhortation and dissuasion. After the introduction one should make a distinction between the goods external to virtue and those actually inherent in virtue, putting it thus: goods external to virtue fall under high birth, strength, beauty and wealth; virtue is divided into wisdom, justice, courage and creditable habits.[a] Those belonging to virtue are justly eulogized, but those external to it are kept in the background, since it is appropriate for the strong and handsome and well-born and rich to receive not praise but congratulation on their good fortune. Having, then, made this distinction, we shall place first after the introduction the genealogy of the person we are speaking of, as that is the fundamental ground of reputation or discredit for human beings, and also for animals; so in eulogizing a human being or

---

[a] Synonym for σωφροσύνη, temperance or soundness of mind.

---

[7] μετὰ δὲ (l. 15) . . . διαλογισάμενοι secl. Ipfelkofer ut secundum *Rhet.* ii. 9 interpolatum. διελόμενοι pro διαλογισάμενοι Sp.

[8] Rac.: εὐλόγως.

1440 b

γενεαλογήσομεν· ὅταν δὲ πάθος ἢ πρᾶγμα ἢ λόγον
ἢ κτῆμα, ἀπ' αὐτῶν εὐθὺς τῶν προσόντων ἐνδόξων
ἐπαινέσομεν.

Γενεαλογεῖν δὲ δεῖ ὧδε. ἐὰν μὲν ὦσιν οἱ
30 πρόγονοι σπουδαῖοι, πάντας ἐξ ἀρχῆς ἀναλαβόντα[1]
μέχρι πρὸς τὸν ἐγκωμιαζόμενον, ἐφ' ἑκάστῳ τῶν
προγόνων κεφαλαιωδῶς ἔνδοξόν τι παρατιθέναι.[2]
ἐὰν δὲ οἱ πρῶτοι μὲν ὦσι σπουδαῖοι, τοὺς δὲ
λοιποὺς συμβεβήκῃ[3] μηδὲν ἀξιόλογον πρᾶξαι, τοὺς
μὲν πρώτους τὸν αὐτὸν τρόπον διεξελθεῖν, τοὺς
35 δὲ φαύλους παραλιπεῖν, προφασισάμενος[4] ὅτι διὰ
πλῆθος τῶν προγόνων οὐ θέλεις λέγων αὐτοὺς
μακρολογεῖν, ἔτι δὲ οὐκ ἄδηλον εἶναι πᾶσιν ὅτι
τοὺς ἐξ ἀγαθῶν γενομένους εἰκός ἐστι τοῖς προ-
γόνοις ὁμοιοῦσθαι. ἐὰν δὲ οἱ παλαιοὶ πρόγονοι
φαῦλοι τυγχάνωσιν ὄντες οἱ δὲ πρὸς αὐτὸν ἔνδοξοι,
40 τούτους δεῖ γενεαλογεῖν καὶ λέγειν ὅτι περὶ μὲν
1441 a ἐκείνων περίεργον ἂν εἴη μακρολογεῖν, τοὺς δὲ
πλησίον γεγονότας τῶν ἐπαινουμένων, τούτους
ὄντας ἀγαθοὺς ἐπιδείξεις, καὶ δῆλον ὡς οἵ γε
τούτων πρόγονοι σπουδαῖοί τινες ἦσαν, οὐ γὰρ
εἰκὸς φανῆναι τοιούτους[5] εἶναι τοὺς[6] ἐκ μοχθηρῶν
5 προγόνων γεγονότας.[7] ἐὰν δὲ μηδὲν ἀπὸ τῶν
προγόνων ἔνδοξον ὑπάρχῃ, λέγε ὡς αὐτός ἐστι
γενναῖος, συμβιβάζων ὡς εὖ γεγόνασι πάντες οἱ
πρὸς[8] ἀρετὴν εὖ πεφυκότες. ἐπιτίμα[9] δὲ καὶ τοῖς
ἄλλοις ὅσοι τοὺς προγόνους ἐπαινοῦσι, λέγων ὅτι

---

[1] Sp.: ἀναλαβόντες.　　　　[2] Finckh: περιτιθέναι.
[3] Sp.: συμβέβηκε.　　　　[4] Usener: προφασιζόμενον.
[5] Rac.: τοὺς τοιούτους καλοὺς ἢ ἀγαθοὺς (καλοὺς ἢ
ἀγαθοὺς εἶναι secl. Kayser).
[6] τοὺς add. Rac.
[7] προγόνων γεγονότας Sp.: προγεγονότας.

1440 b

a domestic animal we shall state their pedigree, although when praising an emotion or action or speech or possession we shall base our approval directly on the creditable qualities that actually belong to it.

The proper way to employ genealogy is this. If the ancestors are men of merit, you must enumerate 30 them all from the beginning down to the person you are eulogizing, and at each of the ancestors summarily mention something to his credit. If the first ones are men of merit but the rest do not happen to have done anything remarkable, you must go through the first ones in the same way but omit the inferior ones, 35 explaining that because of the number of the ancestors you do not wish to make a long story by mentioning them all, and moreover that it is patent to everybody that the scions of a worthy stock naturally resemble their ancestors. If his early ancestors happen to be undistinguished but those near to his own time are famous, you must mention his descent from the latter 40 and say it would be tedious to dwell on the former, 1441 a but that you will show that the immediate predecessors of those you are praising were good men, and that it is quite clear that *their* forefathers must have been men of merit, because it is manifestly unlikely that those born from base ancestors could be of that quality. If he has no ancestral distinction in 5 his favour, say that he himself is a fine fellow, suggesting that all men by nature well-endowed with virtue are 'well-born.' Also rebuke all the other people who praise their ancestors by saying that many

---

8 v.l. πρὸς τὴν.   9 Sp.: ἐπιτιμᾶν.

πολλοὶ προγόνων ἐνδόξων τυχόντες ἀνάξιοι γε-
10 γόνασιν. λέγε δὲ καὶ ὅτι τοῦτον, οὐ τοὺς προγόνους, πρόκειται νῦν ἐγκωμιάζειν. ὁμοιοτρόπως
δὲ καὶ κακολογοῦντα ἐπὶ τῶν μοχθηρῶν προγόνων
ποιητέον τὴν γενεαλογίαν.

Καὶ τοῦτον μὲν τὸν τρόπον ἐν τοῖς ἐπαίνοις καὶ
ταῖς κακολογίαις τὰς γενεαλογίας τακτέον.

15 Εἴ τι δὲ ἔνδοξον αὐτῷ διὰ τὴν τύχην ὑπῆρξε * * *
* * *¹ τοῦτο μόνον διαφυλάττοντα ὅπως πρέποντα
ταῖς ἡλικίαις ἐρεῖς, καὶ μικρά· τοὺς γὰρ παῖδας οὐχ
οὕτω δι᾿ αὐτοὺς ὡς διὰ τοὺς ἐφεστῶτας οἴονται
κοσμίους εἶναι καὶ σώφρονας, διὸ βραχυλογητέον
περὶ αὐτῶν. ὅταν δὲ τοῦτον τὸν τρόπον διέλθῃς,
20 ἐπὶ τελευτῇ τοῦ μέρους ἐνθύμημα καὶ γνώμην
εἰπὼν ὁρίσας² τοῦτο τὸ μέρος, ἐπὶ τῇ τοῦ νεανίσκου
ἡλικίᾳ καὶ τὴν πρόθεσιν ποιήσας καὶ προθέμενος ἢ
τὰ ἔργα τοῦ ἐπαινουμένου ἢ τὸν τρόπον ἢ τὰ ἐπιτηδεύματα, αὔξειν καθάπερ εἴπομεν πρότερον ἐν
ἀρχαῖς ἐπὶ τοῦ ἐγκωμιαστικοῦ εἴδους, διεξιὼν ὅτι
25 ὑπὸ τοῦ³ ἐπαινουμένου ἐν ταύτῃ τῇ ἡλικίᾳ ὄντος τὸ
καὶ τὸ γέγονεν ἔνδοξον, ἢ ὅτι διὰ τοῦτον, ἢ ὅτι διὰ
τοῦ ἐπιτηδεύματος,⁴ ἢ ἐκ τούτου, ἢ ἕνεκα τούτου.
δεῖ δὲ καὶ ἑτέρων νέων ἐνδόξους πράξεις παριστάναι καὶ ὑπερβάλλειν δεικνύναι τὰς τοῦδε τὰς
ἐκείνων, τοῦ μὲν ἑτέρου τἀλάχιστα τῶν ὑπαρχόντων
30 λέγοντα, τοῦ δ᾿ ὑπὸ σοῦ ἐπαινουμένου τὰ μέγιστα.
χρὴ δὲ καὶ παρ᾿ ἄλλα σμικρὰ⁵ ἔνδοξα πράγματα

---

¹ lacunam Sauppe.   ² v.l. ὁρίσαι.
³ v.l. τούτου τοῦ.
⁴ [ἢ ὅτι διὰ τούτου . . . ἐπιτηδεύματος] Sp.
⁵ Finckh: ἄλλοις μικρά.

---

men who have had distinguished ancestors have been
unworthy of them. Also say that the business in 10
hand at the moment is to eulogize the man himself,
and not his ancestors. Similarly in vituperation use
must be made of genealogy in a case of bad ancestry.

This is the way in which to introduce genealogy in
eulogy and vituperation.

If the person possessed some distinction that was 15
due to luck . . .

. . . ^a only taking care to say things suited to their
ages, and say little, for people do not think that
orderly conduct and self-restraint in young people is
due so much to themselves as to those who are in
charge of them, so in speaking about them one must
be brief. When you have gone through the topic in
this way, after terminating this section by enunciating
a consideration and a maxim at the end of the section, 20
when you come to the young person's early manhood
you must state your line, namely either the achievements of the subject of your eulogy, or his character,
or his habits, and amplify them as we said before
at the beginning when dealing with the eulogistic
species of oratory, recounting that this or that distinguished thing was done at this age by the subject 25
of your eulogy or through his agency or owing to his
habit or from his initiation or at his prompting. You
must also compare the distinguished achievements of
other young men and show that they are surpassed
by his, specifying the smallest achievements of the
other youth and the biggest exploits of the one you 30
are praising. And you must make the exploits you

success rather to his own efforts than to fortune.—You must
next describe his habits and way of life beginning from his
earliest years.>

1441 a

παριστάμενα τὰ¹ μέγιστα ὑπὸ σοῦ λεγόμενα οὕτω
μέγαλα φαίνεσθαι. δεῖ² δὲ καὶ εἰκάζοντα τὰς
πράξεις αὔξειν ὧδε· καίτοι ὅστις³ νέος οὕτω φιλόσοφος ἐγένετο, οὗτος⁴ πρεσβύτερος γενόμενος με-
35 γάλην ἂν ἐπίδοσιν σχοίη· ἢ ὅστις⁵ ἐρρωμένως τοὺς
ἐν τοῖς γυμνασίοις ὑπομένει πόνους, σφόδρα τὴν ἐν
τῇ φιλοσοφίᾳ φιλοπονίαν ἀγαπήσει. τοῦτον μὲν
οὖν τὸν τρόπον εἰκάζοντες αὐξήσομεν.

Ὅταν δὲ καὶ τὰ περὶ τὴν ἡλικίαν τοῦ νεανίσκου
διέλθωμεν καὶ ἐπὶ τελευτῇ τούτου τοῦ μέρους
1441 b γνώμας καὶ ἐνθυμήματα τάξωμεν,⁶ ἢ παλιλλογήσαντες συντόμως τὰ προειρημένα ἢ περὶ⁷ τὸ
πρακτικὸν μέρος τελευταῖον ὁρισάμενοι, πάλιν⁸
ἃ διεπράξατο ὁ ὑφ' ἡμῶν ἐγκωμιαζόμενος ἀνὴρ⁹
προθέμενοι, τὴν δικαιοσύνην τάξομεν¹⁰ πρῶτον, καὶ
5 ὁμοιοτρόπως τοῖς προειρημένοις αὐξήσαντες ἥξομεν
ἐπὶ τὴν σοφίαν, ἐὰν ὑπάρχῃ· καὶ ταύτην τὸν αὐτὸν
τρόπον διελθόντες, προθέμενοι τὴν ἀνδρείαν, ἐὰν ᾖ,
καὶ τὴν αὔξησιν ταύτης πάλιν διαδραμόντες, ὅταν
ἐπὶ τελευτῇ τούτου τοῦ μέρους γενώμεθα καὶ πάντα
τὰ εἴδη διεξεληλυθότες ὦμεν, παλιλλογήσαντες ἐν
10 κεφαλαίῳ τὰ προειρημένα, τελευτὴν ἤτοι¹¹ γνώμην
ἢ ἐνθύμημα παντὶ τῷ λόγῳ ἐπιθήσομεν. ἁρμόσει
δ' ἐν τοῖς ἐπαίνοις καὶ πολλοῖς ὀνόμασι περὶ ἕκαστον χρησάμενον μεγαλοπρεπῆ τὴν λέξιν ποιῆσαι.¹²

Τὸν δ' αὐτὸν τρόπον ἐπὶ τῶν μοχθηρῶν πραγ-

---

¹ τὰ add. Sp.   ² Sp.: ἀεί.
³ Finckh: καὶ ποῖός τις aut καὶ ποῖ τις.
⁴ Hammer: ὅς.
⁵ σχοίη . . . ὅστις Sauppe: ἔσχεν καὶ τοιοῦτο (aut
οὕτω) τις.
⁶ v.l. τάξομεν.   ⁷ v.l. παρὰ (locus vix sanus?).
⁸ πάλιν ⟨διέξιμεν⟩ Sauppe.

are narrating seem great by comparing them with
other noteworthy achievements on a small scale.
You must also magnify his deeds by conjecture, thus :
' Yet one who has become such a philosopher when
young is likely to make a great advance when he gets
older,' or ' One who has endured the toils of the 35
gymnasium so sturdily will be an ardent devotee of
the toilsome labour of philosophy.' This is how we
shall magnify his record by using conjecture.

When we have gone through the events of the
youth's early manhood and have ended this section
with maxims and considerations, after either a concise 1441 b
recapitulation of what we have said already or a final
conclusion in respect of the section dealing with
conduct, we shall next set out the achievements of the
person we are praising when an adult. We shall put
first his justice, and after having magnified this in a 5
manner similar to what has been said already, we
shall come to his wisdom, if he possesses that virtue ;
and after going through this in the same way, we shall
set out his courage, if he has it, and having in turn
run through the amplification of this, when we have
reached the conclusion of this section and have
gone through all the species of virtue, we shall 10
recapitulate what we have said before in a summary,
and then affix either a maxim or else a consideration as
a conclusion to the whole speech. In eulogies it will
be appropriate to add dignity to the style by speaking
about each topic with considerable fullness.

We shall compose accusations in the same way,

---

⁹ ἀνὴρ ⟨γενόμενος⟩ ? Rac.
¹⁰ τάξομεν om. v.l.
¹¹ τελευταῖον ἤδη Wurmer.
¹² [ἁρμόσει . . . ποιῆσαι] Ipfelkofer.

15 μάτων κακολογοῦντες¹ τὰς κατηγορίας συστήσομεν.
δεῖ δὲ μὴ σκώπτειν ὃν ἂν κακολογῶμεν, ἀλλὰ
διεξιέναι τὸν βίον αὐτοῦ· μᾶλλον γὰρ οἱ λόγοι τῶν
σκωμμάτων καὶ τοὺς ἀκούοντας πείθουσι καὶ τοὺς
κακολογουμένους λυποῦσιν· τὰ μὲν γὰρ σκώμματα
20 στοχάζεται τῆς ἰδέας ἢ τῆς οὐσίας, οἱ δὲ λόγοι τῶν
ἠθῶν καὶ τῶν τρόπων εἰσὶν οἷον εἰκόνες. φυλάττου
δὲ καὶ τὰς αἰσχρὰς πράξεις μὴ αἰσχροῖς ὀνόμασι
λέγειν, ἵνα μὴ² διαβάλῃς τὸ ἦθος, ἀλλὰ τὰ τοιαῦτα
αἰνιγματωδῶς ἑρμηνεύειν, καὶ ἑτέρων πραγμάτων
ὀνόμασι χρώμενος³ δηλοῦν τὸ πρᾶγμα. χρὴ δὲ καὶ
ἐν ταῖς κακολογίαις εἰρωνεύεσθαι καὶ καταγελᾶν
25 τοῦ ἐναντίου ἐφ' οἷς σεμνύνεται, καὶ ἰδίᾳ μὲν καὶ
ὀλίγων παρόντων ἀτιμάζειν αὐτόν, ἐν δὲ τοῖς
ὄχλοις κοινὰς μάλιστα κατηγορίας λοιδορεῖν· αὔξειν
δὲ καὶ ταπεινοῦν τὸν αὐτὸν τρόπον τὰς κακολογίας
ὅνπερ καὶ τὰ ἐγκώμια.

Περὶ μὲν οὖν τούτων τῶν εἰδῶν ἐντεῦθεν εἰδή-
σομεν τὴν χρῆσιν.

30 XXXVI. Λοιπὸν δ' ἐστὶν ἡμῖν εἶδος τό τε κατηγορικὸν καὶ⁴ τὸ ἐξεταστικόν. ταῦτα πάλιν ὡς ἐν
τῷ δικανικῷ γένει συνθήσομεν καὶ τάξομεν⁵ διέλθωμεν.

Πρῶτον μὲν οὖν ἐν τοῖς προοιμίοις προθήσομεν
τὸ πρᾶγμα περὶ οὗ κατηγορήσομεν ἢ ἀπολογησό-
μεθα, ὥσπερ ἐπὶ τῶν ἄλλων εἰδῶν. προσέχειν
35 δὲ παρακαλέσομεν ἐκ τῶν αὐτῶν ὧν ἐν τῷ προ-

---

¹ v.l. πραγματολογοῦντες.
² [μὴ] ? Rac.
³ Rac.: χρωμένους.
⁴ καὶ ⟨τὸ ἀπολογητικὸν καὶ⟩ Sp.
⁵ Sp.: τάξομεν καὶ.

1441 b

by employing vituperation with reference to wicked 15
actions. We must not scoff at the person we are (2) *Topics*
vituperating, but recount his career ; for narratives *of vitupera-*
carry more conviction with the hearers than scoffs, *tion.*
and also annoy the victim more, since scoffs are aimed
at men's appearance or their possessions, but narratives mirror their characters and manners. Be careful 20
not to designate even his base actions by base names,
in order that you may not traduce his character,[a] but
to indicate such matters allusively, and to reveal
the fact by using words that denote something else.
In vituperations also you should employ irony, and
ridicule your opponent for the things on which he 25
prides himself ; and in private when few people are
present you should try to discredit him, but in crowded
assemblies your abuse should consist chiefly of ordinary charges ; and you must amplify and minimize
vituperations in the same way as eulogies.

As to these species of oratory this will teach us the
mode of employing them.

XXXVI. We still have left the oratory of accusa- 30
tion and that of investigation. Let us in turn discuss *Structure of*
how we shall construct and arrange these species *forensic*
under the forensic genus. *oration.*

First then, as in the case of the other species, we (a) *For the*
shall set out in the introduction the action with which *prosecution :*
our accusation or defence[b] is concerned. And we (1) *Intro-*
shall use the same means to appeal for attention in 35 *duction.*

---

[a] ' In order not to violate conventional feeling ' (Forster).
Perhaps the negative should be omitted, giving ' To discredit
his character, do not openly specify his base actions but
merely hint at them.'
[b] Included as the opposite of accusation and falling into
the same class of oratory ; in the next sentence only defence
is specified.

τρεπτικῷ καὶ ἐν τῷ ἀπολογητικῷ.¹ ἔτι δὲ καὶ περὶ
τῆς εὐμενείας, τῷ μὲν εὖ διακειμένῳ² μηδὲ³ διαβεβλημένῳ τῷ πρὸς αὐτὸν ἢ πρὸς τὸ πρᾶγμα ἢ
1442 a πρὸς τὸν λόγον τοὺς ἀκούοντας δυσχεραίνειν, τὸν
αὐτὸν τρόπον ὡς περὶ ἐκείνων εἴρηται τὴν εὐμένειαν παρασκευαστέον⁴· τῷ δὲ μήτε εὖ μήτε
κακῶς διακειμένῳ⁵ καὶ τῷ⁶ ἢ ἐκ τοῦ παροιχομένου
χρόνου ἢ ἐκ τοῦ παρόντος ἢ δι᾽ ἑαυτὸν ἢ τὸ
5 πρᾶγμα ἢ τὸν λόγον διαβεβλημένῳ ἔνια μὲν μεμιγ-
μένως ἔνια δ᾽ ἰδίως πρὸς εὐμένειαν ποριστέον.⁷

Οὗτος μὲν οὖν ὁ τρόπος ἔσται δι᾽ οὗ τὴν εὐμένειαν παρασκευαστέον. τοὺς μὲν γὰρ μήτε εὖ
μήτε κακῶς διακειμένους αὐτοὺς μὲν συντόμως
ἐπαινετέον καὶ τοὺς ἐναντίους κακολογητέον, δεῖ
10 δὲ αὐτοὺς ἐκ τούτων ἐπαινεῖν ὧν μάλιστα μέτεστι
τοῖς ἀκούουσιν, λέγω δὲ φιλόπολιν φιλέταιρον
εὐχάριστον ἐλεήμονα καὶ τὰ τοιαῦτα, τὸν δ᾽ ἐναντίον
κακολογεῖν ἐκ τούτων ἐφ᾽ οἷς οἱ ἀκούοντες
ὀργιοῦνται, ταῦτα δ᾽ ἐστὶ μισόπολιν μισόφιλον ἀ-
χάριστον ἀνελεήμονα καὶ τὰ τοιαῦτα. χρὴ δὲ καὶ
15 τοὺς δικαστὰς ἐπαίνῳ θεραπεῦσαι ὡς δικασταὶ
δίκαιοι καὶ δεινοί εἰσιν. συμπαραληπτέον δὲ καὶ
τὰς ἐλαττώσεις, εἴ που τῶν ἀντιδίκων κατα-
δεεστέρως ἔχει πρὸς τὸ λέγειν ἢ πράττειν ἢ ἄλλο
τι τῶν περὶ τὸν ἀγῶνα. πρὸς δὲ τούτοις ἐμβλητέον
τό τε δίκαιον καὶ τὸ νόμιμον καὶ τὸ συμφέρον καὶ
20 τὰ τούτοις ἀκόλουθα. τῷ μὲν οὖν μήτε εὖ μήτε

---

¹ ἀποτρεπτικῷ Sp.
² post διακειμένῳ add. ἐκ τοῦ παροιχομένου χρόνου ἢ τοῦ
παρόντος καὶ codd.: del. Sp.
³ Sp.: μήτε.
⁴ Rac.: ποριστέον.
⁵ post διακειμένῳ v.l. add. τὴν εὐμένειαν παρασκευαστέον.

1441 b

defensive oratory as in the oratory of exhortation.
Again, as to goodwill, for a client towards whom the
audience is favourably disposed, and not prejudiced
through being irritated by his personality or his conduct or his speech, goodwill must be secured in the 1442 a
same way as has been described in the former cases.
For one towards whom they are neither favourable
nor unfavourable, and also one against whom they
have been previously or are now prejudiced either on
account of his personality or of his conduct or his
speech, we must produce reasons for goodwill, some 5
in combination and others in detail.

That will be the way in which we must secure goodwill. For when the disposition of the audience is
neither favourable nor unfavourable, we must briefly
praise our clients themselves, while running down
their adversaries. We must praise them for the
qualities that most concern the audience—I mean 10
loyalty to country and friends, gratitude, compassion
and the like ; and we must abuse an adversary for
qualities that will provoke the anger of the audience
—these are disloyalty to country and friends, ingratitude, hardness of heart and so on. We ought also to
court the favour of the jury by praising them for their 15
justice and competence in their office. We must also
bring in any matters in which our client is at a dis-
advantage as compared with the other side with
regard to word or deed or anything else concerning
the suit. In addition we must bring in considerations
of justice, law and expediency and connected matters.
These are the means by which we must secure the 20

---

⁶ καὶ τῷ add. Hammer.
⁷ v.l. om. πρὸς . . . ποριστέον.

1442 a

κακῶς διακειμένῳ ἐκ τούτων ἐν τοῖς δικασταῖς τὴν
εὔνοιαν ποριστέον.

Τῷ δὲ διαβεβλημένῳ, ἐὰν μὲν ἐκ τοῦ παροιχομένου χρόνου αἱ διαβολαὶ ὦσι περὶ τὸν λόγον,[1]
ἴσμεν ὡς δεῖ τὰ τοιαῦτα λύειν ἐκ τῶν προτέρων·
ἐὰν δὲ ἐκ τοῦ παρόντος χρόνου περὶ αὐτὸν τὸν
25 ἄνθρωπον, ἀναγκαῖον διαβεβλῆσθαι ἐὰν ἀπρεπὴς ᾖ
τῷ παρόντι ἀγῶνι ἢ ὑπεναντίος τοῖς ἐγκλήμασιν ἢ
ὁμολογούμενος τῇ κατηγορίᾳ. ἀπρεπὴς μὲν οὖν
γένοιτ᾽ ἂν ἐὰν ἀγωνίζηται νεώτερος ἢ πρεσβύτερος
ὑπὲρ ἄλλου, ὑπεναντίος δὲ ἐάν τις ἰσχυρὸς ὢν
ἀσθενεῖ δικάζηται αἰκίας, ἢ ἐάν τις ὑβριστὴς ὢν
30 ὕβριν ἐγκαλῇ σώφρονι, ἢ ἐάν τις πάνυ πλουσίῳ
δικάζηται πάνυ πένης χρημάτων ἐγκαλῶν. οἱ μὲν
οὖν τοιοῦτοι ὑπεναντίοι εἰσὶ τοῖς ἐγκλήμασιν·
ὁμολογούμενος δ᾽ ἔσται, ἐάν τις ἰσχυρὸς ὢν ὑπὸ
ἀσθενοῦς αἰκίας διώκηται, ἢ ἐάν τις κλέπτης δοκῶν
35 εἶναι κλοπῆς δίκην φεύγῃ· ὅλως δὲ οἱ τὰς περὶ
αὑτῶν δόξας ὁμοιοτρόπους αὑτοῖς ἔχοντες ὁμο-
λογούμενοι τοῖς ἐγκλήμασι δόξουσιν εἶναι. περὶ μὲν
οὖν αὐτὸν τὸν ἄνθρωπον ἐκ τοῦ παρόντος χρόνου
τοιαῦται γενήσονται διαβολαί, αἱ δὲ περὶ τὸ πρᾶγμα
συμβαίνουσαι,[2] ἐάν τις πραγματεύηται πρὸς οἰ-
1442 b κείους φίλους ἢ ξένους ἢ ἰδίους,[3] ἢ περὶ μικρῶν ἢ
αἰσχρῶν· ταῦτα γὰρ ἀδοξίαν τοῖς δικαζομένοις
ποιεῖ.

Πῶς οὖν τὰς διαβολὰς τὰς προειρημένας ἀπο-
λύσομεν, τοῦτο δηλώσω. δύο μὲν δὴ στοιχεῖα

---

[1] [περὶ τὸν λόγον] Sp.   [2] συμβαίνουσι Sp.
[3] [ἢ ἰδίους] Kayser.

goodwill of the jury for persons towards whom they are neither well nor ill disposed.

For a man against whom they are prejudiced, if the prejudices turn on something he has said in the past, we know from what has gone before how to dissipate difficulties of this sort. If the prejudices arise from the present and concern him personally, there is bound to be prejudice against him if his personality is unsuited for the case in progress or incompatible with the accusations he is making or consistent with the charge brought against him. There would be unsuitability if one who was too young or too old appeared on behalf of another ; incompatibility if a strong man sued a weak one for assault, or a violent man brought a charge of violence against a well-behaved one, or a very poor man sued a very rich one on a charge of defrauding him of money : such are cases where the personality of the litigants is incompatible with the charges. There will be compatibility if a strong man is prosecuted for assault by a weak man, or if a charge of theft is brought against a person with a reputation for stealing ; and in general, the charges will be thought to be consistent with the litigants if their reputations tally with their actual personalities. Such are the prejudices that will arise at the time in connexion with the litigant's personality. Prejudices occurring in regard to his action will be raised if a man takes proceedings against relations or guests or private friends, or about petty or discreditable matters : these things bring litigants into disrepute.

I shall now show how we shall get rid of the aforesaid prejudices.   I maintain that there are two elementary

λέγω κοινὰ κατὰ πάντων, τὸ μέν, οἷς ἂν νομίζῃς
5 τοὺς κριτὰς ἐπιπλήξειν, προκαταλάμβανε αὐτοὺς
καὶ ἐπίπληττε· τὸ δὲ ἕτερον εἰ¹ τὰς πράξεις
μάλιστα μὲν εἰς τοὺς ἀντιδίκους ἀποτρέψεις, εἰ δὲ
μή, εἰς ἄλλους τινάς, προφάσει χρώμενος ὅτι οὐχ
ἑκὼν ἀλλ' ὑπὸ τῶν ἀνταγωνιστῶν ἀναγκαζόμενος
εἰς τὸν ἀγῶνα κατέστης. καθ' ἑκάστην δὲ τὴν
10 διαβολὴν τάδε χρὴ προφασίζεσθαι, τὸν μὲν νεώτερον πρεσβυτέρων φίλων ἀπορίαν τῶν ἀγωνιου-
μένων ὑπὲρ αὐτοῦ, ἢ μέγεθος ἀδικημάτων, ἢ
πλῆθος,² ἢ προθεσμίαν χρόνου, ἢ ἄλλο τι τοιοῦτον.
ἐὰν δὲ ὑπὲρ ἄλλου λέγῃς, ῥητέον ὡς διὰ φιλίαν
συνηγορεῖς, ἢ δι' ἔχθραν τοῦ ἀντιδίκου, ἢ διὰ τὸ
15 τοῖς πράγμασι παραγενέσθαι, ἢ διὰ τὸ κοινῇ συμφέρον, ἢ διὰ τὸ ἔρημον εἶναι καὶ ἀδικεῖσθαι ᾧ
συνηγορεῖς. ἐὰν δὲ ὁμολογούμενος τῷ ἐγκλήματι
ἢ ὑπεναντίος τῇ κατηγορίᾳ γένηται,³ τῇ τε προκαταλήψει χρῆσθαι καὶ λέγειν ὡς οὐ δίκαιον καὶ
νόμιμον οὐδὲ συμφέρον ἐκ τῆς ὑπολήψεως ἢ τῆς
20 ὑποψίας κατακρίνειν πρὶν τοῦ πράγματος ἀκοῦσαι.
τὰς μὲν οὖν περὶ τὸν ἄνθρωπον αὐτὸν διαβολὰς
οὕτω λύσομεν, τὰς δὲ περὶ τὸ πρᾶγμα οὕτως
ἀπωσόμεθα, τὴν αἰτίαν εἰς τοὺς ἐναντίους⁴ τρέ-
ποντες, ἢ λοιδορίαν ἐγκαλοῦντες αὐτοῖς ἢ ἀδικίαν
ἢ πλεονεξίαν ἢ φιλονεικίαν ἢ ὀργήν, προφασιζόμενοι
25 ὅτι τοῦ δικαίου δι' ἄλλου τρόπου τυχεῖν ἀδύνατον.
τὰς μὲν οὖν ἰδίας διαβολὰς ἐπὶ τῶν δικαστῶν⁵ οὕτω

---

¹ v.l. εἰς. ² ἢ πλῆθος hic Sp.: infra post χρόνου.
³ γένη, δεῖ Sp.
⁴ Sp.: τὸ ἐναντίον aut τὸν ἐναντίον.
⁵ v.l. δικαστηρίων.

rules that apply to all cases in common. The first rule is this—whatever arguments you think your adversaries will use to make an impression on the judges, anticipate them and make the impression yourself. The second way is if you shift the responsibility for the acts, if possible, on to your opponents, or failing that, on some other persons, pleading that you have become involved in the suit not of your own will but under compulsion from your adversaries. The following excuses must be put forward to correspond with each particular prejudice. A comparatively young man must plead lack of friends to contest the case on his behalf, or the magnitude and number of the offences with which he is charged, or the time-limit fixed, or something else of the sort. If you are speaking on behalf of another person, say that your motive for advocating his cause is friendship, or enmity for his opponent, or your having been present at the events, or the public interest, or your client's isolated position and the wrong that has been done to him. If his personality is consistent with the charge brought against him or not compatible with the charge that he is bringing, employ anticipation, and say that it is unjust and illegal and inexpedient to convict on the strength of an opinion or a suspicion before hearing the facts. This is how we shall dissipate prejudices felt against a man personally. Those that turn on his conduct we shall repulse thus—by turning the blame against his opponents, accusing them either of slander or injustice or cheating or contentiousness or bad temper, pleading that it is impossible to get justice by any other means. This is how we shall dissipate private prejudices in the case of the

1442 b

λύσομεν, τὰς δὲ κοινὰς πᾶσι τοῖς εἴδεσιν, ὡς ἐπὶ
τῶν προτέρων εἰδῶν εἴρηται.

Τάξομεν δὲ τὰ δικανικὰ προοίμια τὸν αὐτὸν
τρόπον ὅνπερ καὶ τὰ δημηγορικά· κατὰ τὸν αὐτὸν
30 δὲ τρόπον[1] καὶ τὰς ἀπαγγελίας ἢ[2] συνάψομεν τῷ
προοιμίῳ ἢ[3] περὶ τὰ μέρη πιστὰς καὶ δικαίας
ἀποφανοῦμεν ἢ αὐτὰς ἐφ'[4] ἑαυτῶν σωματοειδεῖς
ποιησόμεθα.

Τὰ δὲ μετὰ ταῦτα ἔσται βεβαίωσις, ἂν μὲν
ἀντιλέγηται τὰ πράγματα ὑπὸ τῶν ἀντιδίκων, ἐκ
35 τῶν πίστεων, ἂν δὲ ὁμολογῆται, ἐκ τῶν δικαίων καὶ
τῶν συμφερόντων καὶ ἐκ τῶν τούτοις ἀκολούθων.
τάττειν δὲ δεῖ τῶν μὲν πίστεων πρώτας τὰς μαρ-
τυρίας καὶ τὰ ἐκ τῶν βασάνων ἡμῖν ὁμολογηθέντα,
ἂν ὑπάρχῃ. ἔπειτα βεβαιοῦν, ἂν μὲν πιθανὰ ᾖ,
γνώμαις καὶ ἐνθυμήμασιν, ἐὰν δὲ μὴ παντελῶς
1443 a πιθανὰ ᾖ, τῷ εἰκότι, ἔπειτα τοῖς παραδείγμασι καὶ
τοῖς τεκμηρίοις καὶ τοῖς σημείοις καὶ τοῖς ἐλέγχοις,
τελευταῖον δὲ τοῖς ἐνθυμήμασι καὶ ταῖς γνωμο-
λογίαις. ἐὰν δὲ ὁμολογῆται τὰ πράγματα, τὰς μὲν
πίστεις ἐατέον, τῇ δὲ δικαιολογίᾳ ὥσπερ ἐν τοῖς
5 ἔμπροσθεν χρηστέον. καὶ τοῦτον μὲν τὸν τρόπον
βεβαιώσομεν.

Μετὰ δὲ τὴν βεβαίωσιν τὰ πρὸς[5] τοὺς ἀντιδίκους
τάττοντες προκαταληψόμεθα αὐτῶν τὰ ἐπίδοξα
λέγεσθαι. ἐὰν μὲν οὖν ἐξαρνῶνται τὰ πράγματα,[6]
τὰς μὲν ὑφ' ἡμῶν πίστεις εἰρημένας αὐξητέον
10 τὰς δ' ὑπ' ἐκείνων μελλούσας λέγεσθαι διασυρτέον
καὶ ταπεινωτέον. ἐὰν δὲ ὁμολογοῦντες μέλλωσιν[7]

---

[1] v.l. λόγον.   [2] ἢ add. Finckh.
[3] ἢ Finckh: καὶ ἢ.   [4] Pacius: ὑφ'.   [5] v.l. ἐπὶ.
[6] Forster: τὸ πρᾶγμα.   [7] Sp.: ὦσι.

judges; public ones [a] we shall remove by all the methods that have been described, as has been said [b] in the case of the previous species of oratory.

In forensic speeches we shall arrange the introduction in the same way as in parliamentary ones, and we shall also deal in the same way with the narra- 30 tives of facts,[c] either attaching them to the introduction or proving their reliability and justice under the various divisions of the speech, or setting them out as a separate section by themselves.

The next section will be confirmation. This will (2) *Proof of* be based on proofs if the facts are denied by the *charges.* opposite party, but on considerations of justice and 35 expediency and the like if they are admitted. First among the proofs must be placed the evidence of witnesses and confessions that we have obtained by torture, if any be available. Next this evidence must be confirmed by means of maxims and general considerations, if it be convincing, or if not entirely convincing, by probability, and then by examples, 1443 a tokens, signs and refutations, and by considerations and the enunciation of maxims to finish with. If the facts are admitted, proofs may be passed over, and legal arguments employed, as in the earlier passages. This is the way in which we shall effect 5 confirmation.

After confirmation we shall put our case against our (3) *Anticipa-* opponents, anticipating their probable arguments. If *tion of* their line is to deny the acts, we must amplify the *case.* proofs that we have put forward and pull to pieces 10 and minimize those that are going to be put forward by them. If they are going to admit the acts and try

---

[a] ' Those that concern a man's public life ' (Forster).
    [b] 1436 b 37 ff.   [c] *Cf.* 1438 b 24.

ἔννομα καὶ δίκαια ἀποφαίνειν κατὰ τοὺς γεγραμμένους νόμους, οὓς μὲν ἡμεῖς παρεσχόμεθα καὶ τοὺς
ὁμοίους τούτοις δικαίους καὶ καλοὺς καὶ συμ-
φέροντας τῷ κοινῷ τῆς πόλεως καὶ[1] κεκριμένους ὑπὸ
τῶν πολλῶν τοιούτους εἶναι πειρατέον ἐπιδεικνύειν,
15 τοὺς δὲ τῶν ἀντιδίκων τὰ ἐναντία. ἐὰν δὲ μὴ
ἐνδέχηται ταῦτα λέγειν, ὑπομίμνησκε τοὺς δικαστὰς
ὅτι οὐχ ὑπὲρ τοῦ νόμου ἀλλὰ τοῦ πράγματος δικά-
ζουσιν, ὁμόσαντες κατὰ τοὺς νόμους τοὺς κειμένους
τὴν ψῆφον οἴσειν, καὶ δίδασκε ὅτι οὐ νομοθετεῖν
νῦν προσήκει ἀλλ' ἐν ταῖς περὶ τούτων κυρίαις
20 ἡμέραις. ἂν δ' ἡμῖν συμβαίνῃ παρὰ μοχθηροὺς
δοκοῦντας[2] εἶναι νόμους τὸ πρᾶγμα πεπρᾶχθαι,
ῥητέον ὡς οὐ νόμος ἀλλ' ἀνομία τὸ τοιοῦτόν ἐστιν·
ὁ μὲν γὰρ νόμος ἐπὶ τὸ[3] ὠφελεῖν τίθεται, οὗτος δὲ
βλάπτει τὴν πόλιν. ῥητέον δὲ καὶ ὡς οὐ παρα-
25 νομήσουσιν ἂν τούτῳ τῷ νόμῳ ἐναντίαν ψῆφον
θῶνται, ἀλλὰ νομοθετήσουσιν ὥστε μὴ χρῆσθαι
δόγμασι πονηροῖς καὶ παρανόμοις. δεῖ δὲ καὶ
τοῦτο συμβιβάζειν, ὡς οὐδεὶς νόμος κωλύει τὸ
κοινὸν εὖ ποιεῖν, τοὺς δὲ φαύλους νόμους ἀκύρους
ποιεῖν εὐεργετεῖν τὴν πόλιν ἐστίν. περὶ μὲν οὖν
τῶν σαφῶς εἰρημένων νόμων, ὁποίους[4] ἂν αὐτῶν[5]
30 ἔχωμεν, ἐκ τῶν τοιούτων προκαταλαμβάνοντες
ἀντιλέγειν εὐπορήσομεν. περὶ δὲ τῶν ἀμφιβόλων
ἐὰν οὕτως ὑπολαμβάνωσιν ὡς σοὶ συμφέρει, δεῖ
ταῦτα ὑποδεικνύειν· ἂν δ' ὡς ὁ ἐναντίος λέγει, χρὴ
διδάσκειν ὡς ὁ νομοθέτης οὐ[6] τοῦτο διενοεῖτο ἀλλ'[7]
ὃ σὺ λέγεις, καὶ ὅτι συμφέρει αὐτοῖς οὕτω λέγειν

---

[1] καὶ add. Bekker.   [2] v.l. τὸ παρὰ μοχθηροῖς δοκοῦσιν.
[3] v.l. τῷ.   [4] ὁποτέρους ? Rac.   [5] αὐτοῖς Kayser.
[6] οὐ: αὐτὸ Halm.   [7] ἀλλ' add. Sp.

to prove that they were legal and just according to
the laws enacted, we must attempt to show that the
laws adduced by us and those like them are just and
honourable and advantageous to the common weal,
and have been judged to be so by the general body of
the citizens, and that those quoted by the other side 15
are the opposite.   If it is not feasible to take this line,
remind the jury that they are giving judgement not
about the law but about the fact, as they have sworn
that they will give their vote according to the laws
established ; and instruct them that it is not proper
to make laws on the present occasion but on the
regular days appointed for that purpose.   If the 20
position is that the action committed was contrary to
laws that seem to be bad ones, we must say that a
regulation of that sort is not law but the negation of
law, inasmuch as the law is laid down for the public
benefit, but this law is injurious to the state.   And
we must also say that if the jury give a verdict con- 25
travening this law, they will not be acting illegally
but legislating to prevent the execution of resolutions
that are bad and illegal.   Also we must bring forward
the point that no law forbids acting for the good of
the community, and that it is a public service to annul
bad laws.   Such considerations as these will give us 30
plenty to say against our opponent's case in anticipation with regard to laws that are clearly expressed,
whatever class of them we have before us.   About
laws that are ambiguous, if the jury understand them
in the sense favourable to you, you must indicate that
interpretation ; if they accept your opponent's view,
you must explain that the legislator had not that
meaning in mind but the one you put forward, and
that for the law to have your meaning is to their

1443 a

35 τὸν νόμον. ἐὰν δὲ μὴ δυνατὸς ᾖς ἐπὶ τὸ ἐναντίον
μεθιστάναι, δείκνυε ὡς οὐδὲν ἄλλο λέγειν δύναται
ὁ νόμος[1] ἢ ὃ σύ. καὶ περὶ μὲν νόμων, ὡς δεῖ
χρῆσθαι, τοῦτον τὸν τρόπον μετιὼν εὐπορήσεις.

Καθόλου δέ, ἂν ὁμολογήσαντες ἐκ τῶν δικαίων
40 καὶ τῶν νομίμων τὴν ἀπολογίαν ποιεῖσθαι μέλλωσιν, ἐκ τούτων τὰ ἐπίδοξα ῥηθήσεσθαι προκατα-
ληπτέον. ἐὰν δὲ ὁμολογήσαντες συγγνώμης ἀξιῶσι
1443 b τυχεῖν, ὧδε χρὴ περιαιρεῖσθαι τὰ τοιαῦτα τῶν
ἀντιδίκων. πρῶτον μὲν λεκτέον ὡς κακοηθέστερον
ἦν, καὶ ὡς τὰ τοιαῦτα ἐξαμαρτάνειν φασὶν ὅταν
γνωσθῶσιν, ὥστε " εἰ τούτῳ συγγνώμην ἔχετε, καὶ
τοὺς ἄλλους πάντας τῶν τιμωριῶν ἀφήσετε." ἔτι
5 δὲ λέγε ὡς " εἰ τῶν ὁμολογούντων ἐξαμαρτάνειν
ἀποψηφιεῖσθε, πῶς τῶν μὴ ὁμολογούντων κατα-
ψηφιεῖσθε;" λεκτέον δὲ ὅτι " εἰ καὶ ἐξήμαρτεν,
οὐκ ἐμὲ δεῖ διὰ τὴν τούτου ἁμαρτίαν ζημιοῦσθαι."
πρὸς δὲ τούτοις ῥητέον ὡς οὐδὲ ὁ νομοθέτης τοῖς
ἁμαρτάνουσι συγγνώμην ἔχει· οὐκοῦν δίκαιον οὐδὲ
10 τοὺς δικαστὰς κατὰ τοὺς νόμους κρίνοντας. ἐκ μὲν
οὖν τῶν τοιούτων τὰς συγγνώμας περιαιρησόμεθα,
καθάπερ καὶ ἐν ἀρχαῖς δεδηλώκαμεν· συλλήβδην δὲ
τὰ ὑπὸ τῶν ἀντιδίκων μέλλοντα λέγεσθαι καὶ πρὸς
πίστιν καὶ δικαιολογίαν καὶ συγγνώμην ἐκ τῶν
προειρημένων προκαταληψόμεθα.

15 Μετὰ δὲ ταῦτα[2] τὴν αἰτίαν ἀναλογιστέον[3] ἐν
κεφαλαίῳ τοῦ λόγου ὅλου,[4] καὶ συντόμως, ἐὰν
ἐνδέχηται, πρὸς μὲν τοὺς ἐναντίους ἔχθραν ἢ ὀργὴν

---

[1] Kayser: λέγειν ὁ ἐναντίος δύναται νόμος.
[2] v.l. ταύτην.   [3] v.l. ἀναλογητέον.
[4] Kayser: τὸν λόγον ὅλον (μετὰ δὲ ταῦτα τὴν αἰτιολογίαν
παλιλλογητέον ἐν κεφαλαίῳ τοῦ λόγου ὅλου ? Hammer).

1443 a
35

advantage. If you cannot turn the law the other
way round, show that it cannot possibly mean anything else than what you say. If you follow this
method you will have no difficulty as to how to deal
with the point of law.

In general, if your opponents are going to admit
the facts and base their defence on principles of 40
justice and legality, you must anticipate what is
likely to be said under those heads. If while admitting the facts they claim to be granted pardon, this is 1443 b
the way in which you must deprive your adversaries
of pleas of that nature. First you must say that their
conduct was really more unprincipled, and that those
are the sort of offences that they admit when they are
found out, and consequently ' If you pardon this man
you will absolve everybody else too from punishment.'
Further say : ' If you give a verdict of Not guilty on 5
those who confess their offence, how will you be able
to vote Guilty on those who do not confess ? ' And
you must say : ' Even if he is guilty, I ought not to be
punished for his offence.' Furthermore argue that
even the lawgiver does not pardon offenders ; neither,
therefore, is it right for the jury to do so when giving 10
judgement according to the laws. We shall use
arguments like these to deprive our adversaries of
pleas for pardon, as we have also shown at the
beginning ; and generally, we shall anticipate what
our adversaries are going to say to prove their case on
points of principle and in pleading for pardon by
employing the considerations previously stated.

After this, in a summary of the whole speech we 15
must repeat the charge, and if feasible briefly inspire (4) *Recapitu*
the jury with hatred or anger or jealousy against our *lation.*

1443 b

ἢ φθόνον τοῖς δικασταῖς ἐμποιητέον πρὸς δ' ἡμᾶς
φιλίαν ἢ χάριν ἢ ἔλεον. ὅθεν δὲ ταῦτα γίνεται, ἐν
τῷ δημηγορικῷ εἴδει[1] ἐπὶ τῶν προτροπῶν καὶ
20 ἀποτροπῶν εἰρήκαμεν, καὶ ἐν τῷ ἀπολογητικῷ
εἴδει πάλιν ἐπὶ τελευτῆς διέξιμεν.

Τὸν μὲν οὖν πρῶτον λόγον, ἐὰν κατηγορῶμεν ἐν
τοῖς δικανικοῖς, οὕτω συνθήσομεν καὶ τάξομεν.

Ἐὰν δὲ ἀπολογώμεθα, τὸ μὲν προοίμιον ὁμοιοτρόπως τῷ κατηγοροῦντι[2] συστήσομεν, τῶν δὲ
25 κατηγορουμένων ἃ μὲν εἰδέναι τοὺς ἀκούοντας
ἐποίησε, παραλείψομεν, ἃ δὲ δοξάζειν, ταῦτα προθέμενοι μετὰ τὸ προοίμιον διαλύσομεν, τούς τε μάρτυρας καὶ τὰς βασάνους καὶ τοὺς ὅρκους ἀπίστους
ποιήσομεν, ὡς προακήκοας, εἰ μὲν τὰ πράγματα
30 πιστὰ εἴη,[3] τὴν ὑπὲρ αὐτῶν ἀπολογίαν ἐπὶ τὸν
ἐκ τοῦ παραλειπομένου τόπον μεταβιβάζοντες, εἰ
δ' εἶεν οἱ μάρτυρες οἱ βασανισθέντες πιστοί, ἐπὶ
τὸν λόγον ἢ τὴν πρᾶξιν ἢ ὅ τι ἂν ἄλλο ἔχῃς ἐπὶ[4]
τῶν ἐναντίων πιστότατον. ἂν δὲ τὸ λυσιτελὲς ἢ τὸ
ἔθος ἐπιφέρων σοῦ κατηγορήσῃ, ἀπολογοῦ μάλιστα
35 μὲν ὡς ἀλυσιτελές[5] σοί[6] ἐστι τὸ κατηγορούμενον,
εἰ δὲ μή, ὅτι οὐκ εἴθισαι τὰ τοιαῦτα πράττειν οὔτε
σὺ οὔτε οἱ σοὶ ὅμοιοι, ἢ ὅτι οὐ τοῦτον τὸν τρόπον.
τὸ μὲν οὖν εἰκὸς οὕτω λύσεις.

Τὸ δὲ παράδειγμα πρῶτον μέν, ἂν δύνῃ, δείκνυε
ὡς οὐχ ὅμοιόν ἐστι τῷ ἐγκαλουμένῳ, εἰ δὲ μή,
40 ἕτερον φέρε αὐτὸς παράδειγμα ἐκ τῶν ἐναντίων
παρὰ τὸ εἰκὸς γενόμενον. τὸ δὲ τεκμήριον λύε

---

[1] εἴδει Rac.: καὶ (om. nonnulli).
[2] κατηγορικῷ Kayser. [3] Sp.: ῇ. [4] [ἐπὶ] Sp.
[5] Bekker: λυσιτελές. [6] σοί add. Kayser.

---

[a] Cf. ' Cui bono ? ' [b] Cf. 1429 a 21.

opponents and friendship or favour or pity for ourselves. We have said how these feelings are to be
produced when we were dealing with persuasion and
dissuasion in the section on parliamentary oratory, 20
and we shall go over it again in the section at the end
on defence.

This, then, is how we shall construct and arrange
the opening speech in forensic cases if we are for
the prosecution.

If we are for the defence, we shall construct the 25
introduction in the same way as the prosecutor : we
shall pass over charges of which he gave his hearers
convincing proofs, and put forward after our introduction and refute those which he only got them to accept
as probable ; and we shall discredit the witnesses, and
statements made under torture and on oath, in the
way which you have heard already,—if the facts be
convincing, by transposing our defence about them 30
into the form based on omission ; if the witnesses
that have been examined under torture are trustworthy, by passing over to the argument or action
or anything else that is your most convincing point
against your opponents. If his accusation is based on
the ground that you stood to gain by the act,[a] or that
it is your habit, plead in defence, if possible, that the
action you are charged with would not have been
profitable to you, or else that it is not your habit nor 35
the habit of people like you to do such acts, or not to
do them in that way. This is how you will refute the
argument from probability.

In dealing with an example,[b] first show if you can
that it does not resemble the act of which you are
accused, or else yourself produce another example to
the contrary that has occurred against probability. 40

*(b) Forensic
oration for
the defence :
(1) Alleged
actions
disproved,*

φράζων παρ' ἃς αἰτίας ἐναντιωθῆναι συνέβη. τὰς
1444 a δὲ γνώμας καὶ τὰ ἐνθυμήματα ἢ παράδοξα ἀπόφαινε ἢ ἀμφίβολα. τὰ δὲ σημεῖα πλειόνων ὄντα[1]
ἀπόφαινε σημεῖα, καὶ μὴ μόνου τοῦ σοὶ ἐγκαλου-
μένου. καὶ τὰ μὲν τῶν ἐναντίων ἐπὶ τὸ ἐναντίον
ἄγοντες ἢ ἐπὶ τὸ ἀμφίβολον ἀπίθανα τοῦτον τὸν
5 τρόπον καταστήσομεν.

"Αν δὲ ὁμολογῶμεν τὰ ἐγκαλούμενα πεποιηκέναι,
ἐκ τῶν δικαίων καὶ νομίμων μετιόντες ἐννομώτερα
καὶ δικαιότερα τὰ ἡμέτερα ἀποδεικνύναι πειρασό-
μεθα. ἐὰν δὲ μὴ τοῦτο ἐνδέχηται, εἰς ἁμάρτημα ἢ
ἀτύχημα καταφεύγοντας καὶ μικρὰς τὰς βλάβας
10 ἀποφαίνοντας, συγγνώμης τυγχάνειν πειρατέον τὸ
μὲν ἁμαρτάνειν κοινὸν πάντων ἀνθρώπων ἐπι-
δεικνύοντας τὸ δ' ἀδικεῖν ἴδιον τῶν πονηρῶν. λέγε
δὲ ὅτι καὶ ἐπιεικὲς καὶ δίκαιον καὶ συμφέρον ἐστὶ
συγγνώμην ἔχειν ταῖς ἁμαρτίαις· οὐδεὶς γὰρ οἶδεν
ἀνθρώπων εἴ τι τοιοῦτον ἄν[2] αὐτῷ συνεμπέσοι.[3]
15 ἀπόφαινε δὲ[4] καὶ τὸν ἐναντίον, εἴ τι ἐξήμαρτεν,
συγγνώμης τυχεῖν ἀξιώσαντ' ἄν.

Μετὰ δὲ[5] ταῦτα αἱ προκαταλήψεις αἱ ὑπὸ τῶν
ἐναντίων εἰρημέναι. τὰς μὲν οὖν ἄλλας ἐξ αὐτῶν
τῶν πραγμάτων εὐπορήσομεν λύειν· ἐὰν δὲ δια-
βάλλωσιν ἡμᾶς ὡς γεγραμμένους λόγους λέγομεν
20 ἢ λέγειν μελετῶμεν ἢ ὡς ἐπὶ μισθῷ τινι συν-
ηγοροῦμεν, χρὴ πρὸς τὰ τοιαῦτα ὁμόσε βαδίζοντας
εἰρωνεύεσθαι, καὶ περὶ μὲν τῆς γραφῆς λέγειν μὴ
κωλύειν τὸν νόμον ἢ αὐτὸν γεγραμμένα λέγειν ἢ
ἐκεῖνον ἄγραφα· τὸν γὰρ νόμον οὐκ ἐᾶν τοιαῦτα[6]

[1] Sp.: ὄντων.   [2] ἄν add. Rac.   [3] v.l. συνεμπέσῃ.
[4] δὲ add. Rac.   [5] δὲ add. Aldus.   [6] τὰ καὶ τά ? Rac.

[a] Cf. 1430 a 14.

1443 b

Refute a token[a] by giving reasons showing that what
really happened was just the opposite. Maxims and 1444 a
considerations you must show to be either paradoxical
or ambiguous. Signs you must show to indicate a
variety of things, and not only the act of which you are
accused. In this way we shall make our opponents'
arguments unconvincing, by showing that they point
in the opposite direction or that they are ambiguous. 5

If, on the other hand, we admit the actions we are *(2) or justi-*
charged with, we shall take the line of justice and *fied, or palliated :*
legality, and we shall endeavour to prove that our
conduct was more legal and more just. If this is not
feasible, we shall have recourse to the plea of error or
of misfortune, and shall show that the damage done
was small, attempting to obtain forgiveness by 10
pointing out that error is common to all mankind,
whereas wrongdoing is peculiar to the wicked. Say
that to forgive error is reasonable and just and
expedient, because no human being knows whether
something of the kind might not befall himself. And
point out that if your opponent had committed an 15
error he too would have asked for pardon.

After this come the anticipations of our case made *(3) antici-*
in the speeches of our opponents. For the most part *pations answered :*
we shall find no difficulty in rebutting them merely
on the strength of the facts ; but if they try to discredit us by saying that we read our speeches, or
practise them beforehand, or that we are acting as 20
advocates for a reward, we must come to close
quarters with suggestions of that sort, in a tone of
irony, and about writing our speech say that the law
does not forbid one to read a written speech oneself
any more than it forbids one's adversary to speak
without notes ; what the law prohibits is certain

1444 a

πράττειν, λέγειν δὲ ὅπως ἄν τις βούληται συγ-
25 χωρεῖν. ῥητέον δὲ καὶ ὅτι "οὕτως ὁ ἐναντίος οἴεται
μεγάλα ἠδικηκέναι ὥστ᾽ οὐ νομίζει με κατ᾽ ἀξίαν
ἄν¹ κατηγορῆσαι εἰ μὴ γράψαιμι² καὶ πολὺν χρόνον
σκεψαίμην." πρὸς³ μὲν οὖν τὰς τῶν γεγραμμένων
λόγων διαβολὰς οὕτως ἀπαντητέον· ἂν δὲ φάσκωσιν
ἡμᾶς λέγειν μανθάνειν καὶ μελετᾶν, ὁμολογήσαντες
30 ἐροῦμεν "ἡμεῖς μὲν οἱ μανθάνοντες, ὡς φῄς, οὐ
φιλόδικοί ἐσμεν, σὺ δὲ ὁ λέγειν μὴ ἐπιστάμενος καὶ
νῦν ἡμᾶς καὶ πρότερον ἑάλως συκοφαντῶν," ὥστε
λυσιτελὲς φανεῖται τοῖς πολίταις κἀκεῖνον μανθάνειν
ῥητορεύειν· οὐ γὰρ ἄν⁴ οὕτω πονηρὸν οὐδὲ συκο-
35 φάντην αὐτὸν εἶναι. τὸν αὐτὸν δὲ τρόπον κἂν ἡμᾶς
ἐπὶ μισθῷ συνηγορεῖν λέγῃ τις, ὁμολογήσαντες
εἰρωνευσόμεθα, καὶ τὸν αἰτιώμενον ἡμᾶς ἐπι-
δείξομεν ταὐτὸ⁵ ποιοῦντα καὶ τοὺς ἄλλους ἅπαντας.
τῶν δὲ μισθῶν διαίρει⁶ τὰ εἴδη, καὶ λέγε⁷ ὡς οἱ
μὲν ἐπὶ χρήμασιν οἱ δ᾽ ἐπὶ χάρισιν οἱ δ᾽ ἐπὶ τι-
40 μωρίαις οἱ δ᾽ ἐπὶ τιμαῖς συνηγοροῦσιν· σαυτὸν⁸ μὲν
οὖν ἀπόφαινε διὰ χάριν συνηγοροῦντα, τὸν δ᾽
1444 b ἐναντίον λέγε οὐδ᾽ ἐπὶ μικρῷ μισθῷ συνηγορεῖν·
ὅπως γὰρ λάβῃ ἀργύριον ἀδίκως, οὐχ ὅπως μὴ
ἐκτίσῃ, δικάζεται. τῷ αὐτῷ δὲ τρόπῳ⁹ καὶ ἐάν τις
ἡμᾶς δικάζεσθαί τινας λέγῃ διδάσκειν, ἢ λόγους
5 δικανικοὺς συγγράφειν· ἀπόφαινε γὰρ¹⁰ καὶ τοὺς
ἄλλους ἅπαντας, καθ᾽ ὅσον δύνανται, τοὺς φίλους
ὠφελεῖν καὶ διδάσκοντας καὶ συμβουλεύοντας. καὶ
οὕτως ἐντέχνως περὶ τῶν τοιούτων ἀπαντήσεις.

---

¹ ἂν add. Halm.   ² Rac.: γράψοιμι.   ³ Sp.: περὶ.
⁴ ἂν add. Halm.   ⁵ Finckh: τοῦτο.
⁶ Sp.: διαιρεῖν aut διαιροῦ.   ⁷ v.l. λέγειν.
⁸ Sp.: αὑτὸν.   ⁹ τρόπῳ ⟨δεῖ χρῆσθαι⟩ Sp.
¹⁰ ἀποφανοῦμεν Sauppe.

actions—it allows a man to speak as he likes. One should also say : ' My opponent thinks the offences he has committed are of such magnitude that he feels I should not be able to conduct the prosecution adequately if I had not written my speech and given much time to considering it.' This is how to meet misrepresentations about written speeches. If they say that we study and practise speaking, we shall admit the charge, and say : ' We who study speaking, as you say, are not litigious, whereas you who do not know how to make a speech are proved to be bringing a malicious prosecution against us now and to have done so before '—so making it appear that it would be to the advantage of the public if he too studied rhetoric, as he would not be such a rascally blackmailer if he did. In the same way also if someone says that we are acting as advocates for a reward, we shall admit it in an ironical tone, and prove that the person accusing us does the same, and so does everybody else. Also distinguish between the different sorts of reward, and say that some people act as advocates for money, others as a favour, others for revenge, others for honours ; and then show that you yourself are acting as advocate for a favour, but say that your opponent is acting for a reward and not a small one, as he is bringing the case in order to get money dishonestly, not in order to avoid having to pay money. Similarly if someone says we instruct people in legal procedure, or write speeches for lawsuits : show that everybody else also, to the best of his ability, assists his friends with instruction and advice. These will be scientific methods of meeting charges of this sort.

1444 b

¹Χρὴ δὲ καὶ περὶ τὰς ἐρωτήσεις καὶ τὰς ἀπο-
κρίσεις, ὁπόσαι πίπτουσιν εἰς τὰ τοιαῦτα εἴδη, μὴ
10 ῥᾳθύμως ἔχειν, ἀλλὰ διακρίνειν τὰς ὁμολογίας καὶ
τὰς ἀρνήσεις ἐν ταῖς ἀποκρίσεσιν. ὁμολογίαι μὲν
οὖν εἰσὶν αἱ τοιαίδε· '' ἀπέκτεινάς μου τὸν υἱόν;''
'' ἀπέκτεινα πρότερον ἐπ' ἐμὲ σίδηρον αἰρόμενον.''
'' συνέκοψάς μου τὸν υἱόν; '' '' ἔγωγε ἀδίκων χειρῶν
ἄρχοντα.'' '' κατέαξάς μου τὴν κεφαλήν; '' '' ἐγὼ
15 βιαζομένου σου νύκτωρ εἰς τὴν ἐμὴν οἰκίαν εἰσιέναι.'' αἱ μὲν οὖν τοιαῦται ὁμολογίαι τῷ νομίμῳ
πιστεύουσαι ὁμολογοῦνται, αἱ δὲ τοιαίδ' ἀρνήσεις
παρεγκλίνουσι τὸν νόμον· '' ἀπέκτεινάς μου τὸν
υἱόν; '' '' οὐκ ἔγωγε ἀλλ' ὁ νόμος.'' τὰ δὲ
τοιαῦτα πάντα οὕτω δεῖ ὑποκρίνεσθαι,² ὅταν τῶν
νόμων ὁ μὲν κελεύῃ τοῦτο ποιεῖν ὁ δὲ κωλύῃ. τὰ
20 μὲν οὖν πρὸς τοὺς ἀντιδίκους ἐκ τούτων ἁπάντων
συνάξεις.

Μετὰ δὲ ταῦτα παλιλλογία τῶν εἰρημένων ἤδη
σύντομος ἀνάμνησις. χρήσιμος δ' ἐστὶ παρὰ
πάντας τοὺς καιρούς, ὥστε καὶ παρὰ μέρος καὶ
παρὰ εἶδος τῇ παλιλλογίᾳ χρηστέον. μάλιστα δ'
25 ἁρμόττει πρὸς τὰς κατηγορίας καὶ τὰς ἀπολογίας,
ἔτι δὲ παρὰ³ τὰς προτροπὰς καὶ ἀποτροπάς. οὐ
γὰρ μόνον ἀναμνῆσαι δεῖν φαμεν περὶ τῶν εἰρημένων ἐνταῦθα, καθάπερ καὶ ἐπὶ τῶν ἐγκωμίων καὶ
τῶν κακολογιῶν, ἀλλὰ καὶ πρὸς ἡμᾶς τοὺς κριτὰς
εὖ διαθεῖναι καὶ πρὸς τοὺς ἐναντίους κακῶς· διὸ καὶ
30 τελευταῖον τοῦτο τῶν ἐν τῷ λόγῳ μερῶν τάττομεν.
ἔστι δὲ μνημονικὸν ποιεῖν ἐν κεφαλαίῳ ἢ⁴ ἀπολογι-
ζόμενον περὶ τῶν εἰρημένων ἢ διαλογιζόμενον,⁵ ἢ

---

¹ Χρὴ δὲ . . . 20 συνάξεις spuria Ipfelkofer.
² v.l. ἀποκρίνεσθαι.   ³ [παρὰ] Sp.

432

Also one must not be slack about any questions and ⁽⁴⁾ *rhetorical questions;* answers that occur in this class of cases, but in one's ¹⁰ answers one must clearly distinguish what one admits and what one denies. The following are examples of admissions : ' Did you kill my son ? '—' I did kill him, when he drew on me first.' ' Did you give my son a thrashing ? '—' Yes, I did, when he was the aggressor.' ' Did you break my head ? '—' Yes, when you were trying to break into my house at ¹⁵ night.' Such admissions, then, are based in form on the actual terms of the law. Denials like the following give a slight twist to the law : ' Did you kill my son ? '—' No, I did not, but the law did.' All such replies should be made in this manner in cases where one law orders the commission of the act and another law prohibits it. Out of all these examples you will ²⁰ collect modes of replying to your opponents.

After this comes recapitulation—a brief reminder ⁽⁵⁾ *recapitulation;* of what has been said already. This is useful on all occasions, so recapitulation should be employed at every part of a speech and with every kind of speech. It is most suitable for accusations and defences, but ²⁵ also in exhortations and dissuasions. For we say that in these we should not only recapitulate what has been said, as in eulogies and vituperations, but also we ought to make the judges favourably disposed towards ourselves and unfavourably disposed towards our opponents ; and on this account we place this last ³⁰ of the divisions in a speech. A summary reminder may be made either by enumerating the points that have been made or in the form of a calculation ^a or

^a See 1433 b 4.

---

⁴ ἤ add. Rac.   ⁵ ἤ διαλογιζόμενον v.l. om.

1444 b

προσερωτῶντα¹ τῶν μὲν σαυτοῦ τὰ βέλτιστα τῶν
δὲ τῶν² ἐναντίων τὰ φαυλότατα, εἰ δὲ βούλει,
ἐρωτήσεως σχῆμα ποιησάμενος. οἷον δὲ τούτων
35 ἕκαστόν ἐστιν, ἐκ τῶν προτέρων ἴσμεν.

Εὖ δὲ διαθήσομεν πρὸς³ ἡμᾶς καὶ πρὸς³ τοὺς
ἐναντίους κακῶς, ὥσπερ ἐπὶ τῶν προτροπῶν καὶ
ἀποτροπῶν, ἀποφαίνοντες⁴ κεφαλαιωδῶς ἐφ' οἷς εὖ
πεποιήκαμεν τοὺς ἀδικοῦντας ἢ ποιοῦμεν ἢ ποιήσομεν, ἢ αὐτοὶ ἢ οἱ ἡμέτεροι φίλοι, ἢ αὐτοὺς ἢ ὧν
κηδόμενοι τυγχάνουσιν, ἢ πάλιν τοὺς κρίνοντας ἢ
40 αὐτοὺς ἢ ὧν κηδόμενοι τυγχάνουσιν, καὶ διεξιόντες
1445 a αὐτοῖς ὡς νῦν καιρὸς χάριτας ἡμῖν τῶν ὑπ-
ηργμένων ἀποδοῦναι, καὶ πρὸς τούτοις ἐλεεινοὺς
ἡμᾶς αὐτοὺς καθιστάντες, ἐὰν ἐνδέχηται. τοῦτο δὲ
ποιήσομεν ἐπιδεικνύντες ὡς πρὸς τοὺς ἀκούοντας
οἰκείως ἔχομεν καὶ ἀναξίως δυστυχοῦμεν, κακῶς
5 πρότερον πεπονθότες ἢ νῦν πάσχοντες, ἢ πεισόμενοι
ἐὰν μὴ βοηθῶσιν ἡμῖν οὗτοι, ἐὰν δὲ μὴ τοιαῦτα
ὑπάρχῃ, διεξιόντες τίνων ἀγαθῶν ἐστερήμεθα ἢ
στερισκόμεθα, ἢ στερησόμεθα ὀλιγωρηθέντες ὑπὸ
τῶν κρινόντων, ἢ ὡς ἀγαθοῦ μηδέποτε τετυκή-
καμεν⁵ ἢ μὴ τυγχάνομεν⁶, ἢ μὴ τευξόμεθα⁷ μὴ
10 τούτων ἡμῖν συμβοηθησάντων· ἐκ γὰρ τούτων
ἐλεεινοὺς καταστήσομε νήμᾶς αὐτούς, καὶ πρὸς⁸
τοὺς ἀκούοντας εὖ διαθήσομεν.

Διαβαλοῦμεν δὲ τοὺς ἀντιδίκους καὶ φθονεῖσθαι
ποιήσομεν ἐκ τῶν ἐναντίων τούτοις, ἀποφαίνοντες
ὑπὸ τούτων ἢ τῶν τούτοις φίλων τοὺς ἀκούοντας

---

¹ προαιρούμενον Ipfelkofer.   ² τῶν add. Rac.
³ πρὸς bis add. Rac.   ⁴ v.l. ὑποφαίνοντες.
⁵ Rac. (ἐπιτετυχήκαμεν cf. 24 Hammer.): ἐτύχομεν.
⁶ Sp.: ἐπιτυγχάνομεν.

by putting questions as to your own strongest points and your opponent's weakest, and if you like by employing the figure of a direct question.[a] The nature of each of these figures we know from what 35 has been said before.

We shall make them well-disposed towards our-(6) *concili-* selves and ill-disposed towards our opponents in the *ate the* *audience;* same way as in exhortations and dissuasions, by summarily showing on what occasions we or our friends have done or are doing or are going to do good to those who are wronging us or to persons whom they care for, or again to the judges themselves or persons 40 whom the judges care for, and by explaining to them that now there is an opportunity for them to repay us 1445 a a return for the services we have rendered ; and in addition by making ourselves if possible objects of compassion. We shall effect this by demonstrating that we stand in friendly relations with our hearers and that we are undeservedly unfortunate in having been in trouble already or being so now, or going to 5 be if they do not help us, or if such pleas are not available, by recounting what benefits we have been or are being deprived of, or shall be if we are slighted by those judging the case, or how we have never had or have not any good luck, or never shall have if they do not come to our help. By these means we shall 10 make ourselves objects of pity, and put ourselves on good terms with our audience.

We shall discredit our adversaries and make them (7) *discredit* objects of jealousy by the opposite means—by show-*the other* *side.* ing that our hearers themselves or those they care for

[a] On the difference between ἐρωτᾶν and προσερωτᾶν see *Rhet.* 1418 b 39 ff.

---

[7] Sp.: ἐπιτευξόμεθα.   [8] [πρὸς] ? Rac.

15 ἢ αὐτοὺς[1] ἢ ὧν[2] κήδονται κακῶς πεπονθότας ἢ
πάσχοντας ἢ πεισομένους παρὰ τὸ προσῆκον· ἐκ
γὰρ τῶν τοιούτων καὶ μῖσος καὶ ὀργὴν πρὸς αὐτοὺς
ἕξουσιν. ἂν δὲ μὴ ταῦτα ἐνδέχηται, συνάξομεν ἐξ
ὧν φθόνον τοῖς ἀκούουσι κατὰ τῶν ἐναντίων ἐργασό-
μεθα· τὸ γὰρ φθονεῖν πλησίον τοῦ μισεῖν ἐστίν.
20 φθονήσονται δὲ συλλήβδην ἐὰν ἀναξίως αὐτοὺς εὖ
πράττοντας ἀποφαίνωμεν καὶ πρὸς τοὺς ἀκούοντας
ἀλλοτρίως ἔχοντας, διεξιόντες ὡς ἀγαθὰ πολλὰ
πεπόνθασιν ἀδίκως ἢ πάσχουσιν ἢ μέλλουσι
πείσεσθαι, ἢ ἀγαθοῦ οὐδέποτε πρότερον ἐστερή-
θησαν ἢ νῦν οὐ στερίσκονται ἢ οὐ στερήσονται, ἢ
25 κακοῦ οὐδέποτε τετυχηκότες εἰσὶν[3] ἢ νῦν οὐ
τυγχάνοντες, ἢ οὐ τευξόμενοι, ἐὰν μὴ νῦν αὐτοὺς
οἱ κριταὶ κολάσωσιν.

Ἐκ τούτων μὲν οὖν ἐν τοῖς ἐπιλόγοις εὐμειῶς
μὲν πρὸς ἡμᾶς[4] αὐτοὺς κακῶς δὲ πρὸς[5] τοὺς
ἐναντίους διαθήσομεν, ἐκ δὲ τῶν προειρημένων
ἁπάντων ἐντέχνως καὶ τὰς κατηγορίας καὶ τὰς
ἀπολογίας τάξομεν.

30 XXXVII. Τὸ δ' ἐξεταστικὸν εἶδος αὐτὸ μὲν
καθ' ἑαυτὸ οὐ πολλάκις συνίσταται, τοῖς δὲ ἄλλοις
εἴδεσι μίγνυται· καὶ μάλιστα πρὸς τὰς ἀντιλογίας
χρήσιμόν ἐστιν. οὐ μὴν ἀλλ' ὅπως μηδὲ τούτου
τὴν τάξιν ἀγνοῶμεν, ἄν ποθ' ἡμῖν λόγον ἢ βίον
ἢ πρᾶξιν ἀνθρώπων ἢ διοίκησιν πόλεως ἐξετάζειν
35 συμβῇ, διέξειμι[6] καὶ περὶ τούτου κεφαλαιωδῶς.

Φροιμιαστέον μὲν οὖν σχεδὸν ὁμοιοτρόπως τοῖς
διαβεβλημένοις καὶ τοῖς ἐξετάζουσι ταῦτα, ὥστε

---

[1] ἢ αὐτοὺς add. Sp.   [2] ὧν Rac.: ὧν αὐτοὶ.
[3] εἰσὶν add. Halm.   [4] ἡμᾶς add. Rac.
[5] πρὸς add. Rac.   [6] διέξιμεν ? Hammer.

have been or are being or are going to be wrongfully ¹⁵
ill-treated by them or their friends ; for such statements will inspire the audience with hatred and anger
towards them. If this is not possible, we shall adduce considerations that will result in our inspiring our
hearers with jealousy against our opponents; because
jealousy is near to hatred. Speaking generally, they ²⁰
will encounter jealousy if we show that they are pros-
pering undeservedly, and that they are ill-disposed
towards our hearers—we must recount that they have
received or are receiving or are going to receive many
benefits unjustly, or that they have never before been
or are not now being or are not going to be deprived
of some benefit, or that they have never before met
with or are not now meeting with some evil, or will ²⁵
not do so unless the judges punish them now.

By these means in our perorations we shall make
the audience well-disposed towards ourselves and
ill-disposed towards our opponents ; and by all the
methods already stated we shall construct both
speeches in accusation and speeches in defence
scientifically.

XXXVII. The examinational species is not gener- ³⁰
ally employed as a separate composition but in com- *Structure*
bination with the other forms : it is specially useful *of Investiga-*
tional
in meeting contradictions. Nevertheless, in order *oration.*
Introduc-
that we may not be ignorant of the structure of this *tion: points*
form either, in case it ever befalls us to have to *to be treated.* ³⁵
examine the words or life or conduct of individuals or
the administration of a state, I will give a summary
account of this also.

In making an examination of these matters the introduction should be framed on almost the same lines as
in refuting a misrepresentation. We shall therefore

προφάσεις ἐν ἀρχαῖς εὐλόγους ἐνεγκόντες δι᾽ ἃς
δόξομεν εἰκότως τοῦτο ποιεῖν, οὕτως ἐπὶ τὴν
ἐξέτασιν ἥξομεν. ἁρμόσουσι δὲ αἱ τοιαίδε, ἐν μὲν
40 τοῖς πολιτικοῖς συλλόγοις, ὡς οὐ φιλονεικίᾳ
1445 b τοιοῦτο[1] ποιοῦμεν ἀλλ᾽ ὅπως μὴ λάθῃ τοὺς
ἀκούοντας, εἶτα ὅτι ἡμᾶς οὗτοι πρότεροι[2] ἠν-
ώχλησαν· ἐν δὲ τοῖς ἰδίοις ἢ ἔχθρα[3] ἢ τὰ ἤθη[4]
τῶν ἐξεταζομένων φαῦλα ὄντα ἢ φιλία[5] πρὸς τοὺς
ἐξεταζομένους, ὅπως[6] συνέντες[7] ἃ πράττουσι μηκέτι
5 ταῦτα ποιήσωσιν· ἐν δὲ τοῖς δημοσίοις τὸ νόμιμον
καὶ[8] τὸ δίκαιον καὶ[9] τὸ τῷ κοινῷ συμφέρον.

Φροιμιασάμενοι δ᾽ ἐκ τούτων καὶ τῶν τούτοις
ὁμοιοτρόπων, ἐφεξῆς ἕκαστον προτιθέμενοι τῶν
ῥηθέντων ἢ πραχθέντων ἢ διανοηθέντων ἐξετάσο-
μεν, ἐνδεικνύντες αὐτὰ καὶ τοῖς δικαίοις καὶ τοῖς
10 νομίμοις καὶ τοῖς ἰδίᾳ καὶ κοινῇ συμφέρουσιν
ἐναντιούμενα, καὶ πάντα σκοποῦντες, εἴ που αὐτὰ
αὑτοῖς ἐστιν ἐναντία ἢ τοῖς ἔθεσι[10] τῶν χρηστῶν
ἀνθρώπων ἢ τοῖς εἰκόσιν. ἵνα δὲ μὴ μηκύνωμεν
τὸν λόγον καθ᾽ ἓν ἕκαστον λέγοντες, ὅσῳ ἂν
πλείοσι τῶν ἐνδόξων ἐπιτηδευμάτων ἢ πραγμάτων
15 ἢ λόγων ἢ ἐθῶν ἐναντιούμενα τὰ τῶν ἐξεταζομένων
ἀποφαίνωμεν τοῖς ἀκούουσι, τοσούτῳ μᾶλλον οἱ
ἐξεταζόμενοι ἀδοξήσουσιν. δεῖ δὲ πικρῷ τῷ ἤθει
μὴ ἐξετάζειν, ἀλλὰ πραεῖ· τοῦτον γὰρ τὸν τρόπον
οἱ λόγοι γιγνόμενοι πιθανώτεροι φανήσονται τοῖς
ἀκούουσιν, οἱ δὲ λέγοντες αὐτοὺς[11] ἥκιστα δια-
20 βαλοῦσιν. ὅταν δὲ πάντα ἀκριβῶς ἐξητακὼς

---

[1] v.ll. τοῦτο, τὸ τοιοῦτο (τὸ καὶ τὸ? cf. 1444 a 23 Rac.).
[2] v.l. πρότερον
[3] Sp.: ἔχθραν.
[4] Sylburg: ἔθη.
[5] Sp.: φιλίαν.
[6] Sp.: ἢ ὅπως.
[7] Finckh: ἀνέντες.
[8] καὶ add. Rac.
[9] καὶ om. v.l.

begin by producing plausible pretexts that will make
our action appear reasonable, before we proceed
to the examination. The following are examples of
pretexts that will be suitable : in political conferences, 40
that we are acting in this way not from contentious- 1445 b
ness but in order to acquaint our audience with the
facts, and also that our opponents were the aggressors ; in private cases, our motive will be given
as hostile feeling or the bad moral character of the
persons under examination, or friendliness for the
persons under examination, with the intention that if
they understand what they are doing they may not 5
do it any longer ; in public trials, considerations of
law and justice, and the public interest.

These and similar subjects having furnished *Tone and*
material for our introduction, we shall next put for- *bearing.*
ward for examination the various past utterances or
actions or intentions of the persons seriatim, showing
that they run counter to the principles of justice and
law and to private and public interest, and scrutinizing 10
any points in all of them where they are inconsistent
with themselves or with the habits of virtuous people
or with probability. Not to prolong the subject by
going into detail—the greater the number of creditable
pursuits or actions or words or habits to which we can
convince our audience that the pursuits etc. of the 15
persons under examination run counter, the more
those persons will be discredited. The examination
should be conducted in a mild and not a bitter spirit,
because speeches delivered in that manner will appear
more plausible to the audience, and those who deliver
them will arouse least prejudice against themselves.
When you have carefully examined everything and 20

---

¹⁰ Rac. : ἤθεσι.   ¹¹ v.l. αὐτούς.

1445 b

αὐξήσῃς αὐτά, παλιλλογίαν ἐπὶ τῇ τελευτῇ σύντομον ποίησαι[1] καὶ τοὺς ἀκροατὰς περὶ τῶν
εἰρημένων ἀνάμνησον.

Τὰ μὲν οὖν εἴδη πάντα τοῦτον τὸν τρόπον τάττοντες ἐντέχνως αὐτοῖς χρησόμεθα.

XXXVIII. Δεῖ δὲ καὶ λέγοντας καὶ γράφοντας
25 ὅτι μάλιστα πειρᾶσθαι κατὰ τὰ προειρημένα[2]
τοὺς λόγους ἀποδιδόναι, καὶ συνεθίζειν αὐτοὺς
τούτοις ἅπασιν ἐξ ἑτοίμου χρῆσθαι. καὶ περὶ μὲν
τοῦ λέγειν ἐντέχνως καὶ ἐν τοῖς ἰδίοις καὶ ἐν τοῖς
κοινοῖς ἀγῶσι κἂν ταῖς πρὸς τοὺς[3] ἄλλους ὁμιλίαις
ἐντεῦθεν πλείστας καὶ τεχνικωτάτας ἀφορμὰς
30 ἕξομεν· χρὴ δὲ καὶ τὴν ἐπιμέλειαν ποιεῖσθαι μὴ
μόνον περὶ τοὺς λόγους ἀλλὰ καὶ περὶ τὸν βίον τὸν
αὐτοῦ, διακοσμοῦντα ταῖς ἰδέαις ταῖς εἰρημέναις·
συμβάλλεται γὰρ ἡ περὶ τὸν βίον παρασκευὴ καὶ
πρὸς τὸ πείθειν καὶ πρὸς τὸ δόξης ἐπιεικοῦς
τυγχάνειν.

Πρῶτον μὲν οὖν διελέσθαι χρὴ τὰ πράγματα
35 κατὰ τὴν ὅλην τοῦ παιδεύματος διαίρεσιν, ὅ τι
πρῶτον ἢ δεύτερον ἢ τρίτον ἢ τέταρτον μετα-
χειριστέον, εἶτα σαυτοῦ ποιεῖσθαι παρασκευήν,
ὥσπερ ἐν τοῖς προοιμίοις διήλθομεν τὰ περὶ τῶν
ἀκροατῶν. εὐμενῆ[4] μὲν οὖν τὰ περὶ σεαυτὸν
ποιήσεις, ἐὰν οἷς ὁμολογεῖς ἐμμένῃς καὶ δια-
40 φυλάττῃς φίλους τοὺς αὐτοὺς διὰ παντὸς τοῦ βίου,
1446 a καὶ περὶ τῶν ἄλλων ἐπιτηδευμάτων φαίνῃ μὴ
μεθιστάμενος ἀλλ' ἀεὶ τοῖς αὐτοῖς χρώμενος.
προσέξουσι δέ σοι ἐὰν μεγάλας καὶ καλὰς μεταχειρίζῃ πράξεις[5] καὶ τοῖς πολλοῖς συμφερούσας.

---

[1] Sp.: ποίησον.   [2] Sp.: πεπραγμένα.
[3] τοὺς om. v.l.   [4] εὐμενεῖς Finckh.

have amplified your points, conclude by giving a concise repetition, recalling what you have said to your hearers' memory.

This is the way in which we shall arrange all the species in order to employ them scientifically. *Miscellaneous appendix.*

XXXVIII. Both in speaking and in writing we must try to frame our remarks as far as possible in 25 accordance with the rules already stated, and we must train ourselves to employ all of them readily. These rules will supply us with the largest number of resources of the most scientific character for speaking artistically in private and public contests and in social intercourse. And one must also be careful not 30 only about one's speech but also about one's personal conduct, regulating it by the principles that have been stated, because one's manner of life contributes to one's powers of persuasion as well as to the attainment of a good reputation.

First, therefore, you must divide your matter according to the general system of division given 35 by your training, and arrange what topics are to be treated first, second, third or fourth. Next you must prepare your hearers to receive you, as we said in discussing the handling of the audience in the introduction.[a] You will make their feelings towards you favourable if you stand by your agreements and keep the same friends all through your life and generally 40 show yourself not changeable in your habits but 1446 a always keeping to the same principles. And they will hear you with attention if you deal with important and honourable actions[b] and such as are to the public advantage.

---

[a] *Cf.* 1437 a 31 f., 1440 b 4.

[b] v.l. τὰς πράξεις.

1446 a

Εὐμενεῖς δὲ γενόμενοι, ὅταν ἐπὶ τῶν πράξεων
5 γένῃ ὅσαι τῶν κακῶν ἀποτροπὴν ἔχουσι τῶν δ'
ἀγαθῶν παρουσίαν, ταύτας μὲν ὡς συμφερούσας
αὑτοῖς ἀποδέξονται, ὅσαι δὲ τἀναντία παρασκευάζουσιν αὐτῶν, ταύτας ἀποδοκιμάσουσιν.

Ἀντὶ δὲ τοῦ ταχεῖαν καὶ σαφῆ καὶ καθαρὰν καὶ[1]
μὴ ἄπιστον τὴν διήγησιν λέγεσθαι, τὰς πράξεις
10 δεῖ τοιαύτας[2] ποιεῖσθαι. ταχέως μὲν οὖν ἐπι-
τελέσεις ἂν μὴ * * * *, σαφῶς δὲ ἂν μὴ[3] πάντα ἅμα
πράττειν[4] βούλῃ, ἀλλὰ πρότερον τὸ πρῶτον,
ἔπειτα τὸ ἑξῆς· καθαρῶς δὲ ἂν μὴ ταχὺ τῆς
πράξεως παυόμενος ἄλλα πράγματα μεταχειρίζῃ
πρὶν ταύτην ἐπιτελέσαι· μὴ ἀπίστως δὲ ἂν μὴ
15 παρὰ τὸ ἦθος τὸ σαυτοῦ πράττῃς, πρὸς δὲ τούτοις
ἂν μὴ προσποιῇ τοὺς αὐτοὺς ἐχθροὺς καὶ φίλους
εἶναί σοι.

Ἐκ δὲ τῶν πίστεων ληψόμεθα, περὶ ὧν μὲν
ἐπιστήμην ἔχομεν, κατὰ τὴν ταύτης ἐξήγησιν τὰς
πράξεις ἐπιτελεῖν, περὶ ὧν δὲ τυγχάνομεν ἀ-
γνοοῦντες, κατὰ τὸ ὡς ἐπὶ τὸ πολὺ συμβαῖνον·
20 ἀσφαλέστατον γὰρ πράττειν περὶ τῶν οὕτως
ἐχόντων πρὸς τὸ εἰωθὸς ἀποβλέποντας.

Εἰς δὲ τὸν πρὸς τοὺς ἀντιδίκους ἀγῶνα ἐν μὲν
τοῖς λόγοις ἐκ τῶν λελεγμένων ποιήσομεν βε-
βαιότητα περὶ ἡμῶν, ἐν δὲ τοῖς συμβολαίοις τοῦτο
ποιήσομεν ἐὰν κατὰ τοὺς νόμους αὐτὰ μεταχειριζώμεθα τοὺς ἀγράφους καὶ τοὺς γεγραμ-
25 μένους μετὰ μαρτύρων ὡς βελτίστων ὁριζομένοις
χρόνοις.

---

[1] καθαρὰν καὶ add. Rac.   [2] Sp.: ταύτας aut ταῦτα.
[3] * * * * σαφῶς δὲ ἂν μὴ add. Finckh.
[4] Rac.: πάντα πράττειν ἅμα aut πράττειν ἅμα πάντα.

1446 a

The goodwill of your audience having been gained, when you come to practical proposals for securing the avoidance of evils and the provision of benefits, they will accept these as contributing to their own advantage, and they will reject measures that produce the opposite results.

For the purpose of making your exposition rapid, clear, distinct and convincing in style, your practical suggestions must have those qualities. You will get through them rapidly, if you do not * * * *[a]; clearly, if you do not try to treat every point at once, but the first thing first and then the next; distinctly, if you do not quickly drop the subject and take up other matters before you have finished this one; convincingly, if your line of action is not at variance with your own character, and in addition if you do not pretend that the same persons are your enemies and your friends.

From among methods of proof, in matters of which we have knowledge we shall adopt the plan of completing our practical proposals by its guidance; but in matters of which we happen to be ignorant we shall follow the line of what generally occurs, as in such cases it is safest to act with an eye to what is usual.

As regards the issue with our opponents, on a question of words, we shall obtain confirmation in regard to our case from the actual words used; on questions of contracts we shall do so if we deal with them in accordance with written and unwritten laws, with the support of the best available evidence, within fixed limits of time.

---

[a] Some words are clearly lost here in the ms. text, which runs, 'You will get through them rapidly if you do not try to treat every point at once.'

1446 a

Ἐκ δὲ τοῦ ἐπιλόγου περὶ μὲν τῶν λελεγμένων
ἀναμνήσομεν τοὺς ἀκροατὰς[1] τὰ πραχθέντα ἐν
κεφαλαίῳ αὖθις εἰπόντες, περὶ δὲ[2] τῶν πεπραγμένων ἐξ ὧν πράττομεν ἀναμνήσομεν οὕτως,
ἐπειδὰν τὰς αὐτὰς πράξεις ἢ τὰς ὁμοίας μεταχειριζώμεθα ταῖς προτέραις.

30 Φιλικῶς δὲ διακείσονται πρὸς ἡμᾶς ἐὰν πράτ-
τωμεν ἐξ ὧν εὖ πεπονθέναι δόξουσιν ἢ πάσχειν
ἢ πείσεσθαι. μεγάλα δὲ πράξομεν ἐὰν πολλῶν
αἰτίας καὶ καλῶν πράξεις μεταχειριζώμεθα.

Καὶ τοῦτον μὲν τὸν τρόπον χρὴ τὰ κατὰ τὸν βίον
αὐτοῦ παρασκευάζειν, ἐκ δὲ τῆς προτέρας συν-
35 τάξεως περὶ τοὺς λόγους γυμνάζεσθαι.

[Τὰς δὲ θυσίας δεῖ ποιεῖν ὡς προείρηται, πρὸς
μὲν τοὺς[3] θεοὺς ὁσίως, πρὸς δὲ τὰς δαπάνας
μετρίως, πρὸς δὲ τὰς θεωρίας λαμπρῶς, πρὸς δὲ
τοὺς πολίτας ὠφελίμως. καὶ πρὸς μὲν τοὺς θεοὺς
ὁσίως ἕξουσιν ἐὰν κατὰ τὰ πάτρια θύωμεν· πρὸς
1446 b δὲ τὰς δαπάνας μετρίως ἐὰν μὴ τὰ πεμπόμενα
πάντα τοῖς δαπανωμένοις συναναλίσκηται· πρὸς
δὲ τὰς θεωρίας λαμπρῶς ἐὰν μεγαλοπρεπῶς ὦσι
κατεσκευασμένα· πρὸς δὲ τοὺς πολίτας ὠφελίμως
5 ἐὰν ἱππεῖς καὶ ὁπλῖται διεσκευασμένοι συμ-
πέμπωσιν. τὰ μὲν δὴ πρὸς τοὺς θεοὺς οὕτω
γινόμενα ὁσίως ἂν ἔχοι.

Φιλίαν δὲ συστησόμεθα πρὸς τοὺς ὁμοιοτρόπους
ἡμῖν καὶ οἷς ταὐτὰ συμφέρει καὶ οἷς περὶ τὰ
μέγιστα ἀναγκαῖόν ἐστιν ἡμῖν κοινωνεῖν· ἡ γὰρ

---

[1] v.l. λελεγμένων μνημονικοὺς ποιήσομεν.
[2] δὲ hic Finckh : post ὧν aut om. codd.
[3] τοὺς add. Rac.

Under the peroration we shall remind our hearers about what has been said by giving a summary repetition of the facts, while we shall remind them of our past acts by reference to our present actions on the same lines, when we are adopting courses of action that are the same as or similar to our former ones.

They will be favourably disposed towards us if we 30 follow lines of action that they think to have been or to be or to be likely to be conducive to their advantage. Our actions will be important if we embark on policies productive of many and creditable results.

This is the manner in which the orator must regulate his personal conduct. His oratorical training must follow the system previously stated. 35

a [Sacrifices should be performed as has been said *Miscellane-* before, with piety towards the gods, moderation in *ous political* expenses, splendour as a spectacle, and benefit to the *tions.* public. They will be performed with piety towards the gods if we conduct them according to the ancestral ritual ; with moderation in expenditure if the whole 1446 b amount of the contributions is not lavished on the expenses ; with spectacular splendour if they are magnificently equipped ; with public benefit if cavalry and infantry in full equipment join in the 5 procession. Our duties to the gods will be piously performed if carried out in this way.

We shall establish relations of friendship with people with manners like our own, and those with the same interests, and those with whom we are compelled to be in partnership as to matters of the highest

a As to the spuriousness of the following passage see Introduction, p. 265.

τοιαύτη μάλιστα συμμένει φιλία. συμμάχους δὲ
10 δεῖ ποιεῖσθαι τοὺς δικαιοτάτους καὶ τοὺς δύναμιν
πολλὴν ἔχοντας καὶ τοὺς πλησίον κατοικοῦντας,
ἐχθροὺς δὲ τοὺς ἐναντίους τούτοις.

Πόλεμον δὲ αἱρεῖσθαι πρὸς τοὺς ἀδικεῖν ἐπιχειροῦντας τὴν πόλιν ἢ τοὺς φίλους ἢ τοὺς συμμάχους αὐτῆς. τὰς δὲ φυλακὰς ἀναγκαῖον ἔχειν
15 ἢ δι' αὐτῶν ἢ διὰ τῶν συμμάχων ἢ διὰ ξένων,
καὶ· κράτιστον[1] μὲν δι' ἑαυτῶν, δεύτερον δὲ διὰ
τῶν συμμάχων, τρίτον δὲ διὰ ξένων.

Περὶ δὲ πόρου χρημάτων, κράτιστον μὲν ἀπὸ
τῶν ἰδίων προσόδων ἢ κτημάτων, δεύτερον δὲ
ἀπὸ τῶν τιμημάτων, τρίτον δὲ τῶν πενήτων τὰ
σώματα παρεχόντων λειτουργεῖν, τῶν δὲ τεχνιτῶν
20 ὅπλα, τῶν δὲ πλουσίων χρήματα.

Περὶ πολιτείας δέ, δημοκρατία μὲν ἀρίστη ἐν
ᾗ οἱ νόμοι τοῖς ἀρίστοις τὰς τιμὰς ἀπονέμουσι τὸ
δὲ πλῆθος μήτε χειροτονίας μήτε ψηφηφορίας
ἐστέρηται, κακίστη δὲ ἐν ᾗ τῷ πλήθει παρα-
διδόασιν οἱ νόμοι τοὺς πλουτοῦντας ὑβρίζειν. ὀλιγ-
25 αρχιῶν δ' εἰσὶ δύο τρόποι· ἢ γὰρ ἐξ ἑταιρείας ἢ
ἀπὸ τιμημάτων.

Ποιεῖσθαι δὲ συμμάχους ἀναγκαῖόν ἐστιν ὅταν
οἱ πολῖται μὴ τυγχάνωσι δι' ἑαυτῶν δυνατοὶ τὴν
χώραν καὶ τὰ φρουρία φυλάττειν ἢ τοὺς πολεμίους
ἀμύνεσθαι· παρίεσθαι δὲ δεῖ συμμαχίαν ὅταν μὴ
30 ἀνάγκη τις ᾖ ποιεῖσθαι αὐτὴν ἢ μακρὰν τοῖς τόποις
ἀπέχωσι καὶ ἀδύνατοι ὦσι κατὰ τοὺς προσήκοντας
παραγίνεσθαι καιρούς.

Πολίτης δὲ ἀγαθός ἐστιν ὅστις φίλους μὲν
χρησιμωτάτους τῇ πόλει παρασκευάζει ἐχθροὺς
δὲ ἐλαχίστους καὶ ἀσθενεστάτους, καὶ ὅστις προσ-

importance ; for this is the most permanent kind of
friendship. We should form alliances with the
most just and with the very powerful and with those
who are our neighbours, and we should have the
opposite of these as our enemies.

We should levy war against those who attempt to
injure our state or her friends or allies. We must
guard our country either by serving in person or by
means of our allies or of mercenaries—best of all by
personal service, second best by means of allies and
third by mercenaries.

As to financial provisions, the best thing is to derive
funds from our own revenues or estates, second best
from a tax on property, third by means of national
contributions—the poor furnishing bodily service, the
artisans arms, and the rich money.

As to constitution, the best form of democracy is
that in which the laws assign the offices to the best
people while the multitude is not deprived of the
function of voting in parliament and at elections ; the
worst form is that in which the laws hand over the
wealthy to the violence of the multitude. Oligarchy
is of two forms : it is based either on party or on
property-qualifications.

It is necessary to obtain allies on occasions when
the citizens are not able to guard the country and the
forts or to keep off the enemy by their own efforts ;
but an alliance should be forgone when there is no
necessity to form it or when the people concerned are
far distant in locality and unable to come to our aid
at the proper occasions.

A good citizen is one who procures for the state the
most serviceable friends and the fewest and weakest

---

[1] v.l. πρῶτον.

1446 b

ὁδοὺς παρασκευάζει πλείστας τῶν ἰδιωτῶν μηδένα
35 δημεύων, καὶ ὅστις ἑαυτὸν δίκαιον παρέχων τοὺς
ἀδικοῦντάς τι τῶν κοινῶν ἐξετάζει.

Δωροῦνται δὲ πάντες ἐλπίζοντες ὠφεληθήσεσθαι
ἢ τῶν προτέρων εὐεργεσιῶν χάριν ἀποδιδόντες.
ὑπηρετοῦσι δὲ πάντες κέρδους ἕνεκεν ἢ τιμῆς ἢ
ἡδονῆς ἢ φόβου. συναλλάττουσι δὲ πάντες ἢ κατὰ
1447 a προαίρεσιν ἢ ἀκουσίως· αἱ γὰρ πράξεις ἐπι-
τελοῦνται πᾶσαι ἢ διὰ βίας ἢ διὰ πειθοῦς ἢ δι᾽
ἀπάτης ἢ διὰ προφάσεως.

Ἐν δὲ πολέμῳ περιγίνονται πολεμοῦντες ἢ διὰ
τύχην ἢ διὰ σωμάτων πλῆθος ἢ ῥώμην ἢ διὰ
5 χρημάτων εὐπορίαν ἢ διὰ τόπων εὐφυΐαν ἢ δι᾽
ἀρετὴν συμμάχων ἢ διὰ στρατηγοῦ γνώμην.

Ἐγκαταλιπεῖν δὲ τοὺς συμμάχους ὑπολαμβάνουσι δεῖν ἢ διὰ τὸ μᾶλλον συμφέρειν τοῦτο ἢ διὰ
1447 b τὸ καταλύσασθαι τὸν πόλεμον.

Δίκαια δὲ πράττειν ἐστὶ τὸ τοῖς κοινοῖς τῆς
πόλεως ἔθεσιν[1] ἕπεσθαι, τοῖς νόμοις πείθεσθαι,
ταῖς ἰδίαις ὁμολογίαις ἐμμένειν.

Συμφέρει δὲ σώματι μὲν εὐεξία καὶ κάλλος καὶ
5 ῥώμη καὶ ὑγίεια, ψυχῇ δὲ σοφία φρόνησις ἀνδρεία
σωφροσύνη δικαιοσύνη, συναμφοτέροις δὲ τούτοις
χρήματα καὶ φίλοι. ἀσύμφορα δὲ τἀναντία τούτων.
πόλει δὲ συμφέρον πλῆθος πολιτῶν ἀγαθῶν.[2]]

---

[1] v.l. ἤθεσιν.   [2] ἀγαθῶν v.l. om.

1446 b

enemies, and who procures most revenues without
confiscating the property of any private citizen, and
who, while himself behaving justly, exposes those 25
who are injuring some public interest.

Men always give presents in the hope of receiving
some benefit or as a recompense for former good
offices. Services are always rendered for the sake of
profit or honour or pleasure, or from fear. People
always have mutual dealings either from choice or
unwillingly ; for all actions are performed either 1447 a
under compulsion or through persuasion or through
fraud or with some pretext.

In war one side gains the upper hand owing either
to luck or to numbers or efficiency or financial
resources or geographical advantages or to having 5
good allies or a wise commander.

Men think proper to abandon their allies either
because it pays them better to do so or as a means
of bringing the war to an end.   1447 b

Righteous conduct is to follow the common customs
of the state, to obey the laws, to abide by private
contracts.

Bodily advantages are good condition, beauty,
strength, health ; mental advantages are wisdom,
prudence, courage, temperance, justice ; advantage- 5
ous to both mind and body jointly are wealth and
friends. Their opposites are disadvantageous. A
multitude of good citizens is advantageous to the
state.]

INDEX TO PROBLEMS

I.—INDEX NOMINUM

II.—INDEX RERUM

(The references in this index are to Books and Problems)

INDEX TO PROBLEMS

INDEX TO PROBLEMS

INDEX TO RHETORIC TO ALEXANDER

References are to the pages, columns (a and b), and lines of the Berlin edition of Aristotle, 1831, marked in the left-hand margin of the text. The two first figures of the page-numbers are omitted, 20 a to 47 b standing for 1420 a to 1447 b.